Religion in
Canadian Society

Religion in Canadian Society

Edited by
Stewart Crysdale
and
Les Wheatcroft

Macmillan of Canada
Maclean-Hunter Press

ISBN 0-7705-1335-2   cloth

ISBN 0-7705-1336-0   paper

Canadian Cataloguing in Publication Data

Main entry under title:

Religion in Canadian society

Includes bibliographical references.
ISBN 0-7705-1335-2 bd.   ISBN 0-7705-1336-0 pa.

1. Canada—Religion—Addresses, essays, lectures.
2. Canada—Religious life and customs—Addresses,
essays, lectures.   I. Crysdale, Stewart, date.
II. Wheatcroft, Les, 1946-

BL2530.C3R4   200′.971   C76-017059-2

Printed in Canada for the
Macmillan Company of Canada Limited
70 Bond Street
Toronto, Ontario M5B 1X3

Contents

Preface

In view of the historical importance of religion in Canadian society, it is remarkable that this should be the first volume in this country to compile and analyse studies by social scientists on the subject. This may be partly because until the past decade religion has been taken for granted by most Canadians. But profound changes are occurring in this and other social areas. More and more people have become aware of the problematic nature of our parliamentary politics, the fragility of the economy, the environmental and social costs of unrestrained technology, the fallacies of much of the educational system, and the dubiousness of traditional notions about sexual roles. The mood of doubt and apprehension encompassing religion today reflects and augments the questioning which pervades contemporary culture. Now that religion, like other social institutions, is no longer taken for granted, it has assumed a renewed fascination for social scientists.

An inventory of scientific studies of religion in Canada since 1945 (Crysdale and Montminy 1974) revealed that half have been completed since 1964. The majority of these studies are by sociologists, probably because changes in religion are closely related to changes in the dominant value systems and basic patterns of social groups. Since sociology attempts to deal systematically with patterns of relations between individuals and between groups, this discipline is well suited to examine the interaction between religion and other institutions and social processes.

Thus, 23 of the 33 selected studies in this volume fall within the discipline of sociology. Seven of the remainder are in anthropology, two are in history, and one is in political science. But while this book's perspective is largely sociological, its broad focus, regardless of discipline, is on the interaction between religion and other aspects of Canadian society in the process of change.

Twelve of the contributions appear here for the first time—an indication of the growth of scientific interest in religion. Most of the others have been published in sources that are not readily available. Some better known works are not included because they are easily accessible elsewhere. And, of course, many excellent studies have been omitted owing to limitations of space.

The papers selected are representative of the principal areas now being investigated by Canadian social scientists. They illustrate various theoretical approaches and methods of research, and reflect the ethnic and regional variations characteristic of Canadian society. In Part II we examine the place of religion in the life of indigenous peoples, then deal with the pre-industrial period in French-speaking, Roman Catholic Quebec and in English-speaking Protestant Canada West. The adaptation of religion to social change is traced in cultures as different as the Cree in Saskatchewan, the Micmacs in Restigouche, the Eskimo in Keewatin, the Québécois, and the Protestants in central Canada and the West. Of the seven papers dealing with religion in Quebec, three were originally written in French.

The largest section, Part III, treats religion in contemporary life. Of necessity it is a mosaic, highlighting the major areas of current research. These include the religious composition of the population; forms of community in which believers gather; types of religious organization; responses to religious callings; social sources of ecumenism, politics, economics, and social strata; and, finally, youth and socialization.

This book, we hope, will be useful to a wide range of readers, including interested individuals, students, teachers, and social scientists. As an aid to a systematic overview we have prepared a substantial introduction (Part I), reviewing theoretical perspectives, methods of inquiry, the Canadian literature, and continuing problems and issues.

Our indebtedness to contributors and publishers is abundantly clear.

What may not be so obvious is the generosity of authors in agreeing to abridgments and revisions, or in writing and rewriting manuscripts. Readers undoubtedly will share our gratitude to them.

Atkinson College   S.C. and L.W.
York University
Toronto
1976

Religion in
Canadian Society

PART

I

INTRODUCTION

The Analysis
of Religion

Stewart Crysdale
Les Wheatcroft

1. The Problematic Nature of Religion

From the founding of New France there has been in Canada close co-operation between dominant religious organizations and the state. Public ceremonies such as the opening of Parliament have been characterized by prominent roles played by clergy of leading denominations. Churches have often legitimated the existing order and acted as partners with governments in the provision of education, health care, and other social services. As a minor counter-theme, throughout Canadian history religious movements have risen to criticize the prevailing church-state *entente cordiale* and to advocate fundamental social reform.

In the everyday lives of most Canadians, religion—either as a mechanism for integrating individuals into society or as a rallying point for those disaffected with the social structure—has until recently exerted a strong influence. Church membership and attendance for generations have been the preferred form of voluntary association in nearly every Canadian community, and Canadians still attend church more frequently than do people in most parts of the world.

Recently, however, there have been important changes in the place of religion in society and in the lives of many individuals. At the societal level there has been a decline in formal religious activities such as church-going and in the ability of religious bodies to influence governments, other social institutions, and individuals. At the same time, at the personal level, belief, particularly for numerous younger and well educated people, has become a less institutional and more private experience. For many this has meant a decrease in, and for some the complete disappearance of, traditional belief, either as an integrating moral force or as an expression of anxiety and guilt.

For a minority, however, religious faith is a unifying and liberating experience with compelling relevance to all aspects of their lives. For them religion has become a synthesizing force, breaking down traditional divisions which exist within the self and between the self and others. In this way religion unites and gives meaning to the whole of existence (Fallding 1974: 112-14, Chs. 4 and 8). Unfortunately, few social scientists today study the subjective, individual aspects of religions or, for that matter, of other systems of meaning, though beginnings were made by Weber, Freud, and some recent phenomenologists and psychoanalysts.

A decline in traditional religious observance, notably church attendance and donations, after a decade of advance, began in Canada in the late 1950s, especially in large cities and among Protestants. By the early 1970s it had spread to rural regions and towns and had made spectacular inroads among Roman Catholics. While social scientists have not produced much evidence to explain these changes, there has been some discussion of several broad processes of social change which bear particularly on conventional beliefs and practices. We shall mention briefly three of these: secularization, urbanization, and economic and scientific rationalism. Each of these constructs is plagued by conceptual ambiguity, and in this short discussion we can do no more than suggest that they are broad, orienting themes which help in understanding the changes which are taking place in Canadian society.

By secularization we mean (a) an increasing differentiation between religious and other social institutions, (b) an increasing pluralism in systems of ultimate meaning, (c) a heightened tendency for individuals and groups to choose values (or general goals) and beliefs (convictions about truth and ethics) on the basis of particular situations and subjective feelings, and (d) a decline in the influence of traditional religious organizations (Fenn 1970: 135). Examples of secularization are the assumption by the Province of Quebec in 1964 of direct control of education, replacing control by the Roman Church; conflict between Christian socialism and conservative Protestant individualism during the Winnipeg General Strike in 1919; and the widespread use of contraceptive birth control methods among Roman Catholics, in spite of papal directives against them.

Urbanization refers to the multi-faceted process of change in which populations concentrate in towns, cities, and metropolitan areas as opposed to scattered, rural patterns of settlement. Accompanying urbanization, urbanism has become the dominant style of life, involving not only high population density but also heterogeneity in relationships (or the blending of people with various ethnic, religious, political, and economic attributes), frequency of interaction, and accentuated depersonalization (Wirth 1938). One study found that a frequent correlate of highly developed urbanism (as distinct from community size) is liberalism in forms of faith or creed, in heightened tolerance of differing values, beliefs, and behaviour, and in the approval of more public planning (Crysdale 1965). The spread of liberalism leads to the decline of traditional forms of religion and their replacement by agnosticism or atheism, by quietism or withdrawal from all but necessary involvement with worldly affairs, or by more universalistic, diffuse, and often attenuated forms of religious belief and practice.

Finally, heightened economic and scientific rationalism has had a powerful impact on both the social structures and the consciousness of individuals in the past few generations (Habermas 1970: Ch. 6). Rationalism in this sense is sceptical of judgments that are not based on empirical observations. Rationalism in economics stresses cost-benefit efficiency as the supreme standard of right or wrong. But cost-benefit efficiency has paradoxical effects wherever it is applied. On the one hand it standardizes products, services, and facilities so that, given a large measure of democratic polity, people from different socio-economic backgrounds and cultures may share widely in material benefits and in more open social and geographical mobility. The levelling impact of economic rationalism, however, also has serious disadvantages for it often discourages innovation and variation in human thought, feeling, and action. Numerous writers (Ellul 1964, 1970; Grant 1969) are pessimistic about the effects of economic rationalism, because unrestrained technology increases productive capacity at the cost of dehumanizing society. Similarly, scientific rationalism, when extended to social and cultural behaviour (present-day positivism), holds in its thrall many opinion-leaders and decision-makers in education, the mass media, the arts, business, engineering, and advertising, as well as many successful politicians, who rely on expediency rather than principle in order to gain or hold power. The consequences of the conformity exacted by economic and scientific rationalism are everywhere apparent in the banalities of contemporary culture and the mediocrity of bureaucratic performance.

But there are signs of disenchantment with this view of the world among some of the young and increasing numbers of middle-aged people. Lately, several eminent social scientists (Heilbroner 1974) have written pessimistically about the human prospect, obsessed as it is with increasing production and extravagant consumption, distinguished by competing and alienating social structures, threatened by mounting conflict over scarce resources, and disillusioned with the implicit ideal of "liberal" men operating in a "free" world under "beneficent" natural laws. The apparent effects of forces such as secularization, urbanization, and rationalism in heightening boredom, alienation, and meaninglessness are illustrated in the situation of many families. When they must move to an apartment they can afford within some miles of their place of work, their attachments to community and neighbours often become tenuous. Family life and interaction with kin and friends are subject to increased strains, and voluntary associations, including those with the church, decline in practicality and relevance.

Changes in religious association are reflected in the decrease in church attendance between 1956 and 1974, shown in Table 1.

TABLE 1.   Roman Catholic and Protestant Church Attendance in Canada by Percentages, from Gallup Polls, 1956, 1965, and May 1974*

	1956	1965	1974
Roman Catholics	87	83	59
Protestants	43	32	27
National Total	61	55	39

*Determined by responses to this question: "Did you, yourself, happen to attend church or synagogue in the last seven days?" By permission of the Canadian Institute of Public Opinion. (The comparability of these statistics is somewhat weakened because they were gathered in different months for each year.)

While Catholics are still more likely to be weekly church-goers than Protestants, their attendance has slumped more severely over the two decades, from 87 to 59 per cent, compared with the decline among Protestants, from 43 to 27 per cent. Altogether, the totals for Canada fell from 61 to 39 per cent.

Comparisons with trends in the United States are instructive, partly because Gallup Poll data there are more complete than in Canada. A special report on religion in America (Gallup Opinion Index 1975) shows that the slide in church attendance which began in 1956, when the percentage was 46 compared with 49 the year before, came to a halt in 1971 at 40 per cent, where attendance has stabilized. As in Canada, the decline has been dramatic among Roman Catholics, from 71 to 54 per cent between 1964 and 1975; in the same period Protestant attendance fell by one percentage point to 37 for the years 1971 to 1974 and rose again in 1975 to 38 per cent. Among persons 18 to 30 years of age attendance increased slightly from 1973 to 1974, offsetting small decreases among older persons. As a whole, however, attendance in older age groups remains much higher than among young people, regardless of denomination. At the same time, young adults are the most likely to think that religion is becoming more influential, with 37 per cent holding this view in 1974 as against 14 per cent in 1970. Large majorities of persons under 30 claim belief in God (97 per cent), in heaven (84 per cent), and in life after death (71 per cent). And 59 per cent of the same age group say they have a great deal of respect for organized religion.

While we do not have such detailed information for Canadians, it is clear that there is growing interest in the social and ethical implications of religious belief, in the universalistic aspects of faith and practice, in Protestant fundamentalism, Roman Catholic Pentecostalism, Judaic Conservatism, in Eastern religions, and in quasi-religious groups which delve into astrology and other areas of the occult.

The problematic nature of religion in modern societies raises three types of question for social scientists. First, why does religion in some form persist in all types of society, traditional and modern, capitalist, socialist, and totalitarian? Second, in the face of the cogent arguments of secular, scientific, and rational thought, how viable is the central tenet of religion, that there is an ultimate dimension of reality which pertains to the observable, empirical world but also reaches beyond it to realms of thought and experience not subject to scientific validation? And third, what are the relations between religion and other social and cultural institutions and processes?

Inquirers who focus on the first question usually look for some important functions which religion performs for people in social groups which other systems of belief and values cannot perform. (See Section 2 of this chapter, also Durkheim 1915; Davis 1949; Merton 1957; Parsons 1960; O'Dea 1966.)

Some who probe the second type of question, concerning the viability of faith, trace the systems of meaning which grow out of interaction between religion and historical events and directions without investigating the reality behind those meanings. Others, employing the phenomenological approach, attempt to analyse experiences of ultimate reality. (See Section 2 of this chapter, and Crysdale 1961: Part 2; Weber 1963; Berger and Luckmann 1966; Hiller 1969; Bellah 1970: Ch. 15; Berger 1974.)

An example of variation in forms of belief is provided in a 1971 poll of public opinion, presented in Table 2. It showed that 89 per cent of Canadians interviewed believe in a personal God or in "some kind of spirit or vital force in the world". About one-third of this group expressed their faith in a spiritual force rather than a personal God. But the poll also indicates the diversity of belief under modern conditions (Hunt 1972; King and Hunt 1972; Northover 1974).

TABLE 2.   Gallup Poll of Canadians' Belief in God, by Percentages, September 1971*

	CANADA	PROTESTANT	ROMAN CATHOLIC	OTHER FAITHS
1. There is a personal God	60	52	75	41
2. There is some kind of spirit or vital force in the world	29	37	21	28
3. I am not sure if there is a God or vital force in the world	7	8	2	14
4. I am sure there is no God or vital force	2	1	1	10
5. None of them	2	2	1	7
TOTALS	100	100	100	100

*By permission of the Canadian Institute of Public Opinion.

The persistence and viability of religion are also illustrated in two opposing or paradoxical trends in current religious behaviour. On the one hand, there is growing emphasis on the individual or private aspects of faith—what Thomas Luckmann (1967) calls "invisible religion". This may take the form of a belief orientation which normally is not evident but surfaces when a person undergoes a major crisis or a radical change in status and self-image, such as marriage, the birth of a child, severe illness, loss of employment or esteem, and death. Regular church-goers often criticize "carriage Christians" who go to church only for high ceremonies or in emergencies, but the generality of the practice calls attention to an important aspect of contemporary religion. The individual may find all the social supports he needs outside the church for the ordinary routines of family, job, or club, but when life tumbles in and "other helpers flee" he may, for various reasons, turn to spiritual or religious resources.

On the other hand, for some the emphasis is on the implementation of faith and ethics in social and political action (Reinhold Niebuhr 1932; Bennett 1946, 1954; Hutchinson 1953; King 1964, 1967; Malcolm X 1965; Yinger 1970: Chs. 14 and 15; Crysdale, this volume). The involvement of clergy and lay people in drives or demonstrations for civil rights, peace, freedom, brotherhood, and environmental reform is as familiar in these times as were their counterparts' activities in campaigns for personal morality, temperance, and sabbath observance two or three generations ago. How or whether one worships and what life style one follows tend increasingly to be matters of personal choice, but how one acts with regard to public issues, such as discrimination and fair practices in employment and housing, comes under increasing public scrutiny. Thus, paradoxically, religion has become simultaneously more private and more involved with public issues.

The third type of question for inquiry concerns inter-relations of belief and practice on the one hand, and a number of social variables on the other, such as denomination, orthodoxy, ethnicity, region, size of community, social class, level and type of education, occupation, income, age, and sex. (See Section 2 and Crysdale 1965; Stark and Glock 1968.) Thus, belief among Roman Catholics is usually stronger and participation greater for those who are middle-aged, of French origin, and living in Quebec, in towns and small places—regardless of education, income, or occupation. In contrast, among Protestants, regardless of occupation or level of education, belief is stronger and church attendance is higher for those who are past middle age, whose first language is not English, and who live in middle-sized towns and city suburbs (Institute for Behavioural Research, 1974; also Mol, this volume).

Broad differences in the beliefs of Roman Catholics and Protestants are also illustrated in responses to questions in the poll shown in Table 2.

Whereas 75 per cent of Roman Catholics believe in a personal God, the proportion falls to 52 per cent of Protestants and 41 per cent of members of other faiths. Protestants are more inclined to believe that "there is some kind of spirit or vital force in the world" (37 per cent) than are Roman Catholics (21 per cent) or members of other faiths (28 per cent).

The analysis of correlations between religion and other social characteristics has been the most common theme of studies by sociologists in Canada, the United States, and Europe, partly because this sort of question may be stated and investigated fairly simply and accurately by quantitative analysis. Progress in analysing other types of problems concerning the viability and functions of religion in modern society and variations in its interpretation and meaning require the development of more complicated research methods and more sophisticated theories than are currently in vogue.

Before proceeding, we are obliged to clarify the concept of religion, particularly as it is commonly thought of as a social institution. As we will make clear in Section 5, even the definition of religion is a problem, since various social scientists think of it differently. Our concern at this point is not to affirm dogmatically a single definition. In dealing with a realm of human experience which is at the same time personal, social, and cultural, variations are bound to occur. Variations also arise from the focus of a particular study, the perspective of the writer, the form of religion under investigation, and the cultural context (Fallding 1974). But some broad uniformities inhere in religion as it is commonly experienced and as it is usually described and analysed by social scientists (Dobbelaere and Lauwers 1973).

First, religion deals with a sphere of reality which includes but usually extends beyond the present and the tangible (O'Dea 1966). It may or may not have explicit ethical implications for behaviour in the present world: the great historical religions have important consequences for the mundane life, and while some cults and sects affirm the world, others deny present realities and advocate the greatest possible withdrawal from the world. In any case, religions usually emerge and make claims on the sensibilities and judgments of people at the threshold between the natural order of things and that which lies beyond. It is precisely because they believe that ultimate reality is shrouded in impenetrable mystery, which yields only fragments of truth to human intelligibility (and then as often to the approach of faith as to the approach of reason), that many believers think of themselves as religious. Religion, then, tends to deal with the supranatural; that is, it may include this-worldly concerns but it reaches beyond them to a higher order of existence, to spiritual being. In some systems, such as Christianity, Judaism, and Mohammedanism, reference is chiefly to a transcendent God external to human beings, and in others, such as Hinduism and Confucianism, reference is chiefly to an immanent God internal to man and the natural order.

The dualism discussed above, which is inherent in historical religions, leads some recent thinkers to define religion as that system of belief and practice which expresses man's concern with ultimate reality (Tillich 1951: 211 ff.; Glock 1965: Ch. 1; Bellah 1970: Ch. 2). Other writers go further and include under "religion" secular belief systems such as ethical humanism and Maoism. There may be good cultural reasons for thus extending the term, but the disadvantage in doing so is that a broadly inclusive concept hinders the distinction of social structures and behaviour which may be described as "sacred" from those which are "secular". Secular political belief systems may have "religion-like" attributes which serve to legitimate their authority, such as the reverence accorded in the U.S.S.R. to Lenin and his writings and the elite status awarded to party members as "true believers" (McDowell 1974). Also, some aspects of "civil religion" in the United States (Bellah 1967), including deference to the flag, to national heroes, and to the office of the president, have in the past assumed religion-like significance. To some extent the Watergate affair has led to the "desacralization" of the presidency, and evidence of illegal and self-serving activities on the part of the CIA and the FBI have shaken the legitimacy of civil religion in the United States. In any event, national rituals and myths usually stop short of paying allegiance to supranatural authority, as the constitutional documents of both the U.S.S.R. and the U.S.A. make quite clear.

The second widely acknowledged attribute of religion is that its validation is supra-empirical; that is, it is not restricted to events, objects, or social realities which can be observed by the senses. Indeed, according to Emile Durkheim (1915) and many anthropologists (Geertz 1966), religion deals specifically with the sacred as against the profane aspects of existence and must be validated on its own terms, within the context of the sacred. Like secular belief systems, religion asserts its own truth and denies that its creed can be subject to tests that spring from other belief systems, including political and scientific dogmas.

The third central attribute of religion for the purpose of clarifying its definition is that it is intrinsically social. Although this view is not usually contested by social scientists, it is sometimes not given sufficient recognition in explaining idiosyncratic religious behaviour. There is no question that religious experience is highly personal, but all social and cultural behaviour originates within a given context, whether it conforms to or deviates from commonly approved patterns. Obviously, there are wide variations among individuals in their "religiosity" or commitment. Glock and Stark (1965) have measured five dimensions of religiosity in which individuals may differ: degree of participation, level of orthodoxy, intensity of experience or feeling, depth of knowledge, and capacity for translating belief into practice. But while religion is usually, if not essentially, individual, it is also inevitably social. The observation of experiences that are repetitive and common to many persons in varying settings and through succeeding generations leads to generalizations which may be tested and modified, validated, or rejected.

In the development of patterns of thought and action which have broad application and transcend space and time, religions become social institutions. We do not mean by this simply that they are large, formal organizations. A social institution is an approved, accustomed, and enforceable way of dealing with a particular network of basic needs which are broadly accepted as essential for the survival of a society. Examples are politics, which deals with the generation and distribution of power; the economy, which provides goods and services and allocates rewards; science, which develops the knowledge and technology for the management of the environment; and marriage, which replenishes and socializes the population.

As a social institution religion permits people to cope with and to make sense of the inescapable limits of their existence. There are three principal limits or "breaking points": man's eventual *powerlessness* in the face of relentless historical and natural forces, in particular, suffering and death; his *contingency* or uncertainty concerning outcomes which vary from small matters such as moods or feelings to calamities such as famines, plagues, depressions, and wars; and the chronic *scarcity* of material and spiritual resources which thwarts the fulfilment not only of his basic needs for survival such as food and shelter but also of his need for emotional, psychological, and spiritual development and completeness (O'Dea 1966: 4–7). Because these three limits are universal they confront all people in every era with profound questions concerning the meaning of existence.

Social institutions not only express approved ways of dealing with basic needs, but do so with a vigour and thoroughness approaching coercion. Depending on the degree of cultural homogeneity and the extent of the perceived threat to those in power, institutions exert influence either as total authority or as moral suasion. To achieve their ends, both expressively and instrumentally, religions devise subsystems which guide followers in worship, belief, and social relations (Wach 1944).

The first subsystem, worship, provides cultic or ritual occasions when believers may enter into communion with God as the active object of faith. Normally, these are corporate or public occasions in which faith is mutually reinforced, elaborated, and applied. Here religion is expressed and renewed in its root or primal form. The second subsystem, belief, involves the theoretical articulation and application of faith, led by acknowledged experts and subject to the approval of followers to a degree consistent with the historical structure of each religion. The third subsystem, social relations, organizes members with respect to their relations both with each other and with the outside world. Some religions are governed democratically and others by an elitist hierarchy. Some religions have ordained priests or ministers; others have not. Some seek to convert the world, while others accept, reject, or ignore it. In practice, of course, the structures and functions of each of these three subsystems—worship, belief, and social relations—intertwine.

A brief comment on their distinctive emphases will help to clarify the ways in which major social science disciplines analyse religion. Sociologists focus on social systems or specific forms of interaction among individuals and collectivities (Rocher 1972). Political scientists study the distribution of power among social groups and the various means by which power is legitimated (Van Loon and Whittington 1971). Anthropologists emphasize culture, which consists of the transmitted and created techniques, patterns of ideas, values, and other symbolized sets of meanings which shape human activity (Kroeber and Parsons 1958). Psychologists concentrate on individual behaviour and psycho-physiological processes. But all these disciplines attempt to analyse human phenomena. While the specialized approach of each yields knowledge which has vastly enlarged our understanding of religious and other behaviour, we must always remember that scientific knowledge is partial and cannot fully explain human action. It has advantages and limitations in common with the humanities, including history, philosophy, the arts, and theology. When all of these disciplines complement one another, their capacity to explain behaviour is much enhanced. Unfortunately, at present this co-operation is rare and consequently most studies of religion explicate but do not explain behaviour.

2. Theoretical Perspectives

Throughout their development the social sciences have regarded the topic of religion from a variety of theoretical perspectives.[1] These perspectives need not be mutually exclusive; some of the foremost students of religion, such as Max Weber, have synthesized two or more approaches.[2] But each one represents an orientation that is broadly identifiable and engenders a more or less distinctive method of analysis.

(a) The Evolutionary Perspective

Although the idea of an evolution of religious beliefs had been advanced by David Hume in the mid-eighteenth century, it was not until the following century that the evolutionary perspective fully emerged in the social sciences. Despite wide variations in doctrine, generally the nineteenth-century evolutionists agreed that social change is gradual, progressive, and unilinear, that societies can be ranked on a scale of development, with the European ones being the most advanced, and that all societies go through the same stages of development (Demerath and Hammond 1969: 111). Given these assumptions and the corollary that contemporary institutions had originated in primitive societies, the early evolutionists concluded that the essential features of modern societies could be discovered by studying the technologically less developed primitive ones.

The first sociologist to advance an evolutionary perspective in studying religion was August Comte (1798–1857). In his view, the history of humanity involves three stages. The first is the theological stage, in which military and hierarchical social organizations dominate and are coupled with an interpretation of reality characterized by mythical superstition and prejudice. The second is the metaphysical stage, in which democratic and egalitarian social organizations prevail and individuals understand the world by using rational and abstract categories without being able to support their ideas empirically. The third is the positive stage, in which society is ruled by sociologically educated experts and traditional assumptions are replaced by factual knowledge and scientific modes of understanding (Comte 1830–42; O'Dea 1966: 43; Yinger 1970: 95; Scharf 1971: 13–14). Following Comte, a number of nineteenth-century anthropologists used the evolutionary perspective in their search for the origins of religion. Sir Edward Tylor (1871), who defined religion as "belief in spiritual beings", attempted to show that primitive fantasies about the movement of the individual soul in sleep and in death had evolved into complex belief systems. In Tylor's view, religious development went from animism through polytheism to monotheism, with each successive stage indicating mankind's ability to construct more rational explanations (Bellah 1970: 5).

Within the same tradition, Sir James Frazer (1890) conceived of three stages of religious development—magic, religion, and science. According to Frazer, each stage was a rational attempt to deal with the human condition, but magic and religion were inadequate because of faulty logic and insufficient empirical study (Yinger 1970: 72).

Herbert Spencer (1897) advanced a theory of social evolution in which the structure of societies gradually and progressively became differentiated, and religious institutions became separated from political and economic ones. Spencer also claimed that human consciousness underwent a similar process as religious thought became narrowed within a specific institution and scientific reasoning dominated society as a whole (Birnbaum and Lenzer 1969: 7–8).

Critics of nineteenth-century evolutionism argue that this perspective is oversimplified because it posits distinct linear stages, and that it is inaccurate in its descriptions of primitive and modern religious systems. Many primitive societies tended towards monotheism in that they believed in a great or supreme God in addition to numerous spirits or lesser gods. Further, the religious systems of primitive peoples were both more complex and more varied than the evolutionists had believed.

Another criticism focuses on the assumption that there are separate or distinct stages in religious evolution. O'Dea (1966: 43) comments that the "stages" often overlap and are frequently found together in human experience. The persistence of magical and religious beliefs in modern societies supports this contention.

In recent years, the idea of religious evolution has been re-examined. Robert Bellah (1970: 16) states that the focus of analysis should be the religious symbol system. The main line of development here is from compact to differentiated symbolism, with an increasing differentiation between art, science, and other cultural systems on the one hand, and

religious symbolism on the other. These more differentiated symbol systems make demand greater for individual decision and commitment, and
thus heighten religious individualism. Critics of Bellah maintain that the
differentiation of symbolic systems and institutions is itself a transitional
phase resulting from increased intercultural contact, the growing world
population, the emergence of capitalism and socialism, and the rapid
industrialization of the past two centuries.

(b) *The Historical Perspective*

A second theoretical perspective is the historical approach.[3] Nottingham
(1971: 296–7) comments that at the turn of the twentieth century the
German school of historical sociologists used the data of history in a
much more disciplined way than had the evolutionists, by confining their
efforts to testing limited hypotheses concerning religion's role in specific
periods. Max Weber (1864–1920) is the classic exponent of the historical perspective. One of Weber's major contributions was his convic-
tion that the social sciences differed fundamentally from the natural
sciences in that no single historical interpretation can claim to be universal. Weber was primarily concerned with studying the character and
development of European society, and for this purpose he analysed religion as one of its most significant factors.

The principal method by which Weber analysed historical action was
in the application of the concept of ideal types. In this manner he distinguished between exemplary and ethical prophecy; between traditional,
charismatic, and rational-legal religious authority; between church and
sect forms of religious organization; and between mystical and ascetic
theological emphases. Much of Weber's analysis consisted of comparing
a broad range of historical data in terms of the interrelations among these
ideal types.

The merits of the historical approach as advanced by Weber have
been widely debated. Some scholars have charged that his work is full of
historical inaccuracies (Tawney 1926; Samuelsson 1964) and does not
produce sufficient evidence to support its contentions (Robertson 1969:
295). More specifically, Bonhoeffer has argued that Weber's historical
approach is too narrow in examining "almost only religious history in its
general historical or political economic aspects" (quoted in Vrijhof 1967:
31). Samuelsson (1964: 149–50) has attacked Weber for vagueness in
his application of ideal type concepts. They were much too complex and,

at the same time, were narrowly applied by the selection of a single factor for correlation with a vast array of factors in modern civilization.

But in spite of criticisms of Weber's particular mode of historical analysis, this approach remains an important one.[4] Some scholars have continued to address the specific problems which Weber emphasized (Green 1959; Eisenstadt 1968), whereas others have utilized the concepts and methods of the social sciences to focus upon other issues ranging from the social location of Israelite prophecy (Berger 1963) to the role of the Roman Catholic church in French-Canadian society from the founding of New France to the contemporary period (Falardeau 1964).

(c) *The Typological Perspective*

Closely intermingled with the historical approach in origins and application, the typological perspective has become "something of a sociological obsession" (Robertson 1969: 359). In this perspective attempts are made to apply ideal types to patterns of religious organization.

The most influential typological study after Weber was Ernst Troeltsch's *The Social Teaching of the Christian Churches* (1911), which analyses religion in Christian societies during the period between the death of Christ and the modern industrial era. Troeltsch distinguishes three types of religious organization: the church, the sect, and mysticism. The church is universalistic; members are generally born into it. There is an approved theological creed, a professional order of priests or ministers, a formal organization, and a type of worship which tends to be firmly ordered. Churches recognize and often co-operate with other social institutions. The sect is a group whose members make a voluntary decision to join after undergoing conversion. There is usually no formal creed, no professional ministry, little in the way of organization, but there is an intricate pattern of primary relations among members. They may accept, reject, or ignore "the world". Mysticism stresses individual striving for a direct experience of God's presence, purifying the believer both from personal sin and from contamination by material and physical concerns.

Each of these forms of religious organization tends to attract followers from different social classes. According to Troeltsch, the church draws its members from all classes, the sect appeals essentially to the working and lower classes, and mysticism attracts persons from the leisure class.

Troeltsch's typology has inspired considerable work both in the form of specific applications (Niebuhr 1929; Pope 1942; Clark 1948) and in attempts to develop more refined categories (Becker 1932; Mann 1955; Johnson 1963; Wilson 1963; Gustafson 1967; Yinger 1970).

A renowned application is Niebuhr's *The Social Sources of Denominationalism* (1929), an American study which concludes that sectarian religion is always transient and thus sects either die or become churches. This work has been criticized on two grounds: not all groups follow either of Niebuhr's alternatives (Wilson 1967); and some groups are denominational from the outset (Martin 1962).

Yinger (1970: 257–80), elaborating the typological approach, has identified the following types of religious organizations: the universal institutionalized church, the universal diffused church, the ecclesia, the denomination or class church, the established sect, acceptance sects, aggressive sects, avoidance sects, and cults. With respect to sects, Wilson (1963) has distinguished six types: conversionist, revolutionary, introversionist, thaumaturgical, reformist, and utopian. Finally, Ellwood (1973: 13–36) has discussed uniformities and variations among cultic groups.

The typological approach in recent years has come under increasing attack. Yinger (1970: 252) argues that it fails the test of empirical adequacy by not being able to account for the full range of data, that it does not discuss the conditions under which various types of religious organization are most likely to occur, and that it is limited to Christian organizations. Johnson (1957, 1963) points out that the typology is limited in that it is applicable only where sectarian movements, by the fact of there being an established religion, must have a protest character. Eisler (1967: 87) argues that the typological approach "in effect, is an open invitation, if not a demand for subjective, value-laden definitions" and that this is scientifically unacceptable.

Dittes (1971: 375) points out that all typologies contain "a heavy contraband of value judgment that simply will not be sloughed off" and that they suffer from "a formal untidiness—multiple defining categories, carelessly agglutinated, shifting from one discussion to another, not integrated with each other conceptually and manifestly not correlated empirically". Snook (1974: 191–204) says that this perspective lacks cross-cultural applicability and fails to treat religious institutions as multi-dimensional phenomena. Snook then proposes as an alternative the hypothesis "that religious institutions organize religious experience into structures of authority which can be analyzed along four dimensions—symbolism, structure, intensity, and pervasiveness."[5] Despite these criticisms, the typological perspective is still widely used.

(d) The Comparative Perspective

In *The Rules of Sociological Method* Emile Durkheim (1964: 139) wrote that "comparative sociology is not a particular branch of sociology; it is sociology itself." Since then, the main thrust of this perspective has involved the analysis of specific social institutions, with emphasis on the significance of religion for economic organization and social change.[6] Here the most notable figure again is Max Weber, whose best-known book is *The Protestant Ethic and the Spirit of Capitalism* (1904–5). In attempting to understand the influence of Calvinist ethics on the evolution of Western, capitalistic rationalism, he conducted massive inquiries into the religious ethics of other societies (Fischoff 1964: xiii). Weber maintained that ancient Palestine, China, and India had economic bases similar to precapitalist Europe but did not develop that variety of capitalism which maximized rational efficiency in the organization of economic production in a market economy (Parsons 1964: lx). He argued that this mode of capitalism did not emerge elsewhere, in spite of many favourable conditions, because other religious systems did not generate the anxious, thrifty entrepreneur or the intense economic activity which Calvinism fostered. For example, in India, Hinduism supported a caste system which militated against economic change. In China, "nothing conflicted more with the Confucian ideal of gentility than the idea of a 'vocation' " (Weber 1951: 247). "Only in the Occident, particularly where inner-worldly asceticism produced a specific personality type, were sufficient conditions present" (Gerth and Mills 1967: 61).

Much of the comparative analysis in the sociology of religion has followed the Weberian tradition (Eisenstadt 1968). Bellah (1957), for example, studied the religion of Japan, the only Oriental nation that by the beginning of the twentieth century had developed a system of modern capitalism, and found the existence of a religious ethic somewhat similar to the Protestant Ethic in the period just before industrialization.

The comparative approach has been subjected to a number of criticisms. Perhaps its greatest weakness is a tendency to compare what may be incomparable. Sometimes its advocates assume that differences in space and time between societies do not significantly affect the variables which are compared. Or they assume that differences in the subjective meanings of institutions or relationships are unimportant. There is also a tendency towards ethnocentrism, which obscures the need to understand each culture on its own terms.

(e) *Functional Perspectives*

The prevalent perspectives in the social scientific study of religion today are functional ones. They focus on the relation between religion and other principal social institutions, and on the role religion plays in integrating and maintaining the social system as a whole. On another level of analysis, functional theory investigates how religion identifies the individual with a group, supports him in time of crisis, provides elements of identity, and offers the means for overcoming guilt and alienation (O'Dea 1966: 16).

Emile Durkheim (1859–1917) is widely acknowledged as the founder of functionalism in sociological inquiry. Although his study *The Elementary Forms of the Religious Life* (1915) reflects the evolutionary tradition, Durkheim's central contribution lies in demonstrating that, at least in some primitive societies, religion provides cohesion for society. Individuals find in religion the chief way of reaffirming their commitment to moral bonds (Demerath and Hammond 1969: 200). Unlike earlier evolutionary theorists, Durkheim thought that religion emerges from human interaction. In his view, belief in God springs from the exigencies of man's quest for solidarity in society. Ultimately, he states, the act of worship entails the worship of society.[7]

After Durkheim, the functional approach branched into three principal, though interconnected, streams (Rocher 1972: 279). The first of these, *absolute functionalism*, holds that in all civilizations every custom, material object, idea, and belief performs some vital function, accomplishes a task, and contributes to the maintenance of the society as a whole (Malinowski 1931). The second stream is *relative functionalism*, as advanced by Robert K. Merton (1949). This position maintains that, rather than attempting to analyse the contributions to the whole made by cultural or social elements, inquiry should focus on their observable consequences. To this end, Merton advances four new functional concepts: functional alternatives (or equivalents), dysfunctions, manifest functions, and latent functions (Merton 1949; Rocher 1972). The third stream is *structural functionalism*. The starting point here is the society which is perceived both abstractly and totally. Structural functional analysis attempts to answer the question "What essential functions must be fulfilled in order that a society may exist and perpetuate itself?" (Rocher 1972: 280–1). The Parsonian model which posits four basic systemic problems—latency (pattern maintenance), goal attainment, adaptation, and integration—falls into this category (Parsons 1937).

In the sociology of religion, attempts have been made to apply all three functional streams. Malinowski was the chief advocate of the absolutist approach. Nottingham (1954) and O'Dea (1966) adopted relative functionalism to explain the relations between religion and society. And, more recently, Schneider (1970) has attempted to offer a comprehensive structural-functional analysis.

The debate over the merits of the functional perspectives has been sharp, longstanding, and voluminous. The absolutist position of Malinowski has been criticized by Merton (1957: Ch.1) for being based on three questionable postulates: the unity of society, universal functionalism, and indispensability. But Merton's own concepts of functional alternatives and dysfunctions can also be taken to task, the former because of the difficulty of specification in an empirical investigation, and the latter as "a camouflage for implicit value judgements on the part of the observer" (Rocher 1972: 280). Structural functionalism can be criticized for its high level of abstraction, which tends to defy empirical investigation; for its negation of the scientific principle of refutability; and, in its Parsonian form, for its use of only a simple systemic model which relies too heavily on concepts such as equilibrium and homeostasis (Buckley 1967).

Other criticisms of the ways in which functional perspectives are generally applied are directed against tendencies (1) to be ahistorical, (2) to assume that all existing social systems either are well integrated or move towards equilibrium in the long run, (3) to understate the importance of physical coercion and psychological manipulation as integrative mechanisms, (4) to equate the existing order with the best interests of all groups and classes, (5) to de-emphasize the conflict-generating and prophetic aspects of religion, (6) to take for granted that religion or "secular equivalents" are necessary for both individuals and societies, and (7) to suppose that religion performs the same social and psychological functions cross-culturally and in different historical periods.[8]

(f) *Psychoanalytic and Psychological Perspectives*

According to the functional perspective, religion not only integrates society as a whole but serves as a means by which the individual can cope psychologically with fundamental life crises. A radically different analysis of the psychodynamics and social implications of religious experience and expression has been provided by the orthodox Freudian perspective. Freud's first systematic treatise on religion was *Totem and Taboo* (1913), an attempt to explain the origins of religion using nineteenth-century anthropological data. From his work as an analyst, Freud was drawn to religion because of similarities he observed between the reactions of his phobic patients towards the objects they feared and the reported responses of Australian aborigines towards the totemic symbol. Consequently, he concluded that the origins of religion could be explained by the Oedipal drama which religion symbolically expresses, and that all religion essentially is a projection of the child's relationship with his father.

After *Totem and Taboo*, Freud refined and applied his theories concerning religion in two works: *The Future of an Illusion* (1927) and *Moses and Monotheism* (1939). In the former, he shifted focus somewhat from concern with the origins of religion and concentrated on the question "What are the roots of religious sentiments in man and what determines the form such sentiments take?" (Demerath and Hammond 1969: 22). Freud (1928: 30) maintained that the presence in the individual of frustration is the key to the origin of religious sentiments: "The gods retain their threefold task: they must exorcise the terrors of nature, they must reconcile one to the cruelty of fate, particularly as shown in death, and they must make amends for the sufferings and privations that the communal life of culture has imposed on man."

In Freud's view, religious sentiments take the form they do because of similarities between the frustrations encountered by the individual in later life and the familial frustrations experienced in childhood. On the basis of these similarities, Freudian psychiatrists hypothesize that many persons resort to parallel coping mechanisms. According to Fromm (1967: 11–12), "Man copes with threatening forces in the same manner in which he learned to cope with his insecurity in childhood, by relying on, admiring and fearing his father. . . . Thus religion . . . is a repetition of the experience of the child." Since all individuals experience the same kinds of frustration, many psychiatrists infer that religion becomes a shared illusion and a universal obsessional neurosis.

Freud's theories have been attacked because of the limitations of their evolutionary assumptions and the fallacy of psychological reductionism (Eliade 1969: 14–15). In addition, they have been criticized because the anthropological data on which *Totem and Taboo* is based are not reliable (Schmidt 1935) and subsequent research has indicated that the Oedipal drama is not universal (Malinowski 1955). Another criticism holds that Freud's concept of culture is inadequate, for culture is not alien to man but inherent, and often has liberating as well as repressive effects. Yinger (1970: 182) says that "Culture creates and expresses needs; it does not simply repress 'nature'. Group life is also natural, and the manifestations of culture and society in the personality cannot adequately be described as intrusions from outside."

Further, some scholars charge that Freud's theories are too general and do not account for variations among belief systems. Scharf (1971: 91) asks why the balance between male and female deities may differ from one society to another and "why some gods are personal and transcendent, while others are more impersonal and immanent." A final criticism is that Freud generalized about all religions from the limited clinical evidence gathered from his own patients, chiefly wealthy Viennese women.

Of psychologists who studied religion early in this century, William James has had the most lasting influence.[9] Like Freud, James viewed religion as a highly individual, rather than a social, phenomenon, and posited a close relation between neurotic behaviour and some forms of religiosity. However, unlike Freud, James did not feel that all religion is undesirable, and he distinguished between two types of religious experience: that of the "sick soul" and that of the "healthy minded". Further, he was not particularly interested in the origins and processes of religion. For James, the pragmatic philosopher, the ultimate justification of religion lies in its results: whatever the genesis of a religious impulse, if the consequent activities are beneficial to the individual or to society the religion is justified (Clark 1958: 8).

In his classic work *The Varieties of Religious Experience* (1902) James deliberately analysed experiences which would be considered pathological by conventional standards. He believed that through the examination of exceptional mental states one can best understand the meaning of religious feeling. James did not indulge in psychological reductionism, that is, the explanation of religion as constituting merely the expression of an organic or psychological pathology, but, rather, based his approach on radical empiricism. Johnson (1959: 29) points out that James was convinced that nothing is as important as concrete experience. In religion the most vital concerns are ultrarational and are settled not by abstract reasoning but by living experience. James's main thesis is that, although some manifestations of it may be absurd, religion is man's most important function: "The facts of religious experience are not secondary but primary evidence in their own right, and these he will respect for their testimony of invisible realities which they reveal" (Johnson 1959: 29).

James's work on religion has been criticized on a number of grounds: for being more literary and philosophical than psychological, for being vague in many key concepts, for selecting only the more extreme cases for analysis, and for relying on some central assumptions and conclusions of questionable status (Clark 1958: 8–9; Yinger 1970: 144).

A third seminal influence in the psychology of religion has been the work of Carl Jung (1933, 1956, 1958). Although originally a student and associate of Freud, he disagreed with his mentor on many fundamental questions, including the issue of religion. Unlike Freud, who believed that religion is rooted in frustration and that religious behaviour is neurotic, Jung held that all religions are rooted in the collective unconscious of the human race and that religion is an essential human activity. Therefore he concluded that, instead of seeking to explain away religion, psychology should attempt to explain how man reacts to situations which are described as religious (Spinks 1965: 101).

Jung, however, does agree with Freud and James that religion is a product of human experience and that theological concepts, such as God, are formulated from this experience. On the other hand, his concepts of the collective unconscious and of archetypal symbols operating within the unconscious show that his analysis is not as individualistic as Freud's or James's. For Jung, religion arises from the universal unconscious energy of the human race, a source which transcends and yet envelops the individual unconscious. Religious archetypes are universal symbols because they have emerged from the basic conditions of human existence, conditions which are shared by all people everywhere.

Theologians have argued that Jung confuses psychical facts with spiritual realities (Johnson 1959: 13). Some psychologists hold that his approach is more intuitive and mystical than scientific, while others state that he "reduces religion to a psychological phenomenon and at the same time elevates the unconscious to a religious phenomenon" (Fromm 1967: 20).[10]

In recent decades much of the theoretical development of the psychology of religion has been in the form of footnotes to the work of Freud, James, and, to a lesser extent, Jung. There has been, however, a proliferation of empirical research, notably in the United States. One thrust has been to trace relationships between indicators of religiosity and other personality traits. For example, a number of psychologists (e.g. Allport 1960, 1966; Rokeach 1960) report that individuals exhibiting the highest degree of traditional or orthodox religiosity tend also to be the most closed-minded, dogmatic, and prejudiced.[11]

A second concern has been the exploration of linkages among individual religious characteristics, other personality traits, and sociocultural categories. Fromm (1941), for example, found a persistent relation between the Protestant Ethic, the anal character (with its emphasis on obstinacy, orderliness, and parsimony), and attachment to the capitalist system.

A third emphasis in research among psychoanalysts and psychologists has been a serious questioning of the orthodox Freudian notion that religion is an illusion. Brown (1970: 231) writes that the relation between psychoanalysis and religion is not a simple polarity of science and wishful thinking. Rather, the hidden reality which is the central theme in religion is the same as that with which psychoanalysis deals, namely, the unconscious. "Psychoanalysis and religion represent phases in the return of the repressed to human consciousness. Psychoanalysis may claim that it represents a full return of the repressed, and religion only a partial and distorted return. . . . But this superior wisdom does not authorize psychoanalysis to dismiss religion as neurotic."

Among psychoanalysts, Viktor Frankl has developed a therapeutic doctrine, logotherapy, or existential analysis, which goes further and provides a psychoanalytic rationale for religion. According to Frankl (1963: 144, 154, 210), "Man's search for meaning is a primary force and not a rationalization of instinctual drives. . . . Of course, there may be some cases in which an individual's concern with values is really a camouflage of hidden inner conflicts; but, if so, they represent the exceptions from the rule. As soon as we have interpreted religion as being merely a product of psycho-dynamics, in the sense of unconscious motivating forces, we have missed the point and lost sight of the authentic phenomenon."

(g)   *The Marxist Perspective*

Whereas in many other fields of social scientific inquiry the Marxist perspective has been influential, in the study of religion it has been largely ignored or distorted. Like the orthodox Freudian position, Marxism holds that religion is both an illusion and an instrument of repression. For Marx and Engels, in a class society religious belief reinforces the existing inegalitarian economic and social order by encouraging submissiveness with the promise of life after death. Religion thereby prevents the subordinate classes from becoming aware of their relationship to the means of production and from engaging in revolutionary praxis. Marx and Engels (1964: 41–2, 71, 134) wrote: "The religious world is the reflex of the real world [and] religious sentiment is a social product. . . . The abolition of religion as the illusory happiness of the people is required for their real happiness. . . . Religion is the sigh of the oppressed creature, the heart of a heartless world, just as it is the spirit of a spiritless situation. It is the opium of the people."

Yet Marx and Engels maintained that religion, by its emphasis on rewards in an afterlife, contains an implicit criticism of existing society. Further, Engels argued that in certain historical situations, such as the German Peasants' War, religion can encourage class conflict and social transformation.

Nevertheless, as Bellah (1970: 247–8) points out, Marx and Engels' analysis contains elements both of consequential reductionism, that is, the explanation of religion in terms of its functional consequences, and of symbolic reductionism, or the view that religion conceals a hidden reality which the social scientist can discover beneath the overlay of myths and rituals.[12]

Another deficiency in the Marxist perspective is its failure to account satisfactorily for the religious faith of the ruling classes. Scharf (1971: 83–4) observes that Marx and Engels attempted to deal with this problem partly by charging that the ruling classes were hypocritical and practised religion only to persuade the masses to do the same and thus perpetuate their docility. Yet at times they also implied that the ruling classes could be alienated and that in trying to maintain their privileged position they mistakenly came to rely on religious justifications.

(h)   *Non-Marxist Conflict Perspectives*

Given the widespread discord of the contemporary world and the undeniable presence of serious and deepening contradictions in modern and modernizing societies, it is not surprising that the postulate that stability, order, and integration are the prevailing characteristics of nation states is now untenable. This recognition of the ubiquity of social conflict coupled with the growing influence of Marxist and neo-Marxist thought throughout the world has led a number of liberal social scientists who reject some of the tenets of Marxist analysis to construct alternative conflict theories.

Non-Marxist conflict perspectives are rooted largely in the work of Weber and Simmel and earlier in the ideas of Hobbes, Hegel, and other philosophers of the dialectic. At some points there is a convergence between non-Marxist and Marxist thinkers concerning conflict and social change. For example, the notion that conflict with the surrounding social milieu can lead to increased group cohesion (Coser 1964) bears considerable resemblance to Marx's analysis of the conditions which facilitate the development of class consciousness and solidarity.

Incisive studies of religion based on non-Marxist conflict perspectives appeared in the United States in the first decade of this century in the writings of the social gospel movement and later in response to the Depression and the Second World War (Niebuhr 1932, 1955; Pope 1942; May 1949). Recently there has been a renewal of interest in this approach, reflecting the realization among more Americans that they can no longer take their society for granted. Examples are the work of Raab (1964), Hammond and Mitchell (1965), and Hadden (1969).

In Canada the literature also mirrors an ebb and flow of interest in conflict analysis. The earlier endeavours of those involved in the social gospel as it gained new strength during the upheaval of large-scale immigration and the Great Depression is represented by Bland (1920) and by Scott and Vlastos (1936). More recently the theme of conflict has been prominent in the writings of Clark (1948), Crysdale (1961, this volume), and Allen (1973).

Among the more salient non-Marxist conflict theorists is Ralf Dahrendorf (1959). He contends that social structures change chiefly because of conflict between groups on the basis of interest and authority, which determine the distribution of power. Society must be visualized in terms of coercion exercised by the powerful over the weak; instability and change underlie all aspects of human relations; and constraints or efforts to resolve conflict lead to the definition of positions, then to unity and coherence. Social classes are differentiated around the concept of authority, which legitimates the use of force, the dominant class possessing or controlling authority and the subjugated classes seeking it. Conflict, then, is not only inherent in human relations; it is essential for creativity, innovation, and adaptation or fundamental change.

Another conflict theorist, Lewis Coser (1964), draws on the pioneering work of Simmel (1908) to argue that conflict within a group may help to strengthen unity. Whether conflict helps in adaptation depends on the type of issue at stake and the type of structure within which conflict occurs. When conflict does not threaten the basic assumptions, values, and beliefs of the group, it may reinforce the adaptation of norms and power relations. But when conflict touches the deep, crucial values and beliefs of the group, it may disrupt the structure. A safeguard against disruption exists in structural systems which institutionalize and tolerate conflict, such as representative government and democratically governed religious bodies.

Simmel's and Coser's theories may help to explain the different ways churches and sects develop and diminish. Because small, closely knit sectarian groups demand a high frequency of interaction and stress personal involvement, they often suppress conflict until it finally erupts and leads to schism. However, churches, which are more loosely knit, constantly experience conflicts along various lines and, being accustomed to compromise, are able to survive most controversies. In both types of organization, conflict with external elements or forces usually strengthens internal cohesion.

Non-Marxist conflict theories can be criticized on two grounds. First, many non-Marxist theorists frequently criticize Marx for points he didn't make. For example, the idea that the ownership of the means of production and the ensuing production relations determine all other social structures and processes is specifically rejected by Marx's writings on aesthetics and Engel's work on religion. Second, some non-Marxists ignore the entire neo-Marxist tradition (cf. B. Brown 1973). It is an easy task to point out where some of Karl Marx's predictions about the demise of capitalism have erred; it is a more formidable undertaking to dismiss so easily the writings of neo-Marxists such as Wilhelm Reich, Herbert Marcuse, Jürgen Habermas, and Ralph Miliband.

(i) *The Phenomenological Perspective*

In his writings on method Max Weber took a phenomenological approach by regarding the individual as the basic unit of sociological analysis, "the upper limit and sole carrier of meaningful conduct"

(Gerth and Mills 1967: 55). Further, he maintained that behaviour is motivated in the sense that each actor associates a subjective meaning with every act. Given these assumptions, the central task for the social scientist becomes the discovery of the subjective meaning of social action.[13]

Critics of Weber have pointed out his failure to apply this interpretive or phenomenological mode of analysis in his own work and to rely instead on structural explanations "which attempt to account for the motivation of systems of action by their functions as going concerns rather than by the subjective intentions of individuals who act them out" (Gerth and Mills 1967: 57).[14]

An authoritative phenomenologist of religion was van der Leeuw (1890–1950). In his classic work *Religion in Essence and Manifestation* (1933), he set out the following tasks for this perspective. First, the phenomenology of religion assigns names (or defines concepts), for example, sacrifice, prayer, saviour, or myth. In this way it appeals to appearances. Second, it introduces these appearances within its own life and experiences them systematically. Third, it withdraws and attempts to observe what appears, while suspending judgments or evaluations. Fourth, it endeavours to clarify and comprehend what has appeared. Finally, it confronts chaotic "reality", and its still uninterpreted signs, and testifies to what it has understood.

Another important representative of this approach was Rudolf Otto (1869–1937) who, in *The Idea of the Holy* (1917), investigated the non-rational aspects of power and authority in religious experience and their relation to the rational. More recently, Mircea Eliade (1952) writes of the universal search for meaning beyond apparent realities in everyday life which expresses itself in a wide variety of symbols and myths.

The phenomenological approach has been advanced at the theoretical level by Peter Berger and Thomas Luckmann (1966), who focus on the social construction of systems of meaning. Carlos Castaneda (1969) has demonstrated the application of this approach in an account and analysis of his apprenticeship into a different order of reality under the tutelage of a Yaqui Indian shaman.

The major criticism of the phenomenological approach is directed, not against its assertion that the sociologist should attempt to understand the subjective meaning of social action, but rather against the tendency among some practitioners to view this task as the only valid one. Frequently, they seem to forget that the social world of the individual is

influenced by other rules and action systems, specifically power relations and the instrumental action systems of science and technology
(Dreitzel 1970: xix). Another difficulty arises from the rejection or disregard of the possibility of "objective" meaning. Gerth and Mills (1967:
58) note that while Weber wished to restrict the understanding and
interpretation of meaning to the subjective intentions of the actor, in
his actual work he is very much aware of the fact that the results of interactions are not always identical with what the actor intended. For example, the Puritan wished to serve God, but he helped to bring about
modern capitalism.

(j) *Other Analytical Perspectives: Demographic, Sociologie Religieuse, and Ecological*

Three other perspectives used in the sociology of religion will be discussed briefly. The *demographic* approach employs census and survey
data to provide statistical descriptions of the size, composition, and
distribution of religious populations and changes in them through time.
While much of this data on religious groups is valuable, the approach
usually suffers from the absence of a theoretical framework.

Related to the demographic approach is *sociologie religieuse*, a socio-
graphic perspective. Its originator was Gabriel LeBras, a French Catholic who compiled religious statistics, concentrating on demographic
studies of religious observance (Brothers 1967: 13). In recent years
sociologie religieuse has broadened to include the typology and etiology
of religious facts (Poulat 1967: 156). Typical surveys are no longer
confined to the demographic characteristics of those present at church
on a particular Sunday, but examine other questions such as recruitment
to the priesthood and religious communities. This approach tends to be
overly programmatic, serving the administrative needs of churches rather
than asking more fundamental questions about the role and practice of
religion in changing times. However, church-sponsored research in the
United States, Europe, and Canada made important early contributions
to the development of empirical methods in the study of religion.[15]

A less frequently used perspective, the *ecological*, deals with the
distribution of people, activities, and institutions in relation to the environment (Moberg 1962: 27). This perspective has been applied for the
most part to the city, and is principally an outgrowth of the theory of
"natural areas" developed by Park and Burgess at the University of

Chicago, beginning in the 1920s. Park and Burgess maintain that the usual spatial pattern of cities in industrial societies is a series of concentric circles, each with distinctive characteristics, moving out from the hub into more affluent residential areas. The first circle, known as Zone I, consists of the central business district with its commercial and institutional buildings, good hotels, and entertainment centres. Zone II is a transitional area of deteriorating housing, old stores, and new high-rise buildings. Zone III includes lower-class residences, usually multiple units; Zone IV is an area of middle-class, single-family dwellings; and Zone V comprises suburban, upper-class residential areas (Burgess 1925).

In the ecological approach, the industrial city changes partly through the migration of unskilled persons who come from other cities, rural areas, and other countries. They enter the industrial system at the bottom and live in the central slum regions. As they become established they move upward occupationally and outward in the city toward more desirable residential areas, leaving their places in the slums to new arrivals. The principal characteristics of urban areas, however, are thought to remain virtually constant as these populations pass through them. In Zone II these characteristics include low income, poverty, low education, high crime rates, high morbidity and mortality rates, and heightened alienation. Some behavioural traits of people are influenced by experiences in these areas, but these may change when they leave. Because the characteristics remain with the area rather than with the group, it is said that they are ecologically determined (Faris 1944: 741).

The ecological perspective is open to a number of criticisms. In the first place, many of its original hypotheses were not substantiated (Dunham 1955). Some ethnic groups became firmly entrenched in an area and transformed the environment rather than being changed by it. Even in situations where hypotheses seemed at one time to be valid, the changing nature of the contemporary city has illustrated that the theory is historically specific (Weinberg 1967). Examples here are the "renewal" of residential communities in the downtown core, the transplanting of low-income people to the outer suburbs, and the establishment of dispersed urban nuclei in metropolitan areas, linked by rapid transit and expressways.

Finally, the etiology of this perspective is questionable. Early applications frequently failed to take into account geographical mobility and social class as explanatory factors. Further, this approach attempts to explain individual behaviour by relying solely on data gathered at the structural level of analysis. For example, the participation of residents in a given area in worship and church activities may change, not because of social structures, such as age, ethnicity, education, or class, but because of socio-psychological factors, such as alienation or apprehension. The first may result in less participation, while the latter may lead to more participation.

In spite of their limitations, the demographic, *sociologie religieuse*, and ecological approaches, carefully applied and adequately informed by theory, have been helpful in understanding why the position and effectiveness of churches in modern societies, particularly in large cities, have changed.

3. The Present Situation: Theories and Methods of Research

(a) *Clusters of Theories*

In the preceding section we traced the history of theoretical perspectives which have been used in attempts to study religion scientifically. In these attempts the broad aim has been to develop theories that would describe, explain, and predict religion as a persistent, pervasive, and influential social phenomenon. But systematic, tested theories are remarkably sparse. We will discuss some reasons for this at greater length in the section on problems and issues. Meanwhile, we may note that research on religion has been relatively spasmodic. After the pioneering work of Marx, Durkheim, Weber, and Freud three and four generations ago, there was a period of inactivity which gave way to renewed interest only in the past three decades. Further, while there has been some continuity in theory-building, inquirers have often begun with different concepts and premises and used different methods (Merton 1957: Intro.; Kuhn 1962). Finally, no quest could be more complex than for man to look within himself in an effort to analyse the spiritual aspects of his being and to relate them to the more apparent, external conditions of his existence. In this quest the sociology of religion is closely tied with the sociology of knowledge—how we come to form ideas and develop knowledge in relation to the sociocultural environment (Curtis and Petras 1970).

In spite of the absence of broad, well-integrated, empirically validated theories of religion, generalizations growing out of sociological inquiries can be grouped into several clusters. What have been developed are largely theories of the middle range which, as Merton (1957: 5–6) noted, can be tested; which seek to explain behaviour, values, and beliefs in specific social contexts; and which, while not grandly inclusive, are needed for the development of minor working hypotheses in day-to-day routines of research. Limitations of space permit only a brief listing.[16]

Theories which form one cluster deal with the claim that religion has an independent impact on social behaviour in different social contexts (Weber 1963). For example, Driedger and Jacobs in this volume show that Mennonite youth in Canada have a stronger sense of ethnic identity than youth raised in other Germanic groups. And Whitehead learned that youth with religious affiliations are less likely to use drugs than non-affiliated youth. Mol, also in this volume, demonstrates that church attendance varies more with the type of religious belief and practice than it does with indicators of social class such as education, income, and education. Other researchers, however, following Marx, argue that religion does not have a direct, independent impact on behaviour, but, rather, it mediates the "false consciousness" sustained by inegalitarian social structures (Milner and Milner; Warburton, this volume).

A second cluster of middle-range theories has to do with the reasons for the influence of religion on social behaviour. Here two archetypal positions are in tension. One, following Durkheim and the functionalists, holds that religion persists as a powerful factor chiefly because it binds various segments of a society together in the face of strains arising from conflicts between individuals and groups, from external threats, and from the limitations of the human condition. In this view religion is the product of society's need for cohesion and solidarity. The opposing position is that religion may have independent effects on social behaviour and on history which under certain conditions may conserve and integrate a society but under other conditions may disrupt an existing order and help to bring about basic changes. Weber is the key theorist here, and a growing number of social scientists are preoccupied with the central question which concerned him—the search for meaning in an age of secularism, pluralism, and rational, bureaucratic organization. The article by Balikci in this volume is an example of the Durkheimian position. Crysdale's articles in this volume illustrate the Weberian view that under certain conditions religion may serve as an ideological base for challenging the existing order.

Theories which form a third cluster focus on religious organization, following Ernst Troeltsch's threefold typology: church, sect, and mystic or cultic structures. Troeltsch's findings, based on historical analysis in Europe, have, as we have seen, been widely applied and, recently, widely challenged. Wilson (1963, 1967) has shown that, depending on the social situation and their belief system, some sects aim at the transformation of society and thus are amenable to change into churches, while others may ignore or reject the surrounding society and tend either to sustain themselves in opposition or to disappear (Clark 1948; Mann 1955).

But distinctions between types of organization have been based chiefly on the somewhat ambiguous concept of "ideal types", and recent empirical work discloses the theoretical deficiencies of this concept as a basis for wide-ranging typologizing. For example, within some Roman Catholic parishes, especially in urban, middle-class areas and among well-educated members, sect-like behaviour has appeared in the charismatic movement (Harrison 1974). Also within many Protestant churches, at both the national and congregational levels, elements co-exist which represent differing forms of belief and action. Some stress liberal prophecy by aggressively attacking current social issues such as civil rights, fair housing and employment, peace, and environmental reform, while others accent personal pietism by seeking salvation and sanctification through individual repentance, conversion, prayer, and Bible study (Crysdale 1965; Quinley 1974). In this volume, articles by Kallen, Westhues, Moreux, Mann, and Kaill deal with adaptation to change in church-type organizations, while those by Bennett, Bird and Reimer, O'Toole, and Bibby and Brinkerhoff analyse adaptation within sects and cults.

Theories which emphasize the meaning of religion for believers constitute a fourth cluster. Here the unit of analysis is not the organization but individual experience, where the person's ideas evolve in interaction with others. Examples in this volume are the articles by Stryckman and Gaudet and by Sévigny. In this regard phenomenologists such as Berger, Otto, Buber (1958), and van der Leeuw have much to contribute. But, interestingly, so do sociologists who employ the functional approach, such as Luckmann, Glock, and Bellah, and anthropologists such as Levi-Strauss (1968) and Geertz (1966). While theories of this sort are not yet well formulated and are not clearly complementary to each other, the variety of perspectives being used may enhance their significance. One writer (Hodges 1974) has recently argued that assumptions about the supernatural may be usefully considered to be a cultural environmental factor and therefore a causal force in constructing theories, with the provision that these assumptions can be put in the form of postulates. Examples of the causal postulate are the contentions that (a) if people act consistently with beliefs about the supernatural they should develop positive conditioned emotional responses to religious symbols, behaviours, and groups, and (b) the clearer and more accurately a person identifies feedback to his or her religious actions, the more the person will continue with them.

Other evolving theories are located at lower levels of analysis. For example, some theories focus on the process of socialization, in which religious faith and behaviour are transmitted by believers and internalized as valid and binding by children, youth, and converts. Socialization is examined in the articles by Driedger and Peters, Currie, Whitehead, and Sévigny. Recent investigations show that, whereas social class may explain only a small portion of the variance in religious behaviour, socialization in childhood explains over half the variance in religious behaviour among adults and only slightly less among adolescents (McCready 1972; Greeley 1974: 229).

It is clear that theory-building in the sociology of religion draws heavily on generalizations developed in other social contexts. What Durkheim learned about the importance of collective sentiments and representations in maintaining the social cohesion of a society has basic implications for the analysis of religion. Implications also follow from Marx's stress on the social consequences of the control of the means of production for freedom and alienation, and from his stress on the normality of conflict; from Weber's contributions on the power of religious ideas in history and the subjective meaning of social action; from the concept of the unconscious worked out by Freud and his successors; from theories of consistency between beliefs, values, and actions developed by such thinkers as Merton, Festinger (1956, 1957), and Frankl; and from the theory of Parsons, Shils, and colleagues that most members of dominant groups strive for the integration of each part of the social system with other parts and with the whole in patterns of "dynamic equilibrium". While investigators of religion may choose one or more of these general theories as a point of departure, for the purpose of either supporting it or derogating it, they all draw widely on the assumptions, postulates, and generalizations of their predecessors.

(b) *Principal Methods of Research*[17]

When a social scientist has selected a problem for examination he or she usually designs a study to meet the requirements of the scientific method.

Very briefly described, this calls first for the statement of a problem in terms of the causal relations between two or three principal variables. This statement should facilitate the search for an explanation of the relationships that may be tested empirically and objectively. Moreover, the scientific method looks for explanations which persist, with minor variations, in different situations or contexts. In other words, the social scientist attempts to gather systematically information or data about an occurrence which will explain its causes and its consequences in repetitive patterns under controlled or specified conditions. It is hoped that this knowledge will permit the original observer and other researchers, who may replicate the study on the basis of facts gathered in different situations, to make generalizations about all such occurrences. These generalizations should find a place within a theoretical framework that is logically consistent and comprehensive, and thus permit predictions to be made under certain conditions and within ranges of probability which ideally may be stated in advance. By following this method, natural scientists have made giant strides in adding to knowledge about man and the world of things. For reasons already discussed, it is more difficult to apply these methods and to build established theories in the social sciences, where the distinctions between fact and value are sometimes blurred and where subjective meanings are crucial.

Most researchers follow similar steps in designing a study. Often these steps are not clearly set down, but they are implicit in well-designed studies. First the researcher states a problem in such a way as to minimize systematic bias and maximize the possibilities for gathering reliable and valid data to test the propositions or hypotheses. Next, he reviews the literature written by other researchers on relevant topics and discusses the theories on which they rest. He also clarifies his own theoretical perspective and decides on the methods and techniques which seem appropriate, depending on the problem, approach, and research possibilities. Then he hypothesizes the ways in which he expects the major variables to be related to one another and makes it possible actually to conduct the study, defining the major concepts or variables which are interrelated, and specifying the empirical indicators which he will use to measure those variables. Now he collects the facts to test his hypotheses, perhaps by digging out data that already exist in census, survey, documentary, or historical records, or by gathering new data, as in community, small-group, or organizational research, or in a sample survey. When the data are assembled, checked, and classified, the researcher analyses them along the lines of his hypotheses or expectations. This permits him to verify, modify, or reject his hypotheses. He finally prepares a report, interpreting the results for whatever audience he has had in mind.

Eight methods which are widely used in the sociological study of religion are listed below:[18]

Methods Which Analyse Existing Data

Census analysis
Secondary analysis of survey data
Library or documentary research
Historical analysis

Methods Which Collect and Analyse New Data

Community study
Participant observation
Sample survey
Social-psychological study

Before discussing and illustrating these methods, we must point out that in practice most research is not as tidy or complete as our account may suggest. Often a competent researcher may start out with confused notions as to the problem and appropriate theories and methods, and find that a change of direction is necessary part way through. And frequently a complex problem warrants the application of several theories and methods at once.

(i) THE ANALYSIS OF EXISTING DATA

Census questions in Canada, unlike those in the United States, include preferred religious affiliation, and hence provide amply for the analysis of correlations between affiliation and many other social variables. In this volume Kalbach and McVey draw on this source to show how denominations have grown or declined through generations; they elaborate these findings by region, by ethnicity, and by immigration. Hiller challenges a widely held assumption that Alberta is a haven for fundamentalist sects by using census data. Millett (1969, 1971) uses census information to modify the widely used typology of religious organizations by introducing the concept of minority churches. Few inquirers have yet taken advantage of the existing data for census tract analysis (Crysdale 1972), and other rich census resources are largely untapped.

Another underdeveloped mine of quantified data exists in numerous sample surveys that have been conducted for other purposes. Mol and Whitehead in this volume illustrate the usefulness of *secondary analysis* of existing survey data, the former by tracing correlations between church attendance and a number of social variables, cross-tabulated by denominations, and the latter by showing that church-affiliated youth are less apt than others to use drugs.

Library or *documentary* research permits the study of both quantitative and qualitative data to obtain findings about a wide variety of problems. Lucas and Warburton also use existing records for their articles. Students are likely to prepare studies of this sort rather than follow methods that are more elaborate, time-consuming, and expensive. Frequently, however, they limit themselves unduly to the hypotheses and findings discussed in their sources; they should be encouraged to raise questions of their own and to compare alternative explanations (Becker and Gustafson 1968: Chs. 4 and 6).

The *historical* method in sociology differs from library research chiefly in that it is oriented to changing processes and structures across generations. It does not simply consist of a chronology of the past but, as a sociological tool of analysis, it examines patterns of interaction between groups, institutions, beliefs, values, and interests. As in other methods, historical studies should use specific theoretical perspectives which provide possible explanations for the course of events. Evidence should then be gathered systematically and objectively to test the hypotheses. The articles by Falardeau and Moir in this volume are classic examples of this method, the first by a sociologist who uses historical data and the second by a historian who applies sociological perspectives.

There are many historical studies of parishes, diocesan groups, denominations, sects, and orders in French and English Canada which do not meet the criteria of scientific method and hence are excluded from consideration in this volume. Of those based on scientific methods, the most numerous by far are by French-speaking scholars and deal with religion in Quebec (Crysdale and Montminy 1974). This reflects the sharper feelings about religion, society, and nationalism which prevail among the minority Québécois. One of the general findings is that until the 1960s secular and sacred sentiments and structures in Quebec were relatively undifferentiated and complementary (Dumont 1961; Falardeau 1952). It is true that the latter part of the nineteenth century saw bitter conflict between ultramontanists and liberals, but this did not alter the underlying homogeneity of French-language, Catholic culture. Religion had a central place in the political, economic, and other major sectors of Quebec society as well as in the lives of most individuals. The old order changed radically in the 1960s with the emergence of a new middle class consisting of mobile technical and bureaucratic workers centred in large cities, the secularization of education and public welfare, the collapse of the conservative Union Nationale, the rise of separatism, and the spread of liberal, reform sentiments within the church. Most sociological studies show the impact of these historical changes and are preoccupied with the quest for new forms of belief and practice. Some deal with specific aspects of the changing scene, for instance, David's (1969) doctoral thesis, "La grève et le bon Dieu", and Grand'Maison's (1970) inquiry into the relations between religion, on one hand, and the "quiet revolution" and political ideologies, as manifest in nationalism, on the other hand.

The historical method has not been used as extensively in English-language sociology of religion. A notable exception is the work of S. D. Clark (1948), who combined the frontier thesis with the church-sect typology to analyse the place of religion in the development of Canadian communities until 1940. Mann (1955) used the historical along with library and field methods, testing Clark's ideas in an examination of the rise of sects and cults, accompanied by theocratic politics, in Alberta in the 1930s. More recent examples of the historical method are found in this volume in studies by Milner and Milner, Crysdale, Grant, and Westhues. The historian Richard Allen (1971) has made an important recent contribution in tracing the connection between religion and social reform at the height of the social gospel movement, 1914 to 1928.

(ii) THE COLLECTION AND ANALYSIS OF NEW DATA

Until the last decade, the *community study* persisted as the most common method for gathering and analysing new data. Since then, the influx of American sociologists and the refinement of computer techniques have made sample surveys popular. The community study often combines the anthropological concern for inherited institutions, structures, normative patterns, and technology with the sociological interest in the systematic relationships between these and other elements of a society, particularly stratification, power, and control. The boundary between these two disciplines is more blurred than that between others. In particular, the anthropologists' extensive studies of pre-industrial and relatively stable indigenous peoples in Canada, as elsewhere, have added much to a comparative understanding of the place of religion in different cultural contexts. The works of Jenness, Müller, Balikci, Shimpo, Bock, Vallee, and Bennett in this volume are clear evidence of the importance of the anthropological emphasis in community studies. The interweaving of religion with other basic institutions in indigenous societies helps us to grasp the relativity of contemporary patterns, where religion is more specialized and distinct from politics, economics, and other ways modern people have devised to cope with basic common needs.

Two classic studies of Canadian communities show how the place of religion has changed with the growth of industry. The first is Horace Miner's (1939) ethnographic study of St. Denis, a rural Quebec parish where family and other social life was sustained around the church in spite of fundamental changes in the economy brought about by the incapacity of the land to maintain successive generations of large families. The other, a sociological inquiry by Everett C. Hughes (1946), *French Canada in Transition*, shows how the growth of the factory system in a small Quebec city, with more specialization of economic functions and greater differentiation between classes, led to fragmentation between religious groups in separate parishes and between denominations. Examples of the method of community study in this volume are the articles by Hughes and Lucas. In both cases several methods are used. A more typical community study is that by Ishwaran (1971) into the social and economic behaviour of Calvinists in a Dutch-Canadian rural area.

The method of *participant observation* has been more widely practised by anthropologists than by sociologists in the study of religion in Canada. It is especially useful in the analysis of small groups, such as sects, cults, or congregations. The papers here by Bock, by Bird and Reimer, and by O'Toole illustrate its procedures and productivity. Another example is William Shaffir's (1974) *Life in a Religious Community*, an account of the Lubavitcher Chassidim in Montreal. In view of the proliferation of small, intimate religious or parareligious groups at the present time, this method will probably become more widely used. In it the researcher enters directly into the activities of the group, sometimes acknowledging his purpose and sometimes not. He shares their experiences, feelings, fortunes, and views of reality. Problems may arise with respect to objective and accurate reporting because of his identification with the group.

The most common method in recent years, the *sample survey*, permits the gathering of precise and voluminous data in a short time from a carefully drawn sample of a specified population. The data-collecting instrument may be either a self-explanatory questionnaire which is mailed or distributed by hand to the sample, or a schedule of questions which interviewers ask of respondents. Because identical questions are asked of all respondents, it is possible to standardize and quantify the replies. The data may then be readily punched on cards and tabulated by a computer. This method has enhanced research enormously by its precision, controls, comparability of results, speed, and relatively low expense. However, it must be used with care because sometimes the questions do not mean to the respondents what the researcher thinks they do, and frequently important aspects of belief and practice are difficult or perhaps impossible to detect in the formal, structured interview situation. Nevertheless, this has become the most common method in sociological research into religion.

In this volume the following authors use sample surveys: Kallen, Stryckman and Gaudet, Moreux, Kaill, McDonald, Driedger and Peters, Currie, and Sévigny. Crysdale (1965) conducted a national survey of clergy, members, and adherents of the United Church employing survey methodology. Northover (1974) inquired into variations in belief among Roman Catholics in Metropolitan Toronto. These procedures have been widely used in studies of parishes, districts, orders, and college students in both French- and English-speaking Canada. Political scientists (Meisel 1964; Alford 1963) have also relied on survey techniques to gather data on the relations between religion and voting.

Psychosociological inquiries into religious behaviour are much more common in Quebec than in English Canada, where, indeed, the scarcity of psychological studies of religion is remarkable. Most projects of this kind have been conducted at l'Université de Montréal. They have followed three main directions: (1) studies of religious attitudes of small groups and, in particular, of religious organizations, (2) studies of how religious knowledge is communicated among children and adolescents, and (3) studies of psychological symptoms related to the religious conscience. Techniques include surveys of matched groups, depth interviews, Rorschach and thematic apperception tests, Q-sorts, and personality inventory tests. While the articles by Driedger and Peters and by Currie on socialization imply a psychosociological perspective, they use standard survey methods. Only Sévigny among the authors in this volume employs distinctively psychosociological techniques.

4. Overview of Canadian Studies

The variety and scope of scientific studies of religion in Canada have been manifest in the preceding discussion of contemporary theories and methods. In this section we will consider briefly the main differences in emphasis between French- and English-language studies and the principal themes which engage the attention of researchers in both languages.

From the evidence gathered by Crysdale, Montminy, and colleagues (1974) it is clear that works on religion by Francophone social scientists are more numerous and more diverse than those by Anglophones. In both cultures sociologists are the largest contributing group, making up half of those in English Canada and almost half of those in French Canada. In English the next most numerous contributors are anthropologists, then political scientists, followed with a few items each by demographers, planners, historians, psychologists, and economists. In French the second-largest number of projects are in the field of psychology, third are those in anthropology and related disciplines, and fourth are those in social history—all in substantial numbers, followed by a few each in documentation, geography, phenomenology, pedagogy, and pastoral studies.

One may ask why so many political scientists in English Canada have contributed to studies of religion as against almost none in French Canada, and why psychologists have been so productive in the study of religion in French Canada, while their colleagues in English Canada have produced almost no studies of this kind. This lack is all the more surprising when we consider that in sociology as a whole, French-Canadian studies tend more to focus on social structure and on global matters than do English-Canadian studies. Francophone sociologists also tend more than their Anglophone counterparts to participate directly in politics and in public debate (Rocher 1972: 500). It is tempting to accept the facile explanation that individual and university specialties have worked out this way at random, bearing in mind, for example, the considerable work of John Meisel in political science at Queen's University and the high productivity in the psychology of religion at Montreal. However, a more accurate explanation may be found by investigating differences that exist in French- and English-Canadian societies, first in the relations between the institution of religion and other structures, notably politics, in the course of change; and second in the milieu where research takes place. In the narrow scope of these introductory observations it is possible only to suggest explanatory propositions and to leave their testing for other studies.

From references earlier in this chapter, we may note that relations between religion and other social systems, particularly the state, in most parts of English-speaking Protestant Canada have been chronically ambiguous and unstable and at times have flared into conflict. In the 1930s the theologically conservative Social Credit movement swept Alberta, forming the provincial government for over thirty years. During the 1940s the neighbouring province of Saskatchewan saw the Social Gospel movement, grounded in liberal theology, join forces with farm and labour interests to form the first socialist government in English-speaking North America. Also, in the 1930s throughout Canada, though less in the Atlantic provinces, many members of the principal Protestant churches swung toward liberalism in theology and in social and political ethics. The main point is that during these troubled decades substantial numbers of influential English-speaking Protestants threw their support behind innovative political movements and parties (League for Social Reconstruction 1935; Irving 1959). This phenomenon attracted the attention of social scientists in English Canada to interaction between religious affiliation and political behaviour. In the same period in Quebec there were also important political changes, notably the resurgence of nationalism. But even in 1962 when the Créditistes emerged as a right-wing minority party of protest (Pinard 1971), the question of a connection between religion and party preference did not assume importance because the vast majority of Québécois were Roman Catholic.

The milieu in which social research was undertaken was also quite different in French and English regions of the country. Sociology in Quebec had its beginnings in the 1920s and 1930s at Laval and Montreal universities under the strong influence of Catholic theology (Rocher 1970; Falardeau 1974; Lévesque 1974). There was little to distinguish "religious studies" from the study of culture, social organization, or social movements (Falardeau 1962), at least up until 1960. Then came the quiet revolution in Quebec early in the 1960s, and the traditional role of the church in politics and education was sharply criticized from within and without the church. But even then the relative lack of religious differentiation and absence of political radicalism, both in the population generally and among social scientists, meant that there was little interest in research into the relations between religion and politics. Instead, some researchers in French Canada turned their attention to the psychological and social impact on members of religious orders and on laity, particularly youth, of the growing secularization and desacralization of society. In contrast, the social sciences in Anglophone universities came into being in a secular milieu. This fact and the apparent relationship between religious affiliation and political innovation channelled the curiosity of English-speaking social scientists in other directions.

The principal themes of scientific inquiry into religion in Canada will now be considered along the lines followed in Parts II and III of this book. The two main divisions here are (a) through history, and (b) in contemporary life.

(a) Through History

(i) INDIGENOUS RELIGIONS

Anthropological studies in both French and English have disclosed some widespread similarities in religious beliefs and practices among the Indian and Inuit peoples before contact with Europeans (Jenness, this volume; Rousseau 1952, 1954). Jenness comments on a number of these uniformities, such as the inseparability of man and nature, belief in a Supreme Being and in the presence in all objects of a spiritual entity, and belief in the continuity of the individual's spirit after death. However, as Müller points out, the similarities should not obscure the diversities, as the case of the Kwakiutl Indians vividly illustrates.

(ii) THE PRE-INDUSTRIAL PERIOD

Sharp divergences in early forms of religious organization and practices as between French Roman Catholics in Quebec and English-speaking Protestants in Upper Canada are evident in the two articles in this section of the book. While Falardeau writes of the seventeenth-century parish in French Canada, the homogeneity and integration of its beliefs, practices, and structures carried through for several centuries and stand in vivid contrast to the variety and conflicts which Moir traces in the early development of Protestant churches and sects in Upper Canada in the mid-nineteenth century. It is true that Moir writes of Protestantism in a society that even then was beginning to urbanize, with attending complexity in forms and processes; but the rural-urban distinction can explain the historical differences only partially. Much of the variety and conflict in early Protestantism grew out of its insistence on the right of individuals to interpret the Scriptures freely and to act on a general rather than on a particular concept of authority.

(iii) SOCIAL CHANGE AND ADAPTATION

A recurrent theme in the sociology of religion has been the effects of social change on religious organization and on beliefs and practices. S. D. Clark (1948), in *Church and Sect in Canada*, shows how the church form of organization to a large extent was unable to adapt to the needs and interests of settlers in frontier communities and how the churches in these areas were often superseded by sects. Further, some of these sects evolved into churches as their members became more established and their communities more settled. With the opening of more remote frontiers, new sects emerged to take the place of the old. Later, with the passing of the frontier and the emergence of political federation and nationalist sentiment, the church became the dominant form of religious organization, and a number of church unions were formed by the larger denominations. With increasing urbanization and industrialization, social-class differentiation became more pronounced; existing denominations ministered to the successful, while new sectarian groups attracted the poor.

W. E. Mann (1955) refined the typological approach and applied it in a study of the growth of sects and cults in Alberta. He demonstrated that a combination of geographic isolation, evangelical heritage, ethnic diversity, educational deficiencies, and economic instability between 1910 and 1946 led to social upheaval, community disintegration, and religious change. These tendencies were strengthened by the conservatism and rigidity of the major denominations. Sects met the need of many frontier people for social integration, while cults attracted the intellectually curious and psychosomatically ill. The aggressive indigenous leadership of the sects, their organizational flexibility, and their use of new techniques, notably the radio broadcast, broadened their appeal.

Another topic is the response of indigenous peoples to European culture. In some cases attempts have been made to retain traditional religious beliefs and practices, while in others the Christian religion has been adopted with modifications. In this volume Shimpo, Bock, Vallee, and Warburton analyse the dynamics and implications of cultural contact and attempted conquest.

Other studies have treated the effects of social and economic change on the Roman Catholic Church in Quebec society. The studies by Miner (1939) and Hughes (1943) document fundamental changes in community and institutional patterns. With a similar concern, Falardeau (1949) examines changes in the Quebec parish. In the traditional rural parish the *curé* was the secular as well as the religious leader. But in the contemporary urban parish, lay persons do not feel bound to a parochial group but identify with other collectivities. They may join church-sponsored movements which go far beyond the traditional parish structure. Parish churches compete for clientele and the clergy become bureaucratic functionaries.

A few writers have analysed changes in religious organization in Quebec at a higher level of analysis. Guindon (1960) argues that the massive industrialization of the 1930s to 1950s strengthened the position of the traditional religious elites as they became bureaucratic overlords in the burgeoning fields of education, social welfare, and health services. In this volume, Milner and Milner deal with the authoritarian and elitist reaction of the Roman Catholic hierarchy in Quebec to the rumblings of change in the 1930s (see also Kernaghan 1966). E. C. Hughes shows how a layman's movement altered its goals during the Second World War to support nationalism in Quebec (cf. Clement 1972).

In English Canada, there have been a variety of responses to social and economic change, as the work of Clark and Mann illustrates. Varying conditions across the generations were faced in different ways. During the period of extensive western settlement and the upheaval of war, between 1908 and 1918, there was an upsurge of social reform among major Protestant denominations (Crysdale, this volume), whereas during the 1960s, when churches were losing members and influence, the stress in the churches was on renewal and consolidation (Grant, this volume).

(b) *In Contemporary Life*

(i) PEOPLE AND POPULATION

An awareness of the religious characteristics of a population, and of modifications in these characteristics, is a prerequisite to understanding the dynamics of religious organization in any society. In this volume

Kalbach and McVey describe the growth of religious denominations, their regional and rural-urban distributions, and the factors affecting changes in their composition. They show the effects of immigration, natural increase, and intermarriage in different periods. Mol, in this volume, analyses correlates of attendance and finds that members of churches with minority status are more apt to attend regularly than those of churches with majority status (cf. Herberg 1955; Lenski 1961; Greeley 1972).

(ii) FORMS OF COMMUNITY

Interest in some studies focuses on religious behaviour in different kinds of community: simple or complex, rural or urban. The three articles in this section illustrate the various patterns that may emerge. Bennett describes how the Hutterites withdraw as much as possible from the secular world by creating their own farming communities. Lucas shows how social conflicts which characterize single-industry towns are reflected and also generated in competing churches. And Kallen analyses the variations in Judaism which are possible in large, complex metropolitan areas.

Numerous studies of ethnic groups include references to religious behaviour, but because these are oriented around ethnicity rather than religion they do not contribute much to our knowledge of belief and practice in different communities. Other studies are closer to the topic. Driedger (1968, 1972), for instance, finds that almost one-half of the Mennonites in Canada live in cities, for the most part contiguous to rural hinterlands from which they have come. Mennonites adapt to urban communities in three ways, depending on their numbers and the size of the receiving community: by forming "rurban satellites", where they can maintain strong ethnic identity and where churches tend to be conservative; by adhering to "ethnic urbanism", whereby they create social enclaves in big cities by developing schools and occupational groups; and by yielding to "urban accommodation", where, because of the scarcity of members in some cities, pressures are strong to assimilate.

The rural church as such has not been widely studied, although there are numerous reports on dioceses in Quebec and a few in Protestant areas which include rural parishes. Whyte (1966) discusses the plight of country churches owing to depopulation, the secularization of community life, and the loss of effective leadership. Settle (1971) surveyed a rural area in Nova Scotia and found that along with numerous weak congregations there were urgent unmet social needs, such as more recreation facilities and help for school dropouts, as well as problems of unemployment, alcoholism, and poverty. Respondents generally agreed that church mergers or closer co-operation were desirable, but little was accomplished because leaders preferred their traditional and separate ways.

Urbanism as a style of life, we have said, is not restricted to city dwellers. It refers to a social pattern marked by heterogeneous relationships, high density and interaction, rational planning, and considerable mobility. These are characteristic of many city dwellers but are by no means limited to them. As mentioned earlier, Crysdale (1965) found that people in his national sample who were urbane in the above sense also were more liberal than others in beliefs, in tolerance of different ways, and in approval of public planning. Lapointe (1967) also demonstrated that in the diocese of Ste. Anne de la Pocatière people in an urban milieu were more liberal than those in a rural milieu.

(iii) TYPES OF ORGANIZATION

Some contemporary research deals chiefly with religious organization, based partly on the typology of church, sect, and cult, but often going beyond its limitations. Westhues in this volume shows that the Roman Catholic Church in Canada has continued to be effective through changing times because it is flexible and adapts to prevailing social structures and values. In Quebec, where the Roman Catholic Church enjoys majority status, it assumes one stance with respect to other institutions, but in those provinces where it is in a minority situation it assumes a different stance. Parenton (1948) compares the Catholic Church in Quebec with its counterpart in South Louisiana. Because of its minority position, the ethnic heterogeneity of its members, and the rivalry between religious orders, the church in South Louisiana never acquired the power of the church in Quebec.

Bird and Reimer in this volume discuss characteristics of sects and cults in Montreal, which differ extremely from the church type of organization in structure, goals, and practices. O'Toole argues that the concept of sect can be applied to political as well as religious groups. In the cases of two radical political sects he concludes that the latent functions they perform for members in providing them with social identity take pre-

cedence over, and thus prevent the accomplishment of, the public purposes they proclaim.

Many studies have been conducted of denominations, dioceses, and
parishes in Quebec and English Canada which, though chiefly aimed
toward developing practical programs, throw light on problems of adaptation which formally structured churches have in meeting the changing
needs of communities and individuals (Pickering 1963, 1967; Routhier
1964, 1965, 1966; Crysdale 1965, 1966, 1972; Anglican Church of
Canada 1966; Rouleau 1968; Wener 1968; Presbyterian Church in
Canada 1969; Villeneuve 1969; Crysdale and Montminy 1974). The
greater flexibility of sects and cults often permits them to respond to
these needs more effectively (Mann 1955), at least for marginal groups
and in the short run.

(iv) RESPONSES TO RELIGIOUS CALLINGS

How individuals respond to the appeal of religious teaching constitutes
another important theme. While responses are essentially personal and
subjective, they are also socially differentiated into group patterns. Two
patterns are common: (a) leader and follower, priest and lay person; and
(b) conservative and liberal, orthodox and innovative. Because responses
require interpretation and commitment they are manifestations of shared
meanings and thus clearly indicate the subjective core of shared beliefs.
For the same reasons they distinguish between groups of believers, both
within each body of faith and between different denominations and
faiths.

The characteristics of religious leaders, particularly the clergy, have
been examined frequently. S. D. Clark (1948: 34) pointed out that
before 1776 most of the Congregational ministers in Nova Scotia were
upholders of religious orthodoxy, were graduates of the best schools, and
tried to maintain in pioneer settlements the formal religious services
which had been established in New England. They emphasized correct
theological doctrine but in many cases displayed little spirituality. A
major reason why churches lost their appeal in frontier areas was this
reliance on clergy who were socially "above" the population; sects, in
contrast, made good use of indigenous leadership.

The characteristics of leaders have been examined from other perspectives. In *The Vertical Mosaic* (1965), Porter analyses biographical
data on the Anglican and Roman Catholic hierarchies. Most Anglican

bishops were from Great Britain and had diverse social backgrounds. Roman Catholic bishops, in contrast, were Canadian-born and constituted a socially homogeneous group, separate from other elites.

Crysdale (1965) found that United Church clergy tended to be more liberal than lay people in attitudes towards social issues and the role of government in matters pertaining to economic planning and social welfare. Pickering and Blanchard (1967) examined the attitudes and needs of Anglican clergy and discovered that job satisfaction was generally high, although almost one-half experienced considerable loneliness in their work. Johnson and Cornell (1972) analysed the beliefs, expectations, and orientations of North American Protestants towards the church. They found Canadian clergy to be more theologically traditional but less judgmental than lay people. Canadian clergy were slightly more optimistic about the importance of the church in the next ten years than their counterparts in the United States.

In this volume, Stryckman and Gaudet show that some English-speaking Roman Catholic priests view their calling primarily as priestly and administrative, while others emphasize its prophetic and pastoral aspects. Stress on the latter has been legitimated by the theological position of the Second Vatican Council and by the sentiments of many younger lay persons and priests. In an earlier study Stryckman (1970) found similar distinctions among French-speaking priests in Quebec.

A number of investigations have been conducted on the social characteristics and attitudes of the laity. Pickering (1963) learned that members of five Anglican inner-city congregations in Winnipeg, in comparison with the general population, were overly representative of older ages, women, and unmarried persons. Among the men, there were more white-collar than manual workers. Crysdale (1965) found that about one-eighth of United Church laity were strongly liberal in beliefs, five-eighths were moderately liberal, and two-eighths were conservative. Regular worshippers were slightly more liberal than occasional ones in attitudes towards minorities, and active church youths were more liberal than inactive ones. In the church as a whole, there was strong consensus on beliefs concerning the nature and work of God and Jesus Christ, the means of grace, and actions toward others. There was little consensus on the meaning of life, views of salvation, and codes of behaviour.

Johnson and Cornell (1972) learned that their sample of Canadian laity were in much less agreement than Canadian and American clergy and United States laity regarding traditional beliefs. Canadian laity were also less likely to seek divine guidance for decisions in everyday life and had a higher tolerance for ambiguity in their judgments of others.

In this volume the paper by Bibby and Brinkerhoff explores "conversion" into evangelical sects and discovers that the largest number by far are children of members or recruits from similar fundamentalist groups. Moreux studies the quality of commitment among a sample of Catholic lay women in a Quebec parish. She learns that while there continues to be widespread ritual conformity, the intellectual and moral commitment is weak. Hiller investigates another problem related to response. He checks census data for Alberta compared with those of other provinces and finds that they furnish little support for the popular notion of a Bible Belt in that province. He concludes that the stereotype was attached to Alberta, not because of any preponderance of sects, but because fundamentalist ideas were extended to influence political ideology during the Social Credit regime.

(V) SOCIAL SOURCES OF ECUMENISM

Frequently, as we consider above, the interpretation of faith and the commitment it elicits differentiate one religious body from others. But under some circumstances barriers between denominations fall and the spirit of ecumenism prevails. In this volume Mann and Kaill discuss these social circumstances, the former at the level of denominations which came together in church union in 1925, and the latter at the local level of eight congregations (four each of Anglican and United) in central western Ontario. Mann found that, besides historical and theological reasons, socio-economic forces encouraged church union. These included low population density, shortages of clergy, the rise of trade associations which promoted the ideal of unionism, the existence of co-operatives favouring mutual aid, frontier anti-intellectualism which weakened arguments against union, the mood of optimism and liberalism, the growing sense of nationalism in eastern Canada, and the steady expansion of Roman Catholicism which strengthened Protestant interest in a national church.

The more recent study by Kaill shows that the strongest influences on favourable attitudes toward union among laity were perceptions of clergy attitudes and belief in the freedom of expression. Religious considerations did not systematically influence lay attitudes towards union. A footnote may be added from the observation of Clark (1944) that church history, by focusing on unions, has neglected the counter-movements toward sectarian forms of religious organization.

(vi) POLITICS, ECONOMICS, AND SOCIAL CLASS

We mentioned that a major area in the English-language sociology of religion in this country has been the relations between religion and politics, in particular between affiliation and voting behaviour or political preference. Meisel (1956) studied the 1953 federal and 1955 provincial elections in Kingston. He found that in both elections members of the Anglican and United churches disproportionately supported the Progressive Conservatives, while Roman Catholics disproportionately supported the Liberal party. He concluded that when there are no salient political issues the tradition of a religious organization seems to be the decisive factor in voting.

Alford (1963) examined the relations between religious affiliation and class voting from 1945 to 1961 at the federal level and discovered that class voting was higher among Protestants than among Catholics. Further, religious affiliation had a higher correlation with party preference than had class differences within each denomination.

Anderson (1966) studied religious affiliation and voting preference among working-class residents in Hamilton and found that Catholic voters supported Liberals, while Protestant voters supported Progressive Conservatives, that younger age groups were less inclined than older groups to vote according to the tradition of their religion, that the NDP party was supported predominantly by younger, male, Protestant non-attenders, and that religious affiliation was more important than any other variable, including ethnicity, in determining voting preference.

Meisel (1964) edited an anthology on the 1962 federal election, in which a number of researchers examined the relations between religious affiliation and political preference. Alford (1964) produced more evidence that at the national level Roman Catholics vote heavily Liberal, Protestants Conservative, and Jews Liberal. Provinces differed considerably in the degree and direction of the religious factor, but it was always present. Alford also showed that religious voting was more prevalent in older provinces with their history of religious cleavages. But traditional national patterns are not always replicated. Perlin (1964), for example, found that in St. John's, Newfoundland, Protestants voted Liberal and Catholics voted Conservative. He concluded that voting choices in Newfoundland are the function of local rather than national factors.

McDonald's study (reprinted in this volume) of the voting intentions of Ontario residents before the 1968 federal election partially confirms the hypothesis that increases in denominational awareness of group identity and interests will increase the Liberal vote among Catholics and the Conservative vote among Protestants.

Silverstein (1968), reviewing returns for Saskatchewan provincial elections from 1948 to 1964, found that Roman Catholics remained consistently opposed to the CCF and loyal to the Liberals, while United Church members consistently supported the CCF. Also in Saskatchewan, Laskin and Baird (1970) studied factors in voter turnout and political preference in the 1958 federal, 1960 provincial, and 1960 municipal elections in the town of Biggar. Contrary to findings elsewhere, voting preferences of Anglicans tended to be more similar to those of Roman Catholics than to those of United Church members, and variations in religion did not obscure the variations on class lines.

The relations between religion and economic behaviour have also been examined. Here there are two emphases: the role of religious organizations in economic development and the effects of belief on individual economic behaviour. Ryan (1966) studied the influence of religion on economic growth in Quebec from 1896 to 1914. He concluded that the major barriers to economic development were lack of capital, technical knowledge, and entrepreneurs. The relation between religious affiliation and social class is of longstanding interest, as the previously discussed studies by Clark and Mann illustrate.

Other studies have attempted to test Weber's thesis that the Calvinist ethic helped to bring about modern productive capitalism. Lowry (1969) learned that persons living in poor, rural areas in the Maritime provinces were more likely than those living in cities or in more prosperous places to adhere to the Protestant ethic and to traditional beliefs. However, Ishwaran (1971) shows that in a rural, Dutch-Canadian community there is a tendency to downgrade individualism and to accent authoritarianism, thus hindering economic enterprise.

The close interplay among the polity, the economy, and social strata is reflected by the articles chosen for this section. Warburton reasons that racial and cultural discrimination among the dominant European settlers against the Indian peoples was legitimated to a large extent by the missionaries' attempts to convert them. Recently, however, stereotyping and prejudice have been decried by church leaders who have supported demands by Indian peoples for social justice. The paper by Crysdale argues that the Social Gospel movement represented a quest in western Canada for a modern ideology to remedy widely perceived economic and political injustices.

(vii) YOUTH AND SOCIALIZATION

A number of recent studies have probed the effects of religious socialization and commitment among youth, including those in this volume by Driedger and Peters, Whitehead, Currie, and Sévigny. The latter's finding, that French-speaking Catholic youth in their late teens tend to express faith in individual rather than church-oriented terms, is consistent with the few other studies on religious socialization that have been conducted among youth and younger children. Lachance (1955), for example, reports that the internalization of beliefs by children aged five and six depends largely on differences in their cognition and perception. Kurokawa (1969) found in a study of Mennonite mothers and young children in central Ontario that high levels of traditionalism and authoritarianism among mothers were closely correlated with covert symptoms of maladjustment among children and with lower scores of adequacy, personal freedom, and extroversion. Tremblay (1966) discovered in analysing data from a sample of Quebec youth that attitudes of love towards God and towards people varied with three stages in psychological development: pre-adolescence, adolescence, and post-adolescence.

The foregoing brief overview indicates substantial progress in the accumulation of systematic knowledge. But the task of building and testing theories is only beginning. Some of the problems and issues that this task encompasses are outlined in the next section.

5. Problems and Issues

In the opening section of this chapter we argued for a substantive definition of religion which would satisfy the conventions and expectations of two groups: people who every day think and talk about and experience something which they call religion, and social scientists who must have discriminating concepts and theories about the phenomena which they propose to analyse. We maintained that the meaning of the term "religion", to satisfy the expectations of our two types of users, should recognize three principal common aspects. Religion is supranatural, supra-empirical, and social.

This seemingly harmless statement plunges us into a fundamental controversy which students of religion have yet to resolve: What is it? We noted earlier that Tylor (1871), the nineteenth-century anthropologist, said that it was simply "belief in spiritual beings". Durkheim (1915), after reflecting on the functions of religion in holding a society together, said that it was "a unified system of beliefs and practices relative to sacred things set apart and forbidden, beliefs and practices which unite into one single moral community called a church, all those who adhere to them". But this approach does not provide for the individual, subjective aspects of religion, for variations endemic within and between religious systems, or for the disruptive or innovative influence of religion under some conditions and at certain times and places (Crysdale 1973: 273 ff.). The subjective and dynamic qualities of religion are better represented in Luckmann's (1967) definition: "the capacity of the human organism to transcend its biological nature through the construction of objective, morally binding, all embracing universes of meaning".

At least three questions are involved in attempts at defining religion. First, should it be regarded as a real or as a nominal concept? The former has a direct, observable referent, something which can be ascertained by the senses, such as a table. A nominal concept, however, is a more abstract construction which cannot be perceived directly, for example, the ego or superego. Then we may ask, should a definition be substantive or functional (Berger 1974; Dobbelaere and Lauwers 1973)? A substantive definition states what religion is—for instance, a mode of believing, relating with others, and acting in various contexts, as in Luckmann's definition above. A functional definition, in comparison, concerns what religion *does*; as in Durkheim's definition, it may integrate society or help allay anxiety by affirming social and individual meaning. Finally, at what level of analysis should religion be defined? Is religion primarily a group phenomenon with consequences for individuals, as Durkheim suggests, or is it chiefly an individual experience which is shared with others, as Freud prefers? The positions an inquirer may take on these questions is closely linked with how he or she defines religion. This leads to other views such as whether religion should include "secular equivalents", for instance, some political ideologies and ethical humanism.

A second issue is the suitability of theoretical perspectives and methodologies in the sociology of religion. Should sociologists adopt the comparative, historical, functional, conflict, phenomenological, psychoanalytic, or some other, approach? Obviously the observer's own values affect his choice of perspective, but just as important is the fit between the theoretical framework and the problem being investigated. For example, if one is interested in the goals of equal opportunity and democratic decision-making, the conflict framework may be appropriate because it focuses on how interests are affected and power is distributed. If the emphasis is on the development of the institution of religion and its role in different societies, then the comparative or historical framework is useful. The maintenance of religion as a subsystem can be understood clearly from the functional viewpoint. If problems of meaning and identity are crucial, phenomenology has much to contribute. As we have already stated, some sets of problems require the application of more than one theoretical perspective. Similarly, what methods and techniques should one use to explore problems or test hypotheses? Again, the selection will depend on the value orientation of the researcher, the problem he tackles, and the theoretical perspective he thinks most suitable.

The third issue we mention briefly is the assessment of individual religiosity, or intensity of commitment. Who is more religious than another? Even at this basic level, religious behaviour is extremely complex. Its dimensions include belief, observance, knowledge, experience, and ethical action. To measure only one of these dimensions or to give it more weight than another introduces bias and error. Thus, to judge religiosity by church attendance alone clearly would be inadequate. The importance of attendance varies, for example, between Roman Catholics and Unitarians. Again, for Jews rituals in the family circle are of great importance, while for Mennonites and Quakers pacifism is next to godliness. Moreover, how should one measure each dimension of religiosity? Does a single intense religious experience, such as a traumatic, overwhelming vision of the Lord, equal a number of more common experiences, such as a pervading and renewing sense of forgiveness and peace during worship? In assigning weights to one or another element, it is almost impossible to avoid bias, introduced as a result of the perception, cognition, or values of the observer or of the informants. Again, the problem of interpretation arises when we ask identical questions of persons from different cultures or generations or with varied levels of education.

Finally, if all the above problems were solved, we would still have disputes between those who think religion should be analysed as one sector of general knowledge and those who view it as a special field with its own criteria of value, measurement, and claims for legitimacy. Readers may keep these and other issues in mind as they examine the studies which comprise the remainder of this book.

NOTES

1 For the reader interested in intellectual antecedents of the sociological mode of understanding religion, see Birnbaum and Lenzer (1969: 1-5).

2 We are not suggesting here that all theoretical perspectives can be combined. For example, in our view a synthesis of functionalism and Marxism is not possible. For a debate on this point see van den Berghe (1963) and Frank (1966).

3 For a discussion of the differences between social evolution and social change see Guy Rocher (1972: 337-8).

4 The distinction between historical sociology and sociological history is at times arbitrary. Frequently, however, there is a difference of emphasis. In this regard Kai T. Erikson (1970: 332) has stated, "A sociologist is more likely to note the structure of the scene than the character of its leading actors, he is more likely to be interested in the activities of civil society than in the actions of governments, and, in general, he is more likely to be concerned with some underlying pattern in the events he is studying than with the moments of crisis. . . ." For a critique of contemporary historical sociology see Rocher (1972: 336-7).

5 For additional criticisms of the typological approach see Erich Goode (1967, a, b), Demerath and Hammond (1969: 161-2).

6 For a discussion of comparative sociology see Marsh (1967).

7 For a discussion of criticisms of Durkheim's theory and attempts to apply it see Demerath and Hammond (1969: 23-30, 32-7), Scharf (1971: Ch. 5), and Segar (1957).

8 In fairness, it should be emphasized that these are general tendencies among functional theorists. Some attempts have been made to address these criticisms and to alter functional analysis accordingly. For a discussion of these issues see N. J. Demerath and R. A. Peterson (1967).

9 Other influential psychologists of religion producing works in the late nineteenth and early twentieth centuries include Hall (1904), Starbuck (1899), Coe (1900, 1916) and Leuba (1912, 1916).

10 For a methodological critique of Jung, see Fromm (1967: 15-17). For comparisons of Freud and Jung, see Spinks (1965: 100-2) and Johnson (1959: 206-11).

11 For a critique of this research, see the articles in *The Journal for the Scientific Study of Religion* 10, No. 4 (1971): 339-83. Crysdale (1965: 50, 110, 111) found in the national survey of members and adherents of the United Church of Canada that older members who scored high in conventional religiosity also had slightly lower scores in civil liberalism. However, active church members on the whole were more liberal in attitudes towards deviant others than inactive members. Active young people were more liberal than young people who did not attend church regularly.

12 However, the criticism of consequential and symbolic reductionism may be directed towards all theoretical approaches in the scientific study of religion, with the exception of the phenomenological perspective.

13 In Weber's writing "the concept 'social' [is] defined in terms of a relationship between the behavior of two or more people, and the concept 'action' is defined as behavior to which a subjective meaning is attached. A social action, therefore, is an action which is oriented toward the past,

present or future behavior of another person or persons" (Walsh 1967: xxi).

Social scientists conducting phenomenological investigations make a number of assumptions about social reality. First, they regard all symbolic dimensions of culture as being social constructions. Second, they hold that there is a tremendous variety both among and within cultures as to what is assumed to be "real". There is no universally agreed upon "real world" in the social sense. Individuals are socialized to quite different conceptions of the universe, not only in different cultures but also in the various subcultures within differentiated societies. Third, they believe that it is possible to understand "from the inside" the socially constructed reality held by others. And, finally, they maintain that the investigator can seek this knowledge directly through immediate, intuitive apprehension of the experience of others, free from the imposition of prior scientific conceptualization.

14 For a thorough critique and reformulation of Weber's position, see Alfred Schutz (1967).

15 The Bureau of Social and Religious Research (1972) was established in 1941 at Garrett Theological Seminary, Chicago, under the leadership of Murray H. Leiffler. Later, many research institutes appeared under denominational or ecumenical auspices. Examples in Europe are the Institute of the Catholic Church (KASKI) at The Hague and the Reformed Institute at Amsterdam. The Centre de Recherches en Sociologie Religieuse at Laval University, Quebec, has conducted many parish studies and fostered growth in knowledge about religion from various theoretical and methodological viewpoints.

16 Readers who wish to consider more thoroughly some current theories concerning religion may consult such sources as C. Y. Glock and R. Stark (1965), Religion and Society in Tension; T. Luckmann (1967), The Invisible Religion; P. L. Berger (1967), The Sacred Canopy; N. J. Demerath III and P. E. Hammond (1969), Religion in Social Context; R. N. Bellah (1970), Beyond Belief; J. M. Yinger (1970), The Scientific Study of Religion; Susan Budd (1973), Sociologists and Religion; and Harold Fallding (1974), The Sociology of Religion.

17 Helpful texts are available which describe methods of sociological research, including the brief introduction by Leonard Becker Jr. and Clair Gustafson (1968), Encounter with Sociology: The Term Paper. Delbert C. Miller (1970), in Handbook of Research Design and Social Measurement, presents statistical analysis, scales, and indices. Other useful references are Aaron V. Cicourel (1964), Method and Measurement in Sociology; Severyn T. Bruyn (1966), The Human Perspective in Sociology: Participant Observation; and James A. Davis (1971) Elementary Survey Analysis.

Specific reference to methodology in the sociology of religion, in the American context, may be found in Samuel Z. Klausner (1963), Thomas F. O'Dea (1970), Jeffrey K. Hadden and Edward F. Heenan (1970), Richard L. Means (1970), and Gary D. Bouma (1970).

18 Additional methods include content analysis, sociometry, action research, experimental research, interaction process analysis, and systems analysis, but since, with a few exceptions, they have not been used in the study of religion in Canada, we do not discuss them here.

REFERENCES

Alford, Robert
1963   "Religion and Class Voting."
        Party and Society. Chicago:
        Rand, McNally.
1964   "The Social Bases of Political
        Cleavage in 1962." In John
        Meisel, ed., Papers on the 1962

Election. Toronto: University of
Toronto Press.
Allen, Richard
1971   The Social Passion: Religion and
        Social Reform in Canada,
        1914-28. Toronto: University of
        Toronto Press.

Allport, Gordon W.
1960   *Personality and Social Encounter.* Boston: Beacon Press.
1966   "Religious Context of Prejudice." *Journal for the Scientific Study of Religion* 5: 447-57.
Anderson, Grace M.
1966   "Voting Behaviour and the Ethnic Religious Variable." *Canadian Journal of Economics and Political Science* 32, No. 1 (February): 27-37.
Anglican Church of Canada
1966   "Report of Survey among Laymen." Toronto: General Synod.
Becker, Howard
1932   *Systematic Sociology.* New York: John Wiley and Sons.
Becker, Leonard, Jr., and Clair Gustafson
1968   *Encounter with Sociology: The Term Paper.* Berkeley: Glendessary.
Bellah, Robert N.
1957   *Tokugawa Religion.* New York: Free Press.
1967   "Civic Religion in America." *Daedalus* 96, No. 1: 1-21.
1970   *Beyond Belief.* New York: Harper and Row.
Bennett, John C.
1946   *Christian Ethics and Social Policy.* New York: Charles Scribner's Sons.
————, H. R. Bowen, W. A. Brown, Jr., and G. B. Oxnam
1954   *Christian Values and Economic Life.* New York: Harper and Row.
Berger, Peter
1963   "Charisma and Religious Innovation: The Social Location of Israelite Prophecy." *American Sociological Review* 28: 940-50.
1974   "Second Thoughts on Defining Religion." *Journal for the Scientific Study of Religion,* Vol. 13, No. 2 (June).
————,and Thomas Luckmann
1966   *The Social Construction of Reality.* Garden City: Doubleday.
Birnbaum, Norman, and Gertrude Lenzer, eds.

1969   *Sociology and Religion.* Englewood Cliffs, N.J.: Prentice-Hall.
Bland, S. G.
1920   *The New Christianity.* Toronto: McClelland and Stewart.
Bouma, Gary D.
1970   "Assessing the Impact of Religion: A Critical Review." *Sociological Analysis* 31, No. 4 (Winter): 172-9.
Brothers, Joan, ed.
1967   *Readings in the Sociology of Religion.* London: Pergamon Press.
Brown, Bruce
1973   *Marx, Freud, and the Critique of Everyday Life: Toward a Permanent Cultural Revolution.* New York: Monthly Review Press.
Brown, Norman O.
1970   (1959) *Life against Death: The Psychoanalytic Meaning of History.* Middletown: Wesleyan University Press.
Bruyn, Severyn T.
1966   *The Human Perspective in Sociology: The Method of Participant Observation.* Englewood Cliffs, N.J.: Prentice-Hall.
Buber, Martin
1958   *I and Thou,* 2nd edn. Trans. by Ronald G. Smith. New York: Charles Scribner's Sons.
Buckley, Walter
1967   *Sociology and Modern Systems Theory.* Englewood Cliffs, N.J.: Prentice-Hall.
Budd, Susan
1973   *Sociologists and Religion.* London: Collier-Macmillan.
Bureau of Social and Religious Research
1972   *The Story of Research in Sociology of Religion.* Evanston, Ill.: Garrett Theological Seminary.
Burgess, Ernest
1925   "The Growth of the City." In Robert E. Park, Ernest W. Burgess, and Roderick McKenzie, *The City.* Chicago: University of Chicago Press.
Castaneda, Carlos
1969   *The Teachings of Don Juan: A Yaqui Way of Knowledge.* New York: Ballantine Books.
Cicourel, Aaron V.
1964   *Method and Measurement in*

Sociology. New York: Free Press.

Clark, S. D.
1948   *Church and Sect in Canada.* Toronto: University of Toronto Press.
1962   (1944) "Religious Organization and the Rise of the Canadian Nation, 1880-1885." Reprinted in 1962. *The Developing Canadian Community.* Toronto: University of Toronto Press.

Clark, Walter H.
1958   *The Psychology of Religion.* New York: Macmillan.

Clement, Gabriel
1972   *Histoire de l'Action catholique au Canada français.* Commission d'étude sur les laïcs et l'Église. Montréal: Éditions Fides.

Coe, George A.
1900   *The Spiritual Life.* New York: Abingdon Press.
1916   *The Psychology of Religion.* Chicago: University of Chicago Press.

Comte, Auguste
1830–42 *Cours de philosophie positive.* 6 vols. Paris.

Coser, Lewis A.
1964   *The Functions of Social Conflict,* Glencoe: Free Press.

Crysdale, Stewart
1961   *The Industrial Struggle and Protestant Ethics in Canada.* Toronto: Ryerson.
1965   *The Changing Church in Canada: National Survey of the United Church in Canadian Society.* Toronto: United Church of Canada. Portion reprinted in C. Beattie and S. Crysdale, eds., *Sociology Canada: Readings.* Toronto: Butterworth, 1974.
1966   *Churches Where the Action Is!* Toronto: United Church of Canada.
1972   "The Church in Exurbia: A Canadian Case." Paper given at joint meetings of the Society for the Scientific Study of Religion and the Religious Research Association, Boston.
————, and C. Beattie
1973   "Religion and Secularization."

Ch. 14 of *Sociology Canada: An Introductory Text.* Toronto: Butterworth.
————, and J.-P. Montminy, with L. Wheatcroft and H. Urbano,
1974   *La Religion au Canada/Religion in Canada: Annotated Inventory of Scientific Studies of Religion, 1945-1972.* Downsview, Ontario, and Québec, P.Q.: York University and Les Presses de l'Université Laval.

Curtis, James E., and John W. Petras
1970   *The Sociology of Knowledge.* London: Gerald Duckworth.

Dahrendorf, Ralf
1959   *Class and Class Conflict in Industrial Society.* Stanford: Stanford University Press

David, Hélène
1969   "La grève et le bon Dieu." *Sociologie et Sociétés,* Vol. 1, No. 2.

Davis, James A.
1971   *Elementary Survey Analysis.* Englewood Cliffs, N.J.: Prentice-Hall.

Davis, Kingsley
1949   *Human Society.* New York: Macmillan.

Demerath, N. J., and R. A. Peterson, eds.
1967   *System, Change and Conflict.* New York: Free Press.
————,and Phillip E. Hammond
1969   *Religion in Social Context.* New York: Random House.

Dittes, James E.
1971   "Typing the Typologies: Some Parallels in the Career of Church-Sect and Extrinsic-Intrinsic." *Journal for the Scientific Study of Religion* 10, No. 4: 375-83.

Dobbelaere, Karel, and Jan Lauwers
1973   "Definition of Religion—a Sociological Critique." *Social Compass* 20, No. 4: 535-51.

Dreitzel, Hans P., ed.
1970   *Recent Sociology No. 2.* New York: Macmillan.

Driedger, Leo
1968   "A Perspective on Canadian Mennonite Urbanization." *Mennonite Life* 23, No. 4 (October); 147-51.

1972 "Urbanization of Mennonites in Canada." In H. Poettcker and R. Regehr, eds., *Call to Faithfulness: Essays in Canadian Mennonite Studies*. Altona, Man.: D. W. Friesen and Sons.

Dumont, Fernand
1961 "Réflexions sur l'histoire religieuse du Canada français." *l'Église et le Québec*. Montréal: Éditions du Jour.

Dunham, H. Warren
1955 "The Field of Social Psychiatry." In Arnold Rose, ed., *Mental Health and Mental Disorder*. New York: W. W. Norton.

Durkheim, Emile
1915 (1912) *The Elementary Forms of the Religious Life*. Trans. by J. Swain. London: George Allen and Unwin.
1964 (1895) *The Rules of Sociological Method*. Trans. by S. Solovay and J. Mueller. New York: Macmillan.

Eisenstadt, S. N., ed.
1968 *The Protestant Ethic and Modernization: A Comparative View*. New York: Basic Books.

Eister, Allan W.
1967 "Toward a Radical Critique of Church-Sect Typologizing." *Journal for the Scientific Study of Religion* 6, No. 1: 85-90.

Eliade, Mircea
1959 *The Sacred and the Profane*. New York: Harcourt, Brace and World.
1969 (1952) *Images and Symbols*. New York: Sheed and Ward.

Ellul, Jacques
1964 *The Technological Society*. New York: Vintage Books.
1970 *Meaning of the City*. Grand Rapids: Eerdmans.

Ellwood, Robert S.
1973 *Religious and Spiritual Groups in Modern America*. Englewood Cliffs, N.J.: Prentice-Hall.

Erickson, Kai
1970 "Sociology and the Historical Perspective." *American Sociologist*, Vol. 5 (November).

Falardeau, Jean-Charles
1949 "The Parish as an Institutional Type." *Canadian Journal of Economics and Political Science*, Vol. 15, No. 3.
1962 "Les recherches religieuses au Canada français." *Recherches Sociographiques*, Vol. 3, Nos. 1-2.
1964 (1952) "The Role and Importance of the Church in French Canada." In M. Rioux and Y. Martin, eds. *French Canadian Society*, Vol. 1. Toronto: McClelland and Stewart.
1974 "Antécédents, débuts et croissances de la sociologie au Québec." *Recherches Sociographiques* 15, Nos. 2-3 (mai-août): 135-65.

Fallding, Harold
1974 *The Sociology of Religion*. Toronto: McGraw-Hill Ryerson.

Faris, R. E. L.
1944 "Ecological Factors in Human Behavior." In J. McV. Hunt, ed., *Personality and the Behavior Disorders*. New York: Ronald Press.

Fenn, Richard K.
1970 "The Process of Secularization: A Post-Parsonian View." *Journal for the Scientific Study of Religion* 9, No. 2: 117-36.

Festinger, Leon
1957 *A Theory of Cognitive Dissonance*. Evanston, Ill.: Row, Peterson.
———, and Henry Riecken
1956 *When Prophecy Fails*. Minneapolis: University of Minnesota Press.

Fischoff, Ephraim
1963 Translator's Preface, in M. Weber, 1963, pp. ix-xvii.

Frank, André G.
1966 "Functionalism, Dialectics and Synthetics." *Science and Society* (Spring).

Frankl, Viktor E.
1963 (1959) *Man's Search for Meaning*. New York: Pocket Books.

Frazer, James G.
1922 *The Golden Bough*. New York: Macmillan.

Freud, Sigmund
1918 (1913) *Totem and Taboo*. Trans. by A. A. Brill. New York: Moffat Yard.

1928   (1927) *The Future of an Illusion.*
Trans. by W. D. Robertson-
Scott. New York: Horace
Liveright and the Institute of
Psychoanalysis.
1955   (1939) *Moses and Monotheism.*
Trans. by Katherine Jones. New
York: Vintage Press.
Fromm, Erich
1941   *Escape from Freedom.* New
York: Holt, Rinehart and
Winston.
1967   *Psychoanalysis and Religion.*
Toronto: Bantam Books.
Gallup Opinion Index
1975   *Religion in America.* Report 114.
Princeton, N.J.
Geertz, Clifford
1966   "Religion as a Cultural System."
In M. Banton, ed., *Anthropolo-
gical Approaches to the Study
of Religion.* American Sociologi-
cal Association, Monograph No.
3. London: Tavistock.
Gerth, H. H., and C. Wright Mills
1967   *From Max Weber.* New York:
Oxford University Press.
Glock, Charles Y., and Rodney Stark
1965   *Religion and Society in Tension.*
Chicago: Rand, McNally.
Goode, Erich
1967   (a) "Some Critical Observations
on the Church-Sect Dimension."
*Journal for the Scientific Study
of Religion* 6: 69-77.
1967   (b) "Further Reflections on the
Church-Sect Dimension." *Journal
for the Scientific Study of
Religion* 6: 270-5.
Grand'Maison, Jacques
1970   *Nationalisme et Religion.* T.I:
*Nationalisme et Révolution
culturelle*; T. II: *Religion et
Idéologies politiques.* Montréal:
Éditions Beauchemin.
Grant, George
1969   *Technology and Empire.*
Toronto: House of Anansi.
Greeley, Andrew M.
1972   *The Denominational Society.*
Glenview, Ill.: Scott, Foresman.
1974   "Religion in a Secular Society."
Social Research 15, No. 2
(Summer): 226-40.

Green, R. W., ed.
1959   *Protestantism and Capitalism.*
Boston: D. C. Heath.
Guindon, Hubert
1960   "The Social Evolution of Quebec
Reconsidered." *Canadian
Journal of Economics and
Political Science*, Vol. 26
(November).
Gustafson, Paul
1967   "UO-US-PS-PO: A Restatement
of Troeltsch's Church–Sect
Typology." *Journal for the
Scientific Study of Religion* 6:
64-8.
Habermas, Jürgen
1970   *Toward a Rational Society.*
Boston: Beacon Press.
Hadden, Jeffrey K.
1969   *The Gathering Storm in the
Churches.* Garden City:
Doubleday.
————, and Edward F. Heenan
1970   "Empirical Studies in the
Sociology of Religion: An
Assessment of the Past Ten
Years." *Sociological Analysis*
31, No. 3: 154-71.
Hall, G. Stanley
1904   *Adolescence.* New York:
Appleton.
Hammond, Phillip E., and Robert E.
Mitchell
1965   "Segmentation of Radicalism—
the Case of the Protestant
Campus Minister." *American
Journal of Sociology*, Vol. 71,
No. 2.
Harp, John, and James Curtis
1971   "Linguistic Communities and
Sociology: Data from the Can-
adian Case." In J. Gallagher
and R. Lambert, eds., *Social
Process and Institution.* Toronto:
Holt, Rinehart and Winston.
Harrison, Richard I.
1974   "Sources of Recruitment to
Catholic Pentecostalism."
*Journal for the Scientific Study
of Religion* 19, No. 1 (March):
49-64.
Heilbroner, Robert L.
1974   *An Enquiry into the Human
Prospect.* New York: W. W.
Norton.

Herberg, Will
1955 *Protestant–Catholic–Jew*. Garden City: Doubleday.
Hiller, Harry
1969 "The New Theology and the Sociology of Religion." *Canadian Review of Sociology and Anthropology*, Vol. 6, No. 3.
Hodges, Daniel L.
1974 "Breaking a Scientific Taboo: Putting Assumptions about the Supernatural into Scientific Theories of Religion." *Journal for the Scientific Study of Religion* 13, No. 4 (December): 393–408.
Hughes, Everett C.
1943 *French Canada in Transition*. Chicago: University of Chicago Press.
Hunt, Richard A.
1972 "The LAM Scales." *Journal for the Scientific Study of Religion*, Vol. 11, No. 1 (March).
Hutchinson, John A., ed.
1953 *Christian Faith and Social Action*. New York: Charles Scribner's Sons.
Institute for Behavioural Research
1974 "Special Tabulation of Gallup Poll Data on Religious Belief and Practice in Canada." Downsview, Ont.: York University.
Irving, John
1959 *The Social Credit Movement in Alberta*. Toronto: University of Toronto Press.
Ishwaran, K.
1971 "Calvinism and Social Behaviour in a Dutch-Canadian Community." In K. Ishwaran, ed., *The Canadian Family*. Toronto: Holt, Rinehart and Winston.
James, William
1902 *The Varieties of Religious Experience*. New York: Longman's.
Johnson, Benton
1957 "A Critical Appraisal of the Church-Sect Typology." *American Sociological Review* 22, No. 1: 88-92.
1963 "On Church and Sect." *American Sociological Review* 28, No. 4: 539-49.

Johnson, Douglas W., and George W. Cornell
1972 *Punctured Preconceptions: What North American Christians Think about the Church*. New York: Friendship Press.
Johnson, Paul E.
1959 *Psychology of Religion*. Nashville: Abingdon Press.
Jung, Carl G.
1933 *Modern Man in Search of a Soul*. New York: Harcourt, Brace.
1956 *Symbols of Transformation*. New York: Pantheon Books.
1958 *Psychology and Religion: West and East*. New York: Pantheon Books.
Kernaghan, W. D. K.
1966 "Freedom of Religion in Quebec, with Particular Reference to the Jews, Jehovah's Witnesses, and Church-State Relations, 1930-1960." Ph.D. thesis, Duke University.
King, Martin Luther, Jr.
1964 *Why We Can't Wait*. New York: Harper and Row.
1967 *Conscience for Change*. Massey Lectures, 7th Series. Toronto: Canadian Broadcasting Corporation.
King, Morton B., and Richard A. Hunt
1972 "Measuring the Religious Variable: Replication." *Journal for the Scientific Study of Religion*, Vol. 11, No. 3 (September).
Klausner, Samuel Z.
1963 "Methods in Data Collection in Studies of Religion." *Journal for the Scientific Study of Religion* 3, No. 4: 193-203.
Kroeber, A. L., and Talcott Parsons
1958 "The Concepts of Culture and of Social System." *American Sociological Review*, Vol. 23 (October).
Kuhn, Thomas S.
1962 *The Structure of Scientific Revolutions*. Chicago: University of Chicago Press.
Kurokawa, Minako
1969 "Psycho-Social Roles of Mennonite Children in a Changing Society." *Canadian Review of*

Sociology and Anthropology,
Vol. 6, No. 1 (February).

Lachance, Jean-Marie
1955   "Étude sur l'enseignement du
catéchisme d'après les théories
de Jean Piaget." Thèse de
licence en psychologie, Institut
de psychologie de l'Université
de Montréal, non-publiée.

Lapointe, Gérard
1967   *Structures sociales et attitudes
religieuses du diocèse de Sainte-
Anne de la Pocatière*. Québec:
Université Laval, Centre de
Recherches en sociologie
religieuse.

Laskin, Richard, and Peter Baird
1970   "Factors in Voter Turnout and
Party Preference in a Saskatchewan Town." *Canadian Journal
of Political Science* 3, No. 3
(September): 450–62.

League for Social Reconstruction
1935   *Social Planning for Canada*.
Toronto: Thomas Nelson.

Lenski, Gerhard
1961   *The Religious Factor*. Garden
City: Doubleday.

Leuba, James H.
1912   *A Psychological Study of
Religion*. New York: Macmillan.
1916   *The Belief in God and Immortality*. Chicago: Open Court.

Lévesque, Georges-Henri
1974   "Itinéraires sociologiques."
Recherches Sociographiques
15, Nos. 2-3 (May-August):
203-11.

Levi-Strauss, C.
1968   *Structural Anthropology*.
London: Allen Lane. (Translation of *Anthropologie Structur-
ale, 1958.*)

Lowry, Douglas
1969   "Economic Motivation Among
Canadian Calvinists." Unpub-
lished Ph.D. thesis,
Massachusetts Institute of
Technology.

Luckmann, Thomas
1967   *The Invisible Religion*. New
York: Macmillan.

Malcolm X
1965   *Autobiography of Malcolm X*.
New York: Grove Press.

Malinowski, Bronislaw
1931   "Anthropology." *Encyclopaedia
Britannica*.
1955   *Sex and Repression in Savage
Society*. Cleveland: Meridian.

Mann, William E.
1955   *Sect, Cult and Church in Alberta*.
Toronto: University of Toronto
Press.

Marsh, Robert M.
1967   *Comparative Sociology*. New
York: Harcourt, Brace and
World.

Martin, D.A.
1962   "The Denomination." *British
Journal of Sociology* 13
(March): 1-14.

Marx, Gary T.
1967   "Religion: Opiate or Inspiration
of Civil Rights Militancy Among
Negroes?" *American Sociological
Review*, Vol. 32, No. 1 (Feb.).

Marx, Karl, and Friedrich Engels
1964   *On Religion*. New York:
Schocken Books.

May, Henry F.
1949   *Protestant Churches and Industrial America*. New York:
Harper and Brothers.

McCready, William C.
1972   "Faith of Our Fathers: A Study
of the Process of Religious
Socialization." Unpublished
Ph.D. dissertation, University of
Illinois, Circle Campus.

McDowell, Jennifer
1974   "Soviet Civil Ceremonies."
*Journal for the Scientific Study
of Religion* 13, No. 3 (September): 265-79.

Meadows, Dennis
1972   *The Limits To Growth*. Report
for the Club of Rome. New
York: New American Library.

Means, Richard L.
1970   "Methodology for the Sociology
of Religion." *Sociological
Analysis* 31, No. 4: 180-96.

Meisel, John
1956   "Religious Affiliation and Voting Behaviour." *Canadian
Journal of Economics and Political Science* 22, No. 4: 481-96.
1962   ed. *The Canadian Federal Election of 1957*. Toronto: University
of Toronto Press: 139-42.

1964   ed. *Papers on the 1962 Election.* Toronto: University of Toronto Press: Conclusion.

Merton, Robert K.
1957 (1949) *Social Theory and Social Structure.* Glencoe, Ill.: Free Press.

Miller, Delbert C.
1970   *Handbook of Research Design and Social Measurement,* 2nd edn. New York: David McKay.

Millett, David
1969   "A Typology of Religious Organizations Suggested by the Canadian Census." *Sociological Analysis* 30, No. 2: 108-19.

1971   "The Orthodox Church: Ukrainian, Greek, and Syrian." In J. L. Elliott, ed., *Immigrant Groups.* Scarborough, Ont.: Prentice-Hall.

Miner, Horace
1939   *St. Denis: a French-Canadian Parish.* Chicago: University of Chicago Press.

Moberg, David O.
1962   *The Church as a Social Institution.* Englewood Cliffs, N.J.: Prentice-Hall.

Niebuhr, H. Richard
1929   *The Social Sources of Denominationalism.* New York: Henry Holt.

Niebuhr, Reinhold
1932   *Moral Man and Immoral Society.* New York: Charles Scribner's Sons.

1955   *The Self and the Drama of History.* New York: Charles Scribner's Sons.

Northover, Wallace
1974   "Variations in Belief among Roman Catholics." In C. Beattie and S. Crysdale, eds., *Sociology Canada: Readings.* Toronto: Butterworth.

Nottingham, Elizabeth K.
1954   *Religion and Society.* New York: Random House.

1971   *Religion: a Sociological View.* New York: Random House.

O'Dea, Thomas F.
1966   *The Sociology of Religion.* Englewood Cliffs, N.J.: Prentice-Hall.

1970   "The Sociology of Religion

Reconsidered." *Sociological Analysis* 21, No. 3: 145-52.

Otto, Rudolf
1923   (1917) *The Idea of the Holy,* rev. edn. Trans. by John W. Harvey. London: Oxford University Press.

Parenton, Vernon J.
1948   "The Rural French-Speaking People of Quebec and South Louisiana: A Comparative Study of Social Structure and Organization with Emphasis on the Role of the Catholic Church." Ph.D. thesis, Harvard University.

Parsons, Talcott
1937   *The Structure of Social Action.* New York: McGraw-Hill.

1960   *Structure and Process in Modern Society.* New York: Free Press.

1963   "Introduction" in Weber, 1963: xix-lxvii.

Perlin, George
1964   "St. John's West." In John Meisel, ed., *Papers on the 1962 Election.* Toronto: University of Toronto Press.

Pickering, W. S. F.
1963   "The Church in a Changing Society." *Bulletin of the Council for Social Service.* Toronto: Anglican Church of Canada.

————, and J. L. Blanchard
1967   *Taken for Granted: A Survey of the Parish Clergy of the Anglican Church of Canada.* Toronto: General Synod.

Pinard, Maurice
1971   *The Rise of a Third Party: A Study in Crisis Politics.* Englewood Cliffs, N.J.: Prentice-Hall.

Pletsch, Donald J.
1966   "Ecumenism in Two Protestant Churches in Ontario." M.Sc. thesis, University of Guelph.

Pope, Liston
1942   *Millhands and Preachers.* New Haven: Yale University Press.

Porter, John
1965   *The Vertical Mosaic.* Toronto: University of Toronto Press.

Poulat, E.
1967   "Religious Sociology and Its Aims." In J. Brothers, ed., *Readings in the Sociology of Religion.* London: Pergamon.

Presbyterian Church of Canada
1969   "Ministry of the Presbyterian
        Church in Canada." Toronto:
        Committee on Recruitment and
        Vocation.
Quinley, Harold E.
1974   "The Dilemma of an Activist
        Church." *Journal for the Scienti-
        fic Study of Religion* 13, No. 1
        (March): 1-21.
Rebb, Earl, ed.
1964   *Religious Conflict in America.*
        Garden City: Doubleday.
Regenstreif, Peter
1963   "Some Aspects of National
        Party Support in Canada."
        *Canadian Journal of Economics
        and Political Science* 29, No. 1
        (February): 59-74.
1964   "Group Perceptions and the
        Vote." In John Meisel, ed.,
        Papers on the 1962 Election.
        Toronto: University of Toronto
        Press.
Robertson, Roland, ed.
1969   *Sociology of Religion.* Har-
        mondsworth: Penguin.
Rocher, Guy
1970   "The Future of Sociology."
        Paper given at the annual meet-
        ing of the Canadian Sociology
        and Anthropology Association.
        Translated and abstracted in C.
        Beattie and S. Crysdale, *Socio-
        logy Canada: Readings.* 1974.
        Toronto: Butterworth.
1972   *A General Introduction to
        Sociology.* Trans. by Peta
        Sheriff. Toronto: Macmillan of
        Canada.
Rokeach, Milton
1960   *The Open and Closed Mind.*
        New York: Basic Books.
Roszak, Theodore
1968   *The Making of a Counter
        Culture.* Garden City:
        Doubleday.
Rouleau, Jean-Paul
1968   *Chicoutimi: contexte socio-
        religieux et adaptation pastorale.*
        Québec: Université Laval,
        Centre de Recherches en Sociolo-
        gie religieuse.
Rousseau, Jacques
1952   "Persistances päiennes chez les
        Amérindiens de la forêt boreale."

Dans Les Cahiers des Dix, Vol.
17.
1954   "De menus rites päiens de la
        forêt canadienne." Dans *Les
        Cahiers des Dix,* Vol. 19.
Routhier, Francoise
1964   *L'Île d'Orléans.* Québec: Univer-
        sité Laval, Centre de Recherches
        en Sociologie religieuse.
1965   *Jonquière. Kénogami. Arvida:
        contexte socio-religieux et
        adaptation pastorale.* Québec:
        Université Laval, Centre de
        Recherches en Sociologie
        religieuse.
1966   *Zone de Shipshaw-Valin: étude
        de sociographie pastorale.*
        Québec: Université Laval,
        Centre de Recherche en Sociolo-
        gie religieuse.
Ryan, William F.
1966   *The Clergy and Economic
        Growth in Quebec, 1864-1914.*
        Québec: Les Presses de l'Univer-
        sité Laval.
Samuelsson, Kurt
1964   (1957) *Religion and Economic
        Action.* New York: Harper
        Torchbook.
Scharf, Betty R.
1971   *The Sociology of Religion.* New
        York: Harper Torchbook.
Schmidt, Wilhelm
1935   *The Origins and Growth of
        Religion.* London: Methuen.
Schneider, Louis
1970   *Sociological Approach to Reli-
        gion.* New York: John Wiley
        and Sons.
Schutz, Alfred
1967   (1937) *The Phenomenology of
        the Social World.* Trans. by G.
        Walsh and F. Lehnert. Chicago:
        Northwestern University Press.
Schwartz, Mildred
1967   *Public Opinion and Canadian
        Identity.* Berkeley: University
        of California Press.
Scott, R. B. Y., and G. Vlastos, eds.
1936   *Toward the Christian Revolution.*
        Chicago: Willett Clark.
Segar, I.
1957   *Durkheim and His Critics on the
        Sociology of Religion.* New
        York: Columbia University
        Press.

Settle, Lester M.
1971   *The Functional Community and Parish Organization: West Colchester Research Project.* Toronto: Division of Outreach, United Church of Canada.

Shaffir, William
1974   *Life in a Religious Community: The Lubavitcher Chassidim in Montreal.* Toronto: Holt, Rinehart and Winston.

Silverstein, Sandford
1968   "Occupational Class and Voting Behaviour: Electoral Support of a Left-Wing Protest Movement in a Period of Prosperity." In S. M. Lipset, *Agrarian Socialism.* Garden City: Anchor Books.

Simmel, Georg.
1955   (1908) *Conflict and the Web of Group Affiliations.* Trans. by Reinhard Bendix. New York: The Free Press.

Snook, John B.
1974   "An Alternative to Church-Sect." *Journal for the Scientific Study of Religion* 13, No. 2: 191-204.

Spencer, Herbert
1897   *The Principles of Sociology*, 3rd ed. New York: Appleton-Century-Crofts.

Spinks, G. Stephen
1965   *Psychology and Religion.* Boston: Beacon Press.

Starbuck, Edwin D.
1899   *The Psychology of Religion: An Empirical Study of the Growth of Religious Consciousness.* New York: Charles Scribner's Sons.

Stark, Rodney, and Charles Y. Glock
1968   *American Piety: The Nature of Religious Commitment.* Berkeley: University of California Press.

Stryckman, Paul
1970   *Les prêtres du Québec d'aujourd'hui.* Québec: Université Laval, Centre de Recherches en Sociologie religieuse.

Tawney, R. H.
1926   *Religion and the Rise of Capitalism.* New York: Harcourt, Brace and World.

Tillich, Paul
1951   *Systematic Theology*, Vol. 1.

Chicago: University of Chicago Press.

Tremblay, Roland
1966   "Les attitudes de charité chez l'adolescent." Thèse de licence en psychopédagogie, Université Laval, non publiée.

Troeltsch, Ernst
1931   (1911) *The Social Teaching of the Christian Churches.* 2 vols. New York: Macmillan.

Tylor, Edward B.
1924   (1871) *Primitive Culture.* 7th edn. New York: Brentano's.

van den Berghe, Pierre L.
1963   "Dialectic and Functionalism: Toward a Theoretical Synthesis." *American Sociological Review* 28, No. 5: 695-705.

van der Leeuw, G.
1967   (1933) *Religion in Essence and Manifestation.* 2 vols. Trans. by J. E. Turner. Gloucester, Mass.: Peter Smith.

Van Loon, Richard J., and M. S. Whittington
1971   *The Canadian Political System.* Toronto: McGraw-Hill Ryerson.

Villeneuve, Rudolph
1969   "Signs of the Times: A Diocese in Transition." Alexandria, Ont.: Diocese of Alexandria.

Vrijhof, P. H.
1967   "What Is the Sociology of Religion?" In J. Brothers, ed., *Readings in the Sociology of Religion.* London: Pergamon.

Wach, Joachim
1944   *The Sociology of Religion.* Chicago: University of Chicago Press.

Walsh, George
1967   "Introduction" in A. Schutz, 1967, pp. xv-xxix.

Weber, Max
1951   *The Religion of China.* Trans. by H. H. Gerth. New York: Free Press.

1952   *Ancient Judaism.* Trans. by H. H. Gerth and Don Martindale. New York: Free Press.

1958   *The Religion of India.* Trans. by H. H. Gerth and Don Martindale. New York: Free Press.

1958   (1904-5) *The Protestant Ethic and the Spirit of Capitalism.*

Trans. by T. Parsons. New York:
Charles Scribner's Sons.
1963   *The Sociology of Religion.*
Trans. by E. Fischoff. Boston:
Beacon Press.
Weinberg, S. Kirson, ed.
1967   *The Sociology of Mental Dis-
orders.* Chicago: Aldine.
Wener, Normand
1968   *Les catholiques pratiquants et
l'Église de Montréal.* Montréal:
Action Catholique.
Whyte, Donald
1966   "Religion and the Rural
Church." In M. A. Tremblay and
W. J. Anderson, eds., *Rural
Canada in Transition.* Ottawa:

Agricultural Economics Research
Council of Canada.
Wilson, Bryan R.
1963   "Typology of Sects in Dynamic
and Comparative Perspective."
Archiv. Sociol. Relig. 8, No. 16
(July-Dec.) : 49-63.
1967   *Patterns of Sectarianism.*
London: Heinemann.
Wirth, Louis
1938   "Urbanism as a Way of Life."
American Journal of Sociology,
Vol. 44.
Yinger, J. Milton
1970   *The Scientific Study of Religion.*
New York: Macmillan.

THROUGH HISTORY

1.

Indigenous Religions

Canadian Indian Religion*

Diamond Jenness

At a time like the present, when the Christian religion is being openly attacked and in some countries rejected, when men's thoughts are being regimented and directed towards increasing the majesty and power of a new and to some of us a monstrous divinity, the state, it is appropriate that we should consider the thoughts of certain non-Christian peoples [concerning] man's place and purpose in the universe. For religion has been one of the most potent forces in human history, and nowhere was this more apparent than in Canada, a half-continent inhabited, before European settlement, by at least fifty Indian tribes [which although differing widely] in the outward forms of religious observances were nevertheless remarkably uniform in the inner beliefs on which these observances were founded.

The basic doctrine throughout the country was the kinship of man with nature. Europeans tend to set man apart from the outside world: they consider him a special creation of the Deity; endowed with a soul and aspirations that mark him off from everything else. Moreover, they sharply contrast animate with inanimate nature. The Canadian Indian

*Appeared first in *Anthropologica* 1 (1955): 1-17. Published here in abridged form with the kind permission of the author's estate and the publisher.

recognized no such distinctions. To him all nature was one in kind; the rocks on the hillside, the trees of the forests, the animals on land, in the sea, and in the sky, even the stars in the distant heavens, all were endowed with different outward forms, but all alike possessed personalities similar in kind to those of the Indians themselves. Their outward forms were transitory and impermanent, but their personalities, their souls, remained as constant and unchanged as human souls. Thus, the universe of the Indians was filled with spiritual entities all of which claimed the Indians as their kin.

Just as human beings, however, are not all [equally] gifted, so likewise was there variation in the external world. Not only have birds the gift of flight which is denied to human beings, but the eagle soars higher than other birds and surpasses them in strength. A blow that would crush a man makes no impression on hard granite. In the eyes of the Indian these "qualities" inherent in external things were the outward manifestations of spiritual forces. Consequently everything in his cosmos glowed in greater or lesser degree with some spiritual force that might be either friendly or hostile.

Observation revealed no definite grading in this cosmos, no orderly subjection of certain powers to others. Yet clearly some were far mightier, more free and more far-reaching in their influence. Who, for example, could check the forces inherent in the winds, the thunder, mother earth, and the light- and life-giving sun? These awed the Indians with a sense of mystery; and throughout the whole of Canada man held them in special veneration. A few tribes in the north of Canada lingered at this stage of thought. Their universe was a playground for spiritual forces that differed in might from one another, but [that], one and all, acted independently.

Such a conception of the universe [did] not satisfy the majority of the Indians. Just as they demanded order and discipline in their societies, so they found the universe unintelligible unless it was organized on a similar pattern. For every species of plant and animal, therefore, they postulated a ruler or chief with magnified powers, and these in turn they subordinated to still higher powers. The latter were generally vague and nameless, but in some regions the Indians defined them more clearly and gave them such names as the "Rulers of the Four Quarters of the Sky". Above these again, in the belief of many, ruled the sun deity, associated with, but ranking higher than, the moon; and the sun himself was but the visible manifestation, the first deputy, of a still mightier power, the true ruler of the cosmos.

In this way the Indians arrived at the conception of a Supreme Being. Manifestly, their conception of him hardly coincided with the Christian conception. He was not the Great Creator who fashioned the world and directed its course for some divine destiny beyond the intelligence of mortal minds. Neither was he that Supreme Intelligence or Guiding Spirit pervading all matter and all space. Rather, he was the ultimate source of all the power or force in the universe, power that was single and yet divisible, like the radiation of the sun; power that actually was divided, not only among lesser deities, but among all the objects of nature, including man himself.

Christianity, which makes God the fount of all power, makes him also the fount of all goodness. Some of its adherents hold the problem of evil insoluble. Others dispose of it in one of two ways: either they deny its real existence, asserting that what appears evil to human eyes is simply God's way of working and inevitably results in good; or, if they cannot convince themselves that evil is unreal, they postulate a duality in the universe, [to include also] a God of Darkness and Evil. A few tribes in eastern Canada arrived at the second solution, that the world was governed by two Great Spirits, one good and one evil; but [these tribes] too failed to resolve the contradiction which this doctrine entails.

The majority of the Canadian Indians ignored the problem altogether. They accepted without question the existence of evil, and concerned themselves not with its explanation, but with its avoidance. Most of them thought that even the Great Spirit was too remote to trouble himself greatly about human affairs; and while they rendered him lip service, and occasionally approached him in prayer, they directed most of their thoughts to those lesser powers—the spirits of birds and animals, and of the sun, the winds, and the thunder—that seemed to exert a more immediate influence on their daily lives.

These powers, as we have seen, might be either friendly or hostile. Whether they were friendly or merely neutral, the Indian might unwittingly arouse their hostility through his own actions. To avoid this calamity, every tribe evolved in the course of centuries innumerable regulations and taboos that were handed down from one generation to another. It was natural that the most important regulations and taboos should relate to the food supply, since the hunter who offended the spirits of the game animals could hardly hope for success in the chase.

Any violation of these regulations and taboos was sin, and sin inevitably brought punishment on the wrong-doer and his kin unless the unseen powers turned a merciful ear to their prayers and entreaties. Certain tribes in eastern and northern Canada believed that public confession would absolve them from all supernatural penalties. The tribes in southern Ontario, on the other hand, found the road of escape through a scape-goat; they ceremoniously cast their sins on a pure white dog, which they then strangled and burnt as a sacrifice.

Sacrifices were common from the Atlantic to the Pacific, but only rarely did they involve the killing of animals or of human beings. Before attempting to run a dangerous rapid, or to cross a perilous defile in the mountains, the Indians would throw a little tobacco into the water, or add a stick to a pile already raised by previous travellers, in the hope that the supernatural power dwelling in the neighbourhood would grant them safe passage. Sacrifice, however, was never more than an adjunct to prayer, in which the Indians found the true key [which] they believed would unlock the gate to the supernatural world.

There is a world-wide tendency for prayer to become stereotyped, to degenerate into incantations of meaningless or half-meaningless phrases. This rarely happened in Canada, and then mainly in those districts where certain religious rites became the function of a regular priesthood. The daily prayers of the Indian issued from him spontaneously. The supernatural world seemed too real and omnipresent for him to place any trust in unintelligible formulae: he felt constrained to address it from his heart.

He did, however, believe that prayer could be powerfully reinforced by fasting (itself a major sacrifice), especially at the age of adolescence, when the physical and psychological changes in human beings brought them into closer relationship with the unseen forces all around. Throughout most of Canada, boys (and sometimes girls) of tender years fasted and prayed in solitude in the hope of a visitation from the supernatural world. Each tribe had its own notion of the form the visitation would take. Whatever the form the vision assumed, the suppliant was firmly convinced that he had acquired a supernatural guardian whom he could summon to his aid in any dire emergency; and ever afterwards, in compliance with his dream, he carried on his person a dried animal skin, a feather, or perhaps a wisp of hair, as an everpresent assurance of his "blessing".

In this way the Indian, inheriting the doctrine of his spiritual kinship

with nature, sought to enlist its forces for his own protection and welfare. By his prayers and fasting he forged a mystic link between himself
and the supernatural—or, as he himself regarded it—the natural world,
a link so mystic and holy that he rarely dared to reveal the vision that
created it, through fear that the link would be broken. Nor did he strain
the link needlessly by invoking his guardian spirit on every occasion of
distress or difficulty. Too frequent a summons would "wear out the
blessing", and the link might be snapped when perhaps it was most
needed. Hence he called on his guardian spirit only in the greatest crises,
frequently only once or twice in a lifetime. Nevertheless, it was a never-
failing source of strength and confidence. The Indian who faithfully cherished his vision, and obeyed whatever instructions his guardian spirit had
then imparted to him, felt, as it were, protecting wings around him that
would shelter him in any dire emergency.

Not all the amulets that the Indian wore on his clothing or around
his neck symbolized his guardian spirit. Some had a purely magical intention. Just as Europeans have been known to conceal "lucky" coins in
their pockets, so certain Indians carried curiously shaped stones to bring
them good-fortune in their hunting. Amulets of this kind contained their
own magical powers, and could be bought and sold without losing their
supposed efficacy. The amulet symbolizing the guardian spirit, on the
other hand, possessed no more intrinsic value than the crucifix worn by
a Christian priest. It was a token of its owner's relationship with the
spiritual world, a relationship established by his vision; and it could possess no meaning or value to another Indian whose vision was certainly
different.

Many Indians, however, found it difficult to dissociate all virtue from
the guardian-spirit amulet, especially when its owner was unusually successful in life. Those who lived on the plains finally adopted the [belief]
that the "blessing" could be transferred with the symbol, provided the
new owner acquired also a knowledge of the vision and of the songs that
went along with it. In that area the buying and selling of visions became
an established ritual, and a few amulets were enlarged into complex
"bundles" associated with important tribal activities. Their owners in
consequence enjoyed great prestige and ranked among the leading men
in their communities.

Dreams of every kind possessed deep significance to the Indians
because they seemed to free the soul from its bodily shackles and to
permit its association with other spiritual forces. Certain Indians were

more prone to visions than others; in the eyes of their countrymen they were especially favoured by the supernatural powers, which might appear to them unsolicited even in broad daylight and bestow on them faculties not granted to ordinary individuals. These persons then became medicine-men in their communities, credited with power to divine the future and to cause and cure diseases. The majority of the medicine-men, however, were normal individuals who developed a technique by training under other medicine-men, and deliberately induced their visions by long-con-tinued prayer and fasting. They were not quacks (with rare exceptions), for they genuinely believed in their mission and their ability to commune with the unseen world. Some of them, indeed, underwent fearful priva-tions in childhood to equip themselves for their profession.

There were regional variations in the training that medicine-men underwent and in the methods that they employed, but nearly everywhere they pursued their profession in complete independence of one another. Only in Ontario, and in parts of British Columbia, were some of them organized into societies, and even in those places they could not usurp the religious leadership or modify to any appreciable extent the prevail-ing beliefs and practices. In British Columbia they had to subordinate themselves to a clan organization based on a system of castes, while the Ontario tribes were too democratic even to submit unquestioningly to their elected political officers, much less to tolerate a domination of the religious field by any special group. So although medicine-men often attained considerable influence, nowhere did the Indians evolve a power-ful priesthood to direct their religious life. In many of their religious festivals, indeed, the presiding officers were not medicine-men at all, but laymen, either leaders in civil life or officials directly appointed by the people.

The absence of organized priesthoods, and the fluidity of Indian reli-gion, exercised a profound influence on the mythology. Within certain limits, each native had to make his own adjustments to his spiritual world, and thereby develop his own individual tenets and practices. No tribe, therefore, formulated for itself a coherent body of myths or legends that it handed down generation after generation. It is true that there were coherent bodies of myths on the Pacific coast, but these were the pro-perty, not of a tribe, but of individual families, by the same rights of tenure as the houses and the totem-poles; and they were of little concern to other families that cherished their own special myths. Likewise, on the plains, certain myths were individual possessions because they were associated with "medicine" objects, and could not be related except on special occasions, and then only by the owners of those objects. Elsewhere, myths were the common property of entire tribes; but because there was no authority to standardize or teach them, the repertory of the average Indian was small and his versions seldom agreed with those of his fellow tribesmen.

Characteristic of Canadian Indian mythology is the lack of any clear distinction between myths properly so called, quasi-historical traditions, and common folk-tales. This again was a direct outcome of the religion, or rather of that spiritual interpretation of nature on which the religion rested. The Indian believed that the powers of the supernatural world interfered in human affairs just as actively in his own day as in the days of his remote ancestors, and he attributed to their agency any and every event that he was unable to explain on purely physical grounds.

He did, however, make one distinction, one that stands out fairly sharply in the tales of nearly all tribes. It is a distinction between events he attributed to a heroic age before the world assumed its present form, and events he assigned to the world as he knew it in his daily life. In the heroic age, he believed, man could freely communicate with animals and birds, many of which, indeed, were human beings at that time, or else commonly appeared in human garb and were swayed by human thoughts and emotions. The many nature tales, similar to those we find in other lands, hark back to this earlier period. So also does another group of tales more distinctive of the Canadian Indians and of the Indians to the southward, tales of a mighty Trickster and a mighty Transformer, who are sometimes combined into a single character. In these stories the Trickster travels over the world playing pranks on men and birds and animals, but often catching himself in his own toils; while the Transformer destroys or transforms the monsters that ravage mankind, creates new animals for man's benefit, and gives to the land and the waters their present forms.

It is rather surprising, therefore, to find in Canada none of those creation myths that are so common in other parts of the world, myths that ascribe to the will of one great power the genesis of light and darkness, earth and sky. There are myths that purport to explain the origin of the moon and the Milky Way, of certain lakes and rivers, of the caribou and the salmon, and of man himself; but the notion of a First Cause for everything, of a Great Spirit that created *ex nihilo*, as it were, everything that lives or moves or has its being, seems never to have entered the Indian's mind, even in those regions where he acknowledged the existence of a

Supreme Being. He premised, perhaps unconsciously, that nature's greatest phenomena had always coexisted with the Great Spirit, and that to both alike there was neither beginning nor end.

None of his myths, again, are frankly didactic, deliberately designed to inculcate the prevailing morality. It is true that they actually served that purpose in certain regions, and that the moral of a tale was reinforced at times by an explicit epilogue. Yet this seems to have been a mere after-thought, for the whole character of Indian mythology belies its ethical intention. There is no effort, for example, to elevate right above wrong, to encourage the strong to protect the weak, or to represent that the evil-doer will meet with his just reward, either in this life or in the life hereafter.

In the character of the Canadian Indian realism and mysticism blended strangely. Beneath the semblances of external things he pictured beings animated with thoughts and emotions similar to his own, beings that struggled as he did to maintain their places in the arena of life. He did not hesitate to destroy their outward forms, to shoot down the buffalo with his arrow, or to tear up the plant from its native soil; but he extended to all things a certain measure of reverence, as befitted one who himself played a role in the same amphitheatre. The why and the wherefore of the struggle he did not ask, nor did he concern himself greatly with its ultimate outcome. It sufficed for him that he too had been stationed in the arena, and all that he demanded from his religion was assistance to play his part successfully until old age or other forces beyond his control put an end to the struggle. Whether he prayed to the spirit world around him, or turned his eyes upward to the sky god above, he asked for earthly blessings only, health and long life, a loving wife and children, and prosperity for himself and his kin. Not for one moment did he believe that death put an end to all existence; but so dense a fog obscured the after-life, so conflicting were the opinions about it, that he planned his course for an earthly existence only and blindly resigned himself to whatever fate awaited him hereafter.

The Kwakiutl of British Columbia*

Werner Müller

Primitive cultures tend towards individualization, not generalization. With the growth of settled life the basic patterns become more and more complex, from both a linguistic and a religious point of view, so that one village [becomes] set apart from the next by widening cultural differences. This tendency to split, which gives primitive cultures their immense richness and complexity, was brutally cut short by the European invasion of North America.

The extent to which this process can be carried, and the degree of personal identity that can attach to even the smallest unit, is illustrated by the example of the Pacific Coast fishing tribes, which inhabit a narrow coastal strip which lies on the side of the continent furthest from Europe and which continued its evolution relatively undisturbed into the nineteenth century.

On the western side of the continent the division between more advanced and less advanced peoples is the exact reverse of that in the

*Appeared first as "North America", in W. Krickeberg *et al., Pre-Columbian American Religions*, trans. Stanley Davis (London: Weidenfeld and Nicolson, 1968), pp. 210-15. Published here in abridged form with the kind permission of the publisher.

east; here the primitives live in the south and the advanced tribes in the north. What is more, agriculture offers no reliable criterion; the cultural standard attained by the peoples of British Columbia is based not on farming but on fishing.

The fjord coastline between Vancouver and Alaska, with its thousands of islands, brings the sea far inland. Food is there for the taking; there are fish and seals all the year round. With even the most rudimentary equipment, terrible and degrading winter hunger like that experienced by the tribes of inland Canada is impossible in British Columbia. The constant torrential rains produce thick stands of firs and cedars which are as inexhaustible as the fish of the ocean. Between the waters of the innumerable inlets and the steep, dark green wooden slopes lie the villages of the inhabitants. Approaching from the direction of the fjord— there are no other communication routes—one sees, raised a little above the beach, a street of large, low gabled wooden houses. From some of the seaward gables rise massive, elaborately carved poles carved from single tree trunks. On the beach below are brightly painted dugout canoes; with the gaily coloured poles and house gables they give the whole scene an extraordinarily exotic air under the eternally grey skies.[1]

Each house is like a massive wooden citadel. The posts, beams, and planks are of gigantic dimensions, and the impression of excessive size is enhanced by the fact that these structures, approximately thirty feet square, might easily have been constructed quite solidly with much less expenditure of material. The framing inside the gable ends, which are the main supports of the structure, consists of pairs of posts so thick that two men can hardly reach round them. On these rest two immense beams which support only a comparatively light shingle roof. The walls, which consist of planks a handspan thick, are more suitable for a fortress than a mere dwelling. This is the kind of building that a megalithic culture might build if reduced to using wood instead of outside stone blocks: no longer megalithic but megaxylic.

The Pacific Coast culture, so massively embodied in the timber block-houses of its villages, is found all along the coast from Alaska to the mouth of the Columbia River. In the north it gradually gives place to Eskimo culture, and in the south to that of the Californian tribes; but the unity which encompasses all the disparate and fragmentary ethnic groups in the coastal area is remarkable.

The origins of the Pacific tribes are apparent from their languages. There are Athapascan tribes from the Canadian interior such as the

Tlingit, Tshimshian, and Haida; Old Salishan tribes such as the Kwa-kiutl and the Nootka, also from east of the Rockies; and New Salishan tribes such as the Bella Coola, who are the newest arrivals. The Pacific Coast culture crystallized in its purest form among the southern Kwakiutl on Vancouver Island and the adjacent regions of the mainland, and this group will serve as a paradigm of the whole culture.

Here, if anywhere at all, is a primitive culture completely impreg-nated with religious ideas. One has to deal with an ever-present religious control and motivation. The "civilized" division into "Sunday" and "everyday" is completely unknown in undisturbed primitive groups.

The existence of these Pacific fishermen is governed by the rhythm of a bipartite year. In the summer they leave their houses and go to the river estuaries and the entrances to the fjords to catch salmon, or to the forest to gather berries. They live in improvised bark huts and there is little social contact. Only occasional minor festivals interrupt the iso-lated and contemplative existence of each clan and each family.

In November all this changes. The coast is lashed by south-westerly gales, and the Indians return to their villages. Religious life suddenly comes into its own, and one festival follows close upon another. Pipes are played, bullroarers whirled, the roar of the drums is heard from the festal houses, and on the tall carved poles float garlands of fir twigs tied with bast, signifying that the god is present.

Unlike the Pueblo festal calendar, in which some kind of ritual activity is always going on throughout the year,[2] the Pacific Coast year swings from an inactive to an active phase, summer and winter, near to the gods and far from them. The tribe we have chosen as a model, the Kwakiutl, aptly describe the two periods as bachus, "profane", and tsetsaequa, "full of secrets".

The social structure, too, is based on this rhythm; its basic units, the clans and the fraternities, apply to different times of the year. In summer the village community is divided into clans or super-families; in winter, into fraternities or religious societies. But of course the two types of classification apply to exactly the same individuals.

The clans of the Kwakiutl are not based on blood relationships but have a mythical origin. Each clan, which occupies a group of adjacent houses, is considered to stem from a single common ancestor, who descended from the sky or emerged from the underworld or from the ocean, bringing with him the patrimony of the clan: the emblems, masks, dances and names which are peculiar to it.[3]

The clan legend, an extremely important feature of the verbal lore of the Pacific Coast culture, deals in detail with the circumstances in which the clan ancestry or "first one" received these things as gifts from one of the gods. Family history thus constitutes a sort of title deed.[4] This heritage is represented on the carved poles before the doors of the houses and in the paintings on the gables, from which it is possible to read the name, origin, and hereditary possessions of the families concerned. It will be seen that in the course of time the evolution of clan tradition must necessarily have resulted in an immense variety of myths and modes of worship.

Among the goods which make up the heritage of each clan is an immense variety of fantastic masks which represent the finest achievements of the Indian wood carver's art. Considering that the other "hereditary possessions" of the clan consist of dances, emblems, and names, the inheritance system can hardly be said to be based on practical considerations. It is true that each clan also has tangible assets such as its own fishing, hunting, berry-gathering preserves, but the principal emphasis is definitely on the religious values which were gifts of the gods. A sharper contrast can hardly be imagined between Indian and urban culture, between the world of painted masks and the world of share-portfolios, than the difference between the two conceptions of "hereditary possessions".

The winter half of the year is dominated by the ritual fraternities, the members of which have to be specifically initiated. These fraternities are linked with the gods. The pantheon is [unique in several ways]. Pueblo rainmakers and animal gods are schematic and impersonal, and only the mask gods are individualized to any extent in their emblems and functions. But the transcendental beings believed in by the Kwakiutl can with perfect justification be referred to as personal gods. They are individuals with their own distinct functions. This is a rare phenomenon anywhere in North America. The Kwakiutl pantheon is a genuine divine hierarchy, not arranged in accordance with a patriarchal family structure, but based on the four quarters of the horizon.

It would only be confusing to attempt to enumerate all the fabulous lands on the rim of the cosmos in which the Kwakiutl gods have their homes; but one deity deserves special treatment. This is Baxbakwala-nuxsiwae, "the cannibal at the north end of the world".[5] This god, who appears in the form of a man, embodies an institution characteristic of the tribe. He feeds upon human beings. His other names refer to the same subject: "He has eaten someone", "He devours skulls on earth". The cry "hap, hap", "eat, eat!" signals the presence of the god.

Baxbakwalanuxsiwae dwells in the exact north of the world with his family and his retinue. From the openings in the roof of his house there rises red smoke. His wife and his maidservant both catch people for their lord and master to eat. At the door there sits a raven who pecks out the eyes of the corpses as they come in. Also present are the fabulous bird Hochhoku, who cracks the brain pans with his long beak, and a man-eating grizzly bear.

This cannibal god is by no means a remote figure. He dwells at the north end of the world in the summer; but when the autumn storms buffet the houses he comes southward with his retinue towards the dwellings of men. He then lives in the festal houses, appears in person behind a grotesque mask, and dances before the assembled villagers.

The arrival of the god is the signal for the transformation of the social structure. The clans are disbanded and the villagers re-group in fraternities and degrees. Each individual deity has his own adherents: there is a society of votaries of Baxbakwalanuxsiwae, called the *hamatsa*, "devourers"; the wife of the god, the raven, Hochhoku, and the grizzly all have their own fraternities. Membership of these groups is hereditary; each family has the right to introduce its children into its own club. The fraternities have a fixed order of precedence, the hamatsa naturally being the senior society. It is reserved for heads of clans.

As well as this divine world there is also an origin myth—not a creation myth, in which the Kwakiutl are not interested, but the story of the origins of ritual life: Originally there were only animals on earth. They lived on Crooked Beach in two villages; one had Raven and Otter as its chiefs, and the other had Head Wolf as its chief.[6] The two villages hated each other bitterly. The wolves had the winter ritual, i.e. the initiation ceremonies of the hamatsa, to themselves. When they celebrated it for the first time they were surprised by Raven and Otter and killed. Since then the ritual has been the lawful property of the victors, and all the rites performed today are re-enactments of those primordial festivities on Crooked Beach.

After the victory of Raven and Otter there began the second age of the world, in which Raven and Otter acted as "transformers", providing sunlight, filling the rivers with salmon, and regulating the tides and the wind; in short, like the Algonquin and Athapascan culture heroes, Raven and Otter gave mankind the wherewithal to live. Some of the animals now laid aside their animal shape and became human beings, while others remained as they were. On their travels these first human beings, the clan ancestors, received the clan patrimonies as gifts from the gods. The earth gradually took on the appearance that it has today.

The cosmos, like the origin myth, is divided into three levels, with the earth in the middle.[7] On the "other side", above the "upper rim of the clouds", dwell the sun, the dawn, the thunderbird, and many other beings. The underworld is the realm of the dead. A mighty copper pole passes through all three layers and supports the earth and the sky. This cosmic house is the dwelling of gods and men.

The rites, like those of the Pueblo, concentrate on personal deities; the great difference lies in the purpose behind the rites. Whereas the Pueblo gods are servants of life, and bring clouds, rain, snow, happiness, and fruitfulness, for the Kwakiutl life is the servant of the gods. In the winter half of the year, one ritual follows hard upon another; but the purpose is not to beg the supernatural beings for fish, whales, and seals, but to swell the ranks of their votaries by initiating new members into the various fraternities.

For the Pueblo the life of the whole world is at stake, even that of squirrels and trees; but Pacific Coast ceremonialism is concerned only with man. The distinction is the same as that between the Delaware Big House and the central Algonquin medicine hut; in the Big House prayers are offered up for the welfare of the whole world, while the medicine hut concerns itself with the individual novice who is being initiated. This sharp contrast between universalist and individualist forms of worship has a historical origin. The central Algonquin, with their partial conversion to agriculture, are clearly among the newest elements of the Canadian hunting and gathering population; and the linguistic evidence shows the Pacific Coast fishing tribes to have the same origins. The religious patterns of the Canadian forest Indians centre on the individual; and ethnographically speaking, the Pacific Coast tribes of British Columbia are merely their most advanced representatives. Pacific Coast ceremonialism therefore is confined to individual rites; there is no festal calendar relating to such events as the beginning of a new year or the opening of the salmon season.

NOTES

1   Cf. the introductory sections in Müller (1955).

2   See the day-to-day festal calendar in Parsons (1939), pp. 514 sqq.

3 Boas (1889), p. 826; Boas (1890), p. 608. The tribe itself, on the other hand, is a territorial unit; it consists of the descendants of all those clan ancestors who entered the world at a given spot.
4 The Kwakiutl carefully distinguish between clan legends (or family histories) and myths (*nuyam*). As we shall see, the myths are set in an antediluvian world, on Crooked Beach; the clan legends belong to the age after the Flood, when the first human being appeared. Texts of both kinds appear in

Boas (1902-5) and Boas (1906).
5 Concerning Baxbakwalanuxsiwae, see Boas (1897), pp. 394, 396 sqq., 405-6.
6 For a detailed description of the sacred land and its role in Kwakiutl myth and legend see Müller (1955), pp. 41 sqq. Crooked Beach is on Tournour Island, north of Johnstone Strait.
7 For the cosmology see Müller (1955), pp. 15 sqq. The cosmic significance of the post or pole has been discussed by Josef Haekel (1958).

REFERENCES

Boas, Franz
1889 First General Report on the Indians of British Columbia. *Report of the British Association for the Advancement of Science*, pp. 801-93.
1890 Second General Report on the Indians of British Columbia. *Ibid.*, pp. 562-715
1897 The Social Organization and the Secret Societies of the Kwakiutl Indians. *Report of the U.S. National Museum for 1895*, Washington, pp. 311-738.
Boas, Franz, and George Hunt
1902-5 Kwakiutl Texts. *Memoirs of the American Museum of National History*, Vol. 3. Publication of the Jessup North Pacific Expedition.
1906 Kwakiutl Texts Second Series. *Ebenda* 10, pt. I.
Haekel, Josef
1958 Kosmischer Baum und Pfahl in Mythus und Kult der Stämme Nordwestamerikas. *Wiener völkerkundliche Mitteilungen* 6 (Neue Folge 1): 33-81.
Müller, Werner
1955 Weltbild und Kult der Kwakiutl-Indianer. *Studien zur Kulturkunde* 15. Wiesbaden.
Parsons, Elsie Clews
1939 Pueblo Indian Religion, *The University of Chicago Publications in Anthropology, Ethnological Series*. Chicago.

The Netsilik Eskimo[*]

Asen Balikci

Elements of Religion

Religious beliefs and ritual observances had a great influence on Netsilik social life and formed the intellectual basis of its culture. Religion explained the world's past, present, and future states, helped control numerous crisis situations, influenced interpersonal relations, and reduced fear. Essentially the relation of society to nature was mediated by a series of symbolic representations and actions increasing an individual's feeling of security in a hostile environment.

In the following section a brief outline of the main elements of Netsilik religion will be presented, followed by an analysis of the principal functions of local ritual observances. Particular attention will be given to the specific nature of the relations between individuals and supernatural beings and among the supernaturals themselves. It will become clear that while most relations with supernaturals were ambiguous and flexible, certain classes of religious observances were extremely rigid and knew of no alternatives. Further, the influence of certain super-

[*]Appeared first in Asen Balikci, *The Netsilik Eskimo* (Garden City, N.J.: The Natural History Press 1970), Chaps. 10 and 12. Published here in abridged form with the kind permission of the author and the publisher.

naturals affected individual behavior alone, while the power of others concerned society as a whole. And while certain religious activities were thought to be beneficial to the people, others were distinctly malevolent in nature. This dichotomy proves to be the basis of Netsilik morality. Throughout this section the term "religion" will be used in its broadest sense, including such diverse elements as collective religious presentations, individual sorcery practices, and certain native classification systems.

The Netsilik believed that both the vast, cold universe and their individual camps were inhabited by supernatural beings of many different kinds. Most important were the human souls, of which there were three species: personal souls, name souls, and ghosts of deceased men and women. In addition, people were surrounded by amulet spirits with important protective powers. Animals also had souls, some incarnated and some free-floating and ghost-like. Shamans had the ability to harness many of these ghosts for specific tasks as personal protective spirits. Another category of supernaturals that inhabited certain areas of the country included various monsters, giants, and dwarfs, mostly anthropomorphic in nature. Above these various lesser spirits there reigned three major deities: the sea spirit Nuliajuk, the weather god Narssuk, and the moon spirit Tatqeq.

The Netsilik obtained their manly strength mainly from their souls. The human soul was thought to consist of a mysterious yet extremely powerful force. It contained the life force of a human being and gave him the power to act energetically and with determination. The soul strengthened the hunter's capacity to withstand hardship, enabled him to make quick and appropriate decisions, and was generally the source of all will power. Further, the soul gave a man his identity. The soul contributed to good health and animated a man's whole body. It was assumed that a man's soul was similar to his physical appearance both in size and in facial characteristics. Generally the soul resided in the hunter's body, occupying it in its entirety. In some cases of shamanistic acts, however, mention is made of very small human souls, about two inches in height, that evil sorcerers could pull from under their sleeves. These small souls could be given instructions and sent out to enter men's bodies, bringing them great misfortune or death. The belief in these reduced souls was not very widespread in the Netsilik area, however. Netsilik women also had souls, though little is ever mentioned about them.

Though the personal soul was the source of health and energy, it was also vulnerable to attack by evil spirits and malevolent shamans. All physical sickness resulted from evil spirits hurting the human soul by taking abode in the patient's body. The Netsilik knew numerous techniques to protect their souls from these harmful influences. One such practice was to have the soul removed from the body at the very moment of birth. This was done ceremonially by a shaman, who placed the soul under the soapstone lamp of a close relative of the infant, preferably the mother, where it remained forever, free to grow to full strength. The distant location of the soul confused aggressive evil spirits, who were unable to find it in the body they wanted to attack, and so their action was rendered ineffectual.

Human souls, called *inoseq* ("in the liking of man"), were considered immortal and continued their independent existence after the death of the body. If the various taboos associated with death were properly observed, the soul migrated peacefully to one of three afterworlds, where it remained forever. When a breach of a death observance occurred, the soul became an evil spirit, blinded by anger. Instead of leaving for the happy land of the dead, it stayed near camp and might strike indiscriminately against any living person, including relatives. The presence of such evil ghosts was revealed by shamans before, during, or after a disaster. Numerous techniques were used in defense against the invisible attacks of ghosts, the most reliable being the shamanistic practice, to be described later.

Quite distinct from the ordinary human souls were the name souls. Personal names were thought among the Netsilik to possess a personality of their own characterized by great power and a distinct ability to protect the name bearer from any misfortune. In fact, they acted as guardian spirits, highly beneficial to humans. It was therefore in the interest of individuals to acquire as many names as possible, and sometimes a person accumulated up to twelve names and more. No distinction was made between male and female names, which were used indiscriminately. Personal names were drawn from a variety of categories: inanimate objects, animals, and domestic activities.

Hunters valued having many names because of the additional manly strength they gained, while women thought that the many name souls they themselves possessed would make their offspring healthier. The first name soul was acquired sometime before birth and was of special importance. This was associated with the name a woman chose for her baby when having a difficult childbirth. The mother in labor called out various names; if birth was speeded following the mentioning of a particular name, it was assumed that this name soul had entered the infant's body and successfully speeded delivery. Thereafter the child would bear that name. This indicates a belief in reincarnation exclusively concerning name souls and not personal souls. It was rigorously forbidden to kill a newborn infant who was already named.

Three particular animals were distinguished by the power of their souls: seal, caribou, and bear. As with human souls after death, the hunter had to pay homage to the animal he killed by observing a number of rigorous taboos. A failure in any of these observances could turn an animal soul into a crooked spirit, a bloodthirsty monster. Particularly dangerous in this respect were bear souls. Numerous instances of shamanistic behaviour indicate a special association between evil shamans and bear souls. The Netsilik lived in perpetual fear of wandering animal ghosts, since they depended for survival on regularly killing game animals. The very food which was absolutely essential for the survival of society became a source of evil.

Death taboos for dealing with animal souls were the main strategy by which hunting animals became a safe activity. It was thought that the soul of a killed seal for which all death taboos had been properly observed would be greatly pleased by the received attention and would reincarnate in another seal body with the intention of letting itself be killed again by the same hunter. In this sense a careful hunter continuously hunted the same animal. The death taboo about seals not only prevented the soul of a seal from turning crooked by helping it reincarnate, but also ensured continuous successful hunting.

Another very important group of spirits was connected with the various amulets carried by men, women, and children alike. The physical appearance of the amulet was of little significance. The amulet received its supernatural power from the resident spirit exclusively and not because of any physical properties. Practically any small object could serve as an amulet. In the very large collection of Netsilik amulets gathered by Rasmussen (1931: 269–70) at camps near the Magnetic Pole, small parts of various animals were particularly numerous.

Most amulets were attached to the owner's coat to protect him wherever he traveled. Special belts were also worn outside the coat with numerous amulets hanging from it. While most men or women carried up to half a dozen amulets, there were exceptional cases when persons wore a very large number of amulets. Amulets were given to boys and girls by their mothers and considered strictly personal property. Only the owner could benefit from their supernatural power. They were never exchanged or given away. Women did not wear their amulets for their own benefit, but to help the children they would bear. And amulets did not lose their power with time. On the contrary, amulets increased in strength as they grew older, getting more and more powerful as they were inherited by successive generations.

There were three functional categories of amulets. The first was related to subsistence: amulets in this group were intended to bring luck to the hunter. Almost all amulets in this category concerned specific species of game animals, with caribou and seal appearing most fre-quently, followed by salmon, trout, and bear. This of course reflects both the economic importance of the seal and the unreliability of caribou hunting.

The spirits attached to the second category of amulets protected or strengthened various manly qualities not connected with specific hunting abilities. The most general of these aims was to ensure that the owner remained a real man, a proper and stern human being endowed with good health and substantial strength and vigour. More specific objectives were long life, good bearing, a strong stomach, strong shoulders, power-ful arms and fists, protection against headaches, and ability in crafts-manship, fighting, and song dueling. The third category of amulets con-cerned relations between men and the supernaturals themselves. These amulets made the owner clever at shamanizing, protected him against evil spirits, and gave him visions.

Another important class of supernatural beings were the shaman's own protective spirits, called *apersaq* ("helpers") or *tunraq*, the general term designating spirits. Some of these the shaman acquired during his initiation, others he obtained during later practice. The shaman called his spirits before a trance with the help of a special song, and could ask them to perform any number of different tasks. A great variety of things could count as a shaman's helping spirits: human beings, ghosts, ani-mals, elements of nature such as the sun or moon, and a number of monsters and bizarre beings. Their common characteristic was that their energy could be harnessed for the benefit of the officiating shaman.

The Netsilik believed that their country was peopled by a multitude of strange beings, mostly human-like but inevitably endowed with very characteristic supernatural personalities. In size they varied greatly, some being enormous monsters while others were dwarfs. While most had no real ethical characteristics, some were particularly bloodthirsty and dangerous to humans, and others were relatively indifferent to humans.

Many stories and legends were associated with these strange beings. Hunters on the trail could see their fresh tracks, follow them, and, just as they were about to reach them, see the supernatural creatures disappear on the horizon. All Netsilik, however, lived in great fear of some of these evil monsters, especially during the dark winter months. Shamans were frequently called to protect people from being devoured.

Above all these lesser spirits were the three deities: Nuliajuk, Narssuk, and Tatqeq. Nuliajuk, a female deity living in the depth of the sea, was considered the mother of all animals and the mistress of both the sea and the land. Narssuk, the giant baby, was the weather god, master of the wind, rain and snow. Tatqeq, or the moon spirit, was a deity of no great power who was generally well disposed toward mankind.

We can make certain generalizations. First comes the fact that many spirits were personally owned by the people and generally at their service: souls, name souls, shamans' protective spirits, amulet spirits. Even the relationship between persons and animal souls and monsters was direct and concerned only the parties involved. It seems that only the major deities performed functions of collective concern involving society as a whole. With the exception of name souls and amulet spirits, almost all supernatural beings were either openly evil and dangerous or could become such, and these would include human souls that became evil ghosts, animal souls, and shamans' own protective spirits, who could change nature and become bloodthirsty monsters.

Clearly, evil spirits and supernatural beings of uncertain intentions seem to have vastly outnumbered the good souls; even the two major deities were inimical to mankind. The Netsilik thus lived in perpetual fear of sudden attacks by malevolent spirits. Their fears reflected the assumption that spirits controlled both the natural world and the major events in human life.

Religious Activities

The religious activities of the Netsilik can be divided into two main levels of complexity: first, the relatively simple and very numerous minor rituals such as magic words, various observances, taboos, and elementary forms of malevolent magic; and, second, the highly complex body of shamanistic practices. Whenever relevant in the following description, the social implications of symbolic action will be emphasized.

A large number of magic formulae for beneficial purposes were known to the Netsilik. They were addressed either to the various spirits or to human ghosts and souls of dead animals. They were considered personal and very secret property, transmitted from father to son or purchased from a shaman. Their powerful and generally mysterious nature was enhanced by the special language of the shamans with which they were composed. Since nobody was allowed to hear them, they were uttered either early in the morning when one's housemates were still asleep, or far in the country, away from camp and fellow hunters.

A definite characteristic of magic words was their specificity of purpose. Each formula was applicable to one subject only. There were magic words for better hunting in strange lands, for help in caribou hunting, musk-ox and bear hunting, to cure sickness and heal wounds, to facilitate birth, and to give boys strength in competitive games.

Evidently magic formulae performed very similar functions to amulet spirits, though the latter seem to have had a more continuous power. Both were employed to give supernatural help to people in need.

Taboos

The Netsilik knew and rigidly observed a very large number of taboos and rituals. The strict taboo system indeed constituted the cornerstone of their religious life. There were basically two broad categories of taboos, the first concerning hunting activities and game animals (seal, caribou, bears, salmon), the second relating to the critical phases of a person's life cycle (birth and death) and certain physiological functions such as menstruation.

[The] list of taboos could be almost indefinitely lengthened. Why did the Netsilik burden their lives with so many restrictions, some of which were obviously very cumbersome? What is the significance of the taboo system in relation to Netsilik religion considered as a whole? What is the social meaning of these taboos?

No simple or single answer can be given to these questions, but the Netsilik taboos had certain common characteristics that can help us discover their principal functions. First, there were the very important rules separating land from sea animals. As Rasmussen notes (1931: 179): "caribou hunting and sealing must be kept quite distinct. . . ." It has been mentioned that no work on caribou skins was allowed at the sealing camps. It was strictly forbidden to eat lake trout, a land animal, on the same day that one had eaten seal meat. Land and sea animals were kept separate with reference to hunting, utilization of parts, and food consumption. All these observances were really ways to confirm symbolically the separation of the world into two halves: land and sea. This dichotomy was very much in harmony with the character of the Netsilik migration cycle, characterized by a dual form of ecological adaptation. In a sense these separation taboos were a symbolic expression of the dualistic life the Netsilik had to lead.

Second, the majority of taboos concerned activities of the greatest importance to society, namely hunting and childbirth. The survival of society depended on both. Further, and it is possible here to include death, these were issues largely beyond the control of individuals. The hunter on the chase was never certain of a kill. Mothers obviously entertained fears about the survival of their newborn infants, and death could occur practically any time. The taboos thus appear as symbolic provisions destined to control the uncontrollable and to reduce the level of anxiety generated by uncertainties. Of course if things turned really bad the shamans could be called upon for help. Their intervention, however, was occasional and generally depended upon invitation. The application of taboos was of a different order. It was compulsory, no exception was made, and it concerned everyone. It was in this respect that the systemic and ritualistic character of the taboo was most important. The taboo system was the first automatic defense mechanism against uncontrollable and unpredictable dangers. Taboos, then, could function as important psychological control measures for the reduction of anxiety.

Third, taboos were important because the breaking of taboos provided the Netsilik with an understandable reason for tribal misfortunes. Inadvertently or out of weakness, someone breaks a taboo. This angers some evil spirit who brings disaster to a camp fellow, all under the watchful eye of Nuliajuk. The shamans then have to be called with their helping spirits to exorcise the harmful spirit, and everyone feels better about whatever the misfortune was. Strangely, in the Netsilik religious order, the taboo system, which is in a sense the underwriter of the supernatural order, becomes the very source of evil. It is as if, despite continuous efforts to keep things in good order, society fails to control itself at a certain point and generates evil. Here lie the ethical aspects of the taboo system. The ethics of taboo do not concern interpersonal relations, however. They refer to individual misfortunes, or group disasters, or more generally to the relations between society and the supernaturals.

Fourth and most important are the essentially religious aspects of the taboo system. Rasmussen noted that at certain important caribou hunting places and stone weirs some very exacting and different taboos had to be observed, which gave the areas a kind of holy status. It is easy to conclude that many hunting taboos reconfirmed locality sacredness. The majority of hunting taboos referred to the souls of animals, the objective being to appease their anger and ensure future success in hunting. Hunting taboos and animal souls were closely connected, with the result that the observation of the first constantly strengthened the belief in the second. As for childbirth and menstruation taboos, they centered [on] the notion of impurity, particularly female impurity. These taboos guarded society from any danger of pollution. The taboo system worked to strengthen religious beliefs by making the spiritual world omnipresent.

Shamanism

The shaman, or *angatkok*, occupied an important position in Netsilik society. Although in daily life he behaved like an ordinary hunter, he was generally respected and feared for his supernatural powers.

Shamans had control of only one class of spirits, the *tunraqs*. They continued to acquire tunraqs throughout their lives, usually as gifts from other shamans or by the spirits' own volition. Relations between angatkoks and tunraqs were by no means simple; they showed considerable ambivalence, because of the ethical characteristics of certain spirits and their relative autonomy of action. If it is generally true that most powerful shamans were well in control of their tunraqs, there were other tunraqs that were very independent.

As mentioned before, many classes of malevolent supernaturals could bring misfortune to people. Besides the evil ghosts, *tupiliqs* were another important group of evil-intentioned spirits. Round in shape and filled with blood under considerable pressure, they could cause terrible sickness. The tunraqs themselves were more dreaded, however. When a shaman dispatched one of his spirits on an aggressive mission and the tunraq failed to achieve its task, it became a "reversed spirit" or *tunraq kigdloretto*, a blood-thirsty being, blinded by frustration, totally out of control, who generally turned against his master and relatives and brought sickness and death into their camp. Under these circumstances other shamans had to intervene and with their more powerful tunraqs harness the kigdloretto.

Sickness was always caused by evil ghosts and spirits, usually angered by a breach of taboo. These attacked the patient in group formation and took abode in his body. The shaman was then called to chase them away. If the patient died, it was said that the tupiliqs were too numerous for the shaman to kill, or that after the seance, additional evil spirits attacked the patient again.

The main para-shamanistic technique, called *krilaq* ("head lifting"), was widely practiced in the Netsilik area. The *krilasoktoq* ("practitioner of krilaq") did not require any special training and was much weaker than a regular shaman; his technique, although involving the manipulation of spirits, lacked a trance. His spirits, *aperksaqs* ("helping spirits"), were weaker than the tunraqs and not his personal "property". Head lifting was performed generally on the krilasoktoq's wife or on his own leg or on a stone. Angatkoks apparently never practiced krilaq; they disdained the lack of sharp vision and the dilatory action of the krilasoktoq.

Angatkungaruks ("lesser shamans") constituted a third class of curers. Their para-shamanistic technique involved identifying the evil spirit and localizing it in the patient's body. They were helped by some of the weaker tunraqs, though they never possessed them. The angatkungaruk would sit calmly near the patient and after many hesitations declare that he saw the evil spirit and that the latter was leaving the patient. Because of the angatkungaruk's lack of keen vision and inability to control powerful supernaturals, the diagnostic treatment and his encouragements to the patient had to be often repeated. This variety of shaman received no special training, practiced the krilaq technique very rarely, and was incapable of foreseeing future events.

Different from the shamanistic and para-shamanistic techniques described so far was a form of magical practice called *ilisiniq*. It is probable that numerous persons engaged in this evil art in order to bring calamity, paralysis, or death to a secret enemy or to a person disliked or envied. Many manipulative techniques were known, most of them based upon connecting something associated with the enemy to the dead or to menstrual blood: animal bones brought in by the enemy might be stolen and placed in a graveyard; the enemy might be touched with the mitt of a dead man. Some practices were simpler: breaking the bones of the enemy's seal or spitting in front of him. It was essential for all such acts to be accompanied by mental wishes specifying the evil aim desired.

Shamanistic control was frequently used to maintain a balance between people and environment, particularly in case of disaster. Shamanistic practices to attract game belong to this category. Whenever game was unavailable, the krilasoktoq was asked to discover, with the help of his spirits, where the animals were located, while the angatkok's tunraqs more actively directed the game toward the hunters. Frequently a breach of taboo brought the community to the verge of famine, and the shaman had to invite people to make confessions. His spirits informed him in advance of a breach of taboo, but it was essential that culprits confess of their own volition before the shaman could see about increasing the food supply.

Shamanistic acts could control individual or collective crises not necessarily stemming from the physical environment. Crises were generally brought about by breaches of taboo which angered the spirits and caused them to attack humans. All cases of curing may be grouped under this category. A sickness should not be considered, however, a purely individual misfortune; it was a collective crisis. Such is the dependence of people on each other in an extremely harsh environment within a small community that a hunter in bed means probable hunger for the family and lessened chances for the group to catch food; likewise a sick wife leaves the husband with nobody to cook the meat and mend his clothes.

Evil spirits and various classes of monsters might try to attack the people. The whole community often lived in dreadful fear, surrounded by malevolent beings. The intervention of several shamans then became imperative.

Harpoons, ice chisels, and iron needles were important tools, highly prized and difficult to replace. Loss of any of them created a crisis calling for the shaman's help. Harpoons and ice chisels often fell into the sea through seals' breathing holes. The shaman recovered them either by jumping supernaturally into the water through the narrow ice hole, in front of a credulous audience, or by tying them with a thong lowered through the breathing hole; the helping spirits did the rest. Lost needles were directly found by tunraqs.

Numerous shamanistic acts and ilisiniq practices were meant to control interpersonal relations. All aggressive acts, even involving the shaman himself in a competitive or otherwise hostile relation, belong to this category; here, too, we can include his supernatural aid in selecting a mate and in achieving blood revenge.

Interpersonal tensions came about for many different reasons. Jealousy, however, seems to have been the most frequent motivation for aggressive shamanizing.

Irqi was the mother of a grown son, a very poor seal hunter. This boy's meat-sharing partner, Krasovik, used to catch many seals. Krasovik was a much faster runner. Irqi grew jealous and made ilisiniq against Krasovik. The latter, protected by powerful amulets, got only some pains in the legs. The aggressive act turned against the witch and killed her son.

A certain external difficulty may irritate an individual and lead him to aggression.

Atkrartok, a shaman, and Nulialik were traveling together on rough ice. Nulialik became irritated because of the difficult journey and apparently wanted to turn back, to which Atkrartok objected. A fight with knives ensued; they decided to stop using knives but to continue fighting with supernatural means. Nulialik did ilisiniq against the shaman, believing that his opponent was trying to kill him with his tunraq. The evil act turned against Nulialik and killed him. . . .

In traditional times the high incidence of female infanticide caused a considerable sex-ratio imbalance to exist. This made for great difficulties in finding a wife. Steehoven (1959: 40) notes several cases of the murder of husbands by men who wanted to steal their wives. Such murders could be accomplished with supernatural means.

Some shamans considered lying with a particular woman as a necessary part of a shamanistic act. The audience assumed this was a desire of the tunraq. Often, however, the shaman's propositions were rejected.

The people asked Igarataitsok to stop a particularly violent snowstorm. The shaman first desired to lie with two girls. The father of the first agreed immediately, but the husband of the second said: "A tunraq cannot copulate with women."

This attitude was not general with all shamans. Informants agreed, however, that a shaman who desired a particular woman would readily threaten her with imminent sickness in order to attain his aim.

The fourth major category of shamanistic activities includes the large number of shamanistic performances, the obvious or hidden objectives of which are to control the shaman's own position in society, to enhance his prestige.

The shaman was capable of performing strange and wonderful acts upon his own body, and this always in front of an audience. Iksivalitak used to shoot himself with a gun, Qagortingnerk removed his own leg, other angatkoks preferred to pierce themselves with spears and grow beards in a second. People who claim to have seen such performances still speak with awe and admiration about the ability of these shamans.

Finally, there is the large class of outstanding shamanistic achievements, such as journeys to the underworld, travels to the moon, or meetings with strange monsters. These were feats of the most important shamans, to whom they brought considerable prestige.

The most striking characteristic of Netsilik shamanism and associated beliefs was the fusion of good and evil elements. Although the Netsilik distinguished clearly between an evil shamanistic act from its positive counterpart, the same shaman was capable of performing both. This intermixing of good and evil had important social consequences. The possibility of nearly any Netsilik's supposed ability to influence supernaturals for aggressive purposes contributed much to the interpersonal suspicions and hidden hostilities of their society. The individual lived in an atmosphere of suspicion and fear, dreading both the possible secret attacks of his camp fellows and the spirits who might initiate an evil action on their own.

If shamanism was practised as a kind of social control, its ethical ambivalence meant that it was not always very effective. The shaman rarely had full control over the spirits; they could acquire autonomy, attack some individual blindly, and create new enmities altogether, with quite an opposite effect than that desired by the society. Thus, in the imbroglio of fears and accusations, not only existing enmities found free expression but entirely new hostilities could emerge.

The second major function of Netsilik shamanism was perhaps more successful than the social control function. For the Netsilik, the shamans were the people who brought the world together. Environment, spirits, the afterworld, social life—all of these elements were brought together for them into one meaningful whole. Both the components and the acts of shamanism indicate that for varying aims a multiplicity of elements was fused during the shamanistic performances. Elements of nature, the animals of land and sea, snowstorms and thunder, and cracking ice, were brought under the shaman's power. The world of the dead was also present during a seance: deceased relatives were utilized as protective spirits, and evil ghosts fought. Society was also represented, and in two ways; often an audience participated directly in the shamanistic performance, and all shamanistic practices involved the presence of at least part of the community. Basic religious beliefs were also included in the shamanistic complex. In varying situations and for different purposes the shaman integrated these diverse elements into a dynamic unity. In his role as integrator, in a stream of symbolic effusions, the shaman gave meaning to a multiplicity of situations which would have remained inexplicable to society without his intervention (Balikci 1963: 395).

REFERENCES

Balikci, Asen
1963 "Shamanistic Behaviour among the Netsilik Eskimos." South-western Journal of Anthropology 19: 380-96.
Rasmussen, Knud
1931 The Netsilik Eskimos. Reports of the Fifth Thule Expedition, Vol. 8. Copenhagen.

van den Steehoven, Geert
1959 Legal Concepts Among the Netsilik Eskimos of Pelly Bay, N.W.T. Ottawa: Northern Co-ordination and Research Centre, Department of Northern Affairs and National Resources, NCRC-59-3.

2.

The Pre-Industrial Period

The Seventeenth-Century Parish in French Canada*

Jean-Charles Falardeau

Seigniories and Villages

It has been the thesis of Rameau, shared by the nineteenth-century French-Canadian historian, Abbé Henri-Raymond Casgrain, that France in colonizing Canada brought over to the new continent the full complement of her political and religious institutions.[1] This thesis has recently been taken up again by Burton Ledoux.[2] Actually, the situation has not been quite so simple, and it is worthwhile outlining a few of the contrasts and modifications which made the Canadian institutions so unmistakably different from their metropolitan models. Even though it was the ambition of Louis XIV to build a colony that would be an exact replica of France,[3] the land settlement pattern, as well as the type of civil and religious government in Canada, took, in most cases, the shape of institutions well adapted to the conditions of a new country and the needs of a society in the making.

*Appeared first in French under the title "Paroisses de France et de Nouvelle-France au XVIIe siècle", in *Cahiers de l'Ecole des sciences sociales, politiques et économiques de Laval*, Vol. 2, No. 7 (Québec, 1943). Reproduced in part in Marcel Rioux and Yves Martin, eds., *French-Canadian Society*, Vol. 1 (Toronto: McClelland and Stewart, 1964). Reproduced here in abridged form with the kind permission of the author and the publishers.

The first step in the colonization of Canada, the establishment of the seigniories, involved a very important innovation in comparison with continental traditions. Whereas the French feudal system had been a political institution, the Canadian seigniorial system, whose very name implies an adaptation to a new country, appeared essentially, as has been pointed out by Georges Langlois and others before him, as "a purely economic system . . . a method of distributing land and of exploiting it".[4]

The seigniories granted from the time of Talon were all about the same size, with a frontage one league in length along the St. Lawrence or another river, and one league in depth inland. Since the St. Lawrence and the rivers constituted for a long time the only roadways in the colony, each *censitaire* had to have immediate access to them. This also made it easier for him to go fishing. Thus, all the settlers' lots were very narrow and very deep, measuring five or six *arpents* along the river and thirty or forty *arpents* deep. Each settler built his house at the extreme end of his farm facing the river, not far from that of his neighbour, with the result that an uninterrupted string of houses, known as *la côte*, stretched gradually along the St. Lawrence and the rivers. Consequently, "one could have seen nearly every house in Canada, by paddling a canoe up the St. Lawrence and the Richelieu."[5] When all the land along the rivers was occupied, another row or *rang* of houses was built one mile from the coast and parallel to it; later, a second row or *rang* a mile further, and so on. This peculiar arrangement of houses built in a long row made it impossible to have any form of clustered community such as existed in France. In Canada, the *côte* or the *rang* became the natural unit of settlement. The seigniory was a vast rectangle stripped with equidistant *rangs*. The parish itself, a wide territorial framework, could hardly succeed at first in concentrating the population which spread out along the ribbon-like, never-ending roads.

As early as 1663, and on several occasions, Louis XIV ordered the administrators of the colony "to prevent the *habitants* from building their houses on their land but to oblige them to group themselves in villages,[6] and to incite them to observe the by-laws and customs practised in France".[7] Intendant Talon attempted to apply this by-law to the subsequently granted concessions. He tried to oppose "any building [of houses] not grouped in communities—hamlets, villages and boroughs".[8] He even went so far as to plan with great care, in the vicinity of Quebec, six boroughs or villages modelled after the French pattern, that is, with a nucleus of houses in the centre and the fields distributed all around this hub like the spokes of a wheel.[9] These were also the only concentrated communities (*lieux ramassés*) ever established in New France. The Canadian *habitants* kept on building their houses on isolated *rangs* along the St. Lawrence or on the main road.[10] The influence of the environment was stronger than the intentions and edicts of His Majesty.

During the first stages of the colony, only a few Canadian seigniors fulfilled their obligations to bring settlers to their estates. More willing on the battlefield than on their estates, unconcerned or lacking resources or agricultural knowledge, too venturesome or not industrious enough, most of them failed in their rural obligations and contented themselves with holding offices in the local government. They never had any real or lasting influence over the Canadian settler. They never played towards him what Léon Gérin has called the role of "agricultural entrepreneurs".[11] The considerable ascendency which the rural nobleman still exerted in France, and which could have had its counterpart in New France and could have been perfected by a direct action of the seignior on the temporal affairs and on the fate of his settlers, was soon assumed, in his place, by the curé of the parish.

As for the Canadian *habitant*, he was attached to his land, and he cultivated it unrestrainedly with the help of his family. Near him, other *habitants* were engaged in a similar enterprise, and this community of interests, reinforced by the closeness of the houses along the same road, resulted in a tradition of mutual aid such as never existed in rural France. Neighbours helped and visited each other. The *côte* or *rang* soon became the elementary unit of social cohesion. The *rang* is more than a mere road; it refers to the community of *habitants* living alongside. This neighbourhood unity [was] the first spontaneous pattern of rural organization.[12] It persisted, without losing its original strength, long after the founding of the territorial parish. The latter has scarcely been anything more than the grouping of a certain number of *rangs*. Are we not familiar, even today, with the toponymy of the country people who mark differences between various areas of a parish by using expressions such as the *haut* and the *bas*, and even the *haut du haut* and the *bas du bas*?

Apart from family life, neighbourly relations were practically the only type of social activity among the Canadian *habitants*, for whom municipal life, as such, then had no importance or even no meaning at all. Throughout the French régime in Canada, there was no system of local municipal organization. It was the parishes which, though they were religious structures, fulfilled, as they were gradually established, the functions of rural municipalities. Only under exceptional circumstances did the settlers of New France express any interest in the government of the country. "Without any type of organization which could have assembled and governed them," as Gustave Lanctot points out, "they acquired the habit of passively deferring to the ordinances of the intendants, to the orders of the governor and to the edicts of Versailles."[13]

The *habitant* who lived in the country, the real *habitant*, never enjoyed any right of representation or of participation in public affairs. As to his local interests, his seignior, or more often his curé, played the role of mandatory, of counsellor, or of arbitrator. Independent and rather passive, he never felt the need to establish any institution like the rural *communauté* as it existed in seventeenth-century France. All the problems of village life, such as the organization of schools, were solved adequately by the few agents of the local parochial church, especially by the *fabrique*. The municipal interest of the Canadian *habitant* always remained of a strictly parochial character.

The Canadian Proto-parish

The parish was one of the key institutions which the pioneers brought with them to New France. Its development was achieved by a tireless clergy, supported or stimulated by the first ecclesiastical and civil administrators of the country. At the outset, the latter designed a systematic plan for the division of the colony into parochial units long before those areas were actually settled. In fact, the religious organization of the first settlements in New France could only be achieved slowly and under poor conditions. Yet it came closest to realizing the king's wish that colonial institutions should reproduce the metropolitan patterns.

On the arrival of Msgr. de Laval in 1659, there were only three parishes in the colony: Québec, Montréal, and Château-Richer. After the areas of Québec, Trois-Rivières, and Montréal were populated, colonization spread further along the banks of the St. Lawrence. One has only to read the historical monographs of some of the parishes which were founded in New France during the seventeenth century to discover that all of them went through the same heroic early development, enhanced on the one hand by the pluck of the settlers, on the other by the apostolic courage of the priests who had founded them or who had them under their care.

As soon as the settlers moved into an area, sometimes with their seignior, they started clearing the land. The missionary visited them at irregular intervals. Usually, he was lodged by the settlers and celebrated mass either at the seigniorial "manor" or in one of the *habitants'* houses. When the "village" had acquired a certain importance, usually by the time it counted about forty or fifty families, and when a chapel had been built, the inhabitants asked the bishop to send them a resident priest. But [owing] to the large size of the seigniories of the colony, and within each seigniory to the dispersion of the population along the *côtes*, the concentration of the ecclesiastical ministry was difficult to achieve. More-over, the number of priests in the colony was very small. A large number of villages remained during long periods without the visits of the travel-ling curés who each had under their care two, three, five, eight, or even— as in the case of the Abbé Morel who alone ministered to all the southern shore of the St. Lawrence below the city of Quebec—thirteen districts.

Size

At the beginning of the colony, the name of "parish" was thus given to an ill-defined entity in the process of accommodating and adapting itself to a milieu in the making. The first parishes covered immense areas. For example, in 1691 Msgr. de Laval and the intendant had delineated parishes thirty or forty leagues wide.[14] These parishes were more pre-cisely "missions" or parochial districts. A *Plan général de l'état des missions du Canada*, prepared in 1683 at the request of the bishop, enumerates, for the three governments of Québec, Montréal, and Trois-Rivières, a list of seventy-nine villages or towns most of which were only simple missions still in embryo.[15] The same can be said of the forty parochial districts established all at once rather arbitrarily, around 1685, by the vicar-general to Msgr. de Laval and Intendant de Meulles,[16] or finally of the eighty-two new ones determined by the *Règlement des districts de paroisses de la Nouvelle-France* of 1721.[17] Many of those districts, according to Abbé Gosselin, the historian of the Canadian Church, were not yet inhabited: they were simply devised to encourage settlers to come and settle there.[18] Their boundaries mainly served to circumscribe, at a given time, the constituencies under the responsibility of each of the missionary curés. In a memorandum a few years later, Msgr. Dosquet writes as follows: "As soon as the land is cleared and the inhabitants settle down, it is necessary to change the residence of the missionary, to increase the number of parishes, to unite or subdivide them, etc., for the convenience of the population and of the pastors."[19] Almost every parochial district included several "villages" which formed part of either the same seigniory or two or three small seigniories.[20] As the settlement of the colony progressed, the original parochial territories were subdivided into smaller units which corresponded more closely to what we now designate as parishes and which could be exclusively under the care of one curé.[21] During the whole French régime, the establishment of parishes was solely a prerogative of the bishop, who acted in full liberty, without the interference of the State. The old jurisprudence which recognized the rights of the bishop as defined in the Canon Law never ceased to prevail.[22]

Curés

The essential factor, without which a village remained an isolated and imperfect community incapable of ever making any real parochial progress, was the presence of a resident curé. Even more so in Canada than in rural France, the curé was the animator *sine qua non* of parochial life. As soon as the village had its own curé, no longer was it merely a place where the officiating priest stopped along a *côte*, or the sum of a certain number of *rangs*: it became a real parish, that is, a community of faithful identified by a specific territory. The Canadian curé was first the catalytic agent, then the active ferment of the rural parochial community.

Unlike his colleague in France who was attached for life to a given parish, the Canadian curé was always removable at the bishop's pleasure. Such was the decree of Msgr. de Laval, in conformity with the needs of a newly-formed Church, and it was a decree which no subsequent ecclesiastical authorities could, or would even wish to, repeal.[23] Due to the fact that the vast original parochial districts often needed to be modified in accordance with the migrations of the population, spiritual assistance to the new parishes would have been problematic if each curé had been appointed for life to a given territory. But this did not prevent him from living in want. His only official income was the tithe (*la dîme*), definitely set, after many transformations,[24] as the twenty-sixth part of the harvest which had to be paid to him by the settlers. Yet, this was far from yielding an adequate income for him to live on. The tithes of the whole country, in 1700, could have supported, at the most, about ten priests. The *habitants* were poor; during many years, it fell to the royal treasury to assume the responsibility of paying a salary to the Canadian clergy and, at the same time, of financially supporting many parishes. The allowances varied throughout the years, but they had a tendency to stabilize around eight thousand *livres* a year. This amount is repeated as a leitmotif in the correspondence of the intendants. It seems that, without it, the fate of the curés would have been compromised.

The Canadian curés were pastors of communities lacking resources, organization, and, most of the time, local leaders. They soon became also the real leaders of these communities. As in France, they were responsible for the registration of births, marriages, and deaths. They had an intimate knowledge of the life of their parishioners. J.-Edmond Roy reports that all the parishioners of St. Joseph-de-Lauzon sought the help of Curé Boucher, over a period of twenty-five years, for solving any of their problems. "He was consulted every time a transaction was made in the parish. He was a trustee for testaments, he wrote deeds for donations, and prepared any other legal document that his parishioners would care to ask him."[25] Whereas the curés' control over the religious government of the parish continued for many years to be restricted by frequent personal interventions of the bishop,[26] their temporal leadership over the public life of the community continually increased. The inhabitants of the Canadian village had neither a common law, nor a communal assembly nor a municipal council. Very seldom was the seignior among them either to show interest in their wishes or to oppose them. The *conseil de fabrique* (board of wardens), composed of *habitants* who knew little about public affairs, was most of the time controlled by the curé and seldom opposed his views. The right of the inhabitants to inquire into or admonish the curé's administration seems to have been unknown in New France.

Although it was enhanced by such a favourable situation, the prestige of the curé was chiefly due to [his office's] sacerdotal character and to the confidence which the faithful bestowed on him *a priori*. The great majority of the Canadian settlers were Christians for whom the preaching of the Gospel, regular partaking of the Sacraments, and the celebration of the religious services corresponded to a real need. We thus see them, according to the chronicles, claim the presence of the priest and the services of his ministry as soon as they settle somewhere. Thanks to his role as spiritual minister, the curé is also the supreme arbitrator of his homogeneous flock. He is called the "pastor" and it is he who actually presides over and controls their social life. It is around him and under him that they gather as a parochial community. Whenever a parochial church has been built and the weekly high-mass is celebrated regularly, the Sunday *prône* will renew in the Canadian parish an old French tradition which wanted the curé to be the public informant as well as the mentor of his flock—of those he calls his children as they themselves call him their father.

For all these reasons, the curé of the Canadian countryside constituted from the beginning what he has never ceased to be since then, "the strongest link in the parochial life . . . the natural protector and the natural representative of the *habitant*".[27]

Administration of the parish

An important and necessary event in the life of the parish was the building of a church. Because of widespread poverty, this event was usually awaited for a long time. A *Mémoire* of 1660 mentions only eight churches in the government of Québec.[28] In 1685, when Msgr. de Saint-Vallier made his first pastoral round, there were only four stone churches in the whole country.[29] Everywhere "the holy places are covered with straw, extremely dilapidated, without vessels and without vestments."[30] There were very few settlers who could, like those of Rivière-Ouelle, realize soon enough their wish to have "at least a small church"[31] built on a lot which the seignior had given them. The 1769 Edict had granted the seigniors, or some of the prominent inhabitants of the parishes, certain privileges regarding the construction of the parish churches. He who "gave as alms" the capital for the construction of a church and met the total expenditures involved for the building, which had to be of stone, would have the right to be considered the patron founder of the said church, with the right to propose a new curé in case of vacancy.[32] But very few Canadian seigniors were able to meet the cost of building a parish chapel, even a very modest one. Those who were better off, or the more zealous ones, were satisfied to grant the land, and in return they were given a special pew in the church.[33] The building of the first Canadian churches was made possible thanks to grants from the seminaries of Québec and Montréal which were supplemented by royal grants. The *habitants* often contributed the building materials, and they always provided the labour.

As soon as it was sufficiently organized, a parish in New France, as was the case in France, acquired a legal status. As in France, also, the parochial corporate body was made up of the *fabrique* whose statutes and powers were stipulated by the old French law, by the official regulations of the Canon Law, and by a few local customs approved or interpreted by Orders of the Sovereign Council and the directives of the Quebec bishop.[34] The ordinary *conseil de fabrique*, under the chairmanship, by right, of the curé, was composed of three churchwardens (*marguilliers*) who remained in office for three years, but who had to be elected every year by the resident parishioners. They took precedence over each other according to the length of their service, and the senior member, the so-called churchwarden in charge, had to give an account of his managership, at the end of his term, before the *fabrique* proper. The latter was composed of the curé and of all the former and newly-elected churchwardens of the parish.[35] The functions of the Canadian churchwardens were limited to the administration of temporal matters, chiefly as these concerned the properties and assets of the church and the upkeep of the place of worship, without being under the control, as in France, of a parochial general assembly. Their periodical meetings took place at the presbytery, when there was one, or at the sacristy. The resources of the *fabrique*—proceeds from the collection, perquisites, contingent legacies, and proceeds from the annual allocation by auction of the church pews—were meagre. In all cases, the *fabrique* was responsible to the bishop, who was the only judge and arbitrator.

Furthermore, the parochial *fabrique* occasionally took the initiative to build, and assumed the responsibility for, the few primary schools which existed under the French régime. There were about twenty-four of these at the end of the seventeenth century. Most of them were under the direction of religious congregations, especially Les Dames de la Congrégation, or else run by a teacher or the curé.[36] Schooling was free. The expenses for the upkeep of these schools were the responsibility of the inhabitants or, more precisely, of the parochial *fabrique*.

A strict ceremonial regulated a hierarchy of statuses in the life of each of these parochial communities, particularly in the church, the main meeting place of the population. A series of state by-laws and of ecclesiastical statutes sanctioned a scale of honorary privileges to which various local personalities, depending on their rank, were entitled. The seignior, in particular, was from time to time the object of honours quite similar to those customary in France and which are described in a decree of 1709.[37] The seignior on whose land the church was built was the only one recognized in each parish as "high justice". A permanent pew was set aside for him and his family in the most "honorary" place of the church, "on the right, when coming in, four feet from the communion rail". The other places of honour in the church were hierarchically distributed in the same manner. In the second place, in a separate pew, behind that of the seignior, came the militia captain. The third place was that of the churchwardens in the traditional *banc-d'œuvre*. A similar hierarchy prevailed for the religious processions, for the Midsummer Day celebration (*les feux de la Saint-Jean*), for the Sunday distribution of the Holy Bread, of the candles, of the palms, of the ashes: immediately after the curé and the clergy came the seignior, the captain of the *côte*, the judges of the seigniory, if there were any, the churchwardens, and finally the faithful without distinction.[38]

Summary

This sketchy historical account reveals the fundamental process through which the Canadian parish, during the first century of its existence, took shape and strength, while adapting itself patiently to hard conditions. Within a few decades, it would approximate still more closely the ideal which the Catholic clergy has set for the parish everywhere, throughout the centuries: a true community of families, a large family itself.

This indeed was the ideal of the founders of the Canadian Church. Yet, they were compelled to compromise according to circumstances. The seigniorial system preceded any other frame of social life in New France. Just as it is impossible to understand the parish of old France without the village, so one must mention the Canadian seigniory before the parish. On the other hand, the Canadian *habitant* refused the model of the village of France in order to confine himself to the *côte* or to the *rang*. Preoccupied at the beginning with defending himself and with surviving, he had the boundaries of his fields laid out as he pleased, and once the struggles with the Iroquois were over, he took up by himself the task of cultivating sufficient land to meet the needs of his family. As a result of frequent contacts and of exchanging services with neighbours who lived close to him and who shared his ways of life and of thinking, he soon identified himself with this elementary network of social life. [In] the absence, in most cases, of an influential seigniorial manor, there was, at the beginning, no other focus to his ambitions and activities.

The church and the curé he had asked for superimposed a centre which was religious in character on the chequered arrangement of the *côte* and the *rangs*. But the French-Canadian *habitant* did not play, and for that matter was never able to play, at any time, an active role in the life or in the administration of his community. This situation is the reverse of the one which prevailed in the villages and cities of England where the initial organization, the administration, and the success of the municipal life were the immediate concern of the inhabitants.[39] As Léon Gérin points out: "It is not the [Canadian] *habitant* who established the parochial institution; he found it all established, entered into it, was marked by it. He does not dominate the parish, he is dominated by it."[40] He is much less an active and enterprising citizen than a submissive and faithful parishioner. As soon as he has his own church and his own curé who will administer a territory with clearly defined boundaries, this church, even though he may live far from it, will constitute the centre of his social life. The curé will inherit the role and the prestige of the absentee seignior. What the *habitant* will call *his* parish will imply a familiar territory as well as an integrating unit of social life, both religious and municipal. He will have forgotten long ago the name of his seignior, but whenever he will need to identify himself, he will spontaneously add after his surname those of his *rang* and of his parish.

NOTES

1 Rameau, *Une colonie féodale* (Introduction, pp. 22ff.), quoted by Abbé H.-R. Casgrain, *Une paroisse canadienne au XVIIe siècle* (Québec, 1880), p. 185.
2 Burton Ledoux, "French Canada: A Modern Feudal State", *Virginia Quarterly* (Spring, 1941), pp. 206-22.
3 Emile Salone, *La colonisation de la Nouvelle-France: Etude sur les origines de la nation canadienne-française* (Paris, 1906), p. 191.
4 Georges Langlois, *Histoire de la population canadienne-française* (Montréal, 1935), p. 55.
5 Francis Parkman, *France and England in North America* (9 vols.; Boston, 1890-92), Part 4, *The Old Regime in Canada*, p. 236.
6 *Mémoire du Roy au Sieur Talon*, 27 mars 1663. Quoted by G. Lanctot, "La participation du peuple dans le gouvernement de la Nouvelle-France", *Revue trimestrielle canadienne* 15 (septembre 1929): 238.

7 *Mémoire du Roy à M. Talon*, 1669. Quoted by E. Salone, *op. cit.*, p. 191.
8 Talon à Colbert, 1666. Quoted by E. Salone, *op. cit.*, p. 191.
9 F. Parkman, *op. cit.*, pp. 235-6.
10 G. Lanctot, *op. cit.*, p. 238.
11 Léon Gérin, "L'habitant de Saint-Justin, Contribution à la géographie sociale du Canada", in *Mémoires de la Société royale du Canada*, 2e série, 4 (1898): 204.
12 Léon Gérin, *Le type économique et social des Canadiens* (Montréal, 1938), pp. 88-91.
13 G. Lanctot, *op. cit.*, p. 238.
14 E. Salone, *op. cit.*, p. 274.
15 *Mandements des évêques de Québec* 1: 115-28. Quoted by Abbé Ivanhoé Caron, "La colonisation dans la province de Québec sous la domination française (1608-1760)", in *Annuaire statistique de Québec, 1915*, Part II, pp. 57-60.
16 "We found, wrote the intendant, that it was absolutely necessary to map

out all at once 40 parochial districts, the curés thus being compelled to have an eye on their particular parish. . . ." *Rapport de l'intendant de Meulles*, in *Mss de la Nouvelle-France* 4: 180, 338 (Ottawa, Parliamentary Library). quoted by Abbé Auguste Gosselin, *L'Eglise du Canada depuis Mgr de Laval jusqu'à la Conquête* (3 vols.; Québec, 1911), 1: 350.

17 *Edits et Ordonnances* 1: 443. See P.-B. Mignault, *Le droit paroissial* (Montréal, 1893), pp. 38-9; J.-Edmond Roy, *Histoire de la seigneurie de Lauzon* (5 vols.; Lévis, 1897-1904), 1: 94; A. Gosselin, *op. cit.*, 1: 352-3; I. Caron, *op. cit.*, p. 67.

18 A. Gosselin, *op. cit.*, 1: 360.

19 Msgr. Dosquet, "Mémoire sur l'affaire des curés fixés par le chapitre de Québec", quoted by A. Gosselin, *op. cit.*, 2: 188.

20 J.-E. Roy, *op. cit.*, 1: 267; Pierre-G. Roy, "La paroisse et l'habitant canadien sous le régime français", *Catholic Historical Review* 18 (January, 1933): 472. A. Gosselin, *op. cit.*, 1: 356-7. See also Msgr. Dosquet, "Memoire . . .", quoted by A. Gosselin, *op. cit.*, 2: 189.

21 P.-G. Roy, *op. cit.*, p. 473. Msgr. Dosquet, "Memoire . . .", quoted by A. Gosselin, *op. cit.*, 2: 187-8.

22 P.-B. Mignault, *op. cit.*, pp. 4, 38-9; M.-A. Lamarche, o.p., *Notre vie canadienne: Etudes et discours* (Montréal, 1929), ch. 5: "La paroisse gardienne de la vie sociale", pp. 207-8.

23 Msgr. Dosquet, "Mémoire . . .", quoted by A. Gosselin, *op. cit.*, 2: 188.

24 P.-B. Mignault, *op. cit.*, pp. 3, 4,

40, 151, 152, 158, 162, 163.

25 J.-E. Roy, *op. cit.*, 2: 62.

26 Gonzalve Poulin, o.f.m., "L'évolution historico-juridique de l'institution paroissiale au Canada français" [First Part], *Nos Cahiers*, 1, No. 4, (décembre 1936): 309.

27 L. Gérin, *op. cit.*, pp. 103-4.

28 Quoted by J.-E. Roy, *op. cit.*, 1: 265.

29 *Estat présent de l'Eglise et de la colonie française dans la Nouvelle-France*, par M. l'Evêque de Québec (Paris, 1688), p. 55, quoted by E. Salone, *op. cit.*, p. 275.

30 *Ibid.*, p. 57, quoted by E. Salone, *op. cit.*, p. 275.

31 H.-R. Casgrain, *op. cit.*, pp. 79-81.

32 A. Gosselin, *op. cit.*, 1: 190.

33 *Ibid.*, 191.

34 P.-B. Mignault, *op. cit.*, pp. 221-2.

35 *Ibid.*, pp. 225-6, 248, 260.

36 G. Poulin, *op. cit.* [Second Part], *Nos Cahiers* 2, No. 1 (avril 1937): 112.

37 Pierre-G. Roy, *L'Ile d'Orléans* (Québec, 1928), p. 181.

38 A. Gosselin, *op. cit.*, 1: 312-14; P.-G. Roy, *L'Ile d'Orléans*, p. 181; P.-G. Roy, "La paroisse et l'habitant canadien . . .", p. 484.

39 See Beatrice and Sydney Webb, *English Government from the Revolution to the Municipal Corporation* (London, New York and Bombay, 1906-22); *The Parish and the Country* (1906), Book I, *The Parish*, ch. 1, 2.

40 "Monographie du Canada— L'histoire de la colonisation. X. Comment le domaine plein a limité le développement de la race. Conclusions", *La Science sociale* 18 (novembre 1894): 337-8.

Relations Between Church and State in Canada West, 1841 to 1867*

John S. Moir

1. Introduction

In Canada West (formerly Upper Canada, and from 1841 the western half of the newly created United Province of Canada) the problem of the relation of church and state was far from new. The attempt to found a little England complete with an established church had met with strong opposition in the frontier community of Upper Canada, and had been a contributing cause of the recent abortive Rebellion of 1837. But after the union of Upper and Lower Canada the problem took on a new appearance, in part as a result of the Rebellion, in part as a result of the contemporary events in Europe. To the older force of North American frontierism, and its corollary of complete separation of church and state, was added the leaven of nationalism. The full implications of this change did not become evident until the Union was almost a decade old.

Admittedly, the concept of a pre-Confederation Canadian national-ism—a sense of geographic, political, and social identity—requires qualification, for only national interests can create a national spirit. It is

*Appeared first in John S. Moir, *Church and State in Canada West* (Toronto: University of Toronto Press, 1959). Published here in abridged form with the kind permission of the author and the publisher.

a commonplace of Canadian historians to date the birth of Canadian nationalism from the War of 1812–14, which drew both French- and English-speaking Canadians together in defence of their home or native land, but the growth of a true national sentiment was severely retarded by the sense of exile, by the stark reality of colonial status, and by the indigenous parochialism and regionalism of a scattered population in a broad land. Only when Canadian statesmen faced national responsibilities after the achievement of responsible government, and after the railways and telegraph had provided isolated areas with the means of rapid communication, could the parts be welded into a whole. Confederation provided only a framework for political and economic nationalism—the psychological sense of identity was slow in following the flag and trade. "Canadian nationalism differs from the nationalism of the Old World in this, that while they draw their inspiration largely from the past, it draws its inspiration mainly from the future."[1] (Significantly, Troeltsch and Niebuhr describe this forward-looking attitude also as being one mark of the sect, and religious sects played a lively part in Canada West.)

Nevertheless the seeds of nationalism were already planted in the Canadian Union of 1841. Lord Durham's abortive plan for a confederation of British North America had been accepted by many leading Canadians and his famous Report held out this idea of wider union as "the only means of fostering such a national feeling . . . as would effectively counterbalance whatever tendencies may now exist toward separation [from the mother country]."[2] This "means" was not adopted until 1867, but signs of national feeling are not lacking during the Union period. In spite of, and at times because of, all the sectional practices and divisions which grew up to compromise the Union of the Canadas, their union was the necessary precursor to Confederation. In fact Reformers demanded the end of the existing union in the very name of political nationalism and all that term connotes.

The conjunction of political and religious radicalism in Canada West was not accidental, as the groundwork had been well laid during the half-century existence of Upper Canada. The fact that the overwhelming majority of Loyalists and post-Loyalist American settlers who first entered the colony were not members of the Church of England from the start practically nullified the plan to make this an established church. External opposition to Anglican supremacy came from two sources: from the Church of Scotland, which claimed equal rights as a co-establishment in the empire, and from the voluntarists, who demanded the complete separation of state and church in the name of Christianity. Voluntarism in theory denotes the free will of the individual. In practical terms it means voluntary membership and the reliance of churches on the financial and moral support of their adherents, in contradistinction to support or aid from the civil authorities. By its opponents it has been described as "ecclesiastical free trade". It implies by necessity the complete separation of the affairs of religion and politics. The sole duty of the civil magistrate towards Christianity is, then, the protection of religious liberty.

The force of voluntarism in Canada West was a reflection of its important role in the "North American way of life".[3] The strongest supporters of the voluntary principle were, and are, the Baptists. In Canada West voluntarism was an ideal of the majority of Protestant churches— Baptist, Congregational, Methodist, and Presbyterian. The obvious exceptions were the Churches of England and Scotland. The Quakers and other Plain Folk were rendered passive voluntarists by their faith. The Church of Rome, traditionally favourable to establishment, was restricted in its influence by its numerical inferiority in Canada West. It could not hope for ascendancy; it must make the best of its opportunities in a predominantly Protestant province, but, thanks to the Union of 1841, those opportunities were greatly enhanced by the political support which the numerically superior Roman Catholics of Canada East could give their co-religionists in Canada West.

The conflict between the forces of voluntarism and church-statism in Canada West centred largely on two issues—establishment and education. Establishment, in a circumscribed form, was represented by the Clergy Reserves, the forty-four Rectories, and government grants of land and money to a few denominations. In the field of education, church-statism was apparent in the public funds given to denominational colleges and in the existence of denominational separate elementary schools. Those churches which advocated a closer connection with the state demanded special privileges and rights at the expense of the state and other religious bodies. Voluntarists rejected these claims in the name of religious equality. Paradoxically the voluntarists found their strongest ally in the concept of a non-religious statism. For purposes of education the state should be a "collective parent", and for purposes of religion the churches should depend on the voluntary support of their members.

Thus, within the body politic of Canada West, it might be said that two antithetical tendencies were at work. On the one hand was *centrifugal denominationalism*—the tendency of the largest churches to claim a special privileged and protected status as the religious counterpart of the civil authority. On the other hand was *centripetal nationalism*—a force which in Canada West sought to equate all creeds by separating them completely from the world of politics.

In the history of Canada West the period of the Great Ministry of Baldwin and Lafontaine marks a watershed in the development of the relations of church and state. In 1840 the passing of a new Clergy Reserves Act to divide the bulk of the proceeds among a few denominations created a sort of plural establishment, which pleased no one, but which was generally acquiesced in for the sake of peace. The continuing existence of the endowed Anglican Rectories seemed to ensure the quasi-ascendancy of the Church of England. The growth of denominational colleges in the forties led to demands for the sharing of the endowment of the provincial University. This was matched by the voluntarists' demand for the nationalization of King's College, which was monopolizing that ample endowment. At the same time provision for separate Roman Catholic or Protestant elementary schools, as protection from insult, had been made in the educational system which Egerton Ryerson was busy constructing. The claims of the Church of England to have its own schools had been rejected, as had the Church of Scotland's demand for compulsory use of the Bible in classrooms. But extreme voluntarists were not satisfied with decentralized elementary education, and were loudly demanding the abolition of separate schools of all kinds, and total state control of the educational system.

During the decade after Union the resentment of voluntarists and nationalists steadily increased against what they believed to be the growing influence of denominationalism. When the Reform party won the general election of December 1847, the hopes of religious as well as political reformers rose. At last the opportunity had come to establish by constitutional means that civil and religious equality of which they had dreamed so long, and which William Lyon Mackenzie had failed to gain by force of arms. The realization that their party leaders were in fact conservatives at heart came slowly. Grumbling at the slowness of reform mounted steadily, and soon produced the Clear Grit group of advanced reformers. After the retirement of Baldwin and Lafontaine the process of disintegration within the party was hastened by the popular distrust of Francis Hincks, and of his "combination" with certain former Clear Grits.

Considerations, both constitutional and political, frustrated the popular cry for secularization of the Clergy Reserves and abolition of the Rectories for six years. At last, in 1854, the Reserves were secularized; not, however, by Reformers, but by the new Liberal-Conservative party. Centripetal nationalism did not gain a complete victory, for provisions were included, protecting the vested rights of incumbents, which were in essence a compromise with denominationalism. However much this solution disappointed the extremists on both sides, at least it did settle finally this long-vexed problem to the satisfaction of the majority in Canada West. The case of the Rectories was less of a victory for nationalism, because the existing Rectories were permanently maintained.

The Great Ministry acted more positively in the matter of University reform. The "National Endowment" for higher education was in fact nationalized, and every inducement and pressure was used to reduce denominational rivals of the provincial University. Once more thoroughgoing Reform hopes failed of complete realization, for the denominational institutions continued to exist as equals of the state institutions, to receive some government aid, and actually to increase in numbers. The fulfilment of the compromise between denominationalism and nationalism in higher education was not reached in Canada West before Confederation, but the developments after 1850 ensured that neither force would exclude the other from the field. The acceptance of the co-existence of both national and denominational colleges in the province was the first step towards the present solution of general grants and affiliation at Toronto.

Yet only in the field of elementary education did centripetal nationalism suffer a really serious reverse. Here the demand for denominational schools, which the Church of England had brought forward in the forties, was taken up with considerably more success by the Roman Catholics in the fifties and sixties. Thanks to the tremendous influx of Irish Roman Catholics after the potato famine, and to the presence in the United Legislature of the virtually solid Roman Catholic representation from Canada East, the Church of Rome was able to push beyond the original provisions for protection from insult in the elementary schools. Claiming its own denominational schools as a right, the Church of Rome established bit by bit its own system of elementary education. This process was stopped just short of complete educational dualism by the compromise written into the British North America Act, by which Roman Catholic separate schools were placed under the same ultimate control as the common schools of this province. This settlement has been accepted, at least by Protestants, as a final compromise between nationalism and denominationalism in elementary education.

Behind these developments lay a community of outlook on problems of religion and morality which embraced practically all Protestants of Canada West. Generally speaking, the attitude towards such subjects as temperance and Sabbath labour transcended denominational lines, although there was a closer connection of religious reform with political reform than with political conservatism. "Almost all men who are right on the liquor law question," wrote one Reformer, "are also right on the Clergy Reserves question." The end of the Clergy Reserves marked the removal of the last major barrier to this Protestant unity of outlook, and paved the way for the development of a sort of omnibus Protestant denomination, which was not an organization but an attitude. The process of union among the Protestant churches of Ontario began soon after Confederation, and though organic union is still incomplete, the "Protestant outlook" exists today even more certainly than it did in Canada West.

2. Attitudes of Major Denominations

The Church of England

The Church of England was the largest and most influential Christian denomination in Canada West before Confederation. Under the leadership of John Strachan, whose episcopate (1839–67) corresponds almost exactly with the period of this study, the Church of England continued to take a prominent part in the political life of the province, as it had in Upper Canada, seeking to obtain or retain the peculiar privileges which it claimed by virtue of orthodoxy and establishment in England. But its opponents during the Union were numerous. Dissenters had, since the 1820s, been jealous of its privileged position. Although this position was severely circumscribed at the time of Union, Protestants outside the pale of the "Establishment" still clamoured for religious equality, either separately as denominations or collectively as the "underprivileged". To the Church's fear and distrust of dissent was added an unmitigated horror and hatred of the Church of Rome, a sentiment generally shared by all Protestant bodies of that day.

The other external force of opposition to the Church of England was that of the would-be secularizationists, the radicals of Canada West and their willing allies, the Whigs at Westminster. The influence of these two groups rose and fell with the tide of politics. But one source of opposition to Strachan's dreams of ecclesiastical supremacy which only rose, never fell, was much closer to the Bishop's Palace. Within the Church itself a large body of liberal-minded clergy and laity doubted the wisdom of many of John Toronto's policies. Generally speaking, these people were Low Church and Church of Ireland, and their numbers and influence grew rapidly in the late forties as a result of the Oxford Movement and of the increased immigration to Canada. Their stronghold was the peninsula of western Ontario, but they were also to be found throughout the rest of the diocese.

The conflict of Irish Low Churchism *versus* English High Churchism began to appear in the mid-forties and by the time of the founding of Trinity College it had become open warfare. Puseyism and Tractarianism had rent several congregations, and in the field of education Low Churchmen openly opposed Strachan's demand for parochial schools and his control of the "Church University". Both Huron and Wycliffe colleges were established as Low Church rivals of Trinity. And on the score of establishment most of the Low Church element actually favoured secularization. Thus Low Churchmen could generally be classed as Reformers and advanced Conservatives, hardly ever as Tories.

The rapidly expanding need for increased personnel and finances had most serious consequences for the Church of England during the period of the Union. The fact that the Church was not indigenous (it augmented its clergy largely by importing young Englishmen) was complicated by the refusal of the lay immigrants to support their ministers, and by the increasing reluctance of the industrialized mother country to subsidize the Church, particularly in a colony whose separation from the mother country was the topic of popular discussion. At the same time the Church of England in Canada lost its share of the Clergy Reserves. The only solution was to adopt the disagreeable practice of voluntarism, which, once accepted, proved to be the Church's salvation in Canada. The secularization of the Clergy Reserves and the creation of synodical self-government for the Church of England marks the end of its colonial dependence and the beginning of its development as a purely Canadian denomination. The Old World heritage of monopoly was finally abandoned of necessity, in favour of a policy of competition.[4]

Apart from the difference of opinion on liturgy, education, and voluntarism, the Low and High Church groups assumed distinctive social attitudes. The Low Church was at one with dissenters in its abhorrence of gambling, drinking, and all similar sins of the flesh. The mouthpiece of such sentiments, the *Echo and Protestant Episcopal Recorder,* was founded in 1852, and was openly and avowedly anti-Puseyite and anti-Romanist. Strachan's official paper, the *Church,* had suffered from incompetent editors, financial reverses, and popular reaction against its High Churchism ever since its inception in 1837. The *Patriot,* an entirely secular journal, proved in the long run to be a more effective and vocal partisan of Toryism and High Churchism.

The Church of Scotland and Other Presbyterians

The Church of Scotland had long claimed the privileged position of being an established church in Upper Canada, but unlike the Church of England it had failed to gain Imperial recognition before the Union.[5] True, it had received a measure of government assistance, but the collusion of Strachan and successive Lieutenant-Governors had excluded it from any share of the Clergy Reserves. But despite the fact that they were fewer in number than the Anglicans, the men of the Kirk held an equally important place in the councils and affairs of the province.

In the 1830s a movement for the union of the Church of Scotland and the much smaller Synod of the United Secession Church (generally called the United Synod) had begun, but only the chance of sharing in the division of the Clergy Reserves in 1840 finally brought the two bodies together.

If there was one tendency which marked all Presbyterians in Canada more than any other it was their strong individualistic, anti-clerical, and anti-sacerdotal tradition. The power of the laity in church affairs rose from the congregation through the presbytery to the annual synod meeting where the laity were most vocal in defending their freedom from all priestly presumptions. The control of church property was always a focal point for this clash of lay and clerical authority. Thus the creation of Queen's University led to such a struggle within its Board of Trustees, and was followed soon after by a similar conflict over the management of the Kirk's share of the Clergy Reserves.[6]

But the attempt of certain ministers in 1843 to obtain a Temporalities Act favourable to themselves precipitated a major revolt of the laity. Congregations met to denounce the "iniquitous and insidious" scheme of their own clergy and petitioned the Governor General and Parliament against its enactment.[7] "This ought to prove a lesson to the Synod," wrote Hugh Scobie, editor of the *British Colonist.*[8] So it may have done, for never again did the ministers of the Church of Scotland in Canada dare to make such a bare-faced grab for temporal power. The disruption of 1844 marked the turning of the tide of fortune for the Church of Scotland in Canada West. Thereafter the influence and members of that denomination declined in inverse ratio to the success of the Free Church. Not until the eve of Confederation did the Church of Scotland have the number of clergy it possessed before 1844.[9] And not until 1852 could it boast a native-born clergyman. So rapidly did the Free Church expand that in less than seven years it had far outstripped the "Residuary Church" in size, and with its advocacy of national education, religious equality, and "Protestant principles", it assumed the role of leadership among dissenters vacated by the Wesleyan Methodists between 1834 and 1838. It also tended to show an affinity with political reformism.[10]

The only other Presbyterian group of any consequence was the United Presbyterian Church, relatively small in numbers and containing more Irish- and American-born adherents than Scottish. Overtures for union with the Free Church had been offered and received by the United Presbyterians in 1844 but came to naught until 1861, when 70 United Presbyterian ministers joined 163 of the Free Church, together being more than double the number of Church of Scotland ministers.[11] The major cause of the seventeen-year delay in forming this union was, as always among the Presbyterians, the issue of church-state relations rather than any doctrinal difference. The United Presbyterians were voluntarists and denied Christ's Headship over the nations. The Free Church asserted that Christ was Head and could command the civil magistrates' support. By 1861 the Free Church was completely voluntarist in sentiment and the problem of Christ's Headship was solved with one of those typically Canadian compromise resolutions which meant whatever both parties believed it did.[12]

The Wesleyans and Other Methodists

Of all the Christian denominations in Canada West, the Wesleyan Methodists are probably the best known because they are the most written about. Originally organized as part of the Genesee Conference in New York State, they had achieved complete independence in 1829 under the name of Methodist Episcopal Church. At the instigation of the Colonial Office, the British Wesleyans began in the early 1830s to expand their operations from Lower Canada into Upper Canada with the specific objective of acting as an eradicator of (or at least a strong deterrent to) the supposed radical and "republican" tendencies of North American Methodism.[13] To forestall this political manœuvre and prevent the duplication of work by rival organizations, the Canadian body entered into union with the British Conference in 1833. But a minority of the Canadians, correctly sensing some ulterior motive behind the British influx, refused to join and organized another church which retained the name and many of the distinctive features of the Methodist Episcopals.

The union of the British Wesleyans and Canadians into the Wesleyan Methodist Church proved to be an unhappy arrangement because of their differing attitudes regarding the relations of church and state. The Canadians had for years been the most vocal opponents of Anglican supremacy and the advocates of equal religious liberty, whereas the British group retained their traditional deference towards the "Establishment". This difference of outlook became most embarrassing during the Rebellion and finally caused an open rupture when the Clergy Reserves question was revived in 1840. As a result of the British Wesleyans' desire for a share of the Clergy Reserves money the union was dissolved by the British Conference at the very moment when the two Canadas were being reunited.

After six years of the most violent internecine war, during which time both parties were excluded from participation in the Clergy Reserves funds, a new and lasting union was negotiated. This reunion had been influenced by the growth of Tractarianism and Millerism, and by the example of the Evangelical Alliance in England, but the opponents of Methodism credited it to the desire to obtain state aid. Thereafter, though the two parties might not see eye to eye on such problems as state endowments and religious education, they did manage to keep their differences repressed, and to present a seemingly united front on public issues. But the heyday of political radicalism among the Wesleyans passed with the first union in 1834, and after the Union of the Canadas they held to the straight and narrow path of a neutrality which verged [on] conservatism. Only on the University question did they become involved in politics, but this problem, they insisted, was primarily a religious one, and thus they justified their partisanship.

Although Canadian Methodists of all descriptions were essentially voluntarists, the Wesleyans did accept state aid for their educational institutions, much to the disgust of all other branches of Methodism. The policy was inherently self-contradictory and the Wesleyans were never able to find a logical solution to their dilemma. They did, however, maintain with all other Methodists a common attitude on other social problems, being strong advocates of temperance and sabbatarianism.

Of the other Methodist bodies, the largest was always the Methodist Episcopal Church, about one-third the size of the Wesleyans. The circuit-rider tradition of frontier democracy, lay participation in church management, and militant evangelism were maintained by the Episcopals long after their Wesleyan brethren had been "corrupted" with the formalism and respectability of bourgeois urbanization. The other Methodist churches—Bible Christian, New Connexion, and Primitive—were separately insignificant in numbers and influence, and tended to follow the lead of the Methodist Episcopals in their political ideas. The close connection between the left-wing Methodist groups and the anti-Clergy Reserves movement, for instance, is an indisputable fact. Generally speaking, it may be said that all the non-Wesleyan Methodists were inclined to political as well as religious radicalism. Numerically they equalled the Wesleyans, and it is an error to overlook their influence, to equate them with the Wesleyans, or to treat them simply as camp-followers of the Wesleyans by ignoring their differences of opinion. In organization these bodies copied the efficient circuit-district-Conference system of the Wesleyans, and, [as with] the Presbyterians, the main *raison d'être* of every Methodist body was its distinctive approach to the problem of church-state relations.

In conclusion it may be said that there existed a unity of outlook among all the non-Wesleyan Methodists, and that their attitudes were shared by many Canadian Wesleyans. But union with the British Wesleyans and urbanization had modified and compromised the Wesleyan Methodist attitude on the relations of church and state since the era of Upper Canada, and this denomination was to be found in the conservative *via media* during the period of the Union, desperately maintaining a position of neutrality to prevent internal divisions.

The Baptist, Congregationalist, and Smaller Protestant Churches

Despite their relative paucity of numbers, the Baptists of Canada West were unquestionably the most militant, dogmatic, and vocal denomination in a province where these attributes were common property. As the majority of Baptists were of Scottish descent they had much in common with the Free Church, while at the same time they shared with the Congregationalists the traditions and the ideals of English nonconformity. Yet their influence, which probably was greater than their numerical strength would suggest, was seriously vitiated by their strong individualism and two internal lines of division. The Baptist congregations of the Ottawa Valley were usually missions organized from Montreal under strong "old country" influence, whereas the churches in the western peninsula were dominated by and closely allied to the United States Baptists.[14] Across these national lines the issue of open *versus* closed communion cut like a knife, and though the east tended to be open and the west closed, this was only a tendency, not a rule.

The strong individualism which prevented co-operation between these chequered groups also infested particular congregations. Internal dissension was rife within congregations as it was within communions, and the power of the purse was most effectively wielded against any clergyman or cause which did not please individual members. A weak union of the congregations of Canada West collapsed in 1849 after six years of futile effort to combine these autonomous units.

Regardless of this balkanizing tendency among the Baptists, they were completely of one mind on the question of the relation of church and state. Their stand in favour of national education, voluntarism, religious equality, and absolute separation of church and state was uncompromised for more than a century after the Union of the two Canadas, and they yielded first place to none in the advocacy of these ideals.

The history of the Congregationalists of the province has not yet been written, probably because of the scarcity of primary source material. They received no missionary aid from abroad and practically no increase in numbers as a result of immigration. Nevertheless, they played a prominent role in the politico-religious disputes of the period.[15] Though less rigid in their theology than the Baptists, the Congregationalists held the same basic belief in the separation of church and state, and their laymen and clergy were always prominent in the activities of such organizations as the Anti-Clergy Reserves Association.

Closely allied to the Baptists in theology and to the Baptists, Congregationalists, and non-Wesleyan Methodists in politics were several small denominations such as the Disciples of Christ, and the Christians. As the combined numbers of these groups probably did not exceed a thousand, they can be dismissed by lumping them with the other larger voluntarist denominations.

Yet another grouping of denominations comprises the Mennonites, Tunkers, and Quakers. For the purpose of these studies they can be ignored, since their faith precluded their participation in politics. Being non-jurors and pacifists they were virtually disfranchised, although their sympathies undoubtedly lay with the aggregation of voluntarists. Finally, mention should be made of the Lutherans, whose numbers approximately equalled those of the Congregationalists. Lacking any newspaper to express their views and usually unacquainted with the English language, the Lutherans were as quiet as the Quakers. Traditionally they favoured a close connection between religion and the state, and on at least one occasion, by applying for a share of Clergy Reserves funds, they proved themselves untouched by their voluntarist milieu.

The Church of Rome

The Roman Catholic Church in Canada West at the time of Union was smaller than either the Church of England or the Church of Scotland, and about equal to the combined strength of the British and Canadian Wesleyan Methodists. By 1867 the Church of Rome was second to the Church of England, thanks to the great influx of Irish after the potato famine, and was considerably more influential than any other Christian denomination. This power, however, arose not so much from the increased membership in the upper province as from the close religious and political connection with the large Roman Catholic population in Canada East.

Although Upper Canada was predominantly and deliberately a Protestant province, the Roman Catholics had received the same magnanimous treatment there as had the French Canadians after the Conquest. At a time when their religion was proscribed in Britain, Roman Catholics in Upper Canada were receiving financial assistance from the state and denominational privileges which were denied to the dissenters. Yet their inferior status in the Imperial connection limited their power to demand further favours. They could and did receive willingly any emoluments offered by the government, but they could not ask as much as they probably would have desired. After Union, however, the alliance with their co-religionists along the lower St. Lawrence and the sudden and gigantic flood from Ireland greatly improved the political bargaining position of that church. The flood-tide of immigration also necessitated a more extensive and effective organization of the Roman Church in Canada West and the number of sees was repeatedly increased after 1850.

Despite its great size and huge political potential, the Church of Rome maintained a posture and attitude of relative neutrality in the affairs of state in the upper province. It took money from the Protestant Clergy funds when it was offered, but it did not interfere officially with the popular demand for the secularization of the Reserves. Similarly, it stood by as a disinterested observer while the Protestant denominations fought for control of the provincial University endowment. On one major public issue, however, the Church of Rome did stand forth adamantly in demanding what was considered a sacred right. That issue was the separate schools question.

Lest it be mistakenly presumed that there was no other source of friction between the Roman Catholics and Protestants in Canada West than that of sectarian control of elementary education, it must be added at once that the existence of Orangism and a general Protestant antipathy to Rome, accentuated by the "Papal Aggression" controversy, provided a fertile and seemingly eternal source of irritations and petty conflicts for both parties of Christians. But this was more a chronic condition breaking out intermittently as the result of some particular incident, and despite the troubles lurking just below the surface, it was mostly sound and fury signifying little of major importance to the main religio-political problems of Canada West.

NOTES

1   W. S. Wallace, *The Growth of Canadian National Feeling* (Toronto, 1927), p. 41.
2   Sir C. P. Lucas, ed., *Report on the Affairs of British North America,* 3 vols. (Oxford, 1912), 2: 309.
3   Cf. H. Richard Niebuhr, *The Social Sources of Denominationalism* (New York, 1957), Chaps. 6, 7, and S. D. Clark, *Church and Sect in Canada* (Toronto, 1948), Chaps. 5-7.
4   Cf. H. R. Niebuhr, *ibid.,* p. 211.
5   William Gregg, *History of the Presbyterian Church in the Dominion of Canada* (Toronto, 1885), p. 437 *et sqq.*
6   Q.U.A., Queen's University Papers, W. Morris to F. A. Harper, Jan. 1, Feb. 12, 1841.
7   Morris Papers, Hugh Scobie to W. Morris, Nov. 7, 1843; R. B. Sullivan to W. Morris, Nov. 18, 1843; *British Colonist,* Nov. 9 and 14, 1843; *Examiner,* Nov. 22, 1843.
8   Morris Papers, H. Scobie to W. Morris, Nov. 7, 1843.

9   *A Historical and Statistical Report of the Presbyterian Church of Canada . . . for the Year, 1866* (Montreal, 1868), pp. 128, 165-72; Gregg, *History of the Presbyterian Church,* p. 494.
10   Ian Rennie, "The Free Church and Relations of Church and State in Canada, 1844-54", unpublished M.A. thesis, University of Toronto, 1954, pp. 66-7.
11   Gregg, *History of the Presbyterian Church,* p. 494.
12   Anna Ross, *The Man with the Book or Memoirs of "John Ross of Brucefield"* (Toronto, 1897), pp. 76-81.
13   C. B. Sissons, *Life and Letters of Egerton Ryerson,* 2 vols. (Toronto, 1937, 1947), 1: 152-91.
14   G. W. Brown, "The Formative Period of Canadian Protestant Churches", in R. Flenley, ed., *Essays in Canadian History* (Toronto, 1939), p. 364.
15   G. W. Brown, *ibid.,* p. 364.

3.

Social Change
and Adaptation

Native Religion in Sociocultural Change: The Cree and Saulteaux in Southern Saskatchewan, 1830-1900*

Mitsuru Shimpo

1. Introduction

One of the common political tasks of 19th-century Canada and the United States was the opening of the western frontier. During this period governments of both nations used a series of treaties to swindle the native peoples of their territorial rights in order to support the recently arrived white settlers who wished to protect not only their lives but also what they perceived as their private property. The Indians, in contrast, wanted to maintain their nomadic existence which centred on the migrations of the buffalo.

Despite these similarities, the immigrant-native relationships in Canada and the United States differed conspicuously in the amount of overt physical violence involved. In the Canadian prairies there were only a few outright conflicts, namely the incidents of 1816, 1867–70, and 1885–6.[1] One explanation of this phenomenon may lie in differences in the cultural systems among the natives in North America.[2]

Nomadic societies, despite their diversities, share a number of similar features.[3] One similarity is that the religion serves to integrate the socio-

*Prepared for this volume.

cultural system and consequently affects individual behaviour. Hence, an approach which examines the natives' behaviour from the viewpoint of their religion and culture may provide a plausible explanation for their diverse responses to the whites' external challenge. In pursuing this approach, I will follow three steps: (1) outline the natives' socio-cultural system from the 1830s until the 1870s; (2) analyse changes in these conditions from the 1870s until approximately 1900; and (3) discuss the role of religion in the same periods.[4]

2. The Sociocultural Equilibrium among the Plains Cree and Saulteaux before Treaty No. 4 (1874)

On the Canadian prairies in the 19th century, both the Cree and the Saulteaux shared a similar sociocultural system.[5] The following features characterize these two groups before the treaties of the 1870s.

(a) *Politics*

The tribe was not a visible social unit. On the Canadian prairies it was the band which constituted the basic community. The band did not have a clearly defined boundary and its membership was loose. Since the plains Cree and Saulteaux were completely dependent upon the buffalo, its movement affected the physical formation of the band. During the winter, when the buffalo migrated to the northern bush and formed very small herds, the natives organized small hunting parties to follow the animals. In the spring, when the buffalo returned to the plains in large herds, the natives organized their total band for hunting.

The band had an elected chief supported by a group of elected council members. These leaders were the members of a "Warriors' Society" which performed the functions of the government, the court, the police, and the welfare agency. The chief as an individual did not have significant power. He merely announced the collective decisions made by the band council. Except during the group-hunt of buffalos, decisions of the band council did not sharply control the behaviour of individual members. Any member disagreeing with a decision could simply leave and join another band.

(b) *The Economy*

Economic activities may be divided into two categories: production for exchange and production for domestic consumption. The natives trapped fur-bearing animals for the Hudson's Bay Company and received fire-arms, gunpowder, flour, liquor, and other goods which they could not produce themselves. They used the buffalo as their major source of food, clothing, and shelter. In addition, they hunted other animals, fished, and collected wild rice or berries for domestic consumption.

Their cycle of production was the reverse of the settlers'. During the long winter, native hunters desperately struggled to survive in the northern bush. During the warm season the natives enjoyed their social life in the band camp. It was a time to relax because buffalo were relatively abundant.

(c) *Education*

Education was provided by the kin-group. Male relatives took boys on hunting and trapping trips. Female relatives encouraged girls' participation in domestic chores. The educational method emphasized participation and practice. If children succeeded, the adults lavishly praised them. If they failed, the adults laughed at them. The curriculum was directly related to daily life and future responsibilities. If the children failed to master a task, they would be unable to survive. Since the teachers had expertise in these necessary skills, they could easily gain their pupils' respect. The curriculum was so closely related to everyday life that the teachers could almost perfectly socialize the younger generation.

(d) *The Value System and Religion*

The natives of this region held in common cultural values of seniority, courage, autonomy, sharing, and generosity. These values were systematized, were verified by a belief-system, and served to integrate the socio-cultural system. To understand the operation of this value system one needs to be aware of the natives' cosmology. They divided the spiritual world into two spheres: the kingdom of *Kitchi Manitou*, the Great Spirit, and the kingdom of *Michi Manitou,* the Evil Spirit. The former reigned in heaven and on earth, while the latter ruled the underground world. These spirits were omnipotent and omniscient in their own spheres and competed for dominion over man. Since they lived at a distance from the world of men, they created other spirits or *manitous* to help them care for the men under their influence. Most *manitous* were actual game animals but some of them were fictitious ones, such as the thunderbird.

As the universe was ruled by these various *manitous*, the natives were convinced that no one could succeed in any activity unless he had assistance from one of them. Those who sought prestige among the band members particularly needed such help. The dream visitors would come with sympathy when a native was weak or ill only as a result of his devotional efforts in seeking help. Since every *manitou* had a different amount of power as a guardian, the degree of protection which the dreamer would receive varied. If a man accepted the offer of a *manitou* to be his guardian he must not tell others about it. Thus, no one knew who another's *manitou* was or to which camp his *manitou* belonged—that of the Great Spirit or the Evil Spirit—or how much power he had.

In every sphere of life, men relied upon the benevolence of the *manitous*. For example, aged men were believed to have a special blessing. If such a man were insulted or attacked, the guardian *manitou* would take revenge. Thus, seniority was respected partly from fear of the old one's guarding deities. A man had profound personal relations only with the *manitou*—hence the native's personal autonomy. Only when an individual surrendered himself to the *manitou* did he receive his protection and aid. The complete surrender of the self to the spirit would create "courage". His fellows would respect him as a result of his activities. Success in hunting or trapping was interpreted as a reward from the *manitou*. Hence, by generously sharing the fruits, he could both increase his social prestige and demonstrate the amount of protection which he was receiving from his *manitou*.

On the one hand, this religion developed an atomistic tendency in community life. On the other hand, by subscribing to the value of sharing, the natives could maintain their social institutions within a subsistence economy. Their values provided protection, prestige, and security. Also, participation in religious ceremonies integrated the community. Thus, during this period from the 1830s to the 1870s, the natives' sociocultural system maintained a state of equilibrium.

(e) *Conditions Favouring Sociocultural Equilibrium*

At least three conditions enabled the natives to preserve this equilibrium until the 1870s. First, they were geographically isolated from the impact of European industrial civilization in eastern Canada. Second, the natives depended little on a monetary economy. The major resource for their economic survival was the buffalo and not commodities purchased from the Hudson's Bay Company.[6] Finally, as a consequence, they maintained political independence.

3. Changes in Conditions and Consequent Disequilibrium (from 1874 to approximately 1900)

In 1812 the Selkirk Settlement was established on the Red River. There followed a slow migration of whites into the west. In 1821 the Hudson's Bay Company absorbed the North West Company of Montreal and now almost monopolized the western frontier. By 1846 the company had completely halted the American Fur Company's invasion into Canadian territory. In 1867, however, the United States purchased Alaska, and British Columbia was sandwiched between American territory to the north and to the south. "There was no future for the colony so long as it remained an isolated British outpost; every economic consideration seemed to point to annexation by the United States as the only practicable solution."[7] The International Financial Society, which was established in London in 1870, purchased the land and charter of the Hudson's Bay Company in order to establish sovereignty in the west. At the same time, the government of Canada signed a series of treaties with the natives to take away their land legally and to allow the whites to settle the west. Also in the early 1870s, the buffalo herds were slaughtered by white hunters and practically disappeared from the Canadian prairies. Consequently, the natives lost their basic economic resource. Now they had few alternatives to signing Treaty Number Four at Qu'Appelle Lake on September 15, 1874.

(a) *Politics*

This treaty undermined the natives' political independence. They were to be administered under the Indian Act. The boundary of the band became clearly defined and the membership was legally registered by Indian Affairs personnel. The natives had to settle down on the reserve. The chief and elders were still elected by the band members but they were essentially no more than messengers for the Department of Indian Affairs. The government clearly intended to integrate the natives into the dominant society. As a means of achieving this goal, the government told the natives to adopt farming and to send their children to school. The government also encouraged Christian churches to convert the native population.

(b) *The Economy*

The pattern of production activities changed dramatically. The natives were supposed to become farmers. This policy conflicted violently with

their traditional economic behaviour. Hunting was not a secular profession but a sacred one. To become farmers, the natives believed, meant
renouncing hunting, which implied the discarding of the traditional
belief-system. Farming also conflicted with the traditional pattern of
mobility. Instead of roaming the prairies and the northern bush, they
were supposed to settle in a specific location. The seasonal rhythm of
life changed as well. The natives were supposed to rest during the winter
and to work hard during the warmer season. The reward-pattern likewise changed. For hunters, the reward of daily toil was immediate. In
farming, however, one had to wait for half a year, and crops were often
damaged by unstable natural conditions. Further, to be a successful
farmer, one had to possess a considerable amount of specialized knowledge in agricultural matters. For the natives who had accumulated a body
of sophisticated knowledge in hunting, making such a drastic switch was
a difficult task. Finally, the kind of farming the government imposed
upon the natives introduced a qualitatively different set of ideas. Private
ownership of land was, for the people of a hunting and gathering society,
an entirely alien concept.

Because of these difficulties, the results of farming were poor. Under
Treaty Number Four, 24 bands started to adopt the governmental program. In 1885, the most remarkable achievement was observed in one
band of 35 families. According to the existing records, 30 families were
engaged in farming to some extent but more than half of their harvest
(about 800 bushels of crops) was yielded by only two families.

Until the end of the 19th century, the natives could still find some
game animals in the northern bush. When this resource was depleted,
they took advantage of their land resources and cut trees to sell as fire-
wood or fence posts to the whites. They also raised horses and monopolized winter transportation until the railway was built in 1905. At the
time of the construction of the railway, they were employed as unskilled
workers. In return, they began to buy factory-made commodities and
their production and consumption activities became involved in the
monetary economy.

(c) *Education*

After the signing of the treaty, schooling was introduced by the missionaries. Immediately after the settlement of the natives, Roman Catholic,
Anglican, and Presbyterian missionaries were stationed on the reserves.

They learned the Cree language and tried to adapt to the Cree culture as a means of evangelization. In spite of the missionaries' zealous efforts, adult natives did not submit to the "new" religion. The missionaries then changed their strategy. They wished to teach English to native children so that the educated youngsters would eventually read and understand the Bible. In the area I studied, the first school building was erected in 1881 by the Presbyterian Church. The government officials who had promised to give the natives a formal education did not supply the necessary resources of buildings, capital, and teachers; education was provided by the churches.

The new school had a miserable record of attendance. There was no road on the reserve, which was six miles wide and twelve miles long. Some parents took boys on hunting trips and girls were not encouraged to attend school. In this area, the temperature often goes down to 50 or 55 degrees below zero(F.). When the summer came, the teachers took a rest. There was no possibility of reaching students under these circumstances. As an alternative approach, the teachers visited homes and asked nearby children to attend classes. But according to one report, the average attendance rate in 1882 was only 28 per cent of school-age children on the reserve.

The missionaries' teaching method was quite different from the traditional native one. Schoolteachers explained endlessly. The curriculum was not related to the children's lives, and textbooks were hard to understand. The method of discipline included making the victim stand in the corner of the room so that the rest of the class could laugh at him. In the 1890s the church erected a residential school in which the use of the native language was prohibited. If any child used his native tongue, all students in the dormitory were punished.

In addition, the older people did not encourage their youngsters to attend school. They felt threatened by the new body of knowledge which their children were absorbing from the teachers. The children were slipping away from the native socialization process and were developing contempt for their elders. The elderly people whom I interviewed in 1963 almost unanimously responded that even in the 1910s, old folks did not like them to speak English at home, and discouraged them from being too co-operative with teachers.

Teachers were discouraged at the lack of motivation and poor achievement. Parents who wished to maintain their traditional way of life were distressed. Students were torn between two worlds.

(d) *The Value System and Religion*

The ultimate goal of the government has been the integration of the natives into the dominant value system of Canadian society. This policy emphasized less autonomy and more conformity to the norms of formal organizations. Further, Indian Affairs introduced private property to replace joint ownership and this undermined the traditional values of generosity and sharing. However, in spite of these unfavourable conditions, the traditional value system still survived to some extent.

The reaction of most native adults to Christianity was expressed by an old Cree whom I interviewed:[8]

Look at the chapel over there. How many Indians are attending the service on Sunday? I tell you, the religious training at the residential school was very, very strict. In spite of the enormous effort of the missionaries, we have not become true "Christians". Do you know why? I tell you.

I personally think religion is a good thing. Man should be humble before the gods. But we cannot understand what the missionaries are trying to do. We want to make others happy and like to see happy people. When missionaries ask us to attend their service we are willing to attend because we like to see their happy faces. If we attend, however, they tell us that religions other than theirs are all wrong.

According to our grandparents, our ancestors knew that other Indians worshipped different gods from ours, but they never declared that they should not worship these gods. And men of other tribes never criticized our god and asked us to worship their god. In the past, Indians sometimes fought among each other, but they did not interfere with others' religions.

Let us tentatively accept that Christianity is a superior religion to ours. The Bible tells us, "All men are brothers and sisters", "God is love and men are all sinners", and so on. The Bible also tells us that the love of God delivered men from their sin. From the above it follows that men should love each other instead of judging each other. We quite agree with the teaching.

But look at what the missionaries are doing. What they tell us to do is different from what they are actually doing. On this reserve, the Anglican Church has been the only church. According to the missionaries, all other churches but Anglican are wrong. If you go to the neighbouring reserve, the Roman Catholic missionaries will tell you the same thing, claiming that the Roman Catholic Church is the only right one. Under these circumstances, can you believe the missionaries from different churches love each other as their brothers? It seems to me they hate each other as if others are a bunch of devils. And both groups of missionaries continue to preach to Indians to love other men as our brothers. If you are an Indian and listen to them, do you trust them and accept what they preach?

The missionaries say the whites have adhered to Christianity for almost two thousand years. But are the whites practising what the Bible tells them to do?

We feel particularly bitter when the missionaries say all men are created equal. Do whites really believe Indians are equally created by the Christian God? Some whites criticize us that we do not have good education: this is true. As some other whites say, we do not farm as well as the white farmers do. We are more frequently drunken than the whites are. But a number of whites are like some of us. And, even the ignorant, poor, and drunken whites despise us because we are Indians. They look at us as if we Indians are a kind of animal.

If Jesus taught man to treat everybody as an equal person, and if the whites are Christians as the missionaries tend to claim, why do the whites not obey their Lord's commandment and regard Indians as their equals? During the First World War, I joined the army and fought in Europe. Then I saw numerous poor whites. Although they were poor, they treated me as a man. Do you think a poor white is superior to a poor Indian? I cannot understand the white man's logic. The more we observe them, the more we are convinced that the whites do the opposite of what the missionaries around here preached to us.

You may not know this, but our religion is quite close to Christianity. This is why I like Christianity. But I do not like what the whites do. By this I include missionaries. It seems to me that missionaries are concerned with their achievement only, and that they regard the number of Indian converts as the criterion of their achievement. In brief, they use us as a means of their personal success. If this is the case, why should we not use missionaries for our purpose as well? Indeed, we do. When the missionaries promise some gifts, we go to church to get it. When they do not offer anything, we do not go. It is a matter of fact, isn't it?

It seems fair to infer that during the initial period of missionary activity, the natives' reactions toward missionaries might have been even more negative.

The missionaries were confronted with the natives' religion. The political ideology of Indian Affairs conflicted with the natives' cultural values. School education threatened the traditional socialization process. Change from hunting to farming implied a desacralization of work. The natives' belief system was challenged in every sphere of the social system. Throughout this process, what were the roles of the natives' traditional religion and of Christianity?

4. The Role of Religion in the Period of Disequilibrium

I stated in the introduction that Canadian natives peacefully surrendered to the whites' authority and that blood-shedding was minimal. My hypothesis is that the natives' religion played a significant role in this surrender, although religion was by no means the sole condition which explains the situation.

As a response to the series of radical changes in their sociocultural system, one can infer that the natives used their traditional religion as a means of cushioning the impact. In the economic sphere, the natives continued hunting and trapping until the supply of game was exhausted, and then they made a very limited commitment to farming. Their stronger commitment to hunting was closely related to their religious beliefs. All natural phenomena were divided into classes and at the head of each class was an "owner" or "boss". Every animal had an invisible boss who appeared to certain people in dreams and became their guardian.

The guardians sent visible (or actual) animals before their protégés as the game. However skilful the hunters might be, they would kill no game without divine help. Success in hunting was an assurance of divine protection from the supernaturals. At the time of disequilibrium, every member of the social system needed the assurance that he was protected. The sudden disappearance of the buffalo from the prairies was often interpreted as the revelation of the wrath of *manitous,* and natives desperately sought pardon and a sign of divine blessing. The easiest method of obtaining this assurance open to every adult male was hunting. Though the Canadian government offered help in farm development on the reserve, this implied two things to the natives: they had to adopt a secular profession and they had to lose their source of sacred assurance at a time of crisis. This interpretation of events retarded the adoption of farming.

Generally speaking, in traditional societies religion promotes group cohesion, strengthens the moral order, binds individuals to the social order, and provides a source of identity. In times of trial, religion offers solace to the believers. When their social organization was being challenged by the government's programs, the natives wanted to maintain the social order in their own way. Many conditions underlay their sociocultural equilibrium, and religion was one of the most significant factors. Hence, they tried to adhere to their traditional beliefs, demonstrating indifference or hostility towards the religion imported by the whites.

Likewise, the natives wished the younger generation to follow the traditional belief system. In order to maintain their religion, the natives had to retain their language. They believed that *Kitchi Manitou* created human language and that words had spiritual power. It was thought that beyond each form of a word, there was a spirit of that word which might be the equivalent of the "boss" of the animal species. The natives believed that if any powerful or good words were associated with a person the *manitou* of these words would provide help and protection to that person. Accordingly, great significance was attached to names of the natives. School education, as we noted, was aimed at making the children English-speaking, and that posed a threat to the adults.

From the natives' viewpoint, material wealth was visible fruit of divine protection. The more material possessions one could obtain, the stronger was the power of the *manitou*. The whites were immensely rich. Fur traders, civil servants, missionaries, and other whites owned abundant possessions which the natives did not. Hence, the whites must have had extremely powerful *manitous* behind them. Moreover, these *manitous* must have belonged to *Michi Manitou*, because the whites spoiled the natives and made them weak by "fire-water". The natives wished to manipulate the whites who had such horribly powerful *manitous* behind them. Hence, they made some compromises. They accepted the whites' authority in a superficial way. They scratched the surface of the soil to please the whites. They were not violently opposed to sending their children to school, although they did not positively encourage schooling. And they did not go so far as to drive missionaries away from their reserves. The natives were courteous and diplomatic but their commitment to the whites' command was limited. In the bands I studied, I was told that traditional beliefs were still in effect in the 1910s.

The impact of Christianity as a belief system is not known. My data is concerned only with the functioning of missionaries on reserves. The missionaries acted politically as the local interpreters of government policies and programs. The missionaries in the 19th century made sincere efforts to master the natives' language and to understand the native culture. Most of the civil servants did not do this since they assumed that the natives would eventually be assimilated into the dominant culture. The missionaries were less authoritarian than the civil servants, for the former had to establish rapport with the natives to achieve their goals, while the latter were simply representing a powerful bureaucratic organization. Consequently, early records reveal that the natives found it easier to approach the missionaries than the civil servants. Civil servants needed missionaries for two reasons. Since government resources were limited then, they had to depend upon the resources provided by churches. Also, the number of whites on the prairies in this period was very small, so that those who were in charge of administering the Indian Act among the natives found missionaries to be dependable friends who could play the role of mediators in isolated regions.

In the economic sphere, missionaries contributed to bands in two ways. They contributed educational facilities, ran schools, and employed a certain number of natives. Also, through school education, they taught the values of the whites as well as skills in farming. The government's agricultural extension officers looked after the adults only and their method of instruction was blunt and unsuccessful. Missionaries took sufficient time to train young people for farming and they taught girls cooking and homemaking.

The churches provided highly motivated teachers who did their best despite discouraging conditions. Particularly since the churches started residential schools, the missionaries were agents of change among the natives. They introduced new music through hymn singing, new drama through Christmas pageants, new art through religious paintings, a concept of public health through rigid regulation in the residential school, and a host of different ideas through school education.

In summary, Christian churches acted as agents of social change, confronting the traditional systems of value and belief. What the churches did on reserves served to undermine conditions which had maintained the sociocultural system of the natives. The response of the natives was negative, in self-defence, and their religion cushioned the impact of radical change in social conditions.

NOTES

1   On the subject of violence on the American frontier, see Dee Brown, *Bury My Heart at Wounded Knee: An Indian History of the American West* (New York: Holt, Rinehart & Winston, 1971).

2   S. D. Clark has explained the absence of violent protest in western Canada in terms of the earlier, long-range established order by relatively selected whites. See his *Movements of Political Protest in Canada (1640-1840)* (Toronto: University of Toronto Press, 1959). His view, however, tends to emphasize only one side of the total picture: the conditions of the whites. This paper is to supplement this position by focusing on the conditions of the natives.

3   Gerhard Lenski, in *Human Societies: A Macrolevel Introduction to Sociology* (New York: McGraw-Hill, 1970), provides a concise summary in this regard.

4   This paper uses the data I collected during the period from 1963 to 1966. Details are documented in the following reports: Mitsuru Shimpo and Robert Williamson, *Socio-Cultural Disintegration among the Fringe Saulteaux* (Saskatoon: Extension Department, University of Saskatchewan, 1965); Mitsuru Shimpo and André Rénaud, "Cree Childhood on the Canadian Prairies" (unpublished manuscript, 1966); and Mitsuru Shimpo, *Canadian Indian* (Tokyo: Sanseido Publishing Co., 1968) (in Japanese). In the summer of 1974, I obtained a sizable grant to conduct the re-study of these reserves starting from 1975.

5   The following reports were fully or partly consulted in the preparation of this paper:
V. Barnouw, "Acculturation and Personality among the Wisconsin Chippewa", *Memoirs of the American Anthropological Association* 86 (1950): 1-152.
F. Sensmore, "Chippewa Customs", *Bulletin of the Bureau of American Ethnology* 86 (Washington, 1929): 1-204.
A. I. Hallowell, *Culture and Experience* (Philadelphia, 1955).
D. Jenness, *The Ojibwa Indian of Parry Island*, Bulletin of the Canada Department of Mines, National Museum of Canada, Vol. 78 (Ottawa, 1925).
R. H. Lowie, "The Military Societies of the Plains Cree", *Proceedings of the International Congress of Americanists* 31, No. 1 (Paris, 1955): 3-9.
D. Mandelbaum, "The Plains Cree", *Anthropological Papers of the American Museum of National History* 37 (1940): 155-316.
A. Skinner, "Ojibway and Cree of Central Canada", *The American Indians* 10 (New York, 1908): 9-18.

6   This does not mean that the natives were completely autonomous. However, the degree of economic autonomy was close to complete in this period compared with that of the post-treaty period.

7   W. T. Easterbrook and H. G. Aitken, *Canadian Economic History* (Toronto: Macmillan of Canada, 1958) p. 344.

8   Recorded in 1966 on a Cree reserve in southern Saskatchewan.

The Religion of the Micmac Indians of Restigouche[*]

Philip K. Bock

Of the three major institutions on the Reserve—the school, the Agency, and the Church—the one most difficult to evaluate is the Church. The Micmac have been nominally Roman Catholic for almost 350 years. At Restigouche there has been a resident priest for more than 100 years, and a Capuchin monastery for almost 70 years; yet Restigouche is still known as "The Mission", and the priest is officially considered to be a missionary.

The aboriginal faith is dead; any survivals are better treated as fragments of folklore (Wallis and Wallis 1953). Until recently there has been no serious "rival doctrine"; many people are apparently "firm in the faith". There is an Indian choir at High Mass which sings the hymns and responses in Micmac; attendance at Mass is fair; indoctrination of the children would seem to be complete. However, two priests expressed to me their doubts as to the depth of religiosity of the Indians. And there is a subtle difference between the Indians and the French in the quality of their commitment to the Church. It may be due merely to my lack of

*Appeared first in Philip K. Bock, *The Micmac Indians of Restigouche: History and Contemporary Description.* Bulletin 213 (Ottawa: National Museum of Canada, 1966). Published here in abridged form with the kind permission of Information Canada.

acquaintance with Roman Catholic communities in other countries, but the Restigouche Micmac seem more tentative in their commitment, less pious in their outlook, readier to suspect or condemn the priest, less informed concerning their faith, and more "in" than "of" the Church than might be expected after so many years.

Most disturbing to the priests are the drinking, sexual licence, and lack of "financial responsibility" of the Indians, whom they think of as simple and childlike. The Indians, though protesting their faithfulness to their religion, make a sharp distinction between the Church and its priests, whose authoritarian attitudes, meddling, and demands for money they strongly resent. The *curé* is accused of working hand-in-hand with the agent, favouring the French parishioners, being a "businessman", and taking advantage of the Indians: "Did you hear? The priest made $8,000 on Ste. Anne's Day. . . . That used to be a big time for the Indians, but now it's all for the Church."

Of the contemporary priests at the monastery, only old Father P——— is fluent in Micmac, and he commands general respect; but in a recent sermon he felt called upon to remind the people of the special status and authority of the priest as the voice of the Church: "Do not think of the priest as just another man. . . ." This is really a focus of conflict, for in religious as in political affairs, the Micmac find it virtually impossible to accept authority of any kind, certainly not when it is based on some kind of claim of personal superiority.

It is difficult to estimate the effect of religious instruction upon the young, or of priestly exhortation upon the adults. One young man attended the seminary for two years, and two girls started the Holy Rosary novitiate, but none of them entered the religious life. In the absence of any alternative creeds, the attitude of most of the adults seems to be one of passive acceptance.

Participation in the weekly rituals seems to be quite general, but according to Adrien (1954: 74): "attendance at Mass during the week is negligible, there are hardly any adult communicants, and only a few on Sunday."

The missionaries of the seventeenth and eighteenth centuries did their best to create a version of Roman Catholicism which would be suitable for the Indians. This meant introducing prayers, hymns, and catechisms in Micmac, and special devotions, especially to Ste. Anne. They relied heavily upon the Indian women to preserve and teach the tradition to their children during the long parts of the year when the families were away from the church. There is general agreement that, for more than two hundred years, virtually all the Micmac were devoted Roman Catholics, even if their standards of "morality" were not always those of the priests.

Adrien attributes the growth of indifference to religious affairs in part to the cessation of instruction in the Indian language, but also to "Les mêmes facteurs qui tendent à modifier leur culture profane . . . contact d'une civilisation matérialiste en rupture plus ou moins ouverte avec l'esprit du christianisme . . ." (1954: 73). He also notes the presence of two groups with diverse languages and cultures within the parish; indeed, his main suggestion for improving the religious situation is to separate the mission from the larger parish, though he recognizes the infeasibility of this solution since "ce sont les Blancs qui font vivre la paroisse" (financially), and it is unlikely that the Indians would consent to giving up their present church (located in the centre of the reserve) (1954: 78-9).

Adrien feels that "la cohabitation des Indiens avec les Blancs dans la même paroisse contribue à l'effacement graduel des traits spécifiques du catholicisme micmac," and that "l'état de 'guerre froide' subsiste encore longtemps" between the two groups (1954: 79). He also attributes the Indians' "abstentionisme" from the affairs of the Church to their dislike of working with or under the direction of the non-Indians. This is true, but it is only part of the story, for certain actions and attitudes of the missionary-priests have contributed to the alienation of many Indians from the Church.

I shall not be able to go into all the complexities of this situation but shall indicate the five main sources of conflict. These are land, money, favouritism, participation, and authority.

As is true of most American Indian groups, the Restigouche Micmac are extremely sensitive about anything relating to their land. The author's efforts were nearly compromised early in his study when he explained that his intention was to make a "community survey". This was interpreted by some to mean that he was a "surveyor", and in a few days the rumour was widespread that he had come to "divide up the land".

There are many stories current about the origin of the "church lot", but it seems clear that this land was given to the Church by Band authorities some time in the mid-nineteenth century. The missionaries used it as a site for the church building and cemetery, and for their residences, though Father Saucier also ran a small store there in the 1860s.

With the coming of the Capuchin Fathers in 1894, the use of the land became more diversified. The church had burned in 1893, but a new one was soon built, together with a sizeable monastery, and gardens and orchards were cultivated. When the mill opened in 1905, the wharf located at Mission Point became a great centre of activity. The Champoux Company opened a trading store and built houses for non-Indian workers on land leased from the Church. During this period, the convent was also constructed on the church lot.

Though I have no evidence, it seems likely that these developments were resented by many of the Indians. For though the parish priest has regarded the church lot as his own property and as a means to raise revenue for the support of the church and monastery, the Indians still regard it as part of the reserve and particularly resent the presence of the French-Canadian families in the newly renovated houses on "the Flats". Inter-group relations are today marked by coolness and aloofness, but formerly there was a good deal of open hostility.

The new regional school was constructed on the church lot, apparently without prior notification of the Indians. In 1961, the old convent was moved back from the road, and a new dormitory (for Normal School pupils) was built adjoining the school and connecting with it. Tension over this new addition was reflected in arguments over the location of the contractor's shack (which was found to be several feet onto reserve land) and in persistent rumours that the priest was selling portions of the church lot to non-Indians and negotiating to lease a large lot by the highway for the construction of a hospital. Rather than try to understand or sympathize with the Indians' attitudes toward their land (and the uses of the church lot), the priests try to minimize the contribution and the historic claims of the Indians.

Money is a second major point of conflict. The parish priest is responsible for the finances of the parish. Father A———, who left Restigouche in 1961 after fourteen years of residence, was an able administrator who devised a number of means to raise money for the maintenance and improvement of the church. He ran bingo games and raffles and showed movies, made special appeals for various projects, rented houses on "the Flats", opened a skating rink, increased the commercialism of Ste. Anne's Day, and tried to raise various church fees. A constant refrain among the Indians was that "the priest is quite a businessman." One informant said: "I guess they all want money . . . but at least Father A——— shows you something for your dollar: he had the church painted, put in new bells, and fixed up the cemetery." Nevertheless, many Indians were annoyed by the constant appeals for money. They gladly patronized the skating rink, bingo, and movies, but when it came to paying fees for church seats or burial, or making special contributions (other than at the Sunday collections) their attitude was: "We gave that land to the Church with the understanding that we'd never have to pay for seats or for burial; the priest makes plenty from all his businesses, so why should we pay anything?"

The priest's attitude is always the same—the Indians don't understand that it takes money to run a parish. The church was partially burned and has been rebuilt twice in this century. Today it is beautifully decorated, and the monastery is a plain but attractive building with many modern conveniences. All this has doubtless cost a good deal of money. Has it resulted in the alienation of the Indians from the very institution which is supposed to serve them? Perhaps so. One of the nuns was very concerned that I get the "right information", e.g.: "The story got around that the Indians built this church; anyhow, that's what some tourists heard. That's ridiculous. Most of them give only ten cents on Sunday, and there are only five or six paying for their pews." But according to Father Pacifique, the Indians did build a chapel with their own hands in the 1840s. Clearly, some changes have occurred.

Though land and money are the main sources of conflict the factors of favouritism, participation, and authority also contribute to the situation. Many Indians feel that the priest shows favouritism towards the French and other non-Indian peoples in the parish. Father A——— recognized that they sometimes resented his help to the "whites", but felt that the Indians had the government to "look after them", whereas many of the non-Indians had nowhere to turn but to the Church. Though he tried to be impartial, his attitude came out quite clearly in one statement. He said: "I tell them, 'Keep your language and customs but learn to live like French . . . I mean, like *White* people in your homes.' "

The differential participation of Indians and non-Indians in various parish activities is also an important factor. For example, the one religious society (sodality) in the parish—the "Third Order"—is composed entirely of non-Indian women. One group of Micmac men is responsible for running the bingo games in the church basement, and another group intones the Micmac hymns at High Mass and other rituals. But Ste. Anne's Day, formerly the most important social and religious event of the year, has been virtually emptied of its Indian form and content.

Formerly a "big time for the Indians", it has become the main money-raiser for the parish.

Wallis and Wallis quote several descriptions of Ste. Anne's Day celebrations, past and present; they describe it as "the Micmac 'national holiday', which was the union of the aboriginal summer council with the feast of Ste. Anne" (1955: 283). Halleck's description of the celebration at Restigouche in 1868 (quoted above and in Wallis, 1959: 60–1) includes few if any aboriginal features, but it was then an all-Indian affair including church services, feasting, foot races, and dancing. Today, however, the event is totally devoid of Indian content and resembles the celebration of the patron saint's day in many small Roman Catholic communities.

Different conceptions of the authority of the priest over sacred and secular affairs are another major cause of conflict in the community. The Church has had great influence over community affairs for years. We have little reliable information on the years during which the priest was also the agent at Restigouche, but it is fair to assume that this double role generated some conflict. One informant told me with pride that his great-grandfather had in 1890 been instrumental in the removal of a priest who had given a sermon stating that the Indians had to do his bidding.

Many of the conflicts discussed above relate to the question of authority: the priest considers himself the *spiritual leader* of the people in his parish and, as missionary to the Indian population, has special concern for the Indians' religious and moral behaviour; the Indians, however, tend to limit the area of the priest's concern and authority to strictly religious (i.e., ritual) matters, and sometimes even to the physical environment of the church area. Acceptance of leadership is not a characteristic of the Indian group, and attempts by the priest to impose his will upon the people are met with resistance and hostility.

Nevertheless, the Church plays an important part in determining the structure of the community by the ways in which it organizes time and space, and by its patterning of interpersonal behaviour. Most of the people on the Reserve orient their behaviour in accordance with at least some of the beliefs and expectations established by the Church. These include the seven-day week with its day of abstention from work and attendance at Mass; the Church year with its various seasons and sacred holidays; the regular secular activities at the church; the doctrine and cosmology of the Church, including conceptions of heaven, hell, and purgatory, the afterlife, etc.; the life crisis rituals (baptism, marriage, extreme unction); and the obligatory periodic rites (Confession and Communion). Though there is great variability in the details of belief and behaviour, observations and interviews show that these and other conceptions promulgated by the Church have a pervasive effect upon the orientation and behaviour of members of the Community.

The only other religious activity on the Reserve centres in the "Bible Group". This group is composed of members of five families who have broken away from the Roman Catholic Church and set up their own mode of religious belief and practice.

The information obtained from this group is very difficult to evaluate. The group was apparently formed in 1957 when a young Indian named F——— returned to the Reserve, having undergone some kind of religious conversion following a period of discouragement and illness. In a New York hospital he started to read the Bible for the first time and soon found a great improvement in his condition. Returning to the Reserve he began to spread his doctrine, which consisted primarily of a belief in personal literal interpretation of the Old and New Testaments, paired with a violent anti-clericalism. There was also a political component: F——— is a student of law and of Indian history, and he felt that the priest, the agent, and the chief (with the councillors) were in league together against the interests of the people. He ran for chief in the by-election held in December 1957, but of 221 votes cast for the five candidates he received only one vote.

F——— was not successful in convincing his father, who has remained a relatively pious Roman Catholic; but he soon persuaded his mother to convert and (according to most informants) intimidated his younger siblings into accepting his ideas. The four other families in the Bible Group include those of his elder brother, his father's brother's daughter, and two neighbours. (An elderly ex-chief, related to the wife in a neighbour's family, was also involved, but he returned to Roman Catholicism during a serious illness. He has since died.) The Group has no unified theology but engages in the following practices: Bible study (singly and together), healing by prayer, abstention from liquor and from certain foods prohibited by the Old Testament, observances of the Saturday Sabbath and certain Jewish holidays, non-observance of Roman Catholic rituals, and participation in various secular activities—including group picnics, communal gardening, and building of a camp "up in the woods".

In its early days, the Group was associated with the efforts of a local group of Jehovah's Witnesses to evangelize the reserve and, though any direct association is denied by F———, many Indians still refer to these families as "the Jehovah's". Members of the Bible Group make no secret of their anti-clericalism. By forbidding their children to participate in religious exercises at the school and by keeping them out of school on Jewish holidays (the occurrence of which is calculated by a lunar calendar), they point up the close relationship and co-ordination between the Church and the school. Some members make a point of working on Sunday, deliberately hanging out clothes or chopping wood when others are returning home from High Mass. Members of the Bible Group ostentatiously cleared their homes of Catholic images and ritual objects, substituting for them Bibles, lecterns, and displays of magazines or books on religious topics.

Needless to say, the Group has met with considerable opposition. Though most of the Indians do not object to the beliefs of the Bible Group members, they were upset by several incidents involving physical violence within the members' families, by attempts at proselytizing, and by the deliberate ridicule of Roman Catholic beliefs and practices. On one occasion several men of the community banded together to provide moral and financial support for one of F———'s younger brothers, who had been forbidden Confirmation. They bought him the necessary clothes and saw him through the ceremony despite the opposition of the Bible Group.

Matters came to a head in 1959 when the Band Council unanimously passed a resolution calling for the removal of members of the Bible Group from the Reserve. The Agent forwarded this resolution to the Regional Council (noting that the Group had made a nuisance of itself, and that the Council had insisted on passing the resolution). It was immediately disapproved since it was clearly illegal, violating the Indian Act and the civil rights of the Group members. The Group gradually gave up its proselytizing efforts, and the situation became calmer as the members became immersed in their personal affairs.

By 1961, aside from disputes about religious education in the school and about keeping the children out of school on certain holidays, the Group had apparently become an object of amusement rather than hostility. The Church adopted a policy of waiting rather than of prosecution of the "heresy": Father A——— (who was himself a keen student of the Bible) said, "I have given up arguing with them. It does no good—as soon as I show them something they skip to another part of the Bible that has no relation and say, 'What about this? What about this?' " One of the families has drifted toward the Salvation Army; another has adopted a fundamentalist viewpoint under the influence of a radio preacher. The head of one family spent several months in a Quebec mental hospital; he returned to the Reserve with an individual point of view, being extremely sceptical of all established doctrines. His illness confirmed the opinion of many of the other Indians that Group members are "half-cracked".

Although the Group has been limited in its membership, the very fact that it could come into existence on the Reserve, the type of open hostility to established institutions which it manifested, and the reaction of the others to its presence and policy are of the greatest interest.

Briefly, it may be stated that the adults who became involved in the Bible Group were discontented with the religious or political institutions of the Reserve, or held a grudge against both. Whatever one may think of their ideas, there is no doubt that it took courage to stand up to the established institutions and the weight of public opinion. The reaction of the rest of the community indicated that the Group was regarded as more of a nuisance than a threat—few if any of the Indians understood the theological implications of the "heresy", and the priest's decision to ignore the Group has probably contributed to its decline. The Group's policy contained no positive "nativistic" elements and was essentially one of negation. The priests are "devils", the agent, chief, and councillors "a bunch of crooks". One woman, speaking of her years of Roman Catholic worship, said: "I feel foolish when I think of all the things I used to do. Now that I have the Bible, I just put that religion up there on the shelf and look at what I've been through and thank God that I'm out of it."

The emergence of such a minority group may be interpreted in many ways. I prefer to see in it a confirmation of my estimates of discontent and lack of commitment present in the community. Some members have used the Group as a way of defying certain figures in authority, but for others it seems to fill a definite social and intellectual need. Only time will tell whether the Group will continue, or whether it will be succeeded by some other form of protest.

REFERENCES

Adrien, R. P. (O.F.M., Capt.)
1954   "Les Micmacs de Restigouche:
rapport d'une enquête anthropo-
logique sur leur état actuel."
M.A. thesis, Institute of Mis-
sionology, University of Ottawa.
Wallis, Wilson D.
1959   *Historical Background of the
Micmac Indians of Canada.*
Ottawa: National Museum of
Canada, Bulletin No. 173.
————, and Ruth S. Wallis

1953   "Culture Loss and Culture
Change Among the Micmac of
the Canadian Maritime
Provinces, 1912-1950." In
memorial volume to Walker B.
Kline, *Kroeber Anthropological
Society Papers* Nos. 8-9, 100-29.
Berkeley: University of Cali-
fornia Press.
1955   *The Micmac Indians of Eastern
Canada.* Minneapolis: University
of Minnesota Press.

Religion of
the Kabloona and Eskimo*

Frank G. Vallee

In the Baker Lake region when the first missionaries appeared in 1927, the Eskimo religion rested on the assumption that individual and group survival depended on the harnessing of the forces of nature which could not be controlled through technology; these forces could only be harnessed by people with special powers, using magical skills. When it became obvious that the difference between success and failure in bringing down caribou was to a large extent due, not to the magical intervention of the *angakok*, but to the superior technology of the Kabloona [white men], the significance of religion for this crucial aspect of their way of life diminished.

However, the problems of disease, of inexplicable misfortune, of the meaning of life and death remained. Over the decades the Kabloona's answers to these questions would supplant the traditional ones, thus eroding even further the position of the *angakok*. The Kabloona were to demonstrate that they could harness visible and invisible powers to an extent

*Appeared first in F. G. Vallee, *Kabloona and Eskimo in the Central Keewatin* (Ottawa: The Canadian Research Center for Anthropology, Saint Paul University, 1967). Published here in abridged form with the kind permission of the publisher.

undreamed of in the past. In this region there are no records of overt contests between the *angakoks* and the missionaries, such as we read about from other parts of the Arctic (Coccola and King, 1955).

Although today no Eskimo in this region professes openly to be an *angakok* or to believe in such powers, we have never heard an Eskimo scoff at these imputed powers. A common interpretation nowadays given by the few Eskimos who are willing to talk on the subject is that the *angakoks* were possessed by the devil and were thus to be feared. This, incidentally, is the interpretation of at least one of the missionaries. Furthermore, it is a common belief that the evil spirits which possessed the *angakoks* are abroad in the world today, but it is believed that they operate mostly among the Kabloona.

Christian influence among the Eskimos of the Baker Lake region antedated the arrival of the first missionaries here. For one thing, those groups which were in touch with coastal populations were familiar with at least some aspects of Christianity for many decades before the missions were established in the interior. For another, some of the more ardent Christians among the traders and the R.C.M.P. imparted the messages of Christianity to the interior populations, in some places holding prayer meetings and distributing bibles.

Nevertheless the full impact of Christianity was not felt until the arrival of the first missionaries in 1927. In August of that year, the Reverend Mr. Smith of the Anglican Church in Canada arrived at Baker Lake by boat from Chesterfield Inlet. This boat was to return to bring in a Roman Catholic missionary, but it broke down and the latter had to charter another boat, from Eskimo Point, which finally got him to Baker Lake almost a month after the Anglican missionary had arrived.

By this time Mr. Smith "had the names" of most of the Eskimos in the immediate vicinity of the Lake. "Getting the names" appears to have been an informal way of staking prior claims on the potential adherence of non-Christians. This, of course, was only a first step in the conversion process. According to the present-day missionaries, one of whom, Canon W. J. R. James, succeeded Mr. Smith in 1930 and has been the Baker Lake incumbent since that time, a complete conversion would occur only at baptism which, for adults, would occur only when the person expressed a willingness to embrace Christianity.

Both Anglican and Roman Catholic missionaries took special pains to instruct catechists, selected persons who showed more than an ordinary interest in Christianity, the aim being that the catechist should, with or without the aid of the missionary, in turn instruct and lead services among the other Eskimos. Although the Anglican missionary brought a bilingual Eskimo from the Eastern Arctic to assist him, it was understood that both Anglican and Roman Catholic missionaries should learn Eskimo and conduct their services in that language, except for the Roman Catholic Mass, which is sung in Latin.

During the thirties, missionary activity was concentrated on establishing the mission chapels and residences and on converting the folk in the outlying districts. Because the Roman Catholic missionary had few adherents at the settlement, he tended to travel on the land more frequently than his Anglican counterpart. During the mid-thirties the Roman Catholics converted a number of people from the Kazan River region, while the Anglican missionary, on one extended trip to the West and North, converted a large number of Back River people to the Anglican persuasion.

Kabloona informants who are skeptical of the claims of the missionaries that the Eskimos experienced true spiritual conversion refer to some of these converts as "bread and butter" Christians or "ammunition" Christians, suggesting that it was material rewards to be gained from the missionary and the Hudson's Bay Company manager which impelled them to become adherents. However, there is no evidence that these Eskimos received favoured treatment in the material sense because of their conversion.

The most recent group in the region to be converted are the Haningayormiut of the Garry Lake district to the North West of Baker Lake. The story of the conversion of this group by a Roman Catholic missionary is told in a recent publication (Anon., 1957). By the year 1958 almost every adult Eskimo and child in the Baker Lake region had been converted to Christianity. At the R.C.M.P. census of November 1958, about 19 per cent of the Eskimo population was Roman Catholic, the remainder Anglican. In the winter of that year the large number of people evacuated from the Garry Lake famine area comprised mostly Roman Catholics, and because the majority were eventually sent out of the Baker Lake region, the proportion of Roman Catholics in the population declined steeply to its present 10 per cent or so.

The conversion phase completed, Christianity is now the normal condition of the Eskimo population, and it is assumed that children will adhere to the denomination of the parents. Where one member of a family belongs to a particular denomination, it is highly probable that other members of the family also belong. In a few families accidents of fosterage and other conditions have given rise to mixed membership, so that siblings who were fostered by parents of different denominations themselves follow different paths, as do *their* children.

There have also been five mixed marriages during the past fifteen years, in one of which the partners adhere to their original faiths, the children being brought up as Roman Catholics. In the other four, the Roman Catholic partners, all women, ceased practising that faith after marriage and the advent of children, who are being brought up in the Anglican denomination.

Apart from these cases, it is generally true that kinship affiliation coincides with religious affiliation. Conversion to the Anglican from the Roman Catholic faith has occurred in at least seven cases known to the author, four of these being of people who were baptized Roman Catholic in coastal regions but became Anglicans after immigration to Baker Lake. We know of no person who formally adopted the Roman Catholic after having been a member of the Anglican faith.

The Roman Catholics form a minority group in terms of social position as well as in terms of numbers. Not one of them is a prominent Kabloonamiut or settlement leader; in fact, what leadership there is among the settlement Eskimos is provided mostly by men who are prominent in the Anglican congregation, including notably the catechist. The major institutions dealing with the Eskimos, such as the R.C.M.P. and the H.B.C., have been more closely identified with the Anglican than with the Roman Catholic congregation, not through deliberate policy but through the adherence of their officers to the Anglican rather than to the Roman Catholic church and through the intimacy of friendship between the Anglican missionary and these Kabloona. Likewise, the clients of Kabloona patrons, such as the special constables of the R.C.M.P. and the Eskimo assistant of the H.B.C., have been particularly staunch Anglicans.

To the great majority of Eskimos, the Roman Catholic is defined as a deviant, not so much in the pejorative sense as in the sense of a non-conformist who is doing no harm. The public attitude is one of tolerance and, perhaps, wonder. One infers from the way people behave in normal everyday life that the existence of the Roman Catholic minority is of small moment to the majority. We know of no incident where overt hostility was shown between people of the two faiths which could be attributed to out-group rejection.

To some extent the Roman Catholics are segregated from the others. As noted earlier, most Roman Catholic children attend the residential school at Chesterfield. Then, when in the settlement, they normally camp near the Roman Catholic mission and the only permanent residents among the Roman Catholic population have their dwellings within a stone's throw of the mission. Because kinship is the basis for sharing residence in (land) camps and because, as we saw, kinship ties normally coincide with those of religious affiliation, in most camps all members are of the one faith. In fact, there is evidence that it is difficult for a person of one faith who shares a camp with a majority of people of the other faith to maintain his religious identification and practice, for social pressures to conform to the camp norms are evidently strong. In any event there is some residential segregation, and, of course, segregation for actual chapel services, between Roman Catholics and Anglicans. At the same time, there is considerable interaction between members of the two groups, in work teams, in friendship, at dances, movies, and so on. Religion divides for some purposes but is insignificant for others.

The missionaries maintain a respectful, if rather distant, kind of relationship to each other. Officially the two groups have achieved an accommodation; there is no flagrant proselytizing, no pressure put on the members of one group to join the other, no public criticism of the other group. Of course, by their divine terms of reference and vows the missionaries are bound to propagate their faiths, but in practice they are more concerned that potential apostates remain in the denomination than they are with adding new members. One of the primary concerns of the missionaries is that of mixed marriage. Although neither missionary interferes very much in marital arrangements, both are concerned when there is the risk of a member moving out of the faith through marriage to someone of the other denomination. This problem is particularly acute among the Roman Catholics, for because of their small numbers and the discouragement of cousin marriages, they frequently have to seek mates outside their own group.

Few Kabloona anywhere in the Christian world go to their churches as much as do the Eskimos in this region. The average service lasts for one and a half hours and there are six services a week in the Anglican chapel, five a week in the Roman Catholic. This means that most Eskimos, for the majority go to all services, attend chapel services for between seven and ten hours per week. A clergyman here would regard as a backslider an Eskimo who spent only about three or four hours a week in church.

This phenomenal church attendance is indicative of the heavy stress which the Eskimos place on the devotional side of religion, which includes not only attendance at church, but also the reading of prayers and the Bible in the home, abstinence from work and play on Sundays, the closing of dances with a prayer, and so on. In a theological contest between faith on the one hand and good works on the other, the Eskimos in this region would come down strongly on the side of faith, no matter how often the missionaries tell them that faith must be balanced by good works.

Recalling the traditional Eskimo religion, the contemporary stress on observances may be interpreted as continuous with the traditional emphasis on conforming to rules laid down by the spirits. The object in so conforming nowadays is not to ensure an abundant wildlife harvest, but to ward off evil spirits and ensure a happy afterlife. When we say evil spirits, we mean concretely the Devil, or *Satanasi* as the Eskimos call him. Among the contemporary Eskimos there is a belief in possession by the Devil who is intent on destroying the good work of God. *Satanasi* is a substantial person, or rather the spirit of *Satanasi* is manifested in substantial persons, who are thereby endowed with unnatural powers, such as the *angakoks* used to display. The only protection against *Satanasi* is devotion.

Satanasi is especially active in the cities of the South and in such places as Rankin Inlet and Churchill. Under his influence, people forget the important things in life, such as sacred devotions, and concentrate on pleasure, the attainment of wealth, and the corruption of the innocent. They drink, commit adultery, murder, and rob. The South is wonderful in many ways, but it is a dangerous place, for everywhere there are Cities of Sin. It is better to be here at home, where people are poor but safe from *Satanasi*, as long as they observe the rules of the church.

It is evidently believed that in the old days *Satanasi* had much more of an influence over the Eskimos than he has now, for he had possession of the *angakok*, who in turn held the people in fearful thrall. One reason that so many Eskimos have abandoned much of their traditional culture and refrain from passing it on to their children is that they are fearful of objects or practices which had even the remotest connection with the *angakok*. Drumming has virtually disappeared; Eskimo songs sung in concert, as preludes to many séances, are hardly ever heard; stories about the *angakok* are told only in the strictest confidence and never in the presence of children or of fervent church-goers. This abandonment of parts of the traditional culture which seem to smack of *Satanasi* is especially noticeable among those in the settlement who are leading members of the Anglican congregation. These do not even want to talk about such matters and are exceedingly disturbed when people try to induce the Eskimos to discuss shamanism or describe some of the rites.

An illustration may be given to demonstrate this taboo on traditional magic and religion which ramifies out to include lore and song only incidentally connected with the *angakok* of old. We had been in the community only a week when we were invited to attend a meeting of the Eskimo ladies' group. The Kabloona woman who organized and directed these sessions introduced us and told the ladies that we were interested in old things, including songs and stories. We had intended to appear only for the introduction and had not planned to record any songs or stories, but when the Kabloona woman persuaded two elderly sisters to sing a kind of duet we brought in our recorder. This song was followed by another, a hunting song which one woman had learned from her late husband. From the very beginning the Kabloonamiut women from the settlement, and particularly the younger one, dissociated themselves conspicuously from the performance. As the singers warmed to their songs, the older ladies in the audience were quite visibly moved and entered into the spirit of the session by volunteering song after song. As we could speak no Eskimo we had no idea what the ladies were singing. We learned later that they had, in their mounting enthusiasm, progressed from innocent hunting and work songs to songs about sex and thence to shamanistic songs, culminated in a fever of excitement by a demonstration of a séance, which one old lady performed using a tin plate as a drum. As the older ladies grew increasingly absorbed in their performances, the younger married and single women from the settlement grew more and more aloof, carrying on their own conversations in another part of the room.

The next day we learned that two of the old ladies, both widows, had not slept that night, suffering torments of guilt, until they were impelled to rush to the missionary and fall on their knees, confessing to what they had done and asking that he banish *Satanasi* from them. The other ladies also suffered "hangovers" and, filled with remorse, promised never to sing or drum again. We see in this incident not only how the traditional religion and some of its appurtenances have been re-interpreted in terms of the evil past, but also the ambivalence which the older people show in their attitudes to their own traditions. The excessive rejection of things associated with *angakok* suggests what psychoanalysts call compulsive behaviour, in which the person over-rejects something because he secretly fears that the shameful impulse might gain the upper hand.

This illustration brings out the profound influence of the missionary among the Eskimos. He is not simply another Kabloona. He is completely devoted to the Eskimos, speaks their language, intercedes on their behalf. His control is both remote and direct. Everything to do with the Eskimos is his business if he chooses to make it so. In large measure the missionary acts through his Eskimo catechist. The latter not only preaches regularly at chapel among the Anglicans: if people in the community are not behaving according to the rules of the church, he tells them about it, or threatens to tell the missionary about it, which is just as effective a deterrent.

If the missionary's main role is that of general protector, a kind of magnified father image, the catechist's is that of the watchdog, the one who keeps the faithful on their devotional toes. Furthermore, he, rather than the missionary, is taking an increasing interest in how people behave out of chapel. There are signs that some Eskimos are coming to resent the intrusion of the catechist in their affairs. Although the Eskimos were quick to adopt the devotional features of Christianity, they are slower and understandably less eager to adopt those rules of living which were not taboo under the old regime but which form a prominent part of the Christian code: namely, rules about adultery and coveting the neighbour's wife. As far as we could ascertain there is no public approval of extramarital or premarital sex relations among the Eskimos in this region, but there is among many of them a private attitude of tolerance towards sex relations outside marriage. The more ardent church-goers are strictly opposed to such sexual behaviour, however, and the catechist has adopted the practice of warning individuals to desist from sex relations outside marriage. Some of these individuals at least have expressed the opinion that the catechist is overstepping his authority, that it is none of his business, although they agree that it would be in order for the missionary to make it his business. In short, it seems that there is no zone of privacy around the individual which the missionary cannot legitimately invade if he so desires, whereas there are comparatively narrow limits to the zones of privacy which the catechist may invade. This brings up the interesting question of native clergymen. The Anglican Church in Canada has adopted the policy of encouraging the training of Eskimo deacons with a view to eventual ordination. In fact, a Baker Lake resident was the first Eskimo to be ordained in the Anglican Church and is now a missionary at Rankin Inlet (Anon., 1959). Will the Eskimo clergyman be endowed with the same informal influence in the community as the Kabloona missionary enjoys? We would predict on the basis of current trends that the Eskimo clergyman will be expected to act as a spokesman for the Eskimos but that the Eskimos will allocate to him less informal extra-chapel influence than they allocate to the Kabloona missionary.

It is tempting to compare the role of the missionary with that of the *angakoks* when the latter were at the zenith of their powers. There are similarities in the two roles, as we have seen, but there are significant differences also. For one thing, the *angakok* had to keep proving his powers by performing incredible tasks, by making things happen immediately or in the near future. The missionary's supreme test is to guide people to eventual salvation, and his success or failure in this cannot be demonstrated. If the caribou fail, he is not expected to do anything about it; if there is an epidemic, he is expected to comfort the dying and conduct funeral services when he can, but he is not expected to bring the dead back to life or to cast out the spirits which are causing the sickness. He is expected to cast out the spirit which makes people sin and he can demonstrate his effectiveness at this, for penitents who come to him go away feeling cleansed.

The missionary's influence can be expected to diminish as more Eskimos assimilate to Kabloona ways. There are signs that the City of Sin theory, which explains the material inferiority but the moral superiority of the Eskimos over people elsewhere, is undergoing revision as an increasing number of people visit places such as Churchill and Winnipeg without succumbing to the Devil. As the assimilation process advances, we expect a shift in emphasis from the devotional features to the moral and ethical features of Christianity. We expect also that the "poor man's consolation" element in Christianity will be accentuated as the Eskimos come to compare themselves with Kabloona, using the same standards of material well-being, and find themselves relatively poverty stricken. What is meant here is that the Eskimos evaluate themselves and one another in terms of material well-being, education, etc., on a scale which is separate from the scale on which Kabloona are evaluated, as though it were tacitly recognized that a good position on the Eskimo scale would be a poor one on the Kabloona scale. Some of the settlement Eskimos, and especially the teenagers, are tending more to assess their own positions in terms of the same scale used by the Kabloona, a condition which should become typical of the entire population within a generation.

In the meantime, organized religion is of crucial importance to the Eskimos in this region. In these times of sharp and rapid change, the practice and beliefs of their religion serve as steadying influences, a thread of continuity linking the present with the past and the future. It must be remembered that the majority of Eskimos are the offspring of people who are Christian. That is, Christianity is now an integral part of the Eskimo way of life in this region, not just a fad or an importation of fleeting significance. Whether the Eskimo interpretation of Christianity does or does not accord with the interpretations found among the majority of Kabloona, this interpretation serves them well, helps them make sense out of life. The interpretation will in some respects change with the times, as it does with people in every part of the world.

REFERENCE

Coccola, Raymond de, and Paul King
1955   *Ayorama*. Toronto: Oxford
       University Press.

Authoritarianism and Sellout in Quebec in the 1930s*

Sheilagh H. Milner
and Henry Milner

Les Québécois, as Marcel Rioux reminds us, are among the oldest, if not *the* oldest, colonized people. Quebec was settled in the early seventeenth century to serve those who ruled France. The inhabitants, "les Canayens", quickly developed a social structure and culture which reflected that colonial position. Certain aspects of life such as commerce, politics, and war were closed to the participation of the inhabitants. This was the prerogative of the colonial régime.

Matters social, moral, and cultural were the concerns of the inhabitants and life in the row settlements was built around preserving the traditional social patterns. Central was the Church, whose authority in moral and related questions was supreme. The centre of the community became the parish priest, who was responsible for the maintenance of the social structure. Thus even in this early stage the basic pattern is already in evidence. There are two elite forces, one external and the

*Appeared first in Sheilagh H. Milner and Henry Milner, *The Decolonization of Quebec* (Toronto: McClelland and Stewart, 1973). Published here in abridged form with the kind permission of the authors and The Canadian Publishers, McClelland and Stewart Limited, and Carleton University Library Board.

other internal, each acting independently within its own domain supplemented by a process of negotiation, characterized by limited conflict, on items of joint concern.

Any chance that existed for a challenge to the essentially monolithic culture of the Ancien Régime lay at this point in the development of a significant French-speaking liberal commercial class. The British conquest put an end to this possibility. The British, sharing neither religion nor language with the people, permitted the autonomy of the clerical authority in its own sphere to be enhanced. On the other hand the Church succeeded in keeping the Canayens out of politics, commerce, and any potential military action against the new rulers.

This arrangement functioned admirably for both sides until the nineteenth century. At this point a movement arose among some of the more educated of the French Canadians (a group we will refer to as the old middle class), influenced somewhat by the triumph of American Republicanism. Its goals were democratic participation by the people in their political affairs, the liberalization of the society, and the eventual independence of the Quebec state. This movement was crushed militarily by the British in 1837-38 and, afterwards, in the period up to confederation, crushed ideologically and culturally by the Church through excommunication, rigid censorship, and the like.

A new class of English-speaking businessmen centred [on] the railroad interests had gained power in this period, especially in Montreal. It was this group that was the driving force behind confederation, which took place in 1867. Confederation was a minor event in Quebec. Although it provided on paper for greater political representation, its major significance was that it symbolized the transformation of the colonial control of Quebec from political to primarily economic techniques. The culture of survival ("survivance") revolving around the clerical hierarchy was not at all challenged by political change. While outwardly Quebec changed a great deal between confederation and the thirties, as rapid industrialization and urbanization occurred, inwardly it remained basically static. There were certain minor changes; the Church hierarchy, once the remaining "rouge" elements had been suppressed, was able to incorporate the old middle class under its authority. When popular feeling or anger rose in Quebec on one matter or another it was usually channelled into harmless forms of negative nationalist protest. The Riel execution in 1885, followed by the emergence and disappearance of Mercier and the Parti National, is one example.

In 1926 the U.S.A. replaced Britain as the major source of foreign capital in Canada. In this period Quebec produced an important culture, but one which found its ideals and heroes in a romanticized portrayal of the life of the inhabitants of the seventeenth century. The nineteen-twenties, which were a period of relative prosperity, saw a great flowering of cultural expression which, if it had continued, might have given rise to new ideas to challenge the old system and the beliefs on which it rested. The depression and the resultant hardship had the effect of postponing that possibility. Quebec turned even more inwards and looked even more to the past.

During the thirties, the Church and a small elite of lay people trained by the clergy and directly under their influence controlled almost every non-economic aspect of French-Canadian social and cultural life. Throughout Quebec, only one view of the world was presented: the schools, the newspapers, and the magazines explained the depression and analyzed its causes in much the same way, and proposed almost identical solutions. There were very few, if any, French-speaking organizations in the province which did not echo this same analysis while vainly trying to implement the God-given solutions under the direction of this elite. It was virtually impossible for an opposition to develop, for no media would carry its message and all public forums for discussion were dominated by the clergy and lay people who articulated the philosophy it taught. During the latter part of the decade the Padlock Law was imposed so that any groups whose ideas were considered at all threatening were legally restrained from the use of any premises large enough for public meetings.

The depression resulted in a 44 per cent decrease in provincial revenue for Quebec. In 1933, 30 per cent of the province's work force was unemployed.[1] The employment that was available was little improvement over unemployment. The Royal Commission on Price Spreads in 1937 completed an investigation of many large industries. They found incredibly deplorable working conditions alongside an actual increase in the profits of these companies during the depression. The commission cited one example in which a company declared a dividend (in parts) of 80 per cent, but 90 per cent of its employees earned less than $10 per week.[2]

In light of these conditions we turn to the philosophy propounded by the Church and the lay intelligentsia, which together make up what we call the traditional elite, and which dominated social life and thought in Quebec during this period. The Archbishop of Montreal, Monseigneur Gauthier, saw the causes of the depression imbedded in economic liberalism. This philosophy, he said, based on immoral business practices, a materialist conception of money, and the mechanization of jobs needed by men, had the sole objective of profit making.[3] The Archbishop of Quebec deplored the system in which a worker was viewed as a production machine, devoid of human dignity or a soul, and where the company's owners ignored the worker's responsibilities to God and to his family.[4] The Church asserted that the first duty of the proprietors of industry was to pay wages which were sufficient for men to support their large families.[5] Employment of women was opposed, not on the grounds of exploitative working conditions but because the woman's role was seen as one of wife and mother exclusively.

The bishops of Quebec were always careful to distinguish between the system of capitalism, which they defended, and the abuses of the system, which they hinted were the result of the greed which originated in the Protestants' liberalism and materialism.

The role of the state is to stimulate, to sanction, and to orient the work of private initiative, but not to substitute for it. The vitality of professional organizations was thought to be diminished if public powers assume their tasks; furthermore, state intervention to regulate the economy or to mediate poverty was viewed as the beginnings of state capitalism or socialism. All forms of social insurance, of protective tariffs, of old age pensions provided by the state were harmful, for they weakened individual enterprise.

The Church viewed itself and the elite which it had trained as having a duty to care for the lower classes. The privileges and comparative wealth of the elite were acknowledged and justified on the grounds that a superior class such as this was essential to protect and direct the French-Canadian flock.

The hierarchy of the Quebec Church seems to have recognized the possibility of the discontent of the lower classes turning into a clear demand for a radical change in the society. One explanation suggests that this fear forced them to become even more protective of their dominant position. In a more liberal, centralized state the Catholic Church would lose its privileged position and much of its control over education and social welfare. The hierarchy seems to have understood the probable result if the CCF or a party with similar goals were to achieve power and fought hard to avert it. It has commonly been assumed that the CCF failed in Quebec because of the Church's condemnation. [We intend to demonstrate in this work] that it was not the official condemnation but rather the blocking of all forms of discussion, political education, or even of communication of information between the party and the Quebec population which ensured the failure of the CCF and of all left-wing political action. (The English Protestant public image of the CCF did not serve to help its cause either.)

Almost all manner of activity in Quebec during the thirties was to some degree under the control of the Church. By briefly looking at some of the lay organizations which were founded by the Church, we can understand why the development of a viable opposition was impossible. "La Confédération des Travailleurs Catholiques du Canada" (C.T.C.C.) was organized by the Church and the nationalist elite who feared that French-Canadian traditions and customs were threatened by the rapid growth of international unions in Quebec. The C.T.C.C. was a negative response: it was anti-socialist, anti-communist, anti-international, anti-American, anti-Protestant, and anti-neutral.

Membership in the C.T.C.C. was limited to Roman Catholics. Each local was run by an aûmonier, a priest or chaplain whose duty it was to educate the members to be conscious of their Catholic duties in their role as trade unionists. The aûmoniers chose from among the members a select group to participate in special study sessions. Most time was spent in the explanation of papal encyclicals and their application to the practical problems met by the union members. "The meeting of the study group began with a prayer, followed by the reading of the minutes of the last meeting. The chaplain then chose a member from the assembly to read a passage from the encyclical. . . . The reading was followed by a period of discussion in which the members sought to interpret what they had heard read aloud. The chaplain directed the discussion and corrected the errors."[6]

The only economic demand viewed as legitimate for the worker was simply that of a wage sufficient to support his family. Legal strikes were permitted only when all else had failed; sympathy strikes were immoral and thus prohibited. The worker had no access to technical information to aid him in understanding the system of which he found himself a victim. He was prevented from developing skills of argument and of public speaking by the authoritarian role of the chaplain. The idea of the owner as a man with a different role to play in the social order was propounded. The idea of class conflict was violently repudiated, as was the notion of a collectivist economy. Pontifical teachings were used to justify the right of private property.

The movement of "caisses populaires", credit unions, was begun at the turn of the century. Organized on a parish basis, they were meant to teach the virtue of savings and to provide low-interest loans to members. But they provided a more important service. In 1932, the provincial government passed a law, at the urging of the Fédération des Caisses, that all investments must be made within Canada, in the forms of loans to municipalities, to school boards, for the building of churches, cemeteries, etc. In this way the parish priest exercised a good deal of influence on the decisions made.[7] To join the local branch an individual had to swear, "I am a French Canadian and a practising Catholic."

In November of 1929, Adrien Arcand began the fascist review, *Le Goglu*. "L'Ordre Patriotique des Goglus" was founded along with the review. It was a para-military, hierarchical, authoritarian movement dedicated to "general purification, the conservation of our Latin character, our customs and traditions, and to the defence of our rights and privileges".[8]

In 1934, "le Parti National Social Chrétien" was formed primarily by old Goglus. Arcand wrote *The Key to the Mystery*, a violently anti-Semitic pamphlet, which the Nazi party translated and distributed throughout Germany. The family, the natural hierarchy, and the basis of fascism in nationalism and Christianity were common themes for speeches and articles. The party seemed to indulge principally in educating its members and lobbying with both federal and provincial members of parliament. Citizenship was to be granted only to Christians; the Jews were to have no rights to their newly acquired schools in Quebec, and Canada should press for increased imperialistic effort through the Commonwealth.

In 1937 the American Nazi leader finally persuaded Arcand to form a Canadian Nazi party and Arcand became its leader. However, the Nazi party's policies of internationalism and pan-Canadianism were not popular in Quebec. Consequently the party remained on the fringes of political developments in the province.

The Church never condemned Arcand and his followers. Monseigneur Gauthier went only as far as to warn the people that Nazism had many contradictory positions which needed to be clarified. The anti-Semitism of the movement was never mentioned.

This movement is important in understanding this era of Quebec's history. The fact that the traditional elite condoned such activities, and even suggested that attacks upon the fascist movements were diversionary tactics used by communist sympathizers, is significant. The close correspondence between the analysis and solutions proposed by Arcand and those of the traditional elite explains why there was no thought of condemnation.

The Church and the traditional elite promoted their authoritarian policies and ideas by attempting to integrate them into the daily lives of the Québécois in ways and through organizations that we have described and many others. Because the ideology espoused by this elite saw no role for the French Canadian in big business, it condoned the activities of the ruling Liberal party, whose economic program seems to have been little more than selling Quebec to foreign investors at a cheap price. Foreign capitalists were encouraged by the government's minimum of restrictions and control over such matters as public utility rates, corporate financing, and the sale of securities. Grants of land, tax exemptions, and other concessions further promoted the exploitation of raw materials. Social welfare legislation was to be avoided, as it increased taxes, as well as destroying the individual's sense of responsibility and initiative. Groups and individuals seeking guarantees for adequate wages, proper working conditions, and the right to collective bargaining and union organizing were opposed as threats to economic stability.[9] Taschereau, the liberal leader, "regarded the prosperity of the large enterprises as the primary source of general well-being".[10]

In the spring of 1933, an immigrant named Zynchuck was shot by a policemen apparently for no reason. The Protestant Ministerial Association, the Montreal Women's Clubs, and the Delorimier Liberal Reform Club were among the groups demanding an inquiry.[11] Taschereau refused to institute such an inquiry and stated: "Foreigners who are not satisfied to breathe the air of Quebec have but to depart to other lands."[12] The next day in the legislature he paid homage to the Montreal police. In a speech to the Police and Fire Chiefs' Association of Quebec the premier declared: "When public bodies condemn the police and side with aliens, then I say they are wrong. . . . The grilling system has its advantages. When you read that after a sixteen-hour grilling the police were able to get some information in an abduction case, I think those who have done the grilling will say it is a useful way of obtaining information. . . . I even wonder if the man found with a revolver in his hand about to commit a crime should not get life imprisonment."[13]

The editors of *Canadian Forum* aptly summed up the Quebec situation under the Taschereau regime: "cases of police brutality and of callous disregard for the rights of the citizen have multiplied to such an alarming extent in the Province of Quebec recently that the shooting of the unfortunate Zynchuck by a policeman is only one incident among many. It is becoming increasingly clear that Quebec, with the open connivance and approval of the Government of that province, is openly becoming a center of Fascist infection and of the blackest kind of reaction."[14]

[The Liberal party] was supported by almost all English Quebecers, and deeply tied to those at the top. This was the party the English had helped keep in power in the mid-thirties. But the Liberals met an opponent too strong for them—the Church. It seems as if the innumerable directorates held by Taschereau and his cabinet members on the boards of large banks and companies with operations in Quebec alienated the Church. The Church felt that the Liberals were now too tightly connected with the English corporate world and thus not sensitive enough to the demands of the Church. For this error in judging power, Taschereau and his party paid dearly.

In 1933, the Jesuits of L'Ecole Sociale Populaire wrote "Le Programme de restauration sociale". This was an interpretation and program for the practical application of the papal encyclicals *Rerum Novarum* and *Quadragesimo Anno* to the problems of Quebec. "Le Programme" became the basis of the platform for a break-away faction of the Liberal Party, "L'Action Libérale Nationale" (ALN).

The program of L'Action Libérale Nationale was heart-warming to the Church and lay elite. The rural way of life was idealized. Low credit rates, subsidies for some farm markets, assistance in marketing, and the development of small and medium-sized industry to complement farm activity and destroy the "milk trust" were proposed. Co-operatives were to be organized to efficiently compete with and curb the power of large foreign enterprises; to promote rural colonization, roads, schools and churches were to be built in yet unpopulated areas.

Workers were to be guaranteed adequate wages and working conditions. Health insurance, pensions for needy mothers and the aged, and slum clearance programs were described. By "every possible means" the electric, paper, coal, gasoline, and bread trusts were to be destroyed. Conflicts of interest would be ended by prohibiting cabinet ministers from sitting on boards of directors of companies holding government contracts. The upper house was to be abolished.[15] These more progressive elements of the ALN program, however, were never to be implemented.

L'Action Libérale Nationale entered into a coalition with the dormant and ineffective provincial Conservative party. The money, political techniques, and practical knowledge for the new party, the Union Nationale (UN), would be supplied by the Conservatives; popular support, as well as new men and ideas, were to be contributed by L'Action Libérale Nationale. For the election of 1935 the UN fielded candidates in all constituencies, winning 42 of 90 seats. Taschereau and the Liberals had used all manner of corruption, from stealing ballot boxes to beginning public works projects in crucial areas just months before the election and stopping work on them the day after the election, and still just barely sneaked through.

According to the agreement of the coalition, Duplessis, as leader of the Conservative party, was to lead the UN, while Paul Gouin, the leader of L'Action Libérale Nationale, and his colleagues were to form the majority of the cabinet. Duplessis was a shrewd and skilful politician. He immediately forced the re-opening of the Public Accounts Committee and raked the Liberal party over the coals for their mishandling of public funds. Taschereau was forced to resign and the new leader, Godbout, called an election. Duplessis fought the 1936 elections by stirring up nationalist feeling and appealing to the small businessmen and farmers. The corruption of the Liberal party having been exposed, Duplessis was easily voted into power, winning 76 of 90 seats.

Duplessis's economic policy was essentially the same as that of Taschereau, although neither he nor his cabinet ministers ever became as outwardly integrated into the Anglo-capitalist elite. Duplessis carried out almost all of the immediate agrarian reforms suggested in the "Programme de restauration sociale". The Church had been rewarded for its support of the new party.

Duplessis had no more respect for fair electoral practices than had Taschereau. He seems to have shared many of his predecessor's views with regard to the police, to opposition, and to democracy itself. Duplessis was different from Taschereau, in that he did not want to make it as an equal with the English corporate elite. He wanted this group to do its job of developing the province and providing jobs, while paying due respect to the power of the Premier. Similarly, Duplessis saw the Church as having specific functions, such as education, caring for orphans, the aged, the blind, etc. From the Church, too, he sought respect for his power.

There is little doubt that the Church and traditional elite collaborated with Duplessis on the virulent anti-communist campaign which he soon launched. This campaign resulted in a repressive atmosphere in which no opposition to the government or Church was free from being labelled communist. One was either for the status quo or for a communist, atheist revolutionary.

In March 1937 the infamous Padlock Law came into existence. It provided for the padlocking of all premises used for "communist" purposes or wherein communist literature was found. With the definition of communism left sufficiently vague so as to apply to almost any philosophy other than right-wing Catholicism, Duplessis proceeded to use the Padlock Law against any form of opposition to his regime.

Archbishop Gauthier voiced the dominant feeling in the Church hierarchy in his public reaction to such activities: "Prohibition . . . in . . . Montreal of meetings of the Communist Party, and throughout the province the seizure . . . of the evil literature which it spreads. God be praised! We have been very slow to protect ourselves, but at last the public authorities . . . have had the courage to take measures of a pressing necessity. . . . Note the . . . disguises with which Communism covers itself: . . . the campaigns against Fascism, the saving of democratic institutions, freedom of speech and meeting. . . ."[16]

Thus, with the moral support of the Church, Duplessis was able to wage an all-out war against any and all opposition. Policemen, rather than judges or Justices of the Peace, issued warrants. Homes were raided and ransacked to teach people lessons. The machinery of the state was available and used to plug up leaks in the information network—to keep "subversive" ideas and unwelcome facts out of the minds of les Québécois.

Duplessis demonstrated his faith and also eliminated opposition criticism through direct censorship. In 1938 alone the police seized 54,369 papers, 39,317 reviews and books, 23,602 circulars, 15,000 assorted pamphlets, and 4,900 buttons and badges.[17] As Quebec is surrounded only by English-speaking neighbours, this censorship was most effective. The school system, even the universities, was closed to all but Catholic doctrine, and its socio-political corollary, right-wing corporatism.

During all this, Quebec was continuing to industrialize. Anglo-Canadian and American capitalists invested heavily in Quebec. Perhaps most important of all, the new companies appreciated the comparative passivity of the Quebec work force and the repressive labour legislation which allowed them to pay exceptionally low wages with little fear of strikes. The intelligentsia and the Church supported these activities. Accepting the fact that Anglo-Saxons and not French Canadians were destined to be industrialists, they demanded nothing more than that the workers be paid wages sufficient to support their families, and respect for Church holidays and customs. In return, through the c.t.c.c., they would convince the trade unionists of the good faith of the capitalists and use their power and moral authority to block the organizing attempts of the international unions.

The monolithic ideology which reigned throughout Quebec identified the ethnic and cultural distinctiveness of the lower classes as the cause and legitimation of their socio-economic position. All discontent was carefully channelled by the traditional elites away from the true oppressors and, when useful, focused upon two scapegoats—the communists and the Jews. But, herein lies the contradiction within this elite's position. Why was it legitimate for the English to have material wealth at the expense of the French Canadians? The Church did not approve of the capitalists' ideology; they frequently spoke of its non-Christian, evil character. Yet, they forced their own people to accept its legitimacy and tried to eradicate those elements in the society which struggled against it. The reaction of the people of Quebec, apart from a small number of zealots, is quite interesting. The ideology was accepted, not believed; its tenets and commands submitted to, not joyously received. Underneath, the people were aware of its contradictions and futility; yet it was all they had, and so, as true colonials, they submitted for a time.

Thus, the coincidence of interests among the economic, the political, and the traditional elites during the thirties reinforced the power of each within [its] own sphere, rendering them unchallengeable. Its partially contradictory basis meant, however, that sooner or later a crack would show and decline would set in.

The thirties had seen the Ancien Régime, in all its force, repeating a pattern that was centuries old. Military and political colonization was replaced by a predominantly economic form, but the alliance of internal and external elites went on as before. Opposition forces from the outside, the CCF, the Communist party, the international unions, were fought and excluded. Potential internal opposition was neutralized. L'Action Libérale Nationale was co-opted—its progressive platform and leadership cut away, and its support channelled into the reactionary quasi-nationalism of the traditional elite and the Union Nationale. This was not the first time this happened, nor the last time it would be attempted.

NOTES

1 Réal Caux, "Le Parti National Social Chrétien", M.A. Thesis, Laval University, 1958, p. 6.
2 Cited in P. E. Trudeau, ed., La Grève de l'Amiante (Montréal: Editions Cité Libre, 1956), p. 79.
3 Jean Hulliger, L'Enseignement Social d'Evêques Canadien de 1891-1950 (Montréal: Editions Fides, 1958), p. 175.
4 Ibid., p. 176.
5 Ibid., p. 251.
6 Gilles Laflamme, "L'Education Syndicale à la Confédération des Syndicats Nationaux", M.A. Thesis, Laval University, 1968, p. 30.
7 "Les Caisses Populaires", L'Ecole Sociale Populaire, No. 271 (1936), p. 22.
8 Le Goglu, 30 janvier, 1931, quoted in Réal Caux, op. cit., p. 40.

9 See Herbert Quinn, The Union Nationale (Toronto: University of Toronto Press, 1963) pp. 30-4.
10 Quoted in ibid., p. 31.
11 Québecer (Frank Scott), "French Canadian Nationalism", Canadian Forum (March 1936), p. 12.
12 Quoted in E. A. Forsey, "Politics in Quebec", Canadian Forum (June 1933), p. 326.
13 Quoted in ibid.
14 Canadian Forum (June, 1933), p. 323.
15 Herbert Quinn, op. cit., Chap. 4.
16 Quoted in Eugene Forsey, "Under the Padlock", Canadian Forum (May 1938), p. 42.
17 E. A. Forsey, "The Padlock—New Style", Canadian Forum (March 1939), p. 362.

Action Catholique and Nationalism: A Memorandum on the Church and Society in French Canada, 1942

Everett C. Hughes

Introduction, Boston 1974

This essay, published here for the first time, was written in the middle of World War II. I was teaching in the École des Sciences Sociales, Université Laval, at the invitation of the Reverend Georges-Henri Lévesque. The spirit of Quebec City was expressed about that time in a painting by Jean-Paul Lemieux. The city rose from the river to a low-hanging, dark sky. Angels hovered protectively. In the background a squadron of war planes approached in fire and smoke.

Life was quiet enough in Quebec; but the strain between French and English over the war was great beneath the surface. Yet it was possible to get on with classes and with minor research with scarcely a mention of the war. I made many notes on what I thought was the state of things. I did not publish them. In conversation I did try to dissolve the rigid stereotype through which English-Canadian eyes saw the French Canadians. Strange as it may appear, the aim of this essay was, in part, to suggest to English Canadians that they might better not try to persuade French Canadians to support the war more fully.

The French Canadians had voted fairly solidly against conscription into the army. But there were many of them in the volunteer forces. Certainly the French did not like to be told their patriotic duties by English people. It was my impression that French parents did not publicly display evidence of their sons' participation. There was no cult of loyalty to the British Crown as among many English Canadians. Certainly the English Canadians (except for Quebecers, which then meant only people of the city and region of the city) had little idea of the structure of French-Canadian society. I was living a more completely French-Canadian life than I had ever done before. It was a time of discovery for me. The essay was written in large part for myself. In view of certain conversations with Toronto and Ottawa people, I hoped that this statement and others I wrote would convince them that the nature and level of the French-Canadian action during the war was so deeply rooted in the social structure that sentimental propaganda was worse than a waste.

For an excellent introduction to the rise of sociology in Quebec, see "Sociologie au Québec" in Recherches Sociographiques, *Vol. 15, Nos. 2–3, 1974. The volume is devoted entirely to this subject: the articles by Jean-Charles Falardeau and the account by T. R. P. Georges-Henri Lévesque, o.p. Lévesque's account especially throws light on Action Catholique, the social movement in the Province of Quebec, leading up to the founding of the Faculté des Sciences Sociales.*

Québec, 1942, 1943

William Graham Sumner said, in his *Folkways* (p. 96), that sects are at war with the world, that is, with the mores. He also said that "The folkways create status. Membership in the group, kin, family, neighborhood, rank, or class are cases of status. . . . Each case of status is a nucleus of leading interest with the folkways which cluster around it." (p. 67)

These texts, taken in combination, suggest that war upon the mores is of necessity also an attack upon status, upon the social structure. It seems that all societies tend to develop status groups, each of which has its own way of life and its peculiar interests. The mores regulate the relations of these groups to each other. The resulting social order is an organic integration of diverse functioning parts. Crises of various sorts threaten the integration from time to time. When this happens, the relations of status-groups to each other become a matter of conscious concern, and even of conflict. Religious and political sects of intransigent temper appear; their adherents agitate against the social order in the name of various causes and sacred symbols.

In this memorandum concerning contemporary French-Canadian society, the above ideas are applied to relations between the church and the social structure, and to two powerful social movements, Action Catholique and the nationalist movement. While the discussion does not seem to bear much upon the attitudes of French Canadians to the present war, I think that the key to this problem lies precisely in what is here presented.

Relations between the Church and the Social Structure

The Catholic church has, in various times and places, achieved a rather complete integration with the social structure. French-Canadian society is such a case. People of all classes are Catholic; and the church has both implicitly and openly recognized the social classes in various ways.

In the organization of the territorial parish, worldly (profane) status knits closely with church office. The leading men are, or have been, church wardens, although in many urban parishes there are a few men of standing and influence who leave wardenship to more mobile and ambitious people. Leading families hold the best pews, purchased at auction, and pass them on, if they wish, from generation to generation. The seigneurs had the right to the front pew at the right of the center aisle of churches on their domains. Such families may continue to hold this pew in a country parish although they seldom live there. In many parishes, men who are on the make strive for prominent places in church choirs and in parish works. A newly rich man will give large sums to the church, and may receive a papal order for his zeal and gifts. We heard complaints against the Gregorian chant, now being insisted upon by the clergy, because it is purely group singing—and in unison. Gregorian allows no place for solos, or other conspicuous behavior. Individual talent music, however, still has a prominent place at weddings. Its mobility functions, both for the family whose wedding it is and for the musicians, are wittily recognized by everyone.

In both religious and national ceremonial, civil and religious authorities appear side by side. When the Sacred Host is carried through the streets on Corpus Christi—a purely religious fête—the mayor and city councillors appear as the escort of honor. On the national holiday, St. Jean Baptiste, the same configuration of civil, business, and religious dignitaries occurs. At the opening of the provincial legislature, at a eucharistic congress, the consecration of a bishop, a special mass for prayers for victory, and a congress of scholars the same thing happens, the ranks of the ecclesiastical and worldly authorities present depending upon the occasion.[1]

The clergy themselves are not a class, but a *Stand*—a group with a common technique, sense of fraternity, way of living, legal status, and prestige. Being celibate, they cannot become a hereditary class.[2] There are ranks within the clergy, but a man of lowly origin may reach the top. The ranks are partly ecclesiastical and formal, from the arch-bishop—who may be a cardinal—bishops, prelates, canons, on down to the parish curé, the vicars, and humbler chaplains. The strict authority relations are simple in theory: the bishop has authority over all priests in his diocese; the curé, over all in his parish. In informal fact, the hierarchy is very complicated. The bishop of a large diocese centering in a great city has more prestige than a country missionary bishop. The curé of a large and prosperous urban parish of middle- and upper-class people has more prestige than the curé of a lower-class parish. The "country curé" is sometimes spoken of with a touch of condescension; in lauding him for his devotion, people document his lack of prestige.[3]

The regular clergy—those in the Orders—also have their prestige hierarchy. Certain Orders have the reputation of getting "chic" parishes assigned them. Others who are missionaries to the poor are honored with the same dubious compliment as the country clergy. About the cathedral, the seminary, and the university in the city of Quebec, is a large group of priest-professors, prelates, archivists, auxiliaries, and canons; they are a sort of cabinet and court of the archbishop's palace. Priests of this group, and of the more prominent Orders, are widely known among people of standing, wealth, and learning. They lecture to civic bodies, literary clubs, women's organizations, professional associations. They are in the places of honor on great public occasions, while their humbler brethren sit further back among the common people.

The family backgrounds of such men are widely known and commented upon. If a man is made bishop, people immediately talk of who he is. Class references turn up very clearly. The model prelate in the minds of "old Quebecers" was Cardinal Taschereau, who was of one of the province's most aristocratic families. The recently elevated auxiliary bishop is of humble origin, and people talk of it; some doubt whether he is a man of "culture" such as Msgr. Roy, rector of the university, and other dignitaries whom they like. Of the new auxiliary people of family say in one breath, "He is an extreme Action Catholique man"; "His family are nobody"; "He is nationalistic"; "He has no culture"; "He keeps notes on everyone in the university"; "He is an extremist"; "He is a spy", etc.

People of old family recall with pride that an aunt or great-aunt was Superior of the Ursuline convent, where girls of the best families were educated and "finished" for many generations. Such nuns were, in fact, social arbiters and genealogical experts. Of a certain prelate who is liked, it is said, "No, his family was nothing special. But he is a man of great culture." Such remarks are made of people of standing when discussing attitudes toward the war. Priests of "culture" and "good family" support the war and are never "nationalists". "Culture" evidently means something other than mere learning; it indicates a set of acceptable attitudes and manners.

It does not follow that any bishop or prelate would be snubbed—if that were possible—because of his humble origin or lack of "culture". The offices of the church are endowed with too much prestige and power for that.

It seems certain that a change has taken place in the social selection of the clergy, even of the higher clergy, and of the nuns of the more distinguished convents. Although our informants know well the background of previous Superiors of the Ursuline convent, they do not know the family name of the present incumbent and of other nuns now in the house. Recently an Ursuline teaching nun, in scolding a child, remarked that the fact that one's grandmother's name had the prefix "de" was no excuse. The father of the girl wrote a letter to the Superior protesting against attack upon his family name. The nun made some sort of amends to the child. The affair was dismissed among the old families with the remark that the nun was probably some ignorant country girl.

Recently the consecration of a new auxiliary bishop brought nearly all of the French-Canadian bishops to Quebec. The youth of the more recently elevated among them was commented upon a great deal. The comments included emphasis upon "brilliance" in studies and upon humble origins. There is a whole generation of "bright young men" in the episcopacy. "Brilliance" connotes ambition, devotion, and hard work—symbols of mobility; "culture" connotes, rather, grace or manner, and a certain diplomatic and forbearing attitude toward the worldly upper classes.

I have not made a survey of the origins of the bishops of another day. It is possible that the majority of them were always of humble origin and that it was always a matter of comment when the son of an *habitant* became a prince of the church whom all would address as Excellency or Eminence, and to whom all would give the deference of kneeling and kissing his ring. I speak only of the current impression that there has been a change.

The youth of the new bishops implies a short-cutting of the more usual slow rise through the hierarchy. Each such appointment ends the hope of ecclesiastical advancement for older men already in influential posts. Bishoprics are limited in number; the appointment of young men necessarily lowers turnover by lengthening tenure, hence the number who can hope for elevation is reduced. Under the older custom of slow rise, a man spent many years about the archbishop's palace or the university, sharing in the honors and prestige of the ecclesiastical capital, and learning the bearing and attitudes of the higher clergy before he himself became a bishop.

It is possible and probable that young men who have risen abruptly will have assimilated less of the "aristocratic" and "diplomatic" spirit associated with the episcopacy. Certainly their youthful zeal is regarded as something of a threat to existing arrangements between the church and the "world". This fear has been expressed concerning a couple of the newer bishops. It might be expected that in the clergy, as in other hierarchies, "class" aggressions are gradually liquidated in the course of slow and regular advancement, while they remain strong in the young men who rise quickly.[4]

The change seems to be a decline of vocations from the upper classes, which would increase the proportion of clergy of humbler origin. The change in proportion is probably not great, but it is significant insofar as it means a paucity of candidates of higher class for preferment in the hierarchy. Vocations are undoubtedly still—as perhaps always—related to social mobility. The independent farm family and the town lower-middle-class family of some ambition consider it an achievement to get a son into the priesthood.[5] The city working masses and the poor apparently do not aspire to the priesthood; it takes money, school success, and ambition. The upper classes apparently direct their children into secular pursuits. A family on the way up may have a son who gets into the priesthood and who gets ahead in the hierarchy. Certain classical colleges are favored by well-placed and ambitious families. These colleges are especially known as places of training for the university professional courses as well as for candidates for the more "intellectual" priesthood.[6]

The priesthood continues to have a mobility function, but the close alliance between the clergy and families already established in the upper classes is disappearing. A feature of the traditional integration of the church with the social structure was the assumption, on the part of the upper-class laity, that the ranking clergy would be "liberal". That is, that many of the preachments of the church would not be too strictly enjoined upon the upper classes. The Quebec church has long been known as rather puritanical. Certain groups in the church have long encouraged pledges of total abstinence from all alcoholic liquors. In many parishes the curé successfully prevents dancing. The people of the upper classes act as if these movements did not exist. If the curé does not interfere with their ways, the middle and upper classes consider him "liberal", meaning that he has a certain tolerance of their mores. It means also the opposite of nationalistic. The liberal priest does not make embarrassing or undiplomatic statements. He is, in short, not a "fanatic".

Action Catholique

Action Catholique is the name given to an upsurge of piety and social action encouraged by recent popes. Several encyclicals define the movement, set its limits, and urge it upon the clergy and the faithful.

Action Catholique is "the apostolate of the faithful (i.e., laity), who, under the direction of their Bishops, put themselves at the service of the Church and aid Her to fulfill completely Her pastoral ministry".[7] The papal texts stress a more complete collaboration of the laity in the apostolic work of the church. The appeals include many statements of the kind found in sectarian literature generally, namely proofs that Action Catholique was found in the primitive church, where much of the spreading of new faith was done by laymen; the demand that the whole man must be transformed before he can go at this work; the stress on the application of Christian principles to all classes of people.[8]

The movement is, in short, conceived as a livelier and more complete mobilization of the faithful, a sort of revival.

The term *action* is also associated with the "social problem"—the labor problem, the distribution of wealth, city life, housing, poverty, etc. It is Catholicism's attack upon the dangers and evils of modern life.

Action has several opposites which appear frequently in the official literature. They have become almost synonymous, by having in common the character of vices which stand in the way of the good, *action*. One such is "laicism"—the tendency for an increasing number of activities and functions of society to be carried on independently of the church. The word is also applied to the doctrine that any such activity —especially education—should be free of church control. Another opposite is "liberalism", which means laissez-faire in economic activity, with connotations of separation of church and state. The upper classes are supposed to be especially addicted to "liberalism". Along with liberalism goes the conception of "democracy". Democracy as such is not attacked in the official Action texts, but the connection between democracy and liberalism is frequently remarked in the writing of certain priests active in Action. A companion phrase to "laicism" is "neuter". The "neutral" school is that in which no attention is paid to religion or, worse, in which "religion" is said to be a good thing, but the Catholic religion is classed along with others. It is also the *Laïque* school. Ordinary labor unions are also called "neutral", i.e., neutral as regards religion. Since the church considers that the relations of capital and labor involve moral issues, it does not accept the idea of a neutral union. Rotary, Kiwanis, etc., are considered neutral organizations because they concern themselves with social welfare—a moral problem—but without recognizing the "true" religion. A neutral organization might, in fact, have a predominantly or completely Catholic membership.

The commercial newspaper is also "neutral". A good deal of Action Catholique propaganda is directed against this press and supports the idea of a purely Catholic press—*la bonne presse*. In Quebec the ideal has been realized in the daily, *L'Action Catholique*. Subscriptions are solicited openly by the clergy. It is said about Quebec that a certain organization of merchants has agreed to advertise in the newspaper *Action* alone, if *Action* will refuse to accept Jewish advertising. The agreement is supposed to be in effect. In Quebec City this means a boycotting by *Action* of one of the two large department stores.

The movement encourages special Catholic bodies in all of these and many other fields of activity. It does not generally encourage Catholic political parties; it enjoins Catholic Action people to take an active part in politics, adhering always to the Catholic principles, constantly demanding respect for the rights of the church. The good Catholic may belong to any party which "gives the necessary guarantees for defense of the cause and of the rights of the Church". But associations of Catholic youth, etc., organized for Catholic Action should not be political parties or be affiliated with such. Nor should the leaders of such groups be chiefs of parties or of political assemblies.[9] But the individual militant Catholic should interest himself in politics, always putting the claims of the church above all others.

Some Action Catholique leaders constantly speak disparagingly of "politicians" and of "party politicians". This is a common enough theme among people interested in special reforms and causes anywhere in the democratic countries. In this case, there is the difference that the talk emanates from an organization of great power, and from the church which controls education. The younger priests and brothers who teach in the schools and colleges are considered the greatest apostles of Action Catholique. At least by inference they attack the idea of party government.

Let us discuss the relation of this movement to the social structure. "Action Catholique is a veritable apostolate in which participate the Catholics of all social classes who come to unite themselves in thought and action with the centers of sound doctrine and multiple social activity, centers legitimately constituted and consequently receiving the aid and support of the authority of the Bishops."[10] This statement does not appear radical. In other statements there is a more direct suggestion that the middle and upper classes are not as devoted as they should be. In a special encyclical on the priesthood, a recent pope complains of the lack of vocations from these classes, and lays it to their lukewarmness in general, and especially to a direct opposition of parents to having their children enter the priesthood. These are the classes generally suspected of wanting to run their own affairs without too much interference.

Historically, in Quebec, I should say that the relation between the church and the upper classes has been of diplomatic character. Each has been aware of the power of the other. And there has been integration of leadership, with competition. The church has, of course, always had its direct relations with the poor and miserable. But in general, it has been inclined to recognize the class organization of society, with the responsibility of the better-off for the poor. Parish societies have historically had middle- or upper-class leaders. The church, in short, has worked through the medium of those who had lay authority and prestige.

Action Catholique would seem to continue this, if one read only the statement that it is an apostolate of the laity, and those concerning the role of a Catholic élite. But this élite is one of *militant* Catholics— Catholics who take their mission seriously. This the middle and upper classes are accused of not doing. The élite is so because of enthusiasm, devotion, and submission to the will of the church, not because of social position. The leaders of Action Catholique are to be trained in study groups whose members are perhaps recommended by laymen, but accepted finally by the priest who leads the group. All Action Catholique leaders are chosen by the priests.

In the Jepnesse Ouvrière Catholique, which is organized by parishes, the leaders are also chosen by a chaplain. I found that in Cantonville, an industrial town studied in detail, the leaders of this organization were in fact not known by the leading men and families of the parish. A certain uneasiness was felt at this by-passing of the traditional leaders of the community. The church directly, and without use of middle-class leaders, has mobilized a whole class of young people.

At this point another distinction is to be made. There are predominantly, even completely, Catholic organizations which are "profane". The Knights of Columbus is, for example, profane. It is not part of Action Catholique or of general parochial organization. It is organized by lay initiative. Many priests do not like the organization. In response to a direct question, the curé of a large parish divided the associations of his community into those which were parochial or church-sponsored, and those which were profane. He said frankly that the church did not try to organize business and professional men for "social action" and recreation; they have their own organizations. This was a community parish, in which people of all classes are found.

In other parishes, especially in cities, the parishioners may include none of the middle and upper classes. It appears, in Quebec City, that organization of the parish according to the principles of Action Catholique is most nearly complete in lower-middle-class parishes. The prize parish in this regard is St. Charles de Limoilou, a district of small functionaries, clerks, and small-business people. This parish prides itself on having none of the vices of the richer and more chic Haute Ville or of the poorer working-class parishes along the river St. Charles. It has no taverns, no theater, no dance hall; it was the first to have a Caisse Populaire (Parish Mutual Savings Bank), and boasts the most active Action Catholique committee.

In the same city, men of a little more position insist—at least privately—that they do enough "Action Catholique" in their Knights of Columbus chapters and in their various civic and professional organizations; implied is a resentment of clerical pressure to have them take more active part in church-sponsored organizations. In an old and stable working-class parish which is being studied in detail it appears that there is a rather complete set of organizations—political clubs, athletic clubs, unions, etc.—with a lay leadership, and that the Action organizations exist more on paper than as active forces. The leaders of the latter are leaders only by fiat, and not by virtue of any real influence in the community. In short, it is likely that in upper-middle-class and upper-class parishes Action Catholique is slow to develop, and when it does so, it largely takes the form of female piety. In the poorer working-class parishes, Action Catholique is a kind of missionary activity, not integrated with the real organization of the community. Only in the lower-middle-class parish is Action organization and leadership in large measure the real organization and leadership of the community.

Of course, certain of the movements sponsored by the Action spirit are in direct conflict with the interests of the upper classes. The Labor Syndicates (Catholic Labor Unions) and the Parish Mutual Savings Banks and Consumers' Co-operatives run directly against the economic interests of the economically directing classes. The temperance movement strikes at middle- and upper-class mores, although perhaps more so at lower-class ways. The attack upon the commercial press and the implied attack upon traditional political parties strikes also at their interests and at their leadership in public life.

One may detect, then, several reasons for resistance of the middle and upper classes to extreme Action:

1. It generally ignores lay, middle-class leadership.

2. It contains a constant implied criticism of the secular spirit and more easy-going mores of these classes.

3. It organizes certain groups which these classes would prefer not to be organized as such—the working classes in Catholic Unions and in

Catholic Workers' Youth; working and lower-middle classes in Consumers' and Saving Co-operatives.

4. It starts movements which compete with or challenge the economic institutions and leadership of the upper classes.

5. It is generally too "enthusiastic" or "fanatical". Enthusiasm in a cause generally agreed to is always a menace to those who adhere to the same cause, symbols, etc., but in a more moderate way. When the subordinate becomes more enthusiastic than his master he is "insubordinate" in the most fundamental sense of the term. Generally, the leading classes do not mind preaching in season, but they are embarrassed and disturbed by "testifying in and out of season".

In Quebec, the growth of Action Catholique has occurred at the same time as a tremendous growth of town and industrial population. An aspect of this growth has been the growth of influence of the English-speaking factory manager and engineer. The middle- and upper-class French, whose position rests largely on smaller industries, commerce, and the professions, do not share proportionately in the new economic power. At the same time, they identify their interests with those of business and industry closely enough to be disturbed by the movements of labor and poorer classes generally—even though the latter are directed mainly against the "foreign" (English and American) industries and large financial and commercial institutions. It is a little as if their own church—in organizing co-operatives, unions, etc.—were but hastening and intensifying their already great difficulties. For one thing, it seems to rob these classes of their traditional role of leading their own people and of maintaining, for their own people, equitable and equable relations with the English-speaking part of the country.

It is a very ambivalent situation in which these classes find themselves. As if it were not enough to challenge their leadership by organizing the lower classes directly, the church adds to their difficulty by threatening their secular contacts with the larger world, and their lines of communication and collaboration with the more friendly of the English in the Rotary; and by criticizing neutral organizations not only for the poor, but for the middle and upper classes.

Thus, it is not surprising that Action leaders accuse the old upper-class "liberals" of having really become very conservative. The old "liberals" (the young liberals of the 1890s and early 1900s) were in their day in favor of laicizing the schools and making school attendance compulsory. They are said now to want to go slow on both these matters. Lay teachers might organize and want more money; and compulsory school attendance would require additional school facilities and hence also more money. Some of the young Action priests, on the other hand, now want more lay teachers, not on principle, but as a means of getting specialized subjects taught in the schools; and the church now seems to support legislation to make school compulsory. The old liberals are said by these young priests to have an alliance with heads of certain teaching Orders of brothers and nuns to keep things as they are: the lay liberals for fear of taxes and of the social changes which seem encouraged by Action Catholique, the heads of Orders for fear of losing their teaching contracts with school boards.

In the Action Catholique movement there is—as hinted already—an emphasis on youth. A young auxiliary bishop has been appointed to head Action Catholique in the diocese of Quebec. In other dioceses, a young priest is sent to some school to study for a year or two the social problems of the day and the Action organizations designed to meet them; then he returns to his diocese as a special agent of the bishop to carry out the Action program. Such young priests tell tales of the difficulty they have in selling their movements to old country curés, to well-established curés of rich parishes, and sometimes even to the bishop himself. One gets the impression of unanimous lip service to Action Catholique, but also of a good deal of passive resistance on the part of older clergy and clergy in certain higher positions. Even here, Action seems like a short-cutting of traditional hierarchical arrangements and a threat to the authority of the curé in his parish. There has been comment on the number of new bishops who have been elevated before the age of forty; young men who are noted for their enthusiasm for the Action cause rather than for their dignity and their displaying qualities of "princes of the Church".

The Ecole des Sciences Sociales of Laval University was recently mentioned by the new auxiliary bishop of Quebec as a special instrument of Action Catholique, the training place of the young men with the will and the technical knowledge to bring about—in submission to the church—the reforms necessary to make a Christian social order. In general, the students of this school are ardent Action people—full of social zeal, and ready to study society in order to reform it. They want to improve housing and the conditions of workers, to see that proper playgrounds are established and that young delinquents are handled in the most advanced manner; in short, they want to solve all of the traditional problems.

Action Catholique to these young people and to many younger priests means not merely an increase of piety but a great social movement to solve the problems created by modern industrialism. And modern industrialism is, to them, a creation of the English.

Some of the students of this school are of families which, although mobile, are already in the upper middle class. Such students—generally law students at the same time—see in this movement and in the Ecole itself an instrument of security and mobility. They expect to combine law practice with government service in the general field of social welfare—housing, unemployment insurance, pension bureaux, etc. Others of the students are more directly from poorer classes; for them their education prepares them for a lay mission, for the regeneration of French-Canadian society along Catholic lines. They are very aggressive against the upper classes, the ambitious, the rich, and the English. Such students are also mobile, but their personal goals are defined in terms of social reform—the reforms sought by Action Catholique.

Nationalism

All French Canadians are nationalists and, in a certain degree, separatists.

All are nationalists in that they base their living and their political behavior on the assumption that the French Canadians will continue indefinitely to be, as in the past, a people with their own language, system of institutions, world of social relations, and sense of historical identity. The exceptions to this statement are, in the province of Quebec, negligible in number and in influence. Many French Canadians would not like to be called nationalists, since this word indicates a special state of mind and suggests a lack of loyalty to the Canadian government. I use the phrase because there is a tendency on the part of English Canadians, even those who claim to be "sympathetic", to betray, when they do not openly state, that they consider French-Canadian society as a temporary thing, something which will eventually disappear, and that all French Canadians who do not accept the idea of eventual assimilation are "nationalists". Thus, the facts being as they are, all French Canadians correspond to the implied English definition of nationalists.[11]

In the same sense, French Canadians are all separatists in the English implied meaning of the term. For, although in the French-Canadian meaning a separatist is someone who proposes political separation of Quebec from Canada, the English incline to apply the term to those who defend provincial autonomy and who propose to maintain and extend the system of separate institutions.

Practically all French Canadians live their informal social lives in French cliques and circles. They go to French schools from infancy to professional degree. If they are socially mobile, they move up through activity and offices in civic, fraternal, and professional organizations which are French. They seek admittance to social circles above them— but French circles. In certain kinds of careers, the French Canadian may make certain English contacts and be active in mixed associations (Canadian clubs, Rotary, chambers of commerce, golf clubs, etc.); but —except for a very few people—these contacts are on the periphery, rather than at the center, of the field of activity.

However, the successful French Canadian does not want to isolate himself on principle from mixed or predominantly English activities. His interests coincide at certain points with those of English people of like social and economic position. Hence, he fights against the attempt, on the part of Action Catholique, to expand the system of exclusively Catholic organizations to include the interests and activities of the middle class.

This brings us to the connection between Action Catholique and French-Canadian nationalism. Action Catholique, we have said, contemplates a social order consisting of as wide as possible a complement of purely Catholic institutions and associations, all with militant lay leadership closely subject to clerical control. Nationalists contemplate a complete French-Canadian system of organizations. To Action, a mixed organization is one which contains Protestants, Jews, etc., and which must be "indifferent" or "neutral" as regards religion. To the *nationalist* a mixed organization is one which contains English, Jews, etc., and which to do so must be "indifferent" or "neutral" as regards the ethnic question. The Jews are the common term in the two equations. The Protestants of the first equation coincide fairly closely with the English of the second.

There is thus a natural tendency for the term "mixed" and others like it to be used in contexts in which they may refer to Protestant and/ or English. Nationalistic exclusiveness and Action Catholique exclusiveness tend to become one and the same thing, in the minds of both proponents and opponents.[12] Thus, it is with some reason that nationalism and Catholic Action are confused. They draw nourishment, in fact, from the same roots.

This all leads naturally to a comparison of nationalistic with Action Catholique attitudes toward the social structure. Extreme nationalism, like extreme Action, is especially aggressive toward the failings of upper-middle-class and upper-class people. The speeches, essays, and books of Abbé Lionel Groulx, one of the most extreme nationalists, never fail to attack such people for their bridge, golf, dances, and parties. He has made an epithet of the word *chic*; it means an attempt to be "better" than other French Canadians by being like the English. In this, Abbé Groulx is followed by nationalists and by Action people generally. A *chic* parish is one of well-placed people who pay little attention to Action movements and who have their own associations, some of which may be ethnically and religiously mixed.

In nationalism, as in Action, there is the open suggestion that the economically and socially powerful French Canadians "sell out" their nationality and religion alike; or that, at least, they are indifferent to their "patriotic" duties. The people referred to give some grounds for such accusation. For one thing, they show malaise in the presence of extreme nationalism. They have a stake in collaboration between the French and English. Their attempts to explain and justify French-Canadian nationalism to their English acquaintances subjects them to the accusation that they are, themselves, nationalistic. And their association with English people makes them "traitors" in the eyes of the more ardent nationalists among their own people. Another sectarian feature shared by nationalism and Action is a *méfiance* of political parties. The politician must work with his party; the party, to operate in the Dominion government, must be bi-ethnic. It must even include Jews. Hence, the party politician is branded as a compromiser. No words are too vituperative for nationalists to apply to him. A party politician converted to a national "bloc" or "movement" is regarded as a sinner snatched from the burning. Maxime Raymond, long a Liberal member of Parliament, became a nationalistic hero by openly withdrawing from his party to head the "bloc" which is opposing the Canadian war effort.

Finally, like Action, the nationalist movement shows a strong drive for economic and social reform, although their propaganda is directed chiefly against foreign (English and Jewish) domination of Canadian industry and finance.

One would expect, from the above, that the Action press and the nationalist press would be one and the same. This is not quite true, although the Action publications strongly support French-Canadian rights, and the nationalist press overworks its Catholicism. The official newspaper, *L'Action Catholique*, is fairly moderate in its nationalism. It is, after all, the organ of the Cardinal, primate of all Canada. It has a diplomatic role to play. *Le Devoir*, the Montreal nationalist daily, is "officiously" Catholic. It loves to accuse English people of not respecting the Catholic religion and of thereby wounding French Canadians. The nationalist weekly, *La Boussole*,[13] goes further. It ridicules other religions and uses religious prejudices—couched in vulgar language—to make its nationalistic points.

There is every evidence that at the extreme wing of the nationalist movement there exists a semi-secret sect which goes far beyond the official church policy and beyond the Action movement. This group claims to be loyally Catholic. In fact, their protestations of Catholicism are so strong that they contain the hint that less nationalistic people are not as good Catholics as they themselves are. Such an attitude is always suspect to the religious authority.

Thus, while Action and nationalism are one in the minds of many people, and while they root in the same soil of discontent, there are important distinctions between them. The extremists of nationalism show a certain—although hidden—defiance of the church. Action heads up in the church, and its dominating spirit is that of reform—often social reform—inspired and held in check by religious sentiments and by the hierarchy itself.

POSTSCRIPT

My book, *French Canada in Transition*, went to the publisher about the time this essay was written. After the war Action Catholique played a part in developing social consciousness in the Province of Quebec. Many of the young people who were active in it became leaders in other social movements and in politics; some turned to sociology and social journalism. The Quiet Revolution with its less quiet phases followed. The social structure has changed its form considerably.

E.C.H. Boston, 1974

NOTES

1 See my *French Canada in Transition*, Chap. 14, "Religious and Patriotic Ceremony". (Chicago, 1943)

2 For a good statement concerning distinctions between *Stand*, social class, economic class, etc., see Max Weber, *Wirtschaft und Gesellschaft*, chapter on "Stände und Klassen" (Tübingen, 1925). [*Economy and Society*, New York, 1968.] Charles Henry Lea, in *Sacerdotal Celibacy in the Christian Church*, shows how the pious masses and the jealous nobility aided the popes in establishing celibacy and "poverty" among the clergy. In many places priestly families had already become established so far as to pass on benefices and church estates to their children.

3 The farmer-hero of Ringuet's *30 Arpents* (Paris: Flammarion, 1938) is disappointed that, after spending a great deal of money to make his son a priest, the son gets to be nothing more than a vicar in a missionary parish—whose curé is so ascetic that his vicars live on cold potatoes. The farmer and his wife had hoped to boast to their neighbors of their son, curé in some well-known "fat" parish.

4 There is talk that the new auxiliary of Quebec was appointed to clear out "dead wood" and "ecclesiastical ornaments" from the university and seminary hierarchy. A series of family case studies which were written by Laval students contained frequent evidences of "class" aggression of lower and disappointed clergy against both the upper-class laity and the clergy who seek "chic" parishes and preferment.

5 A caricature painting recently done by a young Quebec artist shows a family group of lower middle class. The father is in his vest, but wears a white stiff collar. In the chair of honor sits a grown son in the habit of a lay brother of a minor order. He is unshaven and his costume is rather shabby. He symbolizes the failure of the family to attain its ambition to have a priest among its number. A shabby lay brother is a pretty humble substitute for a priest.

6 It is perhaps significant that the Jesuits have developed the two outstanding "mobility" colleges. The Jesuits are considered an ambitious and "arrivist" order by the Dominicans, Franciscans, and Benedictines. They are accused of using their colleges as recruiting grounds and their alumni as a supporting "bloc".

7 From a letter of Pope Pius XI, quoted in, E. Guerry, *Action Catholique, Textes Pontificaux classés et commentés* (Paris, 1936).

8 *Ibid.*, Chap. 2, *et passim*.

9 *Ibid.*, p. 91, *et passim*.

10 *Ibid.*, p. 8.

11 When one talks to English Canadians about French Canadians they eventually bring up the question of eventual assimilation. They seize upon individual cases as evidences of a beginning of a revolt against the church.

12 I have taken records of Catholic Labor Union rally speeches in which "closed shop" obviously means "closed" to non-French and non-Catholic.

13 Cardinal Villeneuve gave *Le Devoir* a sharp public rebuke this past winter for attempting to define the role of Action Catholique as religious, while *Le Devoir* and other unofficial Catholic papers were to be free to express more strongly the political sentiments of nationalism. A nationalist press is always watched closely by the church, because it may get out of bounds.

Social Awakening Among Protestants, 1872 to 1918*

Stewart Crysdale

Traditionalism was the dominant characteristic of the Canadian Protestant churches before the turn of the century. It was not until the industrial revolution was in full swing in burgeoning eastern cities that some church leaders realized that their responsibility for human welfare must lead them into a prophetic witness in the arenas of politics and economics. By the close of the First World War concern over the plight of growing masses of helpless industrial workers had mounted in some quarters of the churches to a crusade for social justice.

Although Canadian churches before 1906 tended to view social tensions from a rural standpoint and were slow to develop a relevant social ethic, their connection with the masses was closer than in Britain or the United States. The most obvious explanation of this difference is that in many parts of Canada there was practically no interval between the settlement of the frontier and the beginning of industrialization. As railroads were pushed northward and westward and new towns were built, churches and industries grew up together.

*Appeared first as Chapter 2 in Stewart Crysdale, *The Industrial Struggle and Protestant Ethics in Canada* (Toronto: Ryerson Press, 1961). Published here in abridged and revised form with the permission of the author.

In Canada there was little labour violence until feelings ran high in strikes following the First World War. The changing reaction of the churches to critical social changes may be seen in the pronouncements of church courts and in the comments of the religious press.

The Printers' Strike in 1872

The churches without exception opposed the first concerted effort of Canadian labour to win its demands by means of a trade-wide strike. The printers' action in Toronto in 1872 provoked this comment in the Methodists' *Christian Guardian* of March 27:

> While we have a profound sympathy with all honest, working men, and a sincere desire for their comfort and improvement, we seriously question the wisdom and advantage of this movement—especially the strikes to which it is likely to lead.

The Presbyterian press was more unreservedly critical of the printers, and this editorial from the Montreal *Witness* affirmed emphatically the Protestant ethic of individualism:

> No man ever rose above a lowly condition who thought more of his class than his individuality. In this new country, where every man who strives may advance in social power and rank, to teach men subordination to class movements is to deprive them of those noble opportunities for personal advancement which are the peculiar glory and advantage of this continent.[1]

The editor of *The Church Herald*, expressing Church of England views, was even more caustic in his criticism of the printers:

> The printers of the city have seen fit to usurp the control of the offices, an usurpation which needed and secured, by the force of its boldness, united and decided action on the part of those to whom alone that control legitimately belongs,—the Employers. . . .
> As to ourselves, the matter stands thus:—Our men had heretofore declared themselves satisfied with their labour and wages. But the insidious whimperings of a foreign-born League, circulated amongst them, their eyes were blinded under the excuse of opening

them, so that to men *totally* unfit to judge of Canadian peculiarities of Labour, we have to give thanks for this ill-growth of antagonism between it and the Capital.[2]

The Baptist and Congregational presses took no notice of the printers' strike.

Immigration's Challenge, 1882-1914

Thirty years later, the hardships of masses of newcomers in Canadian cities, drawn by the hope of industrial employment, awakened the humanitarian concern of many church leaders. Typical of these was James Woodsworth, Methodist missionary superintendent of the northwest and father of J. S. Woodsworth, the founder in the 1930s of the Socialist party, the Co-operative Commonwealth Federation. The elder Woodsworth and the church generally believed that genuine conversion would lead to "disinterested benevolence" and thence to the solution of social problems. This approach was implied in the name of the standing committee set up to deal with social problems in 1902, "The Board of Temperance, Prohibition and Moral Reform".

A change in emphasis occurred, however, as leaders became convinced that only a radical revision of the social order could solve the evils of industrialism. At the Seventh General Conference of the Methodist Church in 1906 there was strong criticism of the existing competitive order. These views were reiterated in 1910 and given wide circulation. The 1906 statement declared:

We hold that the work of the Church is to set up the Kingdom of God among men, which we understand to be a social order founded on the principles of the Gospel—the Golden Rule, and the Sermon on the Mount—and made possible through the regeneration of men's lives.

We acknowledge with regret that the present social order is far from being an ideal expression of Christian brotherhood, and that the spirit of much of our commercial life is alien to that of the Gospel. We deplore the great evils which have their source in the commercial greed of our times, the money madness which leads men to oppress the unfortunate and to forget their obligations to the higher interests of society. . . . While we admit the right of both labour and capital to guard their interests by combination we condemn the disregard of the rights of the public and the individual which has been shown now by combinations of capital and now by combinations of labour.

While we admit that with the abounding and increasing wealth of our country, it is possible for the rich to grow richer without the poor becoming poorer, we deplore those existing economic conditions which tend to accentuate the inequality of opportunity open to the various classes of the community and to permit, through artificial and unfair conditions, the massing of the larger proportion of the wealth of the country in the hands of the few, with all the attendant economic and political dangers.

When the living wage is not made the first factor in determining the price of manufactured articles and the sweat shop scale of wages is so low that our maidens have set before them the awful choice between hunger and dishonour, and in the factory young children are stunted in mind and body by excessive labour, it is time for Christian citizenship to take up the Master's "whip of small cords" and drive these things from the holy places of our civilization, and for the Church to urge its members who in corporate bodies and otherwise, are served by labour, to keep themselves clear of guilt in these economic relations.[3]

The early years of the twentieth century also saw a drastic change in Presbyterian social policy. At first, under the leadership of men like James Robertson, awakening social concern was directed against moral abuses of the frontier. The General Assembly in 1907 set up a "Standing Committee on Temperance and Other Moral and Social Reforms".[4] The Baptist Convention of Ontario and Quebec also formed a Committee on Temperance and Moral Reform in 1906.[5]

One of the most important aspects of the churches' social awakening in the first two decades of the twentieth century was their effective teamwork to meet the problems of rapid industrialization. The *Proceedings* of the 1908 General Assembly of the Presbyterian Church stated:

The Moral and Social Reform Council of Canada was organized on December 26, 1907, with Archbishop Sweatman, primate of the Church of England, honorary president; Dr. A. Carman, general superintendent of the Methodist Church, president; James Simpson, vice-president of the Trades and Labour Congress of Canada, vice-president; Dr. J. G. Shearer (Presbyterian), secretary; and Mr. Henry Moyle of the Baptist Church, treasurer.

By 1914 the movement, now known as the Social Service Council of Canada, had issued a statement of Christian social principles which was adopted by all of the churches and groups connected with it. In 1917 these included the Church of England, the Presbyterian, Methodist, Baptist, and Congregational Churches, the Evangelical Association, the Dominion Grange and Farmers' Association, the Salvation Army, the Canadian Purity-Education Association, the Christian Men's Federation, the National Council of the Y.M.C.A., the Dominion Council of the Y.W.C.A., the W.C.T.U., the Canadian Council of Agriculture, and the National Council of Provincial Sunday School Associations.

In October, 1918, the new magazine *Social Welfare* was launched. By the end of the year there were twenty-nine units of the Council—eighteen Dominion-wide and eleven provincial. Fourteen provincial secretaries had been appointed and were giving their full time to the work. The active concerns of the Council included temperance, public health, child welfare, housing, amusements and recreation, gambling, education, the care of dependants, and immigration.[6] The Council's work in bringing to bear upon the life of Canada the churches' united and urgent witness was of paramount importance to the emerging social pattern.

Portions of the 1917 statement of principles of the Council bearing directly upon industrialization were as follows:

The Social Service Council of Canada believes in:
The Fatherhood of God and the Brotherhood of man;
The Kingdom of God, and therefore in universal righteousness and social justice through the evangel of Christ;
The saving of not only men but man, not only of the individual but society; . . .
The highest good of all people as the ideal and test of social legislation and institutions.

It is commonly thought that the writings of Walter Rauschenbusch and the historic social pronouncement of 1908 of the Federal Council of Churches in the United States gave initial impetus to the movement among Canadian churches for social justice. Although the American social gospel movement was influential in this country, especially in the second and third decades, there is unmistakable evidence that the movement for reform in Canada was largely indigenous) Rauschenbusch's first influential book, *Christianity and the Social Crisis*, was not published until 1907, but already the agitation among Canadian church leaders had progressed to the point where in that year interdenominational organization occurred. The Methodist Church in Canada made the first of its radical policy statements as early as 1906.

The Methodist and Presbyterian Boards co-operated in the appointment in 1911 of field workers to study urban problems in Montreal, Toronto, Winnipeg, Vancouver, and other centres. The Presbyterian committeee recommended that Christian settlement centres be established in overcrowded and neglected downtown areas, and also that the church press for legislation to improve conditions of housing, employment, education, and welfare. It was in 1911, too, that the name of the committee was changed to the Board of Social Service and Evangelism, showing the new emphasis by placing "social service" first. The year following, it was stated that the wide distribution of the 1911 report had contributed to the awakening of public interest in social questions and the need for righting mounting evils. The 1912 General Assembly was told that slum conditions were multiplying in Canadian cities with the influx of immigrants, and that established churches were not reaching thousands of them, tending rather to move out before the incoming hordes and to seek "more comfortable quarters in the residential suburbs". In 1912 St. Christopher House was opened in Toronto and Chalmers House in Montreal, augmenting the settlement work that had been started a few years before at Robertson Memorial Institute in Winnipeg. Effective lobbying sought Ontario legislation for workmen's compensation, an eight-hour day, minimum wages, and other beneficial labour enactments.

Social awakening came about more slowly in other denominations. The formation of the Moral and Social Reform Council of Canada in Toronto on December 26, 1907, was not so much as mentioned in the Anglican *Canadian Churchman*, in spite of the fact that the Primate, Archbishop Arthur Sweatman, had agreed to act as its first honorary president. In view of the social ferment in the Methodist and Presbyterian churches in Canada in these years, the coolness of the Church of England periodical to demands for social reform is worthy of note. The social conservatism of the Anglican Church in this period of awakening elsewhere is all the more remarkable in the face of the strong Christian socialist movement in England.

The first official cognizance of industrial problems taken by the Congregational Union of Canada was a report of representatives on the Moral and Social Reform Council of Canada to the fifth annual meeting of the Union, held at Kingston in June, 1911.[7] This was four years *after* the Council was formed! The committee reported that it had represented the Congregational churches at the annual meeting of the Council, and that it had participated in the work of its executive. It recommended the use of the reading course in social science prepared by the interchurch Council, but no mention was made of the somewhat radical attitude of the Council to social reform. Instead, close attention was given to the evils of gambling, intemperance, and personal impurity.

Nevertheless, the impact of industrialization was being felt adversely by the Congregationalists. This was evidenced by the chairman's address at the annual meeting in Toronto in 1913.[8] The Rev. G. Ellery Read lamented churches half filled in spite of masses of unchurched people in the growing cities. He roundly castigated indifferent members, and described the great obstacle in the way of the church as the "stubborn indisposition, the determined unwillingness of men to surrender themselves" to the spiritual ideal of life in contrast to the "worldly and material". Mr. Read divided the delinquents into two groups, on one hand the economically successful, who had become slaves "bound hand and foot to the great industrial concerns which they developed", and, on the other hand, those who had become victims of the "awful and appalling poverty, which is prevalent in ghastly and challenging contrast to the enormous wealth possessed by the relatively few".

Notwithstanding a few prophetic figures, the majority within the Congregationalist Church considered such matters to be external to its life and work. Indeed, the Congregational Union refused to be placed on record as favouring social reform on a sweeping scale until it was drawn into the aggressive activities of the Social Service Council of Canada in the post-war period.

Progressive spirits among the Baptists also failed at first to gain headway. The Ontario-Quebec Convention Committee on Temperance and Moral Reform reported in 1908:

We regret that some of our pastors and laymen, in saying that nothing but the Gospel should be presented from the pulpit, apply this to the question of Moral and Social Reform. The Master, however, taught "It is lawful to do well on the Sabbath day," and surely we may follow His example. The gospel of Christian Citizenship may well find a place in the services of the Sabbath.[9]

The name of the committee was changed that year to Moral and Social Reform, indicating the wider nature of the work.

The Baptist Committee endeavoured to reassure the Convention of 1911 that concern for social reform need not "compromise our position as Baptists in relation to the separate functions of Church and State".[10] At the 1912 Convention in Brantford they renewed this plea: "One thing we have decided, and that is that at first our work will be largely a vigorous educational campaign. We will be careful not to enter upon any kind of work which will be in any way out of harmony with New Testament teaching."[11] It seems that even these cautious first steps were hindered from within, for the following complaint was recorded:

Your Committee, although desirous of many reforms and having started at home, in an attempt upon the Executive Committee of this Convention, have sadly failed to get for this work a place upon the programme, such as was so strongly requested last year by the Convention. . . . Accordingly we have not been able to bring to this city a strong and prominent speaker, whose address would have been a great inspiration, and at the same time expressed the views of your Committee, and, we think, the feelings of our people generally. . . .[11]

The Recession of 1913-1915

The recession which began in 1913 brought into focus specific points at which an aroused Christian social conscience could operate for the alleviation of hardships attending rapid industrialization. The Methodist Board of Temperance, Prohibition, and Moral Reform was reorganized in 1914 into the Department of Social Service and Evangelism, marking a change in emphasis. At the annual Conference the same year the Methodist Church declared her belief in concrete principles affecting industrial life, embodied in the following resolutions:

The safeguarding of the right of all people to self-maintenance, and the making of provision against the hardships of unemployment, seasonal employment and all other encroachments;

The securing of protection for workers against the perils of danger-ous machinery and occupational diseases; the making of suitable provision for them if incapacitated by old age, injury, or sickness; and the application of the principles of conciliation and arbitration to industrial disputes;

The abatement and ultimate abolition of poverty, by the protection of the citizen, the home, society and the state, against all moral, social and economic waste;

The recognition of equal rights and complete justice for all men in all stations of life, with obligation to make immediate, earnest and thorough effort to learn, if possible, what changes of law or usage relating to land tenure and taxation, public ownership, and control of natural resources, production and distribution, etc., may or may not be necessary to secure the rights of the people;

(a) The reduction of hours of labour to the lowest practicable point; (b) The payment by every industry of a living wage as a mini-mum, and the highest wage that the industry can afford; (c) Such partnership as can be equitably devised between the employer and the employee;

The observance of the Lord's Day, including the complete release from employment on one day in seven for those employed in labour which is necessarily continuous;

The opportunity for wholesome, healthful recreation, by the esta-blishment of supervised playgrounds; the encouragement of whole-some athletics and every sane method to secure clean sport and amusement.[12]

The first reference to the problem of serious unemployment in the reports of the Presbyterian Board to General Assembly appeared in 1914:

Unemployment has stricken thousands of homes in our cities with poverty and serious suffering, driving some to despair and death. Surely society must find a solution for this uncertainty of our oppor-tunity to work for a living. Is it not the Church's duty to stir the heart and conscience of society to face this question and at any cost solve it?[13]

The hardships of unemployment continuing in spite of the war, both the Presbyterian General Assembly and the Methodist Conference in

1915 recommended concrete action along these lines: (1) a nationwide system of free labour bureaux, to save workless men from "exploitation, deception and robbery at the hands of profit-making labour bureaux sharks"; (2) government public works; (3) getting the needy on to the land, with extended credit, and "withholding from rapacious, speculative control the public domain"; and (4) private citizens taking steps to provide odd jobs.[14]

Hard times and shrinking revenues brought about the amalgamation of the Presbyterian Boards of Home Missions and Social Service in 1915. Nevertheless, the report of the new Board for the year 1915–1916 recorded progress in several fields. The churches' crusade had finally achieved prohibition of the manufacture and sale of liquor in all of Canada except Quebec, and headway was being made with progressive labour legislation. For several years the General Assembly had turned its heavy guns on the widespread graft in government war contracts and in party patronage, and now two Royal Commissions were conducting investigations which would lead to the removal of the civil service from political partisanship.

World War I, 1914-1918

The heroic tragedy of the World War of 1914–1918 fanned a bright flame of social idealism. In this revival the churches exerted a strong influence. The spirit of the day was expressed in the 1915 report of the Presbyterian Board of Social Service and Evangelism:

This is the day of democracy—Christian democracy! There has been, and there is, *a great social awakening!* Perhaps no agencies have done more under God to bring this about than the church departments of Social Service.[15]

The Methodists went further than any other denomination in giving specific expression to this idealism. The 1918 report of their Committee on Social Service and Evangelism made the following declaration:

(1) *Special Privilege Condemned:* We declare all special privilege not based on useful service to the community, to be a violation of the principle of justice, which is the foundation of democracy.

(2) *Democratic Commercial Organization:* We declare that

forms of industrial organization should be developed which call labour to a voice in the management and a share in the profits and risks of business. All forms of autocratic organization of business should be discouraged. We call attention to the remarkable and unchallenged success of the co-operative stores, factories and steamship lines of England and Scotland, as great examples of democracy in business.

(3) *Profits of Labour and Capital*: We declare it to be unChristian to accept profits when labourers do not receive a living wage, or when capital receives disproportionate returns as compared with labour.

(4) *Old Age Insurance*: We recommend Old Age Insurance on a national scale, in which the annuity paid shall be based upon the average earnings of the country, each year of a man's effective life.

(5) *Unearned Wealth*: We condemn speculation in land, grain, foodstuffs and natural resources, as well as the frequent capture of unearned wealth through over-capitalization of commercial enterprise.

(6) *Profiteering*: As the people are virtual partners in every business enterprise, we condemn that profiteering which takes out of them profits not justified by the value or cost of the service rendered. We recommend the enactment of legislation which shall secure to labour a fair wage adequate to a proper standard of living, and to the business a fair profit adequate for its continuance, and to the public all returns in excess of these.

(7) *Nationalization of Natural Resources*: We are in favour of the nationalization of our natural resources, such as mines, water-power, fisheries, forests, and means of communication, transportation and public utilities on which all people depend. . . .

(8) *Sympathy with Labour*: As followers of the Carpenter of Nazareth, we sympathetically seek to understand the problems of life as they confront the claims of labour in Canada, and thus rightly estimate the pleas they make for justice, and find in them allies in the struggle, to realize the ends of fair play, humanity and brotherhood.[16]

This statement is a most radical renunciation of *laissez-faire* capitalism, and represents a remarkable about-face from the 1872 conservatism of the Methodist Church.

A similar change is observable in the social thought of the other churches, though in lesser degree. General Synod of the Church of England in 1908 had appointed representatives to the Moral and Social Reform Council of Canada, but the church as a whole remained uncommitted until 1911, when a standing Committee on Moral and Social Reform was appointed by General Synod, meeting in London. This committee held three meetings between 1911 and September 1915, when it submitted its first report to General Synod, in Toronto. It recommended that the Church of England in Canada take its full share of responsibility for bearing social witness to the faith in the rapidly changing industrial situation. In response, General Synod enacted a canon creating a Council for Social Service. It was a first step, although failure to provide a budget sorely restricted effective action.[17]

The first occasion on which the ethical problems of industrialization received thorough consideration by the Church of England in Canada was at the General Synod of 1918. The Council for Social Service recommended the adoption of the declaration of principles enunciated by the Federal Council of the Churches of Christ in America upon its formation in 1908. This the 1918 Synod did. Now committed to a more progressive social policy, the Church of England in Canada, under the vigorous leadership of such men as Archdeacon C. L. Ingles and Rev. Dr. L. N. Tucker, entered upon an increasingly active program of nation-wide organization and distribution of literature.

An incisive criticism of the basic social ills of industrialized Canada was expressed by the Council for Social Service in its 1918 report. Modern civilization, the report stated, had come to rest on three false concepts—individualism, competition, and materialism.

Summary

Summarizing the position of the churches on social questions up to 1918, we detect in the foregoing survey two stages. These are by no means hard and fast, either chronologically or by denomination. Indeed, the earlier individualistic notions are still to be found in all churches, and conversely, even in the earliest days there were flashes of strong social consciousness. Nevertheless, there are two fairly clear stages in this early period. The first, from 1872 to 1905, was an interval of gradual change in social structure; labour unions, big business, and the state gathered power with increasing momentum. In this phase the churches tended to favour the *status quo* and generally were socially lethargic. The "Protestant ethic" of individualism, glorifying personal freedom, and stressing the sufficiency of personal conversion, was joined to nineteenth-century economic idealism, which exalted free enterprise and the operation of "natural" laws such as supply and demand.

The second stage burst upon Canada like a northern storm. In the short space of twelve years between 1906 and 1918 fundamental changes occurred in the Canadian economy and in the attitudes of the three largest non-Roman churches—the Methodist, Presbyterian, and Church of England. The Methodist statements of 1906 and 1918 were the most radical, calling for fundamental changes in the social system—public ownership of basic industries, a fair wage as the first charge against production, regulation of profits, and legally established social security measures. Presbyterian policy did not go so far in demanding state control, but it called for a recognition of the workers' right to share equally with capital in the fruits of production. The Church of England, though not nearly so prominent in social action, approximated the Presbyterian Church's position at this time. The Baptists gave tacit approval, after much urging, to a new sense of social responsibility, but declined to come to grips with specific issues raised by the emergence of huge power groups in modern society. This was in the main also the position of the Congregationalists, Lutherans, Salvationists, and others.

Certain circumstances tended to produce an effective impact by the churches upon Canadian society in this formative period from 1906 to 1918.

1.   There was practically no interval between the settlement of many new towns in northern and western Canada and the emergence of industrialization. In these communities, in contrast to established cities and towns, there was less opportunity for the churches to become strongly class-conscious. They grew up with the industrial communities, and were closely identified in this early period with the human problems of industry. To some extent this was also true of expanding parts of cities in eastern Canada, although there the hardening of class strata was further advanced, and militated against the mingling of social classes within the churches as freely as in frontier communities.

2.   Following the completion of the Canadian Pacific Railway to the west coast in 1885 and the opening of vast new territory for settlement, mass immigration took place. In the nine years after 1905, over two and a half million strangers flooded in. The three largest denominations were extremely active in welcoming them and helping them get settled. This

kept the churches and large numbers of the common people in close touch with each other.

3.   A new theological emphasis at the turn of the century tended to focus the churches' thought upon the application of the Gospel in meeting the social needs of men.

4.   The relationship beween church and state in Canada from the beginning of the English era also favoured the growth of a closer connection between the forces of religion and the human problems of industry. The unwillingness of England in the Constitutional Act of 1791 to designate any one denomination as the established church and the final disposition of the Clergy Reserves left the churches on their own resources. They were dependent upon the freewill support of the people, and as the working class and, later, the new middle class, grew more numerous and influential, they had an important part in shaping the policies and social programs of churches.

There was not in Canada a wide acceptance of the notion of a "middle wall of separation" between church and state such as Jefferson had enunciated in the United States. Rather, the relationship between crown and cross in Canada was one of co-operation. Canada from the beginning was officially a Christian nation, and parliaments and courts owed allegiance to Christ as final sovereign. The constitutional monarch at coronation promised to defend the faith. The consequence was that while the churches were not swayed unduly by political influences, and thus were free from ultra-conservatism, they often enjoyed the favour of the state.

5.   The policy of the Protestant denominations encouraged the participation of laymen in church courts, and a measure of flexibility in forms of worship enabled them to adapt in some degree to the needs and interests of pioneers and newcomers in amorphous communities.

6.   Another favourable factor was the able leadership of men of prophetic vision in the first decades of this century. The establishment of strong Boards of Social Service and Evangelism under their guidance provided effective leadership within the churches in social study and action.

7.   Early close collaboration between Protestant denominations in the Social Service Council of Canada, beginning in 1907, was another primary source of the strong influence of the churches in the early formative period of industrialization. The Council's leadership within the churches, its public influence, and its effective use of lobbying before pub-

lic bodies brought it into the arenas where important social decisions were being made.

8.   Leaders in the new social sciences in Canada were taught in universities largely under the influence of a social philosophy favourable to the Christian faith. There was not the tendency in Canada to absolutize the secular social sciences that prevailed in the early decades of this century in the United States.

9.   It must not be forgotten that federal social policy, in particular, had to take into account the strong Roman Catholic sentiment of Quebec. The solidarity of the Roman Church in French Canada was an inconspicuous, though extremely important, factor in the shaping of the public conscience to deal with the problems of industrialization. While the Catholic Church leaned toward conservatism and stability in political and economic theory, it also insisted upon a Christian view of man in the development of the state's role in the social process. A curious paradox existed, in which the Protestant ethic of individualism, tending toward *laissez-faire*, was tempered by the Roman view of benevolence in public policy. One form of conservatism, largely individualistic, was countered by another—corporateness. This view did not so much arise from demands among lay people as become propagated by the hierarchy. The over-all effect of Roman Catholic influence thus was to keep the Church —both Roman and, indirectly, Protestant—close to the centre of developments.

10.   The labour movement in Canada did not withdraw from other social groupings to the same degree as in the United States or Britain. For example, labour in Canada, in spite of sustained pressure, until very recently refused to become identified with any one political party, in contrast with the usual experience elsewhere. Prominent labour leaders in Canada were often active churchmen, and frequently they were appointed to governmental posts having to do with labour or welfare matters.

11.   From the start of the industrial period many political and governmental leaders have been closely associated with the church. For example, the first Deputy Minister of Labour for Ontario in 1915 was Dr. W. A. Riddell, formerly a Presbyterian divinity student and later a United Church layman. Riddell was one of several young men appointed by the Presbyterian and Methodist churches to conduct surveys of new urban communities before the war. Wilfrid Laurier was a devout Roman Catholic and Mackenzie King was a staunch Presbyterian.

It may be concluded that the period from 1906 to 1918—the most formative from the point of view of economic expansion, growth of power groups, and the determination of Canadian social policy as a compromise between free enterprise and state control—bore the strong imprint of the church. The vision of this young country growing into a Christian nation where the Lord would have "dominion from sea to sea and from the river unto the ends of the earth"[18] had assumed for many in the churches the dimensions of a crusade.

NOTES

1 Quoting *The Witness* (Halifax, April 20, 1872).
2 March 28, 1872.
3 *Journal of Proceedings*, Seventh General Conference, Methodist Church, 1906, pp. 274-6.
4 *Proceedings*, Thirty-Third General Assembly, Presbyterian Church, p. 56.
5 *Baptist Year Book*, 1906, p. 165.
6 *Report of the Board of Home Missions and Social Service*, Presbyterian Church, 1918-1919, p. 10.
7 *The Canadian Congregational Year Book*, 1911-1912, Toronto, p. 57.
8 *The Canadian Congregational Year Book*, 1913-1914, pp. 26 ff.
9 *Baptist Year Book*, 1908, p. 206.
10 *Baptist Year Book*, 1911, pp. 180-1.
11 *Baptist Year Book*, 1912, p. 237.
12 Report of Committee on Social Service and Evangelism, *Journal of Proceedings*, Ninth General Conference, Methodist Church, 1914, p. 402.
13 *Acts and Proceedings*, Presbyterian Church, p. 322.
14 *Acts and Proceedings*, p. 359.
15 P. 14.
16 Pp. 341-2.
17 *Journal of Proceedings*, p. 257.
18 Psalm 72.

A Decade of Ferment:
Canadian Churches in the 1960s*

John Webster Grant

Few suspected when the 1960s began that the decade would bring notable surprises in Canadian church life. Suburbanites continued to support their congregations, following a pattern set shortly after the Second World War, and most of them could point with pride to well-equipped church "plants" that were still almost the last word in ecclesiastical design. Since few of these buildings were yet paid for, a large proportion of the time and effort they could spare for church activities was devoted to the raising of money. The wider life of the church was comparatively devoid of excitement. National and regional bodies passed numerous resolutions, but with a sense that they had already achieved consensus on the most important issues and had ample time to dispose of the rest. The easing of the cold war and the end of the McCarthy era in the United States led to a general cooling of passions, except among a few ban-the-bombers who seemed to most of their colleagues to be making more noise than the peril warranted. The Canadian pew was still comfortable, and the chief complaint of preachers was that they heard so few complaints.

*Appeared first as Chapter 9 in John Webster Grant, *The Church in the Canadian Era* (Toronto: McGraw-Hill Ryerson, 1972). Published here in abridged form with the kind permission of the author and the publisher.

Past the Peak

Already, however, there was mounting evidence that the foundations of the church's recently achieved popularity were not so solid as they looked. Alumni of the swollen Sunday schools of the previous decade, although not conspicuously in revolt against the church, showed little enthusiasm for its youth programs. In 1958 the moderator of the United Church had observed among them considerable interest in personal religion but also exposure to "an endless relativity in faith and morals".[1] Their elders were beginning to complain, after years of faithful attendance, that they found it difficult to grasp the significance of rituals and sometimes even the meaning of sermons. Articulate discontent was still largely confined to the younger clergy, who struggled to relate the traditional roles in which they were often cast to the technical society in which they had to play them. Clearly, however, the religious boom had already passed its peak. Attendance at worship was levelling off, and financial campaigns were no longer almost automatically successful.

Despite the general calm on the religious scene there were indications that the churches recognized that the bulk of their members had moved away from traditional patterns. In 1960 the general council of the United Church, while continuing to urge total abstinence from alcoholic beverages as "the wisest and safest course", admitted that some responsible members conscientiously practised moderation instead.[2] In a sense this had always been the church's position, but the balanced presentation of arguments on both sides represented a significant break with the past. Later in the same month Arthur Packman became the United Church's first "padre of the pubs", and a report that he had sipped a glass of shandy with his parishioners created surprisingly little consternation. In Quebec the death of Duplessis in 1959 and the accession to power of the Liberals under Jean Lesage in 1960 presaged a series of changes that would make the Catholic Church something other than the inescapable presence it had been hitherto, and far-seeing leaders of the church already recognized that its traditional attitude of paternalism was no longer appropriate. Anglicans were slower to sense the passing of Victorian Canada but had a sudden awakening in 1963 when overseas delegates to a worldwide Anglican Congress at Toronto served notice that the patterns of western Christendom were irretrievably broken. From that time their church seemed more willing to reconsider traditional positions. In 1965, for example, it moved to relax a rule that had forbidden its clergy to remarry divorced persons under any circumstances.[3]

Programs of Modernization

The changes of which the public became dimly aware at the beginning of the decade seemed few in number and modest in scale. In fact they were the first tokens of a major process of internal reconstruction that was engaging the attention of a large number of concerned churchmen. Since church leaders were most conscious of inadequacy in communicating their message, they concentrated at first on improvements in the expression and transmission of the Christian faith. The Anglicans issued a revised *Book of Common Prayer* in 1959. The Presbyterians approved in 1964, after considerable debate, a *Book of Common Order* that departed more radically from customary practice. A United Church committee on worship [produced] new Service Books in 1969. The United Church and the Presbyterians began work on new hymn books. Preachers experimented with dialogue sermons and congregational "buzz groups". Most major denominations issued or imported from the United States new curricula of Christian education. Church broadcasters, who lacked the resources for large-scale television production, began to cooperate closely with the CBC and with private producers. In all these areas there was a subtle change of emphasis about 1960 from the refurbishing of the church's image to the search for a better understanding of the church's message.

As they reviewed their programs the churches found it necessary to take a harder look than before at the constituencies for which these programs were intended. Baptists, who had customarily thought of their congregations as gathered out of society, began to conduct careful surveys of the communities in which they worked. In 1962 the Anglicans set up a Unit of Research and Field Study in order to gather more reliable information about their people; its first major project was a survey of the attitudes of the clergy.[4] The United Church, which had inherited from its components a disproportionate number of small rural congregations, was forced to take the automobile age more seriously after 1958 when a decline in farm income speeded up the depopulation of the countryside. Church courts used their authority to combine pastoral charges, and in some localities historic but dilapidated meeting houses gave way to well-equipped consolidated churches. Inner-city congregations, which usually consisted mainly of loyal families who had long since moved their homes to the suburbs, began to give more attention to those who now lived near their churches. In many cases, however, ministers had to contend with congregational resistance to types of service that showed little promise of attracting new members or increased financial support. Voluntary congregational organizations for particular age and sex groups, most of which had been founded to meet the needs of an earlier era, came in for thorough re-examination.

As piecemeal reconstruction proceeded, the need for coordination became apparent. Long-range planning committees became a regular feature of the larger denominations. The United Church grouped its boards into divisions, while the Anglicans contrived to do away with their departmental structure altogether. The resurgence of regionalism in Canada was reflected in attempts to decentralize the process of decision-making. The weakness of most experiments in restructuring ecclesiastical bureaucracies was that those who proposed them thought mainly in terms of doing more effectively what the church was already doing rather than of examining critically the role of the church in an increasingly secular-ized Canada. Attention was focused on the latter problem largely by the discontent of ministers who were no longer certain of the relevance of their traditional functions but apprehensive at the prospect of becoming "mere cogs in a lifeless machine". A search for new avenues of service led to the foundation of the Canadian Council for Supervised Pastoral Education in 1965 and the Canadian Urban Training Project in 1966.

Vatican II

Roman Catholics were the last to undertake major reforms, but they soon outstripped all others. The impulse came mainly from the Second Vatican Council, which was convened in 1962 at the call of Pope John XXIII and held its final sessions in 1965 during the pontificate of Paul VI. The Canadian bishops, unlike their counterparts in most other countries, had met annually for consultation since 1943 in what came to be called the Canadian Catholic Conference. Thus accustomed to teamwork, they were able to press their ideas systematically through successive stages of debate. Canadians also accepted the decrees and general spirit of the council with an alacrity that was by no means universal in the United States. Even before the final session, the shape of the church in Canada was changing with a speed that startled Catholics and Protestants alike.

One result of Vatican II was to initiate a program of modernization similar to that which was already going on in most Protestant churches. *Aggiornamento* or "updating" was the term used by Pope John XXIII, and its progress was all the more dramatic because so much of it needed to be done. Celebration of mass in the vernacular was the aspect of modernization that was most immediately visible to the general public. Equally significant were other reforms of worship—greater participation by the people in hymns and responses, the downgrading of pious devotional practices that distracted individuals from common worship, and the adoption by priests of the basilican posture in which they faced the rest of the congregation across the altar. Christian education, which had been almost unaffected by modern pedagogical methods, began to take on a new look. Previous catechisms had been in a stilted question-and-answer form suitable for memorization. They were gradually replaced during the 1960s by a new series of textbooks in French and English that undertook to deal with questions actually asked by modern children. Clerical training now began to emphasize theological dialogue and to encourage awareness of secular academic disciplines as well as of other religions.[5]

"Collegiality" was one of the key words of the Vatican Council. Strictly speaking, it referred to the association of bishops, acting collectively as a "college" with the pope, in the government of the church. In practice, its popularity encouraged a great deal of consultation at all levels. The Canadian Catholic Conference, with a growing secretariat that included both priests and laymen, was able to make decisions that would previously have had to be referred to Rome. Bishops began to consult priests, and sometimes the laity, before making clerical appointments. Parish councils gave the laity a larger voice in local programs. Paternalism in missions overseas and among native peoples was given a further blow.

The Extension of Dialogue

As the churches turned their attention from expansion to reappraisal, their enthusiasm for ecumenicity began to revive. The preparation of new liturgies and curricula revealed unexpected areas of agreement, as well as a virtual identity in contemporary trends. Surveys of the constituency indicated that many Canadians chose their denominations almost at random and that comparatively few took their peculiar principles seriously.

The most exciting ecumenical development of the decade was the dramatic entry of the Roman Catholic Church into conversation with other communions after four centuries of controversy or silence. Insistence on submission to Rome as a condition of union had seemed to make Catholic participation in the ecumenical movement *a priori* impossible, and several popes had plainly said so. The council promulgated decrees on Ecumenism and on Other Religions that were couched in terms friendly to non-Catholics. Vatican II made such a difference, indeed, that it rendered obsolete all previous accounts of the ecumenical movement.

Whatever hesitations there might be in some other countries, most Canadians were ready to make up old religious quarrels. Joint worship services began in 1965. Groups for the discussion of outstanding issues met in some of the larger cities, but lost their glamour as informal contacts became more frequent. Soon one took for granted the presence of Catholic scholars in theological societies, of priests in ministerial associations, and of seminarians in the activities of the Ecumenical Institute. A sharp exchange in 1962 on the Ontario school issue showed that renewed friendship did not solve all problems, but such differences of opinion would increasingly be resolved by direct encounter and not made occasions for appeals to popular prejudice. Perhaps the most startling evidence of this trend was the institution in 1967 of joint counselling by Catholic priests and Protestant ministers of couples contemplating mixed marriages.[6]

Towards Church Union

The new ecumenical climate brought fresh encouragement to those who for many years had been trying to negotiate formal unions of churches. Those that actually took place in Canada during the 1960s were, in a sense, overflows from the United States. In 1967 the Canada district of the American Lutheran Church became the Evangelical Lutheran Church of Canada, and in the same year this body collaborated with the Lutheran Church of America to form the Lutheran Council in Canada. Another American union that would affect Canadians was proposed between the Methodists and the Evangelical United Brethren Church. The Western Canada conference [of the latter], which was extremely conservative in theology and evangelistic approach, arranged to remain separate while receiving aid from the American Methodists. The more liberal Canada conference in the east, which had begun to discuss union with the Canadian Wesleyans before Confederation, would become part of the United Church of Canada shortly after its centennial.

Conversations between the Anglican and United churches, after almost breaking down in 1958, were resumed in 1960 with new committees. Both churches felt a renewed sense of urgency, and a study guide entitled *Growth in Understanding* was widely circulated.

On June 1, 1965, after years of frustration and deadlock, the official committees were at last able to issue a statement of principles on which an organic union of the two churches might be based. The initial public response was favourable, and with scarcely a dissenting voice the Anglican general synod of 1965 accepted the *Principles* as a basis on which the details of union might be worked out.[7] The general council of the United Church in September 1966 approved the *Principles* in language that was intended to be as positive as the Anglican resolution of the previous year, but only after a vigorous debate during which amendments had been offered in bewildering variety.[8] By 1967 the process of refinement was under way and in 1969 the Christian Church (Disciples of Christ) joined the conversations. [Progress towards union, however, received a severe set-back in 1975 when the Anglican House of Bishops recommended a delay in proceedings. Eds.]

Meanwhile, churches were quietly beginning to do together many things they had previously done separately. In a number of new suburbs and industrial towns several denominations combined to erect buildings for common use. Roman Catholic and Protestant seminarians organized a national conference of theological students, under the aegis of the Ecumenical Institute, that attempted to be not only interdenominational but bilingual. In Newfoundland, where education had always followed strictly denominational lines, the Anglicans, the United Church, and the Salvation Army agreed to consolidate their educational facilities and organization. A broadly representative committee on the Church in Industrial Society laid plans for a congress in 1968.

Less visible to the general public than organized cooperation was an emerging pattern of informal consultation across denominational lines. Experts in Christian education or in family life discovered that they shared more concerns with their opposite numbers in other churches than with colleagues who specialized in different areas. The approach of the major churches to the mass media became practically a single operation, to the astonishment of more denominationally bound Americans. Workers in the inner city were brought together by common problems and by common complaints of indifference at headquarters. Theological teachers began to work out joint curricula.

Rebellion and Experiment

As if the astonishing developments of the early 1960s were not enough for church members to absorb, towards the middle of the decade the pace of change suddenly speeded up. The initiative in innovation, which up to this point had remained firmly in the hands of church leaders, passed to impatient and often younger critics. What had begun as an orderly process of reform began to look more like a revolution. The attack on complacency in the pew succeeded beyond the wildest dreams of those who had launched it. Young people, many of whom were sensitive to the apparent aimlessness of bourgeois society and aroused to indignation by the civil rights struggle in the United States, had no difficulty in believing that the church was irrelevant and inept. Even many older people confessed, when their opinions were sought, that they found little meaning in many aspects of the church's worship and program.

Criticism of the church in Quebec constituted a distinct chapter in the story of dissent, and clergy, religious, and laity vied to outdo each other in irreverence towards a hitherto sacrosanct institution. Frère Untel—Brother Anonymous to English readers—became a national figure overnight by poking fun at the religious orders who imposed their monastic inhibitions on the schoolchildren of the province.[9] Although promptly whisked off to France for further study, he returned as Brother Pierre-Jerôme Desbien to take a serious part in the reform of Quebec education. *Maintenant*, a Dominican magazine that had long taken a radical line, survived the brief removal of its editor and became more influential than ever. Students in the conservative classical colleges were reputed to be the most trenchant critics of the church, but they were closely rivalled by nuns.

On the more positive side, a wave of experimentation demonstrated that alternative methods and ideas were available to the church if it wished to adopt them. The chaotic state of Catholic liturgy in the wake of the Vatican Council made worship a particularly inviting field for innovation. Masses were invaded by electric guitars, singing nuns contributed to a new repertoire of folk hymns, and serious liturgists explored the use of new idioms of music and language. Protestants took up the

Catholic practice of addressing God as "you" and found that as a result they had to revamp their whole vocabulary of worship.

New Lines of Cleavage

Among all the churches there appeared a new line of fissure that bore little relation to traditional denominational and party differences, a good deal more to those of age and ecclesiastical status. Demands quickly followed for the more effective representation of groups that felt themselves to be deprived of power in the church—the laity generally, but especially women, youth, and ethnic minorities. Hierarchical and conciliar churches alike were pressed to institute participatory democracy.

Two main streams of influence affected theology in the 1960s. One, which might be called existential, dominated the thought of many Protestants. It made much of Dietrich Bonhoeffer's vision of a "religionless" Christianity in which man, freed by the gospel from the tyranny of idols of his own fashioning, would devote himself without embarrassment to the attainment of his own creaturely and therefore secular ends. Bonhoeffer's vision, which in some aspects recalled Nietzsche's assertion that man "come of age" had outgrown his need of supernatural aid, gave rise in turn to Harvey Cox's celebration of the secular city on the one hand and to various "death of God" theologies on the other. Another line of thought, which affected the pronouncements of the Vatican Council and profoundly influenced most progressive Catholics, was impatient of all distinctions between the sacred and the profane. It leaned heavily on A. N. Whitehead's "process" philosophy, Paul Tillich's definition of God as "the ground of all being", and the evolutionary theology of Teilhard de Chardin. The former position virtually eliminated the concept of the sacred, the latter that of the secular, but John Robinson attempted to combine the two in his *Honest to God* and his avid readers apparently sensed no incongruity. Whatever their divergences, both approaches at least made possible a view of the world as open to human initiative and innovation rather than as programmed in advance to a precise goal.

Varied Responses to Change

Change was greeted in some quarters with enthusiastic approval, in others with hostility and even shock, and in still others with scepticism or an almost complete lack of interest. The initiative for the overhaul of church structures that began about 1960 came almost entirely from the more highly educated and more socially mobile segments of the middle class. Much less enthusiasm for experiment was evident among farmers, blue-collar workers, and well-established business men.

In local congregations, where the church impinged most directly on the lives of its members, awareness of innovation varied greatly from denomination to denomination. Roman Catholics could not escape change. They participated each Sunday in a simplified and readily intelligible mass, absorbed the new ecumenical atmosphere, and gradually became accustomed to their new freedom to talk back. In Quebec, where the social structure had depended for stability on the absolutes of the Catholic faith, the novel spectacle of officially sponsored self-criticism induced what one pair of clerical dropouts described as a kind of *traumatisme national*.[10]

Conservative evangelicals were in some ways affected least of all, less even than they had been by the affluence of the 1950s. Attacks on constituted authority and deviations from conventional morality were to them symptoms of a society in full flight from the obedience it owed to God, while the advent of new theologies and the inauguration of dialogue with Rome were further proofs of the long-suspected apostasy of the conventional Protestant churches. If the conservative denominations changed their posture at all, it was in the direction of seeking not merely to rescue individuals from the damning effects of worldliness but to provide an alternate set of values for the nation. They began to show interest for the first time in serious projects of general education, especially at the secondary and university levels.

The Disestablishment of Religion

In English-speaking areas of Canada the unofficial establishment of Christianity had virtually come to an end by 1960, although it would take time for many people to adjust mentally to a situation in which churches were no longer moral policemen but pressure groups or even interest groups. Where further retreat was forced upon the church in these areas during the decade it was usually for financial rather than ideological reasons. Roman Catholics, who, outside Quebec, had moved seriously into the field of higher education only after the Second World War, were the first to admit that the price tag was too high. Both money and disagreements over policy were factors in persuading Maritime Baptists to relinquish control of Acadia University in 1966. Surviving church colleges depended increasingly on government support, and the institution of the Ontario Tax Foundation Plan in 1964 brought long-delayed relief to the hard-pressed Catholic schools of Ontario. The contribution of the churches to social welfare, although still considerable, could no longer be compared in scale with that of governments or of specialized secular agencies.

In Quebec, where despite secularizing trends the Catholic Church had maintained unimpaired its position in society, the accession in 1960 of the Lesage administration inaugurated a new era in the relations of church and state. One of the first acts of the new government was to institute a study of education. In 1963 and 1964 the [Parent] commission submitted reports that proposed sweeping changes in educational procedure and in teacher training. Its most daring proposal was for the establishment of a ministry of education, which the church had always opposed as an invasion of its prerogatives. An amended bill was passed unanimously by the legislature early in 1964. Another signal of change was the taxing of religious communities that engaged in business. Rural Quebec was not ready for secularization at such a pace, and the Union Nationale swept back to power in 1966. A process had begun, however, that would not readily be reversed. The influence of the church was a steadily diminishing factor in Quebec politics, and priests were rapidly being displaced from positions of power in normal schools, labour unions, and cooperatives.

By the 1960s ethnic "prejudices and antipathies" were stronger than ever, and even French-Canadian Protestants were urging that French should be recognized as the official language of Quebec.[11] Religion, by contrast, had ceased to be a serious factor in national disunity. French-Canadian nationalism in Quebec, although supported by many Catholics, was no longer in any sense a religious crusade. The churches, if one may judge by the submissions of the three largest of them to the Laurendeau-Dunton commission, were solidly on the side of bilingualism and biculturalism.[12]

Loss and Gain

Questioning and criticism weakened the convictions of many Christians and led others to reject their faith altogether. Membership failed to keep pace with growth in population, attendance at church and Sunday school declined, and money was steadily more difficult to raise. Recruiting for church work fell off sharply, except among conservative evangelicals, while ministers, priests, and religious deserted their posts in alarming numbers. Those who remained in the church were constantly reminded of their failings by critics both within and without. The church was no longer the keeper of the nation's conscience, and few Canadians seemed to regret its dethronement. On the other hand, it had become one of the places where the action was—especially if you were a Roman Catholic. There was gain as well as loss in the exchange. The church's former role as mentor and guide to the nation had inspired it to raise up statesmen and prophets, but it had also laden it with a heavy weight of institutional responsibility. Having shed most of its political power it could, if it would, concentrate on its primary task of offering good news to the people.

NOTES

1   J. S. Thomson, "The State of the Church Now—a Moderatorial Report", *The United Church Observer*, October 15, 1958.

2   *Proceedings of the 19th General Council of The United Church of Canada, 1960*, p. 183.

3   *Journal of Proceedings of the 22nd Session of the General Synod of The Anglican Church of Canada, 1965*, pp. 114-17. In accordance with regular procedure, the change took effect only after confirmation at the 23rd Session in 1967: *Journal* (1967), pp. 25-8.

4   The results were published in W. S. F. Pickering and J. L. Blanchard, *Taken for Granted: A Survey of the Parish Clergy of the Anglican Church of Canada* (Toronto: The General Synod, 1967).

5   See Elliott B. Allen, CSB, "The Roman Catholic Seminary: Changing Perspectives in Theological Education", *Canadian Journal of Theology* 14, No. 3 (July 1968): 159-68.

6   Edward L. Bader, "New Approaches to Interfaith Marriage: A Report", *The Ecumenist* 6, No. 5 (July-August 1968): 172-4.

7   *Journal of Proceedings of the 22nd Session of the General Synod of The Anglican Church of Canada, 1965*, p. 23.

8   *Record of Proceedings of the 22nd General Council of The United Church of Canada, 1966*, pp. 52, 54.

9   *Les Insolences de Frère Untel* (Montréal: Les Editions de l'Homme, 1960); translated into English as *The Impertinences of Brother Anonymous* (Montreal: Harvest House, 1962).

10   Charles Lambert and Roméo Bouchard, *Deux Prêtres en Colère* (Montréal: Editions du Jour, 1968), p. 8.

11   *Breaking the Barriers*, Report of the Board of Evangelism and Social Service of The United Church of Canada, 1964, p. 216.

12   For the Roman Catholic position, see Jean Hulliger, *l'Enseignement Social des Evêques Canadiens de 1891 à 1950*, p. 165. The Anglican brief is printed in full in the *Bulletin* of the Council for Social Service of the Anglican Church of Canada, No. 191 (June 1965). A manuscript of the United Church brief, submitted over the signature of Eugene A. Forsey, is at United Church House.

PART III

RELIGION IN
CONTEMPORARY LIFE

1.

People and Population

Religious Composition of the Canadian Population*

W.E. Kalbach
W.W. McVey

The early scattered settlements in the New World took on the cultural complexion of the immigrants' national origins. As would be expected, French settlements reflected the dominant influence of the Roman Catholic Church, while those communities established by immigrants from the British Isles were characteristically Protestant. In the latter case, the degree of religious homogeneity was probably much less than might appear on the surface in view of the many denominations to be found within the Protestant community. In any event, the religious balance depended upon the relative size of migrant streams coming from Protestant and Catholic areas in Europe and their patterns of settlement. Emphasis on Roman Catholic–Protestant dualism in Canada's history should obscure neither the high degree of religious homogeneity which existed in some areas nor the extent of diversity between areas.

Information on religious composition of early settlements in Canada is sketchy, but it can be presumed that during the period of French domination Roman Catholics were predominant. This is borne out by

*Appeared first as Chapter 7 in W. E. Kalbach and W. W. McVey, Jr., *The Demographic Bases of Canadian Society* (Toronto: McGraw-Hill Ryerson Ltd., 1971). Published here in revised and abridged form with the kind permission of the authors and the publisher.

the earliest detailed information resulting from the census of Lower
Canada in 1831, which indicated that three-fourths of the approximately
half-million inhabitants were Roman Catholic. As may be seen in Table
1, of the six other specific denominations reported, the next largest numbers were affiliated with the Church of England and the Church of
Scotland. Other censuses clearly indicate that Roman Catholics did not
enjoy this same degree of dominance in other areas of settlement. Further
west, in the Territory of Assiniboia, for example, a census of 460 family
heads in the two settlements of Red River and Grantown showed that
only a slight majority, or 57 per cent, were Roman Catholics.[1]

TABLE 1.   Population of Lower Canada by Religious
Denominations, 1831

DENOMINATION	NUMBER	PER CENT
Roman Catholic	412,717	74.6
Church of England	34,620	6.3
Church of Scotland	15,069	2.7
Presbyterian	7,810	1.4
Methodist	7,018	1.3
Baptist	2,461	0.4
Jewish	107	—
Other	5,577	1.0
Not given	67,755	12.3
TOTAL	553,134	100.0

SOURCE: *Census of Canada, 1870-71,* Vol. 4, Ottawa: 1876, Table III, p. 109.

While data are lacking for Upper Canada, the 1842 census suggests
that most of the several hundred thousand people in this area were non-
Catholic. Protestants were dominant in Nova Scotia as early as 1767,
when the census of that year reported 84.6 per cent Protestant.[2] A later
and more detailed census in 1827 revealed that Presbyterians constituted
the largest Protestant denomination with 30.4 per cent, followed by the
Church of England with 23.2 per cent, and Baptists with 16.0 per cent.
Methodists comprised 7.6 per cent of the population, while the Dissenters, with 3.6 per cent, outnumbered the Lutherans, with 2.4 per
cent.[3]

The first comprehensive reports on the religious character of the
population for both Upper and Lower Canada took place in the censuses
of 1842 and 1844 respectively. As these provide the earliest comparison

between the major areas of French and British settlement, the distributions are presented in Table 2. The contrast is striking, with Roman
Catholics comprising 82.1 per cent of the population of Lower Canada
in 1844, compared to just 13.4 per cent for Upper Canada in 1842. While
most of the major Protestant denominations were represented in Lower
Canada, their numbers were relatively small. For example, the second
largest denomination in Lower Canada, the Church of England, accounted for only 6.2 per cent, compared to 22.1 per cent in Upper
Canada, where they were the single largest denomination. The second
largest group in Upper Canada was the Church of Scotland, with 16.0
per cent. All Presbyterian churches combined amounted to 19.9 per cent,
compared to 17.0 per cent for all Methodist groups.

TABLE 2.   Population by Religious Denomination for Upper Canada, 1842,
and Lower Canada, 1844.

DENOMINATION	UPPER CANADA, 1842		LOWER CANADA, 1844	
	NUMBER	PER CENT	NUMBER	PER CENT
Baptist	16,411	3.4	4,063	0.6
Roman Catholic	65,203	13.4	572,439	82.1
Church of England	107,791	22.1	43,527	6.2
Congregational	4,253	0.9	3,906	0.6
Jewish	1,105	0.2	154	0.0*
Lutheran	4,524	0.9	101	0.0*
Methodist:				
British Wesleyan	23,342	4.8	10,797	1.6
Canadian	32,315	6.6	2,993	0.4
Episcopal	20,125	4.1	719	0.1
Other	7,141	1.5	1,315	0.2
Moravian	1,778	0.4	—	—
Presbyterian:				
Church of Scotland	77,929	16.0	26,702	3.8
Other Presbyterian	18,220	3.7	5,279	0.8
Dutch Reform	946	0.2	—	—
Quaker	5,200	1.1	—	—
Other Denominations	19,422	4.0	6,291	0.9
No response	81,348	16.7	18,798	2.7
TOTAL	487,053	100.0	697,084	100.0

Source: *Census of Canada, 1870-71,* Vol. 4, Ottawa: 1876, pp. 135 and 147.
*Less than 0.05 per cent.

Many of the early churches established in Canada maintained ties with their parent organizations in Europe but, as national consciousness began to emerge, efforts in the direction of national independence increased. S. D. Clark has argued that the movement towards union and autonomy, beginning as early as 1824 for the Methodists and culminating in the United Church of Canada in 1925, was part of a general movement towards national autonomy that characterized all forms of association.[4] However, Clark points out that movement towards union and autonomy which was evident among the larger denominations left many divisions and new sects in its wake.[5]

Analysis of religious organization in Canada using census data is difficult, at best, since it is not practical to identify all religious groups. An unfortunate consequence is the misleading impression of simplicity of structure presented by use of the major denominational categories since this obscures hundreds of smaller religious bodies. Not only is diversity hidden within the "other" category, but it is also hidden within the major categories. As late as 1942, *The Vital Statistics Instruction Manual* for Canada, containing instructions for coding religious affiliations stated on marriage, death, and birth certificates, listed forty-five types of Lutheran groups. While there is undoubtedly considerable overlap, differences are illustrated by such terms as American Lutheran, German Reform, Lutheran Evangelical, Zwinglian, and Zion Lutheran.[6]

Growth of Religious Denominations in Canada

The census of 1871, four years after Confederation, shows that 42.9 per cent of the population were Roman Catholics. For Quebec, the percentage was 85.7 per cent, or just slightly higher than for Lower Canada in 1844. Catholics were also proportionately more numerous in Ontario, with 17.1 per cent compared to 13.4 per cent in 1842. Methodists and Presbyterians were approximately equal in number for Canada as a whole; but in Ontario the Methodists were somewhat larger, the proportions being 28.8 and 22.2 per cent respectively.[7]

Between 1871 and 1901, the Catholic and Anglican proportions continued to decline. The former decreased slightly to 41.7 per cent and the latter to 12.8 per cent. On the other hand, Lutherans, Methodists, and other religious denominations increased in proportion.

Trends in size for the eight principal denominations in 1971 are presented in Figure 1 for the period 1901 to 1971. Anglicans increased at

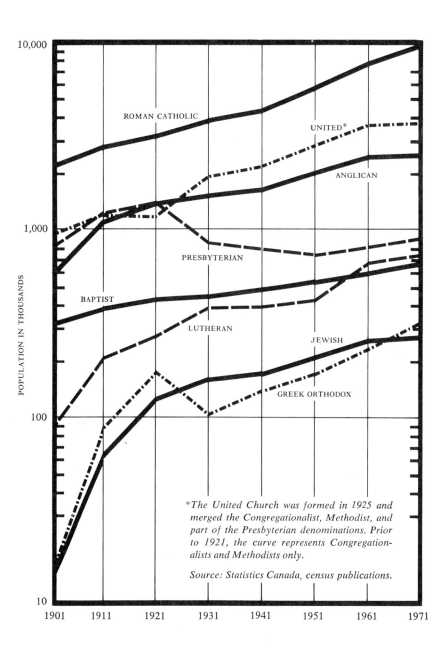

POPULATION IN THOUSANDS

10,000

ROMAN CATHOLIC

UNITED*

ANGLICAN

1,000

PRESBYTERIAN

BAPTIST

LUTHERAN

JEWISH

GREEK ORTHODOX

100

*The United Church was formed in 1925 and merged the Congregationalist, Methodist, and part of the Presbyterian denominations. Prior to 1921, the curve represents Congregationalists and Methodists only.

Source: Statistics Canada, census publications.

10

1901   1911   1921   1931   1941   1951   1961   1971

a more rapid rate than Catholics before 1921, and at a slower rate between 1921 and 1961. Not directly apparent from Figure 1 is the fact that in 1921, the proportion of Anglicans in the population reached its maximum of 16.1 per cent, while the proportion of Roman Catholics was at its minimum level of 38.7 per cent. After 1921 the Anglican rate of growth never again exceeded that of the Roman Catholic, and while they continued to increase in numbers, the numerical increase was not sufficient to prevent a decline in relative size. By 1971, Anglicans constituted only 11.8 per cent of the total, while Roman Catholics reached 46.2 per cent.

Erratic growth curves for Presbyterians and the United Church of Canada between 1921 and 1931 reflect the upheaval and aftermath of the merger of Methodists, Congregationalists, and part of the Presbyterian denominations. Whereas the growth rate for the United Church increased during each of the three decades subsequent to its inception, the number of Presbyterians declined until 1951, after which their numbers showed small increases. As would be expected, the proportion of Presbyterians declined sharply from 16.1 to 8.4 per cent as a result of the formation of the United Church, and thereafter their proportion continued to decline, reaching 4.0 per cent in 1971. Methodists and Congregationalists ceased to exist in any significant numbers, while the United Church increased from just over two million to three and three-quarter million in 1971. However, their proportion of the total population increased only perceptibly, from 19.5 per cent in 1931 to 20.5 per cent in 1951, before declining throughout the subsequent twenty-year period, reaching 17.5 per cent in 1971.

That segment of the population claiming Judaic affiliation reached 1.0 per cent of the total in 1911. By 1931, the Jewish proportion reached 1.5 per cent, where it stayed until 1951. Subsequently, Jewish growth rate has fallen below that for Canada as a whole, and the proportion has declined, reaching 1.3 per cent in 1971. Since the Jews are a highly urbanized and educated population, and as such have the low fertility associated with these characteristics, their continued growth has been maintained primarily through immigration.

The Baptists were the sixth largest denomination in Canada in 1971. However, since their rate of growth has been continually below that for all denominations combined, the proportion who were Baptists has steadily declined, from 5.9 per cent in 1901 to 3.1 per cent in 1971. The drop in numbers between 1921 and 1931 for Greek Orthodox, shown in

Figure 1, has no sociological relevance, as it is simply a consequence of having removed approximately 187,000 Ukrainian (Greek) Catholics in the latter year from the category which had previously included both groups. Since 1951, its growth has been sufficiently strong to exceed the national average, and increase its proportionate share from 1.2 to 1.5 per cent.

Minor Religious Denominations

A number of smaller religious groups have been visible in Canadian census data for close to one hundred years, but most made their statistical debut at the beginning of the twentieth century during large-scale European immigration. However, as early as the 1871 census, 6,202 Adventists, 539 Mormons, 2,289 Unitarians, and 62,874 members of other miscellaneous denominations were enumerated. Two other groups increased to the point where separate recognition was given in the published census reports prior to 1901. In 1881, Churches of Christ, Disciples, accounted for 20,253 persons, and in 1891, members of the Salvation Army were separated from the "other" category and 14,131 were listed.

The 1971 census revealed other changes which perhaps have significance beyond that of fortuitous omission or inclusion. The Hutterites, for example, were reported separately for the first time, numbering 13,650, compared to the 168,150 Mennonites with whom they had previously shared census billing. The Christian Reformed Church, with some 83,400 persons and showing a 34 per cent increase over the decade, was also considered sufficiently important, along with the Church of the Nazarene, to be included in the historical summary table of the 1971 census publication dealing with religious denominations. Nothing, however, quite matched the spectacular increase of 157 per cent recorded by the Jehovah's Witnesses during the last intercensal decade.

Small denominational populations are especially susceptible to demographic processes as well as to social, economic, and political events. Any decline in numbers, not matched by new conversions, can prove fatal to small groups.

The fact that unusually large numbers reported themselves as having no religion at the time of the 1971 census requires some comment. While those doing so have been increasing since 1941, the phenomenal increase

TABLE 3. Adherents of Specified Smaller Religious Denominations, Canada, 1901–1971

DENOMINATION	1901	1911	1921	1931	1941	1951	1961	1971
Adventist	8,092	10,462	14,200	16,058	18,485	21,398	25,999	28,585
Brethren in Christ	—	—	—	—	—	—	16,256	21,380
Buddhist	10,531	10,072	11,316	15,921	15,676	8,184	11,611	16,175
Christian & Missionary Alliance	—	128	283	3,560	4,214	6,396	18,006	23,630
Christian Reformed	—	—	—	—	—	—	62,257	83,385
Christian Science	2,644	5,099	13,856	18,499	20,261	20,795	19,466	—
Churches of Christ, Disciples	17,250	14,610	13,125	15,831	21,260	14,920	19,512	16,405
Church of the Nazarene	—	—	—	—	—	—	13,412	13,590
Confucian	5,171	14,652	27,185	24,253	22,282	5,791	5,089	2,165
Doukhobor	8,858	10,616	12,674	14,978	16,878	13,175	13,234	9,165
Evangelical United Brethren	—	—	—	—	—	—	27,079	—
Free Methodist Church	—	—	—	7,740	8,805	8,921	14,245	19,245
Hutterite	—	—	—	—	—	—	—	13,650
Jehovah's Witnesses	101	938	6,689	13,582	7,007	34,596	68,018	174,805
Mennonite[a]	31,949	44,972	58,874	88,837	111,554	125,938	152,452	168,150
Mormon	7,061	16,115	19,657	22,041	25,328	32,888	50,016	66,635
Pentecostal	—	515	7,012	26,349	57,742	95,131	143,877	220,390
Plymouth Brethren	—	—	—	—	—	—	12,326	5,300
Salvation Army	10,360	18,909	24,771	30,773	33,609	70,275	92,054	119,665
Ukrainian (Greek) Catholic	[b]	[b]	[b]	186,879[c]	185,948[c]	191,051[c]	189,653[c]	227,730[c]
Unitarian	2,032	3,275	4,943	4,453	5,584	3,517	15,062	21,000
No religion	6,193	26,893	21,819	21,155	19,161	59,679	94,763	929,575

Source: *Censuses of Canada, 1951, 1961,* and *1971.*
a Includes Hutterite except in 1971.
b "Greek Catholic" and "Greek Orthodox" combined under "Greek Church".
c Includes "Other Greek Catholic".
—Dashes indicate data not published.

for the 1961–71 decade possibly reflects, in part, significant changes in the enumeration procedures. Unlike the 1961 census, the self-enumeration procedures used in urban areas in 1971 listed "no religion" on the census schedules as one of the thirteen specific choices open to the respondent. In addition, the absence of interviewers in the urban areas could have made it easier for urban residents to give what might ordinarily be considered to be a socially unacceptable answer. Whatever other factors were involved, the changes in procedures would make direct comparisons between the 1961 and 1971 figures inadvisable.

Regional Distribution

If the various religious denominations were evenly distributed throughout Canada, each province would have the same proportion as in the total population. Thus the larger provinces, by virtue of their larger size, would tend to have more of each denomination than the smaller ones. But the important question here is to what extent specific religious denominations tend to be over- or under-represented in each of the provinces relative to their proportion of the national total. Given that religion is an important dimension of ethnicity for most groups in Canada, it is not surprising that many religious denominations have regional patterns similar to those for ethnic populations (Table 4).

The most obvious concentration in 1971 is the Roman Catholics in Quebec, who account for about 52 per cent of all Catholics in Canada and who constitute 87 per cent of that province's population, compared to 46 per cent for the country as a whole. Another 26 per cent were living in Ontario in 1971, but this represented only 33 per cent of that province's population. The only other area with an over-representation of Roman Catholics was New Brunswick, where they comprised 52 per cent of the total. Members of Greek Orthodox and Ukrainian Catholic Churches were heavily concentrated in the Prairies, with the former located more in Saskatchewan and Alberta and the latter more in Manitoba and Saskatchewan.

Anglicans, relative to provincial populations, had their highest concentrations in the Northwest Territories, the Yukon, Newfoundland, and British Columbia. Anglicans constituted about 16 per cent of Ontario's population, compared to 12 per cent for Canada. The highest relative concentrations of United Church people were in the West, especially Saskatchewan, Alberta, and Manitoba. Presbyterians who did not join

TABLE 4. Percentage Distribution of the Population by Religious Denominations for Provinces, 1971

DENOMINATION	Can.	Nfld.	P.E.I.	N.S.	N.B.	Que.	Ont.	Man.	Sask.	Alta.	B.C.	Yuk.	N.W.T.
Adventist	0.1	0.1	0.1	0.2	0.1	—	0.1	0.1	0.2	0.3	0.3	0.1	—
Anglican	11.8	27.7	6.2	17.2	10.9	3.0	15.8	12.4	9.4	10.5	17.7	25.3	36.4
Baptist	3.1	0.2	5.7	12.7	14.0	0.6	3.7	1.9	1.6	3.1	3.0	4.8	1.1
Brethren in Christ	0.1	0.1	0.2	—	—	—	0.2	—	0.1	0.1	0.1	—	—
Buddhist	0.1	—	—	—	—	—	0.1	0.1	—	0.1	0.3	0.1	—
Christian & Missionary Alliance	0.1	—	—	—	—	—	0.1	0.1	0.5	0.3	0.3	—	0.1
Christian Reformed	0.4	—	0.2	0.1	—	—	0.7	0.2	—	0.8	0.5	0.1	0.1
Churches of Christ, Disciples	0.1	—	0.8	0.1	0.1	—	0.1	0.1	0.2	0.1	0.1	0.1	0.1
Church of the Nazarene	0.1	—	0.5	0.1	0.1	—	0.1	—	0.1	0.2	0.1	0.2	0.1
Confucian	—	—	—	—	—	—	—	—	—	—	—	0.1	—
Doukhobor	—	—	—	—	—	—	—	—	0.2	—	0.3	—	—
Free Methodist	0.1	—	—	—	—	—	0.2	0.1	0.1	0.1	0.1	0.1	—
Greek Orthodox	1.5	—	—	0.2	0.1	1.0	1.7	2.6	2.9	2.9	0.9	0.9	0.5
Hutterite	0.1	—	—	—	—	—	—	0.5	0.2	0.4	—	—	—
Jehovah's Witnesses	0.8	0.4	0.4	0.6	0.4	0.3	0.9	0.9	1.1	1.1	1.9	3.2	1.5

Religion												
Jewish	1.3	—	0.3	0.1	1.8	1.6	1.9	0.2	0.4	0.4	0.1	0.1
Lutheran	3.3	0.1	1.5	0.3	0.4	3.5	6.6	9.8	8.2	5.5	5.0	2.1
Mennonite	0.8	—	—	—	—	0.5	6.0	2.8	0.9	1.2	0.3	0.1
Mormon	0.3	0.1	0.1	—	—	0.2	0.1	0.3	1.9	0.6	0.4	0.3
Pentecostal	1.0	5.5	0.9	2.7	0.1	1.0	1.0	1.3	1.4	1.6	1.1	2.0
Plymouth Brethren	—	—	—	—	—	—	—	—	—	0.1	—	—
Presbyterian	4.0	0.6	5.1	2.1	0.9	7.0	3.1	2.2	3.5	4.6	3.8	1.3
Roman Catholic	46.2	36.6	36.3	52.2	86.7	33.3	24.6	27.9	24.0	18.7	25.4	41.3
Salvation Army	0.6	7.9	0.6	0.3	0.1	0.6	0.3	0.4	0.3	0.5	0.2	0.1
Ukrainian Catholic	1.1	—	0.1	0.1	0.4	0.7	5.8	3.7	2.5	0.5	0.5	0.3
Unitarian	0.1	—	—	0.1	—	0.1	0.1	0.1	0.1	0.2	0.2	0.1
United Church	17.5	19.5	20.6	13.4	2.9	21.8	26.0	29.6	28.1	24.6	16.9	8.6
Others	1.2	0.8	0.7	0.8	0.3	1.4	1.1	1.3	2.0	2.6	2.5	0.8
No Religion	4.3	0.4	2.4	1.9	1.3	4.5	4.3	3.7	6.7	13.1	8.8	2.9
TOTAL	100.0	100.0	100.0	100.0	100.0	100.0	100.0	100.0	100.0	100.0	100.0	100.0

Source: Statistics Canada, *1971 Census of Canada*, Bul.1.3-3, Table 11.
—Dashes indicate less than 0.05.

in forming the United Church were most heavily concentrated in Prince Edward Island and to a considerably lesser extent in Ontario.

Lutherans were found primarily west of Ontario and in the Yukon, while Baptists were more concentrated in the Atlantic Provinces. Among other lesser Protestant denominations there were considerable variations in distribution. The Salvation Army was most highly concentrated in Newfoundland, where they comprised 8 per cent of the population compared to 0.6 per cent for Canada as a whole. Others, like the Churches of Christ, Disciples, were situated mostly in both the Maritimes and the western Prairie provinces. Pentecostals had their heaviest concentration in Newfoundland, followed by New Brunswick, Northwest Territories, and British Columbia. Other smaller groups were located primarily in the West, for example, Adventists, Christian Scientists, Doukhobors, Jehovah's Witnesses, Mennonites, and Mormons.

Of the non-Christian denominations, the Jews had their highest relative concentrations in Manitoba, Quebec, and Ontario respectively. Oriental religions, such as Confucian and Buddhist, were primarily found in Alberta and British Columbia, with lesser concentrations in Ontario, Manitoba, and the Yukon.

Rural-Urban Distributions

Generally, regional settlement patterns appear to be closely associated with the degree of urbanization experienced by specific denominations, with those settling primarily in the Prairies and the Maritimes being less urbanized than the population as a whole. The Jews were almost completely urban, with 99 per cent living in urban areas in 1971. Presbyterians, Anglicans, Greek Orthodox, and Roman Catholics were urban above the average for the country as a whole (76 per cent), although both the Anglicans and Roman Catholics, each with 78 per cent in urban areas, were only slightly above the national ratio. The United Church, Lutherans, and Baptists all fell below the average, with 72, 72, and 68 per cent respectively.

Of the denominations shown in Table 5, only the Buddhists and Confucians, in addition to the five already mentioned above, had urban proportions higher than those for the country as a whole. In addition, 81 per cent of those indicating that they had no religion resided in urban places.

Data in Table 5 show that, with the exception of Roman Catholics,

TABLE 5. Rank Order of Population by Urban Percentage for Religious Denominations, Showing Distribution by Urban Size Groups and Types of Rural Areas, Canada, 1971

DENOMINATION	RANK ORDER	TOTAL	URBAN TOTAL	100,000 and over	30,000 to 99,999	10,000 to 29,999	Under 10,000	RURAL NON-FARM	RURAL FARM
Jewish	1	100.0	99.2	95.7	1.7	0.9	0.8	0.6	0.2
Buddhist & Confucian	2	100.0	89.0	72.3	8.5	3.1	5.1	7.0	4.0
Greek Orthodox	3	100.0	85.9	73.9	3.5	3.5	5.0	6.3	7.8
No Religion	4	100.0	80.7	59.9	6.1	7.0	7.6	14.9	4.4
Presbyterian	5	100.0	79.6	49.6	9.3	10.1	10.6	14.3	6.1
Anglican	6.5	100.0	77.9	49.4	8.8	8.5	11.2	18.5	3.6
Roman Catholic	6.5	100.0	77.9	47.2	10.3	8.2	12.2	16.6	5.5
Other	8	100.0	74.9	51.8	6.8	7.1	9.3	17.1	8.0
Jehovah's Witnesses	9	100.0	74.3	49.9	6.9	7.9	9.7	19.3	6.4
Mormon	10	100.0	73.8	37.9	11.3	7.8	16.7	16.0	10.2
Salvation Army	11	100.0	73.7	31.4	11.1	10.1	21.0	24.6	1.7
Christian & Missionary Alliance	12	100.0	73.2	39.5	7.8	14.9	11.0	14.4	12.4
Ukrainian Catholic	13	100.0	73.0	55.2	4.8	5.0	8.1	11.9	15.1
Lutheran	14	100.0	72.4	48.6	5.4	8.0	10.3	15.9	11.8
United Church	15	100.0	71.7	41.7	8.4	8.6	12.9	19.3	9.0
Baptist	16	100.0	68.5	36.6	11.0	8.4	12.5	25.0	6.5
Penetcostal	17	100.0	63.5	31.0	8.3	7.8	16.3	29.2	7.4
Churches of Christ, Disciples	18	100.0	63.2	31.2	8.0	12.2	11.8	26.6	10.2
Adventist	19	100.0	61.3	40.4	6.9	5.4	8.5	25.0	13.8
Christian Reformed	20	100.0	57.4	30.4	8.7	9.6	8.8	18.7	23.9
Mennonite	21	100.0	47.2	26.5	1.6	6.5	12.6	22.9	29.8
Hutterite	22	100.0	4.9	3.5	0.4	0.4	0.7	4.7	90.5
TOTAL		100.0	76.2	47.5	9.0	8.1	11.6	17.2	6.6

Source: Statistics Canada, *1971 Census of Canada*, Bul.1.3-3, Table 11.

those denominations with above-average proportions residing in urban areas tended to have disproportionately greater numbers living in the larger urban areas of 100,000 population and over. Roman Catholics exceeded the average for Canada because of slightly larger proportions residing in urban places under 100,000 population. By way of contrast, Adventists, Christian Reformed, Mennonites, Hutterites, and Ukrainian Catholics have more than double the national average living on rural farms. Pentecostals tend to be concentrated in the rural non-farm category and in smaller urban areas under 10,000, while the Salvation Army and Baptists tend to be concentrated in rural non-farm and urban places up to 100,000 in population.

Factors Affecting Changes in Religious Composition

Each religious denomination is made up of native- and foreign-born components that vary in age-sex structure. For the native born, probably the most important factor affecting their size is natural increase and ability to retain children within their denomination. For the foreign born, growth is assured only if the number of net migrants exceeds the numbers dying plus those dropping out of the church. The absence of reliable data concerning conversion prevents analysis of its significance. Marriage patterns tend to support the existing religious structure. As recently as in 1967, approximately two-thirds of all couples married were of the same denomination.[8] However, other studies have pointed to an increase in interfaith marriages between Protestants, Catholics, and Jews since 1921.[9]

Immigration

Data presented in Table 6 show the number and percentage of foreign born for the major religious denominations for each of the decennial censuses since 1951. All groups, except Ukrainian Catholics, increased their numbers between 1951 and 1961, when heavy immigration exceeded the combined effects of mortality and emigration. However, the gains in foreign born were sufficient only in four of the major denominations to exceed the native-born growth rate and produce an increase in their proportion of the total. Percentage increases during the decade 1951–61 were highest for Roman Catholics, Greek Orthodox, and Lutherans.

During the decade 1961–71, the numbers of Anglicans, Jewish,

TABLE 6. Number and Percentage of Foreign Born for Major Religious Denominations, Canada: 1951, 1961, and 1971

DENOMINATION	1951 TOTAL	1951 FOREIGN BORN NUMBER	1951 PER CENT	1961 TOTAL	1961 FOREIGN BORN NUMBER	1961 PER CENT	1971 TOTAL	1971 FOREIGN BORN NUMBER	1971 PER CENT
Anglican	2,060,720	487,400	23.6	2,409,068	510,980	21.2	2,543,175	469,075	18.4
Baptist	519,585	62,372	12.0	593,553	69,274	11.7	667,240	75,440	11.3
Greek Orthodox	172,271	70,209	40.8	239,766	111,629	46.6	316,605	155,950	49.3
Jewish	204,836	91,096	44.5	254,368	104,636	41.1	276,025	104,230	37.8
Lutheran	444,923	164,696	37.0	662,744	272,848	41.2	715,745	245,650	34.3
Presbyterian	781,747	184,886	23.6	818,558	193,932	23.7	872,330	202,915	23.3
Roman Catholic	6,069,496	434,289	7.2	8,342,826	886,111	10.6	9,974,890	1,178,540	11.8
Ukrainian Catholic*	191,051	74,386	38.9	189,653	63,951	33.7	227,730	58,645	25.8
United Church	2,867,271	332,962	11.6	3,664,008	381,436	10.4	3,768,800	305,820	8.1
All others	697,529	157,615	22.6	1,063,703	249,466	23.5	2,205,770	499,270	22.6
Totals	14,009,429	2,059,911	14.7	18,238,247	2,844,263	15.6	21,568,310	3,295,535	15.2

Source: Statistics Canada, *1971 Census of Canada*, Bul.1.4-12, Tbl. 33; and W. E. Kalbach, *The Impact of Immigration on Canada's Population*, Ottawa: The Queen's Printer, 1970, Table 2.17.

*Includes Greek Catholic.

Lutheran, and United Church foreign born actually declined, while the increase in numbers for Baptists and Presbyterians was not sufficient to increase their proportions of foreign born. Of the major denominations shown, only the Greek Orthodox and the Roman Catholics continued to show relative increases as a result of continuing immigration. The proportion of foreign born belonging to all Catholic denominations combined increased from 28 to 42 per cent during the twenty years following the 1951 census. Clearly, immigration during the 1950s and 1960s favoured the Catholic denominations.

Natural Increase

There are few data to test any hypothesis as to the existence of significant religious differentials in age-sex specific mortality. However, unless the differences are considerable, the important factor is the age-sex structure. An older population will produce more deaths relative to births than a young population, so that certain denominations with many members beyond the child-bearing ages will tend to have lower rates of increase than others with young populations. Thus, the age structure can provide evidence as to the relative balance between births and deaths, and the growth potential. High fertility levels tend to produce high proportions of the population under fifteen years of age, and relatively small numbers sixty-five years and over. Conversely, those denominations with low fertility will have larger proportions in the older age groups.

In the case of religious populations, a person may join through conversion or sever his affiliation, or the membership may change drastically through reorganization, as was the case in the establishment of the United Church. The Presbyterians who did not join the new church were undoubtedly many of the older members who would not make the change. The unusually large proportion of Presbyterians who are sixty-five years of age and over cannot be explained in terms of low fertility alone. The Jewish population, which had a smaller proportion under fifteen years of age, also had a lower proportion sixty-five years and over.

The effects of varying levels of fertility and mortality on a population's age and sex structure may be seen by examining the population pyramids in Figure 2. The size of the age group under five years in ratio to the number of women in the child-bearing years fifteen to forty-four provides an estimate of effective fertility. It is apparent from Figure 2, as well as from Table 7, that the Hutterites in 1971 were by far the most

FIGURE 2 Age and Sex Composition, Selected Religious Denominations, Canada: 1971

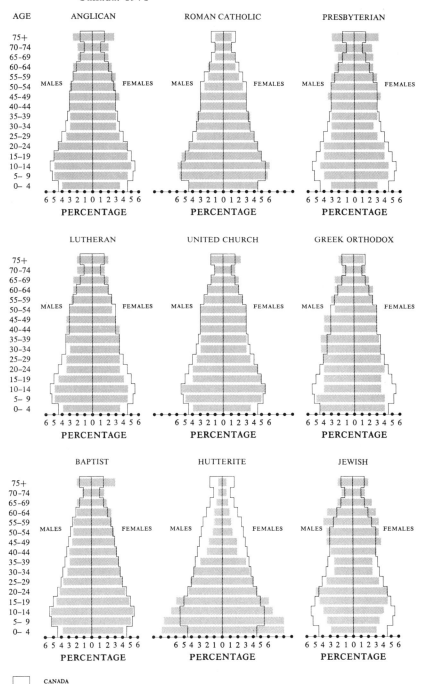

fertile. The Salvation Army, Mennonites, Mormons, and Pentecostals also had high fertility populations, and all but the latter have exceeded the Roman Catholic child-woman ratios since 1951. It is equally apparent from these data that the Jewish, and the Presbyterians, among others, have low fertility profiles. Furthermore, in the case of the Jews, both in 1961 and 1971, and in most of the denominations since 1961, the declining proportions in the five-year age groups under fifteen years reflect the general decline in fertility. However, there are other factors which can produce a similar effect, for example, young families with small children may cease to identify themselves with any religious denomination. Many of those reporting themselves as having no religion in 1971 had rather high child-woman ratios.

TABLE 7.   Number of Children 0-4 Years of Age per 1,000 Women 15-44 Years of Age, by Religious Denomination for Canada, 1951, 1961, and 1971

DENOMINATION	1951	1961	1971
Hutterite	—	—	745
Salvation Army	696	696	493
Pentecostal	583	652	469
Mennonite	581	712	467
Mormon	638	713	439
Roman Catholic	616	666	403
Greek Orthodox	383	426	396
Churches of Christ, Disciples	509	564	382
Baptist	510	565	372
United Church of Canada	529	574	358
Anglican Church of Canada	525	533	358
Adventist	466	531	349
Ukrainian (Greek) Catholic	415	501	349
Lutheran	440	533	343
Presbyterian	441	487	322
Confucian and Buddhist	375	557	304
Jewish	444	421	292
Christian Science	341	365	—
TOTAL	555	606	390

Source: Dominion Bureau of Statistics, *1961 Census of Canada*, Bul.7.1-11, Table IX; and, Statistics Canada, *1971 Census of Canada*, Bul.1.4-4, Table 7.
—Dash indicates data not available.

Inferences as to the relative fertility levels for the various denominations, illustrated in Figure 2, are consistent with, and supported by, the child-woman ratios in Table 7. Interestingly, all groups but the Jews showed increasing fertility between 1951 and 1961, and every group, with the possible exception of the Hutterites, showed the effects of the significant fertility decline of the 1960s. Here too, perhaps, is the clue to the decline of the Christian Scientists. Their child-woman ratio was the lowest in both 1951 and 1961, and, like other groups with low ratios, they had a high proportion of their population over forty-five years of age. In fact, they had the highest proportion of older persons of any denomination in 1961. In 1971, four of the denominations with the lowest child-woman ratios had the largest proportions forty-five years of age and over, ranging from 32 to 39 per cent of their total populations.

Roman Catholics, like the French-origin population, of which they constitute the major share, have depended heavily on natural increase for continued growth. The small part played by immigration is reflected both in the fact that only 12 per cent of Roman Catholics were foreign born in 1971, and in the fact that the proportion of foreign born among Ukrainian Catholics had declined from 39 per cent in 1951 to 26 per cent in 1971. More surprising, perhaps, is the extent to which Mormons, Mennonites, and the Salvation Army have appeared to rely on high fertility to maintain their numbers. Barring other attenuating factors, these denominations can be expected to increase their proportionate share through fertility at a faster rate than other denominations. The overall effect on the balance between Catholic and other denominations will be rather insignificant, as these high fertility groups are relatively small. The proportion of Catholics among the native born has remained relatively constant since 1951, when it was 49 per cent, compared to 50 per cent in both 1961 and 1971. The trend in the foreign-born population has been towards an increasing proportion of Catholics, with the proportion of Catholics among the foreign born increasing rapidly between 1951 and 1971, from 28 to 42 per cent. Given a continuation of these trends, Canada may well have a Catholic majority by the time of the 1981 census.

NOTES

1 *Census of Canada, 1870-71*, Vol. 4 (Ottawa, 1876), "Census of Assiniboia, 1831, Table III", p. 105.
2 *Ibid.*, Table II.
3 *Ibid.*, p. 94.
4 S. D. Clark, *The Developing Canadian Community* (Toronto: University of Toronto Press, 1962), pp. 115-17.

5 Clark presents a very interesting analysis of the efforts to achieve unity among the major denominations and the emergence of religious sects as a concomitant of success in achieving union, autonomy, and social status. See his discussion in *The Developing Canadian Community*, pp. 117-30.
6 By way of further illustration, the

general Presbyterian category had 23 identifiable groups, including Calvinists, Burning Bush, MacDonaldites, etc. The general residual category "Other" included 124 different entries among which were such groups as the Amana Society, Anglo-Israelites, Druids, Evening Lights, Johannites, Rosicrucians, Round Church, and Theosophists.

7   Dominion Bureau of Statistics, *1961 Census of Canada*, Bul.7.1-11, Table 1.

8   Dominion Bureau of Statistics, *Vital Statistics, 1967*, Table M7.

9   D. M. Heer, "The Trend of Interfaith Marriages in Canada: 1922-1957", *American Sociological Review* 27, No. 2 (April, 1962): 245-50.

Major Correlates
of Churchgoing in Canada*

Hans Mol

National church attendance data in Canada have been either not available or not thoroughly analysed. This paper attempts to close the gap
through the secondary analysis of data from a major national study. The
theoretical frame of reference for the interpretation of these data is the
"identity" theory of religion in which it is assumed that religion sacralizes
identity and that objectification, commitment, ritual, and myth are the
mechanisms of this sacralization process (Mol 1974).

The available church attendance figures either are confined to specific
localities or regions or are restricted to one denomination. If they are
national, they do not provide crucial cross-tabulations (Dawson and
Younge 1940: 221; Dumont and Fortin 1960: 501; Crysdale 1965: 103;
MacRae 1969: 148, 167; Hiller 1972: 155). Donald R. Whyte (1968:
578-9), using answers from a January 1960 Gallup Poll, mentions that
55.7 per cent of the Canadian population attended church or synagogue
regularly (61.9 per cent rural farm; 50.5 rural non-farm; 55.6 urban).
He points to regional differences: 58.0 per cent in the Atlantic region,
79.6 per cent in Quebec, 49.4 per cent in Ontario, 44.7 per cent in the
Prairie region, and 30.1 per cent in British Columbia did attend church

*Prepared for this volume.

or synagogue regularly. The problem with the earlier studies is that the samples are generally unrepresentative, and the problem with the 1968 study is that denominational differences are hidden behind the regional figures. The absence of denominational breakdown is also a deficiency of the recent Gallup reports. Yet these have the advantage of being comparable with the national figures of 1956, 1965, 1970, and 1974. The question addressed to a representative sample of Canadian adults was: "Did you yourself happen to go to church (or synagogue) in the last seven days?" In 1956, 61 per cent said that they did go, in 1965 55 per cent, in 1970 44 per cent, and in 1974 39 per cent, showing a severe drop of 22 percentage points over the past 18 years.

Most of the disadvantages of these previous studies and reports can be overcome through a secondary analysis of the very detailed and comprehensive 1965 Canadian National Election Study. (The data used in this paper were made available by the inter-university consortium for political research. They were originally collected by Philip Converse, John Meisel, Maurice Pinard, Peter Regenstreif, and Mildred Schwartz. Neither the original collectors of the data nor the consortium bear any responsibility for the analyses or interpretations presented here.) Individuals interviewed in this study form a stratified, cross-sectional, probability sample of the Canadian population eligible to vote in 1965. The sample of 2118 Canadians is analysed by denomination and by church attendance (with those who go at least twice a month—usually weekly —grouped together as "regular" and those who go never, or a few times a year, or at best once a month, as "irregular"). These variables in turn have been cross-tabulated by sex, age, education, income, occupation, size of community, and preferred political party.

Denomination

In 1965 one-half the Canadian population (50.2 per cent) reported that they went to church regularly (at least twice a month—usually weekly). The other half (49.8 per cent) went irregularly, if at all. Yet this information tells us little, as it could be the reflection of a dominant characteristic of one large denomination or of regional populations. As Table 1 shows, Protestants are much less likely to be regular attenders than Catholics, and English-speaking Catholics in turn are less regular than French-speaking ones.

TABLE 1. Percentage of Church Attendance by Denomination, 1965

CHURCH ATTENDANCE	PRESBY- TERIAN	UNITED	ANG- LICAN	ENG- LISH CATHO- LIC	FRENCH CATHO- LIC	OTHER	TOTAL
Regular	24.3	22.7	19.2	68.9	87.8	33.8	50.2
Irregular	75.7	77.3	80.8	31.1	12.2	66.2	49.8
TOTALS	100.	100.	100.	100.	100.	100.	100.
NUMBERS	(103)	(474)	(245)	(283)	(619)	(331)	(2055)

How do these figures compare with church attendance records in other countries? Few Catholic nations in the world have as high church attendance as French Canada. It is interesting that the only nation with higher church attendance, Ireland (Ward 1972: 297-8), like French Canada, has a history of close alliance between the Catholic Church and a national identity threatened or felt to be threatened by a Protestant English overlord.

Church attendance by English-speaking Catholics in Canada is comparable to that in countries where Catholics are, or were, in the minority and where Catholic identity could not be taken for granted and had to be defended. Attendance by Catholics in such countries as Australia (Mol 1971: 14), England (Martin 1972: 232), Netherlands (Laeyendecker 1972: 335), New Zealand (Mol 1972: 371), South Africa (Higgins 1972: 449), and the U.S.A. (Lazerwitz 1964: 430; Alston 1971: 234) was in the second half of the sixties generally in the neighbourhood of 60 to 70 per cent. By contrast, church attendance by Catholics in such traditionally Catholic countries as France (Isambert 1972: 180), Italy (Acquaviva 1972: 308), Portugal (Querido 1972: 428), and Spain (Almerich 1972: 469 ff.) was much lower and appears to be much more strongly determined by internal divisions, such as class levels.

Attendance among Protestants in Canada also fits an international pattern. Other things remaining the same, it is everywhere much lower than Catholic attendance. Protestant individualism seems to reduce the hold of the institutional church, as compared with Catholic collectivism. Yet, as with Catholics, attendance rises where identity is heightened because of minority status. In Lutheran countries such as Denmark (Thorgaard 1972: 136), Finland (Seppanen 1972: 155), Norway (Vogt 1972: 393), and Sweden (Gustafsson 1972: 487), average church attendance is below 5 per cent of the population. Attendance among Anglicans in England is also in this range. But wherever Protestant sects in any part of the world have a strong identity in what they regard as an essentially hostile camp, church attendance is high. In Canada the dominantly middle- or upper-class denominations, such as Presbyterian, United, Anglican fit neither of these two patterns. The middle classes uphold the status quo rather than defend a radical position, as the sects do. Yet their churches have to compete with other organizations and systems of meaning, in contrast with the state churches of say, Scandinavia. Thus, attendance among Protestants in Canada, like that among Protestants in the U.S.A., Australia, and New Zealand, is relatively strong because of their competitive position and in spite of their high status.

Sex

The Canadian population is not different from those in other Western industrialized nations in that more women than men attend church. Of the men in the sample whose church-going habits were recorded, 44.8 per cent proved to be regular, compared with 55.2 per cent of women. As Table 2 shows, this observation is true for all denominations. (In order to keep the cells reasonably large, Presbyterians were included in "Others" in all tables in which more than two variables appear.)

TABLE 2.   Percentages of Regular Church Attenders by Denomination and Sex

	UNITED	ANGLICAN	ENGLISH CATHOLIC	FRENCH CATHOLIC	OTHERS
Males	18.3	9.6	60.4	85.2	28.5
	(219)	(114)	(121)	(305)	(231)
Females	26.7	27.5	75.4	90.8	37.9
	(255)	(131)	(162)	(314)	(203)

Note: Figures in brackets represent frequencies.

Why would there be a difference between men and women? Argyle (1958: 78-9) makes a number of suggestions. Women have more guilt feelings, he says, or girls prefer fathers and are therefore more attracted to a deity presented as a fatherly male. Glock, Ringer, and Babbie (1967: 43-5) think that females are more heavily involved in the family, and for that reason are more church-oriented. While the church has maintained its strong ties with the family, its involvement in the occupational spheres of the males has weakened. Glock and his colleagues also mention that women have more time to devote to church. There are a number of weaknesses in these arguments, one being that women tend also to engage more in private prayer, suggesting that we need a more inclusive explanation than proclivity towards, or time for, institutional involvement. It may be somewhat closer to the mark to think about both religion and women in Western societies as traditionally preoccupied with conflict-resolving, emotionally healing, integrative, and expressive functions, whereas men are more involved in competitive, differentiating, and instrumental activities (Mol 1971: 31).

Age

As with sex, the over-all age differences in church-going are relatively small. In the 21-to-30 age group, regular attenders comprise 45.6 per cent; in the 31-to-40 group 51.3 per cent; 41-to-50, 50.1 per cent; 51-to-60, 49.0 per cent; and 61 and over, 56.2 per cent. Grouping the three middle categories together, we get the following age differences by denomination (Table 3).

TABLE 3. Percentages of Regular Church Attenders by Denomination and Age

AGE	UNITED	ANGLICAN	ENGLISH CATHOLIC	FRENCH CATHOLIC	OTHERS
21–30	14.2	10.2	53.9	83.7	20.7
	(84)	(49)	(63)	(158)	(87)
31–60	20.1	20.0	71.7	90.3	30.4
	(293)	(145)	(184)	(359)	(253)
60+	40.4	27.8	77.5	87.1	45.7
	(89)	(48)	(31)	(101)	(92)

Note: Figures in brackets represent frequencies.

However small the over-all differences between the age categories, they are unmistakable for most denominations. With the exception of French Catholics, the older people attend church more than the younger ones. The slightly lower figure for French Catholics over 60 may be because in a denomination where church-going is strongly normative only the incapacitated and elderly infirm stay at home. Age makes a difference in denominations and countries where church attendance is at a low ebb, but there are slight differences in denominations where church attendance is very strong (Mol 1971: 40).

Education

The over-all relations between education and church attendance are irregular (Table 4). Of those with less than eight years of schooling 58.9 per cent could be classified as regular attenders; of those with between nine and twelve years of schooling, 44.6 per cent; of those with thirteen or more years of schooling, 49.5 per cent. As the French-speaking Catholics are strongly over-represented in the first group (45 per cent) in comparison with the second group (22 per cent) and the third (20 per cent), and as the French Catholics are by far the best church-goers, one might expect those with least education to be regular church-goers.

TABLE 4.   Percentages of Regular Church Attenders by Denomination and Education

YEARS OF SCHOOLING	UNITED	ANGLICAN	ENGLISH CATHOLIC	FRENCH CATHOLIC	OTHERS
−8	24.0	14.9	65.5	86.7	33.1
	(100)	(47)	(87)	(341)	(175)
9−12	18.8	12.8	69.1	90.1	29.1
	(270)	(132)	(152)	(203)	(182)
13+	31.7	34.8	75.0	88.0	33.7
	(104)	(66)	(44)	(75)	(77)

Note: Figures in brackets represent frequencies.

In fact, when denomination is held constant, those with the most education tend most to be regular church-goers. The tendency is weak, however, and the differences are not statistically significant in most instances. Yet the tendency is in accordance with the correlation between higher education and better church attendance in such countries as Austria (Bogensberger and Zulehner 1972: 57), Belgium (Houtart 1972: 76), West Germany (Kehrer 1972: 197), Switzerland (Campiche 1972: 520), and the U.S.A. (Alston 1971: 235). The fact that in Canada the denomination to which one belongs is much more significant for church attendance patterns than the amount of education one has received suggests that the educational and religious subsystems function largely independently of one another. Yet the strength of the Catholic subsystem and its hold on members enhances its capacity to socialize the young in its own school system (see for the U.S.A. Greeley and Rossi 1966, and for Australia Mol 1971: 183-96).

Income

As with education, it appears at first sight (Table 5) that adults in families with a total income in 1964 of less than $4000 had a better church attendance record (54.9 per cent being regular) than those with incomes of between $4000 and $7000 (49.7 per cent) and those with incomes over $7000 (43.9 per cent). Yet again the over-representation of French-speaking Catholics in the lower income bracket obscures the significance of the denominational variable, for French Catholics contain 38 per cent of those with the lowest incomes, 28 per cent of the middle group, and 20 per cent of those with higher incomes.

TABLE 5. Percentages of Regular Church Attenders by Denomination and Family Income

FAMILY INCOME	UNITED	ANGLICAN	ENGLISH CATHOLIC	FRENCH CATHOLIC	OTHERS
−$4000	25.4	21.8	64.9	85.4	35.6
	(114)	(69)	(77)	(254)	(149)
$4000−7000	23.0	11.8	67.1	90.5	30.8
	(208)	(85)	(134)	(242)	(182)
$7000+	20.8	26.8	73.8	88.2	28.8
	(144)	(82)	(65)	(93)	(87)

In Table 5 the significant differences are between Protestants, English Catholics, and French Catholics when income is held constant, and not between income groups when denomination is held constant.

Occupation

The over-all percentages of regular church-goers among the various occupational groupings vary moderately from farmers (58.9 per cent), pensioners and widows (57.3 per cent), and professionals (56.0 per cent), who are all above average, to managers (48.8 per cent), unskilled (48.6 per cent), skilled (47.5 per cent), clerical (47.2 per cent), service (43.8 per cent), and sales (42.2 per cent). But when denomination is held constant and occupations are collapsed into three categories, a different pattern emerges. One reason why the evidence in Table 6 differs from the first sentence of this section is that managers were under-represented (23.4 per cent) and the unskilled over-represented (40.6 per cent) in the French Catholic subsample (which comprised 29.2 per cent of the total sample).

TABLE 6.   Percentages of Regular Church Attenders by Denomination and
Occupation

OCCUPATION	UNITED	ANGLICAN	ENGLISH CATHOLIC	FRENCH CATHOLIC	OTHERS
Professionals, managers, farmers	30.1 (136)	25.4 (63)	76.0 (75)	93.9 (147)	34.7 (124)
White-collar, clerical, and sales	19.8 (91)	23.1 (52)	74.3 (35)	91.9 (74)	25.6 (43)
Blue-collar, skilled, unskilled, service	12.4 (177)	9.7 (93)	60.5 (134)	86.3 (306)	28.0 (207)

Blue-collar workers are less involved in the major Protestant denominations, more in English Catholicism, and most of all in French Catholicism. Blue-collar workers are also well represented among regular worshippers in "Other" denominations, partly because they include sectarian
churches. It has been stated that blue-collar workers are "alienated"
from the churches (Woodsworth 1911: 155-74), but this is probably an
overly general statement (Crysdale 1961). It is more appropriate to
speak of alienation in describing the attitude of workers to churches in
some European countries such as Spain (Almerich 1972: 469), or Finland (Seppanen 1972: 166), where church attendance among the working class is almost negligible in contrast with that among the bourgeoisie.
However, in such "new" countries as Canada, Australia, New Zealand,
and the United States neither the middle nor the working class has
become strongly disparate in ideology or life style, partly because of
actual and expected social mobility between the classes. As a consequence, Marxist ideology has not had the social base or vehicle for
growth in the "newer" democracies that it had in European countries
such as France, Italy, and Spain. It also means that class identity, as
expressed by such indicators as education, income, and occupation, has
not been as strong as denominational identity. It is probably for such
reasons that the significant differences in church attendance are between
the denominations rather than between socio-economic variables like
education, income, and occupation.

Size of Community

Size of community seems to make a greater difference in church-going than do socio-economic factors (Table 7). Among those living in cities with more than 100,000 inhabitants 38.9 per cent of the entire sample were regular attenders, whereas among those living in towns or cities with a population between 2500 and 100,000, 61.9 per cent were regular worshippers. In villages with fewer than 2500 inhabitants and in rural areas, 52.5 per cent attended at least twice a month.

TABLE 7.   Percentages of Regular Church Attenders by Denomination and Size of Community

SIZE OF COMMUNITY	UNITED	ANGLICAN	ENGLISH CATHOLIC	FRENCH CATHOLIC	OTHERS
City with more than 100,000 inhabitants	17.3 (197)	18.7 (123)	59.4 (96)	83.3 (168)	24.9 (193)
Town or city with between 2500 and 100,000 inhabitants	29.4 (109)	21.9 (73)	73.8 (103)	90.7 (268)	37.0 (100)
Village with fewer than 2500 inhabitants or rural area	25.3 (166)	17.4 (46)	73.8 (84)	88.3 (180)	37.4 (139)

Yet Table 7, controlling for denomination, shows that the difference between cities, towns, and villages is rather small. The difference in attendance between cities and towns is reduced to an average of about 10 percentage points, and the difference between town and villages becomes insignificant. One reason for this reduction again appears to be the over-representation of French Catholics in towns (41 per cent) as compared with cities (22 per cent) and villages (29 per cent). The rural-urban difference in church attendance is usually much more pronounced in Europe than in the newer countries. The European literature on church-going notes the better attendance in rural areas. (See for Austria, Bogensberger and Zulehner 1972: 56; for Belgium, Houtart 1972: 73; for Denmark, Thorgaard 1972: 138; for West Germany, Kehrer 1972:

197; for England, Martin 1972: 233; for Ireland, Ward 1972: 297; for Italy, Acquaviva 1972: 317; for the Netherlands, Laeyendecker 1972: 335; for Spain, Almerich 1972: 466; for Sweden, Gustafsson 1972: 497; for Switzerland, Campiche 1972: 516.) One of the reasons why the rural-urban difference tends to be more pronounced in the older countries may be the convergence of the local church with local identity in European villages (Christian 1972). In the newer countries denominational competition, and consequently denominational identity, tend to offset rather than converge with local community feeling.

Political Party Preference

In the 1965 election study the question was asked: "Generally speaking, do you usually think of yourself as Conservative, Liberal, Social Credit, Créditiste, NDP, Union Nationale, or what?". Among respondents who named the three major parties, the percentage of regular church-attenders among Liberals (60.9 per cent) was considerably higher than among Conservatives (39.1 per cent) or the NDP (34 per cent). This result comes as no surprise to those familiar with Canadian voting patterns. The association between Catholics and the Liberal party has been pointed out by many scholars (Meisel 1956: 486; Laponce 1958: 256; Alford 1964: 213, Engelmann and Schwartz 1971: 48; McDonald 1971: 169; Jacek et al. 1972: 196). One can therefore expect an over-representation of Catholics among Liberals (59 per cent) and a corresponding under-representation of Catholics among the Conservative (21 per cent) and NDP (29 per cent) parties (Table 8).

TABLE 8.   Percentages of Regular Church Attenders by Denomination and Political Party

PARTY IDENTIFICATION	UNITED	ANGLICAN	ENGLISH CATHOLIC	FRENCH CATHOLIC	OTHERS
Conservative	24.7	23.1	64.6	83.3	41.5
	(194)	(104)	(48)	(66)	(123)
Liberal	30.4	23.8	71.7	90.1	24.8
	(125)	(63)	(166)	(262)	(141)
NDP	20.0	9.5	56.5	74.3	23.8
	(55)	(21)	(23)	(35)	(63)

When denomination is "held constant" (Table 8) there is little difference between the percentages of regular church-goers among Conservatives and Liberals. There is a tendency for the percentage to increase among Catholics who are Liberals and for "Others" who prefer the Conservative party (McDonald 1969: 134; Anderson 1966: 33). Regular church-going is lowest amongst those in any denomination who prefer the New Democratic Party. As in most other Western countries, left-wing parties tend to be perceived as demanding a kind of commitment which is akin to religious sentiment. Moreover, the integrative function of the traditional religious organizations for both social and personal identity predisposes the believer to accept meaning in terms of the status quo and to tie divergent perceptions together in terms of future salvation (Mol 1971: 300).

Conclusion

We should not over-estimate church-going as a measure of religiosity. Belief, private prayer, religious experience, and ethical patterns are, for an increasing number of persons, equally or more important dimensions of religious orientation. Yet church-going is an observable, easily measured indicator of commitment to a church or denomination.

Two major observations can be made about church-going in Canada. The first is that, contrary to the European experience, church attendance does not vary much according to socio-economic variables (education, income, occupation). This may mean that a relatively weak class identity has not been able to overshadow and determine denominational identity.

The second general observation is that the greatest variation in church-going is related to denomination. Although since 1965 Canadian church attendance has declined, the rates in French Canada are still probably the highest in the world. Secondary analysis of Gallup Poll data shows that in April 1970 26.4 per cent of Protestants, 55.6 per cent of English-speaking Catholics, and 71.4 per cent of French-speaking Catholics had attended church on the previous Sunday. The corresponding figures for May 1974 were 24.4 per cent, 48.5 per cent, and 62.4 per cent. Although these data are not altogether comparable to the data analysed in this article, they suggest that the severest drop in attendance between 1965 and 1974 took place among French-speaking Catholics, followed by English-speaking Catholics, rather than among Protestants. Yet in the 1970 poll, 32.9 per cent of Protestants said that they went to church less often than they did five years ago, as compared with 8.2 per cent who said that they went more often. The comparable figures for English-speaking Catholics were 23.6 per cent and 5.6 per cent, and for French-speaking Catholics 30.4 per cent and 3.6 per cent. Even with this considerable decrease, attendance rates for Quebec are still high compared with many other countries. They may be related to the role of the Catholic Church in Quebec as the principal strong sacralizer of the culture of an embattled minority for almost three centuries. The lesser, but still high, attendance rate for English-speaking Catholics is comparable to rates in other nations where Catholicism has to compete with other denominations. The attendance rate for Protestants is much higher than comparable figures for Protestant countries in Europe with denominational monopolies, but much lower than the Catholic figures in multi-denominational countries. This may reflect the individualistic character of Protestantism, which since the time of the Reformation has emphasized salvation through the faith of the individual. As a consequence, commitment to the church as the mediator of salvation has declined.

REFERENCES

Acquaviva, Sabino
1972   "Italy." In Hans Mol, Margaret Hetherton, and Margaret Henty, eds., *Western Religion*, pp. 305-24. The Hague: Mouton.
Alford, Robert
1964   "The Social Bases of Political Cleavage in 1962." In John Meisel, ed., *Papers on the 1962 Election*, pp. 203-34. Toronto: University of Toronto Press.
Almerich, Paulina
1972   "Spain." In Hans Mol, Margaret Hetherton, and Margaret Henty, eds., *Western Religion*, pp. 459-77. The Hague: Mouton.
Alston, John P.
1971   "Social Variables Associated with Church Attendance, 1965 and 1969: Evidence from National Polls." *Journal for the Scientific Study of Religion* 10, No. 3 (Fall): 233-6.
Anderson, Grace M.
1966   "Voting Behaviour and the Ethnic-Religious Variable: A Study of a Federal Election in Hamilton, Ontario." *Canadian*

Journal of Economics and Political Science 32: 27-37.
Argyle, Michael
1958   *Religious Behaviour*. London: Routledge and Kegan Paul.
Bogensberger, Hugo, and Paul Zulehner
1972   "Austria." In Hans Mol, Margaret Hetherton, and Margaret Henty, eds., *Western Religion*, pp. 47-66. The Hague: Mouton.
Campiche, Roland, J.
1972   "Switzerland." In Hans Mol, Margaret Hetherton, and Margaret Henty, eds., *Western Religion*, pp. 511-28. The Hague: Mouton.
Christian, William A., Jr.
1972   *Person and God in a Spanish Valley*. New York: Seminar Press.
Crysdale, Stewart
1961   *The Industrial Struggle and Protestant Ethic in Canada*. Toronto: Ryerson.
1965   *The Changing Church in Canada*. Toronto: United Church Publishing House.

Dawson, C. A., and E. R. Younge
1940 *Pioneering in the Prairie Provinces: The Social Side of the Settlement Process.* Toronto: Macmillan.

Dumont, Fernand, and Gerald Fortin
1960 "Un sondage de pratique religieuse en milieu urbain." *Recherches Sociographiques* 1, No. 4: 500-2.

Engelmann, F. C., and M. A. Schwartz
1971 *Political Parties and the Canadian Social Structure.* Scarborough, Ont.: Prentice-Hall.

Glock, Charles Y., Benjamin B. Ringer, and Earl R. Babie
1967 *To Comfort and to Challenge.* Berkeley: University of California Press.

Greeley, Andrew M., and Peter H. Rossi
1966 *The Education of Catholic Americans.* Chicago: Aldine.

Gustafsson, Berndt
1972 "Sweden." In Hans Mol, Margaret Hetherton, and Margaret Henty, eds., *Western Religion*, pp. 479-510. The Hague: Mouton.

Higgins, Edward
1972 "South Africa." In Hans Mol, Margaret Hetherton, and Margaret Henty, eds., *Western Religion*, pp. 437-58. The Hague: Mouton.

Hiller, Harry H.
1972 "A Critical Analysis of the Role of Religion in a Canadian Populist Movement: The Emergence and Dominance of the Social Credit Party in Alberta." Unpublished Ph.D. dissertation, McMaster University.

Houtart, François
1972 "Belgium." In Hans Mol, Margaret Hetherton, and Margaret Henty, eds., *Western Religion*, pp. 67-82. The Hague: Mouton.

Isambert, François A.
1972 "France." In Hans Mol, Margaret Hetherton, and Margaret Henty, eds., *Western Religion*, pp. 175-87. The Hague: Mouton.

Jacek, Henry, John McDonough, Ronald Shimizu, and Patrick Smith
1972 "The Congruence of Federal-Provincial Campaign Activity in Party Organizations: The Influence of Recruitment Patterns in Three Hamilton Ridings." *Canadian Journal of Political Science* 5, No. 2 (June): 190-205.

Kehrer, Günther
1972 "Germany: Federal Republic." In Hans Mol, Margaret Hetherton, and Margaret Henty, eds., *Western Religion*, pp. 189-212. The Hague: Mouton.

Laeyendecker, Leo
1972 "The Netherlands." In Hans Mol, Margaret Hetherton, and Margaret Henty, eds., *Western Religion*, pp. 325-63. The Hague: Mouton.

Laponce, J. A.
1958 "The Religious Background of Canadian M.P.'s." *Political Studies* 6, No. 3: 253-8.

Lazerwitz, Bernard
1964 "Religion and Social Structure in the United States." In Louis Schneider, ed., *Religion, Culture and Society*, pp. 426-39. New York: Wiley.

MacRae, Peter H.
1969 "The Anglican Church and the Ecumenical Movement in New Brunswick." Unpublished M.A. thesis, University of New Brunswick.

Martin, David
1972 "Great Britain: England." In Hans Mol, Margaret Hetherton, and Margaret Henty, eds., *Western Religion*, pp. 229-47. The Hague: Mouton.

McDonald, Lynn
1969 "Religion and Voting: A Study of the 1968 Canadian Federal Election in Ontario." *Canadian Review of Sociology and Anthropology* 6, No. 3 (August): 129-44.

1971 "Attitude Organization and Voting Behaviour in Canada." *Canadian Review of Sociology and Anthropology* 8, No. 3 (August): 164-84.

Meisel, John

1956 "Religious Affiliation and Electoral Behaviour: A Case Study." *Canadian Journal of Economics and Political Science* 22, No. 4 (November): 481-96.

Mol, Johannis (Hans) J.

1971 *Religion in Australia.* Melbourne: Nelson.

1972 "New Zealand." In Hans Mol, Margaret Hetherton, and Margaret Henty, eds., *Western Religion*, pp. 365-79. The Hague: Mouton.

1974 "The Sacralization of Identity." In Margaret S. Archer, ed., *Current Research in Sociology*, pp. 267-82. The Hague: Mouton.

Querido, Augusto

1972 "Portugal." In Hans Mol, Margaret Hetherton, and Margaret Henty, eds., *Western Religion*, pp. 427-36. The Hague: Mouton.

Seppanen, Paavo

1972 "Finland." In Hans Mol, Margaret Hetherton, and Margaret Henty, eds., *Western*

Religion, pp. 143-73. The Hague: Mouton.

Thorgaard, Jorgen

1972 "Denmark." In Hans Mol, Margaret Hetherton, and Margaret Henty, eds., *Western Religion*, pp. 135-41. The Hague: Mouton.

Vogt, Edvard, D.

1972 "Norway." In Hans Mol, Margaret Hetherton, and Margaret Henty, eds., *Western Religion*, pp. 135-41. The Hague: Mouton.

Ward, Conor K.

1972 "Ireland." In Hans Mol, Margaret Hetherton, and Margaret Henty, eds., *Western Religion*, pp. 295-303. The Hague: Mouton.

Whyte, Donald R.

1968 "Religion and the Rural Church." In Bernard Blishen, Frank Jones, Kaspar Naegele, and John Porter, eds., *Canadian Society*, pp. 574-89. Toronto: Macmillan.

Woodsworth, J. S.

1911 *My Neighbour.* Toronto: Methodist Church.

2.

Forms of Community

The Hutterites:
A Communal Sect*

John W. Bennett

Hutterites are one of the three major surviving sectarian groups of Anabaptist Christians; the others are the Mennonites, who have been at least partly assimilated into the Protestant order of sects, and the separatist Amish, a semi-communal and extremely conservative wing of the Mennonite faith. The Hutterites are the only group among the three who have rigorously preserved the communal frame of existence, which requires that all important property be shared by the entire community, and the children raised mainly by the collective institutions of the colony. The economy is that of a large, diversified agricultural enterprise, and all Hutterites are farmers, since no satisfactory way has been found to exist communally in an urban-industrial setting. Hutterian beliefs include strong injunctions against extensive involvement with the "outside"— that is, the majority society—since to Hutterites, it is not only tempting and corrupting in its pursuit of money and personal gratification, but also un-Christian, having fallen away from the original teachings of Christ. Hutterites belong to that ancient tradition that visualizes a perfect Chris-

*First appeared in John W. Bennett, *Plains People: Adaptive Strategy and Agrarian Life in the Great Plains* (Chicago: Aldine, 1969). Published here in abridged form with the kind permission of the author and the publisher.

tian society—not in Heaven, but here on earth, within the capabilities of men. There is therefore a basic paradox in Hutterian ideals: while the world must be avoided, because it is defiling of the true Christian way, it also must be dealt with successfully, in order to preserve the Hutterian faith and further the mission of Christ.

The Hutterian settlement of the Jasper region [which was founded in 1952] represents the most economically successful human settlement in the region's 70-odd years of Euro-American settlement, in terms of range and diversity of use of natural resources and indices of productivity. In general, it is also the most successful in terms of combining high productivity with a conservationist program for resources. The Brethren are efficient farmers not only because of their skilled management and intensive use of machinery, but also because of their ability to control consumption in order to fulfill their ideal of austerity, which incidentally provides them with substantial investment capital. The combination of a relatively large labor force with quantities of machinery and tools, plus their practice of nearly all branches of agriculture, provides them with a balanced "economy of scale".

[The Hutterites moved to Alberta from South Dakota in 1918], when the American government tried to draft them into the Army and local patriots mistakenly harassed them as German enemies. Canada invited them to settle in the Prairie Provinces. The South Dakota colonies were abandoned, but taken in trust by the state government, which later sold them back to Manitoba Hutterites in the 1920s. Most Hutterites today live in Canada, but a substantial and growing number are found in both the Dakotas and Montana. The Province of Alberta has the largest number of colonies.

The recent move into Saskatchewan was prompted by difficulties the Brethren had with the Alberta provincial government. Throughout their history, the Brethren have experienced oppression and martyrdom. Alberta, like some United States state governments, has attempted to restrict the number of colonies, and the practice of establishment of new colonies. The Hutterites divide their colony settlements in two when the population reaches from 125 to 130, because they have found that communal social life is difficult to manage with larger numbers, and that economic conditions in the northern Plains make it hard to support more people on the land available to them, at the desired level of consumption. While the Alberta government attempts to prevent this budding process have been revised and partly rejected by the courts, shortages of land added to the need to move elsewhere. Saskatchewan has been more cordial; it has established a special commission to assist Hutterites to find colony sites, and incidentally to work with them to prevent saturation of particular districts. A number of colonies have been persuaded to move north, to the forest frontier, to help develop this pioneer region of the Province. The group of colonies in the Jasper region were the first Hutterites to appear in Saskatchewan.

Beliefs

The principal doctrinal difference that set Anabaptists apart from other Christian groups was the rejection of the practice of infant baptism. Anabaptists spurned the practice of baptizing infants as unfair and contrary to Christ's teachings and the practices of the early church, which only accepted adults into the faith. Infants and children are conceived by Anabaptists to be too immature to understand the meaning and significance of Christianity. While this issue generated much heat, it is now fully accepted insofar as the regular Baptists are regarded as part of the Protestant order. The Baptists were English analogs to Anabaptism, but appeared in a different social setting and lacked the social revolutionary zeal. In any case, no Hutterite is baptized until he or she is about twenty years old, and voluntarily requests it.

   In all likelihood the real issues behind [the historical persecution of Anabaptists] concerned their other beliefs. The sects seriously proposed to establish the Golden Age in the guise of true Christianity, and rejected the official churches as corrupt. They regarded the State as evil; war as intolerable; taxation as unfair and for the Devil's purposes; contemporary culture as sinful and tempting. Modern Hutterite beliefs continue in this pattern, but show a number of compromises which mirror the Brethren's own remarkable ability to flourish in the world when conditions permit. Hutterites refuse to take political office, or legal oaths, and are not supposed to vote—but they have voted in local elections when their interests were involved. While they believe that the State is corrupt, they enjoin their followers to obey its laws and pay its taxes. They continue to resist military service and in the United States Hutterite boys now serve in conscientious-objector conservation camps (the Brethren refused even this in earlier years). They avoid non-Hutterite society, but are taking an increasing part in charitable activities in local communities, and are mingling with the local people in informal contexts. They continue to practise consumption austerity, although the level of living of the colonies has been rising in recent years. The Community of Goods—the term Hutterites use to refer to their communal property system—still functions effectively, although covert individual accumulation of possessions often appears in many colonies. The Brethren forbid themselves to engage in usury or profit-making industry, but may sell agricultural products for whatever they can get, and drive a hard bargain on anything they want to buy.

Thus the basic Hutterite beliefs are really a blueprint for a particular way of life. Their purely religious ideas are not exceptional: they use Luther's translation of the Bible, and their general Christian dogma is for all practical purposes identical with that of most fundamentalist or Pentecostal sects. But the important thing about Hutterite beliefs is the fact that they are all qualified either by "yes, but" statements, or by modifications of practice. This is a reflection of the basic paradox in Hutterian life pointed to earlier: while the Brethren must avoid the World, they must also learn to use its rules and procedures in order to survive.

The Hutterian acceptance of modern technology is another instance of this compromise policy. Machinery, power equipment, refrigeration, central propane heating, the very latest farming implements, large modern workshops, station wagons (usually one only to a colony, however, to control trips to town), are the stock in trade of every colony. One colony owned four latest-model grain combines with air-conditioned cabs; another had a shower room with stainless-steel walls. These are all cases of "collective consumption", not individual, and thus the Hutterites preserve their basic personal austerity. The acquirement of expensive equipment is needed or defended on the grounds that the colony system must compete in an increasingly high-cost agricultural economy which emphasizes capital requirements over labor; consequently the utmost efficiency of operation is sought. There is truth in this view, since the Hutterites do support a much larger number of people on given units of land and other resources than individual farmers.

Hutterites have very large families and have the fastest rate of population increase of any social group in North America. Population growth, and the press toward enterprise efficiency, forced them to adopt modern machinery in the 1920s, like other Great Plains farmers.

The Jasper Settlement

When Hutterites establish new colonies, they do so with great efficiency and skill, because they have a conscious blueprint for domestic and farming institutions. The colony is a world in itself, a kind of portable village, with essential equipment, funds, and labor force. The Brethren usually have enough cash to buy most of the land they need for the first decade or so of colony existence, and these large land purchases have the effect of providing a more adequate share of natural resources in this exceedingly variable environment.

Hutterites believe that colonies should not be too close together, since this tends to encourage resentment and opposition among the non-Hutterites, and also creates competitive relationships among the colonies themselves, in their local sales of farm produce. The six Jasper colonies were located at varying distances from one another, but those west of Jasper town were very close together—most of them had joint land boundaries. This group of four were too close together by Hutterite standards, but this happened because of available land.

The population of the six Jasper colonies in 1964 was about 550 men, women, and children, or about seven per cent of the total population of the Jasper region. This represented an average per-colony increase of forty-two per cent over the population of each group in the first year of its settlement. Demographers have found that Hutterite population doubles every sixteen years, and since colonies split when the population reaches about 150, the maximum population of the Jasper colonies would be about 900. This will probably never be reached, because colonies are dividing at increasingly lower population levels. In any case, one may assume that the Hutterian population will probably level off at about ten per cent of the total regional population, assuming no important additional growth in the non-Hutterian [sector].

A total of fifty-five farms were sold to the Hutterites in order to acquire the land for their colonies, but most of the former owners retired into Jasper town. Considering the fact that between 1946 and 1960 a total of 685 Jasper farming enterprises disappeared from the census totals, the fraction purchased by the Brethren was small, and would not justify the oft-heard criticism of the Hutterites as driving out local farmers.

However, the local impact of these sales can be great: in the area west of town, the four colonies there bought forty-four farms in an area of approximately 162 square miles, or about one-third of all farms in this district. At the time of the study, the land purchases of the four colonies were not complete, and additional farm sales could be expected. Eventually about one-half or more of all the farms in this district could be expected to go to the Hutterites. By 1965, the colonies controlled about four per cent of all land in any form of agricultural production in the Jasper region.

The six Jasper colonies in some respects formed a region within a region insofar as the Brethren had more to do with each other than with non-Hutterites. However, the amount and kind of relationships among the colonies was influenced by several factors. The first we shall consider is the branch of the sect a particular colony may belong to. All Hutterites are divided into three branches, based on the three groups or waves of immigrants coming from Russia to North America in the 1870s. Two of these branches (or *Leute*, as the Hutterites call them)—the Darius and the Lehrer—were represented in Jasper: two colonies of Lehrer and four of Darius. Hutterites marry only inside of their *Leute*, and the customs of the *Leute* differ slightly (for example, Lehrer men use buttons on their clothes; Darius men have hooks and eyes). Other things being equal, Brethren of the same *Leute* associated together more than with members of the other branch. Where, however, two colonies of different *Leute* were very close together, they would tend to have more relations than with their fellow-*Leute* colonies located at a distance. Hutterites exchange machinery and labor; jointly plan and design new agricultural ventures; attend each other's weddings and funerals; let their young people associate together for courtship; and have other associations of a type to be expected between what are, in effect, farming villages of a European type.

Family and Marriage

Hutterites respect the nuclear family of parents and children, and provide private apartments of three or four rooms for each such unit in the row houses they customarily build. Marriages are expected to be love matches, and considerable care is taken to bring young people together in order to find compatible mates. At marriage, each couple is provided with such basic necessities as furniture, a clock, and a sewing machine for the wife to make the family clothing. Children are usually born in the local hospital—Hutterites greatly respect the need for health and professional medical care (in the sixteenth century they had their own doctors). The children are raised wholly by the parents and older siblings until the age of three, when the colony school system takes over, but even so, children always sleep in their parents' apartment. Children also attend the public school, built by the colony on its premises, and taught by a local school teacher from town. Schooling stops at the eighth grade.

The most important kinship grouping in Hutterite colony society is the group of male siblings of each nuclear family. These boys retain their affectual ties on into adulthood, and often they may constitute a kind of brother-clique which can have considerable importance in the operation of the colony, since a group of such brothers may have managerial positions in the various agricultural activities, and can function as a voting block in colony assemblies. This brother group is, in fact, the only important clique-like structure in Hutterite society.

Each Hutterite is also a member of an extended patrimonial family, which always cuts across two or more colonies because of the fission process. Relationships among the relatives of these big families are about the same as one finds in non-Hutterite farming or ranching society in Jasper; for example, when visiting another colony, a Hutterite will be given a bed in his relative's apartment.

The basic problem of kinship in Hutterite colonies stems from the collective and communal way of life. The most important group in Hutterite society is not the kin, but the communal village. Hutterites work together; go to church as a group; the men and women eat at separate tables; the children are raised communally. Various means have been developed by the Hutterites to control kinship and other forms of factionalism: manipulation of functional job and task assignment such as rotation of jobs, in order to break up cliques; discouragement or prevention of nepotism (a son following in his father's job); and discipline by the minister.

Colony Organization

Figure 1 diagrams the instrumental structure of a typical Jasper colony —and for Hutterite colonies everywhere, since there are no significant departures from this chartered plan. It is a complex type of organization for a relatively small group, but communal life and big enterprises require complex organization. The plan is moreover identical with the structure of the Moravian colonies in the sixteenth century. Hutterites found out early how to organize their large diversified enterprises, and the people in them, and they have never changed. This is due not only to the Hutterite reliance on dogma, but also to the fact that the plan is actually an extremely efficient way of operating a combined group of

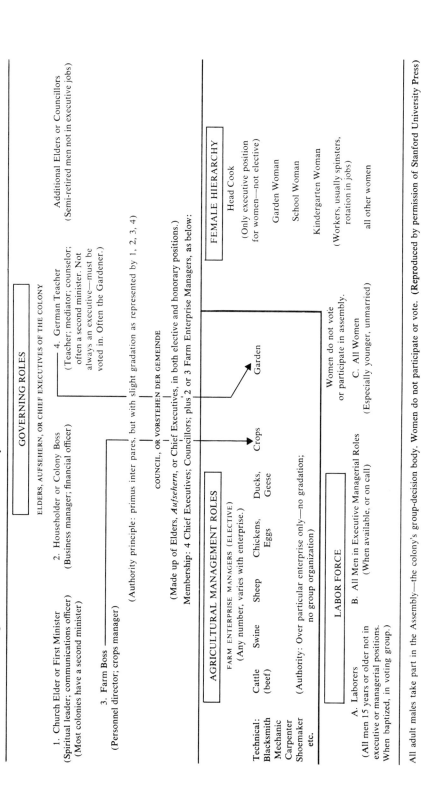

GOVERNING ROLES

ELDERS, AUFSEHERN, OR CHIEF EXECUTIVES OF THE COLONY

1. Church Elder or First Minister
(Spiritual leader; communications officer)
(Most colonies have a second minister)

2. Householder or Colony Boss
(Business manager; financial officer)

4. German Teacher
(Teacher; mediator; counselor; often a second minister. Not always an executive—must be voted in. Often the Gardener.)

Additional Elders or Councillors
(Semi-retired men not in executive jobs)

3. Farm Boss
(Personnel director; crops manager)

(Authority principle: primus inter pares, but with slight gradation as represented by 1, 2, 3, 4)

COUNCIL, OR VORSTEHEN DER GEMEINDE

(Made up of Elders, Aufsehern, or Chief Executives, in both elective and honorary positions.)

Membership: 4 Chief Executives; Councillors; plus 2 or 3 Farm Enterprise Managers, as below:

AGRICULTURAL MANAGEMENT ROLES

FARM ENTERPRISE MANAGERS (ELECTIVE)
(Any number, varies with enterprise.)

Technical:	Cattle	Swine	Sheep	Chickens,	Ducks,	Crops	Garden
Blacksmith	(beef)			Eggs	Geese		
Mechanic							
Carpenter							
Shoemaker							
etc.							

(Authority: Over particular enterprise only—no gradation; no group organization)

LABOR FORCE

A. Laborers
(All men 15 years or older not in executive or managerial positions. When baptized, in voting group.)

B. All Men in Executive Managerial Roles
(When available, or on call)

C. All Women
(Especially younger, unmarried)

Women do not vote or participate in assembly.

FEMALE HIERARCHY

Head Cook
(Only executive position for women—not elective)

Garden Woman

School Woman

Kindergarten Woman

(Workers, usually spinsters, rotation in jobs)

all other women

All adult males take part in the Assembly—the colony's group-decision body. Women do not participate or vote. (Reproduced by permission of Stanford University Press) diverse agricultural activities. The Israeli kibbutz, a modern communal agricultural enterprise, is organized in an almost identical fashion. The kibbutz did not copy the colony—it is simply that there are really a limited number of ways of organizing a communal agrarian system.

In Figure 1, one can see that colony leadership has two principal levels: the Elders or Executives at the top and the Managers just below them. Two positions combine both levels: the Farm Boss and the German Teachers. The former is in charge of the field crops on the managerial level but, because of the large amount of labor expended on crops, he is also a general personnel director and task organizer on the Executive level. The German Teacher (not always an Executive) is usually the Garden Man on the managerial level. This is so because the garden is always close to the buildings and is worked by the women. The Teacher also directs the women who run the nursery school and kindergarten and is around the colony premises all day long. There is also a Council that functions more or less on the Executive level, although usually one to three Managers may be members. The Council discusses important issues to be brought before the Assembly, which consists of all baptized male members—in effect, all men twenty years or older.

The labor force consists of all members of the colony, male and female, although Executives and Managers may be excused from ordinary labor when they must perform their assigned tasks. In every colony there are a number of men who are neither Executives nor Managers, but usually these are the younger men. One reason for the practice of colony division is to give all men a good chance at becoming leaders, so as to maintain commitment and a feeling of responsibility. It has been found that the majority of men who leave Hutterian life permanently (actually the number is very small) are those who have not been elected to leadership position and who believe they never will be.

The women constitute a separate category in Hutterian society. Hutterites believe that women are subordinate to men, although men have an obligation to cherish and defend them. Actually women can play an important informal role in Hutterian life, often exercising considerable influence on their husbands. The Head Cook is the only woman with what might be considered managerial responsibility, and she is the only woman who is elected to office. In most of the Jasper colonies the Cook was the wife of the Householder or General Manager, since this facilitated the technical and financial planning involved in the commissary. The women who worked in the kindergarten and nursery school were often spinsters, of whom each colony had two or more.

The Executives are graded in authority as represented by the numeri-cal order of the roles at the top of the chart. The Church Elder, or chief minister, is the most important figure. His duties are not only to conduct church services (often with the assistance of a second minister) but also to maintain communications in the colony, discipline offenders, main-tain the faith, and in general function as a paterfamilias. The House-holder, or manager and financial expert, is second in authority, and in some contexts of colony affairs is superior to the minister. He manages the entire economic operation and also represents the colony in its deal-ings with outsiders. We have already discussed the Farm Boss and the Teachers. The retired Elders are older men who are no longer in execu-tive or managerial positions, but whose advice and counsel is frequently sought. In a church service or a colony business assembly meeting, all the Elder-Executives sit on a bench behind the table which serves as an "altar" and face the entire congregation. Thus the functional operation of the colony, and its religious identity, are merged in the arrangement. This is, perhaps, the most fundamental fact of Hutterian life. Religion and daily life are blended: religion defines this way of life, and its con-duct is a manifestation of religion.

The activities of the Hutterian colony are organized on the basis of what we have called "managed democracy", meaning by this term a combination of egalitarian group decision and patriarchal authority. It is hard for the average North American to conceive of this combination, since by definition the two are supposed to be opposites. However, human beings can adapt to almost any amount of contradiction providing they want to. Hutterites have no theory of "democracy" or "patriarchy": they simply carry on the business of Christian brotherhood with ideas devel-oped in the sixteenth century. Thus, Hutterites elect every man to office in an assembly meeting, but they believe that such election is the will of God, and that therefore once elected, a man has considerable authority. Every man is supposed to be treated alike so far as possessions go, but the executives have a few more privileges and of course much more authority. All issues are supposed to be openly discussed and fairly voted on by all the men, but most issues are thoroughly thrashed out in infor-mal caucuses by the leaders before being brought to the vote.

The development of the farming enterprises is in the hands of the managers, who are expected to run their operations with considerable autonomy. However, in order to get the equipment they need, or to make improvements, they must present a sound case to the executives and the Council, and eventually to the assembly. They must be able to take failure without complaint or resentment. The managers are in a *de facto* competitive situation, but are not allowed to compete openly or scheme against each other or against the executives. A degree of competition is covertly acknowledged by Hutterites, and is known to be a spur to accomplishment, but this must never be openly acknowledged since it is against the tenets of an egalitarian brotherhood. There is always some temptation for managers to run their activities for their own profit. However, the small size of the colony makes clandestine dealings very difficult and the communal conscience is a strong deterrent.

Another process difficult for the outsider to comprehend is the presence of high motivation to achieve on the part of most Hutterite men, in the absence of the usual incentives to such motivation in the majority society: competition and material rewards. The question is not easy to answer because there is a *degree* of marginal or covert competition, differential rewards, and recognition of a man's need to "rise" in responsibility. Nevertheless, Hutterian society manages to obtain great efficiency and dedication to hard work from its men and women with only minimal development of the kinds of incentives common to the "outside". The most general answer to the question of "how" is simply the intensive socialization of every Hutterite in the principles of group welfare, and in the religious ideal of brotherhood as fulfillment of the mission of Christ.

Relations with the Jasper Community

Hutterites are seldom welcomed by the local inhabitants of Great Plains communities, who fear their powerful competition, irresistible ability to buy land, and alleged failure to spend money with local merchants. Most of these accusations are misleading, insofar as Hutterites add greatly to local productivity, buy large quantities of special equipment, and do not artificially inflate land values. Their presence in an agrarian community has about the same effect as large corporative farms might have.

But the non-Hutterites in Jasper had other criticisms as well. They noted that the Hutterites stood aloof from the rest of society and social relations, and refused to take part in the churches and in politics, hence were not fully participating members in the community. This was a source of considerable anxiety in Jasper, where great store was set on friendly, neighborly interaction, on the basis of old frontier values. Hutterites seemed to belong to another race, another world—their presence meant just so much less social interaction in a region already concerned with a loss of the satisfying social life of the old days.

Hutterites were not only aware of these criticisms, but recognized that their sectarian apartness did indeed create a barrier to participation. Most of the Jasper colonies were making special efforts to find ways of interacting in Jasper society without compromising their principles. The Brethren liked to wander around town during their frequent business trips, talking to merchants and dealers, or local government officials, taking an occasional drink in the beer hall, or visiting the homes of acquaintances. Some Hutterites tried to become experts on local history and traditions, in an effort to identify with the community leaders. The colonies made occasional cash contributions to a few of the local charities and the regional hospital. All of the colonies made an effort to help their small-farmer neighbors, and lent a hand whenever it was needed. Farmers and ranchers in the vicinity of the colonies were generally accepting of the Brethren, and even enjoyed their company, although those who felt that they were ticketed for absorption by land purchases often showed marked resentment.

The Future

As time passes, will the Hutterites change their ways? We have commented on Hutterian attitude toward change, in particular how they are able to modify their "instrumental" (economic and technical) culture while preserving their dogma, customs, and social organization. They are able to do this because the instrumental side of life is defined as a means to an end: maintenance of the Hutterite social system and beliefs.

However this may be, living in a rich, individualistic world is a constant source of temptation, and Hutterites, especially the young, are by no means immune. Even more important is the fact of prosperity: the efficiency of these people can create financial problems in reverse: too much money, and corresponding inducements to increase the level of living.

Perhaps more important than the question of cultural change is the one of expansion. Land is disappearing; sooner or later the Hutterites will have to find ways of either losing people by defection and education, or controlling their reproduction. It is not difficult to see colonies like those in the Jasper region becoming permanent settlements which no longer divide when population grows, but [which] send out some of their young people into the outer world to find their own way, and to carry a modified version of the Hutterian beliefs into secular society.

Religious Differentiation and Conflict in Single-Industry Communities[*]

Rex A. Lucas

"This town is run by the Orange Lodge and the Masons," one Roman Catholic respondent said indignantly. In another community, a Protestant said, "This is a priest-ridden place." The frequence of spontaneous derogatory religious references in interviews suggests that the long, tough roots of sectarianism are found in Canadian small towns.

These roots do not begin during the construction stage when religion is not crucially important in the lives of the workers. Bradwin, for instance, states: "The Church has never properly appraised the campman. Even until very recent years a whole hinterland is placed under one superintendent. He is expected to cover an area bigger than France and Germany put together."[1] Once wives and children move into the community, however, some provision is made for permanent church and schooling. One by one, churches are built as sufficient people from each denomination gather. The importance of differences in belief, creed, form of service, ritual, church architecture, Bible, prayer, and funda-

*First appeared as Chapter 13, "Churches", in Rex A. Lucas, *Minetown, Milltown, Railtown* (Toronto: University of Toronto Press, 1971). Published here in abridged form with the kind permission of the author and the publisher.

mental assumptions are illustrated in the rarity of a community church shared by all Protestant denominations, even in the smallest community, and equally vividly by the rules of endogamy and exogamy maintained by Roman Catholics and Protestants. Assertions of firmly-held fundamental abstract principle are at work here, not convenience or rational and logical arrangements.[2] [Since Vatican II and the decline in church attendance which began in the late 1960s, there have been more instances of community churches or common use of one building in remote new industrial towns. *Eds.*]

An additional reason for the accentuated sectarianism in small communities of single industry probably stems from the varied roles the churches play. In an urban centre, with a plethora of activities under a wide range of sponsorships, segmented roles, and opportunities for anonymity, the over-all importance of particular churches is not as discernible.

The Schools

Most small towns, more conspicuously than cities, have their schooling split along religious lines. This means that families associate with different school systems and the youth of the community are brought up in separate, distinct, and often rival, educational systems. This major and significant cleavage in the social life of Canadian communities has not been given adequate attention. There are infrequent crossings of religious lines for educational purposes, transfers are discouraged on both sides of the religious fence, and often severe sanctions are imposed. Carlton notes one example:

[Catholic] parents who sent children to the public school were on occasion denounced by name from the pulpit or were denied communion. A French Catholic woman dwelling on the outskirts of [the community] with a family of six found herself on relief following her husband's desertion. In order to avoid the high cost of the separate school education which included the purchase of texts she transferred her children to the public school. At her next confession she was told by the priest that she might not receive communion and that she was to consider herself excommunicated. This woman has not since attended church. (This is not a unique case. The researchers encountered several cases of such discipline and were informed that the sanction of excommunication had been regularly invoked during the period in question.)[3]

The Basis of Religious Cleavage

It is unclear what great threats are involved in this community cleavage, so delicately balanced with unwritten and often unspoken rules. During interviews, direct questions elicit stories of the out-group which, although local, represents national or international grand conspiracy. It seems enough to mention some social sin committed by a "dogan", while hinting at a conspiracy in the Roman Catholic marriage regulations designed to swallow up the Protestants; on the other hand, Catholics are not quite sure whether the economic dominance of the Protestants is connected with schemes of the Orange or Masonic lodges or some other nefarious group. The activities of youth are often segregated on moral grounds; there are enough differences in the religious and social attitudes of Catholics and Protestants to justify this. The lack of a blue-law conscience on the part of Catholics, permitting them to dance or play bridge on Sundays, is anathema to fundamentalist Protestants; easy physical contact among youth at dances alarms many priests. Indistinct notions of confession, confirmation, total immersion at Baptism, and such practices, all augment the shared lore that the in-group has about the out-group. In addition the religious denominations incorporate competing ethnic groups.

Catholics are seen as reproducing at a greater rate, marrying earlier, and posing a population threat to Protestants. Many Protestants resent the alleged claim that there is no salvation outside the Roman Catholic Church. They feel that the supernatural power of holy oils, water, candles, medals, and relics is at best mumbo-jumbo, and at worst a cruel racket. The same can be said of mass money for the souls of the dead. The more sophisticated are concerned with the infallibility of the Pope. The transubstantiation of bread and wine at the Eucharist, the immaculate conception, the assumption of Mary into Heaven, and the role of priest either as intermediary or as confessor are looked upon as alien.

Freemasonry is seen by Roman Catholics as conspiratorial, atheistic, and aggressively anti-Catholic. The Bible in the hands of anyone introduces the anarchy and blasphemy associated with some of the fundamentalist Protestant sects who recognize preachers with no theological training. The controversies regarding the Jehovah's Witnesses are well known.[4]

Intermarriage

Differences of theological belief and practice have existed for centuries, and people have become inured to them by and large. But there are current issues, and these are important because they affect role relationships directly.

The attitude of the Roman Church to mixed marriages is, to Protestants, a scandal. If the marriage is not performed by a Roman priest, the Church declares it void and invalid; the parties are living in sin and their children are illegitimate. The civil law says otherwise, but in marriage the Church claims a higher authority than the state. The mental anguish of the Catholic partner may be imagined. When, however, the Protestant partner agrees to have the marriage solemnized by a Catholic priest, he must make a number of serious concessions: a dispensation must be bought; the wedding cannot take place in church and there can be no music or any other sign of rejoicing; the Protestant partner must sign a witnessed document that all children of the marriage must be brought up as Catholics, even if the Catholic partner dies; the Catholic partner must sign a promise to try to win the Protestant partner to Catholicism; and the Protestant partner must agree to take religious instruction from the priest.[5]

It is not surprising that there has been tremendous resistance to marriage between Protestant and Roman Catholic. Parents discourage close social association between Protestant and Catholic children; they are particularly unhappy if a Protestant and Catholic start "going steady". Budding romances are watched with great interest by all concerned, and the engagement and marriage of such a pair is considered as a tragedy by many in the community. On occasion, feuds begin, families do not speak, and the couple marry without benefit of parents' blessing. If youth follow these rules of endogamy (and exogamy) the number of potential marriage-mates in the community is cut considerably.

Ethnicity and Religion

Ethnic differences add to the threat of religion when, for instance, Catholic stands for French instead of Irish. Religious opposition becomes augmented with cultural and linguistic rivalry. Under these conditions one group feels severely threatened by the other. In many small communities the Anglican Church is known as "the English Church", the Catholic Church as the "French Church". Somehow, then, the future of the family, the culture, the way of life, is felt to be threatened by the opposing religious out-group. These threats are made quite explicit in the family and are perpetuated in the Church; many parents say, "Of course I hope you will choose the man you love, but I do hope he will be of our religion."

There are a few situations in which religious groups come together. One is often the golf course; in a small community, a nine-hole golf course is a luxury, and all golfers, Protestant, Catholic, priest, or clergyman, are welcomed. One of the few times that all the clergy of the town assemble in one place is when support is needed for a vote on the wet/dry issue. The clergy co-operate similarly to warn each other about, for example, an underaged local couple who are trying to get married; desperate youths will often go from one member of the clergy to another, regardless of denomination, in the hope that one will perform the ceremony.

Protestant Denominationalism

So far, our consideration has been focused on the split between Roman Catholics and Protestants. The Protestants are divided into a number of denominations: Anglicans, United Church, Presbyterians, Lutherans, Baptists, Evangelical, Salvation Army, and so on. There are at least two Protestant denominations in most communities. Experiments with a Protestant community church are usually short-lived.

Each Protestant denomination has its own church buildings and organizations for its own congregation. Each denomination forms an in-group which is in competition with all other Protestant denominations, as well as Roman Catholics. But there is more feeling of kinship, albeit distant, among the various Protestant denominations than between each Protestant denomination and the Roman Catholics.

Even though each denomination provides an in-group, each of these, in turn, splits internally. So within the Anglican Church, high Anglicans disagree with low Anglicans on the singing and responses and the choral order of service; in the United Church the ex-Methodists disagree with the ex-Presbyterians on the order of service and the activities appropriate for young people; the Baptists split between "hard shell" Baptists and liberal Baptists, and so on. These feuds are carried on within each church family, as it were, and are often much more acrimonious than the cleavages between denominations in the community.

Religious differences in the community become structured through social usage in such a way as usually to prevent open conflict. In contrast, the disputes within the church family, like all families, are more open and are prone to arise at any time. Two important occasions permit the drawing of fine lines and the joining of battle. The first is the annual congregational meeting when reports are received and policies discussed and questions asked; the second is the choice of a new clergyman. The choice of a new clergyman is most important because his background, whether conservative or liberal, high or low, influences the development of the church during his tenure in office.

Similar difficulties assail the Roman Catholic Church, although the conflict within a parish is usually along ethnic lines. The Roman Catholic church often incorporates a wide range of ethnic and cultural groups—Irish, English, Italian, German, and so on. When a parish is made up of both French and Irish Catholics there is considerable conflict; under these conditions it makes a strategic difference if the priest is French-speaking or English-speaking. Controversies regarding lay teachers versus members of the teaching orders in the Catholic school, the maintenance of a convent, the physical upkeep of the church, the model of car and living arrangements of the priest, and whether the vacations are appropriate to the salary of the priest are all discussed by parishioners. The ethnic divisions within the church probably will take on more significance with the shift to the vernacular mass.

Activities Associated with Church

Community cleavages are accentuated because the church is the focal point of much social activity; under its umbrella many voluntary associations serve various age groups. Although there is some crossing of religious lines, it is infrequent, and related to the amount of religious content of the programmes. Thus, a great number of the activities for the town's young people, much of the choir music, women's organizations, teas, and suppers are carried on under religious auspices. The churches provide a ready made in-group, as well as the all-important physical facilities for club activities. In this way, then, the members of a denomination are brought together in active interaction; cliques of friends and close associates form along denominational lines.

Religious auspices take in activities that are usually considered non-denominational, such as Girl Guides, Brownies, Boy Scouts, and Wolf Cubs. Even when these groups hold their meetings on "neutral" territory —that is, town property rather than a church basement—Catholic children are often asked to withdraw by their own religious authorities. Sports teams, because they arise out of school or church organizations, are split denominationally. Recreation centres, even when built by community enterprise and directed by a professional recreational expert, have encountered great difficulties because of religious cleavage.

In addition, the churches are of importance in the one-industry community because they routinely sponsor activities to "raise money". The activities—whether variety concerts, Shamrock Day teas, June garden parties, AYPA plays, rummage sales, or sales of cakes and fancy work— all have the additional function of bringing people together to work in groups. These co-operative efforts are not unstructured, and each person takes his appointed place. Members of other denominations ritualistically attend these affairs. The time, effort, and materials donated by the sponsoring individuals usually exceed the returns from the money-raising bee, but the social cohesion encouraged by co-operative activity remains. In a community where there is seldom "anything new", where there is little recreation apart from the do-it-yourself variety, the church takes on an important role.

The churches, then, provide a regrouping which is different from the structuring of the company hierarchy. They also provide the bases for a social life and cliques that go beyond either association within occupational level and with neighbours, or community-sponsored recreation. Although the churches provide in-groups and out-groups, social life is so structured that there is seldom open conflict.

Religious cleavage tends to be a product of local citizen demands, rather than of the dictates of the particular denomination. There are many possible illustrations of this point, but none more effective than an interview (in French) with a French-Canadian Roman Catholic bishop, reputed to be "liberal". During a courtesy call discussion, he turned to the writer and said,

Tell me, what are your impressions of the area. I must confess to you that I do not know what is going on in my diocese. You must remember that local farm boys go into the priesthood. They are local and rural, they attend the local seminary, they reinforce their local ideas, and become local parish priests. They distrust me because I came from outside the district. No one ever tells me anything. I am a prisoner in my own palace. I know that the information they give me is erroneous. How do you, as a social scientist, view what is happening in the area? I know that the priests are bound to be conservative, but what else?

Political Activities Associated with Church

In over 100 communities of single industry, in which interviews were carried out, there were no indications of a union vote, but respondents in every community noted the religious vote. The significance of voting along religious lines depended a good deal upon the proportion of Catholics and Protestants in the community. As long as one group had a considerable majority, voters tended to vote along religious lines, permitting either a token or reasonable representation for the minority. When, however, the percentage of Catholics and Protestants ranged between forty and sixty the issue was much more difficult to resolve. Many found themselves, as voters so often do at provincial and federal elections, torn between the man as an individual and the group that he symbolized. In these cases, an informal and tacit agreement on a religious division of labour on the town council emerges. One comment illustrates this:

> As far as a religious vote is concerned—shall we say that religious feeling is always there, but it is usually dormant? But it does not take very much to raise an issue so that voting and all sorts of activities go along religious lines. We have all sorts of tacit agreements. If there is a Catholic Mayor we have a Protestant Deputy Mayor selected from the aldermen or with a Protestant Mayor we have a Roman Catholic Deputy.

S. D. Clark long ago related religion and politics in Canada's development.[6] Alford reminds us that this process is still going on;[7] Englemann and Schwartz suggest that the political relevance of religion has always existed throughout Canada's history: "Of all the factors dividing Canadians in their political outlook and behaviour, religion is uppermost in importance. Yet there has never been a specifically religious party in Canada, such as the Christian Democrats, nor one dominated by anti-religious sentiments."[8] Part of their explanation is that "Religious issues do not normally become national, since the areas in which they are most likely to arise—child welfare, the solemnization of marriage, divorce, and education—are all under provincial jurisdiction."[9] It is in the community, particularly the small community, where the religious issues become significant, not so much in terms of principles, but in conflicting norms and daily interaction. There are several reasons for this. Many religious principles have little significance until they are worked out in interpersonal relationships. Despite the social rather than theological emphasis noted in church activities, the participants are part of a sub-culture with many distinctive and basic values.[10] These basic assumptions, these implicit "givens" concerning individual rights, spiritual authority, and the like, are challenged when members of two sub-cultures contemplate intermarriage. Rules of endogamy and exogamy are basic to most cultures, groups, and families, and are not lightly put aside.

The second major reason for predicting that religious differences will continue to be very important in the small community arises out of the first. The value differences lead to patterned activities, so that the community becomes structured along religious lines. The institutionalization of religion in such structures as the school and church leads to its perpetuation. When a great number of social activities are carried out along denominational lines, the religious structuring of the community becomes much more pervasive. Unlike city-dwellers, the citizens have few alternative activities, even if they seek them. Religion has great salience as reflected in the fact that it, rather than position in the stratification system, is reflected in local voting.

Seen from a much broader point of view over a long period of time, religious conflicts can be regarded as religious and social movements. On the day-to-day activity level of the community of single industry, however, the broad sweep of social movements becomes lost in the religious complexities of personal relationships. The heritage from outside is made up of the beliefs, stereotypes, and assumptions associated with each denomination. The kinds of religious differences just described are of great importance because fully half of the population of Canada lives in the religiously-charged context of communities of 30,000 or less. The small religiously-homogeneous community is rare, and will become more so. A homogeneous community such as Miner's St. Denis may still be found in rural Quebec, along the "French Shore" of Nova Scotia, in small fishing villages or (Baptist) agricultural villages in the Annapolis Valley, but homogeneity is incompatible with industrialization.

NOTES

1 E. W. Bradwin, *Bunkhouse Man: A Study of Work and Play in the Camps of Canada 1903-1914* (New York, 1928), pp. 265-6. S. D. Clark comments on the indifference toward the church in early mining camps and the inability of the established church to adapt to instability (S. D. Clark, *The Social Development of Canada*, (Toronto, 1942), especially pp. 373 and 216.

2 Religious differences and conflict have had a long and continuing history in Canada. This topic has been one of the continuing interests of S. D. Clark (*Church and Sect in Canada*, Toronto, 1948; *The Developing Canadian Community*, 2nd ed., Toronto, 1962; *The Social Development of Canada*). Documentation of conflict and seeds of conflict is found on pp. 222, 306, and 375-9 of the last-mentioned volume.

3 Richard A. Carlton, "Differential Education in a Bilingual Community". Unpublished Ph.D. thesis, University of Toronto, 1967, pp. 60-1.

4 For a fuller discussion, see Watson Kirkconnell, "Religion and Philosophy: An English-Canadian Point of View", and T. R. P. Louis-M. Regis, o.p., "La Religion et la philosophie au Canada français", in Mason Wade., ed., *Canadian Dualism* (Toronto, 1960), pp. 41-77. Related works include Clark, *Church and Sect in Canada*; R. C. S. Crysdale, *The Industrial Struggle and Protestant Ethics in Canada* (Toronto, 1961); Jean-Charles Falardeau, "The Parish as an Institutional Type",

Canadian Journal of Economics and Political Science 15 (Aug. 1949): 353-67; E. C. Hughes, *French Canada in Transition* (Chicago, 1943); H. Miner, *St. Denis* (Chicago, 1939); Jean-Charles Falardeau, "Role et importance de l'Église au Canada français", *Esprit*, 20e année (Paris, 1952), 2e semestre, pp. 214-29; S. D. Clark, *Movements of Political Protest in Canada, 1640-1840* (Toronto, 1949); W. E. Mann, *Sect, Cult and Church in Alberta* (Toronto, 1955); Hugh Herbison, "Doukhobor Religion", in H. B. Hawthorn, ed., *The Doukhobors of British Columbia* (Toronto, 1955), Chap. 4; John A. Irving, *The Social Credit Movement in Alberta* (Toronto, 1959).

5 Watson Kirkconnell, "Religion and Philosophy: An English-Canadian Point of View", in Wade, ed., *Canadian Dualism*, p. 54. These regulations have been slightly modified since this was written; the stigma still remains.

6 See Clark, *Church and Sect in Canada*, and *Movements of Political Protest in Canada 1640-1840*.

7 See Alford, *Party and Society*, p. 230.

8 See F. C. Engelmann and Mildred A. Schwartz, *Political Parties and the Canadian Social Structure* (Toronto, 1967), p. 58.

9 *Ibid.*, p. 59.

10 For a discussion of churches and cemeteries in communities of single industry, see Institute of Local Government, Queen's University, *Single-Enterprise Communities in Canada* (Ottawa, 1953), pp. 191-200.

Synagogues in Transition:
Religious Revival or Ethnic Survival?*

Evelyn Kallen

It has long been taken for granted that a correlation exists between Orthodox, Conservative, or Reform synagogue affiliation and class and status divisions among North American Jews (Sodden 1962: 100). Bloom (1942), Warner and Lunt (1941), Warner and Srole (1954), Koenig (1942), Minnes (1953), Bergal (1955), Polsky (1958), and Weinryb (1958) all presented evidence that, following immigration, length of residence in America, upward socio-economic mobility, and the progressive acculturation and assimilation of the generations were accompanied by a shifting from Orthodox to Conservative to Reform synagogues. These findings were to some extent challenged by Sklare (1955: 28), who suggested that because of the rapid economic mobility and growing cultural homogeneity of the American Jew, concomitant with his concentration in the middle class, the various types of synagogues now had to compete for the same clientele. Sklare maintains as a primary assumption that Judaism constitutes an "ethnic church" and that, in the case of Conservative Judaism, ethnic goals provide a con-

*From Chapter 7 of Evelyn (Latowsky) Kallen, "Three Toronto Synagogues: A Comparative Study of Religious Systems in Transition", Ph.D. dissertation, University of Toronto, 1969. Published here in abridged and revised form with the kind permission of the author.

temporary substitute for religious motivations. Glazer (1957) voices the opinion of many authors that in this rejection of the religious *vis-à-vis* the ethnic imperative there exists a "mysterious" factor of Jewish cohesiveness yet to be isolated. Whereas it is possible to separate religion from ethnicity for other groups, it is not possible in the case of the Jews.

Contrary to the views of Glazer *et al*, my own research among three contemporary synagogues in Toronto indicates that the two factors, religion and ethnicity, *can* be separated. Moreover, I will argue in this paper that the so-called "mysterious factor of Jewish cohesiveness" hinges precisely on the articulation between these two factors within the context of contemporary synagogue affiliation.

It is my contention that the contemporary synagogue provides the vehicle *par excellence* for positive ethnic identification. Of the two factors, religion and ethnicity, it is the religious factor which appears to be the more flexible in adapting itself to contemporary Orthodox, Conservative, and Reform orientations among congregants. The ethnic factor, on the other hand, provides the underlying foundation with which all varieties of Judaic religious expression must ultimately articulate. The question now arises: just how do the religious and ethnic factors articulate? How does the synagogue, in its contemporary denominational variety, provide a common positive focus for Jewish ethnic identification, and what is the significance of the variations on the Jewish theme in the context of a contemporary urban community such as Toronto?

Parsons (1966: 21-2) suggests that of prime importance among processes of social change is the *enhancement of adaptive capacity*. In the process of *differentiation*, a single social unit, category, or sub-system divides into units or systems which differ in both structure and functional significance for the wider system, *Enhancement of adaptive capacity*, in this instance, implies an increase in the newly differentiated unit's capacity for performing its primary function, as compared to the performance of that function in the previous, more diffuse structure.

The differentiation of the Judaic religious component from its previous, more diffuse Jewish ethnic/religious structure can be seen, in Parsonian terms, as having thus enhanced its adaptive capacity in the context of the contemporary urban community of Toronto. To the extent that Jewish congregants in Toronto differ in status-orientation—from the polar extremes of the Torah-oriented Orthodox to the atheistic Reform—these variations have been met by the differentiation of three religious denominational forms from their common ethnic base. Contemporary Orthodox, Conservative, and Reform Judaism represent (in this order) a continuum in terms of degree of differentiation of the religious from the ethnic component.

If we view contemporary synagogue affiliations in terms of an *ethnic assimilation continuum*[1] from ultra-traditional Orthodoxy to ultra-liberal Reform, we find that the degree of traditionalism tends to coincide with the degree of ethnic identity. In modern Orthodoxy the ethnic and religious factors are largely merged; Judaism, as in the *shtetl*, is a way of life and the degree of ethnic/religious identity is high. In Conservative and Reform Judaism the religious factor has become far more differentiated from its ethnic base, and ethnic identity is somewhat weaker—to the greatest degree in the case of Reform.

As indicated in Figure 1, the continuum from orthodox-Orthodox to reform-Reform among the three congregations investigated in this study shows a concentration in the middle ranks tending towards Conservatism. It is predicted, on the basis of this study, that religious affiliation among Toronto Jewry will move towards a broader-based Conservatism—whether or not particular congregations are so labelled—and

---

FIGURE 1.   Religious Variation on an Ethnic Assimilation Continuum, Toronto Jewry (1967–9)

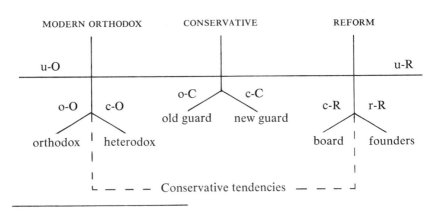

O—Orthodox   U—Ultra
C—Conservative M—Modern
R—Reform

that the orthodox-Orthodox and reform-Reform grouping will become peripheral.

Yinger (1966: 96) suggests that in contemporary America "continued identification with Judaism is possible, for many people, only if it does not conflict with new identifications with nation, with occupational group, and other reference groups that have become important to them. Thus, there is change and there is continuity; there is continued identification with a religion that is progressively more similar to those around it and more congruent with its setting and the non-religious inclinations of its adherents."

According to Hansen's "principle of third-generation interest" (1938: 9–10): "What the son wishes to forget, the grandson wishes to remember." Herberg (1960), following Hansen, suggests that in America the second generation, in their attempt to slough off evidences of foreign origin, rejected their ethnic heritage, and to a lesser degree the ethnic church associated with it. The third generation, on the other hand, secure in their Americanness, sought a focus for their identity within this very broad American context and in so doing turned back to their heritage: thus religion became the focal point of ethnic affiliations.

Within the Jewish congregations which I studied in Toronto, this "return to religion" has occurred among second- as well as third-generation congregants. In Toronto, contrary to Herberg's thesis, which was applied to American Jews, the second generation have not forgotten their Jewish ethnic heritage. They have, in fact, led the way in adapting the traditional Judaic system to the socio-economic milieu of contemporary Toronto. As Yinger suggests, contemporary Judaism has become, in varying degrees, Protestantized, urbanized, and secularized. In Toronto both second- and third-generation Jews have followed Hansen's rule: they have turned to religious associational affiliation as the focal point for their ethnic identity.

The evidence suggests that this apparent difference in generational orientation between Canadian and American Jews is a function of similar historical forces impinging upon North American Jews from without but interacting with a different generation in each case. By the time the first heavy wave of Eastern European/Jewish immigration reached Toronto (1890–1920), many second-generation American Jews were already well on their way to becoming fully Americanized. With the Second World War and the advent of Nazi policies, it became increasingly apparent, even to the very Americanized Jew, that no matter how carefully he changed his name, bobbed his nose, or married into the non-Jewish elite, he could never fully assimilate. But with the end of the war came the promise and then the reality of fulfilment of an ancient Judaic prophecy: the establishment of the State of Israel—a focal point for Jewish identification the world over. Given this boost to their ethnic security, more and more North American Jews returned to their Jewish heritage. That the ensuing forms of Judaic religious expression—Orthodox, Conservative, and Reform—tended to be far more acculturated to dominant ways among American Jews than among Canadian Jews probably reflects not only the differences in prevailing national ideologies (melting pot as opposed to multiculturalism or mosaic) but differences in the generations who "turned back". In the United States they were very Americanized third- and fourth-generation Jews; in Canada they were second-generation Jews still ethnically insecure. Despite these differences, however, the return to religion provided for American and Canadian Jew alike a positive focus for Jewish ethnic identification.

Lewin (1948: 192) contends that in every status grouping some strata are culturally more central, i.e. ideal or typical of group values, traditions, and habits, and other strata culturally more peripheral. Members of the core or central strata, I would suggest, can be said to be *positively identified*, i.e. to look to their particular status category as their primary reference group. Members of the peripheral strata, by contrast, can be said to be *negatively identified*, i.e. to look beyond their particular ethnic grouping to another, usually more dominant, group as their primary reference group.

Lewin (1948: 194–5) points out that, although every grouping contains a number of social strata, there are certain differences between the typical structure of a "privileged" (dominant or majority) and "underprivileged" (subordinate or minority) grouping: the forces acting on the individual members of a subordinate group are directed away from the central area toward the periphery of the group, and, if possible, toward the still higher status of the majority. He further suggests that minority members would leave the group if the barriers set up by the majority did not prevent them from doing so. The group structure of a subordinate status group is therefore considered to be that of a people fundamentally turned against themselves, i.e. *negatively identified* with their status category. The strength and solidarity of the minority group depend ultimately on the balance of forces, positive and negative, within the group. (See Figure 2.)

FIGURE 2 Resolving Social Conflicts
(From K. Lewin, *Resolving Social Conflicts* [1948], Fig. xxvi)

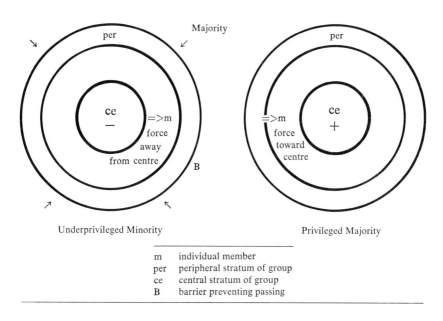

Underprivileged Minority   Privileged Majority

m	individual member
per	peripheral stratum of group
ce	central stratum of group
B	barrier preventing passing

FIGURE 3 Ethnic Minority in Transition: Toronto Jewry (1967–9)

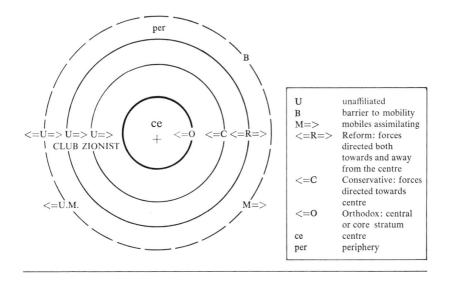

U	unaffiliated
B	barrier to mobility
M=>	mobiles assimilating
<=R=>	Reform: forces directed both towards and away from the centre
<=C	Conservative: forces directed towards centre
<=O	Orthodox: central or core stratum
ce	centre
per	periphery

The synagogue study demonstrated clearly that among Jewish congregants in contemporary Toronto, the balance of forces has changed from negative to positive in ethnic identification and that, concomitantly, the internal structure of the Jewish/ethnic group bears little resemblance to Lewin's model (Figure 2). In Toronto synagogues there were core strata (albeit minimal) of positively identified members upholding and, indeed, as Lewin (1948: 192) points out, over-rating traditional codes and patterns, and they have provided the internal forces of ethnic continuity with which external forces have interacted to create a positive balance in ethnic identification within the group.

The primary external forces influencing ethnic identification have been both positive and negative. The negative forces are those of discrimination against and persecution of the ethnic minority by members of the dominant society. Personal experiences of anti-Semitism in Toronto were compounded by the annihilation of six million fellow-Jews in Germany under the Nazi regime and the latent threat that "It *can* happen here." Positive forces are the perceived lessening of barriers to upward mobility within dominant institutions, particularly within the economic sphere, and to a limited degree in the area of inter-personal or primary relations between members of dominant and subordinate (Jewish) ethnic groups. The greatest boosts, however, to positive ethnic identification have been the establishment of the State of Israel in 1948 and the swift victory of Israel in the Israeli-Arab War of June 1967, with the concomitant rise in status of world Jewry.

Lewin (1948: 163–6) suggests that members of a subordinate minority are typically ambivalent towards it: they react negatively towards minority group values which conflict with dominant group values, yet have a positive sense of identification with fellow minority group members *as such* in terms of sharing a common fate. The study of Toronto synagogues seems to show that the transition from negative to positive identity within the Jewish ethnic group proceeded apace with the resolution of this ambivalence. This was accomplished through the incorporation into the structure of the subordinate group of those codes and patterns of the dominant group which had high-status (elitist) implications.

Lewin appears to have looked at the question of minority group relations as an either/or proposition: members either accepted the core codes and patterns of their ethnic group and identified positively with it as their primary reference group, or they accepted the dominant ethnic majority as their primary reference group and attempted to gain membership within or become absorbed into it. What appears to have happened within the Jewish ethnic membership in Toronto is not absorption (total assimilation) but partial integration: assimilation in public, dominant institutions, with maintenance of ethnic distinctiveness in private religious and secular Jewish institutions. Given the fact of core and peripheral membership in the Jewish ethnic group, what has developed is an internal system of stratification *differentiated* in terms of degree of acceptance and incorporation of majority codes and patterns, and *legitimated* through religious associational affiliation. The internal status system can be said to be stratified ideally into three categories: Orthodox, Conservative, and Reform, each differing essentially in status-orientation.

The Orthodox represent the core membership, the traditionalists, attempting to maintain and perpetuate ethnic and religious codes and patterns and incorporating only peripherally majority ways. For the Orthodox, the core Orthodox sub-stratum remains primary as reference group. The Conservatives are the middle sub-stratum, maintaining a nostalgic attachment to certain core Orthodox codes and patterns, but increasingly incorporating majority ways. These members look primarily to the ethnic group as a whole as primary reference group. The Reform are the peripheral sub-stratum, the marginals, and potential mobiles. Unlike the Orthodox and Conservative, whose ethnic identification is essentially positive, Reform members are ambivalent, shifting situationally from positive to negative in ethnic identification. In this sub-stratum, only those Judaic and ethnic codes and patterns which do not conflict with the high-status ideals of the dominant Anglo-Canadian elite are acceptable, and dominant group codes and patterns assume priority. By incorporating and stressing the intellectual, humanistic, and universalistic aspects of both subordinate and dominant codes and patterns, both reference groups are maintained simultaneously as primary. Thus Reform membership serves to legitimate marginal ethnic status (see Figure 3).

Although the trend among Toronto Jewry towards synagogue-building and membership indicates that the religious association is increasingly becoming the focal point for Jewish ethnic identification, *not all* Jews are religiously affiliated. It should be noted that, as indicated in Figure 3, those Jews who choose *not* to affiliate with a contemporary synagogue are also to be found at varying points within the sub-strata of the ethnic grouping. Those who choose an ideological ethnic alternative, such as a Jewish Zionist or Socialist organization, can probably be said to be positively identified more strongly than members of a private Jewish social and recreational club, and so are located closer to the centre. Similarly, those peripheral Jews who remain Jewish "in name only" can probably be distinguished from unaffiliated mobiles who attempt to assimilate fully.

Despite a continuing trend towards relaxation of barriers to upward mobility in the socio-economic sphere of dominant institutions and to some extent within status ranks in contemporary Toronto as well, a process of change from negative to positive identity is taking place within the Jewish ethnic group. It is predicted, on the basis of the synagogue study, that structural changes within the ethnic group, concomitant with differentiation of the traditional Judaic ideal into Orthodox, Conservative, and Reform sub-strata, will continue to draw members from the periphery towards the centre through acculturation to dominant group codes and patterns. It is further suggested that the resultant increase in intra-ethnic interaction will serve to strengthen bonds of ethnic solidarity and for the majority of members effectively prevent defection through primary assimilation. This latter hypothesis is, however, based on two major assumptions: (1) the continued viability of the State of Israel, and (2) the continued barrier to upward social mobility within status ranks in Toronto, that is, non-acceptance by the dominant group of members of the ethnic minority as social equals in the private sphere of primary relations.

Two interrelated problems stimulated the research upon which the synagogue study was based. The first question concerned the so-called "religious revival" (Herberg 1960: 1-4) in contemporary North America, particularly as evidenced among Jews. The second question, specific to the Jewish group, concerned the growing trend to Conservative Judaism in synagogue affiliation.

In spite of the narrow range of my field research, it seems clear that the "religious revival" among contemporary North American Jews represents in essence an ethnic revival—a shift from negative to positive ethnic identification. The religious association has become a status symbol serving to legitimate positive ethnic identity and to fulfil ethnic goals.

The trend to Conservativism is also strongly linked to the shift from negative to positive identity. For the majority of contemporary North American Jews, traditional Orthodox codes and patterns are too far removed from the ways of the dominant group to provide a positive focus for ethnic identification. Reform, on the other hand, is too ambivalent to provide a positive focus for most Jews. Conservativism, the middle-of-the-road, has the widest appeal in that it combines tradition and change. Conservativism, in other words, maintains core ethnic and religious codes and patterns, yet increasingly incorporates high-status elements from the dominant society. For increasing numbers of contemporary North American Jews, Conservative Judaism seems to be providing the most meaningful positive focus for ethnic identification. Moreover, among those apparently dedicated to Orthodox and Reform congregations through declared membership, there are, in fact, large numbers whose status-orientation places them in the ranks of Conservativism.

NOTES

1   The idea of a continuum in contemporary synagogue affiliation, as opposed to a sharp dividing line between Orthodox, Conservative, and Reform denominational forms, has also been suggested by Sodden (1962).

REFERENCES

Bergal, E. E.
1955   *Urban Sociology.*
Bloom, L.
1942   "The Jews of Buna." In I. Graeber and S. H. Britt, *Jews in a Gentile World.* New York: Macmillan.
Douglass, H. P.
1924   *The St. Louis Church Survey.*
Glazer, N.
1957   *American Judaism.* Chicago: Chicago: University of Chicago Press.
Hansen, M. L.
1938   *The Problem of the Third Generation.* Rock Island, Ill.: Augustana Historical Society.
Herberg, W.
1960   *Protestant, Catholic, Jew.* Garden City: Anchor Books.
Koenig, S.
1942   "The Socio-economic Structure of an American Jewish Community." In I. Graeber and S. H. Britt, *Jews in a Gentile World.* New York: Macmillan.
Lewin, K.
1948   *Resolving Social Conflicts.* New York: Harper and Brothers.

Minnes, M. S.
1953   "Cleavage in Women's Organizations." *American Sociological Review,* Vol. 18 (February).
Parsons, T.
1964   *The Social System.* New York: Free Press.
1966   *Societies: Evolutionary and Comparative Perspectives.* Englewood Cliffs, N.J.: Prentice-Hall.
Polsky, H. W.
1958   "A Study of Orthodoxy in Milwaukee." In M. Sklare, ed., *The Jews.* New York: Free Press.
Sklare, M.
1955   *Conservative Judaism.* New York: Free Press.
Sodden, J.
1962   "The Impact of Urbanization on the Synagogue." Unpublished Ph.D. dissertation, New York University.
Warner, W. L., and P. S. Lunt
1941   *The Social Life of a Modern Community.* Yankee City Series, Vol. 3. New Haven: Yale University Press.

Warner, W.L., and L. Srole
1954   *The Social Systems of American Ethnic Groups.* Yankee City Series, Vol. 3. New Haven: Yale University Press.
Weinryb, B. D.
1958   "Jewish Immigration and Accommodation to America." In M. Sklare, ed., *The Jews.* New York: Free Press.
Yinger, J. M.
1966   *Sociology Looks at Religion.* New York: Macmillan.

3.

Types of Organization

The Adaptation of the Roman Catholic Church in Canadian Society*

Kenneth Westhues

In British North America, the Roman Catholic Church confronted colonial governments which not only gave their allegiance to the head of a different religion (the English monarch) but also, in some respects, persecuted the Church of Rome. The Catholic population in the colonies, while comparatively large, was composed of the conquered French, newly converted Indians, settlers from Ireland and Scotland, and other relatively poor and powerless elements. Today, little more than a century after Confederation, the Catholic Church finds virtually no restrictions on its activities. It is now the largest single denomination in every province east of Manitoba, and embraces nearly a quarter of the population in the west. In half the provinces, the church has unique rights to operate separate schools. Given the difficulties which the Catholic Church initially faced, it has carved out for itself a remarkably secure niche in the Canadian nation.

*Prepared for this volume. The research on which this paper is based was supported by Canada Council Grant No. S73-0293. Grateful acknowledgement is made to E. Burrill and V. Paddy, who served as research assistants for the study, and to P. A. Westhues, G. L. Gold, S. Clark, O. K. White, P. R. Sinclair, C. F. Grindstaff, and C. Levine, all of whom offered critical comments on earlier drafts of this paper.

The purpose of this essay is to give, from the point of view of organizational analysis, a brief portrayal of the mode of adaptation of the Catholic Church to Canadian society. A variety of historical sources are drawn upon, especially those concerning the church outside Quebec. Relatively little research has been done on the church in English Canada, especially as compared to Quebec,[1] with the result that Catholicism in this country is often regarded as mainly a French-Canadian phenomenon. By an intentional emphasis on the other provinces, I want to show that the much-discussed role of the church in Quebec is not unique to that province, but rather forms part of a more general national pattern. By way of introduction, the following paragraphs describe some basic properties of the church under study.

The Catholic Church as an Organization

From a sociological perspective, the Catholic Church is first of all an organization with a leader, a hierarchy of authority, a chain of command, goals, an ideology, functionaries, and all the other properties of organizations. This church conforms to the classic definition of an organization, "a system of consciously coordinated activities or forces of two or more persons".[2]

As an organization, this church differs from most other Christian religious bodies in two broad ways: its multinational character and its particular religious outlook. Milton Yinger has distinguished between the "universal church" and the "ecclesia". By the former is meant a church which manages to transcend national, ethnic, and class boundaries and to incorporate a variety of religious tendencies; by the latter is meant a church which is established in, but limited to, a particular nation or class.[3] To Yinger, the Catholic Church is the purest example of the former type; the Lutheran, Anglican, and Russian Orthodox Churches tend toward the ideal type of ecclesia. According to Catholic belief, nations, governments, classes, and cultures exist in a secular order which is distinct from that of the church and to which the church can never be tied or subject. While Rome encourages adaptation to the political and cultural conditions of various nations and social sectors, such adaptation is permissible only for the sake of achieving the distinctive goals of the church as a whole.

The second basic way in which the Catholic Church differs from most other Christian bodies concerns its belief system. Catholic beliefs can be broadly distinguished from those of Protestant churches by their emphasis on the social nature of man. In the Catholic tradition, the gift of redemption comes to the individual only through the church and its sacraments. Hence the fundamental reality is not the individual but the church, often termed the "Mystical Body of Christ". In the Protestant tradition, by contrast, the gift of redemption comes to the individual directly; what is fundamentally real is the relationship of the individual to God, while the Protestant Church serves not as a mediator between God and men but as an association of believers. In this basic theological difference lies the key to understanding differences in behaviour of Catholic and Protestant Churches in the secular world.[4]

The particularly social and anti-individualistic nature of Catholic theology is reflected in its attitude toward social institutions, of which three deserve particular mention here: the economy, the polity, and education. Above all, Catholic theology deplores a competitive spirit, one which seeks individual advancement and the furtherance of individual self-interest. This is the other side of the coin which Weber described with respect to Protestantism.[5] The individualism and competition of a capitalistic economic order have an affinity with Protestant theology, but an antagonism to Catholic theology. In the Catholic system of stratification, high status is given, not to independent and successful entrepreneurs, but to those who sacrifice their personal desires and subject themselves most perfectly to the God-given authority of the church. While the accumulation of property or power is not regarded as inherently evil—as the wealth of many religious orders and of the church itself attests[6]—the property or power should belong to the community and should be used for the communal good.

The political order, from the viewpoint of Catholic theology, must also reflect man's social nature. A system in which individual politicians compete for the votes of electors who are themselves motivated by self-interest is hardly regarded as appropriate. Political power, like that of the church in the religious sphere, is believed to come not from men but from God; as a result, the yardstick by which a government is to be measured is the extent to which it uses its authority as God intended. The liberal capitalist definition of good government as "that which governs least" is quite distant from the Catholic conception, which portrays good government as that which directs men to live according to the will of God—as defined by the Gospels, tradition, and church pronouncements.

The church's attitude toward education conforms as well to the corporate and communitarian thrust of its theology. Education is not regarded as an experimental laboratory in which ideas are tested one against the other so that students may choose. On the contrary, education is considered the process of inculcating in youth the truth of the human situation, the core of which is the belief that only through the church can man properly reciprocate God's gift of life to him. Thus, schools in which children are taught some other specific religion are scarcely more abhorrent to the Catholic Church than are schools in which children learn about several religions so that they may choose.

The basic goal of the church is to realize, to the greatest extent possible, the kind of organic Catholic community through which, according to its theology, the redemptive work of Christ can be completed. More specifically, the church seeks to involve as many people as possible in its sacramental life. Lest the church in a given nation be a drain on the spiritual budget of the international church, it seeks the establishment of a native clergy, of native communities of monks and nuns, and of energetic religious orders, which are able to keep the laity strong in the faith and involved in the organizational life of the church. The church tries as well to ensure that in every country it should have sufficient control over the educational system to ensure that Catholic youth are educated according to Catholic theology. It is also necessary, of course, to acquire sufficient financial resources to achieve the more fundamental purposes. Finally, the accomplishment of all these goals presupposes that the church have a co-operative relationship with the government, at least to the extent that the latter will not interfere with the church's pursuit of its own organizational ambitions.

In the terminology of the anthropologist Frederik Barth, the hierarchy appointed by the Vatican to a particular nation is expected to act as an entrepreneur on behalf of the church in the face of that nation's cultural and political order.[7] Through a series of transactions with the host society, the bishops assigned to it are expected to secure the eventual and enduring integration of the church as a central institution within that society. The remainder of this paper concerns the manner in which the Catholic Church has achieved integration into that society which evolved from British North America.

Adaptation to Canada in Comparative Perspective

The conquest of the Americas by European powers from the sixteenth to the eighteenth century opened up new opportunities for the Catholic Church to accomplish its global purposes. Hence, its functionaries in each of the conquering nations sought to engage in such transactions as would ensure for the church the most complete integration in the various societies of the new world. In none of them did it fail completely. None the less, the modes of adaptation and integration varied considerably.

Throughout Latin America, the Catholic Church achieved integration through *unique recognition*. As the Belgian sociologist François Houtart has noted, the concept of *Cristianidad* was intimately linked with the concept of *Hispanidad*; political conquest by Spain and Portugal was inextricably interwoven with religious conquest by the Catholic Church.[8] When new nations were formed in South America, the Catholic Church easily assumed the status of the official national religion. While the extent of formal control by South American bishops has varied in different countries at different times, the church has not lost even to the present day its status as the *de facto* religion. Not surprisingly, South American societies bear the imprint of a Catholic definition of the world: communitarian culture, lack of individualism and competition, relative absence of democratic politics, and educational systems directed more to the arts than to the sciences.

In striking contrast to its South American neighbours, the United States gave to the Catholic Church the freedom to exist but the status of absolute *non-recognition*. Certainly nowhere in western Europe or the Americas did the church confront an environment more hostile to its basic outlook on the world. American society was founded as a utopian experiment in democracy, one which enshrined rugged individualism and relentless competition as national values. The United States became a seedbed of experimentation and pragmatism, of liberal capitalism and individual rights. From its inception it defined church and state as separate, and reduced religious denominations to the status of voluntary associations whose viability was dependent upon the individual choice of their members. Such a status, as well as the basic societal organization, was, and remains, wholly congruent with the Protestant worldview.

The United States is usually characterized as a society of denominational pluralism and religious freedom.[9] This characterization is correct, however, only within the basic parameters of the political and social structure of the country; these parameters are themselves at variance with Catholic theology. The ideal Catholic cannot *choose* which church best suits his needs. Thus, in order to protect immigrant Catholics from the dangers of a threatening milieu, the American church was compelled to create in the United States an insular "sub-society" of Catholic schools, hospitals, orphanages, and other organizations, all privately funded from Catholic sources.[10] Some two centuries after the founding of the United States, the American church displays on the one hand a continuing preservation of Catholic character within an insular organization, and on the other hand steady assimilation into the basically Protestant values of American society.

Andrew Greeley has included Canada along with the United States among those few countries in the western world in which denominational pluralism exists.[11] The fact that Catholics in Canada constitute only a minority of the population is, indeed, a point of similarity with their American neighbours. The position of the church, however, is only partially measured by the percentage of the population it can count as members; its position is better measured by the extent to which it succeeds in realizing the organic Catholic community proclaimed in its theology. By this criterion, Canadian society has given to the Catholic Church a far more favourable status than has American society. It is a status of *partial recognition*, according to which the church is permitted to function as something more than a voluntary association, though not as an official religion in the Latin American tradition.[12]

The critical transactions between church and society, those which were to determine the status of the church in Canada for centuries to come, occurred in the decades immediately following the conquest of Quebec by the British in 1760.[13] At that time, virtually the entire Catholic population was in the newly conquered French colony; the ecclesiastical organization was concentrated there as well, with the bishop of Quebec City having jurisdiction over all of present-day Canada. Throughout the period of French rule, the Quebec church had chafed under the attempts of the colonial government to control it. With the conquest, that government departed, leaving the bishop and some 138 priests as the surviving agents of social control and organization among the *habitants*. The fundamental transaction that occurred in the ensuing decades amounted to an exchange of loyalty to the British Crown on the part of the church in return for recognition of the church's authority on the part of the Crown. The British were separated from their new French subjects by the deep chasm of language and culture; if the church, using its moral power over the *habitants*, could help to prevent revolt, recognition of the papist bishop and his control over the meagre educational system were a small price to pay for such assistance.

The willingness of the British government to tolerate the church and use it for its own purposes is generally regarded as shrewd politics. The acceptance of British rule by Bishop Briand and his successors, however, is often looked upon as an act of betrayal of the French Canadians. This is true within a world-view which values self-government and political autonomy, but inaccurate from the viewpoint of the central tenets of Catholic theology. The Quebec church was interested in the political system less as an entity in itself than as a constraint within which it had to operate. If British rule would permit greater realization of the goals of the church—which it did in most respects—then it was preferable to French rule. Since the church had discouraged political participation and democracy under the French, there was nothing lost in discouraging the same practices under the British. The founding transaction between the church and the new colonial regime was a bargain for both sides, given their respective goals.

In its initial interaction with the British, the church established itself as a broker or intermediary between the Catholic subjects of the Crown and the Crown itself. This role, defined in the first instance in Quebec, was simply extended in so far as possible to the other colonies, as Catholic immigrants began to settle in them.

Two principal indices may be pointed out of the partial recognition and role of broker accorded to the church in Canadian society. First was the de facto right given to the hierarchy of making direct representations to the highest levels of the federal and provincial governments. That such a right existed for the bishops in Quebec is common knowledge; its existence in English Canada is less well known. A second index of the special status of the church was the provision of public funds for separate Catholic educational systems. These two indices are intimately related, of course, since the importance of separate education for maintaining the strength of the church made it the most common subject of negotiations between governments and the hierarchy. While no attempt can be made here to portray the special status of the church across the provinces, the history of education in the anglophone regions illustrates the fact that the power and recognition accorded to the church were not limited to the Province of Quebec.[14]

Although exact percentages are impossible to calculate, one can safely estimate that today, between two-thirds and three-quarters of Catholic children in English Canada are enrolled in publicly supported schools directly or indirectly controlled by the Catholic Church. No other religious body in Canada enjoys such special prerogatives in education. Nor are these prerogatives limited to the elementary and secondary levels. Through a variety of arrangements, Catholic colleges affiliated with provincial universities in Alberta, Saskatchewan, and Ontario enjoy some measure of tax support, as do Catholic universities in the Maritimes. In Newfoundland, the boards of directors of provincially supported Catholic colleges are appointed by the bishops of the province.

Explaining the Canadian Mode of Adaptation

If it is clear that the Catholic Church succeeded in securing at least partial recognition from the non-Catholic governments of Britain and then of Canada, and in integrating itself quite successfully into Canadian society, the question remains of why this was possible. An adequate answer to this question must rest fundamentally on certain organizational qualities of this multi-national church. The Catholic Church has functioned throughout its history on a principle of decentralization. Its bishops are regarded as more than subjects of the pope; rather, they are, in theological terms, successors to the apostles. Each bishop is regarded as having the same power in his own diocese as the college of bishops headed by the pope has over the international church. Each diocese is thought to be the embodiment of the church founded by Jesus, not just a subunit of the church as a whole. It was mentioned earlier that the church regards itself as the sole possessor of the power of mediating between God and men; here it must be stressed that each bishop is considered to possess the fullness of that power.[15]

The organizational implication of this theological definition of the bishop's role is that he has considerable freedom to adapt to local conditions. If Catholic bishops demonstrate, for the most part, remarkable compliance with Rome, it is less because of a centralized hierarchy of authority than because of what may be termed *value-integration*.[16] By this term is meant the existence among bishops of such commonality with respect to basic theology, basic values, and union with Rome, that acquiescence to Vatican wishes seldom requires the threat of sanctions; because of ideological agreement, decentralization is possible. The commonality of theology and values is assured through the process of selection of priests for the episcopacy. They are not popularly elected, nor is it permitted for a priest overtly to promote his own candidacy. Rather, future bishops are selected by Rome on the recommendation of incumbent bishops who have themselves demonstrated firm commitment to Rome and its theology. In Canada, as in other countries, the decentralized structure based on value-integration has permitted the nation's bishops to behave aggressively and creatively in adapting to native culture and politics, while at the same time never deviating from allegiance to the core of Catholic theology or to the Vatican itself.

If decentralization is an important key to understanding the success of the church, of nearly equal importance is the discipline by which the church is able to control the behaviour not only of its clergy but also of its lay membership. With respect to the clergy, the rule of celibacy implies that the priest's commitment to the church will not be compromised by competing attachments to a wife or children; the priest's loyalty is undivided, a fact which places him at the nearly total disposal of his superiors.[17] With respect to both clergy and laity, the church's definition of itself as the sole mediator between God and men permits it to impose sanctions impossible to Protestant religious bodies. If man's gift of himself to God occurs only through the church, excommunication by the church means that the gift of self cannot be given and that damnation is all but inevitable. The church's control is sufficient—assuming the laity are successfully persuaded of Catholic theology—to influence greatly behaviour in the voting booth and in the public forum. It is this control which the church used as a resource with which to bargain with federal and provincial governments in Canada.[18]

A third quality upon which the church's international success has hinged is the network of religious orders of both men and women. These orders, like the Jesuits, the Oblates, or the Sisters of Charity, are outside the formal chain of command of pope, bishops, and parish priests. They are organizations directly responsible to the Vatican which supplement the work of bishops and parish priests wherever the need arises. In missionary work, in all levels of education, in the publication of books and periodicals, and in a host of activities both within and outside the basic diocesan and parochial structure, the religious orders have served as special task forces, quickly and easily mobilized to accomplish immediate goals of the church.

A decentralized organization, effective mechanisms to ensure clerical and lay commitment, and an efficient supplementary structure of religious orders are three aspects of the multi-national church which were critical in its successful integration into Canadian society. These factors, however, were not particular to the Canadian experience. What remains is to delimit those factors which resulted in the distinct mode of adaptation of the church to Canadian society. Two broad categories of variables may be distinguished, those characterizing the internal organization of the church and those characterizing its environment.[19] The following paragraphs will describe two principal characteristics internal to the church in Canada (indigenity and ethnic identification) and two salient qualities of its societal milieu (vertical pluralism and corporatist character).

Indigenity

By this term is meant the relatively quick development in the church in Canada of a native clergy and hierarchy, so that its organization in Canada came rapidly to be perceived as indigenous rather than foreign. In this respect the British conquest of Quebec was of benefit to the church; the clergy who identified with France returned home, leaving the Quebec church under the control of a bishop and priests whose attachment was more to Quebec than to France.[20] The decades of isolation from France which followed the conquest helped to confirm a distinctly Canadian identity in the church, one which enabled it both to win more effectively the loyalty of the Quebec people and to bargain more successfully with the British (and later the federal) government. This situation was altogether in contrast to that, for example, in Haiti, where continued French domination of the church (particularly at the hierarchical level) resulted in distrust and resentment of it by the native Haitian government.[21]

It was not only in Quebec, however, that the church quickly became indigenous. In 1893, nearly forty years before Britain granted representative government to Newfoundland, a native Newfoundlander was appointed archbishop of St. John's.[22] The first bishop of Charlottetown, consecrated in 1821, was the son of a farmer who had arrived in the first immigration of Scottish Catholics to the island.[23] A similar policy of making the church indigenous was followed throughout Canada. Porter has shown that by 1952, more than 90 per cent of Catholic bishops in this country were native-born (as opposed, interestingly, to only 40 per cent of Anglican bishops). Porter concluded that the "Catholic bishops know their communities through having grown up in them and are, therefore, able to articulate a Catholic view about Canada which has meaning for the Catholic population of Canada."[24]

Ethnic Identification

Throughout Canadian history, the Catholic population has been composed of members of ethnic minorities. Among these, the largest was the French-Canadian minority, separated from its British conqueror by the boundaries of culture, language, and religion. Second were the Irish and Scottish Catholic minorities of the eastern provinces and Ontario. The third set of Catholic minorities is the result of immigration in the nineteenth and twentieth centuries from Poland, Italy, the Ukraine, Germany, Portugal, as well as the British Isles and other European countries. What has characterized the Catholic population throughout Canadian history has been strong ethnic identification and gross under-representation in the economic, social, and political elites.[25]

The response of the church to the minority ethnic statuses of the Catholic population has been, for the most part, to identify itself with these statuses. Such identification has been clearest in Quebec, where the church regarded language and religion as mutually reinforcing. It appeared as well, however, in other parts of Canada. For the Scottish Catholics of Prince Edward Island and Cape Breton, the church provided Scottish-Canadian bishops and priests of local origin. For the Irish Catholics of Nova Scotia, southern New Brunswick, and Ontario, bishops and priests of the same ethnic origin were appointed. When Ukrainian immigrants began to settle on the prairies in the 1890s, Ukrainian priests were sent to minister to them.[26]

In the present day, the church continues to adapt its parochial organization to the needs of immigrants. As a result, most Canadian cities include parishes specifically designated as Italian, Portuguese, Lithuanian, Hungarian, Slovak, and so forth, which serve the various Catholic minorities. The maintenance of such national parishes represents shrewd adaptation to the pluralistic and multi-cultural nature of Canadian society; in the United States, by contrast, a society far more assimilationist in nature, the church has similarly adapted itself by phasing out national parishes as quickly as the immigrants can melt into the American mainstream. It appears likely that while appropriate adaptation has occurred in both countries, the Canadian variant has better served the church's own goals. By reinforcing the traditional Catholic cultures of the immigrants' countries of origin, the church is more successful in preserving an orthodox Catholic mentality than is the case when it allows Catholics to assimilate into a basically Protestant or secular culture, attempting at the same time to preserve the core of Catholic orthodoxy.[27]

Vertical Pluralism

The indigenity and ethnic identification of the Canadian church would not have resulted in its successful integration into Canadian society without a certain congruity between such behaviour on its part and the expectations of the Canadian ruling elite. In order to understand this congruity, it is useful to conceptualize Canadian society as a collection of marginally autonomous minority groups presided over by a dominant elite in whose hands rests the bulk of political and economic power. In Porter's classic study, clear evidence is presented of the extent to which differences in social class coincide with differences in ethnicity and religion.

Smith and Kornberg, in their comparative study of ethnicity in the United States and Canada, measured the extent of residential segregation in four cities, two in each of the countries. Surprisingly, they found residential segregation *lower* in Canada than in the United States, but political segregation higher. In the United States, they observed that immigrant groups became involved in the political structure and used it for their own upward mobility within, and integration into, the American structure of power. In Canada, by contrast, political leaders from the dominant British elite were able to exploit ethnic differences but still keep centres of power impervious to the involvement of the ethnic groups themselves. Smith and Kornberg concluded that multi-culturalism remains a policy in Canada "because those who benefit from the situation—the Canadian political elite—want it to be maintained."[28]

The implications of such an analysis of Canadian society for the present study are clear. It was in the interests of the Canadian ruling class to encourage relatively self-contained ethnic communities removed from participation in the elite structure of Canadian politics. With respect not only to the French, but to other ethnic minorities as well, the elite could keep itself in power by making enough concessions to non-elites that they would remain in their own isolated and relatively non-threatening enclaves. Such an arrangement satisfied the needs of the church as well, since it would gain few if any advantages from the development of a secular political consciousness among its members. The church's broker role, effectively agreed upon by the British government and the church for the governance of Quebec, was simply extended in principle to the Catholic minorities in the rest of the young Canadian nation. The fact that this role was in the interests of both parties is basic to an explanation of why the church enjoys the partial recognition it does in modern Canada.

Corporatist Character

Closely related to the "vertical mosaic" characterization of Canadian society is the notion that in its structure, Canada has been more corporatist and less individualistic than the United States. With respect to pre-conquest French Canada, Eccles has pointed out that this society rested on a principle of unity, not diversity; its inhabitants were regarded as parts of an organic whole under the guidance of the French monarchy and the Catholic Church.[29] What needs to be added is that British rule did not succeed in destroying this corporatist character but only in placing it in the context of a new empire. The colonial status of Canada, its immense size and harsh climate, and the particular requirements of its economy, forced governments in Ottawa and the provinces to behave as something more than referees in a free economic and social game. The result was a higher degree of centralized power and a lower degree of individual autonomy than in the southern half of the continent.

This corporate quality of Canadian society was more congruent with the needs of the Catholic Church than the religious differences between Britain and Rome would suggest. It helped to prevent a clear separation of church and state from being institutionalized in the Canadian nation. Further, once the Catholic Church had secured recognition as a Canadian institution in the British North America Act, the way was open for continuing negotiation with governments on a range of issues. When the federal government was dealing in a formal way with other large organizations, like the Canadian Pacific Railroad, there was nothing out of character in the church's insisting on similar recognition. The corporate character of Canadian society meant that the Catholic bishops were able to act as more than an informal pressure group; rather, as a legitimate institution in the political and social fabric of the nation.

What this section has been intended to show is that the special status enjoyed by the Catholic Church in Canada, particularly with respect to education, must be attributed on the one hand to the sophisticated organizational structure and policy of the Canadian church, and on the other hand to the elitist and corporatist nature of Canadian society. The church wisely took advantage of the role it could play most effectively for the rulers of Canada, that of securing the loyalty of minority groups to the Crown and to the developing Canadian nation. In return it exacted special privileges for itself. These privileges, to some extent incorporated into law and otherwise confirmed by tradition, have persisted.

Conclusion

The purpose of this essay has been to delineate and explain the partial recognition accorded to the Catholic Church in Canada. This purpose has necessitated a consideration of the colonial origins of the country, since the current status of the church is principally the result of the circumstances of the eighteenth and nineteenth centuries. If many Canadians today regard the separate school systems of some provinces as an anachronism, and if today's Catholics increasingly consider themselves full-fledged Canadians, instead of members of a somewhat separate and excluded minority, these attitudes do not prevent the separate schools from continuing to exist, nor have they been able to propel Catholic Canadians into proportionate representation in the economic, political, or social elites of the country. Social institutions and patterns of stratification are not subject to instant alteration in response to attitudinal shifts in the population. They are controlled—and hence explained—at first inspection by the contemporary structure of power, but more fundamentally by the tradition of past generations, which, in Marx's words, "weighs like a mountain on the mind of the living".[30]

Canadian cultural history has been marked, none the less, by increasing democratization, and this process has done much to reduce the special status of the Catholic Church. In 1896, the church's right to separate schools in Manitoba was lost chiefly because the Catholics of Quebec disobeyed their bishops and voted for the Liberal Party of Wilfrid Laurier, who could appeal to them on the basis of ethnicity alone.[31] It can be said in general that the more Catholics have themselves become involved in mainstream Canadian political and economic life, the less they have relied on the church as their intermediary and the more willing they have become to reduce it to the status of a voluntary association. As this process has occurred, Canadian Catholics have become less willing to accept the church in its traditional role of absolute moral authority. This fact is clearest with respect to the widespread use by Catholic women of church-condemned birth control techniques.[32] In this respect, as in others, Canadian Catholics have come to regard their religion as a private matter, dependent upon their free and voluntary membership—an attitude quite in harmony with the Protestant conception of the relationship between God and men.

In the present day, therefore, the Catholic Church in Canada appears to have lost, for the most part, its principal resource in negotiations with its host society, namely its moral authority over Catholic people.[33] Governments realize that bishops cannot deliver the votes of Catholic people, and church and state have grown more separate. The result is that the privileges which belong to the church in Canada today are held more by tradition than by the contemporary popular will. This fact constitutes a grave concern for the modern church, as it seeks new ways of regaining relevance to principal sectors of Canadian society.

NOTES

1 See, for instance, the extensive studies on the Quebec church by J.-C. Falardeau, Fernand Dumont, Raymond Lemieux, and others at Laval University's Centre de Recherches en Sociologie Religieuse.

2 C. Bernard, *The Functions of the Executive* (Cambridge, Mass.: Harvard University Press, 1938), p. 73.

3 J. M. Yinger, *Religion, Society and the Individual* (New York: Macmillan, 1957).

4 This and the following paragraphs are based principally on the analysis of Christian religions offered by W. Stark, *The Sociology of Religion*, Vol. 3 (London: Routledge, 1967); for a concise statement in similar terms, see T. Parsons, "Religion in Post-Industrial America: the Problem of Secularization", *Social Research* 41 (Summer 1974): 193-225. Individualistic elements in Catholicism are due in great part to the persistence of a charismatic and mystical tradition in the church; for a discussion, see W. Stark, "The Routinization of Charisma: a Consideration of Catholicism", *Sociological Analysis* 26 (Winter 1965): 203-11.

5 M. Weber, *The Protestant Ethic and the Spirit of Capitalism* (London: Unwin, 1930).

6 For perhaps the only careful analysis of the material wealth of the church, see C. Pallenberg, *Vatican Finances* (Penguin Books, 1973).

7 See Frederik Barth, *Models of Social Organization* (London: Royal Anthropological Institute Occasional Paper No. 23, 1966).

8 François Houtart, *The Challenge to Change* (New York: Sheed and Ward, 1964), p. 129.

9 A recent example is A. M. Greeley, *The Denominational Society* (Glenview, Ill.: Scott, Foresman, 1972).

10 See K. Westhues, "An Elaboration and Test of a Secularization Hypothesis in Terms of Open-Systems Theory of Organization", *Social Forces* 49 (March 1971): 460-9.

11 Greeley, *op. cit.*, p. 1.

12 See J.-C. Falardeau, "The Role and Importance of the Church in French Canada", in M. Rioux and Y. Martin, *French Canadian Society*, Vol. 1 (Toronto: McClelland & Stewart, 1969).

13 For a succinct statement of the critical events, see *ibid.*

14 Detailed analyses of separate schools have been performed by G. M. Weir, *The Separate School Question in Canada* (Toronto: Ryerson, 1934), and C.B. Sissons, *Church and State in Canadian Education* (Toronto: Ryerson, 1959). See also various articles published in the *Canadian Catholic Historical Association Study Sessions* (CCHASS). See especially P. J. Kennedy, "The Church in Newfoundland", CCHASS (1952), pp. 37-48; and G. A. Frecker, "The Origins of the Confessional School System in Newfoundland", CCHASS (1971), pp. 1-18.

Among studies of the church in Nova Scotia are the following: Sister Francis Xavier, "Educational Legislation in Nova Scotia and the Catholics", CCHASS (1957), pp. 63-74; D. B.

Flemming, "Archbishop Thomas L. Connolly, Godfather of Confederation", CCHASS (1970), pp. 67-84; and A. A. Johnston, *A History of the Catholic Church in Eastern Nova Scotia*, Vols. 1 and 2 (Antigonish: St. Francis Xavier University Press, 1960). Concerning Prince Edward Island, see especially J. C. MacMillan, *The History of the Catholic Church in Prince Edward Island from 1835 to 1891* (Quebec, 1913); and E. J. Mullally, "A Sketch of the Life and Times of the Right Rev. Angus Bernard MacEachern, the first Bishop of the Diocese of Charlotte-town", CCHASS (1945-46), pp. 71-106. For an excellent analysis of the church in New Brunswick during the last half-century, see P. M. Toner, "The New Brunswick Schools Question", CCHASS (1970), pp. 85-96. For Manitoba, see especially L. Clark, *The Manitoba School Question* (Toronto: Copp Clark, 1968).

15 See the "Decree on the Bishops' Pastoral Office in the Church", in W. M. Abbott, ed., *The Documents of Vatican II* (New York: Guild, 1966).

16 G. L. Wamsley has spelled out the workings of decentralized admin-istration through value-integration with respect to a very different organization; see his *Selective Service and a Chang-ing America* (Columbus, Ohio: Charles F. Merrill, 1969).

17 See L. Coser, "The Social Functions of Eunuchism", *American Sociolo-gical Review* 29 (December 1964): 880-6. For a more general analysis of commitment mechanisms in organiza-tions, see R. M. Kanter, "Commitment and Social Organization: a Study of Commitment Mechanisms in Utopian Communities", *American Sociological Review* 35 (August 1968): 499-517.

18 The examples are numerous. In 1884, the Archbishop of Quebec forbade Catholic workers to join the Knights of Labour (D. J. McDougall, "Cardinal Manning and the Social Problem", CCHASS (1957), pp. 53-62). In 1896, in the same archdiocese, the leading Liberal Party newspaper was banned by the church (Sissons, *op. cit.*,

p. 196). The Liberal Party itself was initially looked upon by the Canadian church as an expression of the philosophy which Pius IX condemned in 1864, in the *Syllabus of Errors*.

19 This analysis relates to the schema for the study of organizations developed by Zald; see M. N. Zald and G. L. Wamsley, *The Political Economy of Public Organizations* (Boston: D.C. Heath, 1973).

20 Falardeau, *op. cit.*, p. 346.

21 See D. Nicholls, "Politics and Religion in Haiti", *Canadian Journal of Political Science* 3 (Sep-tember 1970): 400-14.

22 Kennedy, *op. cit.*, pp. 37-48.

23 Mullally, *op. cit.*, pp. 71-106.

24 J. Porter, *The Vertical Mosaic* (Toronto: University of Toronto Press, 1965), p. 516.

25 *Ibid.*, pp. 289 and 389-90.

26 See A. Roborecky, "A Short Histori-cal Summary of the Ukrainian Catholics in Canada", CCHASS (1949), pp. 25-36.

27 Concerning the role of religion in ethnic-group persistence in Canada, see R. Breton, "Institutional Complete-ness of Ethnic Communities and Per-sonal Relations to Immigrants", *American Journal of Sociology* 70 (1964): 193-205; and L. Driedger and G. Church, "Residential Segregation and Institutional Completeness: A Comparison of Ethnic Minorities", *Canadian Review of Sociology and Anthropology* 11 (1974): 30-52.

28 J. Smith and A. Kornberg, "Some Considerations Bearing Upon Com-parative Research in Canada and the United States", *Sociology* 3 (1969): 341-57.

29 W. J. Eccles, *Canadian Society During the French Regime* (Mon-treal: Harvest House, 1968).

30 Quoted in E. Wilson, *Sociology* (Hammond, Ill.: Dorsey, 1966), p. 52.

31 See Sissons, *op. cit.*, Chap. 3.

32 See T. R. Balakrishnan, J. F. Kantner, and J. D. Allingham, *Fertility and Family Planning in a*

Canadian Metropolis (Montreal: McGill-Queen's University Press, 1975), and E. Lapierre-Adamcyk and Nichole Marcil-Gratton, "La Contraception au Québec", paper presented at the Annual Meeting of the Canadian Association for Sociology and Anthropology, Toronto, 1974.

33 Such is not the case in all countries; for an instance of both the retention of power by the church and its use of that power for the purpose of social change, see K. Westhues, "The Established Church as an Agent of Change", *Sociological Analysis* 34 (Summer 1973): 106-23.

New Religious and Para-religious Movements in Montreal*

Frederick Bird
William Reimer

During the past year we initiated a comparative study of new religious and para-religious movements in the Montreal area. Our research to date has focused on two questions: in what ways are the people participating in these movements engaged in religious activity, and in what ways are their activities in these movements new in comparison with dominant religious and cultural traditions of the West?

Our immediate concern has been methodological. There is a circularity between the concepts which we use to identify these groups as "religious" and "new" and the corresponding activities and groups which we choose to study. And contrariwise, decisions about which groups and activities to study may influence our definition of religiousness and newness.

We interviewed persons in about twenty "new religious" and "para-religious" movements. From these interviews we obtained a fairly exten-

*Revised from a paper presented to the Association for the Sociology of Religion, Montreal, 1974, with the kind permission of the authors. Other researchers for this project included the following students of Sir George Williams University: Steve Paull, Susan Palmer, High Shankland, Bill Wheeler, Bruce Barnes, Hymie Blutchitz, and Darrell Leavitt. Faculty helping with the research included Sheila McDonough, Charles Davis, John Rossner, and David Miller. Research for this project was in part made possible by a grant from the Ministry of Education, Government of Quebec.

sive description of their groups, their practices and rituals, their beliefs and purposes. We developed index forms to collect this information and attempted as far as possible to describe these movements from the perspective of their adherents.[1]

Further, we conducted field studies in several of these groups including Subud, Shatki, and the Divine Light Mission. In co-operation with the Integral Yoga Institute we surveyed about half the membership with regard to changes in beliefs, use of drugs, and well-being as a result of yoga exercises. In co-operation with the Transcendental Meditation Society, we conducted a pilot study of the effects of meditation on anxiety reduction and dogmatism.

Before analysing these movements it is well to note their immense diversity. Some are monastic, while most are not. Some are occult, some pentecostal, some self-consciously scientific, others self-consciously anti-intellectual; some developed by contemporary magi, others quite old and traditional.

A   In What Ways Are These Groups Religious?

There is no simple answer as to whether these movements are religious. The issue is complicated at the outset because a large number of the groups were noticeably concerned to describe themselves as being neither religions nor religious, even though they might use traditional religious rituals or symbols. As a result of our initial investigation, we dealt with this not as one, but as three questions.

1.   To What Extent Are These Groups Religious, Para-religious, or Non-religious?

We adopted the broad labels of "religious" and "para-religious" to identify these groups because we recognized that many of their participants do not define their reasons for participating in religious terms. Persons may meditate twice daily with a TM mantra and at the same time reverently attend all the high holy day festivities of the local synagogue. When we asked a sample of the participants of the Integral Yoga Institute their primary reasons for practising yoga, overwhelmingly they answered that they hoped to learn to relax and to improve their mental health and physical well-being. Only among the most active adherents was there any relatively significant interest in seeking the goal of Samadhi.

We are not interested in labelling as "religious" those groups which claim to be non-religious, but we find the issue more complex than simply polling members. Many so-identified non-religious groups use traditional religious language and rituals. Moreover, we have discovered that it is often quite impossible to make a firm judgment on this question for a particular movement because core members may have quite different views from those who are more peripheral. The former are more likely to explain their participation in more traditional religious language.

Our concern, therefore, has been to identify several aspects of religiosity, which vary in saliency from group to group. We have identified six such dimensions.

(a)   Does the group designate itself as "religious"? Few of these groups identify themselves as distinct *religions*; rather, they tend to identify themselves as being "religious" or "non-religious".

(b)   Do the adherents use the language of traditional religious movements to describe their goals and activities? Answers to this question vary, especially since some groups selectively use some traditional terms and images. It is worth noting that those groups which are more self-consciously religious according to these two criteria usually finance themselves with pledges, donations, and gifts, whereas the more self-consciously secular groups rely much more heavily on fees.[2]

In relation to the next three dimensions, almost all of the movements generally appear to be religious.

(c)   Do the adherents make use of traditional religious ritual and techniques? That is, do they use chants, mantras, breathing exercises, testimonials, mandala, or meditation?

(d)   Do the adherents revere the leader-founder of their movements as an inspired exemplary or ethical prophet? A tension is noticeable in several groups between a scientific and secular posture and a reverence for the charismatic founder, between the rational and charismatic legitimation of the movement.

(e)   Do the adherents follow the rituals and techniques of the group in order to tap what they conceive of as some immanent source of power? Adherents respond quite variably to the final indicator.

(f)   To what extent does participation in the group and its rituals become central to the adherents' whole way of life? For some persons their regular periods of meditation, classes in hatha yoga, or participation in prayer meetings are far from central activities. Rather, these activities represent a kind of break with everyday routines and a time for re-creating. But no clear, coherent, explicit world view necessarily accompanies these periods of meditation.[3] Many persons, however, identify and re-affirm their basic orientation towards life and the meaning of their existence in relation to these images and activities.

There seems to be some correspondence between these movements which identify themselves as religious groups and use religious language and those groups which develop particular conceptions of the general order of existence. However, it is not always possible to make clear-cut distinctions.

2.   In What Ways Are These Groups Cultic or Sectarian?

In his *Sociology of Religion* Weber (1963: Ch. 10) identified three "ideal type" means by which the adherents of some groups may seek salvation: by the faithful performance of certain obligatory rituals; by the performance of certain kinds of moral actions; or by techniques employed for the purpose of self-deification. In the first two types, the aim of religious activity is to develop or maintain a "right" relationship to the sacred. Often in these cases the religious actors seek to overcome some kind of "sin" or the effects of bad karma in order to achieve some eventual state of salvation. These kinds of orientations differ markedly from the orientation of those who seek to realize some form of immediate higher and more peaceful state of consciousness, not by overcoming the world and nature, but by neutralizing these influences. In the latter instance, Weber (1963: 55) noted, the goals of these persons may be stated in quite worldly terms in relation to "the self-interest of those who crave salvation". What these mystics seek is some kind of self-authenticating, intrinsically valuable, self-transcending experience in relation to some form of sacred power either within or beyond the self. Eister (1972), Ellwood (1973b), and Mann (1955) have used the term "cult" to distinguish these mystically oriented movements. Ellwood (1973b: 25) describes a cult as "a movement grounded in the ecstatic experience (rather than doctrinal message, social protest, or the like) and concerned with perpetuating that experience".

This ideal-typical distinction between cultic and sectarian groups corresponded relatively well with the contrast between the mystically oriented groups like the Meher Baba movement, and more sectarian movements like the Jesus movement or Baha'i. These latter movements exhibit several parallel characteristics in spite of their difference in belief:

both strongly emphasize their respective doctrines, both have developed the whole range of religious rituals, both conceive of themselves as religions rather than simply as movements with religious aspects, both have considerable interest in reforming the moral conduct of their adherents, both make sharp distinctions between what they consider to be good and evil practices, and both seek converts and not just interested adherents (Ellwood 1973a; Harder *et al.* 1972; Robbins 1973; Adamson 1974).[4]

We used several criteria to identify the cultic-mystical aspects of these movements as against some ascetic-sectarian concern.

(a)   The kind of goal the adherents seek. Do they seek (i) some form of immediate, self-validating, self-enhancing, self-transcending experience? or (ii) to establish and maintain a right relationship with the Holy as defined by certain doctrines?

At this point it is worth noting that the special or higher state of consciousness which these movements variously seek to foster occurs only when persons make a break with everyday consciousness. This alternative mystic state of consciousness may be distinguished from the hypnotic, dreaming, fanciful, or playful states of mind—all of which also differ from everyday consciousness—by the fact that the self in these states of mind consciously seeks to become open to its deeper, preconscious dimensions. The words self-transcending were used to describe the mystic experience because what the mystic seeks is to transcend the anxious self, so identified with its particular roles and limits, and to experience the self as a unified, anxiety-free, larger Self.

(b)   Attitude towards the world. Do adherents seek (i) ways to neutralize the influence of the world and the flesh, or (ii) to overcome the world and the temptations of the flesh?

(c)   Source of stress. What factors are primarily emphasized as the source of present discomfort and stress: (i) ignorance or lack of knowledge about one's real self, or (ii) "sin", and "bad karma"?

(d)   Role of rituals. (i) To what extent is the focus of ritual activities on therapeutic rituals which the adherents hope to become increasingly skilled in exercising? (ii) In contrast, to what extent do these groups attempt to utilize the whole range of ritual for initiations, rites of passage, the cycle of seasons, and worship?

(e)   Membership. To what extent is the group (i) inclusive at its periphery (although fairly inclusive in relation to the core group of more experienced members), or (ii) exclusive?

In relation to these criteria, these movements generally exhibit a mystical, cultic orientation, although ascetic and sectarian features are not altogether absent, particularly in groups such as the Divine Light Mission and the Krishna Consciousness Society. Both of these groups encourage their adherents to develop an appropriate relation of devotion to their respective avatars, both have formed fairly exclusive core congregations, and both have developed some of the traditional cycle of rituals for rites of passage and changing seasons. Yet neither of these groups primarily emphasizes doctrine, seeks to master the world of themselves, or seeks to overcome some kind of evil or sin within the self.

3.   In What Ways Are These Groups Mystically Oriented?

These groups quite differently envision the state of higher consciousness which they seek. This point needs to be discussed because of the tendency to over-generalize about mystic experiences. Some have argued that at the highest levels of realization the ecstatic state of trance is equivalent to the clear, restful illumination of zazen or samadhi. However, at more proximate levels of realization these states of mind vary markedly in relation to physiological measures of brain-wave activity, in relation to rituals and techniques used to realize these states of mind, and in relation to the self-conscious awareness of the self (Fischer 1971; Goleman 1972). In his study of yoga, Eliade (1958; Lewis 1971) notes the contrast between the enstatic, quiet, restful, and lucid state of consciousness of the yogin and the ecstatic, trancelike, and energetic state of consciousness of the shaman. This contrast between the enstatic consciousness and ecstatic consciousness provides a relevant standard for comparing the various kinds of states of consciousness which the groups hope to help their adherents realize. Certainly, those who participate in Subud and in the Charismatic Renewal Movement seek an ecstatic state of mind, while those who practise Zen, yoga, or Transcendental Meditation seek to realize a contrasting enstatic state of mind.

Many adherents seek to realize higher, more beneficent states of consciousness which cannot adequately be described by this contrast between ecstatic and enstatic states of mind. Many adherents seek to develop certain kinds of psychic powers of divining, mind-reading, or healing, or the ability to endure unusual stresses, or to have visions, and/ or "see" the world in new ways. These kinds of psychic powers have at times been developed by persons achieving enstatic and ecstatic states of mind, but they have also been pursued somewhat independently. Some mystic traditions, like the yoga tradition or the tradition of Christian mystics, have discouraged persons from becoming preoccupied with developing these kinds of psychic powers partly because as a result these persons become less interested in the mystic goal itself. The groups we have studied have not placed much emphasis on the development of such psychic powers. Yet many of them in somewhat less dramatic fashion seek to help their participants develop certain kinds of latent psychic powers variously identified as "creative intelligence" or the "potential self".

Many adherents of these groups seek to achieve a centred, one-pointed state of mind by focusing their attention in reverent devotion and mystic piety on the inspired prophet of their movement. The Jesus Movement, the Divine Light Mission, and the Krishna Consciousness Society explicitly encourage this kind of devotion. Other movements implicitly encourage at least limited forms of this kind of piety, partly perhaps because of the felt needs of the adherents, partly because of transference, and partly because of the loyalty to the movement which this kind of devotion helps to sustain.

This list of various states of higher consciousness is meant to be suggestive. What we have observed thus far is that these groups not only utilize different techniques but also seek to realize somewhat different goals.

B   To What Extent Are These Groups New?

The relative originality and uniqueness of these mystically oriented cultic movements has probably been overstressed by the press, by many of the adherents of these groups, and by researchers seeking to validate the significance of their research.[5] For centuries some religious groups have been using mantra and breathing exercises, have been chanting, have worshipped human avatars, and have cultivated the ability to have states of dissociation. Moreover, these techniques of self-divinization have been practised in the West as well as in south and east Asia. There have been influential mystical movements both within and alongside Christianity and Judaism. Certainly within the past century a number of mystic cultic movements have developed in North America. Moreover, many of these earlier groups are still active today. It can also be argued that the interest in Oriental religions is not a new experience for North Americans, since

Transcendentalists expressed interest in the Oriental religions during the nineteenth century and several religious movements originating in Asia, for instance the Vedanta Society, have been active for almost two generations.

It has been suggested that these contemporary mystic cults are new in the sense that the kinds of values and norms they uphold not only differ from the dominant values and norms of our culture and of the traditional Christian and Jewish religions but also challenge these values and norms. It has been proposed that these movements are in some sense counter-cultural. Such claims are ordinarily over-stated. Some of these movements, like the Charismatic Renewal Movement, the yoga centres, and even the Divine Light Mission, have gone out of their way to indicate their support for and adherence to the salient values of the culture. The newspaper ads for TM or for Silva Mind Control assert the interest of these groups in helping people to lead happy, successful, anxiety-free lives. Moreover, even some of the more esoteric groups, like the Krishna Consciousness Society, Eckaner Cult, Scientology, and Subud, seem to aim directly or indirectly at socializing their adherents into the dominant values of the society (Johnson 1961; Snelling 1972). In so far as some of these groups speak in utopian terms about a coming age of peace they represent a contemporary expression of a utopian and millenarian tradition that has been prominent at various points in the history of North American society.

Although the popular portrayal of the new quality of these groups is often exaggerated, they do appear to have some new aspects.

1.   These movements express a new optimistic world view, not in their Pelagian confidence about the capacity of individuals to free and redeem themselves, but in trusting the efficacy of certain rituals and spiritual techniques. The goal is described in this-worldly terms as "happiness". While most religions have had some element of this-worldliness in so far as adherents seek assurance, consolation, and affirmation of the general order of existence, adherents of these groups seek immediate happiness or psychological contentment for its own sake. Overwhelmingly, participants in the Integral Yoga Institute identified relaxation and mental and physical well-being as the reasons for learning yogic postures and exercises. Guru Maharj Ji promises bliss and peace of mind to his followers. In this sense these groups express the strong contemporary emphasis on the pursuit of happiness, along with frustration in achieving this goal (Rashke 1973).

2.   In addition, many of the participants in these groups value the

ritual processes and symbolic images of these movements as means of orienting themselves in the world, with little or no interest in identifying the ontological or objective basis for their own subjective experiences. Adherents of Transcendental Meditation are not told to analyse the character of reality, which makes it possible for meditation on a Sanskrit word to reduce anxiety. Most practitioners of yoga express disinterest in knowing anything about the traditional Hindu philosophy associated with the exercises and postures they are learning. Followers of Subud have experiences of dissociation, which they come to feel are central and vital to their lives, but they are cautioned not to analyse these experiences. Such examples could be multiplied. The disinterest in metaphysics and in developing any kind of rational, philosophical framework is thus combined with considerable confidence in various techniques and rituals as efficacious means to achieve desired goals (Noel 1973).

3.   These movements may be "new" in the sense that they are attempting to articulate a somewhat different view of the relation of ordinary consciousness to the subconscious dimensions of the human mind. Unlike the psychoanalytic view, these movements describe the subconscious as a potential source for altered and qualitatively higher dimensions of consciousness. In this context what is in common is the interest in having experiences of non-ordinary consciousness. These experiences, they say, are not responses to libidinal drives, but are attempts to gain a greater sense of oneness and integrity and to overcome the split between the inner and external selves.[6]

4.   The interest of participants in these movements reflects a relatively new, expanding concern for what we might call the pursuit of the therapeutic. The word "therapy" is often and ordinarily used to define the process of curing diseases or ailments. We do not mean to use the term in this sense, but rather point to the interest in what Philip Rieff calls a "manipulated sense of well-being" (Rieff 1966: 139; Schwartz 1974). Interest in what is therapeutic in this way concerns the achievement of a relatively unambiguous feeling of personal well-being, not on the basis of one's moral endeavours, but by the stylized use and manipulation of various symbolic and ritual processes and personal interactions.

The goal remains a kind of personal, subjective adjustment comparable to the goal of various kinds of psychotherapy. However, unlike those who turn to psychoanalysis or confession, most adherents seek to achieve this state of psychic well-being without having to go through the anxiety involved in exploration and recitation of past trauma.

The focus of attention is not a new world view, philosophy, or metaphysic, but symbolic forms and actions as a means by which one can achieve the goal or state of well-being. Symbols seem to be evaluated from a practical or aesthetic perspective rather than from an ontological or logical perspective.[7]

We might speculate on the possible origins for this pursuit of the therapeutic.

(a)   The development of the youth culture. Having grown up in households with much care and attention, and then moving into a world that seems personally unconcerned, there may be an interest in recapturing the innocence, the spontaneity, the freedom, of the pre-oedipal child, who, living in some ways beyond good and evil, affirms Self as an unrepressed whole.[8] However, as Peter Berger and colleagues point out, "We think it quite erroneous to say that contemporary youth is rebelling against father figures. On the contrary, the rebellion is against the absence of paternal solicitude in the large bureaucratic structures. If anything, youth is *in search* of plausible father figures. The empirical evidence on the generally happy relations between campus rebels and their parents would seem to bear out our view" (Berger 1974: 242). Correlated with the image of the playful, free child is the image of the solicitous parental environment. Our research data suggest that for many persons one of the factors they appreciate most about the groups they belong to is the sense of personal concern and interest they receive from other adherents.[9]

(b)   A religious interest in the therapeutic is sparked by drug experiences, together with frustrations with traditional piety and morality. (Thus far we have no clear evidence about the extent to which adherents of these movements were encouraged to participate in these groups on account of good, bad, or indifferent drug experiences. To be sure, a goodly portion of the adherents of the Integral Yoga Institute who filled out our questionnaire and who have previously used marijuana were no longer using marijuana since they began yoga (nearly 50 per cent). However, a closer analysis of the data revealed that most of these previous marijuana users had made a decision to stop using this drug before or at the same time as they decided to enroll in yoga classes.)

(c)   Adherence to, but frustration with, the North American dream of happiness and success. Like those of the New Thought Movement, many of the adherents of these groups seem quite concerned to achieve, and to do so with a minimum degree of anxiety.[10]

5.   The interest in these movements reflects a new, much more pluralistic religious situation for North America. Not only is there a wider

range of religiously oriented movements competing for adherents, but also, they do not necessarily require an exclusive adherence. Given the exclusivism of Judaism and Christianity, this is a new cultural situation, although not entirely dissimilar to the cultural situation of the Hellenistic Age.[11]

NOTES

1   The groups surveyed were the Greatheart Buddhist monastery, Tai Chi Chuan, Transcendental Meditation, the Sivananda Yoga Center, the Integral Yoga Institute, the Divine Light Mission, Shakti, Psycho-synthesis, the Eckaner Cult, the Krishna Consciousness Society, a Subud group, a Gurdjieff group, the Self-Realization Fellowship, a Theosophy group, the Ajapa Breath Foundation, a Sri Chinmoy fellowship, a group of followers of Swami Shyam, a Nichirin Shoshun group, a local Baha'i fellowship, and a group of persons involved in the Charismatic Renewal Movement.

2   Those movements that seemed to be self-consciously religious by these criteria were the Greatheart Buddhist monastery, the Krishna Consciousness Society, the Divine Light Mission, the followers of Sri Chinmoy, and the Charismatic Renewal Movement. All of these groups primarily finance themselves from the donations and work of their participants. In contrast, the following groups seemed to be self-consciously non-religious: Tai Chi Chuan, Transcendental Meditation, the Sivananda Yoga Center. All of these groups primarily finance themselves from fees. There are some other parallel contrasts. In the former groups personal devotion to a master is encouraged, while such devotion is de-emphasized in, although not absent from, the latter groups. Adherents of the former groups describe their goals in self-consciously religious words such as Samadhi, Sazen, Bliss, Spiritual Awakening, or God-consciousness, whereas the latter groups tend to describe their goals in self-consciously secular language, such as relaxation, personal effectiveness, less anxiety, or increased productivity.

3   There is considerable evidence that the more involved adherents of the yoga groups or Transcendental Meditation in fact do begin to identify their values and norms in relation to aspects of fairly distinct world views. In TM, meditators are encouraged to participate in periodic retreats, at which time intensive periods of meditation and yoga exercises are interspersed with viewings of video-tape messages from Maharishi Mahesh Yogi. Such sessions tend to encourage the development of certain similar identifiable ways of looking at the world. One of the researchers felt that TM encouraged a relatively clear belief system that was dogmatically held by the more active adherents. Using a Rokeach Dogmatism scale—Form E (Rokeach)—the researcher concluded that "The results of the study support previous literature which has shown that the practice of TM can lead to greater autonomic stability and to a rapid rate of habituation to stressful stimuli. . . . However, the findings of this experiment also show the group of experienced meditators to be significantly more dogmatic than the control group who expressed no interest in TM." (See also Campbell 1974.)

4   The observation about conversion reflects a judgment made several decades ago by Arthur Darby Nock about the mystery cults of the Hellenistic age in contrast to the religions of Judaism and Christianity (Nock 1933: Chaps. 1 and 2).

5   See, e.g., Harrison Pope, Jr., The Road East: America's New Discovery of Eastern Wisdom: "It [these movements] also represents a massive new opposition to technology and science, even a rejection of the philosophical foundations of western

thought." For a more balanced judgment, see Tiryakian (1972).

6 A preliminary investigation of these issues was prepared by Bill Wheeler, one of our researchers, for our study in a paper, "Religion and Altered States of Consciousness", 1974. For relevant literature, see: Goleman 1971, Naranjo 1971, Ornstein 1972, Tart 1969.

7 There is considerable evidence for this hypothesis: (i) a number of the groups, such as TM, the yoga groups, Scientology, and Silva Mind Control, quite consciously seek adherents by claiming to help people live happier, less anxious, more effective and productive lives, not by changing their values or character but by helping them to tap their own undeveloped resources; (ii) adherents of several of the groups we studied, for instance a Gurdjieff group, the Divine Light Mission, and Shakti, explained that the appeal of these groups for them arose out of their promises to help them become more integrated, self-assured persons. Overwhelmingly the adherents of the Integral Yoga Institute said that what they hoped to gain from their classes was a more relaxed and peaceful state of mind and body (Paull 1974, Palmer 1974, Leavitt 1974, Snelling 1972, Needleman 1974, pp. 16-18).

8 We might describe this as a Nietzschian's fantasy: see *Thus Spoke Zarathustra,* Part one, three, metamorphosis, "Why must the preying lion still become a child? The child is innocence and forgetting, a new beginning, a game, a self-propelled wheel, a first movement, a sacred 'Yes', for the game of creation, my brothers, a sacred 'Yes' is heeded: The spirit now wills his own will, and he who has been lost to the world now conquers his own world." (Nietzsche 1954, p. 139).

9 Participants in the Integral Yoga Institute, Divine Light Mission, Krishna Consciousness Society, and Shakti expressed these unsolicited sentiments to researchers.

10 Other possible factors helping to give rise to this perceived interest in the pursuit of the thereapeutic:

(a) An experienced trauma of relativism-pluralism incurred by living in the midst of a world of conflicting values and personal desires may have created an interest in, and search for, a still but sure point;

(b) Disenchantment with the "politics" of government, business, family— i.e. with the collective decision-making processes—and a sense of fatalism may create a search for smaller groups which are both easier to understand and control, and invested with a sense of importance;

(c) Frustration or disenchantment with drugs or sex experiences may create a search for other forms of ecstatic experiences.

11 Whether these movements are gnostic or not is another question which we will attempt to assess. In the diffuse way in which Voeglin uses the term, these groups are gnostic, but so are many other political, philosophic, and cultural movements of the twentieth century (Voeglin 1969).

However, in the more focused sense in which Jonas and Grant describe gnosticism, the groups often reflect a parallel antinomian disenchantment with the orders of this world as meaningless and humanly alien, and an interest in the redemption of the inner, spiritual self (Jonas 1961, Grant 1959). It is, however, difficult to make meaningful comparisons between these contemporary religious and para-religious movements and the gnostic movements of the Hellenistic Age, because thus far most of the studies of gnostic religions have focused on their beliefs and imagery rather than on their organizational and ritual patterns.

REFERENCES

Adamson, Hugh
1974   "Revelation in Islam and Baha'i." M.A. thesis, Sir George Williams University.

Berger, Peter, Brigitte Berger, and Hansfried Kellner

1974 *The Homeless Mind: Moderni-*
zation and Consciousness. New
York: Random House.
Campbell, Colin
1974 "Transcendence Is as American
as Ralph Waldo Emerson."
Psychology Today, April,
pp. 37-8.
Eister, Alan
1972 "An Outline of a Structural
Theory of Cults." *Journal for*
the Scientific Study of Religion,
Vol. II, No. 4 (December).
Eliade, Mircea
1958 *Yoga, Immortality and Free-*
dom. Trans. by Willard Trask.
Chaps. 2 and 8. Princeton:
Princeton University Press.
Ellwood, Robert S.
1973a *One Way: The Jesus Movement*
and Its Meaning. Englewood
Cliffs: Prentice-Hall.
1973b *Religious and Spiritual Groups*
in Modern America. Englewood
Cliffs: Prentice-Hall.
Fingarette, Herbert
1967 *The Self in Transformation*,
Chaps. 1, 2, 5, 7. New York:
Harper and Row.
Fischer, Roland
1971 "A Cartography of Ecstatic and
Meditative States." *Science* 174:
897-904.
Geertz, Clifford
1966 "Religion as a Cultural System."
In Michael Banton, ed.,
Anthropological Approaches to
the Study of Religion. London:
Tavistock.
Goleman, Daniel
1971 "Meditation as Metatherapy:
Hypotheses Towards a Proposed
Fifth State of Consciousness."
Journal of Transpersonal
Psychology 3, No. 1: 1-25.
1972 "The Buddha on Meditation and
States of Consciousness: Part
I, The Teachings; and Part II:
A Typology of Meditation
Techniques." *Journal of Trans-*
personal Psychology, Vol. 4,
Nos. 1 and 2.
Grant, Robert M.
1959 *Gnosticism and Early*
Christianity. 2nd edn. New

York: Columbia University
Press.
Harder, Mary White, James T.
Richardson, and Robert
Simmonds
1972 "Jesus People." *Psychology*
Today, December, pp. 45-50,
110, 112, 113.
Johnson, Benton
1961 "Do Holiness Sects Socialize in
Dominant Values?" *Social*
Forces 39 (May): 309-16.
Jonas, Hans
1961 *The Gnostic Religion.* 2nd edn.,
rev'd. Boston: Beacon.
Lewis, Ioan
1971 *Ecstatic Religion: An*
Anthropological Study of Spirit
Possession and Shamanism.
Middlesex: Penguin.
Mann, W. E.
1955 *Sect, Cult and Church in*
Alberta. Toronto: University of
Toronto Press.
Naranjo, Claudio, and Robert E.
Ornstein
1971 *On the Psychology of*
Meditation. New York: Viking.
Needleman, Jacob
1974 *The New Religions.* Garden
City: Doubleday.
Nietzsche, Friedrich
1954 *Thus Spoke Zarathustra.* In The
Portable Nietzsche, ed. Walter
Kaufman. New York: Viking.
Nock, Arthur Darby
1933 *Conversion.* London: Oxford
University Press.
Noel, Daniel C.
1973 "Fact, Fiction, and Post-Modern
Faith: Carlos Castaneda and
the Incredibly Shrinking Credi-
bility Gap." *Philosophy of*
Religion and Theology. Pre-
printed papers for the Annual
Meeting of the American
Academy of Religion.
Ornstein, Jack
1972 *The Psychology of Conscious-*
ness. New York: Viking.
Palmer, Susan
1974 "Field Survey Report on Shakti."
Unpublished paper.
Paull, Steve
1974 "Doctor Steve of the Divine

Light Mission." Unpublished paper.

Pope, Harrison, Jr.
1974 *The Road East: America's New Discovery of Eastern Wisdom.* Boston: Beacon.

Raschke, Carl
1973 "The Asian Invasion of American Religion: Creative Innovation or New Gnosticism." *Philosophy of Religion and Theology.* Pre-printed papers for the Annual Meeting of the American Academy of Religion.

Rieff, Philip
1966 *The Triumph of the Therapeutic: Uses of Faith after Freud.* New York: Harper and Row.

Robbins, Thomas, Dick Anthony, and Thomas Curtis
1973 "Eastern Mysticism, the Jesus Movement, and the Crisis of Values." Unpublished paper.

Rokeach, Milton, and A. A. Eglash
1956 "A Scale for Measuring Intellectual Convictions." *Journal of Social Psychology*: 135-41.

Schwartz, Gary
1974 "TM Relaxes Some People and Makes Them Feel Better." *Psychology Today*, April, pp. 39-44.

Snelling, Clarence, and Oliver Whitley
1972 "Problem Solving Behavior in Religious and Para-Religious Groups." Paper prepared for the annual meetings of the Society for the Scientific Study of Religion.

Tart, Charles, ed.
1969 *Altered States of Consciousness.* Garden City: Doubleday.

Tiryakian, Edward A.
1972 "Toward the Sociology of Esoteric Culture." *American Journal of Sociology* 78, No. 3: 491-512.

Troeltsch, Ernst
1931 *The Social Teaching of the Christian Churches*, Vol. 2. Trans. by E. Wyon, New York: Harper and Row.

Voeglin, Eric
1969 *Science, Politics and Gnosticism.* Chicago: Henry Regency.

Weber, Max
1963 *The Sociology of Religion.* Trans. by Ephraim Fischoff. Boston: Beacon.

Wheeler, Bill
1974 "Religion and Altered States of Consciousness." Unpublished paper.

Sectarianism in Politics:
The Internationalists and the Socialist
Labour Party*

Roger O'Toole

In recent years public attention has been drawn to the growth of many small social movements which in various ways express behaviour that counters dominant culture. Though their activities may be religious, political, therapeutic, musical, aesthetic, ecstatic, scientistic, or paramilitary, such groups are similar in form and indicate that the concept "sect" may be useful in their sociological analysis. Two decades have passed since Peter Berger observed: "On the modern scene we find the dynamics of sectarianism at work in places far removed from religion proper—in politics, art, literature, and even within the sacred precincts of science itself."[1]

Generally unknown to social scientists working within the Weber-Troeltsch-Niebuhr tradition of studies in the church-sect typology, there exist two distinct "underground traditions" in the analysis of sectarianism. These traditions, which may be labelled "Marxist" and "collective behaviour", emphasize the relations between religious sects and other forms of sectarianism, and place particular importance upon the political sect.

*Prepared for this volume.

The Marxist Tradition

Karl Marx and Friedrich Engels laid the foundations of a perspective which emphasizes the sect's place in social evolution, stresses its historical importance as the embryonic form of the mass movement of social change, and writes its epitaph as a significant social form in the modern era.[2] Engels in particular stresses the continuity between religious and political sectarianism as forms of social protest:

> One good thing, however, Ernest Renan has said: "When you want to get a distinct idea of what the first Christian communities were, do not compare them to the parish congregations of our day; they were rather like local sections of the International Working Man's Association." And this is correct. Christianity got hold of the masses, exactly as modern socialism does, under the shape of a variety of sects.[3]

From its beginnings in the writings of Marx and Engels the notion of the sect as taking religious *or political* form and of the religious sect as a "pre-political" formation may be traced to our own day. The serious student of sectarianism cannot afford to ignore the relevant works of such writers as Eduard Bernstein,[4] Ernest Belfort Bax,[5] Karl Kautsky,[6] Max Beer,[7] Leon Trotsky,[8] and James P. Cannon.[9] Similarly, the imprint of the Marxian tradition of sect analysis may be observed in the works of ex-Marxists such as Daniel Bell[10] and Lewis S. Feuer,[11] as well as in Peter Worsley's[12] and E. J. Hobsbawm's[13] Marxist studies of millenarianism.

The Collective Behaviour Tradition

Robert Ezra Park[14] is the central figure in the "collective behaviour" tradition of sect analysis, for through him a lineage may be traced back to Scipio Sighele,[15] Gustave Le Bon,[16] and Georg Simmel,[17] and down to such writers as Lyford P. Edwards,[18] Ellsworth Faris,[19] Herbert Blumer,[20] Kurt and Gladys Lang,[21] and Lewis A. Coser.[22] In this tradition the sect is perceived as a structural form which varies in content. While for Park and Blumer sects are essentially *religious or political* in content, Kurt and Gladys Lang adopt an even broader perspective:

> In the framework of sociological analysis, the term sectarian has other than religious connotations. As long as the population within a society is heterogeneous, schisms may occur over any matter that is sufficiently important to aggravate emotions. Understandably, where

religion is the dominant value, any consciousness of difference among sectors of the population is apt to express itself in religious terms. Other kinds of sectarian associations crystallize around any one of many political, intellectual, or cultural interests—provided, of course, that these concerns are central and that they arouse in the sectarian the feeling that he is not granted full expression within recognized institutions.[23]

Writers in this tradition follow Sighele's lead in viewing the sect as the nucleus of the mass movement of social protest and as a major unit in the analysis of social change. Thus, Park observes: "Every revolution seems likely to have its origin in a sect, ordinarily a political sect. It is in the ferment and fervour of sectarian life that new ideas and new ideals of life take form and make themselves articulate."[24] More recently, the Langs have viewed the sect as no less than "the fundament for efforts at general social reconstruction".[25]

It is impossible to provide here more than the briefest sketch of the alternative traditions of sect analysis. Even this cursory treatment should indicate, however, that sociologists of religion can profit from investigation of these long-established perspectives. This assertion may be underlined by consideration of the most recent appeal by a sociologist of religion for a broadening of the context of sect analysis.

In an acute critique of the standard literature on church and sect, Benton Johnson[26] questions some central assumptions of the "mainstream" approach to the study of sectarianism. Most significant is his attack on the tendency "to see sect growth as a kind of selling-out process" and his condemnation of sociologists of religion for a failure to see "that a sect might be able to impose its own will, or a part of its own will, on society". Drawing on an essay by Stephen Berger,[27] he asserts that "sects can and do act as the leading edge of social transformation." In giving emphasis to the possible *impact* of the sect upon the wider society, Johnson applauds Berger's attempt to link "Weber's analysis of sects with the study of aggressive change-seeking movements in general" and approves a perspective which rejects traditional boundaries and embraces the study of political as well as religious sects. It is evident from the brief outline of "underground" traditions of sect analysis given above that Johnson, Berger, and those sociologists of religion who follow their lead must investigate the Marxian and the collective behaviour perspectives on sectarianism.

It is not suggested here that the work of scholars associated with the "underground" traditions is intellectually superior to that of writers in the "mainstream" tradition. Indeed, much work in the Marxist and collective behaviour traditions is interesting precisely because of the disagreements and errors upon which it is based. It is maintained, however, that consideration of the literature in all traditions in the study of sectarianism should be an urgent and indispensable prelude at this time to new investigations of this phenomenon.

Such consolidation and codification should enable the scholar to avoid errors previously compounded by the mutual unawareness of writers in different traditions, and ought to encourage fresh lines of enquiry in new research. In particular, knowledge of the variety of sectarian formations in different institutional settings should be a discouragement to the kinds of oversimplification and stereotyping which have been apparent, on occasion, in all the traditions of sect analysis. The discussion here of a single example of such oversimplification will emphasize this point.

Oversimplification of religious behaviour occurs not least among sociologists of religion, but R. E. Park's distinction between religious and political sects certainly does little justice to the diversity and complexity of the religious sectarian experience. After noting their basic similarity, he argues:

> The essential difference between the two seems to be that religious sects, in describing their programme as "a way of life" almost always project their life policies and the Utopias they hope to achieve beyond the limits of human experience and control. This makes life in this world merely a preparation for a world that is to come.
>
> Political sects, on the other hand, are determined that such heavens as they hope for will be achieved presently, on this earth, and, as far as possible, here and now. In the long run this distinction involves a profound difference. The political sects—i.e. the anarchists, socialists, communists, etc.—have a programme of action— radical action. The religious groups—like the Quakers, Shakers, Holy Rollers, and others—are just as radical but, as far as political action is concerned, they are passive and resigned. . . . They accept the universe and make no great effort to change existing political and social conditions. . . . They are concerned about their souls rather more than they are about politics.[28]

Worsley's perception of the "pre-political" nature of religious millenarianism casts grave doubt on the neat simplicity of Park's dichotomy.[29] Yet, while Park's view of religion would now be seen as naive
and simplistic, his conception of politics remains unassailed. In the work
of Worsley and Hobsbawm, no less than that of Park, political activity is
presented as the exemplary form of "rational" or "instrumental" activity.
Thorough investigation of the available literature on sectarianism from
all three traditions should not only dispel the myth of a totally "irrational" religion, but should also caution against the perpetuation of a
myth of a totally "rational" politics. The weakness of such oversimplifi-
cations may be demonstrated most effectively by the presentation of solid,
empirical evidence to the contrary. Thus, a short discussion of some
material from a study of political sects in Canada may not only call into
question the wisdom of adopting an "over-rationalized conception of
politics", but may throw new light on the relationship between the political sect and its religious counterpart.[30]

Sects in Politics: Two Brief Case Studies

The Internationalists

The Internationalists are the members of a political sect founded in
Canada in the 1960s and formally dedicated to revolution in accordance
with the thought of Chairman Mao Tse-tung. Essentially Maoists in the
style of the individuals portrayed in Jean-Luc Godard's film *La Chinoise*,
they are mainly university students from middle-class backgrounds.
While their ideology may be summed up by their declaration that they
"uncritically and loyally follow Chairman Mao",[31] the Internationalists
also owe allegiance to the founder of their sect, a Punjabi intellectual
resident in Canada, whom they term a "revolutionary teacher and . . .
revolutionary in all aspects of his life".[32]

Members of this sect claim to be successfully building a mass movement and intensively proselytizing in order to increase their numbers.
Close scrutiny of the sect casts doubt upon this claim and belies Internationalist assertions that they are a large, growing "new-democratic"
movement of "broad masses of the Canadian people".

Despite their avowals that expansion of the group is desirable, necessary, and occurring, Internationalists leave an impression that they are
only concerned with expansion and progress "on paper" and in their

grandiose pronouncements. Indeed, members of the sect seem to be more concerned with purity than proselytization, with exclusivism rather than expansion, and appear content with minimal growth in membership. Investigation of Internationalist proselytization activities suggests that it would be superficial to view these as simply genuine attempts to gain support and recruits. Rather, these activities might be better interpreted as occasions on which sect members are able to assert proudly their status as members of an elite, in the face of representatives of the wider society, and on which they may experience the honour of persecution at the hands of the "anti-conscious" and unrighteous.

Certainly, to most outsiders who have been in contact with them, the Internationalists appear as an arrogant, intolerant exclusivist group whose frequent appeals for "discussion" and "co-operation" fail to disguise their real nature as a small, self-satisfied, self-proclaimed elite, whose official humility masks a deep pride. Even a sympathetic observer notes:

> . . . I reacted against the aggressive attitudes of members of the group . . . to individuals, myself being one, not directly associated with it. . . . the tone of approach of the Internationalists served to alienate more than endear. . . . they seemed to equate rejection of their criticisms as the mark of ignorance or satisfaction with the system outside the group; they did not seem to accept anyone to be in a transient stage, they seemed to make no allowances for people without the necessary intellect to evaluate their attitude to their immediate context. . . . In a word, they seemed intolerant, a closed circle.[33]

Observation of Internationalist proselytization activities, including literature selling, pamphlet distribution, and public meetings, confirms the assertion that the approach of sect members seems calculated "to alienate more than endear". At times, the Internationalists act quite overtly as a small, exclusivist "closed circle" by turning away from the world, identifying their own group as "the masses", spurning "bourgeois publicity", and engaging only in unpublicized meetings designated "strictly by invitation only".

In such circumstances, it seems mistaken to view the commitment of Internationalists as maintained on the basis of their satisfaction in involvement with a growing social movement. Rather, those who remain within the sect might better be considered as gaining satisfaction from the *sectarian experience itself*, an experience actually very different from that portrayed in Internationalist descriptions of a grand alliance of oppressed and progressive people.

A clue to the real rewards experienced by members of this sect may be found in the writings of the sect's founder, for, referring to the fact that "some Internationalists derive a kind of security from their 'new society' ", he notes:

> For many people, the Internationalists have become a new historical crib, a new perspective through which they can rationalize their position in nearly all circumstances; they can say that "I am an Internationalist, therefore I am a developing person by definition." . . . the malaise of the Internationalists can be thought of in this way: they reinforce their own personalities within the group, and derive satisfaction from being called rebels outside of it.[34]

The outside observer should accept and extend this perception, viewing the sect as an "expressive" rather than "instrumental" movement, which provides its members with an *alternative* to the world rather than the *means* of changing it. Members of this sect appear to derive satisfaction from being part of a small, politically isolated, cognitive and moral elite, a closed circle with a certain notoriety in the outside world. Sharing a distinct sense of reality derived from "facts" in which "relevant things [are] relevant and irrelevant things irrelevant",[35] the Internationalists accord themselves an elevated status further enhanced by its exclusive nature and its rarity.

This sect may be interpreted as offering a closed environment in which members and the significance of their acts are totally transformed. Within it, certain young intellectuals attain cognitive certainty, a sense of status and moral worth, a feeling of comradeship and "belonging", and an awareness of "meaning" in life. Thus, rather than viewing this sect as a means to an end, it may be better understood as an end-in-itself.

The Socialist Labour Party

The Socialist Labour Party can claim the distinction of being the oldest Marxist organization in North America, with over eighty years of continuous activity. It is a living fossil, a small sect surviving as a relic of a once larger and more powerful organization, in the manner of such similar organizations as the modern IWW and the Socialist Party of Great Britain".[36] Although it ceased to be an effective North American political force by 1914, this sect survives in the 1970s in the form of tiny groups scattered throughout major cities. In contrast to the Internationalists, the SLP is composed of working men from middle to old age. Politically ineffectual and largely unknown, the Socialist Labour Party regards itself as the only "genuine" Marxist organization in the world, founded as it is on the distinctive doctrine of "Marxism–De Leonism", and proclaims proudly: "The SLP stands alone in the clarity of its idea of how socialism must be constituted, and, equally important, how the workers . . . must organize to get it."[37]

Although it declares its satisfaction with a condition of smallness and isolation, the SLP also claims to "spread the message of socialism by conducting a ceaseless, vigorous programme of socialist education among the workers".[38] It states:

This educational programme is carried on by every legitimate means available to the Socialist Labour Party—public lectures; study classes; widespread distribution of leaflets; street sales of pamphlets and its official organ, the *Weekly People*; as well as the use of radio and television whenever and wherever possible.[39]

Underlining this professed emphasis on proselytization, the sect announces: "We do not seek to develop mere bookworms or barren philosophers. Men of *action* are the need of the hour."[40] The SLP is at pains to document its missionary activities in precise detail, and such entries as the following typically appear in its regular Canadian publication:

One of the highlights . . . was a trip made to Oshawa, Ontario . . . under the direction of National Office. 3,235 leaflets and 54 back copies of the *Socialist Press Bulletin* and *Weekly People* were distributed on this occasion.[41]

A Daniel De Leon Commemoration public meeting was held on December 14th. In honour of the occasion Comrade —— delivered a thought-provoking address entitled "The Issue is Survival" to a small but attentive audience.[42]

However, the close observer is aware that rational bookkeeping methods are never applied to the *results* of proselytization, and that "a small but

attentive audience" denotes a handful of individuals, mostly sect members. He learns also that when "literature distribution continues to result
in a good number of write-in enquiries, personal visits and phone calls to
Section Headquarters in search of further information" a maximum of
one or two responses is involved. Thus, SLP members appear to be meeting disappointment and keeping their spirits up by transforming their
failure into mild success.

Certainly, the sect disguises the failure of its proselytizing activities
by emphasizing the energy and diligence with which they are carried out
rather than their results, and by stressing the potential effect of such
endeavours. Yet, a simple conception of SLP proselytization as a sincere,
though unsuccessful, attempt to spread the De Leonist word and to seek
recruits to the sect seems ill-founded. Plausible though it is, a view of
SLP members engaging in earnest proselytization and coming to terms
with failure and disappointment by the construction of a rationalization
which demonstrates their "success" is not supported by close analysis.
Indeed, far from engaging in the energetic activity of which they boast,
SLP members appear to be merely going through the motions of educational and propaganda activities, and, moreover, seem to aim many such
activities at targets which virtually guarantee their failure. The members
of the sect may be interpreted as maintaining what Robin Williams terms
a cultural fiction:

> A cultural fiction exists whenever there is a cultural description,
> explanation, or normative prescription that is both *generally accepted*
> *as a norm and is typically followed* in conduct but is at the same
> time markedly at variance with the subjective conceptions or inclina-
> tions of participants in the pattern, or with certain objective, scientific
> knowledge.[43]

It may be suggested that participants in the sect's proselytization
activity are not really disappointed by its failure, firstly because they are
aware that "objectively" it has little chance of success, and, secondly,
because it goes against their "subjective inclinations". This point may be
illustrated in the context of the main form of SLP proselytization: the
anonymous distribution of leaflets which present the basic ideas of the
sect. Compared to the sophisticated canvassing and propaganda techniques used by many modern political groups, SLP leafleting seems
traditionalistic, uneconomical, unproductive, and rather shame-faced.

Leaving bundles of literature in the lobbies of apartment buildings or behind the windscreen wipers of cars parked at shopping centres assures failure by a calculated avoidance of the most strategic targets. Leaflets are never distributed in factories or outside their gates, a situation which parallels the refusal of sect members to present their ideas in a trade-union setting. In this context, SLP members appear to be paying lip-service to the goal of proselytization, and their insistence that they "do the best they can", given their numbers and resources, is unconvincing. The challenge of snatching recruits from the enemy's lair by directing a leafleting campaign towards factory workers, for example, seems to impress SLP members less than the possible hostility which they might encounter. The writer asked a leading member of the sect which leaflets had been chosen for distribution on a recent leafleting campaign and the reasons for this choice. Rather than replying in political terms by stating that, for example, a particular issue was important or timely and that a certain leaflet dealt with it, he stated: "We decided we'd better get rid of this pile as they were beginning to yellow. They've been around for some time and we decided we'd better move them."[44]

The lack of enthusiasm of SLP members for whole-hearted proselytization seems apparent also in their attitude to "firebrands". Although the sect claims to seek "men of action", its members express great hostility towards those who can be labelled with this well-established SLP epithet. One sect member expressed his sentiments thus:

The sort of people we don't want in the movement are "firebrands". *They're* going to shape-up the movement, they're going to put it into action, and so on! A friend of mine was just like that but he burned himself out, they always do—burn themselves out—and then drop out of politics because they get disillusioned. We generally tell these guys—"Look, *calm down*, that's not the way we work in the SLP!" For us, building a revolution is slow, painstaking work—there's no big drama. Unless someone is willing to submit to the discipline of the party and drop all these ideas . . . we tell him to get out. The party can do without him!

Consideration of SLP leafleting activity and its attitude to zealous activism leads the informed observer to view with scepticism the sect's claims to energetic involvement in "spreading the word". Rather than the frantic, widespread, urgent activity portrayed by sect members, an outsider sees half-hearted, ritualistic, and traditionalistic attempts at proselytization. SLP members appear to be play-acting a role as revolutionary evangelists and their activities constitute a pseudo-proselytization aimed, at best, at maintaining the sect at its present strength. Despite their avowed aim of carrying "the life-giving principles and programmes of Marxism–De Leonism, the one hope of humanity, the beacon light"[45] to the working class, the activities of members of the sect seem less than heroic.

Some indication of the reason for SLP members' reluctance to engage in a genuine, whole-hearted attempt to spread the word may be gained by closer analysis of the emphasis placed by them on the fellowship to be found within their sect. A leading Canadian SLP member said:

I've been in the party for twenty years, and I've held on to the party ideas—and God knows, it's been a hard job at times to hang on to them with the pressures of work and life—and I've been tempted just to let it all go. . . . But I'd come here [to SLP Headquarters] and talk to the other SLP fellows, and do you know, that was a real help in meeting all the problems.

Although this statement illustrates the effect of group reinforcement on individual ideological commitment, it is more interesting for its demonstration of a sect member's awareness that his relationship to SLP comrades helped him meet the problems which he identifies with the pressures of work and life. Other SLP members confirm that the sect provides a warm, supportive environment in which private troubles may be shared with sympathetic listeners: " . . . no matter what pressures get you down in work and life—and they get us all at times—you'll find that belonging to the SLP will make you able to live with those pressures better and to get over them."

The emphasis given to fellowship by the SLP is shown in published reports of the sect's activities, for accounts of public meetings and leaflet distribution are accompanied by items which appear odd as progress reports of an avowedly revolutionary organization:

The section held its annual picnic on Sunday, August 2 . . . the weather was excellent and forty comrades and friends from Toronto, Hamilton and as far away as Buffalo, Detroit and Ohio enjoyed a fine day of SLP fellowship. Games were held for the women and children and plenty of corn on the cob was available.[46]

The attempt to infuse a serious purpose into such activities by an appeal for funds appears to emphasize rather than deny their essentially social nature. The best-attended sect activities are similar to those of non-revolutionary voluntary associations such as veteran and church groups. These events provide a congenial, familial atmosphere in which individuals may experience a sense of belonging.

SLP emphasis on fellowship is the cornerstone of the sect's existence in terms of which members' lack of concern with changing the sectarian *status quo* may be most fully understood. SLP members gain satisfaction from belonging to a cognitive and moral elite, but this is sustained by their satisfaction with the sect as an oasis, a place of refuge from the pressures of the outside world. The SLP, like the Internationalists, appears to be best understood as providing an alternative to the world rather than a means of changing it, as an expressive rather than an instrumental movement. For its members the movement is everything, the final goal nothing.[47]

Conclusion

This brief discussion of two avowedly political sects suggests the perils of rashly stereotyping political activity, and demonstrates that the search for communion may be located in a political context as well as in the religious sect. Its perspective on proselytization underlines the necessity for closer investigation of such activity in particular and diverse sectarian contexts, and should interest students of both religious and political sects. Further, it lends support to David Martin's important critique of the Niebuhr thesis.[48] The contention that the denominalization process is *atypical* is strengthened by evidence that certain *political* sects resist such a process and strive successfully to remain small and exclusive communions.

Despite its brevity, this essay seeks to respond to Roland Robertson's call for "a fundamental reconsideration of the type of work which is done by sociologists in the field of religion",[49] and to encourage other sociologists of religion to relate their work to that of scholars in other fields.

NOTES

1   Peter L. Berger, "The Sociological Study of Sectarianism", *Social Research* 21, No. 4 (Winter 1954): 467.

2   For discussion of sects in the writings of Marx and Engels, see Karl Marx and Friedrich Engels, *On*

Britain (Moscow: Foreign Languages Publishing House, 1953); *Selected Correspondence* (Moscow: Foreign Languages Publishing House, 1956); *Selected Works*, 2 vols. (Moscow: Foreign Languages Publishing House, 1958); *On Religion* (Moscow: Foreign Languages Publishing House, 1958); and Lewis S. Feuer, ed., *Marx and Engels: Basic Writings on Politics and Philosophy* (Garden City, N.Y.: Doubleday Anchor Books), 1959.

3   Friedrich Engels in *On Religion*, pp. 205-6. See also p. 318.

4   Eduard Bernstein, *Von der Secte zur Partei* (Jena: Eugen Diedrichs, 1911); *My Years of Exile: Reminiscences of a Socialist*, trans. Miall (London: Leonard Parsons, 1921) (see especially pp. 161, 96-7, and 222-3); *Cromwell and Communism: Socialism and Democracy in the Great English Revolution*, trans. Stenning (New York: Schocken Books, 1963; first published in Germany, 1895).

5   Ernest Belfort Bax, *The Social Side of the Reformation in Germany*, 3 vols. (London: Swan Sonnenschein and Co., 1894, 1899, and 1903).

6   Karl Kautsky, *Communism in Central Europe at the Time of the Reformation*, trans. Mulliken (London: T. Fisher Unwin, 1897), especially pp. 1-28; and *The Foundations of Christianity*, trans. Mins (New York: Russell and Russell, 1953; first published in Germany, 1908).

7   Max Beer, *A History of British Socialism*, 2 vols. (London: G. Bell and Sons, 1919); and *Social Struggles and Socialist Forerunners*, trans. Stenning (New York: International Publishers, 1929).

8   Leon Trotsky, *The Death Agony of Capitalism and the Tasks of the Fourth International* (New York: Pioneer Publishers, 1964; first published 1938), pp. 55-7; and *Against the Stream!* (London: W. I. R. Publications, 1966), pp. 3-9.

9   James P. Cannon, *The History of American Trotskyism* (New York: Pioneer Publishers, 1944), pp. 189-215; *The Struggle for a Proletarian Party* (New York: Pioneer Publishers, 1943); *Letters from Prison* (New York:

Merit Publishers, 1968), pp. 89-93.

10 Daniel Bell, "Marxian Socialism in the United States", in D. D. Egbert and S. Persons, eds., *Socialism and American Life* 1 (Princeton, N.J.: Princeton University Press, 1952): 213-405.

11 Lewis S. Feuer, "Marxism and the Hegemony of the Intellectual Class", *Transactions of the Fifth World Congress of Sociology* 4 (1964): 83-96; "Marxisms—How Many?" *Problems of Communism* 13, No. 2 (1964): 55-7.

12 Peter Worsley, *The Trumpet Shall Sound* (London: MacGibbon and Kee, 1957).

13 E. J. Hobsbawm, *Primitive Rebels* (New York: The Norton Library, 1965; first published 1959).

14 R. E. Park, "Characteristics of the Sect", in R. H. Turner, ed., *On Social Control and Collective Behaviour: Selected Papers* (Chicago: University of Chicago Press, 1967), pp. 240-8 (essay first published, 1932); R. H. Park and E. W. Burgess, *Introduction to the Science of Sociology* (Chicago: University of Chicago Press, 1924), pp. 240-8.

15 Scipio Sighele, *Psychologie des Sectes* (Paris: V. Giard and E. Brière, 1898). A translation of sections of this work is to be found in Park and Burgess, *op. cit.*, pp. 202-7.

16 Gustave Le Bon, *The Crowd: A Study of the Popular Mind* (New York: The Viking Press, 1960), pp. 155-65 (first published in French, 1895); *The Psychology of Socialism* (Wells, Vermont: Fraser Publishing Co., 1965), pp. 37-39, 85-103 (first published in English, 1899).

17 Georg Simmel, *Conflict and the Web of Group-Affiliations*, trans. Wolff and Bendix (Glencoe: The Free Press, 1955); Kurt H. Wolff, ed., *The Sociology of Georg Simmel* (Glencoe: The Free Press, 1950), pp. 307-76.

18 Lyford P. Edwards, *The Natural History of Revolution* (Chicago: University of Chicago Press, 1970) (first published 1927).

19 Ellsworth Faris, "The Sect and the Sectarian", *American Sociological Society Papers and Proceedings* 22 (1927): 144-58.

20 Herbert Blumer, "Social Movements", in A. M. Lee, ed., *Principles
of Sociology* (New York: Barnes and
Noble Inc., 1951), pp. 202-16.
21 Kurt Lang and Gladys Engel Lang,
Collective Dynamics (New York:
Thomas Y. Crowell Co., 1961), pp. 179-
206.
22 Lewis A. Coser, "Sects and Sec-
tarians", *Dissent* 1, No. 4 (1954):
360-9. See also Lewis A. Coser, *Men of
Ideas* (New York: The Free Press,
1965), pp. 99-109.
23 Lang and Lang, *op. cit.,* p. 182.
24 Park, *op. cit.,* p. 245.
25 Lang and Lang, *op. cit.,* p. 202.
26 Benton Johnson, "Church and Sect
Revisited", *Journal for the Scientific
Study of Religion* 10 (1971): 124-37.
27 Stephen Berger, "The Sects and the
Breakthrough into the Modern
World: On the Centrality of Sects to
Weber's Protestant Ethic Thesis"
(mimeographed paper presented to
annual meeting of the Midwest Sociological Society, 1970).
28 Park, *op. cit.,* pp. 243-4.
29 Worsley, *op. cit.,* pp. 221-56.
30 For discussions of the "instrumental-
expressive" distinction in relation to
social movements, see Park and Burgess,
op. cit., pp. 870-4, and Lang and Lang,
op. cit., pp. 500-11. See the perceptive
discussion of "rationality-irrationality"
in Joseph R. Gusfield, *Symbolic Crusade*
(Urbana, Illinois: University of Illinois
Press, 1963), p. 179. See also R. H.
Turner and L. M. Killian, *Collective
Behaviour* (Englewood Cliffs, N.J.:
Prentice-Hall, 1957), p. 431.
The case studies in the present paper
are based upon materials gathered by
the author in Toronto, Canada, in
1968-69.
31 *Mass Line* (an Internationalist publication) 2, No. 26, (1970): 2.
32 *Mass Line* 1, No. 10 (1969): 29.
33 *Words International* (an Internationalist publication) 1, No. 2 (1967): 3.
34 *Necessity for Change!* (Dublin: The
Internationalists, 1967).
35 *Ibid.,* pp. 7 and 22.
36 See S. Holbrook, "Last of the
Wobblies", *The American Mercury*
62 (1946): 462-8, for a discussion of

the IWW. On the SPGB, see G. Thayer,
The British Political Fringe: A Profile
(London: Anthony Blond, 1965): 148-
50. See also R. J. Alexander, "Splinter
Groups in American Politics", *Social
Research* 20 (1953): 288-9.
37 *Socialist Labour Party: Position and
Programme* (leaflet published during
1960s).
38 *Socialism: Questions Most Frequently Asked and Their Answers*
(New York: New York Labour News
Co., the SLP Publishing Outlet, 1967),
p. 60.
39 *Ibid.,* pp. 59-60.
40 Arnold Peterson, National Secretary
of the SLP of America, 1914-69, in
a document presented to all new members. Quoted in Eric Hass, *The Science
of Socialism: A Home Study Course*
(New York: New York Labour News
Co., 1967), p. 59.
41 *Socialist Press Bulletin* (official
organ of the SLP of Canada),
August 1969, p. 5.
42 *Socialist Press Bulletin,* January
1970, p. 6.
43 Robin M. Williams, Jr., *American
Society* (New York: Alfred A.
Knopf, 1961), p. 391.
44 See George Thayer, *op. cit.,* p. 150,
for comment on the yellowing literature of the Socialist Party of Great
Britain.
45 *Socialist Press Bulletin,* June 1970,
p. 5.
46 *Socialist Press Bulletin,* September
1970, p. 6.
47 This famous phrase of Bernstein's is
used here in a different sense from
that intended by its originator. See
Eduard Bernstein, *Evolutionary
Socialism* (New York: Schocken Books,
1961), pp. xxix and 202 (first published 1899).
48 See H. Richard Niebuhr, *The Social
Sources of Denominationalism*
(Cleveland: World Publishing Co.,
1957; first published 1929); and David
Martin, "The Denomination", *British
Journal of Sociology* 13 (1962): 1-14.
49 Roland Robertson, *The Sociological
Interpretation of Religion* (New
York: Schocken Books, 1970), p. 241.

4.

Responses to
Religious Callings

Priests Under Stress*

Paul Stryckman
Robert Gaudet

Three constant elements make up the role-set of the priest in the Church:
the cult (sacraments and liturgy), the Word (teaching and preaching),
and the pastoral ministry (government and formation of community).
Sociologists of religion teach us that the cult is always the determining
element in the different sacerdotal functions (M. Weber, 1964: 28-30;
J. Wach 1955: 324-30). We consider this, therefore, as being consti-
tutive of the role of the priest. But this cultic activity involves two very
different types of priests according to the order of priority established
among these three elements: one type, if the cult is seen as the principle
of authority; the other, if the cult is seen as the expression of the symbolic
action of the Word of faith.

In the first type, if the cult is seen as the principle of authority and
function, the priest is inclined to see himself as the official representative
of the Church, and a specialist in the liturgy and the sacraments. The
stress is laid on the instrumental role of the priest. The emphasis rests
on an image of the priest (and of the Church) whose action is sacred

*Appeared first in *Priests in Canada 1971* (Québec: Centre de Recherches
en Sociologie Religieuse, Université Laval). Published here in abridged and
revised form with the kind permission of the authors and the publisher.

and whose authority is hierarchic—a "priestly-administrator" type. In the second type, if the cult is seen as the expression of the symbolic action of the Word of faith, the emphasis is on the expressive role of the priest inasmuch as he is both a witness to and a prophet of the Christian message. The priest is not exclusively occupied with the sacred functions or with administrative tasks, but his role is seen as a ministry of service in the ecclesiastical community. From this second type emerges an image of the priest and of the Church whose action is prophetic and whose authority is defined as diaconal—a "prophet-servant" type. These two typologies are in no way intended to take on a theological meaning or a particular exegesis. They are meant to be descriptive, not normative. Also, we stress the fact that they are meant to summarize an emphasis among the important sub-roles of the priest and not to exclude any of them. [H. Richard Niebuhr (1956: 58–63) used a similar approach, but his typology is applied to differentiate the ministries among Christian churches through history with a greater emphasis on the theological aspects of such a process. Eds.]

These two models or typologies can apply to different aspects of change in the life of the priest. We can relate them to changes in thought or behaviour (or, in other terms, to changes in ideology and pastoral practice). In this way we can discover how the priests define themselves in terms of what they believe and what they do, and at the same time discover the present tendencies among the clergy in the changing, post-conciliar Church.

In October 1970 we mailed 1,643 questionnaires to the sample of English-speaking priests. Some 61 per cent of the diocesan priests (558) and 54 per cent of the religious (389) completed and returned the questionnaire. [From the results we cannot conclude simply] that priests in general have moved from one [type] to the other. An important distinction we must make is between the priests' *ideology* and their *behaviour* or pastoral practice. From the point of view of their desire and vision of the priesthood we find that priests in general are concerned with preaching the Word and with the formation of community, and they seem very dedicated to the service of the people. We find rather sharp differences, however, in some places concerning where and how this service should be exercised.

From the point of view of their present activity and pastoral practice, the priests themselves describe their image in priestly-administrator terms. Celebrating Mass, attending to the sacramental needs of the people, administration, and fund raising are the dominant components of their own self-image. We must not be too quick to say that all this will change because the priests want it to, and because their desire for the future is expressed in prophet-servant terms, for we recall that the present administrator image exists even though the majority of priests gave reasons [for commitment] at the time of ordination which were [expressed] in prophet-servant terms. Apparently what we see is evidence of the simple fact that thought and desire are not in harmony with practice.

1. Ideological Orientation

Looking at the priests' ideological orientation in general, we find two different dynamics at work. In one area we discover that there is a noticeable shift in orientation in the liturgy and celebrating Mass. The Mass is the central cultic activity in the priests' role and spiritual life, but we find that it has taken on a new focus at the heart of the Christian community. Priests want to give more emphasis in their ministry to preparing for and preaching the Word, developing Christian community among the laity, and making the liturgy meaningful than they do to celebrating Mass. In a sense, they give the Mass a new image, [not] that of being the cultic activity of the Church's official representative on behalf of the people, [but] that of being the cultic expression of the people themselves in which they discover and celebrate their unity. This shift is also reflected in the fact that about one-half of the priests want to eliminate the Sunday obligation under pain of sin, and the majority of them want to eliminate Mass stipends. Both of these actions suggest that the priests want at least to reduce the emphasis on the Church's legislation or directives concerning the Mass and to allow greater room for spontaneous response on the part of the people.

Another dynamic that we find within the ideological orientation of the priests is that the prophet-servant tendency is directed more towards the interior of the Christian community than outside the present Church structure. For example, while priests desire more involvement in social issues than there is now, this desire, together with the interest in ecumenical activities and experimental ministries, takes second place to their concern for the already existing community. We see, too, that priests are much more in favour of the idea of developing a specialty within the lines of their regular ministry (e.g. priest-specialists within the parishes) than they are of developing a professional competence in secular areas outside the lines of their regular ministry. The majority of religious priests, however, think that they will become more involved in secular jobs. Younger priests differ from the others in that as a group they are stronger in their desire for the expressive roles of the priests both within the existing community and outside it.

One of the elements involved in the dynamics of this interior change within the Church structure is that of democratization in the decision-making process. When we look at the priests' expectations of this change, we discover that they look more towards the presbyterium than towards the laity for developing a common responsibility in the Church. Priests look more towards the priests' senate as an influential body in the diocese than towards the pastoral council. One-third of the priests think the laity should have "very much" influence concerning changes in the liturgy and the use of diocesan money, and only 12 per cent of the priests think that the laity should have "very much" influence in the appointment of pastors and the selection of bishops.

Our point is that in terms of ideology we find that most priests had at ordination, and continue to have now, a prophet-servant image of the priesthood, but that today there is a new concern and desire to translate this into communal terms, to express it more within the Christian community than outside it, and to place more hope in the presbyterium than in the laity for its effective realization.

As for the religious priests, there is some evidence that the changes in religious life have been more radical than among the diocesan clergy. While we find in general that the long-range view of religious priests is positive and creative, we find wide differences between younger and older religious concerning their experience of the vows and their judgment as to the place of the vows in religious life. Religious under 50 have changed more in their underlying pattern of ideology between the time of ordination and today than any other group of priests. The shift towards the prophet-servant type has been greater among them than among the diocesan priests and even among the religious over 50. The majority of all religious priests find obedience the mainstay of religious life, and find that poverty needs most to be reinterpreted and updated in practice. But whereas priests over 35 find obedience the most personally enriching and poverty the least enriching, priests under 35 say just the opposite. They find poverty the most personally enriching and obedience the least enriching. What we find is that the experience of the younger priests concerning the vows does not correspond to their judgment about the importance of the vows, whereas with the older priests it does. Some 39 per cent of all the priests find chastity the most difficult of all the vows to observe (the percentage rises to 45 per cent for priests 35 and under). The vow of chastity has a special position inasmuch as it is rated the most difficult to observe and yet at the same time is judged to give a lower degree of spiritual enrichment than either of the other two vows. One feels that religious priests almost avoid raising questions about chastity. This silence is noteworthy, especially when we see the other two vows being discussed so widely, and when we remember that the priests do not consider chastity the mainstay of religious life. One might expect to find evidence of a desire to change this aspect of religious life in the future, but whether this develops will depend in large part on how the celibacy crisis among the diocesan clergy is resolved.

2. Changes in Pastoral Practice

Looking at the level of behaviour and pastoral practice, the priests describe themselves in the image of the priestly-administrator type. Our question now is to discover in what areas and to what degree this is in fact changing, and whether or not the areas of effective change correspond to the areas of desired change.

(a) Typology of Individual and Institutional Change

To do this, we suggest a framework for considering the data further. This will permit us to take into account that not only priests are in a process of change, but the institution of the Church itself can be changing as well. This means that the institutional Church, through her official representatives, also can be examining and re-defining former positions, laws, and policies. If we define the process of change by three positions, namely, traditional, questioning, and re-defined, we can apply these stages both to the priests and to the official Church. It would be possible, for example, that the Church has re-defined a former law (e.g. abstinence on Friday), but that a priest does not accept the new legislation and rigidly follows the old law. In this case the priest could be considered deviant. The same expression can be used for a priest who, on his own, has re-defined a traditional law which the Church has not changed. Here again we could say the priest is deviant. It is possible to have many other combinations of these stages of change. To mention one, both the priest and the official Church could be questioning an issue, in which case we would have a state of normlessness, where criteria and official norms for behaviour are lacking on the part of the Church, and where a social basis and legitimacy for action are lacking on the part of the priest.

It is evident that at the formal canonical level the questioning phase does not apply to the official Church. Previous legislation is not suspended until a new decision has been arrived at. But at the level of attitudes and discussion, a questioning phase can exist in the Church (*Decree on the Ministry and Life of Priests*, No. 22). A formal change is always a post factum recognition of such a process. But in practice we know that this questioning phase can sometimes be exaggerated if individuals think that change is imminent, and act as if the change were already in effect. With this framework we can consider the dynamic of change which is active in the relationship between the individuals and the institution. We will look at two dimensions of this dynamic, namely the areas of conflict and tension, and the signs of stability which we find.

(b) *Areas of Conflict and Tension*

The Canadian priests did not need a research study to know that the celibacy issue is one of the main areas of conflict in the Church, and that there are wide differences among younger and older priests concerning celibacy and many other issues. We find that there are other major areas where there are sharp differences of opinion between the priests in general and the Church organization: namely, some aspects of sacramental discipline, some traditional moral principles, and some aspects of the present situation in the diocesan structure.

Priests are dissatisfied with the image that they [currently] have, the traditional spiritual practices no longer nourish their spiritual lives, and about one-fifth of them have thought seriously of leaving within the last three years.

We discover that the age factor seems the most useful variable for describing the differences among priests, rather than the diocesan-religious difference, the geographic region, or the priest's occupation. While the age factor is important, we cannot say simply that one generation is opposed to another generation. On nearly all the questions we find a progression of agreement or disagreement that speaks not so much of a gap as of a curve.

[The discussion of] celibacy gives some measure of the priests' opposition to the present Church legislation. Some 53 per cent are in favour of allowing priests to marry and to remain active in the ministry, 83 per cent are in favour of the ordination of married men, and two-thirds think that the celibacy law will be changed. An analysis of these general percentages shows that, except for the ordination of married men, the priests over 50 and under 50 hold opposing views: 55 per cent of the younger priests say that the celibacy law seriously limits personal freedom, whereas the majority of priests over 50 deny this. Priests under 50 are in favour of optional celibacy and they think the law will be changed, whereas priests over 50 are opposed to optional celibacy and do not think the law will be changed. What we find important also is that the majority of traditional reasons offered by the Church for celibacy do not receive legitimation and a social basis for support from the young priests. The young priests agree to celibacy's practical values in providing freedom to serve the people and availability for assignment, but these practical reasons would appear to be no longer sufficient. Otherwise, why all the discussion? Either the priests find that these reasons are not sufficient grounds on which to commit themselves to a celibate life, or perhaps the Church itself has not found ministries which maximize the opportunities provided by a celibate clergy.

It is obvious that neither has the Church changed its traditional position on celibacy, nor have the young priests re-defined their position in practice. In relation to the typology just suggested, the younger priests are in a questioning phase, to say the least, and the older priests and the official Church maintain the traditional position. However, younger priests are anticipating a re-defined phase, inasmuch as, in attitude if not in practice, they see the Church changing and think that the celibacy law eventually will be changed. We must recognize that one of the limitations of our research is that we did not study those priests who made an actual re-definition of their situation by either resigning from or leaving the active ministry in order to marry.

From a sociological point of view we would expect to find re-defined positions first appearing in individual cases and private sectors before finding them in the public domain and receiving wider social legitimacy. In the area of sacramental discipline, as mentioned before, we find that one-half of the priests are in favour of eliminating the Sunday obligation under pain of sin. We find, too, that in their pastoral practice 38 per cent of the priests would give Communion privately to a person civilly divorced and remarried, and 22 per cent would do it publicly. In these cases these priests would appear to move beyond the letter of the present legislation in the Church, and to have re-defined their practice in the light of pastoral circumstances.

On two moral principles we find the priests in opposition to the traditional teaching of the Church. Some 72 per cent of the priests think that the traditional position of Catholic moral theology on the gravity of masturbation should be modified, and 62 per cent of the priests think that ligation of the fallopian tubes (as sterilization) should be allowed for therapeutic reasons.

One of the areas where there has been a great deal of change in recent years has been in the organization of the diocese. The *Motu Proprio Ecclesiae Sanctae* re-invented the role of the senate and gave it consultative power in the decision-making process of the diocese. Among priests 34 per cent now define the function of their senate in these terms, and 26 per cent think that the senate has less than a consultative role. We find, however, that the priests want to go beyond the official directives of the *Motu Proprio* and give the senate an even greater role in the formation of diocesan policy. Some 57 per cent of the priests are in favour of the senate's being "democratic" in function, a shift from the consultative function. They recognize that the bishop is the most influential person in the diocese and they want him to remain that way, but they want the influence of the chancery officials and consultors to decrease.

(c) *Signs of Stability*

It would be incomplete to end our remarks with a discussion of the areas of conflict and tension between the clergy and the institutional Church without mentioning as well the other side of the coin. The survey has revealed some remarkable areas of stability and loyalty which must be taken into account if one is to attempt an accurate judgment of the situation. The celibacy issue has put greater strain on priests and on the Church in recent years than any other crisis, and many observers read from this an imminent disintegration of the institution and a stampede of priests leaving the priesthood. Our results give us a different picture. We find that, even if the law of celibacy does *not* change, 68 per cent of the diocesan priests and 77 per cent of the religious say they will "definitely remain celibate". On the other hand, we find that if the law of celibacy *does* change, 4 per cent of the clergy say that they will "definitely marry". Many will find this figure surprisingly low. It is interesting to notice in comparison with this that 1 per cent of the priests say they will "definitely marry" even if the present legislation continues.

We find, too, that the level of job satisfaction is very high among priests. Of the total, 55 per cent express a high degree of satisfaction in their job. This job satisfaction is a measure of personal satisfaction that the priest feels towards his present work. It is a measure of subjective attitude, and does not imply a judgment on the value of the work in relation to the effectiveness of the priest's ministry or the needs of the milieu. Actually the figure of 55 per cent could be considered a low estimate. Further analysis reveals that 76 per cent of the priests describe their job more in terms of satisfaction than in terms of dissatisfaction.

Another important result which supports the degree of satisfaction that priests have is the fact that, if they were given the chance to do it all over again, three-quarters of the priests would enter the same diocese or congregation. There is little desire to enter another diocese or congregation, and there is little desire for diocesan priests to become religious or for religious to become diocesan.

3.   Partial Renewal?

In what direction is the Church heading today? In view of all we have said in this report we look upon the changes that have taken place as a partial renewal. We consider that this partial renewal applies both to the ideological orientation and to the level of pastoral practice. First of all, at the level of ideological orientation, by "renewal" we mean that there has been a shift in the image and expectation of the priests to a greater emphasis on the prophet-servant role. Secondly, we say "partial" because this new orientation remains within the lines of the regular priestly ministry and is primarily directed towards the interior of the existing Christian community rather than outside it.

At the level of pastoral practice, we find that the "renewal" is not very evident, since the priests still look on themselves [as having] a priestly-administrator image. We say here, too, that the renewal is "partial" because we have more evidence of rejection of some former practices than we have evidence of openness and discovery of new ministries. One of the serious limitations of our research is that it is easier to obtain systematic information at the level of expectation, desire, and image than it is at the level of actual behaviour and practice. Our judgments are based on what the priests tell us they do, and not on first-hand observation.

[We have] the impression that the priests are in the questioning phase of our typology of change, but with this difference, that at the ideological level they are closer to a re-defined position than they are in their behaviour. We say this because the behaviour consists more of a [predisposition] to reject some traditional activities and ministries than in an attempt to create and discover new ones. This tendency towards rejection of existing patterns of behaviour tends to produce a condition of normlessness and demoralization.

The direction of the future would seem to be a matter of choice. The greatest obstacle we see is that the level of imagination, experimentation, and even audacity appears low. It is almost as though the socialization of the clergy, the integration process in the institution, and the control system have been too effective. In our judgment, the most hopeful sign is the dynamic trend towards participation and greater sharing at all levels of life and government, even at the levels of major policy.

However, we make two observations about the direction of the momentum of greater participation in the Christian community and the diocesan government. First, we think it must look more towards the laity in the interior of the Christian community, and secondly, we think it must be more open and creative to respond to new forms of ministry that arise outside the Church structure. Both of these areas seem to be somewhat by-passed in the present dynamism of development. Our analysis confirms the conclusions frequently arrived at in other research on organizations based on a "goal model", comparing official purposes or ideologies of the organization with effectiveness or actual changes (A. Etzioni 1960). This observation brings up an important question that is beyond the scope of this report. What are the actual effects of Vatican II's decrees in the ecclesiastical organization, apart from the official goals set up in these documents?

REFERENCES

Niebuhr, H. Richard
1956 The Purpose of the Church and
      Its Ministry. New York: Harper
      and Row.
Etzioni, Amitai
1960 "Two Approaches to Organiza-
      tional Analysis: A Critique and
      a Suggestion." In Administrative

Science Quarterly 5, No. 2:
      257-8.
Wach, Joachim
1955 Sociologie de la Religion. Paris:
      Z. Payot.
Weber, Max
1963 The Sociology of Religion.
      Boston: Beacon.

The Circulation of the Saints*

Reginald W. Bibby
Merlin B. Brinkerhoff

In their *American Piety*, published in 1968, Stark and Glock presented data which suggest that people are moving out of denominations "which are still foursquare for traditional orthodoxy" and into "churches with more liberal, modernized theologies" (Stark and Glock 1968: 189). Their findings, which came from a large sample of San Francisco area laymen, seemed to point toward overall membership gains for the liberal denominations at the expense of the more conservative churches.

But we now know that this is not occurring. Since 1965 many of the relatively liberal Protestant denominations in the United States and Canada have actually reported net *losses* in membership. In Canada, for example, losses have been reported by the United Church, the Anglicans, and the Presbyterians. In the United States declines have been recorded by the Episcopalians, the United Methodists, the United Presbyterians, and the United Church of Christ. In the same period, however, the more

*Appeared first as R. W. Bibby and M. B. Brinkerhoff, "The Circulation of the Saints: A Study of People Who Join Conservative Churches", in *Journal for the Scientific Study of Religion* 12 (September 1973): 273-83. Published here with the kind permission of the authors and the publisher. The authors wish to express appreciation to Professors John Finney, Harry H. Hiller, and Armand Mauss for critical comments and suggestions on earlier drafts.

conservative or sect-like Protestant denominations have reported *increases* in membership. Bodies such as the Jehovah's Witnesses, Mormons, Seventh-Day Adventists, Southern Baptists, Nazarenes, and the various Pentecostal denominations, have all reported impressive numerical gains.[1] So clear is the current trend that it has already provoked an agonized stock-taking in liberal church circles. In a recent book, Dean Kelley (1972) attributed much of the relative success of the conservative churches to their ability to provide a religion which furnishes people with answers to the question of ultimate meaning, places demands on them, and calls forth personal commitment.

Why do recent membership trends contradict the patterns reported by Stark and Glock? Many questions will have to be answered before convincing explanations can be advanced. Among other things, a close and careful look needs to be taken at the pattern of accessions and defections over time among churches of a variety of theological orientations. Many sociologists have raised questions about the reliability and validity of official church statistics (Stark and Glock 1968: 199–203; Demerath and Hammond 1969: 120–1). Stark and Glock have complained that "there are no published (and we know of no unpublished) statistics on the extent or patterns of intra-Protestant denominational switching" (1968: 183). This paper will make a modest beginning toward the information we need for a more accurate understanding of differential church growth. It will take a close look at one aspect of this problem, namely the sources from which conservative churches draw their new members.

Review of Literature

Kunz and Brinkerhoff (1970: 217–18), in contrasting the growth patterns of Mormons and American Baptists, point out that there are three general means by which a church might add members: (1) reaffiliation, (2) birth, and (3) conversion, a generalization which receives support from the existing literature. However, while the importance of these three sources has been hypothesized, limited empirical research has been reported.

Membership Through Reaffiliation: The Return of the "Saints"

It is widely recognized that many people joining churches have previous histories of involvement with religious groups. Often they are the geographically mobile, who spontaneously reaffiliate with the same types of religious groups as they relocate in new areas. For example, Holt (1940), Hoult (1958), Mann (1962), and Moberg (1962) have drawn attention to the relationship between the rise of city churches and rural-urban church member migration, while many writers, including Niebuhr (1929), Herberg (1955), and Mann (1962), have emphasized the relationship between membership growth and ethnic migration. Given the sheer fact of geographic mobility among contemporary North Americans, it should hardly be surprising that religious membership reaffiliation should be a common phenomenon (Demerath and Hammond 1969: 184).

Moreover, it is extremely likely that many individuals will move from one church to another within a city for such varied reasons as physical mobility or dislike of the minister. For example, Mann (1962: 33, 55) found that the evangelical groups in Alberta grew through the addition of people from other Protestant congregations, capitalizing on apparent discontent over the relaxing of moral standards and the modernism controversy.[2] Niebuhr (1929: 133ff) wrote about the same process in the development of Protestantism on the American frontier. We have already mentioned Stark and Glock's data on denominational "switching". More recently, Mueller (1971) has also investigated interdenominational mobility.

Finally, it would appear that some reaffiliating members are restoring their membership after a period of relative inactivity within the denomination. In sum, we argue that many of the new additions to evangelical churches are actually reaffiliates, or "saints" from within the evangelical tradition.

Membership Through Birth: The Conversion of Children

Troeltsch (1931: 331ff) and other church-sect typologists have noted that one manner in which the sect differs from the church is that its members are not born into it. In his discussion of conversionist sects, Wilson (1959: 11) states that the recruitment of the second generation is also an important aspect of evangelism. Along with Niebuhr (1929: 19ff) and Pope (1942: 120), he suggests an important relationship between second-generation converts and religious group development. Yinger (1970: 130–1) also points out that many are drawn to religion through family socialization. As Allport (1950: 35) notes, in some instances the influence of the parents upon their children may not "come to fruition" for years, yet is nonetheless very real. Somewhat surprisingly, religious writers and churchmen, when speaking of new converts who join churches, seldom differentiate between the children of members and other new additions. For example, it is a common procedure in denominational record-keeping to list "baptisms" (or one of the formal means to enter the organization) without indicating whether those baptized are "outsiders" or the children of members. While the children of church members who join churches may sometimes be counted as "the fruits of evangelism", they clearly come from within the religious community. It may be misleading to consider them as proselytes when they are really the offspring of evangelicals. Given this source of members, it follows that birth-rate variations between denominations may have a direct influence on the number of candidates for membership.

Membership Through Proselytism: The Conversion of "Sinners"

Evangelical churches have the explicit goal of evangelizing or "spreading the gospel". That is, they are attempting to convert "sinners". While proselytizing is accepted as a fact of religious life, the social science literature contains few studies which deal with the subject. Attention has commonly been given only to the social and psychological characteristics of converts to religious groups and movements (see, for example, Beynon 1938; Holt 1940; Hoffer 1951; Glock and Stark 1965; Lofland 1966; Monaghan 1967; Nelson 1972; and Seggar and Kunz 1972). But little is known empirically concerning the actual incidence of proselytism, the "success" proselytizing groups have, and the proportion of proselytes within religious groups. The limited empirical studies known to the authors (Hostetler, 1954; Blumstock 1968; Gerlach and Hine 1968; Nelson 1972) suggest that alleged proselytes usually have a church background and that actual proselytism is negligible.

In summary, then, we would argue that there are three broad manners in which religious organizations grow. Many new members are actually reaffiliating, moving from one congregation of a denomination to another, or uniting with the same congregation after a prolonged period of lapse. A second group of new members are young persons who, having parents who already "profess faith", come from *within* the religious community. And finally, the third manner in which churches grow is through proselytism, whereby outsiders, or "sinners", are brought into the group.

Background and Methodology

Using these three major sources of new members, the authors sought to explore the question of who it is that conservative Protestant congregations are adding to their membership rolls. They examined the membership additions of a sample of evangelical churches which claim to be proselyte-minded, located in a western Canadian city with a population of about 415,000. The city is reported to be one of the major centers of evangelical activity in Canada. When the study was conducted in the spring of 1971, the city had over 80 evangelical congregations embracing over 30,000 members and adherents.[3] In addition, it both housed and was proximate to a number of prominent evangelical Bible schools.

The decision was made to study 20 of the churches, based on the belief that this would be a sufficiently large sample to provide answers to the main questions being raised. It further represented a number which could be handled within the time and resource limits of the study. The sample of 20 churches, along with 10 alternates, was randomly selected from a list of 81 churches associated with the city's Evangelical Ministerial Association. The sample was confined to this Association because these churches explicitly profess to be "proselyte-minded", and it clearly defines the population being studied.

The random sample was selected on a probability basis, with all churches having an equal chance of inclusion. The sample churches comprised six Baptist, five Pentecostal, three Nazarene, two Missionary, two Salvation Army, one Christian and Missionary Alliance, and one Plymouth Brethren congregation. Ten of the churches were considered predominantly middle class, while 10 were working class.[4] The formal commitment of the churches to proselytism was checked through responses to items in a questionnaire administered to five leaders from each of the 20 churches.

Membership additions over the period 1966 through 1970 were examined, as we noted earlier,[5] since these years represent a time of evangelical growth in the midst of extensive decline for many other churches. A five-year period was used in order to minimize the biasing effects of "peak" years or "off" years.

In late April of 1971, the ministers of the 20 churches in the sample were contacted in person, had the study interpreted to them, and agreed to prepare a list of members who had been added to their respective churches over the 1966–70 period. This list included members who had since had their names removed from the church roll (e.g., transfers out).[6]

In May the authors conducted a second interview, at which time the membership additions were classified into the three aforementioned source categories by the ministers and their secretaries. At this time, additional specific information was also gathered on the members classified as proselytes.

Those new members who were recognized to be evangelicals upon initially attending a given conservative church were classed as "members through reaffiliation" (e.g., transfers; members received on "profession of faith"; those reinstated, including "backsliders"). That is, these are persons who had previously been considered evangelicals. Those who had been converted during the time they had attended the particular church being examined were divided into two subtypes: "birth-type converts" designated those who had "had at least one evangelical parent or guardian prior to age ten", in essence describing the children of evangelicals;[7] "proselyte-type converts" referred to those who "had not had at least one evangelical parent or guardian prior to age ten," in essence describing converts from outside the evangelical community.[8]

The Findings

Over the five-year period 1966–70, the number of membership additions reported by the 20 churches totalled 1,532. Of this figure, 1,104 (72 per cent) came through reaffiliation, 284 (18 per cent) through birth-type conversion, and 132 (9 per cent) through proselyte-type conversion. Only 12 new members (1 per cent) could not be classified (see Table 1). Clearly the most common source of new members is former members, with birth a distant second, and proselytism third.

When the sources of new members are examined with respect to denomination (see Table 2), the overall trend continues with only one exception: the Salvation Army churches received into membership a higher proportion of proselyte than birth-type converts. A tentative explanation for this is suggested below, where size and social class of membership are discussed. It is interesting to observe that from a denominational standpoint, the highly publicized proselytizing image of groups like the Pentecostals and Nazarenes is not borne out by the data. These denominations draw a very heavy proportion of their new members from the evangelical ranks. Instead, it is the Salvation Army that stands out as containing the largest proportion of proselyte-type converts among its new entrants.

TABLE 1.   The Number of Each Type of Membership Addition for the 20 Churches

GENERAL CHURCH NAME	MEMBER- SHIP SIZE*	ENTERING BY REAFFIL- IATION	BIRTH	PROSE- LYTE	UN- KNOWN	TOTAL	TOTAL
Alliance	453	104	28	18		46	150
Missionary A	22	5	0	0		0	5
Missionary B	85	30	0	0		0	30
Nazarene A	40	13	3	4		7	20
Nazarene B	142	37	5	1	1	7	44
Nazarene C	55	23	5	2		7	30
Non-Union Baptist A	14	23	0	0		0	23
Non-Union Baptist B	141	59	20	5		25	84
Non-Union Baptist C	72	101	10	6	2	18	119
Non-Union Baptist D	35	21	0	1	1	2	23
Pentecostal A	41	31	1	0		1	32
Pentecostal B	67	44	10	4		14	58
Pentecostal C	18	19	0	0		0	19
Pentecostal D	47	7	6	9		15	22
Pentecostal E	35	19	3	0	1	4	23
Plymouth Brethren	142	93	31	6		37	130
Salvation Army A	18	7	2	7		9	16
Salvation Army B	204	86	9	18		27	113
Union Baptist A	185	80	23	9	2	34	114
Union Baptist B	1672	302	128	42	5	175	477
TOTALS: NUMBERS		1104	284	132	12	428	1532
%		(72.1)	(18.5)	(8.6)	(.8)	(27.9)	(100)

*Size represents the average membership over 1966-70.

There are some rather interesting findings with respect to social class. First, concerning size, the ten middle-class churches had a median membership of 142, while the median for the ten working-class churches was only 38. In a ranking of the 20 churches by size, the nine largest churches and the eleventh largest church were all middle-class congregations. Second, the middle-class groups admitted a far larger number of new members than did their working-class counterparts, both over all and within each source category (see Table 3). Third, while both classes admitted approximately the same proportion of proselytes, the middle-class churches added a higher proportion of their members through birth. With respect to reaffiliation, the larger, middle-class groups would seem to have a distinct resource advantage over the smaller, working-class churches in competing for mobile church members. Therefore, it

TABLE 2. Types of Membership Addition According to Denomination, by Percentage

		CONVERSION				TOTALS
	% BY	%	%	%	%	%
DENOMINATION	REAFFILIATION	BIRTH	PROSELYTE	UNKNOWN	TOTAL	N*
Alliance	69	19	12		31	100
	(104)	(28)	(18)		(46)	(150)
Missionary	100	0	0		0	100
	(35)	(0)	(0)		(0)	(35)
Nazarene	78	14	7	1	22	100
	(73)	(13)	(7)	(1)	(21)	(94)
Non-Union	82	12	5	1	18	100
Baptist	(204)	(30)	(12)	(3)	(45)	(249)
Pentecostal	78	13	8	1	22	100
	(120)	(20)	(13)	(1)	(34)	(154)
Plymouth	72	24	4		28	100
Brethren	(93)	(31)	(6)		(37)	(130)
Salvation Army	72	9	19		28	100
	(93)	(11)	(25)		(36)	(129)
Union Baptist	65	25	9	1	35	100
	(382)	(151)	(51)	(7)	(209)	(591)
TOTAL NUMBERS	(1104)	(284)	(132)	(12)	(428)	(1532)

*N is shown in parentheses.

TABLE 3.* Types of Membership Addition According to Class, by Percentage†

		CONVERSION				TOTALS
	% BY	%	%	%	%	
CLASS	REAFFILIATION	BIRTH	PROSELYTE	UNKNOWN	TOTAL	%
Middle Class	70	20	9	1	30	100
	(929)	(269)	(111)	(10)	(390)	(1319)
Working Class	82	7	10	1	18	100
	(175)	(15)	(21)	(2)	(38)	(213)
TOTAL NUMBERS	(1104)	(284)	(132)	(12)	(428)	(1532)

*Yule's Q = .32. This suggests a moderately strong relationship between social class and additions by reaffiliation vs. conversion.
†The number of persons in each cell is in parenthesis.

would be expected that the middle-class congregations would admit a fairly large proportion of geographically and socially mobile evangelicals. The greater proportion of birth additions for the middle-class churches might reflect a younger age structure with more offspring from which to recruit. It could also be that the working-class groups are losing their youth, through factors such as secularization and upward mobility, with some "switching" to other religious groups, including the middle-class evangelical churches.

A more detailed analysis of the 132 proselyte additions illustrated that the vast majority had some previous involvement in non-evangelical church life. Of the 118 for whom information was available, 25 per cent (30) had been members of non-Protestant bodies (18 were former Catholics) and 46 per cent (54) had been members of moderate or liberal Protestant congregations. Thus, over 70 per cent of the proselytes were people with previous church background. Consequently, of the 1,532 new members admitted to the 20 churches over the five-year period, less than two per cent were drawn from the "religious nones". Of further relevance to the question of outreach beyond the evangelical community, it was found that some 32 per cent (42) of the 132 proselytes were either engaged or married to evangelicals at the time of their conversion, including one-quarter (6) of those with no previous church background.[9]

Discussion

The findings indicate that these conservative churches are adding new members primarily through a kind of circulation process by which evangelicals move from one church to another. To a lesser extent, new additions are the offspring of members reared in an evangelical culture. What these denominations commonly describe as "converts" are more accurately "switchers" from other denominations (cf. Stark and Glock, 1968: 183–203). Moreover, religious intermarriage appears to be one of the crucial factors in the decision to switch. It seems likely that relatively few new members of evangelical churches come from outside the Christian community.

These findings suggest that Dean Kelley's assertion (1972) that conservative churches are growing primarily because of the "meaning, demand, and commitment" they provide is in need of qualification. We can conclude that the bulk of the growth reported by the evangelical churches we investigated came about through the reaffiliation of previous members and the recruitment of the children of evangelicals. "Switching", or proselytism, is the *least* important source of new members for these conservative churches. This suggests that conservative church growth is mainly a matter of *retaining* those who are already familiar with evangelical culture. It is not, in North America at least, a matter of making significant inroads outside that culture. The "meaning, demand, and commitment" Kelley talks about may be more compelling incentives for people brought up in an evangelical culture than for people who have been brought up in other subcultures.

This line of reasoning suggests that a close look should be taken at how well moderate and liberal churches are able to retain their members and the children of their members. Recent drops in liberal church membership may reflect a lessening ability to hold onto people who are geographically mobile.[10] It may also reflect a lessening ability to retain offspring. In this connection it should be noted that differential birth rates may be an important unexplored factor in the growth rates of liberal and conservative churches. A religion with a high birth rate that is able to retain a large proportion of its children obviously has a growth advantage over a religion with a lower birth rate and lesser ability to keep its children. In fact, the former religion may be able to "export" a considerable share of its members and its children to the latter without sacrificing its higher growth rate. To be specific, conservative churches could be growing faster than liberal churches while losing more members to liberal churches than they receive in return. If this in indeed the case, then Stark and Glock's findings are perfectly consistent with recent statistics showing that liberal churches are losing members and conservative churches are gaining them.

Conclusion

Obviously future research is needed which will empirically explore some of the hypotheses stimulated by the present findings. Relative to the more liberal groups, do conservative churches in fact retain more of their geographically mobile members? Do they produce and retain a larger number of their offspring? Why is the proselytizing level so relatively low, in view of the apparent extensive evangelistic attempts of the churches? Given the three sources of new members, what kind of a proportional balance seems related to growth and general viability? And what are the correlates of various proportional arrangements? Much theoretical and empirical work is also required to understand adequately the social and cultural conditions affecting the relative predominance of each of the three sources of new members. For example, the present study needs to be repeated in other areas with different religious histories and different kinds and proportions of religious groups. One would imagine that the same patterns of membership additions found in this western Canadian city would be found in other areas where conservative Protestantism is strong (e.g., Alabama): much growth through reaffiliation and birth-type evangelism, relatively little by proselytism. However, in places where proselytizing religious groups are relatively small in number (e.g., in certain foreign mission fields), proselytism logically must take place at least initially if extensive expansion is to occur. Yet it may be true that when membership size reaches a certain level, proselytizing attempts decrease, largely because it is possible for a congregation or denomination to carry out its "commission to reach the lost" (and hence legitimize its ministry) in much easier ways—namely, reaffiliation and birth-type evangelism. Broadly speaking, it may be true that the proportion of additions through proselytism is inversely related to the overall size of a religious grouping within a given social setting (e.g., conservative Protestants in Alberta, Mormons in Utah).

While this study has concentrated on one particular proselytizing religious subculture, it is anticipated that the perspective we have developed will be useful in the analysis of membership additions to other religious groups and perhaps to voluntary associations in general.

NOTES

1   Documentation of this assertion can be found, for example, in the annually published *Yearbook of American Churches* (National Council of Churches) for United States churches and in Tipp and Winter (1970) for Canadian churches. For an excellent summary of these divergent growth trends, see Dean M. Kelley (1972: 1-35).

2   Admittedly, the line between "change of membership due to such discontents" and the "change due to proselytism" may appear thin for some church organizations. However, our discussion below suggests that the line may be fairly clear for the evangelical churches.

3   This congregational figure is limited only to those evangelical denominations affiliated, through their ministers, with the city's Evangelical Ministerial Association. It is recognized that evangelicals certainly are found in other denominations beside those which are traditionally linked with evangelicalism. Thus the figure cited here may be a very modest estimate of the number of evangelically oriented Protestants in this western Canadian city.

4   The criteria used in determining the predominant social class of the congregations included ecological location within the city, general occupational levels of the parishioners, and the type of training received by the minister(s).

5 Seventeen of the 20 churches in the sample reported membership growth between 1966 and 1970. The overall net gain was an even 600 members. This gain is perhaps somewhat more impressive when it is recognized that the largest of the two Baptist Union churches "pruned deadwood" from its rolls in 1966, producing a net loss that year of 214 members for that Baptist congregation.

6 It must be made clear that this study is not one of net growth, because persons who left the church for any reason were not studied. Rather, it merely explores the manners in which people enter church membership. Theoretically, a person could be counted several times as he transferred from one church to another.

7 Such an age figure was chosen somewhat arbitrarily, but in the belief that it would adequately cover the crucial years of familial socializing influence. Obviously this category included both those who had known relatively continuous involvement in church life over the years, and those

whose involvement over time had been intermittent.

8 If children were converted at essentially the same time as their parents, they were classified "proselyte-type" converts.

9 With regard to the question of time lapse between time of conversion and formal membership, all but 10 of the new proselyte members had been converted after 1965; three had been converted before 1960. Thus the majority (92 per cent) of the converts took out membership relatively soon after their conversion.

10 It is interesting to note that some conservative churches have "covenants" that explicitly require their geographically mobile members to unite quickly with a new congregation. A common evangelical covenant includes the statement: "we engage that when we remove from this place, we will speedily seek opportunity to unite with some other church, in whose fellowship we can carry out the spirit of this covenant and the principles of God's Word" (*Canadian Baptist Minister's Handbook*: 6).

REFERENCES

Allport, Gordon W.
1950 *The Individual and His Religion.* New York: Macmillan.
Argyle, Michael
1958 *Religious Behaviour.* London: Routledge and Kegan Paul.
Autrey, C. E.
1959 *Basic Evangelism.* Grand Rapids: Zondervan.
Beynon, Erdmann D.
1938 "The Voodoo Cult among Negro Migrants to Detroit." *American Journal of Sociology* 43 (May): 894-907.
Blumstock, Robert
1968 "Fundamentalism, Prejudice and Mission to the Jews." *Canadian Review of Sociology and Anthropology* 5 (February): 27-35.
Chastain, Theron
1953 *We Can Win Others.* Philadelphia: Judson Press.

Demerath, N. J. III, and Phillip E. Hammond
1969 *Religion in Social Context.* New York: Random House.
Gerlach, Luther P., and Virginia H. Hine
1968 "Five Factors Crucial to the Growth and Spread of a Modern Religious Movement." *Journal for the Scientific Study of Religion* 7 (Spring): 23-40.
Glock, Charles Y., and Rodney Stark
1965 *Religion and Society in Tension.* Chicago: Rand McNally.
Herberg, Will
1955 *Protestant-Catholic-Jew.* Garden City, N.Y.: Doubleday.
Hoffer, Eric
1951 *The True Believer.* New York: Harper and Row.
Holt, John B.
1940 "Holiness Religion: Cultural Shock and Social Reorganiza-

tion." *American Sociological Review* 5 (October): 740-7.

Hostetler, John A.
1954 "Religious Mobility in a Sect Group: The Mennonite Church." *Rural Sociology* 19 (September): 244-55.

Hoult, Thomas
1958 *The Sociology of Religion.* New York: Holt, Rinehart and Winston.

Kelley, Dean M.
1972 *Why Conservative Churches Are Growing.* New York: Harper and Row.

Kephart, William
1963 "Experimental Family Organization: An Historico-cultural Report on the Oneida Community." *Journal of Marriage and Family Living* 25: 261-71.

Kunz, Phillip R., and Merlin B. Brinkerhoff
1970 "Growth in Religious Organizations: A Comparative Study." *Social Science* 45 (October): 215-22.

Lofland, John
1966 *Doomsday Cult.* Englewood Cliffs, N.J.: Prentice-Hall.

Mann, W. E.
1962 *Sect. Cult. and Church in Alberta.* Toronto: University of Toronto Press.

Moberg, David
1962 *The Church as a Social Institution.* Englewood Cliffs, N. J.: Prentice-Hall.

Monaghan, Robert R.
1967 "Three Faces of the True Believer: Motivations for Attending a Fundamentalist Church." *Journal for the Scientific Study of Religion* 6 (Fall): 236-45.

Mueller, Samuel A.
1971 "Dimensions of Interdenominational Mobility in the United States." *Journal for the Scientific Study of Religion* 10 (Summer): 76-84.

Nelson, Geoffrey K.
1972 "The Membership of a Cult: The Spiritualists National Union." *Review of Religious Research* 13 (Spring): 170-7.

Niebuhr, H. R.
1929 *The Social Sources of Denominationalism.* New York: Holt.

Pope, Liston
1942 *Millhands and Preachers.* New Haven: Yale University Press.

Seggar, John, and Phillip R. Kunz
1972 "Conversion: Evaluation of a Step-like Process for Problem Solving." *Review of Religious Research* 13 (Spring): 178-84.

Stark, Rodney, and Charles Y. Glock
1968 *American Piety: The Nature of Religious Commitment.* Berkeley: University of California Press.

Tipp, Charles, and Terry Winter
1970 "The Christian Church in Canada: A Survey of Protestant Churches and Organizations." Unpublished manuscript, Ottawa.

Troeltsch, Ernest
1931 *The Social Teachings of the Christian Churches,* 2 vols. New York: Macmillan.

Weber, Max
1964 *Sociology of Religion.* Boston: Beacon Press.

Wilson, Bryan R.
1959 "An Analysis of Sect Development." *American Sociological Review* 24 (February): 3-15.

Yinger, Milton
1970 *The Scientific Study of Religion.* New York: Macmillan.

The End of a Religion?*

Colette Moreux

In [this chapter] we shall try to undertake two simultaneous operations:
1. We shall consider our female informants as no longer only expressing regulated, individual cases in relation to their adherence to Catholicism, but as the spokesmen for social types differing in age, civil status, profession, rural or urban origin, and level of education. Understanding of the religious aspect of our parish should be widened through the results of this discussion.
2. These people will be considered as representatives not only of a particular parish, Saint-Pierre,[1] but of the French Canadians as an ethnic group, of which we consider they are a fairly representative sample. In doing this, we shall try to make several generalizations about the present and future state of the development of Catholicism in Quebec.

Age and Civil Status
Our informants defined the religious development of a woman through different periods of her life as follows:

*Appeared first as Chapter 19 in Gerald L. Gold and Marc-Adélard Tremblay, *Communities and Culture in French Canada* (Toronto: Holt, Rinehart and Winston, 1973). From *Fin d'une religion?* (Montréal: Les Presses de l'Université de Montréal, 1969). Published here, with abridgements, with the kind permission of the author and the publisher.

At the age of eleven or twelve, we all want to be religious, but the desire passes. When you are young, you are a bit foolish, you think of other things. When you have children, you have to be careful, you have to teach them religion; later, they can do what they like, but they can't reproach us for it. When you are old, you have more time for devotions.

In practice, the old people are the basis of the traditionalist devout and pious categories; their religion is the strongest in external observances, but is perhaps also the least abstract. They hold the most orthodox theoretical beliefs, although they may be somewhat limited, and with few exceptions, they are also the ones for whom the transcendental aspects of the sacred interact most with the secular. This age group is intimately associated with the occupational category of workers and their relatives, which also partly explains some characteristics of their religious attitude. The old people are also the ones who form the basic membership in associations, although they do not occupy leadership roles and barely participate in associational activities.

The youngest age group is marked by its extreme positions; young girls who were born in the village and have never left it differ in no way from the most hard-line old traditionalists, even if the rigidity of their attitude has not yet been mellowed by experience. At the other extreme of our continuum are young village girls who, through their studies or professions, are familiar with the city and often live there part of the week; some reject Catholicism and all the values of their original culture, whereas others borrow avant-garde forms from it, which again is a means of rejecting their culture. On the other hand, young girls whose parents come from the city are much more moderate and most of them may be placed in the modernist group.

No matter what type they belong to, single girls assert themselves both on the purely religious and on the moral level. But, as soon as they marry, their personalities stabilize, even if they are very young; they practise less if they formerly practised extensively, and they return to religion if they had left it; their secular life is also compromised. As is usually the case in all Christian groups, married people between twenty-five and forty[2] are the least religious: this is the category in which we find the least number of devout and the greatest number of modal people. The pious (traditionalist or modernist) are less sincere than their counterparts in the other two age categories. In short, in this group, variations between different degrees of piety and between the modern or traditional forms of Catholicism are less distinct.

On account of the population structure, this last age group is mainly composed of representatives from the new population, which also explains their attitude.

Degree of Social Integration: New or Old Population

The separation between the two types of population is one of the most clearcut. Only five people in the new population belong to the devout and pious type out of the thirty-seven in the sample group, whereas nineteen representatives of the old population out of the fifty-three in the sample group are among the modal and associative; in other respects, modernists and traditionalists correspond almost point for point to the categories of new and old populations. The differences are to be found almost entirely on the level of practice. Therefore, social integration only uses religious channels indirectly, as parish associations are never used as intermediaries and any feeling of a parochial communion is virtually nonexistent.

However, there is a difference in integration in the parish: the older members feel they belong, as for them it is both a group to belong to and a reference point. The "in-group" in this instance is the family, which remains the only social point of reference as its ramifications gradually spread throughout the village and the parish; anyone outside this group arouses no interest. On the contrary, in the new population, although the family is reduced to a nuclear group, it is still the only group of vital importance, but one looks beyond this group to the "out-group" which, as Merton says,[3] is attractive. For the new population, the "out-group" will certainly not be the village, whose inhabitants appear to be uninteresting, nor will it be the parish, but more distant worlds such as Montreal and the whole North American culture.

Also, whereas natives of the village show a certain rigidity and extremism in their convictions, no matter what their orientation has been, the new population is marked by a universalization of norms[4] that never fails to strike sociologists of urban groups: everything is permitted, everything is understood, and pluralism is a criterion of perfection. But this tolerance is passive; it is an "acceptance of" and never a "participation in". These people, perhaps as a parallel to Protestantism, allow and practise a Catholicism whose rites are reduced to a minimum; nevertheless, they maintain the "security attitude"[5] of their faith.

Whether it be in respect of religion or morals, the new population is marked by a taste for ease, which is completely opposite to the supporters of Groulx's canon of the "sense of suffering",[6] at least to those for whom valuing effort was linked to the feeling of religious transcendence. The new population can still reproach the old for such inclinations as its superstitions and its bigotry. However, the old population cannot forgive the new for the way in which it is secularizing Catholicism with an almost self-confessed social conformism, a morality without punishment, and a clinical approach to religious affiliation. One of our informant's slogans —*religion is like brushing your teeth*—is close to the one that Herberg reports was posted in American subways: *Go to church, and you will feel good.*

This conciliatory concept of religion, accompanied by general material well-being, is rapidly winning over the old population through the influence of younger age groups as they marry, that is, as they attain complete socialization. A standardization in this direction is foreseeable in the short term.

Social Strata

The occupational spread of our sample is not wide enough to give us a precise idea of the religious attitude in relation to all occupations followed by the population of Saint-Pierre. For example, there is only one apple-grower's wife and four people connected with services and recreational occupations. Furthermore, as the preceding example well illustrates, we have grouped together professions that are somewhat dissimilar, thus limiting the number of variables. The variable of profession is interrelated with other variables so that the scope of our conclusions is limited.[7] Distinctions [between one professional group and another] can be summarized as follows: manual workers and the industrial commercial classes show a strong attachment to the Church; their level of practice is higher, although more collective in the second group and more intimate in the first. There are similar differences in the membership of parish associations and in the traditionalist forms of moral and religious concepts. The workers seem to be more motivated by obedience to orders from the Church and the local clergy; merchants and industrialists seem to act more from a sense of conformity and social discipline, as their economic and spiritual goals are closely interrelated. Members of the liberal professions, employees, and owners of restaurants and garages[8] show greater independence in respect of religion, both in its parochial and in its personal form; however, the most uncommon forms (intellectual and mystical) of Catholicism are found in this group.

These results run counter to those generally observed: why do classes of manual labourers remain faithful to the Church, whereas the liberal professions, a social stratum that is usually allied to the Church, seem more dissociated? The history of the province and its religion can partly answer this question. We must refer to the explanation provided by Pin and Isambert[9] for the religious disaffection of working classes in Europe, but we must reverse it. We know that the clergy and the liberal professions have long been adversaries, whereas the alliance between the Church and the people dates back more than a hundred years and was strengthened with the rise of clerical ideology. While the upper classes are identified as being the social conscience and soul in bourgeois societies in Western Europe, in French Canada the *race** are *paysans*, the rural craftsmen and small merchants from whom the majority of priests come: the "little man" knows who he is and also knows that he *is* French Canada; he *is* also the French-Canadian Church. Whereas in Western Europe the priest is also an "intellectual bourgeois",[10] in Quebec he remains closely related to the "little man", even if he enjoys a higher level of material comfort. Every *paysan* can always reasonably believe that his son might rise to the priesthood. Moreover, the clergy [has been in competition] with members of the liberal professions for leadership. Certainly, anticlericalism does not wholly prejudice the religious attitude of an individual or a group, but, whether it precedes or follows irreligiousness,[11] it is closely linked to it.

This traditional attachment to the Church and Catholicism by the French-Canadian *paysannerie* is reflected directly in the attitude of the workers' wives whom we studied: they and their husbands are still *paysans*. As far as our female informants are concerned, for example, sixty-six have parents who are both from rural areas, and fifty were themselves born in the country; the figures are probably about the same for their husbands. It is true that many have lived in the city for a time before

*Editor's note. This term is frequently used in French-Canadian popular literature to denote cultural ancestry and should not be taken in its biological or even anthropological sense.

returning to Saint-Pierre. Even if, as Le Bras states, it is only necessary to set foot in the station of a large city in order to lose the faith,[12] there remains a difference between the woman from Brittany in Montparnasse Station and a Gaspésienne arriving in Montreal; the Bretonne immediately finds a number of antireligious and areligious ideologies to which she will transfer her feeling of bewilderment and her disappointment at being uprooted, whereas the Gaspésienne will not encounter any such ideologies, for they do not exist in Montreal.

On the contrary, as we have also noted, members of the liberal professions have always fed on foreign ideological sources by such means as books and travel, which are not available to the lower classes. We should also note the influence of existential philosophies and the ethic of the absurd, which affect the most highly educated sector of the population, that is, the members of the liberal professions.

Another professional category which presents an interesting form of religiousness is the bourgeoisie, especially merchants and industrialists, who are in very close contact with the Anglo-Saxon ethnic group and who mask an almost total absence of religious motivation and practice with abundant rationalizations. Thus, the women of this class no longer own rosaries because their unesthetic qualities offend them; they will only have "a solid gold statuette". They do not pray, but they have some "very elaborate thoughts" on divine matters, and even if they practise very little, "it does not mean that they do not possess a highly valued religion or a marvellous faith which is at the centre of [their] life." Although they are now over fifty, the four people in our sample group who come in this category were all aware of birth-control methods and used them right from the beginning of their marriages; women of the same age from lower social strata ignored these methods, and very few would have dared to use them twenty years ago. In short, these four people are the only ones who showed anything like an overt feeling of social superiority, by speaking in pitying or amused terms about their "poor little housekeepers" or about the neighbouring apple-grower who is "so nice, but not at all the type of person with whom we are used to keeping company".

These few informants, none of whom were originally from the parish, are opposed to the traditionalist conformity of the local commercial and industrial bourgeoisie, one of whose main concerns seems to be keeping in line with the bulk of the population. Do they represent the beginning of a true social class with its homogeneity, consciousness of self, and pride in its wealth?

Level of Education

Just as the social strata are not strongly differentiated, educational levels are also not spread over a very wide scale. The few years of study that separate a public school teacher or a nurse from an office worker or a factory worker are not, at first sight, reflected in the behaviour and pre-occupations of different informants. Only those who have gone through a *cours classique* (classical college) seem to maintain some intellectual activities later on, but never to any great extent.

Generally, the most educated people adhere to the forms of practice, ideology, and religious ethics we have defined as modernist; the less educated follow the traditionalist form. From the point of view of intensity of religious adherence, the most educated prefer to divide themselves into two extreme categories, modernist and pious, and detached, whereas the less educated are often pious and devout traditionalists. The majority of the modal responses corresponds to people with an average level of education. As was the case for the other variables, educational level correlates with the subjects' age, professional group, etc.

If we consider the pious-modernist group as those who conform most closely to present official trends in Catholicism, it must be added that, at least in Saint-Pierre, these forms are accessible to no more than half a dozen people who are educated members of the liberal professions, that is, an intellectual aristocracy. The traditional vocation of French-Canadian Catholicism, a religion of the masses, seems to have undergone a reversal; another indication of this would be the strong interest in intellectual and religious orders to the detriment of the parochial clergy. Do contemporary trends in Catholic ideology, which remove the irrational characteristics from religion in order to, as Allport says, rid it of its "infantilism", not risk driving away the faithful, whose "maturity" has not reached the heights of such an "elaborate" faith? If, to take up Poulat's statement, the "believable" must now take into account the "knowable", does it not also risk being defined as a function of itself and reducing the sphere of the sacred to a philosophy in which the rational elements could suffocate the *mysterium tremendum* which has for so long seemed to be the essence of religion? Even if we adopt Poulat's optimism, according to which a change can only be for the better,[13] or that of Le Bras, who prefers a small number of aware and rational Catholics to a large number who practise mechanically and who are thus almost survivors of paganism,[14] we can ask ourselves if, for any religion, an ideological betterment which may, perhaps, only be relative is adequate compensation for a decrease in the number of faithful followers. In Saint-Pierre, there certainly do not appear to be any official signs of religious disaffection, if the desire of the faithful to belong to Catholicism and the importance placed on the practice of it are taken as criteria. But the number of people who have left the traditionalist and therefore irrational and "infantile" forms of Catholicism, without having progressed to a deepening of their faith as a result, leaves us wary. The informed and educated faithful could perhaps reconcile a religious belief that is both stripped down and at the same time rich in emotional content; but, for the rest of the flock, an impersonal infinity, a divine love without concrete benefits, and a moral code without chastisement or reward will remain a dead letter.

If contemporary Catholicism were to be faced with the problem of educating the faithful and rebuilding its structures, it is conceivable that the problem might be resolved in a few decades. But, by trying desperately to take away from the dogmas and practices of Catholicism the elements which conflict with contemporary rationality, will it not result in the Church destroying the very concept of religion?

In any case, the Church can hardly be considered responsible for this "desacredization" of Catholicism; by adopting modernist attitudes, it is only trying to adapt to a situation we constantly observed in our research. We are now going to return to a brief survey of the characteristics of the type of Catholicism most common among our female informants and try to evaluate the corrosive force of religion's modernism and, consequently, the state of local Catholicism.

Catholicism is a religion which postulates the existence of a personal sacred principle, God, and from that, the recognition of a state different from the temporal, terrestrial condition of human sensibility. The very nature of God (god-love) and the duality of human nature (existence of an eternal incorporeal soul) enable man to rise after death to a state close to the divine absolute; realization of this goal presupposes that certain conditions were observed on earth that are known to a body of religious officials through revelation and tradition, the forms of which they teach the faithful. A just body of rules determines man's attitude to God: recognition of his existence, his love, and gifts. The Christian concept corresponds fairly closely to Cazeneuve's definition of the sacred:[15] faith in a transcendent being and communion with that being. A second type of precept is for the reciprocal behaviour of man: he must reproduce

God's way of being for his fellow creatures, and express the love each one must bear for his neighbour.

With our female informants, an almost total ignorance of Catholic dogmas is accompanied by a doctrinal liberty which leads innocently to heterodoxy. This indifference to the theoretical fundamentals of religion goes as far as the divine principle itself: belief in God remains firm, but his attributes and personality have lost much of their importance. What then becomes blurred is the fear or hope of an eternal being who punishes or rewards his creatures according to merit. All the concepts (miracle, mystery) which go beyond the limits of human understanding are suspect; manifestations of the infinite divine are limited by man's understanding and intelligence.

Religious objectives and motives are no longer more important than terrestrial or human concerns. What is called secularization of Catholicism veils a weakened sense of the divine transcendence: if God is not depicted "in a beautiful sunset" or "in the songs of birds on a balcony", it voluntarily becomes a conscious motive of the individual to integrate with the group, or a symbolic recognition of the collective force and existence. Its relationship with the Americanized God described by Herberg cannot be completely proven but it expresses the complete abandon of the individual to the collective will which limits all his affectionate and intellectual horizons. It is the centre of a philosophy in which terrestrial or tangible values have taken precedence over spiritual preoccupations. This easy, pragmatic, and rational ethic is a component of an other-directed personality.

The central idea of Christianity—the love owed to God by the faithful in exchange for his love—never held anything but a secondary and theoretical place here. During the course of our research, only three or four female informants seemed to have internalized this idea; on the other hand, in French Canada, the lack of emotional response was traditionally compensated for by demanding and vigorous practice. Earlier it was noted that participation in various denominations is decreasing, and this is reflected in several accounts of Sunday observance throughout the province. This can be seen in the attitudes of our female informants and those revealed by opinion polls among school populations[16] which clearly show less feeling of obligation with respect to practice. When it exists, it is rarely religious but is a conscious part of a social or family order.

Certain Christian writers and public opinion often consider this relative abandoning of strict ritualism as a proof of the progress and purification of popular religious feeling. It is certainly not a question of measuring the quality of belonging to a faith by cultural conformity, but when it is abandoned without being replaced by another form of religious vitality, is it not a sign of secularization?

There would, however, seem to be progress as far as morals are concerned in Saint-Pierre, which is as much a result of the return to sources brought about by the Canadian Church, after what is generally considered here as a century-long error, as it is a response to the enthusiastic adherence of the majority of the faithful to the *aggiornamento*. Instead of cowed obedience to negative rules, the Catholic should show a thoughtful and free adherence to his own standards of conduct which encourage the development of his personality. The rehabilitation of joy as a moral value especially seems to be a rediscovery of the profound sense of Christianity after the anathema which has overtaken it for so long.

What stage is the Church now at? Let us first note that the Church's direct influence—for example, the respect for the rules it has decreed in the areas of sexual and family morals—is hardly alive any more. The survival of some precepts is due to their social utility, and neither the fear of the priest nor the sense of a discipline freely acquiesced to as a religious ethic continue to be operative.

Finally, the principle of charity, the strict application of which is basic to the entire Christian moral structure, seems to be emphasized once again and is often referred to. But we have, in fact, noted that this demanding virtue is, as usual, only possible for a small number of people, independently of their traditionalist or modernist ideological choice. On the other hand, the most widespread attitude in the group emerges as a spirit of tolerance which, although lacking the power of dynamic love, can promote a positive lifestyle, a sort of second-best communal principle, in the groups who hold this attitude.

In the present case, it is not, therefore, a question of a variation on the theme of Christian love, but an institutionalization of its decline. Although traditional rural communities have never valued tolerance much, it remained, at least in theory, compatible with the small size of the group and it could be counted on [in view of] the vital need of individuals to know each other and to count on each other's support. Urban proliferation and the corresponding ease with which one can ignore one's neighbours make the norms for peaceful coexistence quite adequate. The present ideology of tolerance might be functional, but does this means of conveying it not sound like a mutilation of the original message of Catholicism?

It is not appropriate to speak of religious disaffection in the case of Saint-Pierre, or in that of French Canada as a whole: the importance of practice, that is, of a conscious will to adhere to the Catholic faith, bears witness to this fact. The bell curve which would represent the distribution of our female informants through seven types of religious practice shows that the Church's norms concerning worship are definitely alive and socially acceptable: few people practise completely; few detach themselves completely; most take a middle position.

The nonexistence of ideologies or of irreligious or areligious pressure groups, the cultural isolation of the province, and the confusion about religious and social conventions are all elements which act in the same way: providing the individual's security, justifying his beliefs, and preventing the crystallization of tendencies to indifference or religious detachment. We have seen how the eleven members of our sample group who were detached from religion had little more in common than a number of social and family problems; religious anticonformism is always negative and guilt-ridden and is not yet a sociological characteristic. For the moment at least, it is hardly likely to develop on the level of the masses of the faithful.

Sociologically, there may well exist as many types of Catholicism as types of societies, and each one, in spite of its peculiarities, is in line with orthodox Catholicism. But do the liberties noted here not border on deviation, especially in respect of fundamental points of doctrine, in particular that of the divine transcendence? To what extent can a religion evolve from its origin, or adapt itself to secular society without losing its specificity? In what way does this philosophy of immanence, in vogue in our community, still merit the name of religion?

This vulnerability, which has tendencies that could be grouped together under the theme of modernity, affects the Church hierarchy as much as its faithful followers. Particularly disquieting are the Church's own doctrinal hesitations and its desire for change, which disturbs traditionalist good will without wholly reassuring others' desires for reform. In fact, the uneasiness brought to light by Church officials is not reassuring: the declining recruitment rate in monasteries and the priesthood and the abandonment of the religious and ecclesiastic state are recent and serious problems in Quebec. The secular world is being put on an equal footing with the formerly well-protected ecclesiastical hierarchy through a questioning of the religious state, its definition of itself, and its place in a secular society (for example, celibacy and the economic role of priests); the evidence is in the number and fervour of comments aroused by these questions both in the press and in the home.

This spectacle of a Church in crisis is tragic for the faithful who had for centuries found her to be a fortress of authority and security. As they are perturbed themselves, they cannot help [carrying] their anguish and disappointment to the Church, which can no longer do anything for them and seems itself to be seeking help. Moderate but frequent anticlericalism, which attacks the incompetence of members of the clergy rather than the traditional taste for money, is no longer only restricted to the liberal bourgeois class, where it is conventional, but has won over more moderate people, especially the younger generation. The usual historic relationship between anticlericalism and irreligion is once again asserting itself.

Finally, we have often stated that the Catholic administrative ranks are incapable of controlling and structuring the collective life of the faithful. This retreat from religious influence, which goes hand in hand with the secularization and the anticlericalism about which we have just spoken, is another cause for worry. We have shown several times that if the parish still represents a community, in the sense that Gurvitch intended,[17] for the old population, it is no more than a mass for the new population. This introduces one of the problems most often alluded to in the sociology of religions: can the parish still serve as a framework for the religious and social life of a group and for the individuals constituting it? The answer is negative for the parish of Saint-Pierre, as it is made up of three different communities, and even on the level of the village, which will soon make up a parish of its own, it remains doubtful. But if this basic social and religious cell no longer corresponds to present conditions, it is difficult to see on what basis the Church could build its action. The absence of any viable primary group other than the nuclear family makes an illusion of the development of the type of "religious subcommunities" suggested by Lenski as a replacement for rural communities.[18]

Thus, even in the privileged case of French Canada, the community based on faith no longer acts as a principle of cohesion or of action in collective life, or else it only acts in a superficial way. Essentially secular values are being progressively established and structured by institutions which are increasingly freed of confessionals and clerical personnel.

The generations which have already reached adulthood certainly suffer from the present state of transition, but their mental concepts are formed and their vision of the world will hardly change. The education of youth, as it now appears, torn between contradictory tendencies and brutally subjected to imported family and scholarly teachings whose main criterion for quality is novelty, leaves one uncertain about the religious and moral development of the next generations.

NOTES

1 Saint-Pierre is a pseudonym for a town in the region of greater Montreal.
2 See, for example, E. Pin, *Pratique religieuse et classes sociales dans une paroisse urbaine (Saint-Pothin à Lyon)* (Paris: Spes. 1956), p. 444; J. H. Fichter, *Southern Parish*, Vol. 1, *Dynamics of a City Church* (Chicago: University of Chicago Press, 1951), p. 283; J. H. Fichter, *Social Relations in the Urban Parish* (Chicago: University of Chicago Press, 1954), p. 264.
3 R. K. Merton, *Eléments de théorie et de méthodes sociologiques* (Paris: Plon, 1965), p. 234.
4 H. Carrier, *Psycho-sociologie de l'appartenance religieuse* (Rome: Presses de l'Université Grégorienne, 1960), p. 175. David Riesman speaks of the tolerance and passivity of the other-directed in *The Lonely Crowd*, abridged ed. (New Haven: Yale University Press), pp. 188ff.
5 Marcel Rioux, "Remarques sur l'éducation secondaire", *Cité Libre*, No. 8 (November, 1953), p. 34.
6 Lionel Groulx, *Les chemins de l'avenir* (Montreal: Fides, 1964), p. 164.
7 However, a calculation of correlations seemed to us to be superfluous, because, for such low numbers, this information would certainly have been less helpful than the qualitative knowledge we have of our female informants.
8 Restaurant and garage workers do not usually have the same attitudes as other merchants. They differ from the latter group in that most of them are not originally from Saint-Pierre

and do not stay there very long.
9 F. A. Isambert, *Christianisme et classe ouvrière* (Paris: Casterman, 1961), pp. 204ff.; and Pin, *op. cit.*
10 H. Carrier, "Le rôle des groupes de référence dans l'interprétation des attitudes religieuses", *SC* 7, No. 2 (1960): 146.
11 Isambert, *op. cit.*, pp. 239ff.
12 G. Le Bras, "La sociologie religieuse parmi les sciences humaines", *Recherches et débats du centre catholique des intellectuels français*, No. 25, *Sociologie et religion* (Paris: Desclée de Bronwer, 1958), pp. 447-51.
13 E. Poulat, "La société religieuse et le problème du changement", *Revue française de sociologie* 7, No. 3 (1966): 295.
14 Le Bras, *op. cit.*, pp. 451-2.
15 Editor's note. Jean Cazeneuve, *Sociologie du rite* (Paris: Les Presses Universitaires de France, 1970).
16 For example, research by Father Lauvière on students from forty French-Canadian colleges (1959), research by Father Montminy on students from forty-two French-Canadian colleges (1965), and content analysis by Mme Henripin of essays written by 188 boys aged eighteen to twenty (1966).
17 G. Gurvitch, *Vocation actuelle de la sociologie; vers une sociologie différentielle* (Paris: Presses Universitaires de France, 1950), pp. 143-78.
18 G. Lenski, *The Religious Factor: A Sociological Study of Religion's Impact on Politics, Economics, and Family Life* (New York: Doubleday, 1963), pp. 335-6.

Alberta and the
Bible Belt Stereotype*

Harry H. Hiller

The phrase "Bible Belt" has become part of common parlance and describes population traits and behaviour pertaining to religion that appear to be dominant in a given region. Sociologists generally have ignored the term as a conceptual and descriptive category and have left its use to journalists and the public at large. Nevertheless, the term occasionally arises in the academic literature. For example, Birkby (1966) writes about the U.S. Supreme Court rulings on prayer and Bible readings in the schools and refers to Tennessee as a Bible Belt. While not using the term directly, W. E. Mann (1955) pointed out the predominance of fundamentalism in Alberta in the 1940s. Alberta provides a good case for testing the usefulness and validity of designating an area as a Bible Belt and for examining the question of how such an area may differ from others. Statistical data will be used to determine whether there is any demographic basis for the designation. It will be argued that the phrase is sociologically significant, not only because it tells us some-

*A revision of a paper entitled "The Bible Belt Sterotype: Sociological Fact or Fiction?", presented at the annual meetings of the Society for the Scientific Study of Religion, Washington, D.C., October, 1974. The author acknowledges the assistance of Les Krawee and Wayne Whittaker. Published here with the kind permission of the author.

thing about a given region, but also because it informs us about the attitudes of those who apply the label.

It should be acknowledged that the notion of a Bible Belt is a stereotype. This means that there is an assumption of relative uniformity in outlook or worldview among all or most people in a given location. It is a judgment about people that oversimplifies complex traits by focusing on a few which appear to be dominant to the beholder.

A Check for Demographic Verification

One implication in the use of the term Bible Belt is that the area being discussed, when compared with other areas, contains a predominance of religious groups stressing Biblical literalism. We may test this assumption empirically where census data on religion are available. In the United States this is difficult to do, since the only data on religious identification are supplied by religious organizations themselves (National Council of Churches, Yearbook of American Churches). It is difficult to compare membership statistics because definitions and methods vary (Demerath and Hammond 1969: 119–23), and denominational statistics tell us nothing about the religious affiliations or preferences of non-members.

In Canada the national census provides a body of data on the religious preferences of the whole population. The Canadian census asks "What is your religion?", whereas such questions are not permitted in the United States census. Canadian respondents are encouraged to name a specific denomination regardless of their membership or level of participation. Respondents can also indicate whether their preference is other than those listed and whether they have no religion. Provinces or regions can then be compared to determine differences in religious preference.

These data tell us nothing, of course, about the intensity of religious commitment, which is an important variable. In addition, we lack indicators of the theological stance of the respondent. Biblical literalism is found in many religious groups and not only in those commonly identified as sectarian, and the census data do not allow us to identify these intra-denominational differences. Nevertheless, the census gives us comparative data which enable us to determine whether certain provinces are over-represented with particular denominational preferences. Such over-representativeness might be a contributing factor in the emergence of a Bible Belt stereotype.

TABLE 1. Total Number and Percentage of Religious Preference Indicated for Selected Provinces, 1941

	ALBERTA		ONTARIO		SASKATCHEWAN		BRITISH COLUMBIA		NOVA SCOTIA	
	TOTAL	%	TOTAL	%	TOTAL	%	TOTAL	%	TOTAL	%
Adventist	4,697	.58	2,913	.07	3,510	.39	2,803	.34	1,357	.23
Anglican	113,279	14.22	815,413	21.52	117,674	13.13	245,531	30.02	103,393	17.88
Baptist	32,268	4.05	192,915	5.09	19,460	2.17	29,780	3.64	89,272	15.44
Brethren and United Brethren	1,046	.13	9,693	.25	1,014	.11	1,660	.20	184	.03
Christian	1,372	.17	3,101	.08	1,654	.18	710	.08	251	.04
Christian Science	1,713	.21	8,388	.22	1,114	.12	5,843	.71	272	.04
Church of Christ	2,103	.26	9,743	.26	1,912	.21	650	.07	2,037	.35
Confucian and Buddhist	2,172	.27	2,682	.07	1,573	.16	29,137	3.56	102	.01
Evangelical Church	4,165	.52	24,025	.63	4,130	.46	1,737	.21	373	.06
Greek Orthodox	34,991	4.39	28,383	.74	37,699	4.20	5,198	.63	347	.06

International Bible Students Association	1,010	.12	1,649	.04	2,028	.22	836	.10	271	.04
Jewish	4,052	.50	69,217	1.82	4,076	.45	3,235	.18	2,167	.37
Lutheran	84,630	10.62	104,111	2.74	104,717	11.68	41,772	5.10	9,104	1.57
Mennonite	12,097	1.51	22,219	.58	32,511	3.62	5,105	.62	23	.00
Mormon	14,960	1.87	7,141	.18	1,365	.15	1,281	.15	52	.00
Pentecostal	8,451	1.06	21,053	.55	8,294	.92	5,235	.64	1,848	.31
Presbyterian	68,910	8.65	433,708	11.45	54,856	6.12	94,300	11.53	47,415	8.20
Protestant (other than stated)	917	.11	3,156	.08	641	.07	768	.09	216	.37
Roman Catholic	191,343	24.03	882,369	23.29	243,734	27.20	113,282	13.85	188,994	32.69
Salvation Army	2,103	.26	18,289	.48	1,966	.21	3,880	.47	3,003	.51
United Church	193,664	24.32	1,073,425	28.34	230,495	25.72	200,817	24.55	124,301	21.56
Other	14,768	1.85	47,507	1.25	20,464	2.28	22,107	2.70	1,551	.26
Not Stated	1,458	.18	6,243	.16	1,165	.13	2,194	.26	1,479	.25
TOTALS		99.88		99.89		99.90		99.70		100.27

Source: Compiled from *Census of Canada, 1941*, Dominion Bureau of Statistics, Vol. III, pp. 204, 214-29.

In *Sect, Cult, and Church in Alberta*, W. E. Mann (1955: 3) argues that in comparison with neighbouring provinces, Alberta has a profusion of religious organizations. He lists 35 sects found in Alberta in 1946 and gives approximate membership figures which he concludes make up about 20 per cent of the population of Alberta. In another account, H. H. Walsh (1956: 315) asserts that Ontario may have a greater variety of sects than Alberta, but that they have less influence because they are a lower percentage of the population. We will examine these views in the light of the 1941 and 1971 census data.

Table 1 presents religious preferences, comparing Alberta with her immediate neighbours Saskatchewan and British Columbia, with Canada's most populous province Ontario, and with a Maritime province quite similar to Alberta—Nova Scotia. The table is based on 1941 data —around the time that Mann and Walsh argued for an exceptionally sectarian population in Alberta. Small sectarian bodies like Nazarenes or Church of God are not listed separately, but we can assume that their affiliates would have listed themselves under "Other" or, perhaps, "Baptist". In any case, when the largest groups (each with over 4 per cent of the population) are added together (Anglican, Baptist, Greek Orthodox, Lutheran, Presbyterian, Roman Catholic, and United Church), over 85 per cent of Alberta's population can be accounted for. All the other provinces in the table have similar proportions of these major groups. Therefore, it is clear that there was not much regional variation in religious affiliation.

However, there is variation in group strength from province to province. Most of the groups are considerably stronger in absolute numbers in Ontario. Alberta does stand out with respect to minority ethnic-religious groups, namely, Greek Orthodox, German and Scandinavian Lutherans, and Mormons.

To present this material in shorthand in one table, a location quotient was constructed (Lester 1966: 25; Alexander 1963: 594–5). The formula for the location quotient is:

$$LQ = \frac{D_1}{P_1} \times 100 \div \frac{D_2}{P_2} \times 100$$

($D_1 =$ group total in the province; $D_2 =$ group total in Canada; $P_1 =$ total population of the province; $P_2 =$ total population of Canada.)

The location quotient measures the degree to which a particular group is over- or under-represented in a region as compared with the rest of the nation. A numerical value less than 1.00 indicates that the province has less than its share of members of that group, whereas a number more than 1.00 indicates that the region has more than its share. No consistent pattern emerges from this analysis (Table 2). The three groups mentioned above do show high levels of representation; the score for Mormons, for example, is 8.90. However, in absolute numbers the over-representation of Mormons is only 14,960. A high location quotient in this instance, then, merely means that the small number of

TABLE 2. Location Quotient Representing the Comparative Distribution of Religious Groups in Selected Provinces, 1941

	ALBERTA	ONTARIO	SASKAT-CHEWAN	BRITISH COLUMBIA	NOVA SCOTIA
Adventist	3.62	.43	2.43	2.12	1.43
Anglican	.93	1.41	.86	1.97	1.17
Baptist	.96	1.21	.51	.86	3.67
Brethren and United Brethren	1.00	1.92	.84	1.53	.23
Christian	2.42	1.41	2.57	1.14	.57
Christian Science	1.23	1.29	.70	4.17	.23
Church of Christ	1.44	1.44	1.16	.38	1.94
Confucian and Buddhist	.84	.21	.50	11.12	.03
Evangelical Church	1.62	1.96	1.43	.65	.18
Greek Orthodox	3.62	.6l	3.47	.52	.04
International Bible Students Association	2.00	.66	3.66	1.66	.66
Jewish	.34	1.24	.30	.12	.25
Lutheran	3.05	.78	3.35	1.46	.45
Mennonite	1.57	.60	3.77	.64	.00
Mormon	8.90	.85	.71	.71	.00
Pentecostal	2.12	1.10	1.84	1.28	.62
Presbyterian	1.20	1.59	.85	1.60	1.13
Protestant (other than stated)	1.22	.88	.77	1.00	4.11
Roman Catholic	.55	.53	.62	.31	.75
Salvation Army	.89	1.65	.72	1.62	1.75
United Church	1.26	1.47	1.34	1.28	1.12
Other	1.76	1.19	2.17	2.57	.24
Not Stated	1.28	1.14	.92	1.85	1.78

Source: Computed from *Census of Canada, 1941,* Dominion Bureau of Statistics, Vol. III, pp. 204, 214-29.

TABLE 3. Total Number and Percentage of Religious Preference Indicated for Selected Provinces, 1971

	ALBERTA		ONTARIO		SASKATCHEWAN		BRITISH COLUMBIA		NOVA SCOTIA	
	TOTAL	%	TOTAL	%	TOTAL	%	TOTAL	%	TOTAL	%
Adventist	5,210	.32	9,215	.12	2,285	.25	7,190	.33	1,305	.17
Anglican	170,230	10.50	1,220,535	15.84	87,210	9.42	386,670	17.70	135,695	17.20
Baptist	49,710	3.10	283,400	3.68	15,000	1.62	64,835	2.97	100,350	12.72
Brethren in Christ	865	.05	14,585	.19	575	.06	2,920	.13	260	.03
Buddhist	2,280	.14	5,610	.07	140	.02	6,130	.28	55	.007
Christian and Missionary Alliance	5,520	.34	6,625	.09	4,290	.46	5,610	.26	190	.02
Christian Reformed	13,420	.82	54,660	.71	355	.04	11,460	.52	910	.12
Churches of Christ, Disciples	2,400	.15	7,060	.09	1,490	.16	1,370	.06	1,165	.15
Church of Nazarene	3,930	.24	4,545	.06	935	.10	1,885	.09	715	.09
Confucian	130	.01	370	.005	220	.02	950	.04	25	.003
Doukhobor	200	.01	175	.002	1,675	.18	6,720	.30	5	.0006
Free Methodist	1,200	.07	13,190	.17	1,205	.13	1,860	.09	190	.02

Greek Orthodox	47,165	2.90	134,465	1.75	26,675	2.88	20,525	.94	1,580	.20		
Hutterite	6,100	.37	260	.003	2,215	.24	75	.003	30	.004		
Jehovah's Witnesses	17,930	1.10	67,710	.88	9,880	1.07	42,315	1.94	4,960	.63		
Jewish	6,260	.38	125,315	1.63	1,765	.19	9,715	.44	2,175	.28		
Lutheran	133,045	8.17	267,225	3.47	90,850	9.81	120,335	5.51	11,570	1.47		
Mennonite	14,645	.90	40,115	.52	26,315	2.84	26,520	1.21	90	.01		
Mormon	31,085	1.91	16,810	.22	2,455	.27	12,670	.58	775	.09		
Pentecostal	23,100	1.42	76,630	.99	12,375	1.34	35,225	1.61	6,865	.87		
Plymouth Brethren	300	.02	2,650	.34	210	.02	1,720	.08	90	.01		
Presbyterian	57,185	3.51	540,035	7.01	20,805	2.25	100,940	4.62	40,380	5.12		
Roman Catholic	391,390	24.04	2,568,695	33.35	258,630	27.92	408,330	18.70	286,320	36.29		
Salvation Army	4,645	.29	43,840	.57	3,295	.36	11,885	.54	4,755	.60		
Ukrainian Catholic	41,065	2.52	56,730	.74	34,175	3.69	11,310	.52	745	.09		
Unitarian	1,730	.11	9,220	.12	580	.06	4,755	.22	340	.04		
United Church	456,925	28.62	1,682,820	21.85	274,285	29.61	537,565	24.61	162,885	20.65		
Other	31,780	1.95	106,930	1.39	12,290	1.33	55,995	2.56	5,335	.68		
No Religion	108,410	6.66	343,685	4.46	34,090	3.68	287,115	13.14	19,185	2.43		
TOTALS	1,627,875		7,703,105		926,245		2,184,620		788,960			

Source: Compiled from *Census of Canada, 1971*, Vol. I, Part 3, Statistics Canada (92-724).

Mormons in Canada at that time was likely to be concentrated in Alberta. While it is not usual to speak of Mormons as fundamentalists, it is possible that their life-style contributed to the notion that Alberta was a Bible Belt in spite of the fact that they consisted of only 1.87 per cent of the population. Some Lutherans (particularly Missouri Synod) and Baptists also were characterized by fundamentalist thinking and behaviour, but blanket assumptions cannot be made. Baptists are slightly under-represented in Alberta, while the Adventists and Pentecostals are slightly over-represented; but in absolute numbers the totals are small.

Tables 3 and 4 give the same type of data based on the 1971 census.

TABLE 4.   Location Quotient Representing the Comparative Distribution of Religious Groups in Selected Provinces, 1971

	ALBERTA	ONTARIO	SASKAT-CHEWAN	BRITISH COLUMBIA	NOVA SCOTIA
Adventist	2.46	.92	1.92	2.54	1.31
Anglican	.89	1.34	.80	1.50	1.46
Baptist	.99	1.19	.42	.76	3.26
Buddhist	1.87	.93	.27	3.73	.093
Christian Reformed	2.10	1.82	.10	1.33	.31
Christian and Missionary Alliance	3.09	.82	4.18	2.36	.18
Church of Christ Disciples	1.88	1.13	2.00	.75	1.88
Confucian	1.00	.50	2.00	.50	.04
Doukhobor	.25	.050	4.50	7.50	.015
Free Methodist	.78	1.89	1.44	1.00	.22
Greek Orthodox	1.97	1.19	1.96	.64	.14
Hutterite	6.17	.05	4.00	.05	.67
Jehovah's Witnesses	1.36	1.09	.81	2.40	.78
Jewish	.30	1.27	.15	.34	.22
Lutheran	2.46	1.05	2.95	1.66	.44
Mennonite	1.15	.67	3.64	1.55	.01
Mormon	6.16	.71	.87	1.87	.30
Pentecostal	1.40	.97	1.31	1.58	.85
Presbyterian	.87	1.74	.56	1.14	1.27
Roman Catholic	.52	.72	.60	.40	.78
Salvation Army	.53	1.04	.65	.98	1.09
Ukrainian Catholic	2.38	.70	3.48	.49	.08
Unitarian	1.22	1.33	.67	2.44	.44
United Church	1.64	1.25	1.69	1.41	1.18
Other	1.43	1.02	.98	1.88	.50
No Religion	1.55	1.03	.86	3.06	.57

Source: Computed from *Census of Canada, 1971*, Vol. I, Part 3, Statistics Canada, (92-724).

Interestingly, the new category of "No Religion" was relatively high in Alberta. There are no other significant differences among the provinces that have not already been noted for 1941, in spite of the fact that some of the larger denominations decreased their percentage of the provincial population.

The conclusion is that there are limited demographic data to support the notion that Alberta is exceptionally sectarian in terms of over-representation of fundamentalist denominations, and therefore more of a Bible Belt than other provinces. There is partial support for the idea that some minority organizations are stronger in western Canada than in central Canada or in the Maritimes. But when we look at absolute numbers the significance is slight. Thus, in the demography of Canadian society, the notion of a Bible Belt is more fiction than fact.

We are still left with the necessity of determining the origin and meaning of the phrase "Bible Belt". We would argue that the basic determinants of the Bible Belt stereotype are certain events with religious overtones within the regional culture that attract national attention and build a regional image.

The Regional Culture Hypothesis

The regional culture hypothesis suggests that events having religious overtones and attracting national attention cause people outside a region to infer that such activity is typical of all persons in that region.

Mann (1955: 82) and Rennie (1974) note the proliferation of Bible schools in Alberta, including the Prairie Bible Institute, which in 1947 had the largest enrolment of any theological college in North America. The fact that the school drew students from all over the continent has seemed to be of less importance to the general public than its location in Alberta. Most of the other Bible schools in Alberta serviced at least all of the western provinces and were located in that province partly because it was more populous and to some extent more prosperous than the other western provinces. The presence of these schools in Alberta, particularly the Prairie Bible Institute, with its world-wide reputation, drew attention to the apparent strength of fundamentalism in the province.

Perhaps the most important occurrence highlighting fundamentalism in Alberta was the fact that in the dark night of the depression of the 1930s a charismatic former high school principal combined powerful, prophetic preaching with Social Credit monetary theory. As a popular lay preacher and religious broadcaster, William Aberhart introduced

Social Credit ideas into his Sunday afternoon broadcasts. Through his dynamic personality, organizational ability, and the hope he offered impoverished Albertans, his economic theories caught fire (Irving 1959). In a wave of populist politics, Aberhart and his Social Credit Party were swept into power in 1935. Upon Aberhart's death, he was succeeded by Ernest Manning, who maintained the same religious convictions, although he was more discreet in mixing them with politics. The Social Credit government ruled Alberta from 1935 to 1971 (Long and Quo 1972). References to Aberhart as "Bible Bill" (Neatby 1972: 113ff.) and the religious activity of the party leaders perpetuated the notion in some circles that most Albertans must have had similar convictions. The rise to power of such a maverick group with an unorthodox monetary theory generated considerable national and international attention and fostered the stereotype.

It is not, then, fundamentalist beliefs and activities such as spirited singing, hell-fire preaching, and ascetic practices (Dorough 1974) that produce a Bible Belt, for these activities may be found elsewhere. What seems to evoke the stereotype more than anything else is the prominent transfer of fundamentalist activity to spheres of life other than religion. When fundamentalist belief is imposed on politics, education, and liquor laws, for example, and cherished or tolerated by influential residents of an area, then the label "Bible Belt" is apt to stick.

Conclusion

Peter Berger (1969: 107) reminds us that at the social-structural level, secularization means the removal of sectors of society from religious domination. In a secular society, religion often tends to be narrowed to a special sphere of activity and influence, and may become operative chiefly at the private, personal level. When the norms of a secular society are violated in a particular region, and religion of a fundamentalist variety extends its influence to other sectors of society, then the Bible Belt stereotype may emerge. Thus, the concept of a Bible Belt is a sociological fact and not just a fiction, but the bases for its origin are somewhat different from those generally supposed.

REFERENCES

Alexander, John W.
1963   *Economic Geography.* Engle-
        wood Cliffs: Prentice-Hall.

Berger, Peter C.
1969   *The Sacred Canopy: Elements
        of a Sociological Theory of*

Religion. Garden City: Double-
day.
Birkby, Robert H.
1966 "The Supreme Court and the
Bible Belt: Tennessee Reaction
to the 'Schempp' Decision."
*Midwest Journal of Political
Science* 10: 304-19.
Clark, S. D.
1948 *Church and Sect in Canada.*
Toronto: University of Toronto
Press.
Demerath, N. J., and P. E. Hammond
1969 *Religion in Social Context:
Tradition and Transition.* New
York: Random House.
Dorough, C. Dwight
1974 *The Bible Belt Mystique.* New
York: Harper and Row.
Irving, John A.
1959 *The Social Credit Movement in
Alberta.* Toronto: University
of Toronto Press.
Lester, G. A.
1966 "The Distribution of Religious

Groups in Alberta, 1961."
Unpublished M.A. thesis, Uni-
versity of Alberta.
Long, J. A., and F. Q. Quo
1972 "Alberta: One Party
Dominance." In Martin Robin,
ed., *Canadian Provincial Politics.*
Scarborough: Prentice-Hall.
Mann, W. E.
1955 *Sect, Cult, and Church in
Alberta.* Toronto: University of
Toronto Press.
Neatby, H. Blair
1972 *The Politics of Chaos: Canada in
the Thirties.* Toronto:
Macmillan.
Rennie, Ian S.
1974 "The Doctrine of Man in the
Canadian Bible Belt." Mimeo-
graphed paper. Vancouver:
Regents College.
Walsh, H. H.
1956 *The Christian Church in
Canada.* Toronto: Ryerson.

5.

Social Sources
of Ecumenism

The Canadian Church Union, 1925*

W. E. Mann

On June 10, 1925, twenty-one years after the first official joint meeting to discuss organic union, the Methodists, many Presbyterians, and the Congregationalists came together to form the United Church of Canada. By this union was established the largest Protestant denomination in Canada, numbering in the 1971 census 3,768,800 followers, or 17.7 per cent of the population.

Early Glimpses of Nontheological Factors

As early as 1899 the General Assembly of the Presbyterian Church, recognizing the vast problems of ministering to sparse populations, officially stated its approval of co-operation with other churches in new fields. When union proposals were launched in 1902 at the quadrennial gathering of the Methodist Church in Winnipeg, a local editor commented that "the Methodists would discover that their future in Canada was linked up with their future in the western provinces."[1]

*Appeared first as Chapter 8 in Nils Ehrenstrom and Walter G. Muelder, eds., *Institutionalism and Church Unity* (New York: Association Press, 1963). Published here in revised and abridged form with the kind permission of the author and the publisher.

Dr. Bryce, a Presbyterian fraternal delegate to the conference, emphasized the many things the two churches had in common, among them a common form of church government, the common experience of opposition to the Anglican Clergy Reserves in Ontario, and a somewhat similar stand on the prohibition of alcoholic beverages. Dr. Patrick, Principal of (the Presbyterian) Manitoba College, after noting that "the history of the Canadian Church had been a history of unions and consolidations", and spontaneously appealing for organic unity, concluded by asking, "Has not the time come for further advance into a great national church?" A day or two later, the Conference passed a memorable declaration in favor of church union among the Protestant Churches in Canada, and then proceeded to invite the Congregational and Presbyterian Churches to begin negotiations.[2]

The Negotiations Period, 1904–1925

Subsequent developments clarified both the difficulties of union and the sociological forces active in the general ecclesiastical situation. In 1904 both the Congregationalists and the Presbyterians appointed Committees to study a Basis of Union, and meetings were held annually with the Methodists in a Joint Committee. Although they were invited in a general way, two churches—the Baptists and the Anglicans—never took part in the negotiations. Whereas "The Regular and Free Baptists in the Maritimes had been united in a Convention in 1906 and the new body expressed a willingness to confer on a federal union,"[3] the Baptist Convention of Ontario and Quebec, after appointing a committee which met briefly with the Joint Committee, drew up a statement denying "that organic union of all Christians is an essential condition of Christian unity."

This response discouraged negotiations with the Maritime convention and ended matters. In 1908 the Anglicans took up the question at their General Synod, and there authorized the appointment of a committee, but demanded that it adhere to the requirements of the Lambeth Quadrilateral. The Joint Committee for their part found the necessity of accepting episcopacy a barrier to serious negotiations, but said the door was open if ever this stipulation were made less rigorous. After 1921, when the Anglican General Synod accepted the modified version of the 1920 Lambeth statement on the ministry, with certain reservations regarding preaching and the episcopacy, the Primate invited the Methodists and Presbyterians to a conference, but formal negotiations never materialized before 1925.

Nontheological factors doubtless played an important role in depressing Anglican and Baptist interest in early union proposals. For instance, Anglican congregations were often separated from Methodists by a higher social standing, especially in central Canada. Their congregational life was also strongly tradition-bound and their clergy largely recruited at this time from the Old Country. Many nonconformist ministers were both Canadian born and trained, and thus shared a much different viewpoint upon their church and ministry. Such social factors thus served to cut the Anglican Church, still rigorously divided into over twenty dioceses and preserving a strong link with Britain, from serious negotiations with the Methodists and to a lesser extent with the Presbyterians. The Baptists, on the other hand, were more working-class in their following and also much less bureaucratic in their institutional arrangements than either the Methodists or the Presbyterians.

At an early stage a Presbyterian minority showed reluctance to go beyond increased co-operation on Home Mission Fields, but Methodist enthusiasm for union proposals grew quickly, resulting in 1911 in an overwhelmingly favorable vote.

At the same time, Presbyterian opposition in the General Assembly gradually grew and hardened. In 1910, a vote of the Assembly was taken which strongly favored the Basis of Union, and a resolution was then passed designed to seek initially a vote of the presbyteries rather than of the whole membership. This move aroused certain feelings of injustice and led to organized opposition, especially since it repudiated various earlier statements by "unionist" leaders that no action would be taken without full support. Then, the whole membership was polled, late in 1911, and the results showed 113,000 members and 37,175 adherents in favor of, and 50,753 members besides 14,174 adherents opposed to, union. In 1913, undeterred by the large dissenting vote, "the majority of the Assembly, urged on by 'unionist' leaders, resolved to press forward."[4] In reaction, a group of delegates formed "The General Committee of the Organization for the Preservation and Continuation of the Presbyterian Church in Canada", which shortly numbered 170 ministers and more than five hundred leading laymen.[5]

In 1916 by a large majority the General Assembly decided to proceed to union. This decision aroused further resentment and the continuing group held "a nationwide convocation and reorganized their defence as 'The Presbyterian Church Association' ".[6] Controversy was intense for a year until a truce in negotiations was called for the duration of the war. When in 1921 the Assembly again voted for union by an 80 per cent majority, the Presbyterian Association was revived and in 1923 became fully institutionalized, hiring an executive secretary, a general organizer, and four "lieutenants". The Association began a fiery pamphlet war, organized its supporters in every synod, presbytery, and congregation, and even placed large advertisements in newspapers. Women supporters made house-to-house canvasses, and a card-signing campaign won 114,000 signatures. In reaction, the "unionists" appointed a bureau of publicity; and in 1923 this became "merged in a bureau of literature, information and public meetings of the Joint Committee, and the literature was issued not alone in the name of the Presbyterian Church but of all three churches."[7] Controversy became intense and bitter, and split congregation after congregation. A final vote of the Presbyterians was taken in 1923, but "because of the disputes, later settled or never settled . . . it is difficult to offer an adequate summary."[8] According to Silcox, "if one were to add together the total votes by ballot, it would result in 122,966 (52 per cent) to 114,298 (48 per cent) in favor of Union."[9] Dr. E. Scott, a Presbyterian writer, asserts the vote was 113,000 for and 114,000 against.[10] Other ways of calculating the results, including congregations voting by resolution, or entering union by default, give the "unionist" 178,630.[11] In terms of congregations, "one-fourth of all those in self-sustaining charges did not enter the Union . . . while more than nine-tenths of all aid-receiving churches [did]."[12] The final step was the passage of legislation in both Canada's federal House of Commons and provincial legislatures to set up the new church. This also involved a fierce struggle and left its own legacy of bitterness.

Historical Influences prior to 1902

Certain ecclesiastical developments prior to 1902 played a significant part in readying the ground for union discussions. For instance, a series of unions within the Methodist and Presbyterian churches in both the Maritimes and Ontario throughout the nineteenth century established the practicality of union efforts and gave the term "Church Union" much popularity. "A widely read pamphlet by Dr. W. T. Gunn showed that the Presbyterian Church was itself the result of nine, the Methodist Church the result of eight, and the Congregational of four [unions]."[13] It seems clear, as Silcox says, that "every successful consolidation of religious groups in the same denominational family stimulated interest in, and hope for, a larger union of all Protestantism. . . . If nothing succeeds like success, nothing promoted church union in Canada like the actual achievement of various unions of churches."[14]

The popularity of church union before 1902 is further attested by the existence of a somewhat amorphous church union movement. Thus, in 1901, "there were already 267 union churches in Canada and 554 union Sunday Schools. Most of these were . . . in Ontario. These union enterprises had nothing whatever to do with the local union churches . . . afterward developed especially in the West."[15] Also, a number of societies and associations formed in the nineteenth century fostered co-operative endeavors between Protestants and developed institutionalized relationships of trust and mutual co-operation.

Protestant churches also were early united on issues of moral and social reform. Thus, for Sunday observance, there was formed in 1888 the Lord's Day Alliance, which appointed its own field secretary in 1899. In the university field, the federation of denominational colleges in 1887 in the University of Toronto was a signal step in co-operative intellectual activity.

Several other ecclesiastical developments in the pre-1902 period are worthy of mention. Beginning in the late 1860s the main Protestant denominations began the practice of sending fraternal delegates to the annual meetings of the other churches. These clergy habitually stressed points of agreement and occasionally made actual suggestions regarding church union. "Their visits dramatized the get together movement; their impact . . . over a period of years [was] considerable."[16]

These beginnings were abortive, as were discussions in 1886 on co-operation between Presbyterians and Methodists in sparsely settled areas and a resolution passed in the same year by the Anglican House of Bishops appointing a committee to conduct union discussions with other denominations. Nonetheless, such procedures and official expressions of interest doubtless helped to ease the way for serious deliberations later.

[A consideration of the three denominations' self-images will clarify the preceding historical analysis.] The Congregationalist self-image was dominated by a democratic, individualistic, and liberal orientation, a concern for lay opinion and for Congregational smallness *vis-à-vis* other Canadian Protestant groups and especially for its proportionate numeri-

cal decline within the Canadian population. (In 1871, they represented
.63 per cent of the total population, in 1921 only .35 per cent.) Few
clergy could see it contributing much by itself to the Canadian scene, but
many saw union as providing an opportunity to belong to a big influential church as well as a way out of pressing financial problems.[17]

In the Methodist self-image a vigorous concern for the world's
salvation, an emphasis upon practical adjustment to the needs of the
missionary situation, and a certain flexibility of approach, figured promi-
nently. Historical tradition and rigid theological or ceremonial formula-
tions had little weight. Among the clergy, such ideas as denominational
and missionary advance, adjustment to local needs, and sensitivity to
public and world opinion were prominent in the self-image. Finally, an
acceptance of congregational and ministerial obedience under the district
superintendent along with the four-year clergy rotation system is worthy
of mention.

Certain elements in the Presbyterian self-image doubtless contributed
to their split over union. Among these are a history of schismatic hold-outs
exemplified by the Church of Scotland and the Free Church, a pride in
resistance to Erastian pressures as well as in traditions of democratic
liberty, and opposition to officialdom. In addition, a certain accent upon
creeds and theological dogma institutionalized in the Westminster Confession and upon legal and procedural order formalized in church courts
was important. An emphasis upon individualistic thinking and a relatively high social status within the Canadian community, especially in
central Canada, were also [significant]. In sum, Presbyterianism constituted perhaps the most influential Protestant denomination in the Dominion—influential in scholarship, in general culture, in numbers, in
the wealth and success of the members ". . . such was their assured
position and they faced the future hopefully."[18] Finally among the clergy,
theological erudition and rigidity, respect for order and established prece-
dent, and pride in Presbyterian tradition loomed large.

The great majority of Presbyterians were of Scottish origin. Social
or class alignments in local communities often went along with jealousies
or rivalries between Presbyterians and Methodists. Distrust of the English
who dominated Methodism in Canada, and love for Scottish independence were sentiments which doubtless played a significant role in the
anti-union decisions of many Presbyterians. A certain apprehension of
clerical hierarchy among the clergy, specifically the powers of the district
superintendent, may be noted. Coincident with growing Presbyterian

votes against union was an increasing regionalism in the Canadian economy. "By 1913, the open frontier had disappeared"[19] and the postwar period saw a "decline in the unifying influence of national policies and growing diversity of regional interest."[20] This economic trend was related to the fact that opposition to union was slight on the prairies, fairly weak in the Maritimes, and strongest in Central Canada. The Ontario situation was doubtless associated with the high social status of many Presbyterian congregations in Central Canada.

Unitive Factors within the Churches, 1902–1925

We may now proceed to examine the dynamic institutional forces which, in spite of substantial Presbyterian opposition, swept the church union movement to its consummation. These consisted in the main of two developments, originally distinctive, which converged and produced, before 1925, over 3,000 "union" congregations in 1245 charges in both Western Canada and Ontario. Beginning in 1908, and significantly in Saskatchewan, there emerged independent union churches, founding themselves upon the Basis of Union worked out by the Joint Committee in that same year.

Provincial gatherings of union church representatives began in 1916, three presbyteries were formed, and three organizers appointed. These actions led, after considerable debate, to the appointment of an Advisory Council from the negotiating churches, which advised on tenure of property, status of ministers, and the like. The unofficial function of this Council was to delay the growth and independent institutionalization of these union congregations, pending union. "There was apparently some talk of an independent church in the West, and this was apparently what the denominational leaders . . . really feared."[21]

The second development began in 1911 when the Home Mission Committees of the two main churches reached an agreement not to compete in new territory, nor to plant new congregations within six miles of each other. "From that date, Presbyterians in some places became Methodists and Methodists in some places became Presbyterians."[22] This was an autocratic type of plan which meant, in effect, that the religious affiliation of many Westerners was decided according to the railway stations. As one church historian points out, "Such a plan was made possible and endurable only by the hope of Church Union."[23]

Some attention should be paid to nontheological factors of a permissive character which contributed indirectly to the union of 1925. First is the fact that the accepted form of church government in the three denominations, though not exactly the same, was such as to raise no great barrier to merging. Also, this common form of church government, with its absence of rigid clerical hierarchy, permitted all three denominations to be quite sensitive to lay opinion and initiative.

A second facilitating factor was the common Protestant ethos. This included a similar outlook in respect to the sacraments and the role of the ministry. Related here, too, is [the denominations'] general similarity in social standing in the Canadian community and also in educational requirements for the clergy. Each denomination had reached the status of a national church. Contrariwise, the Baptists, though sharing a Protestant ethos, had yet to achieve this national status. Their common self-image, too, as that of a "denomination" rather than an historical church, undoubtedly facilitated co-operative and unitive activity.

Factors of organizational structure and outlook also played a part. None of the denominations by 1925 had yet developed an extensive bureaucracy whose officials were liable to personal loss from the economies of unification. The smallness of the bureaucracy is related to Canada's geography, which strung out congregations along a 3,000-mile line, making the overhead costs of a centralized bureaucratic apparatus largely prohibitive at this stage. At the same time the anticipated expansion of the country and its churches seemed to guarantee career openings for most if not all of the professional leaders whose positions might be threatened at union's consummation. All three churches had, by the turn of the century, broken their legal ties with their mother churches in the U.S. or in England. Confederation in 1867 and succeeding national developments, as well as the Great War, had upgraded indigenous values and institutions and weakened sentimental links with Europe, thus allowing independence to these ecclesiastic institutions. Also, by 1925, these churches had to a large extent achieved a Canadian-born ministry, so that important decisions were now in the hands of a predominantly indigenous clergy.

Influential Socio-economic Forces

From a socio-economic standpoint, union may be viewed as an attempt to meet the insistent demands of geography and economics on the prairies, where in 1925, "outside the cities there were comparatively few places in any of the four provinces where Presbyterians and Methodists maintained competitive churches."[24] In effect the geography of the West as well as its economic development led to social conditions which greatly hampered the expansion of denominational-based ministries. Although settlers poured into the prairies after the turn of the century, the density of population in the prairies was only 1.87 persons to the square mile. For the most part these people lived very isolated lives, each family squatting on its quarter-section of 160 acres. Roads were very poor and the long, severe winters were especially isolating. The isolation was increased by great diversity of language and culture. The early towns were originally only small groups of frame buildings near railway lines and grain elevators. The work of ministers under these circumstances posed problems unknown in eastern congregations familiar with compact settlements, better communications, and an easier climate.

The planlessness of the early settlement period meant that many immigrants settled on poor land, and soon had to move further west. One-third of the three million settlers who came to Canada between 1895 and 1914 returned home or migrated to the U. S. This mobility of population made for social instability and hindered the building up of well-organized communities. The introduction of mechanized farming after the Great War also contributed to population movement, and increased social isolation by making larger farm holdings common.

A crucial problem was securing enough clergy to man the many new congregations. Before 1900 this was serious, but with the flood of new immigration up to 1914, the demands for new clergy became quite unmanageable. In this period the annual reports of all the major religions, including the Roman Catholics, speak of serious shortages of clergy.

The small and scattered nature of the settlements also meant that few rural congregations attained self-support. Financial help from Eastern Canada and from abroad was needed in ever-increasing amounts. Periodic crop failures after 1910 often made it impossible for even well-organized congregations to pay their minister's salary, and additional burdens were placed on Home Mission funds.

In the face of this situation, competition for supporters among churches of similar ethos appeared to many lay people both a scandal and an economic waste. Among the idealistic the cry was for more effective use of resources, for "good stewardship" of men and money, to facilitate opening up "new works". As Canada's economic historian, H. A. Innis, observes: "The peculiar character of the Canadian economy with its emphasis upon overhead costs has been largely responsible for a persistent trend toward unity."[25]

Two institutional trends in the field of business were probably [influential]. First, in the opening decade of the twentieth century the merger movement swept Canada. "Large primary and secondary producers . . . endeavored to integrate vertically with complementary concerns in order to extend their control over sources of raw materials."[26] A second and corollary development was the rise of the trade association.

Concern for economy spurred the cause of union, but specific social developments within many prairie communities combined to undermine denominational loyalties. The uprooting of Westerners from settled communities in the U. S., Eastern Canada, or Europe often weakened their allegiance to early religious ties, all the more when they settled in districts seldom or never served by a Christian minister. After years of inability to attend any church service, only those most devoted to their beliefs refused to attend services offered by Protestant ministers of other denominations than their own. Meantime, in the larger or less remote centers where several churches coexisted, the highly independent, tradition-free frontier social climate, combined with the great mixture of creeds and nationalities, provided a social atmosphere more favorable to exploring new churches than to strict adherence to childhood allegiances. The continuing social mobility of Westerners, incessantly moving westward in the search for economic security, weakened old social ties, while the need to secure status in one's new community fostered participation in secular activities and community-creating associations. In this situation strict denominationalism often appeared as a barrier both to social organization and to community "progress", especially for the laity.

Social and Cultural Climate

A major characteristic of the newly developing communities in the West was institutions stressing co-operation and mutual aid. Such institutions developed more or less spontaneously to meet conditions of desperate economic need or social organization posed by problems of climate, marketing, or settlement. They reflected a deep concern for aids to material security in the face of great threats and instabilities.

In the period 1900–1925, western farmers created a whole series of co-operative enterprises and in so doing developed both a philosophy and a value system in which co-operation and mutual aid ranked high. Among literally dozens of organizations, the following may serve as examples: The Territorial Grain Growers, a producers' co-operative, formed in 1901; the United Farmers of Alberta, an organization for political action, founded in 1909; and the Saskatchewan Co-operative Elevator Company, set up to aid sellers of grain, established in 1911.

The magnitude and effectiveness of these farmers' co-operative enterprises seemed to point a finger at the pettiness and weakness of the poor and divided churches. Whether this judgment was right or wrong, it sprang from an experience of success in the secular world. Joint co-operative activity brought together people of diverse ethnic and religious backgrounds and led many (of the men especially) to believe that their religious divisions were archaic and alien to prairie life. Out of convictions like these came the rapid development of local union churches.

Frontier devaluation of intellectual disciplines and distinctions was also a significant element in the prevailing social climate. Frontier life provided neither the time nor the facilities for education in doctrinal subtleties.

The social mood of the West between 1900 and 1925 was largely optimistic and liberal, and was fired by boom developments in wheat, oil, and natural gas. In theology, this optimistic spirit found expression in the emerging liberalism of the twenties. Liberal professors teaching in Saskatoon, Winnipeg, and Toronto, in both the Methodist and Presbyterian churches, tended to share a common world view and a common optimistic ethos. They saw church union as a progressive movement and came out strongly for it.

While extremely powerful nontheological forces fostered the church union movement on the prairies, somewhat similar influences emerged in the East. Many people in Ontario, little removed from the frontier stage in 1910, were hardly less concerned than Westerners with practical results and economy. Economic arguments weighed heavily, although counterbalancing forces of tradition, conservatism, and entrenched denominationalism were vigorous. The success of previous church unions was also impressive.

In the period 1900–1925 Eastern Canada was exhibiting a growing sense of nationalism. With the Laurier government of 1896 had come the British preferences, the stimulus of East-West trade, the wheat boom; gradually the idea that the twentieth century belonged to Canada took

root. The great burst of new immigration after 1900, the unifying common tasks and problems of settling the frontier, and the Great War
served to strengthen the impulse to nationalism.

Protestant interest in a national church was partly a reaction to the
steady expansion of Roman Catholicism, especially that of French
Canada. Eastern Protestants were very sensitive to Roman Catholic
political power, and had organized before 1902 several specifically
Anti-Roman organizations which vigilantly scrutinized Roman Catholic
actions and expansion.[27] World War I tended to clarify the country's
basic cleavage along ethnic and religious lines and strengthened both the
French and English varieties of nationalist sentiment.

Conclusion

Certain emphases in the United Church structure stand out suggestively:
a tendency to pragmatic as opposed to theological concerns; a flexibility
of adjustment to new social developments exceeding that of other
non-Roman denominations, not unrelated to the predominance of ex-
Methodists in key posts; a deep strain of moralism, associated with a
widening range of social concern, particularly at headquarters level; a
continuing zeal for union with non-Roman bodies; a fast-developing and
large Toronto-based bureaucracy, associated with higher professional
and academic standards among the clergy; notable success in money
raising, building of new churches, particularly in suburbia, and the utilization of mass media; some strengthening of self-appraisal as the national
Protestant church; attempts to clarify uncertainties regarding basic doctrines by periodic theological "White Papers", combined with a new
interest in theology on the part of many clergy; a firm alliance with the
respectable Anglo-Saxon middle classes along with some success, especially in the prairies, in assimilating European immigrants.

These trends underline the rather influential role of pragmatic and
sociological considerations in union, their consequences for building up a
"national" church, and something of the price exacted by accommodation
to such forces in order to meet the challenge of the social needs of the
Western Provinces.

NOTES

1   C. E. Silcox, *Church Union in
    Canada: Its Causes and Conse-
    quences*, p. 120.

2   E. L. Morrow, *Church Union in
    Canada: Its History, Motives,
    Doctrines and Government*, p. 15.

3 Silcox, p. 131.
4 E. Scott, *Church Union and the Presbyterian Church in Canada*, p. 52.
5 *Ibid.*, p. 53.
6 *Ibid.*, p. 56.
7 Silcox, p. 195.
8 *Ibid.*, p. 281.
9 *Ibid.*, p. 281.
10 "These figures are based upon returns received at the offices of the Presbyterian Church in Canada." Scott, p. 60.
11 Silcox, p. 281.
12 *Ibid.*, p. 282.
13 *Ibid.*, p. 25.
14 *Ibid.*, p. 103.
15 *Ibid.*, p. 74.
16 *Ibid.*, p. 105.
17 *Ibid.*, p. 181.
18 *Ibid.*, pp. 69-70.
19 *Report of Canadian Royal Commission, 1938* (Ottawa: Queen's Printer, 1938), Book 1, Ch. 3, p. 87.
20 *Ibid.*, p. 97.
21 Silcox, p. 224.
22 E. M. House, "Century Plant in Canada", *The Christian Century*, Vol. 62, May 16, 1945.

23 E. H. Oliver, *His Dominion of Canada* (Toronto: United Church Publishing House, 1932), p. 138.
24 Silcox, p. 295.
25 H. A. Innis's Introduction in H. A. Innis and A. F. M. Plumptre, *The Canadian Economy and Its Problems* (Toronto: University of Toronto Press, 1934), p. 21.
26 O. J. McDiarmid, *Commercial Policy in the Canadian Economy* (Cambridge: Harvard University Press, 1946), p. 243.
27 For all Canada the Catholic percentage rose from 39.4 per cent in 1911 to 46.1 per cent in 1951. It shows a steady growth in every decade, after 1941, if we remember to combine the Roman Catholic and Greek Catholic figures from the census. Lumping of Greek Orthodox and Greek Catholic adherents in the early decades of the century serves to hide the total Catholic strength from the unobservant. (Later censuses show that well over 60 per cent of the combined Greek Catholic and Greek Orthodox total represents Greek Catholic strength.)

REFERENCES

Chalmers, Randolph Carleton
1945 *See the Christ Stand! A Study in Doctrine in the United Church of Canada.* Toronto: Ryerson Press.
Clark, Samuel Delbert
1948 *Church and Sect in Canada.* Toronto: University of Toronto Press.
Mann, William Edward
1955 *Sect, Cult, and Church in Alberta.* Toronto: University of Toronto Press.
Morrison, George M.
1956 "The United Church of Canada: Ecumenical or Economic Necessity?" Unpublished B.D. thesis, Emmanuel College, University of Toronto.
Morrow, E. Lloyd
1923 *Church Union in Canada: Its History, Motives, Doctrines and*

Government. Toronto: Thomas Allen.
Riddell, John Henry
1946 *Methodism in the West.* Toronto: Ryerson Press.
Scott, Ephraim
1928 *Church Union and the Presbyterian Church in Canada.* Montreal: John Lovell.
Silcox, Claris Edwin
1933 *Church Union in Canada: Its Causes and Consequences.* New York: Institute of Social and Religious Research.
Slosser, Gaius Jackson
1929 *Christian Unity: Its History and Challenge in All Communions, in All Lands.* London and New York: E. P. Dutton.
Walsh, Henry Horace
1956 *The Christian Church in Canada.* Toronto: Ryerson Press.

The Impact of Clerical Attitudes and Liberalism on Ecumenism*

Robert C. Kaill

The primary concern of this study is with the social factors which influence lay attitudes toward church union, rather than with the relative strength of support for the plan within the two denominations. Nevertheless, notice must be taken of the organizational context within which adherents of the two bodies make decisions and formulate attitudes. It might be assumed initially that because of the episcopal structure, emphasis on historical liturgies, and strong sense of tradition characterizing Anglicanism, members would perceive the merger plan as an overt threat to their religious identity. On the other hand, the Anglican Church has been in a state of relative numerical decline in Canada for more than a decade, and this might create a cross-pressure in favour of union (Dominion Bureau of Statistics, 1961: 924–546). On the surface, the issue appears much less ambiguous for United Churchmen, since their denomination is a product of merger and claims to be not only a "united" but a "uniting church" (United Church of Canada, *Manual,* 1962: 6).

*Appeared first in Robert C. Kaill, "Ecumenism, Clergy Influence and Liberalism: An Investigation into the Sources of Lay Support for Church Union", in the *Canadian Review of Sociology and Anthropology*, Vol. 8, No. 3, 1971. Published here in abridged form with the kind permission of the Canadian Sociology and Anthropology Association and the author.

This claim may, however, be little more than an idealized definition of the situation. Since routinization and rationalization are ubiquitous organizational processes, it must be assumed that after forty-five years of existence, many United Church adherents are unmindful of their denomination's lofty aims, and feel an emotional attachment to it differing little from that of Anglicans. On [this] basis there is no sound theoretical ground for predicting the extent of support for merger in either of the two religious groups.

In seeking to identify the factors predisposing members to accept or reject the union proposal, the claim of Demerath and Hammond (1969: 221) that ecumenism represents primarily a response to the pressures under which modern urban congregations exist offers a point of departure. This explanation of ecumenical behaviour might be appropriate when disintegration appears imminent, but such a threat is by no means apparent in the two groups under study. There has been a moderate decline in participation, but budgets continue to be met and routine operations are not curtailed. It is, therefore, assumed that anxiety over congregational survival is not a primary source of support for merger. The first hypothesis states that pessimism concerning the church's future is not significantly correlated with approval of church union.

A more convincing argument may be made for treating liberalism as the primary source of the ecumenical spirit. [Yinger] (1957: 224) argues that religious groups which preach the social gospel are the same ones that advocate interfaith co-operation and merger. Other writers (Demerath and Hammond 1969: 221) have pointed to the historically coincidental emergence of ecumenism and the social gospel in America. Further evidence of this relationship is provided by the fact that practically all mergers that have taken place have involved liberal Protestant denominations (Salisbury 1964: 299–314). Liberally inclined churches view religious organizations instrumentally, as vehicles of social amelioration.

But, as sociologists have good reason to appreciate, liberalism is a complex and elusive phenomenon, exhibiting secular as well as sacred dimensions. Rokeach (1960), for example, considers "open-mindedness" to be an important aspect of liberalism. This is particularly relevant for the present investigation, since merger of these two religious groups is certain to involve changes in several facets of church life. In formulating their attitudes toward the proposed merger, adherents will be compelled to choose between preservation of familiar religious patterns, and the acceptance of new forms and structures. Hence, openness to innovation must be considered a further component of the liberal spirit for purposes of this study. Finally, liberalism also has politico-economic dimensions, usually expressed in leftist leanings, although many would insist on excluding doctrinal socialism on the ground that it represents an inflexible position incongruent with the liberal spirit. For this reason, Lipset (1960: 101–2) has distinguished between "economic" and "non-economic" liberalism, including in the latter category concern for liberties and tolerance, a phenomenon which has been operationalized in this design as "belief in freedom of expression", following Stouffer's classic study of liberalism in the United States. (Twelve of Stouffer's fifteen items comprising his tolerance scale measured the respondent's willingness to grant freedom of expression to those with whom he disagreed.) Economic liberalism, on the other hand, connotes a negative attitude toward the free-enterprise economic system, coupled with advocacy of welfare-type legislation.

In the present investigation, the church union proposal is considered an expression of non-economic liberalism, and it is anticipated that respondents who favour the plan will be predominantly middle and upper class liberals in the non-economic sense, whereas working class respondents will exhibit less enthusiasm for union and more for economic liberalist principles.

From the foregoing analysis, the following hypotheses have been elicited, specifying the relationships between each dimension of liberalism and attitudes toward the proposed union: (a) that there is a positive correlation between religious liberalism and approval of church union; (b) that there is a positive correlation between belief in freedom of expression and approval of church union; (c) that there is a positive correlation between acceptance of innovation and approval of church union; and (d) that there is a negative correlation between economic liberalism and approval of union. It is also anticipated that respondents who approve of union will exhibit other characteristics commonly associated with liberalism, including higher than average socio-economic status, multiple memberships in secular voluntary associations, and relative youthfulness.

A second factor which might reasonably be expected to influence attitudes of church adherents toward the merger proposal is the position taken on the issue by the clergy. Numerous theoretical and empirical studies have been carried out on the clergy role and the nature of its authority. There have, however, been few empirical attempts to measure the power of the clergy over lay members of their congregations. Utilizing a structural approach, Vernon (1947: 190–1) conceives of a continuum of power ranging from congregationalist clergy at one pole, exerting least power, to episcopal priests at the other, wielding most. In the context of the present study, the Anglican priest exceeds the United Church minister in structural authority by virtue of his episcopal ordination and non-democratic form of government at the congregational level. From this analysis, two hypotheses have been elicited: (a) that both Anglican and United Church clergy influence the attitudes of laymen with respect to church union; (b) that the influence of Anglican priests on lay attitudes toward church union exceeds that of United Church ministers.

Apart from these major theoretical considerations, there are certain other factors which may significantly influence lay attitudes toward church merger, but about which little relevant evidence is available. First, there is the effect of ethnicity to be considered. A somewhat analogous problem concerns the effect of family denominational solidarity or discontinuity on union attitudes. Finally, there is the question of commitment. Does the union proposal receive greater support from the more or less committed? The answers to these questions will be explored, although no formal hypotheses have been formulated.

Research Design

The sample consisted of 408 active adherents of two urban and two town parishes of each denomination in central western Ontario, a total of eight congregations. Active adherents are defined as persons who attended church services at least once in the past year. [Questionnaires] were passed out to worshippers in stamped, self-addressed envelopes as they left the church buildings. To minimize bias, distribution took place on the same date in all eight churches. The clergy also read prepared statements emphasizing the importance of having all viewpoints represented. This procedure combines some aspects of group administration with mailing technique, and probably accounts for the unusually high response rate of approximately 69 per cent. Denominational composition of the sample was 35 per cent Anglican, 60 per cent United Church and 5 per cent Other, representing a ratio of Anglicans to United Churchmen of 3.5:6, closely approximating the national ratio of 3.4:5.3 (Dominion Bureau of Statistics, 1961). Similarly, the sex and rural-urban distribution of the sample did not differ significantly from the parameters of the national population. The age characteristics of the sample are of particular interest in view of the prevailing belief that older persons are over-represented in religious activities. Unfortunately, differential grouping of the data between the research design and census records does not permit exact comparison, but inspection clearly supports the above postulate, younger people being under-represented and the more elderly over-represented, although the discrepancy does not appear to be above five per cent in any of the three categories into which age groups were divided.

Socio-economic status is also of concern, since several studies (Mann 1963: 171–94; Allingham 1962: 32–3) have indicated that Anglicans enjoy a somewhat higher status than adherents of the United Church. The data of the present study confirm this finding, but again the difference is below the level of statistical significance. When compared with national figures, the total sample proves to be well above the mean. When, however, it is recalled that socio-economic status was measured by formal education and occupation, this inconsistency is understandable in view of the large proportion of university faculty members (14 per cent) included in the sample. Further, since this variable is not significantly related to the phenomena under investigation, this sampling bias does not invalidate the findings of the study. In general, then, despite the localized nature of the sample, it exhibits a fairly high degree of representativeness of the national population.

The questionnaire was entirely structured, consisting of 38 Likert-type items, about half the number used in the pre-test phase, the remainder having been eliminated on the basis of item analysis. In attitude studies, the question of single versus multiple measures is particularly crucial, since the relative validity of each item as a true indicator of the attitude under study is always problematic (Blalock 1969: 111). For this reason, multiple indicators were used for all major attitudinal variables, items being combined additively.

Denominationally, the relative approval rate is as shown in Table 1. United Church respondents exhibit significantly higher approval of the merger plan than Anglican. Our research problem now is to explain that difference.

Before examining the data in terms of the formal hypotheses of the study, we shall dispose of the incidental issues raised in the theoretical model. With respect to occupation, it had been anticipated that farmers

TABLE 1. Denominational Approval of Church Union

ATTITUDE TOWARD UNION	ANGLICAN (PER CENT)	UNITED CHURCH (PER CENT)
Approve	48	63
Neutral	20	15
Disapprove	32	22
N	(146)	(248)

Chi-square = 7.88 < .02.

would exhibit lower educational levels, fewer liberal characteristics, and less enthusiasm for merger than other occupational groups. While the data confirm the first premise, this group exhibited mean levels of liberalism and support for union. The data may be interpreted to mean either that farmers who adhere to town or urban congregations internalize the social values of the dominant group, or, conversely, liberally oriented farmers gravitate toward such churches because of the more compatible ideological milieu. With respect to residence, the data indicate some minor positive relationship between community size and approval of union.

The data tend to support the first hypothesis which postulated no relationship between pessimism over the church's future and approval of union (see Table 2). This composite variable had three components, representing anxiety over (1) financial difficulties, (2) recruitment of suitable clergy, and (3) the church's appeal to youth. Item analysis revealed that concern over financial problems exhibited the lowest correlation with the other two items, and with approval of union. Where pessimism about the future does produce a willingness to accept denominational merger, it is the difficulty of clergy recruitment and of holding

TABLE 2. Effect of Pessimism over the Church's Future on Approval of Church Union

ATTITUDE TOWARD UNION	DEGREE OF PESSIMISM		
	HIGH (PER CENT)	MEDIUM (PER CENT)	LOW (PER CENT)
Approve	62	53	58
Neutral	13	23	17
Disapprove	25	24	25
N	(194)	(79)	(132)

Chi-square = 4.06 > 0.40.

the interest of young people that is chiefly functional. This relationship holds for adherents of both denominations, every age group, and all socio-economic statuses.

The first positive proposition of the theoretical model argued that the proposal to merge the Anglican and United churches is an expression of the liberalist spirit. The concept of liberalism was refined into four constituent dimensions—religious liberalism, belief in freedom of expression, acceptance of innovation, and economic liberalism, following the theoretical outline.

The religious liberalism variable was comprised of five questionnaire items. The questions referred to the theological content of belief (doctrine of the Trinity and the divinity of Christ), degree of emphasis on other-worldly matters (attainment of heaven in the next life and mystical experiences in this), and stress on social action (support for the resolution of social evils through collective action rather than by individual conversion). While this composite variable exhibited relatively high internal validity, neither the whole variable nor any of the items was significantly related with approval of church union. Where organizational identity is at stake, religious liberals tend to behave no differently than others.

The "innovation" dimension of liberalism consisted of three items (see Table 3), each of which required the respondent to choose between the retention of familiar religious traditions and change. Again, neither singly nor as a composite measure were these indicators correlated with support for union. However, the statistical relationship between the two variables does provide valuable insight into respondents' attachment to traditional forms of religious expression, and therefore warrants examination. Only fifty-eight respondents (14 per cent) were prepared to

TABLE 3.   Relationship Between Acceptance of Innovation and Approval of Church Union

	ACCEPTANCE OF INNOVATION		
ATTITUDE TOWARD UNION	HIGH (PER CENT)	MEDIUM (PER CENT)	LOW (PER CENT)
Approve	65	66	59
Neutral	13	16	17
Disapprove	22	18	24
N	(58)	(104)	(240)

Chi-square $= 2.38 > 0.50$.

approve change involving the sacrifice of familiar religious forms, while 240 (60 per cent) opted for tradition. The response pattern is approximately the same for adherents of both Anglican and United churches. Since more than half of the total sample approved the union proposal, it is evident that most of them assumed that merger could be achieved without substantial change at the congregational level. Recalling that at present there are significant liturgical and structural differences between the two religious groups, it is apparent that those who favour church merger anticipate either that the new church will permit wide variation in procedures at the congregational level, or that their bargaining agents will be strong enough to impose their present forms on the other uniting group. We must conclude that traditionalism does not deter adherents of either religious group from approving the merger proposal.

The third liberal variable concerned belief in freedom of expression and consisted of two items, one referring to the treatment of Communists in our society, and the other relating to censorship of movies. This composite variable showed a highly significant correlation with support for church union (see Table 4). This relationship between belief in freedom of expression and support for church union holds when controlled for all available theoretically relevant structural variables. In every age category, those who believe most in freedom of expression are also most in favour of church union.

If this liberal quality predisposes people to support church union, United Church adherents should exhibit more of it than Anglicans, since they have shown a significantly higher union approval rate. The data in Table 5 further confirm the hypothesis that civil liberalism and approval of union are positively related, Anglicans exhibiting a greater reluctance to permit freedom of expression to dissenters than United Churchmen.

TABLE 4. Relationship Between Belief in Freedom of Expression and Approval of Church Union

ATTITUDE TOWARD UNION	BELIEF IN FREEDOM OF EXPRESSION		
	HIGH (PER CENT)	MEDIUM (PER CENT)	LOW (PER CENT)
Approve	73	65	29
Neutral	16	19	18
Disapprove	11	16	53
N	(231)	(43)	(126)

Chi-square $= 87.31 > 0.001$.

TABLE 5.   Comparison of United Church and Anglican
Respondents on Belief in Freedom of Expression

	DENOMINATION	
BELIEF IN FREEDOM OF EXPRESSION	ANGLICAN (PER CENT)	UNITED CHURCH (PER CENT)
High	44	64
Medium	13	10
Low	43	26
N	(140)	(236)

Chi-square = 13.59 < 0.01.

The final liberal variable, economic liberalism, exhibited a negative correlation with the dependent variable as predicted (see Table 6). The economic liberalism variable consisted of two questions, one of which suggested that the free enterprise system "favours" the rich and discriminates against the poor, while the other recommended that the government "control and operate all vital industries, such as mining, railways and airlines". The negative relationship between this variable and approval of church merger indicated in [Table 6] persisted when controls were run on several structural variables. In all categories of socio-economic status, support for economic liberalism is inversely related to approval of church union.

The fact that belief in freedom of expression and rejection of economic liberalism both correlate highly with the dependent variable is by no means fortuitous, since in western society the free enterprise system connotes freedom of choice and decision-making, while government control of industry tends to be associated with restriction of individual freedom. This interpretation gains further empirical support from the high

TABLE 6.   Relationship Between Economic Liberalism and
Approval of Church Union

	BELIEF IN ECONOMIC LIBERALISM		
ATTITUDE TOWARD UNION	HIGH (PER CENT)	MEDIUM (PER CENT)	LOW (PER CENT)
Approve	37	57	68
Neutral	16	22	14
Disapprove	47	21	18
N	(88)	(131)	(183)

Chi-square = 37.84 < 0.001.

statistical correlation between these two liberal variables. For this reason, in the remainder of the paper, the former composite variable, "belief in freedom of expression" only, will be used in statistical correlations to represent civil liberalism.

We are now forced to ask the more difficult theoretical question, why commitment to freedom of expression and economic behaviour should lead to approval of a plan to unite two autonomous religious bodies. A clue to the nature of this relationship is available from the earlier observation that a majority of those who approve the plan appear to favour preservation of traditional forms of religious expression. [The liberal's] approval of church union, therefore, suggests that he has been convinced that the merger plans envisage some type of loose federation permitting preservation of existing forms of religious expression at the local level.

The final major hypothesis concerns the influence of clergy on lay approval of church union. Clergy attitude toward the plan was measured in terms of lay perception, each respondent being asked to indicate where his pastor stood on the issue. Only 17 per cent (n = 24) of Anglican respondents believe their pastors favour church union, compared with 36 per cent (n = 87) of United Church subjects, thus establishing an unmistakable link between perception of clergy attitude and rate of denominational approval of the plan. A significant statistical correlation is evident between these two variables within both denominational groups. On the other hand, there is no significant difference in strength of clergy influence between the two denominations. It should be noted that this influence is weaker among younger parishioners than among other members of the sample.

The statistical relationship between perception of clergy attitude and lay approval of union holds for the entire sample, except the under-thirty age group. The data do not provide evidence to indicate whether this outcome is to be interpreted as a function of age differential or of changing attitudes toward clergy authority. In spite of this age group exception, it remains true that for the sample as a whole there is a strong positive correlation between perception of clergy approval of merger and lay support for it.

We have now identified two theoretically independent variables highly correlated with approval of church union. To measure the relative strength of each on the dependent variable it is only necessary to cross-tabulate either one against approval of union, while controlling for the other (Rosenberg, 1968: 169–78). Perception of clergy attitude has a slightly greater effect on respondent approval rate than belief in freedom of expression. When they operate conjointly, more than four out of five respondents (83 per cent) approve church union, whereas when both are absent fewer than one out of five (18 per cent) do so.

Conclusion

These findings will be of direct interest to those concerned with the ecumenical movement, but they also carry more general implications relating to other forms of religious behaviour. It should be noted, for example, that the sources of approval are not theological, nor even essentially religious, since, as we have seen, such considerations bear no significant statistical relationship to the dependent variable. Mol's (1969: 23–31) similar finding in his Australian study reinforces the reliability of this conclusion. This observed relationship, coupled with recognition of the crucial importance of merger for lay organizational identity, provides impressive theoretical and empirical bases for the proposition that *purely religious considerations do not systematically influence lay attitudes toward questions of religious organizational structure.* Other more general attitudes having to do with such issues as individual or group freedom of expression and autonomy appear to have more direct predictive value.

The effect of clergy endorsement as the most powerful single factor generating lay approval was to a considerable extent neutralized by the fact that most members of the sample were not convinced of their pastors' support for the merger plan. This finding is in sharp conflict with Wilson's (1966: 125) contention that among clergy, ecumenism has become "a new faith—something to believe in", and that "a mass conversion of the clergy" to this movement has taken place. Our data suggest that either no such "mass conversion" has occurred among Anglican or United Church clergy in Canada, or, if these leaders are enthusiastic ecumenists, there has been a remarkable breakdown of communication between the pulpit and the pew.

Finally, it might be speculated that the strength of the liberal spirit among United Church adherents is largely a product of their church's history, since it has had to live with diversity from the time of its inception. Not only did the union of 1925 bring together three powerful religious traditions into a single organizational entity, but the melding process was further confounded by the adoption of a form of government which protected the autonomy of both congregation and clergy (Silcox 1933: ch. 10). Hence a healthy respect for dissent was a condition of organizational survival. Our data suggest that adherents have learned the lesson well. For Anglicans, the story is quite otherwise. Having an episcopal form of government, and being the inheritors of a long tradition of liturgical conformity, members of that religious group have been exposed in their religious life to the value of propriety rather than compromise, a cumulative group experience which has undoubtedly made its contribution to the outcome of this investigation.

REFERENCES

Allingham, J. D.
1962   "Religious Affiliation and Social Class in Ontario." Unpublished M.A. thesis, McMaster University.
Blalock, H. M.
1969   "Estimating Measurement Error Using Multiple Indicators and Several Points in Time." *American Sociological Review* 35: 101-11.
Christianity Today
1962   6: 741-2.
Demerath, J., and R. Hammond
1969   *Religion in Social Context*. New York: Random House.
Dominion Bureau of Statistics
1961   *Census of Canada*. Catalogue 924-546, Part 2. Ottawa: Queen's Printer.
Hatt, P. K.
1950   "Occupations and Social Stratification." *American Journal of Sociology* 55: 533-43.
Herberg, Will
1956   *Protestant-Catholic-Jew*. New York: Doubleday.
Latourette, K. S.
1953   *A History of Christianity*. New York: Harper and Row.
Lenski, G.
1961   *The Religious Factor*. New York: Doubleday.
Lipset, S. M.
1960   *Political Man*. New York: Doubleday.

Mann, W. E.
1963   "The Canadian Church Union." In Nils Ehrenstrom and Walter G. Muelder, eds., *Institutionalism and Church Union*. New York: Association Press.
Mol, J. J.
1969   "The Merger Attempts of the Australian Churches." *Ecumenical Review* 21: 23-31.
Rodger, P.
1965   "Toward the Wholeness of the Church." *Ecumenical Review* 17: 146-56.
Rokeach, Milton
1960   *The Open and Closed Mind*. New York: Basic Books.
Rosenberg, M.
1968   *The Logic of Survey Analysis*. New York: Basic Books.
Salisbury, W. S.
1964   *Religion in American Culture*. Homewood, Ill.: Dorsey.
Silcox, C. E.
1933   *Church Union in Canada*. New York: Institute of Social and Religious Research.
Stouffer, S.
1963   *Communism, Conformity and Civil Liberties*. Gloucester: Peter Smith.
Troeltsch, E.
1931   *The Social Teachings of the Christian Churches*. New York: Macmillan.

The United Church of Canada
1962   *The Manual.*
Vernon, G. M.
1947   *Sociology of Religion.* New
        York: McGraw-Hill.
Walsh, H. H.
1956   *The Christian Church of Canada.*
        Toronto: Ryerson Press.
Weber, Max
1930   *The Protestant Ethic and the
        Spirit of Capitalism.* New York:
        George Allen and Unwin.

Weber, Max
1947   *The Theory of Social and
        Economic Organization.* New
        York: Oxford University Press.
Wilson, Bryan
1966   *Religion in Secular Society.*
        London: C. A. Watts.
Yinger, J. M.
1957   *Religion, Society and the Indi-
        vidual.* New York: Macmillan.
Yinger, J. M.
1970   *The Scientific Study of Religion.*
        London: Macmillan.

6.

Politics, Economics, and Social Strata

Religion and the Control of Native Peoples*

T. Rennie Warburton

The focus in this paper is on religion as a means of maintaining and legitimating the control of native people by Canadians of European origin. Religion is examined in terms of its relation to political and economic patterns and to the use of power by the dominant groups to maintain their superior position (Dawe 1970). The theoretical perspective, then, is dialectical and is aimed at diverting attention away from religion as a source of values and normative consensus towards a study of its place in the structure of social control. In this there are excellent precedents in the work of Marx and Weber. Marx thought of religion as contributing to alienation because, as an instrument of social control, it supported an oppressive system of production which prevented the working classes from exercising fully their creative capacities for labour and decision-making and thus from realizing their potential in social experience. Weber was concerned with the complementary relations between social strata and religious beliefs and practices. In his comparative studies of world religions, he analyzed how belief systems sometimes enabled ruling

*Prepared for this volume. Thanks are due to Robert B. Lane and Derek G. Smith for helpful comments on an earlier draft.

groups to perpetuate their authority and at other times motivated emerging groups to establish new forms of legitimate authority.

The phenomenological approach of scholars like Peter Berger also has important implications for studying the relationship between religion and other institutional patterns. Berger (1967: 12) stresses the active manner in which people construct religious and social reality. At the same time he recognizes the coercive influence which social institutions exert over their members. And he indicates how in most societies methods have emerged to hide the "constructed character" of the institutional order. People are persuaded that participation in ritual meets their personal needs and puts them in harmony with the universe which was established by sacred powers. This enables some to forget that their social order "was established by men and continues to be dependent on the consent of men". Without implying that social orders are consciously produced, Berger thus acknowledges the role of some leaders who maintain the *status quo* by endowing it with a sacred quality. We might add that although leaders may mitigate dissent, pressures for change can increase as the disestablished become aware of the man-made character of the existing order and of its injustices.

To say that every social situation includes a power dimension is stating the obvious, but to raise the question of who creates, manages, and controls the typical social situations in which religion operates, and with what consequences, becomes theoretically and practically cogent. Giddens (1968: 264), discussing Parsons' analysis of power, says that a critical aspect of power is that it is always exercised over someone. Religion as a form of power has been paid little attention, and has rarely been examined from the standpoint of the interests of those who directly or indirectly control or support religious institutions whose influence on other elements of a society is frequently considerable.

Religion, then, may be analyzed as an integral part of socially constructed meaning systems and, because the interests of dominant groups are frequently bound up with these meaning systems, religion may come to serve as an important mechanism of social control. This approach is capable of illuminating the relation between religion and phenomena like economic development, nationalism, and social and ethnic stratification—for example, the position of indigenous people in contemporary Canadian society.

The place of religion in the social and economic development of

Canada is an old theme. Sociologists such as S. D. Clark and John Porter have observed some links between the political economy and religion. Clark (1948, 1962) refers to "economic-political-ecclesiastical" control and to a "theocratic-ecclesiastical" system which was supported at provincial and national levels. Porter (1965) has studied one religious elite and mentions those values which legitimate the prestige and moral authority of the holders of power posts. He agrees that religion has helped to make Canadian culture more conservative than its American counterpart (Porter 1965; Lipset 1965; Clark 1962). Hubert Guindon (1960) has commented on how the involvement of Quebec clergy in capitalist and bureaucratic enterprise helped them to retain their elite status.

To illustrate this theoretical perspective, we will discuss the position of the native peoples in Canadian society, and some ways in which the religious activities and religiously based norms and beliefs of Euro-Canadians appear to have maintained it. The position of the native peoples of Canada as a dependent class, or, in Carsten's words, a "class segment", in Canadian society is due to many aspects of their historical relationships with Euro-Canadians (Carstens 1971: 139). It is difficult to isolate the religious component of Euro-Canadian culture from other elements, especially values concerning education, hygiene, work, and respectability. In roles such as missionary, trader, law-enforcement officer, government official, teacher, and social worker, non-natives have carried an alien culture to aboriginal peoples and have sought to control their situation and behaviour in various ways. According to Dawe (1970: 213), a situation is controlled when actors "impose meaning on it by acting upon it" and when they impose their "definition upon other actors in that situation". Our problem, therefore, is to ask what part Christianity has played in the imposition of meanings on the situation of Canadian native peoples.

In broad terms the question might be answered by examining the teachings and beliefs of the various Christian organizations which have established a foothold among the native peoples. But the problem goes much further. Christianity is also associated in Canadian society with ways of interpreting people's conduct, ways of defining the contact between Euro-Canadians and aboriginal peoples, and ways of sorting them into a stratification system. Vallee (1971: 150) has said that "on just about every index of prestige, power, and command over valued resources, the native peoples of Canada are the least advantaged." He has described relationships between native and outside groups in Northern Canada as "asymmetrical, with the outside group in the dominant, patronizing position, and the native group in the subordinate position" (1971: 152). While the degree of segmentation is not always clear and is blurred by the increasing urban migration of many young Indian people, the relationship is similar throughout other parts of the country (Dosman 1972).

Like many Europeans who migrated and conquered aboriginal peoples throughout the world, those who came to Canada brought with them certain ideas about the superiority of their religion and civilization. Largely because of their ethnocentric perceptions, these ideas were reinforced as a result of their encounters with Canadian native peoples. The churches frequently had an important influence on decisions made concerning these peoples, especially in education. These policies were part of plans for the development of the economy and society. As a result, the processes of colonization, urbanization, and industrialization were intricately interwoven with the propagation of Christianity. Christianity was allied with the goals of pioneer leaders in social development.

Religious agents were often used by organizations and agencies such as the Hudson's Bay Company, the RCMP, and governments of the time (Clark 1962; Ferguson 1970; Morton 1973). Clark has illustrated the use of law enforcement and the role of the centralized churches in controlling behaviour in frontier communities. Measures to deal with the problems of ensuring that populations would fit into a political order and an economic system by upholding the law, performing duties as citizens, entering the work force, and becoming permanent and stable members of communities, were seen to be imperative for the advancement of an industrial society.

Schutz (1970: 120) has drawn attention to the process of typification as a means of understanding how groups define one another and enable their members to interpret their own behaviour and that of members of other groups. "Unique individual actions of unique human beings" are transformed into "typical functions of typical social roles, originating in typical motives aimed at bringing about typical ends".

Some of these processes have been examined by Klapp (1962: 7), who refers to a "stock of type images which society maintains", in which "social types comprise a system, more or less stable though ever-changing as the typing process acts on particular individuals, audiences, and human relations. We see an invisible network of rules, an informal structure, registered in symbolic residues of language—the way people think and talk about others." By casting native people as social types and as deviant in the sense of not complying with the normative expectations of Euro-Canadians, the latter's sense of cultural identity and moral respectability has been reinforced.

What sorts of typification process have occurred in native/non-native relationships, especially those that have enabled the Euro-Canadians to remain dominant, and, for present purposes, to what degree are such typifications grounded in Christian beliefs and values?

Foremost among the official bearers of the Christian religion were the missionaries (Walsh 1956, Ch. 17; Grant 1972: 35). Although their behaviour towards native peoples varied considerably from one denomination, and, indeed, from one individual missionary, to another, like their counterparts who moved into other parts of the non-European world, they took with them the belief that Christianity was the sole true religion and that European civilization was the most advanced in the world. While many of them took the trouble to learn the local language and culture to achieve conversions more efficiently and even to minimize cultural disruption, many were ignorant of the role and importance of culture in the lives and communities of aboriginal peoples. They branded native religions as remnants of barbarism, heathenism, and paganism which had to be rooted out if the Christian gospel were to be preached and "sinners" and "savages" converted. Commenting on the impact of missionaries on northern peoples, Vallee (1971: 154) claimed that "only those aspects of the way of life which were judged as inimical to Christianity were to be transformed." The Potlatch Law of 1884 was partly a product of missionaries' demands for the prohibition of a ceremonial feast which was an integral part of a people's cultural identity (La Violette 1973: 40–2; Hawthorn 1960: 37). What were thought to be irrational, even bestial, forms of behaviour at feasting and dancing ceremonies were considered by many missionaries as inimical to the spread of civilization and Christianity. They showed little respect for the religions of native peoples (Manuel and Posluns 1974: 137). Such stereotyping has influenced the attitudes of many powerful Euro-Canadian agents and has led directly to repressive measures (Dosman 1972: 20).

Closely related to general moral downgrading was the typing of Amerindians as illiterate peoples in need of western education. They did not have a written language in early times of contact, and, although in a number of instances clergy and missionaries developed native written languages, the churches generally used education as an instrument for conversion. This situation frequently implied the destruction of native languages and cultures, as well as the classification of native people as inferior.

Until the widespread move towards integrated and non-denominational education in the 1960s, the educational system for native peoples was dominated by the churches. The survey of ideologies among the churches given in the Hawthorn Report revealed a "chaotic situation" and "the greater the educational resources possessed by a church or the greater its investment in Indian education, the greater its anxiety to maintain the *status quo*" (Hawthorn 1967: 61). Not until 1947 did the federal government begin to develop a public school system for the north, and up to this point "Eskimos depended mainly on mission schools affiliated with the Anglican and Roman Catholic churches. The classes served only a minute fraction of the native children, and emphasized religious instruction far more than secular skills" (Davis and Krauter 1971: 28). One survey showed that, in 1944, 93 per cent of children in the Mackenzie Delta and western Arctic were receiving no formal education. Indian children were sometimes punished in residential schools for using their own languages. The motives of the church educators were doubtless sincere. They were convinced of the paramount need for cultural change through education and the inculcation of Euro-Canadian values so that students might return to their people and teach them the ways of Western civilization.

The middle-class position of many of the carrying agents of Euro-Canadian culture is reflected in typifications of native peoples according to which they judged them to be incapable of conforming to the "Protestant Ethic" with its norms of thrift, punctuality, sobriety, and industriousness. For example, the consumption of alcohol by native peoples has been deplored widely by moral guardians. Fondness for alcohol among native peoples has been seen as a major hindrance to developing self-control, moral responsibility, and rationally calculating, restrained behaviour (Dailey 1968). When drinking activity has been accompanied by dancing, chanting, and the revival of aboriginal social practices, the typification of the native person as lacking self-control, as giving way too readily to "primitive" instincts, has been reinforced.

Another typification which refers to "laziness" also reflects the Protestant Ethic (Lower 1954: 129ff.). The level of unemployment and job instability of Indians is high. Frequently they lose jobs because they do not meet the expectations of white employers and fellow workers regarding punctuality and working capacity. Moral comparisons and judgments are made. As a result, Indians become typed as "lazy" or "unreliable" (Canadian Corrections Association 1967). While it may be argued that non-religious factors in Euro-Canadian culture are operating here, there is certainly a link between work ethics, respectability, and religiosity in the minds of many Euro-Canadians, especially powerholders like judges and employers (Lower 1954).

When mention is made of poverty in Canada, attention is often drawn to the plight of the native peoples. On most measures they fall into a category below the so-called "poverty line" (Hawthorn 1967; Adams et al., 1971). This situation reflects certain objective economic facts. It also results in a process of typification whereby the connotations of the term "poor" in Euro-Canadian culture are applied to native peoples. The middle-class work ethic and the notion of responsible behaviour in educational contexts and in family life are brought to bear when the Euro-Canadian compares himself with his less successful counterpart, whether white or native. Voluntary agencies for helping the poor were built on nineteenth-century notions of charity which churches cultivated as a means of expressing the brotherly love of Christian ethics. Although many of these activities have been taken over by the state, the persistence of organized appeals for charity suggest that there is a large residue of charitable attitudes among the Canadian middle classes towards the "poor". These attitudes are to a great extent religiously rooted. Since the native peoples are obliged to receive private and public welfare benefits to a greater extent than others, they are kept in a state of dependency. But this system of welfare payments is often criticized by Euro-Canadians as being too generous towards native peoples (Parsons 1970: 25; Bennett 1971: 111). The devastating effect of Euro-Canadian culture on the position of these peoples is nowhere more apparent than at this point. This conflict between the ethics of charity and work is just one example of how different applications of the Christian belief system, together with denominational pluralism, have generated considerable confusion among non-Christian peoples; and this confusion, without being intended by Europeans, has increased the aboriginals' dependency (Manuel and Posluns 1974: 137).

At the present time, new typifications are appearing which have to do with the concept of "multiculturalism". According to these notions, native peoples are encouraged to preserve and develop indigenous cultures. Liberal elements in churches have supported the drive of native people for greater independence in recent years, and there have been suggestions that their cultural rights should become embodied in the legal system (Manuel and Posluns 1974: 232ff.; Hendry 1969: 15). Nonetheless, as activist, even militant, political behaviour on the part of Indian people increases, there is a danger that they will be typed as "fanatics" and "extremists", labels which have derogatory connotations in middle-class Canada. As a rule the churches openly support violence only when nation-states are at war. The middle classes, whether active in churches or not, are not likely to look favourably on attempts to secure social change by violent means. The widespread opposition to left-wing politics by the dominant religious elements in Canada has been broken only by the reformist ambitions of the Social Gospel movement.

Another question bearing on social control concerns the relationship between the degree of Christianization among native peoples and levels of political activism. Marxian premises can lead to the hypothesis that the more religious a group is the less involved it will be in struggling for a better socio-economic position. Religion, in this perspective, sidetracks the energy of alienated people into activities which provide psychological compensation and gratification but which do little to improve their economic and political position. The criticisms of religion by some political activists such as Harold Cardinal (1969) seem to support such a hypothesis. In contrast, however, the current revival of aboriginal religion appears to accompany a wave of renewed political activism. Obviously, the connection between religion and political reform or radicalism needs to be investigated more thoroughly.

Some scholars and government officials claim that missionaries have encouraged and helped to develop political activity among native peoples (Shankel 1945). That the Reverend Peter Kelly was a founding member of the Native Brotherhood of British Columbia is evidence of the churches' involvement (La Violette 1973: 156). There are also many examples of missionaries instructing native peoples in agricultural methods (Patterson 1972: 124–5).

Recent public statements by the social service branches of Canadian churches express profound distress over reactionary features in Canadian society which hinder equal justice and opportunity. Many of their leaders are strongly committed to developing alternative forms of social organization by means of community development, participatory democracy, and forms of social experimentation which depart from the *status quo*.

The Hendry Report commissioned by the Anglican Church includes among its top priorities "changes in basic attitudes, but also attitudes toward other churches working with native peoples and toward other agencies, including government. This clearly indicates that the Anglican Church of Canada must be prepared to collaborate with other organizations, but on the basis of critical assessment and whatever social or political action may be required" (Hendry 1969: 91). The report also draws attention to the legal situation of native peoples. It raises "the possibility of establishing some new principles of law, of breaking new ground in the relationship between Euro-Canadian (or other invading peoples) and aboriginal inhabitants. Among these principles might be an acknowledgement of the right of aboriginal peoples to have their laws, customs, and territories respected, or compensation granted for loss or impairment of any of these rights and institutions; and the payment of compensation for socio-cultural damage or dislocation, and the institution of effective mediating and rehabilitative measures when such damage and dislocation is caused" (Hendry 1969: 15). What could prove to be a major step in this direction was taken in November 1974 when the Cree people of the James Bay area won a settlement from the Quebec government for an amount reported to be about $150,000,000 in compensation for land to be flooded for power development, along with the right of participation in decisions affecting resettlement and the control of remaining resources. Such measures could represent a fundamental shift in the definition of the situation on the part of the dominant white group, which would lead to a basic change in the balance of power. But many Indian organizations across the country have strong doubts about the James Bay Cree settlement. It could ultimately increase their position of dependency.

The relationship between organized Christianity and the Canadian system of social stratification, then, is not a simple one. The foregoing brief and admittedly one-sided discussion is not intended to be a thorough study of the situation, but is aimed at illustrating the fruitfulness of approaching religion as a basic element in the development of a society's power structure. In the past the organized churches have maintained the domination and patronization of native peoples by Euro-Canadians. More recently, the large, orthodox denominations have advocated radical changes. But official statements and resolutions do not necessarily represent the views of diverse rank-and-file supporters.

The position of native people in Canada is becoming more acute and demanding. Recent events in Kenora, Cache Creek, and Calgary, the caravan to Ottawa, and the land claims of northern native peoples form a pattern which could lead to political, social, and economic changes in their position. The outcome will depend partly on the reformulation of meanings, definitions of the situation, and attitudes of Euro-Canadians. Public opinion with regard to Indian land claims is at present far from sympathetic, for reasons related to the main theme of this essay. Any ultimately satisfactory resolution of the situation will require a considerable redistribution of Canada's economic resources, a concrete extension of social opportunities, and, most important, the discovery of a method of enabling native peoples to make decisions about their own future. They will secure a place of worth and dignity in Canada only if the cultural meanings and attitudes discussed here are changed.

REFERENCES

Adams, I., et al.
1971   The Real Poverty Report.
        Edmonton: M. G. Hurtig.
Bennett, John W.
1971   "A Cree Indian Reserve." In
        J. L. Elliott, ed., Minority
        Canadians, Vol. 1. Native
        Peoples. Scarborough, Ont.:
        Prentice-Hall of Canada.
Berger, P.
1967   The Sacred Canopy. New York:
        Doubleday.
Canadian Corrections Association
1967   Indians and the Law. Ottawa:
        Canadian Welfare Council.
Cardinal, Harold
1969   The Unjust Society. Edmonton:
        M. G. Hurtig.
Carstens, Peter
1971   "Coercion and Change." In
        R. J. Ossenberg, ed., Canadian
        Society: Pluralism, Change and
        Conflict. Scarborough, Ont.:
        Prentice-Hall.
Clark, S. D.
1948   Church and Sect in Canada.
        Toronto: University of Toronto
        Press.
1962   The Developing Canadian
        Community. Toronto: University
        of Toronto Press.
Dailey, R. C.
1968   "The Role of Alcohol among
        North American Indian Tribes

as Reported in the Jesuit Rela-
        tions." Anthropologica, Vol. 10,
        No. 1.
Davis, M., and J. F. Krauter
1971   The Other Canadians. Toronto:
        Methuen.
Dawe, A.
1970   "The Two Sociologies." British
        Journal of Sociology 21, No. 2:
        207-18.
Dosman, E. J.
1972   Indians: The Urban Dilemma.
        Toronto: McClelland and
        Stewart.
Ferguson, J.
1970   "Social Change in the Western
        Arctic." In W. E. Mann, ed.,
        Social and Cultural Change in
        Canada 1: 27-50. Toronto: Copp
        Clark.
Giddens, A.
1968   " 'Power' in the Recent Writings
        of Talcott Parsons." Sociology
        2, No. 3: 257-72.
Grant, J. W.
1972   The Church in the Canadian
        Era. Toronto: McGraw-Hill
        Ryerson.
Guindon, Hubert
1960   "The Social Evolution of
        Quebec Reconsidered." Canadian
        Journal of Economics and
        Political Science 26 (Novem-
        ber): 533-51.

Hawthorn, H., *et al.*
1960   *The Indians of British Columbia.*
         University of Toronto Press
         and the University of British
         Columbia.
Hawthorn, H., ed.
1967   *A Survey of Contemporary
         Indians of Canada.* Vol. 11.
         Ottawa: Indian Affairs Branch.
Hendry, C. E.
1969   *Beyond Traplines.* Toronto:
         Maracle Press.
Klapp, O.
1962   *Heroes, Villains and Fools.*
         Englewood Cliffs, N.J.:
         Prentice-Hall.
La Violette, F. E.
1973   *The Struggle for Survival.*
         Toronto: University of Toronto
         Press.
Lipset, S. M.
1965   "Revolution and Counter Revo-
         lution: The United States and
         Canada." In T. Ford, ed., *The
         Revolutionary Theme in Con-
         temporary America.* University
         of Kentucky Press.
Lower, A. R. M.
1954   *This Most Famous Stream.*
         Toronto: Ryerson Press.
Manuel, G., and M. Posluns
1974   *The Fourth World.* Don Mills,
         Ont.: Collier-Macmillan.
Morton, A. S.
1973   *A History of the Canadian West
         to 1870–71.* Second Edition.

         L. G. Thomas, ed., Toronto:
         University of Toronto Press.
Parsons, G. P.
1970   *Arctic Suburb: A Look at the
         North's Newcomers.* MDRP.8.
         Ottawa: Northern Science
         Research Group, Department of
         Indian Affairs and Northern
         Development.
Patterson, E. P.
1972   *The Canadian Indian: A History
         Since 1500.* Don Mills, Ont.:
         Collier-Macmillan.
Porter, J.
1965   *The Vertical Mosaic.* Toronto:
         University of Toronto Press.
Schutz, A.
1970   *On Phenomenology and Social
         Relations.* Helmut R. Wagner,
         ed., Chicago: University of
         Chicago Press.
Shankel, G. E.
1945   "The Development of Indian
         Policy in British Columbia."
         Unpublished Ph.D. Thesis, Uni-
         versity of Washington, Seattle.
Vallee, F.
1971   "The Emerging Northern
         Mosaic." Ch. 7 in R. J. Ossen-
         berg, ed., *Canadian Society:
         Pluralism, Change and Conflict.*
         Scarborough, Ont.: Prentice-
         Hall.
Walsh, H. H.
1956   *The Christian Church in Canada.*
         Toronto: Ryerson Press.

The Sociology of the Social Gospel: Quest for a Modern Ideology*

Stewart Crysdale

1. The Rise of the New Liberalism

The contribution of the Social Gospel to Canadian development in the first four decades of this century is to be examined here as an aspect of a widespread quest for an ideology that would accord with contemporary social realities. Although this quest assumed certain forms that were peculiar to Canada, especially in Saskatchewan, where special needs arose, the general social and cultural background was shared by western, modernizing societies. The classical liberal ideology, which in the mid-nineteenth century was expressed in economic terms by Adam Smith's doctrine of *laissez-faire,* was no longer acceptable to many people, especially those whose status had become lowered or threatened. The social problems which accompanied industrialism in the nineteenth and early twentieth centuries—disorganized urbanization, intolerable working conditions, widespread unemployment, bad housing, and poor

*Based on a paper presented at a Conference on the Social Gospel in Canada at the University of Saskatchewan, Regina, March 1973. An expanded form of this paper appears in Richard Allen, ed., *The Social Gospel in Canada,* The Museum of Man Mercury Series (Ottawa: National Museums of Canada, 1975), Chap. 9, pp. 263-89.

health, in contrast with huge fortunes made by the economic elite—
destroyed earlier illusions of a benevolent, unseen Hand at work in
the unfolding of all history. Men could no longer take their societies for
granted. The writings of Karl Marx and others, advocating the replacement of the capitalist system by socialism or communism, gripped the
imagination of reformers and formed a basis for some influential alternative ideologies.

About the same time in several western countries, including Britain
and later the United States and Canada, a more progressive form of
liberalism arose. This provided the intellectual basis for another alternative ideology, less incisive than communism, but, as events proved, more
congenial for middle and upper classes in most western, pluralistic societies. A central tenet of this ideology was that man should vigorously
seek mastery of his natural and social environment. Joined with the
traditional humanistic-theistic faith was a new belief in the ability of
applied science to bring about the Millennium. For some the latter
replaced the former, but for the majority religion and science lurked in
the inner recesses of faith in uneasy balance.

The new liberalism was expressed in systematic theological form
notably by Albrecht Ritschl. It was applied to economic and political
life in Britain by the early Christian socialists, F. D. Maurice, John M.
Ludlow, and Charles Kingsley, among others. Although their ideas at the
mid-nineteenth century did not attract a large following, they reappeared
in subsequent decades in several forms, including the co-operative movement. But it took the rise of the Labour Party and the thrust of secular,
socialist thought in Britain to develop a significant measure of popular
support for the new liberalism.

In the United States, Christian socialism was unable to attract a significant following. Rather, the rise of the new liberal ideology there took
the form of a distinctive type of Social Gospel which called into question
the abusive excesses of free enterprise but did not challenge the fundamental tenets of capitalism. The Social Gospel became a social movement, though a diffuse one, among middle-class American church people
in the first two decades of the twentieth century. It lacked a single, clear-
cut focus in spite of the strong, reformative writings and addresses of
leaders such as Washington Gladden, George F. Peabody, and Walter
Rauschenbusch (1907). Nevertheless, a host of religious leaders became
convinced that the traditional emphasis on individual salvation and piety
fell short of expressing the whole gospel, which was also concerned with
men's everyday life together. The largely unregulated expansion of the

economy, which resulted in the enrichment of a few and the exploitation of multitudes, must be modified by a larger measure of public control and by the self-governance of leaders in private enterprise who would implement the teachings of Jesus and His Kingdom of justice, brotherhood, and love (Obenhaus 1965: 18–23; Hutchinson 1953: 8–12).

This reliance on individual initiative and voluntary rectitude, in effect, was not too different from classical liberalism. It flourished principally in the United States, one may speculate, because of rapid expansion there, sustained by a growing, enterprising population which was engaged in subduing enormous natural resources. Although the Social Gospel in the United States failed to engender what might be called a new ideology, it did contribute to a broadening of the role of the churches in American life. The movement engendered a measure of support among church bodies for emerging labour organizations, agricultural reform, and the provision of social services for low-income workers, the aged, and the infirm. One consequence was the formation of the Federal Council of Churches and its liaison with labour and moderate reform groups. The Social Gospel in the United States also quickened social consciousness and stimulated the early development of sociological enquiry into the causes and effects of social processes and structures (Obenhaus 1965: 20–3).

By comparison with its course in Britain and the United States, the Social Gospel in western Canada was more closely linked with the social and political forces which sought a radical departure from traditional, liberal ideology. Although the thrust of the Canadian movement as a distinct entity was largely spent by the end of the second decade of this century, it played an influential role in initiating and legitimating socialist ideology in the 1930s and 1940s. By that time, while the movement had dispersed, its values, beliefs, and norms had become familiar in liberal and radical circles and were incorporated into the platform of the new Co-operative Commonwealth Federation (the socialist-democratic group which later became the New Democratic Party). Indeed, some of the moderate proposals of the Social Gospel were adopted also by the old major parties, the Liberals and later the Progressive Conservatives.

2. An Historical-Experiential Perspective and Typology of Response to Change

The Social Gospel eludes a simple and inclusive definition. It is a term which can be applied to a wide variety of individuals and groups who emphasize one aspect of Christian belief—the responsibility of each person for his neighbours and for the development of just social and political institutions. The Social Gospel gathered sufficient momentum in Canada in the 1910s and 1920s to comprise a social movement.

A social movement arises when large numbers of persons feel that some of the central values and structures of the prevailing order are no longer able to meet their essential needs and they agree, more or less, upon a program of reform, revolution, or salvation. Social movements aim at changing the social order on a large scale and at a high level of norms, values, and ideology. They have long-term goals and centre around a continuing core of leaders (Crysdale and Beattie 1973: 43). The Social Gospel in Canada was reformist in that it did not reject all the dominant values and norms of society, but in some quarters, especially in Saskatchewan, it was also radical, if not revolutionary, in its purposes and program. It proposed a fundamental change in the social structure, namely the transfer of ownership of natural and capital resources from private into public hands. A particular role of the Social Gospel in the Canadian West, then, was to re-interpret the central values or goals of justice and brotherhood, which had deep religious sanctions, and to reject what radical Social Gospel leaders and adherents considered to be an outmoded secular value or goal—the amassing of private fortunes through the individual ownership of the means of production. It did not go as far as communism, for it retained the religious basis of ultimate authority, and existing forms of constitutional and parliamentary democracy as the valid means of government. Moreover, it rejected the communist belief in class conflict as the primary dynamic for historical evolution. Rather, in its western-Canadian form, it espoused moderate, parliamentary socialism.

This discussion assumes that religious beliefs and behaviour represent a reality in history and social experience that is valid in its own right and is not reducible to functions of the biological, economic, or political needs and actions of men and groups. Apart from this perspective, it is not possible to understand phenomena such as the Social Gospel, their meanings for the persons or actors involved, and their implications for the values, norms, and structures of the society of which they form a part (Berger and Luckmann 1966; Bellah 1970: Chs. 2 and 15; O'Dea 1966).

This perspective, which may be called historical-experiential, takes religion at its face value because of the consequences it has for human behaviour and thus for social processes and structures. The attempts by Freud to reduce religion to an illusion which would give way to a social reality conceived on a higher plan of biological and rational need-fulfilment, by Durkheim to explain religion in terms of its functional necessity in holding society together, and by Marx to predict its demise along with capitalism which had created it are all posited on an over-simplification of human experiences and of the perceptions of the realities which men construct. In every society and age there are many who seek a set of beliefs which are non-empirical and thus not subject to quantitative proof, beliefs whose ultimate reference is beyond the fragmentary experiences of time, space, and the senses, yet which seek expression and partial validation within those experiences.

The Social Gospel, as it emerged in the Canadian West, expressed for its believers an over-arching framework of meaning that was needed in a social situation where the old ideologies and social structures were no longer valid. It promised not only to resolve the economic and political issues of the times through its programs of common action, but to link the individual with society in a positive, fulfilling manner that was consistent with basic beliefs.

It is arguable that the emphasis of the Social Gospel on the problems of society rather than on the problems of the individual was the result of growing secularization, and thus represented another diminution in the influence and validity of religion in the scientific age. But such theologians as Paul Tillich (1951), Harvey Cox (1965), and John T. Robinson (1963) hold that, while in the past religion rested on supernatural, otherworldly foundations, its secularity today represents an outgrowth of Christian teaching which stresses man's responsibility for moral action in the present situation. Similarly, Thomas Luckmann (1967) reasons that religion in modern societies often rests not on supernatural sources of legitimation but on whatever beliefs may assume dominance. Sometimes a secular religion emerges which legitimates a political or economic ideology or a humanitarian set of values. John Porter (1965: Ch. 15) observes that in complex nation-states the problems of cohesion and maintenance of basic values are so great that ideologies are necessary to hold them together. These ideologies are essentially transcendent, whether their orientation is towards heaven, towards an inward, spiritual condition, or towards a secular, ideal society or utopia. "Value systems," Porter writes, "particularly at the level of popular consumption, appear always to be dominated by super-empirical, religious modes of thought, even in societies with a rational science and an industrial economy" (1965: 458).

It is important for the purposes of analysis to distinguish between religion as such and ideology. In the broad sense in which it is discussed here, religion, to draw on Charles Glock and Rodney Stark (1965: 4), refers to what people hold to be sacred and "comprises an institutionalized system of symbols, beliefs, values, and practices focused on questions of ultimate meaning". An ideology, on the other hand, is a set of interdependent values and beliefs, affirmed by members of a social system, which express and justify a particular set of religious, economic, or political values and structures. Sometimes, as in simple, closed societies, religion and ideology may be coterminous, but in complex societies, the historic world religions are too broad, universal, and transcendent to be identical with national or even international ideologies. Frequently, some religious groups are in conflict with one or more aspects of the prevailing ideology. This was the case, we suggest, with the Social Gospel, particularly in western Canada.

The Social Gospel had some of the qualities of the world-affirming, critical, and innovative sect. It did not resemble a pure type of sect because its believers were widely scattered and heterogeneous; they came from different religious and ethnic backgrounds. But the more radical among them joined in protest against the excesses of private enterprise, against the weakness or obduracy of the old parties and the federal and provincial governments, and against the complacency and worldly compromises of the majority of church members. In many cases, Social Gospel devotees left pulpits and pews and took up active positions in labour organizations, political parties, education, research, and social work. Often they were bound together by study and action groups, by personal communications, and by periodicals. They also provided sacred legitimation for the socialist reorganization of society. From the 1920s on, however, the sect-like attributes of the Social Gospel gave way to more formal structures in political organizations, in the profession of social work, and in liberal or reform elements within the mainline churches, notably the Methodist and, later, after its formation in 1925, the United Church of Canada.

3. The Special Case of the Social Gospel in Saskatchewan

The Social Gospel at the national level had a brief, varied, and influential career.* The only area, however, where public sentiment swung strongly to the left was Saskatchewan. There the seeds of the Social Gospel and the sympathy of British settlers for labour and socialism were nourished by a combination of other factors and brought to a head by the failure of the wheat crop and the collapse of the world markets and economy. This convergence of factors led western proponents of the Social Gospel along radical lines and prepared the way for a populist, and, later, a socialist, political movement.

Here we may list the social, economic, and political conditions which provided a fertile bed for the radical elements of the Social Gospel, and which generated in Saskatchewan a new, socialist ideology as an option for Canadian society.

The Prairies provided one of the last rural frontiers for settlement in North America in the opening decades of the twentieth century. Across its plains and into its new towns flooded several hundred thousand newcomers from many ethnic and cultural backgrounds, imbued with the hope of establishing successful farms, businesses, and professions. Widespread common goals and interests provided the first condition for the rise of a social movement and the forging of a new ideology.

The building of new towns, roads, schools, churches, and telephone systems brought people together and fostered secondary associations. These were undergirded by neighbourhood and kinship ties between overlapping circles of people. Through reciprocal helpfulness and support, in work bees, and in sharing happy and tragic events, a strong sense of common identity emerged.

A large proportion of newcomers in Saskatchewan were of British stock, with heightened class consciousness. Many of them were receptive to the ideas of the British Fabian socialists. At the same time, when the Great Depression struck in neighbouring Alberta, the politically conservative but economically radical Social Credit movement swept into power in 1935 under the charismatic preaching and political leadership of a Baptist—William Aberhart (Mann 1955; Irving 1959). An important difference between the political situation of the two provinces, according to the Graysons (1974), was that in the 1935 Alberta election, parties in opposition to the Social Credit had lost credibility—the United Farmers' leader was involved in a sex scandal—and the CCF had not yet gained force. In Saskatchewan by 1944 the CCF was the only credible alternative, as the monetary reforms promised by the Social Credit in

---

*See Crysdale, "Social Awakening among Protestants, 1872-1918", in this volume, also 1961, *The Industrial Struggle and Protestant Ethics in Canada* (Toronto: Ryerson Press).

1935 had been blocked by federal opposition. Moreover, whereas Alberta had William Aberhart, the CCF in Saskatchewan had its own charismatic leader—Tommy Douglas, a Baptist minister turned politician-reformer. His skills in strategy, intellectual capacity, and oratory, his tireless campaigning, and his self-sacrificing commitment were big assets in the CCF victory.

In Saskatchewan especially, at regional and provincial levels, economic and political institutions were built around the wheat economy, with links at the grassroots level. The introduction of new species of wheat, new farming methods and techniques, and the establishment of marketing organizations, credit unions, and co-operatives bound the new population into a cohesive whole. Lipset (1968) has documented the remarkably high level of participation in secondary organizations of various sorts at the local, regional, and provincial levels. All of this helped enormously in the espousal of a new ideology and a religious-political movement when a major crisis appeared.

The rise of indigenous agricultural organizations with economic and political purposes followed the rapid growth of the wheat economy. These assumed the nature of populist movements, linked with similar movements in the American west, when it became apparent that the farmers would have to stand together and fight for concessions from federal governments, banks, mortgage corporations, and railways (Allen 1971). Early in their social experience the farmers and townspeople learned the realities of economic and political conflict.

Isolation from the established centres of financial and political power in Ontario and Quebec sharpened the westerners' sense of unity and polarity, even before the Great Depression. This isolation was not only a matter of two thousand miles; it was also apparent in economic and political interests and in life-styles. Careless (1954) has drawn attention to the strong influence of metropolitan centres in shaping Canadian society—notably Montreal, Toronto, and more recently Vancouver. The conflicts which emerged between the rural hinterland and metropolitan centres of power have been traced by Davis (1971). These were largely unresolved in the early decades of this century and contributed to the growing desire of westerners for radical change.

Reference has already been made to the widespread modification of classical liberalism to emphasize justice and equalitarianism in the late nineteenth and early twentieth centuries. Unrestrained individualism fell into disrepute and was tempered by a moderate collectivism, although, as noted, this trend was offset, particularly in the United States, by the drive towards individual achievement in mastering the environment. In Canada, however, expansion has been marked consistently by greater reliance on public, governmental participation or control. This dependence was manifest particularly in Saskatchewan, where public action was required to sell and transport huge crops abroad. If governments could see that railroads and port facilities were built and marketing services provided, why could they not also manage the development of other resources for the common good? The Social Gospel encouraged this reasoning with its emphasis on social rather than individual aspects of religion (Clark 1948: 431).

Against the background of these factors, the disaster of the World Depression of 1929 to 1940 and the successive droughts of the early 1930s were powerful catalysts in bringing about a general demand for profound social change. The failure of former governments to remedy widespread poverty and hardship and the untiring efforts of farm, labour, and religious proponents of socialism in Saskatchewan finally won a majority of electors in 1944, and the first socialist government in North America came into power.

The diffuse character of the Social Gospel permitted it to have a wide variety of consequences. On the one hand, persons of left-wing persuasion in farming, labour, small businesses, and churches united to develop strong support for populist and then socialist endeavours. On the other hand, persons in secular groups and churches who also were imbued with social consciousness but whose political leanings were more conservative devoted their energies to ameliorative programs such as moral reform, temperance, and social welfare. But while the Social Gospel stimulated a diversity of progressive action it could not sustain itself as a unified movement. By 1928, as Richard Allen (1971) records, it had peaked and begun to fragment and disappear. Its effects continued, nevertheless, for some years, for example, in the work of the Fellowship for a Christian Social Order, begun in 1931, and the publication in 1936 of *Toward the Christian Revolution*, edited by R. B. Y. Scott and Gregory Vlastos.

In summary, the Social Gospel contributed to the emergence of the socialist ideology in Saskatchewan in the following ways.

(a) It specified the common needs of the population for a new political philosophy and an economic program on a wide scale to cope with new conditions, namely, the breakdown of capitalism under the blows of world depression and the incapacity of traditional political parties to initiate large-scale efforts to re-organize the means of production, marketing, and distribution of benefits and rewards.

(b) It compared the realities of the present—the injustices of inequitable rewards and opportunities as between social classes and regions—with the realities of the ideal commonwealth, modelled on the teachings of Jesus Christ and the Old Testament prophets. This contrast had the effect of legitimating the socialist ideology and platform by reference to divine authority, which was recognized with varying degrees of faith and with different interpretations by most of the population.

(c) It redefined the social situation, bringing into one camp people of different ethnic, occupational, and religious backgrounds on the basis of their common needs, and offering them, in place of disillusionment and despair, the promise and hope of a better society, a New Jerusalem of their own making. Through this vision, which was reinforced by day-to-day committee meetings, organizational chores, and public rallies, the people assumed a common identity, relating to the ideal future rather than to the discredited past and the unpromising present.

REFERENCES

Allen, Richard
1971   *The Social Passion.* Toronto: University of Toronto Press.
Bellah, Robert
1970   *Beyond Belief.* New York: Harper and Row.
Berger, Peter, and Thomas Luckmann
1966   *The Social Construction of Reality.* Garden City: Doubleday.
Bland, Salem
1920   *The New Christianity.* Toronto: McClelland and Stewart.
Careless, J. M. S.
1954   "Frontierism, Metropolitanism, and Canadian History." *Canadian Historical Review*, Vol. 35, No. 1 (March).
Clark, S. D.
1948   *Church and Sect in Canada.* Toronto: University of Toronto Press.
Cox, Harvey
1965   *The Secular City.* Don Mills, Ont.: Collier-Macmillan.

Crysdale, Stewart
1961   *The Industrial Struggle and Protestant Ethics in Canada.* Toronto: Ryerson Press.
———, and Christopher Beattie
1973   *Sociology Canada.* Toronto: Butterworth.
Davis, Arthur K.
1971   "Canadian Society and History as Hinterland Versus Metropolis." In R. J. Ossenberg, ed., *Canadian Society: Pluralism, Change, and Conflict.* Scarborough, Ont.: Prentice-Hall.
Glock, Charles, and Rodney Stark
1965   *Religion and Society in Tension.* Chicago: Rand McNally.
Hutchinson, John A., ed.
1953   *Christian Faith and Social Action.* New York: Charles Scribner's Sons.
Irving, John A.
1959   *The Social Credit Movement in Alberta.* Toronto: University of Toronto Press.

Lipset, Seymour M.
1968   (1950) *Agrarian Socialism.*
        New York: Doubleday.
Luckmann, Thomas
1967   *The Invisible Religion.* London:
        Macmillan.
Mann, W. E.
1955   *Sect, Cult and Church in Alberta.*
        Toronto: University of Toronto
        Press.
Obenhaus, Victor
1965   *Ethics For an Industrial Age.*
        New York: Harper and Row.
O'Dea, Thomas F.
1966   *The Sociology of Religion.*
        Englewood Cliffs, N.J.: Prentice-
        Hall.

Porter, John
1965   *The Vertical Mosaic.* Toronto:
        University of Toronto Press.
Rauschenbusch, Walter
1907   *Christianity and the Social
        Crisis.* London: Macmillan.
Robinson, John T.
1963   *Honest to God.* London: SCM
        Press.
Scott, R. B. Y., and Gregory Vlastos
1936   eds., *Towards the Christian
        Revolution.* Chicago: Willett
        Clarke.
Tillich, Paul
1951   *Systematic Theology,* Vol. 1.
        Chicago: University of Chicago
        Press.

Religion and Voting:
The 1968 Federal Election in Ontario*

Lynn McDonald

An Overview

In Canada, research has shown voting preferences to be invariably associated with religious affiliation, and that association is at least as strong as, or stronger than, those between voting and any other variable, such as social class or ethnicity (Alford 1963; Anderson 1966; Regenstreif 1965; Gagne and Regenstreif 1967; Meisel 1956; Cameron 1966). Religious affiliation has also been found to have an important association with voting preferences wherever the subject of voting has been studied —in the United States, Europe, and the Commonwealth countries for the most part. The Canadian pattern is unusual only in that religion has an even greater influence than it has in other countries, and that social class (which is the most important influence on voting in most countries) is of less importance than religion in explaining Canadian voting behaviour.

Religious differences are particularly known to affect the social life of rural areas and small towns of Ontario. People have long been sus-

*Appeared first in Lynn McDonald, "Religion and Voting: A Study of the 1968 Canadian Federal Election in Ontario", in *Canadian Review of Sociology and Anthropology* 6, No. 3 (1969): 129-44. Published here in abridged form with the kind permission of the author and the publisher.

picious of the power and evil motivation of the other side. The Orange Lodge, an important organization for years in Ontario, is still active if no longer powerful. In Meisel's Kingston study one-quarter of the people voting Conservative offered, without being asked directly, anti-French or anti-Catholic reasons for their party preference (Meisel 1956).

Marriage across religious lines, although increasing, is still relatively uncommon. In Ontario, only 20 per cent of Protestants and 15 per cent of Catholics marry outside their religion (Heer 1962). This is lower than in the United States, where estimates range between 30 and 50 per cent for Catholics marrying outside their church (Chancellor and Manahan 1955; Duvall and Hill 1953).

In other words, the lines between Protestants and Catholics are fairly well drawn and the groups are relatively homogeneous. Despite the fact that Ontario is a highly urban, industrial province, it should provide a reasonable setting for testing of hypotheses on religious influence.

Although the association of religion and voting is well established, it is curious that very little empirical work has been done to ascertain how or why religion has such an influence. And, despite the fact that religion is the most important variable affecting voting in Canada, there have been only a few studies exploring the nature of religious influence here (Meisel 1956; Anderson 1966; Gagne and Regenstreif 1967).

In this paper we shall examine the relationship of several dimensions of religion to voting. These can be grouped to provide three basic types of explanation.

1. Religious groups are in effect interest groups. Just as occupational groups have different interests and pursue different political goals, the religious groups have different interests, and accordingly they lean to different parties to advance their goals. Religious groups in Canada differ with respect to social class and ethnic composition as well as ideology and ritual. Social class and ethnic group status, of course, affect the stake members have in society, giving the members of the religious groups cause to support different political parties. Given the durability of party identification, the present religion-voting association could be a carry-over from earlier conditions and could even occur without current (or with only minimal) social class and ethnic differences.

2. The various religious groups may have some distinctive beliefs that affect their political orientations. Concern about Catholic separate schools could make Catholics support the Liberal Party, and disapproval of the separate system could make some Protestants favour the Con-

servative. The Protestant religion, through a greater emphasis on individual responsibility, may stimulate attitudes of economic conservatism, and eventually a disproportionately Conservative vote.

3. Finally, a simple reason (though only an explanation in a superficial sense) may be that people vote for the candidate of their own religion where they have a choice. Since the Liberal Party typically runs more Catholics and fewer Protestants than the Conservative, and the Conservative Party more Protestant and fewer Catholics than the Liberal, this could account for the existing voting pattern. It would then be necessary to explain why voters considered it important to vote for a candidate of their own religion—which brings us back to the first two points.

The Data

The data are drawn from a larger survey conducted at the time of the 25 June 1968 federal election. Interviews were obtained from 1,916 eligible voters living in Ontario. The five northernmost constituencies, which contain 4.6 per cent of the population, were excluded, as the cost of fieldwork would have been prohibitive. The interviews were conducted in the respondents' homes, mostly in the three weeks preceding the election, the remainder in July and early August. The survey fieldwork was carried out by a commercial market research firm.

Two samples were drawn,[1] both from the voters' list compiled for the Ontario provincial election of October, 1967. One was a stratified (by community size) random sample from which 1,424 eligible voters, or 75.5 per cent of the original sample, were actually interviewed. The second was an additional sample of French-speaking persons in the ten counties with the highest proportion of Franco-Ontarians, which account for 74 per cent of the French-speaking population of Ontario. The yield in this sample, which required a screening interview first to find out if there was a French-speaking voter in the household, was 88.9 per cent.

A comparison of voting intentions given in the survey with actual election results is shown in Table 1.

Clearly, the sample is very similar to its population, the electorate. However, the Liberal vote was higher amongst respondents interviewed after the election than before, presumably because of the bandwagon effect of the Liberal victory. Voters interviewed after the election have been kept in the analysis, as their elimination would have made the

TABLE 1. Voting Intentions of Ontario Residents

	STATED VOTING INTENTIONS (PER CENT)	POPULAR VOTE (PER CENT)
Conservative	33	33
Liberal	50	47
NDP	17	20
N	1,020[a]	2,785,264

[a]Includes respondents interviewed before the election, and only in the general sample.

sample unrepresentative in terms of region. The effect of the over-reporting of Liberal voting is to diminish correlations slightly.

Before we go on to test the hypothesis on the effect of the various components of religiosity we should first show the effect of religious affiliation itself. Table 2 indicates that Catholics vote disproportionately Liberal, Protestants Conservative, the consistent finding of Canadian voting studies.

The Effect of Religious Group Interests

Politics is essentially the struggle between the haves and the have-nots. Where political parties are organized, this cleavage is reflected in the party system.

The Liberal Party in Canada is the particular representative of have-not interests in terms of religion and ethnicity. However, in social class terms, its supporters actually constitute a representative cross-section of Canadian society, making it a party of neither the weak nor the strong. But religion and ethnicity in Canada have particularly strong social class implications.

Non-Protestants and persons of non-British background are substantially under-represented in the economic, political, and judicial elites of Canada (Porter 1965). As people of this background do have a common disadvantage, there is some scope for religious and ethnic cleavage (which largely reinforce each other) to be of importance in Canadian politics. Religious affiliation does affect one's basic power position in society; Protestants are disproportionately in a position they wish to preserve, Catholics in a position they wish to improve.

TABLE 2.   Religious Affiliation and Federal Voting

	PROTESTANT	RC	JEW[b]	NO RELIGION[b]	PROTESTANT-RC DIFFERENCE
GENERAL SAMPLE (per cent)[d]					
British middle class					
Conservative	46.1	27.4	—	12.8	18.7[c]
Liberal	46.5	65.2	—	73.1	18.7[c]
NDP	7.4	7.4	—	14.1	—
Non-British middle class					
Conservative	39.5	12.7	6.2	13.1	26.8[c]
Liberal	46.0	78.1	93.8	59.5	32.1[c]
NDP	14.6	9.2	0.0	27.3	5.4
British working class					
Conservative	37.5	18.6	—	18.8	18.9[c]
Liberal	36.3	62.1	—	41.5	25.8[c]
NDP	26.2	19.2	—	39.7	7.0
Non-British working class					
Conservative	29.9	6.7	0.0	17.0	23.2[c]
Liberal	34.9	82.9	100.0	35.6	48.0[c]
NDP	35.2	10.3	0.0	47.3	24.9[c]

$N = 1,558$.

[a]Since the cases are weighted, the usual statistical tests cannot be applied. Instead, variances were computed for the proportions in the following tables. The difference between two proportions can be considered statistically significant if it is at least as great as twice the standard deviation of the difference. This note also applies to Tables 3, 4, 6, and 8.

[b]These figures are given for illustration only; the numbers are too low to be statistically significant.

[c]Statistically significant differences.

[d]There were not enough French-Canadian Protestants for any Protestant-Catholic comparison to be made within the French sample.

The Liberal Party's Catholic, non-British associations are well enough known that it is legitimate to assume that people of that background make the association between their status and the Liberal Party. The Liberal Party has run non-Wasp candidates more than the Conservative. The Liberal Party has encouraged immigration from non-Wasp countries more than the Conservative, another factor which publicizes the Liberal–non-Wasp association.

The NDP is ineligible for much of the have-not vote of Catholics it might otherwise merit on social class grounds. It still has something of a reputation, on account of its materialistic doctrines, for being an anti-Catholic if not anti-Christian movement. Indeed, in Montreal until 1944 it was officially a sin for a Catholic to vote for the predecessor of the

NDP, the CCF (Ballantyne 1963). Consequently the Liberal Party may get some of its support from Catholics by default.

Hypothesis 1: Religious Group Identification and Voting

We shall hypothesize that anything that increases Catholic awareness of their group identity and interests will increase the Liberal vote amongst Catholics, and anything that increases Protestant awareness of their group identity and interests will increase their Conservative voting.

The specific indicators of religious group involvement are: membership in parish and other church organizations; communalism (Lenski 1961: 23);[2] anti-Catholic attitudes;[3] social distance from Catholics;[4] frequency of attendance at services.[5]

Two other indicators of more traditional aspects of religiosity have also been included so that the effects of social involvement can be compared with those of non-social dimensions. These are: devotionalism (Lenski 1961: 57)[6] and orthodoxy (Lenski 1961: 56).[7] There should be a higher Liberal vote among the more committed Catholics, and a higher Conservative vote among the more committed Protestants than among the less committed groups respectively. NDP voting should be higher among less committed Protestants and Catholics.

There is only partial support for these hypotheses. Religious communalism failed to be significantly associated with voting behaviour. Church attendance did show some association, especially in the French sample and among Protestants in the general sample. This variable (the only one to have been put to a test previously in Canada) has already been shown to have some effect on voting (Gagne and Regenstreif 1967; Anderson 1966; Meisel 1964).

Membership in parish organizations had a significant association in the French sample, and in one group in the general sample. Membership in any kind of organization with a religious connection (such as the Masons, and Orange Lodge) had an effect in the general sample, but not in the French.

Devotionalism was not related to voting behaviour, but orthodoxy was as strongly associated as the social involvement indices. Thus, there is at least one dimension of religiosity, apart from social relationships, associated with voting choices.

One further test of the social involvement hypothesis could be made. If social involvement affects voting, then differences between Protestants and Catholics in voting preferences should be greater among those who are highly committed to their group than between those who are less committed. A test of this proposition requires controlling for extent of involvement, as well as ethnicity and social class, and making religious affiliation the independent variable. When differences in voting in the low-involvement group were subtracted from the differences in voting found in the high-involvement group, Protestant-Catholic differences were found to be strong in both the high- and the low-commitment groups. The differences were substantially stronger in the more committed group only in the case of church attendance. Consequently, this hypothesis must be rejected.

The Effect of Religion Through Specific Issues

Religious differences put people on different sides of disputes over certain issues. This may be due to certain social aspects of religion as discussed above, or for reasons of doctrine, or for some other reason. Although the issue itself may ultimately be solved to the reasonable satisfaction of all parties, there is a tendency for people to continue to support the side they took during the actual crisis. The issue of concern for our purposes is that of separate school education.

Historical studies of early Canadian politics are replete with instances of inter-religious struggles over education. Over the years, the parties have advocated different positions at different times in different provinces. There have been compromises on both sides. There have been internal disputes as well. One of the most bitter and long-lasting of the disputes, the Manitoba schools question, saw Laurier, the Liberal leader and a Catholic, opposed to the Conservatives and the Catholic bishops. However, even with certain qualifications, the Liberal Party has generally supported the Catholic position and the Conservative Party the Protestant. The Liberals have favoured either a separate school system or at least some public support for the Catholic schools or other accommodation to Catholic education. The Conservative Party has more often favoured a completely non-sectarian public school system, with no public support for any school outside it. The issue is an old one, clearly ante-dating Confederation. The BNA Act attempted to avoid religious conflict over schools by guaranteeing minority religious groups with already established schools the right to continue to have them. At the present time there are either separate school systems or some method of assigning public tax support to separate schools in all the provinces but British Columbia.

However, conflict has erupted to some extent in most provinces at some time. In only two of the provinces, however, has the schools question caused prolonged and bitter division—Ontario and Manitoba. Both these disputes became national issues of long-lasting importance. The Ontario question, which was a problem of language as well as of religion, created immensely bitter feelings which affected French-English, Catholic-Protestant relations in other matters. The conflict was fought in the courts, the House of Commons, the provincial legislature, and local school boards for years. The profoundly divisive conscription issue in 1917 was made more critical by the conflict over the schools issue during the preceding five years. The federal elections of 1919 and 1921 were affected by the issue also.

The major conflicts took place decades ago. However, there have been enough minor events in the intervening years to ensure that the problems have not been forgotten. British Columbia Catholics still work intermittently for some public support for their parochial schools. Ontario Catholics are presently trying to extend the separate school system, which now ends at grade ten, through to the end of high school. Opposition to this attempt has come mainly from the Orange Lodge.

Issues of very great importance affect voting patterns long after they cease to be critical as issues. The effects of the Depression on voting in the United States were still easily noticeable in the 1950s, and are probably still of some importance (Campbell 1960). The conscription issue in Canada in 1917 caused a major realignment in voting patterns, which has never since been reversed. (The Diefenbaker swing in 1958 brought some of the Quebec vote back to the Conservative Party, but only temporarily.)

We cannot ascertain whether or not the struggle over schools affected people's party identification at the time of one or other of these crises. We can hypothesize that people's present views on separate school support is associated with their present voting preferences, a weak proxy for the question of interest.

Hypothesis 2: Opinions on Separate School Support and Voting

It is hypothesized that there will be a higher proportion of Conservative voting and lower Liberal voting among persons opposed to increased financial support for separate schools than those who favour it, controlling for religion, ethnicity, and social class.

The data show that this issue did not have the predicted association. Protestants who opposed the extension of financial aid to Catholic separate schools were no more likely to vote Conservative in the 1968 federal election than those who approved it. Catholics who wanted to see this aid extended were no more likely to vote Liberal than those who were satisfied with the present level. However, since education is a matter of provincial jurisdiction, any effect of views on separate schools might be at the provincial level. But the relationship of provincial voting choices and attitudes on separate schools was in fact no greater than at the federal.

The Effect of "Protestant Ethic" Attitudes

Religious affiliation could affect voting through intervening attitudes on the welfare state. Protestants may subscribe more to the protestant ethic, one of the consequences of which could be political and economic conservatism. Lenski found Protestant-Catholic differences in a number of these respects in the Detroit Area Study (Lenski 1961). However, in this study Protestants were only very marginally less favourable to welfare state provisions than Catholics. Consequently, analysis as to the effect of welfare state attitudes on voting would have been pointless.

Religious differences clearly do not appear to have had any association with voting through orientations on specific issues. So far, the effect of religion has been seen to occur almost entirely through the social aspects of involvement in a religious group.

The Effect of the Candidate's Religion

Political parties believe that if they run a Catholic candidate he will draw Catholic voters from other parties but may lose former Protestant supporters, while a Protestant will draw Protestant voters, or at least lose Catholic voters. Although the hypothesis could not be more simple, it is difficult to test. Since the Conservative and New Democratic parties do not run many Catholic candidates, it is difficult to compare the relative drawing power of Catholic and Protestant candidates.

The hypotheses have to be broken down into several particular comparisons.

Hypothesis 3: The Candidate's Religion and Voting

(a) That among Catholics there will be a higher proportion voting for Liberal candidates who are Catholic than for Liberal candidates who are Protestant, for Conservative candidates who are Catholic than for Conservative who are Protestant, and for NDP who are Catholic than for NDP who are Protestant.

(b) That among Protestants there will be a higher proportion voting for Conservative candidates who are Protestant than for Conservative candidates who are Catholic, for Liberal candidates who are Protestant than for Liberal who are Catholic, and for NDP who are Protestant than for NDP who are Catholic.

These hypotheses are clearly disconfirmed by the data. The lack of popularity of Catholic Conservatives among Catholic voters is explainable in that seven of the nine Catholic Conservatives were running against Catholic Liberals. However, basically the data show that voters did not prefer a candidate of their own religion over a candidate of another. Protestants voted more often for Protestant candidates than Catholic, but that is because Protestants are disproportionately Conservative and the Conservative Party runs mostly Protestants. When the Conservative Party runs a Catholic he will get the same support as a Protestant. The religion of the candidate may have had an effect earlier in forming party identification; and that is an important question that this research simply cannot answer. At the moment the religion of the candidate does not appear to have any measurable effect.

It is widely believed, by candidates and campaign managers even more fervently than by the public, that candidates of no religion are suspect to believers of all religious persuasions. Some candidates said they had no religious affiliation but did not want this information released (with their names attached to it). Several specifically said they thought they would lose votes if their lack of church membership were widely known. Most candidates do state a religion on the personal information they release, and many mention activity in church organizations as well.

There were enough candidates in the NDP stating no religion that the hypothesis that the irreligious candidate fares worse than the religious could be tested, at least to a degree. This could not be done for the Liberal and Conservative parties.

(c) It is hypothesized that amongst Catholics and Protestants alike there will be a lower proportion voting for NDP candidates of no religion than for candidates stating a religion. This hypothesis is also discon-firmed. The irreligious candidates were no less favoured than the religious. The Jewish NDP candidates actually did the best, and the Pro-testant clergymen the worst (among both Catholics and Protestants). However, as the numbers involved here are especially small, not much weight should be put on these remarks.

Voting at the Provincial Level

The question whether religious affiliation affects provincial voting in the same way as federal has never been examined in much detail. Except for Meisel's Kingston constituency study, voting studies have dealt only with federal or provincial elections (1956). That study found higher Conser-vative voting amongst Catholics at the provincial level than at the federal, but did not focus on the federal-provincial comparison.

It would be reasonable to expect religious differences to be more important at the provincial level than at the federal. Education is under provincial jurisdiction, and the dispute over Catholic education has been the main issue that has set Catholics and Protestants against each other in Canada.

Hypothesis 4: The Relative Effects of Religion at the Provincial and Federal Levels

It is hypothesized that Protestant-Catholic differences in voting prefer-ences will be stronger at the provincial level than at the federal—Catho-lics disproportionately preferring the Liberal Party, Protestants, the Con-servative. The provincial data show that the effect is of the same type as at the federal level, and of about the same strength. The hypothesis that it would be greater at the provincial level must be rejected. More Catho-lics vote Conservative at the provincial level than at the federal, but so do more Protestants. More Protestants vote Liberal federally than they do provincially, but so do Catholics.

Conclusions

We have considered three ways that religion could be associated with voting behaviour: through the strengthening of commitment to a distinct social group with distinct interests, through separating members of those groups on specific issues, and through the religion of the candidates run-

ning. The specific issues (support for the Catholic separate school system, and attitudes on the welfare state) showed no measurable effect at
all. The religion of the candidate showed some influence, however, only
in a hypothetical municipal level election. The religion of the candidates
in the 1968 federal election appeared to have had no effect. The candidate's religion is not strong enough an inducement to break the effect of
party identification. (It is, of course, possible that the religion of candidates running in the past might have influenced the initial formation of
party identification, a point on which we could gather no information.)

The dimension of religiosity having the strongest association with
voting proved to be social involvement in the religious community,
although even here more of the predicted relationships failed to appear
than actually did. The process of socializing informally, off church premises, presumably made people more aware of their secular, socio-economic interests. For Catholics this heightened awareness of the interests
of working class people, and for Protestants this increased awareness of
the interests of business and professional people.

Religious differences have the same kind and degree of effect on
voting at the provincial level as at the federal.

The list of non-findings in this study turns out to be longer than the
list of findings. Insofar as that is the case, the research has failed to meet
its objectives. The material has not taken us very far in answering the
fundamental question about the nature of the effect of religion, although
it has given some direction on the choice of variables for further work.
It suggests that such obvious and convenient explanations as issues and
the religion of the candidate should be avoided. It indicates that the
area to explore further for increasing understanding of the religious effect
is that of social involvement.

NOTES

1 By Dr. Ivan Fellegi of the Dominion
   Bureau of Statistics.
2 Degree to which relationships with
   friends and relatives are within own
   religious group.
3 The construction of this index is
   described in another paper, "Attitudes and Voting: A Study of the 1968
   Canadian Federal Election in Ontario",
   1969. The items on the index are:
   Catholics tend to be less objective in
   their thinking than Protestants; Protestants who go to the public schools are

bound to be more tolerant than Catholics who go to the Catholic separate
schools; if you had to choose between
having the top leaders in the country
all Catholic or all Protestant, it would
be better to have them all Protestant;
Catholics here are more prejudiced
against Protestants than Protestants
are against Catholics; what kind of
financial support do you think the
government should give the Catholic
separate schools in Ontario?
4 The Bogardus social distance con-

cept is followed here (1933). Respondents were asked to sort cards on to a board marked into three sections of distance they would want to have from the person described on the card. The hypothetical persons described included all combinations of Protestant or Catholic, French, English, or Italian Canadian, and doctor or truck driver. The religious social distance score is the distance preferred from Catholics minus distance preferred from Protestants.

5   Church attendance is treated here as a social dimension, although it is more than that. Previous studies have shown social class membership and membership in formal organizations generally to be associated with frequency of church attendance (Glock 1965: 188; Fukuyama 1961: 16; Demerath 1965). Also Lenski found attendance to increase with Americanization (1963: 45). Thus it would seem reasonable to group attendance with the social variables rather than with devotionalism or orthodoxy.

6   Frequency of prayer and frequency with which God's help is sought in important decisions.

7   Belief in: God, as Heavenly Father, life after death, hell, saviour, answered prayers, and God's expectation of weekly formal worship.

REFERENCES

Alford, R. R.
1963   *Party and Society*. Chicago: Rand McNally.
Anderson, G. M.
1966   "Voting Behaviour and the Ethnic-religious Variable: A Study of a Federal Election in Hamilton, Ontario." *Canadian Journal of Economics and Political Science* 32: 27-37.
Ballantyne, Murray G.
1963   "The Catholic Church and the CCF." Historical Association Report.
Bogardus, E.S.
1933   "A Social Distance Scale." *Sociology and Social Research* 17: 265-71.
Cameron, D. M.
1966   "An Electoral Analysis of Democratic Socialism in Ontario: CCF-NDP voting patterns, 1934–1963." Unpublished Phil. M. thesis, University of Toronto.
Campbell, Angus, *et al.*
1960   *The American Voter*. New York: John Wiley.
Chancellor, L. E., and T. P. Monahan
1955   "Religious Preference and Interreligious Mixtures in Marriages and Divorces in Iowa." *American Journal of Sociology* 61: 233-9.
Courtney, John C., ed.
1967   *Voting in Canada*. Scarborough, Ont.: Prentice-Hall.

Demerath, N. J., III
1965   *Social Class in American Protestantism*. Chicago: Rand, McNally.
Duvall, E. M., and R. Hill
1953   *When You Marry*. New York: D. C. Heath.
Fukuyama, Yoshio
1961   *Styles of Church Membership*. New York: United Church Board for Homeland Ministries.
Gagne, Wallace, and Peter Regenstreif
1967   "Some Aspects of New Democratic Party Urban Support in 1965." Mimeo, University of Rochester.
Glock, Charles Y., and Rodney Stark
1965   *Religion and Society in Tension*. Chicago: Rand McNally.
Heer, D. M.
1962   "The Trend of Interfaith Marriages in Canada: 1922–1957." *American Sociological Review* 27: 245-55.
Lenski, Gerhard
1961   *The Religious Factor*. Garden City: Anchor.
Lipset, S. M.
1968   *Revolution and Counterrevolution*. New York: Basic Books.
Meisel, John
1956   "Religious Affiliation and Electoral Behaviour: A Case Study." *Canadian Journal of Economics*

and Political Science 22: 481-96.

Meisel, John, ed.

1964   *Papers on the 1962 Election.*
Toronto: University of Toronto
Press.

Meisel, John, and Gilles Paquet

1962–   "Some Quantitative Analyses of
1963   Canadian Election Results: An
Exercise in the Testing of
Hypotheses." Papers and Proceedings of the Canadian

Political Science Association
Conference on Statistics.

Porter, John

1965   *The Vertical Mosaic.* Toronto:
University of Toronto Press.

Regenstreif, Peter

1965   *The Diefenbaker Interlude.*
Toronto: Longmans.

Sissons, C. B.

1959   *Church and State in Canadian
Education.* Toronto: Ryerson.

7.

Youth and Socialization

Ethnic Identity among Mennonite and Other Students of German Heritage*

Leo Driedger
Jacob Peters

Various studies suggest that the Mennonites have a distinctive sense of identity (Peters 1959; Thiessen 1966; Lederach 1971). In this paper we test the proposition that the identity of Mennonite students in Manitoba will be significantly stronger than that of other German-speaking students.

If the Mennonite identity, as measured, is stronger than that of other German-speaking students, then we ask: How might this be explained? The sociological literature on the assimilation of minorities, beginning with Park, holds that because of the industrial-urbanization process which pervades our society most subcultures tend to disappear. This theory suggests that minorities find new opportunities for advancement in socio-economic status through more education, better jobs, and higher incomes. Our question is whether these assimilation processes do actually undermine subcultural identity in the case of the Mennonite, as compared to the other German-speaking students.

*Abridged and revised from *The Mennonite Quarterly Review*, Vol. 47, No. 3, July 1973. Published here by permission of the authors and the publisher. This research was made possible by a grant from the Canada Council (S69-1445). The authors wish to thank K. W. Taylor of the University of Manitoba for statistical insights.

On the basis of various studies which often present inconsistent findings, we hypothesize the following:

1. Mennonite identity will be significantly greater than that of other German students, as measured by language use, endogamy, choice of friends, and participation in religion, parochial education, and ethnic organizations (Driedger).

2. Size of community (Thiessen, Just), socio-economic status (Frenkel-Brunswick, Banton, Peters), and generation in Canada (Frenkel-Brunswick, Nahirney and Fishman, Kloss, Peters, Lazerwitz and Rowitz, Gans, Lenski, Hansen, Herberg) will not be significantly associated with ethnic identity.

3. Institutional completeness will be positively associated with maintenance of identity (Breton, Driedger).

Methodology

The Sample

The sample of 160 German students, which represented 15 per cent of the estimated total German undergraduate student population, was taken from the University of Manitoba Ethnic Survey sample (Driedger 1972). Respondents were selected randomly. The sample comprised 93 males and 67 females, with a median age of 20 years. Approximately two-thirds of the students were reared in an urban environment (lived seven years or more in a community of 1,000 plus). The majority (75 per cent) of the students came from lower socio-economic families, based on Blishen's socio-economic index for occupations in Canada (1967).

The Instrument

To measure social structural correlates of ethnic identity the questionnaire included a series of Likert-type questions. In a study using factor analysis Driedger (1972) developed six factors to measure ethnic cultural identity: religious participation, endogamy, use of ingroup language, participation in ethnic organizations, amount of parochial education, and choice of friends. Four items were designed for each of these factors.

To assess students' behaviour, in addition to their attitudes on the six factors, one behavioural variable for each factor was chosen. Attendance at church services twice a month or more by the respondent indicated activity in religion. No exogamous marriage by any of the siblings in the respondent's family was taken as a measure of endogamy. Conversing in the German language with parents at home was considered an indicator of ethnic language use. One or more memberships in ethnic voluntary organizations indicated organizational activity; any attendance by the respondent in parochial school was a measure of parochial education, and ingroup choice of over half of their five best friends was a measure of ethnic friendship. The above questions were selected from the instrument to measure behavioural aspects of ethnic cultural identity.

Findings

Religious Differentiations

Of the six factors associated with ethnic identity (Table 1), involvement in voluntary organizations seems to be weakest, followed by use of the German language. Religious attendance, endogamy, and parochial education showed up most strongly for most of the groups. Attitudes were quite consistent with behaviour on religion and parochial education, in most cases. In the case of voluntary organizations, favourable attitudes were much higher than actual involvement. This finding may suggest that youth are open to such involvement, but they do not have the time, or organizations do not offer attractive programs. In the case of endogamy the case was reversed, with much stronger association with behaviour than with attitudes.

There are considerable denominational variations in regard to the six identity factors. The Mennonites rank first or second highest in all six factors with respect to both behaviour and attitude. With the exception of endogamy, Germans belonging to the United Church rank lowest in behaviour, although in many cases their attitudes tend to be more favourable.

Data in Table 1 support the notion that Mennonites have a stronger ethnic identity than other German groups. A comparison of Mennonites and non-Mennonite Germans in Table 2 tends to confirm their distinctiveness (Lederach 1971). Mennonites rank higher than other Germans combined on all six factors in both attitudinal and behavioural aspects of cultural identity. Behavioural patterns in church attendance, endogamy, and choice of ingroup friends indicated strong Mennonite identity. Attendance at parochial schools and use of language with their parents

TABLE 1. Association Between Six Ethnic Identity Factors, Comparing German Students in Several Denominations

(Percentages)

GERMAN DENOMI-NATIONS	GROUP N	RELIGION		ENDOGAMY		IDENTITY FACTORS LANGUAGE		VOLUNTARY ORGANIZATIONS		PAROCHIAL EDUCATION		FRIENDS	
		Behaviour	Attitudes	Behaviour	Attitudes	Behaviour	Attitudes	Behaviour	Attitudes	Behaviour	Attitudes	Behaviour	Attitudes
Mennonite	57	78.9	84.2	78.9	31.6	43.9	56.1	24.6	68.4	52.6	77.2	77.2	28.1
Baptist	7	85.7	71.4	71.4	14.3	14.3	57.1	28.6	71.4	42.9	14.3	28.6	28.6
Roman Catholic	10	60.0	70.0	60.0	0.0	20.0	20.0	20.0	40.0	70.0	70.0	10.0	10.0
Lutheran	39	43.6	69.2	46.2	5.1	10.3	28.2	12.8	66.7	46.2	35.9	10.3	5.1
United Church	10	20.0	50.0	80.0	10.0	0.0	50.0	10.0	30.0	40.0	40.0	0.0	20.0
Other or No Religion	36	36.1	36.1	38.9	13.9	22.2	30.6	8.3	36.1	25.0	25.0	16.7	5.6
TOTAL	160												

TABLE 2. Association Between Six Ethnic Identity Factors, Comparing Mennonite and Other German Students

(Percentages)

GERMAN GROUP	IDENTITY FACTORS											
	RELIGION		ENDOGAMY		LANGUAGE		VOLUNTARY ORGANIZATIONS		PAROCHIAL EDUCATION		FRIENDS	
	Behaviour	Attitudes	Behaviour	Attitudes	Behaviour	Attitudes	Behaviour	Attitudes	Behaviour	Attitudes	Behaviour	Attitudes
Mennonite (57)	78.9	84.2	78.9	31.6	43.9	56.1	24.6	68.4	52.6	77.2	77.2	28.1
Other German (102)	43.1	55.9	50.0	8.8	14.7	32.4	12.7	50.0	40.2	34.3	12.7	8.8
χ^2	17.60‡	11.39‡	10.56†	12.07‡	14.77‡	7.61†	2.73	5.27*	1.81	24.70‡	63.27‡	9.50†
Gamma	0.66	0.61	0.57	0.66	0.64	0.46	0.38	0.41	0.25	0.73	0.92	0.62

*P < .05
†P < .01
‡P < .001

were somewhat less, and participation in ethnic organizations seemed to be minimal. Mennonites generally took part to a larger degree than others in ingroup organizations, chose more ingroup friends, attended religious activities more, and used the German language more than other Germans. Only in parochial school attendance and participation in voluntary organizations do other Germans come close to Mennonite involvement.

Mennonites also rank higher than other Germans in attitudinal aspects of each factor, although the pattern varies somewhat. Mennonite attitudes toward religion and language are quite consistent with their involvement. Their attitudes toward choice of ingroup friends and endogamy are most inconsistent, in that they are much more liberal, perhaps opening the way to wider interaction and intermarriage in the future.

Assimilation Theories

Theories of assimilation regard industrialization and urbanization as major reasons for decline in ethnic identity. Such influences as community size, upward mobility, and generation in Canada are usually examined to account for differences in identity.

1. COMMUNITY SIZE

Of the 20 religious groups included in the 1971 census, the Mennonites were the most rural. However, they are moving to the cities in large numbers (Driedger 1968). Data in Table 3 indicate that for non-Mennonites rural-urban differences are statistically insignificant for the associations between all six factors and ethnic identity. Ingroup choice of friends and attitudes toward ingroup choice, however, show a trend toward higher involvement by rural people. Rural-urban differences among Mennonite students for the specified relationships are also statistically insignificant. Community size does not sufficiently differentiate either the Mennonites or the other Germans in terms of ethnic identity.

2. SOCIO-ECONOMIC STATUS

Proponents of assimilation theory would argue that as individuals become upwardly mobile they have more diverse contacts, resulting in loss of identity. Data for non-Mennonites indicate that socio-economic differentiations are statistically insignificant on all six factors.[1] There is a

TABLE 3. Association Between Six Ethnic Identity Factors, Comparing Mennonite and Other German Students and Community Size

(Percentages)

IDENTITY FACTORS

COMMUNITY SIZE	RELIGION		ENDOGAMY		LANGUAGE		VOLUNTARY ORGANIZATIONS		PAROCHIAL EDUCATION		FRIENDS	
	Behaviour	Attitudes	Behaviour	Attitudes	Behaviour	Attitudes	Behaviour	Attitudes	Behaviour	Attitudes	Behaviour	Attitudes
Mennonites												
Rural (30)	76.7	83.3	76.6	31.0	51.7	53.3	31.0	72.4	56.7	80.0	83.3	31.0
Urban (26)	80.8	84.6	84.0	34.6	36.0	61.5	19.2	69.2	50.0	76.9	69.2	26.9
χ^2	.00	.05	.11	.00	.78	.12	.48	.00	.05	.00	.86	.00
Gamma	.12	.05	.23	.08	-.31	.17	-.31	-.08	-.07	-.09	-.38	-.09
Non-Mennonites												
Rural (35)	54.3	65.7	45.7	11.4	18.8	31.4	8.6	51.4	40.0	37.1	22.9	17.1
Urban (66)	37.9	52.3	57.4	7.7	12.5	33.3	15.9	50.8	39.4	33.8	7.6	4.5
χ^2	.88	1.17	.79	.07	.26	.00	.50	.02	.02	.01	3.50	3.05
Gamma	-.32	-.27	.23	-.22	-.24	.04	.33	-.01	-.01	-.07	-.57	-.63

$P < .05$

trend for those of lower class to aspire to more parochial education and to use German somewhat more.

The only statistically significant differentiation is that Mennonites of higher class have attended parochial schools more. Those with greater means are better able to afford private education. The trend is for the higher classes to be more active in church attendance and to have more ingroup friends and fewer voluntary organization memberships. Again, however, socio-economic status seems to be of minimal importance for identity, except for greater parochial school involvement among Mennonites of higher status. We need to look elsewhere for an explanation for Mennonite identity.

3. GENERATION IN CANADA

Does length of residence in Canada have a bearing on the strength of ethnic and religious identity? Hansen (1952) has suggested that first-generation immigrants retain much of their culture, which their children wish to forget and in which their grandchildren again become interested. Proponents of assimilation would suggest that identity declines with time, so that third-generation Canadians will score lower on identity than first-generation immigrants. Do the data support these theories?

Data do not provide clear evidence for either of these theories.[2] Among non-Mennonites there is a significant loss of German-language use and attitudinal support for such use. Among Mennonites also there is a tendency for decline in the use of the German language. Endogamy, religious participation, and parochial school attendance are maintained through the generations. The data in general do not support either the Hansen or the assimilation theories for the Mennonites, and only support them minimally for other Germans.

Institutional Completeness

The assimilation approach, as indicated by community size, socio-economic status, and generation in Canada, does not seem to be a convincing explanation of German student identity. There may have been loss of identity by Germans in general, but this does not account for extensive maintenance of identity among Mennonites. How can this differentiation be explained?

The Breton (1964) theory of institutional completeness seems to hold some promise. It is argued that when an ethno-religious group institutionalizes some of its activities, it retains its identity despite differences in rural-urban background, socio-economic status, and length of time in Canada. Previous studies support the positive function of institutions (Driedger 1973; Driedger and Church 1974). Breton used the number of churches, publications, and welfare institutions as criteria for institutional completeness. These three will be used, plus parochial educational institutions. Publications are broadened to include radio and television media, and welfare institutions are broadened to include other voluntary organizations.

1. CHURCHES

All churches, rural and urban, with a membership of 75 per cent of German descent or more were included. A total of 213 churches of German descent were found in Manitoba. Of these 45 were urban and 167 were rural. The breakdown by denominations can be found in Table 4. Of the 135 Mennonite churches, 108 (80 per cent) were rural and 27 (20 per cent) were urban. The 64 German churches of other denominations included 59 in rural and 19 in urban areas of Manitoba.

Two-thirds of the German churches in Manitoba were Mennonite (64 per cent). Moreover, whereas community size did not seem to be an important factor in differentiating ethnic identity, it may be that with such a large rural Mennonite church hinterland feeding membership into the city, Mennonites tend to perpetuate homogeneity longer and to a greater extent than other Germans do. Mennonite churches in urban areas, however, are also well established and it may be that they will continue to support dynamic religious identity by strong church institutions.

2. PAROCHIAL SCHOOLS

Private schools, like churches, require considerable effort for support in finances and organization. Ethnic and religious groups must be able to maintain sufficient group solidarity in order to organize schools and attract students.

A survey of educational institutions in Manitoba run by groups of German descent included two colleges, three high schools, three Bible schools, and one elementary school. Eight of the schools were operated by the Mennonites and only one elementary school was run by the Ger-

TABLE 4. Comparison of Mennonite and Other German Groups, by Institutional Completeness

GERMAN GROUPS	STUDENT GROUP N	CHURCH MEMBERS N	NUMBER OF INSTITUTIONS			
			CHURCHES	PAROCHIAL SCHOOLS	VOLUNTARY ORGANIZATIONS	MEDIA
German Mennonites	57	20,000	27 Urban 108 Rural	3 Bible schools 3 High schools 2 Colleges	11 Welfare 3 Other	1 Radio station 5 Newspapers
Other Germans (Baptist, Lutheran, Roman Catholic, United Church, etc.)	66	15,000	19 Urban 59 Rural	1 Elementary school	6 Welfare	0
General Other Germans	36		0	0	5	2 Newspapers

man Catholics. One high school and three Bible schools were in rural areas, while the two colleges, two high schools, and one elementary school were located in Winnipeg.

That an ethnic group of 57,000 Mennonites in Manitoba was able to operate eight private schools, with a combined Manitoba student population of almost 1,000 above the elementary level, attests to strong Mennonite solidarity. There were no German Lutheran, Baptist, or United Church private schools.

3. ETHNIC ORGANIZATIONS

Of a total of 25 German organizations, 14 belong to the Mennonites, three to the Lutherans, three to other religious groups, and five to non-religious groups. The Lutheran organizations included a world relief organization, an insurance company, and a retirement home; two served their ingroup and one served others.

The 14 Mennonite organizations included three which rendered services for outgroups such as world relief, offenders, and urban Indians. Four homes for the aged, a benevolent society, and an historical society served members of the ingroup largely, and four organizations, including a travel service, hospital, credit union, mental hospital, and museum, were open to both ingroup and outgroup members. There was a wide variety of Mennonite services and organizations.

4. ETHNIC MEDIA

Ethnic means of communication, such as newspapers, radio, and television, were considered another criterion of group solidarity. The Mennonites went heavily into weekly newspapers in Manitoba, including two all-German (*Die Steinbach Post* and *Die Rundschau*), two all-English (*The Carillon* and *The Altona Echo*), and one English and German paper (*The Mennonite Mirror*). The three English papers are confined to Manitoba readers, while the two German papers have a wider Canadian, Mexican, and South American readership. None of the other German denominations printed papers in Manitoba. Two general non-religious papers are printed in Winnipeg—*Der Courier* and the *German Canadian Business Review*.

Although the institutional completeness approach is a crude measurement of ethnic solidarity, it seems clear from the data that Mennonite development of religious, educational, voluntary, and communications organizations is substantially greater than that of other German religious denominations, whereas the membership difference is not greater. This is especially true in the areas of parochial education and ethnic media. Mennonite voluntary organizations are twice as numerous in a variety of services. About twice as many Mennonite churches as all other German churches combined may be misleading, since Catholic and Lutheran churches on the average may be somewhat larger; nevertheless the data here also suggest greater Mennonite institutional completeness.

Summary and Conclusions

The data indicate that Mennonite university students in Manitoba hold significantly more positive attitudes toward their ingroup and also participate more in the institutions of that group than other German students do. This study also shows that community size, socio-economic status, and generation in Canada are limited in their ability to explain greater Mennonite identity. Institutional completeness seemed to be associated with stronger identity, and appeared to apply particularly to Mennonites. The authors suspect that institutional completeness is the product of ideological and social psychological factors which are nourished within the ingroup which these institutions support. Further study of these factors is needed. The study clearly shows that when Germans are studied in Manitoba, the Mennonites must be "controlled". To include the Mennonites under the German category can greatly increase identity, perhaps disproportionately to the findings of German identity elsewhere in Canada. The Mennonites could be treated as a separate group like the Jews wherever in Canada they are represented in significant numbers.

NOTES

1 See Table 5 of the original article for the statistical data on socio-economic status.

2 See Table 6 of the original article for the statistical data on third-generation Canadians.

REFERENCES

Banton, Michael
1967 *Race Relations*. London: Tavistock.
Blishen, Bernard
1967 "A Socio-Economic Index for Occupations in Canada."

Canadian Review of Sociology and Anthropology 4: 41-53.
Breton, Raymond
1964 "Institutional Completeness of Ethnic Communities and the Personal Relations to Immi-

grants." *American Journal of Sociology* 70: 193-205.

Driedger, Leo, ed.
1968   *Mennonites in Urban Canada. Proceedings of the Conference on Urbanization of Mennonites in Canada.* Winnipeg: University of Manitoba.
1972   "In Search of Cultural Identity Factors: A Comparison of Ethnic Students." Paper presented to the annual meetings of the Canadian Sociology and Anthropology Association in Montreal. *Canadian Review of Sociology and Anthropology,* Vol. 12, 1975.
1973   "Impelled Group Migration: Minority Struggle to Maintain Institutional Completeness." *International Migration Review* 7: 257-69.
1974   "Doctrinal Belief: A Major Factor in the Differential Perception of Social Issues." *Sociological Quarterly* 15: 66-80.

Driedger, Leo, and Glenn Church
1974   "Residential Segregation and Institutional Completeness: A Comparison of Ethnic Minorities." *Canadian Review of Sociology and Anthropology* 11: 30-52.

Frenkel-Brunswick, Else
1952   "Interaction of Psychological and Sociological Factors in Political Behavior." *American Political Science Review* 46: 44-65.

Gans, Herbert J.
1956   "American Jewry: Present and Future." *Commentary* 21: 555-63.

Hansen, Marcus L.
1952   "The Problem of the Third Generation Immigrant." *Commentary* 14: 492-500.

Herberg, Will
1955   *Protestant-Catholic-Jew.* New York: Doubleday.

Just, L. Roy
1953   "An Analysis of the Social

Distance Reactions of Students from Three Major American Mennonite Groups." In *Proceedings of the Ninth Conference on Mennonite Educational and Cultural Problems,* pp. 71-7. Hesston, Kansas. June 18–19.

Kloss, Heinz
1966   "German-American Language Maintenance Efforts." In Joshua A. Fishman *et al., Language Loyalty in the United States,* pp. 206-52. The Hague: Mouton.

Lazerwitz, Bernard, and Louis Rowitz
1964   "The Three-Generation Hypothesis." *American Journal of Sociology* 69: 529-38.

Lederach, Paul M.
1971   *Mennonite Youth.* Scottdale, Penn.: Herald Press.

Lenski, Gerhard
1961   *The Religious Factor.* New York: Doubleday.

Nahirney, Vladimir, and Joshua A. Fishman
1965   "American Immigrant Groups: Ethnic Identification and the Problem of Generations." *Sociological Review* 13: 311-23.

Peters, F. C.
1959   "Comparison of Attitudes and Values Expressed by Mennonite and Non-Mennonite College Students." Unpublished dissertation, Department of Educational Psychology and the Graduate School of the University of Kansas.

Peters, Jacob
1971   "The Association of Religious Affiliation, Socio-Economic Status, Generation and Segregation with German Ethnocentrism." Unpublished M.A. thesis, University of Manitoba.

Thiessen, Irmgard
1966   "Values and Personality Characteristics of Mennonites in Manitoba." *Mennonite Quarterly Review* 40: 48-61.

Belonging, Commitment, and Early Socialization in a Western City*

Raymond F. Currie

Introduction

In the 1971 Canadian census a little fewer than one million persons (4.3 per cent of the population) stated that they had "no religion".[1] The increase in this category over a twenty-year period has been substantial. Millett (1969: 118) has established that 62,000 (.004 per cent) Canadians reported "no religion" in 1951, compared to 100,000 (.58 per cent) in 1961.

The relatively high rate of expressed religious identification should not necessarily be considered a sign of serious religious commitment. In 1973 the Canadian Institute of Public Opinion reported that 50 per cent of Canadian adults considered that organized religion was a relevant part of their lives. About two-thirds (63 per cent) of those 50 years of age and over said that organized religion was relevant to them, but the same proportion of those between 18 and 29 said that it was not. Polls

*This is a revised and abridged version of a paper presented at the annual meeting of the Society for the Scientific Study of Religion, San Francisco, 1973. The research was made possible by a grant from the University of Manitoba Research Grants Committee, whose support is gratefully acknowledged. The author also wishes to thank Professors Charlene Thacker and Leo Driedger for their critical assistance. Published here with the kind permission of the author.

also indicate that regular church attendance is declining. Weekly attendance of adults in Canada dropped from 67 per cent in 1946 to 55 per cent in 1965 and was 39 per cent in 1974.[2] The decline in traditional forms of religion commitment in both Canada and the United States has been substantiated by a number of studies (Hoge 1969; Rapport Dumont 1971; Wuthnow and Glock 1973). Religious commitment, then, appears to have declined more dramatically than religious belonging.

However, one cannot assume that belonging without commitment always represents a decline in commitment for the individual. A substantial proportion of the population who belong may never have had a strong religious commitment. Socialization to religious belonging without socialization to religious commitment may have become rather common.

There is, indeed, literature which treats socialization as one of the major sources of religious involvement. Allport, Gillespie, and Young (1948), as well as Yinger (1970: 130), have found that students trained in religion report that they need religion; their need is, in fact, in direct proportion to the degree of early influence. This socialization to religious commitment is usually associated with socialization to belonging. Bibby and Brinkerhoff (1973) report that even in evangelical groups which tend to stress conversion as a pre-condition of belonging converts tend to be children of evangelical parents. On the other hand, socialization to belonging may not include socialization to religious commitment. Moberg (1962: 430) discusses the difficulties in upholding the standard of a committed or converted membership: "Conversion tends to be 'watered down' with the passage of time until its operational definition fits the actual experiences produced in the group." Thus, more people become members of religious groups simply because they are born into them.

Lenski (1961: 18) and, more recently, Greeley (1972) suggest reasons why belonging may be maintained independently of religious commitment. Greeley has described the United States and Canada as denominational societies. Religion provides not only meaning in the lives of its practitioners but also a sense of belonging. Denominations are means of social differentiation, quasi-gemeinschaft institutions, and "belonging-providing ethnic groups"[3] which help the individual to identify and locate himself in the larger social structure. Greeley supports this theory of the importance of belonging by pointing to the high rates of intramarriage among members of a denomination (69 per cent in Canada in 1967; a slight decline from 71 per cent in 1957), the extent of interaction with members of one's own denomination, and systematic differences in religious beliefs.

Regardless of what the future holds, there are clear indications that belonging has functions which do not relate to religious commitment. In view of this fact, it is useful to establish the extent to which socialization to religious belonging occurs independently of socialization to religious commitment, and under what conditions belonging survives without commitment. The three following propositions are particularly suitable for investigation.

Propositions

1. *Socialization to Commitment Will Include Socialization to Belonging*

Durkheim points out that we do not find a single religion without a church (1965: 59). He distinguishes religion from magic precisely by the system of social relationships which religion requires. However, he recognizes the possibility of "private religions" which may arise and become the pre-eminent form of religious life in the future. Parsons suggests that "in the final analysis, religion is an individual matter . . . ; the nature of the social structuring of religion should be regarded as empirically problematic" (1960: 303). Without attempting to resolve this larger issue, there are indications that the religious commitment of individuals does not always include the dimension of belonging. Vernon (1968) has presented data indicating that religious "nones" (i.e., those who do not belong to a formal church) do exhibit other religious characteristics, such as belief, participation in formal religious activities, and religious experiences. He does not indicate whether or not these respondents were socialized to commitment without belonging. Since, historically, religion has been a collective phenomenon, one would expect that early socialization to commitment would include belonging in a high proportion of cases. Furthermore, cases of commitment without belonging would most likely reflect loss of previous membership through disenchantment with established religious organizations rather than absence of membership in the early period of socialization.

2. *Belonging May Not Involve Religious Commitment and May Not Have Involved Socialization to Commitment*

The possibility of belonging without commitment has long been recognized in the sociology of religion. In fact, involuntary birthright is almost by definition one of the characteristics of church membership, while voluntary conversion is one of the trademarks of the sects. Nevertheless, Bouma (1973) shows that the vast majority of research on the Protestant ethic suffers from the fact that it compares those who belong to different religious groups without investigating whether or not the belonging is associated with specific religious beliefs. Such research [makes the dubious assumption] that belonging is an indicator of religious commitment. This is also the case for many studies that simply "control for religion" by asking whether the respondents are Catholic, Protestant, or Jewish. Data on church membership can be demonstrated to be decidedly inadequate as a measure of religiosity if belonging and commitment can be shown to be independent dimensions.

Some research, of course, does recognize various dimensions of religiosity. Glock and Stark (1965)[4] describe five dimensions: ideological (commitment to beliefs), intellectual (knowledge of church teachings), ritualistic (overt behaviour traditionally defined as religious), experiential (feelings and emotions of a religious nature), and consequential (the effect of the other four dimensions applied to the secular world). One problem in this type of religious research is that even when a number of dimensions are recognized, the tendency is to analyze church member samples. If non-affiliated respondents were included in samples, a more convincing test of the independence of belonging and commitment could be made.

The proposition stated above focuses on the extent to which nominal membership without commitment has become the norm in early socialization and on the extent that belonging survives without commitment. A consideration of some of the conditions under which belonging is likely to survive without commitment leads to the final proposition.

3. *The Socialization to Belonging without Commitment and the Survival of Belonging without Commitment Will Vary according to the Church-Sect Typology*

This proposition is almost a test of the continuing viability of the church-sect typology as a useful sociological tool of analysis. More specifically, it is a test of the Bibby and Brinkerhoff (1974) position that, while sources of religious involvement will vary within churches and sects, some sources are more likely to predominate in one rather than the other. Socialization to belonging without commitment should occur most frequently in church-like groups, since, unlike the sects, they do not require a conversion experience.

The survival of belonging without commitment is also a matter for discussion. Bibby and Brinkerhoff (1974) have referred to *accommodation* as religious involvement because of social pressures from parents, friends, a spouse, or the presence of children. It is used more broadly here to designate belonging without commitment at an age when an alternative is possible. It could arise in cases where belonging was not associated with early socialization to commitment or in cases where commitment had declined. The evangelical thrust of sectarian groups would lead one to expect that they would be less accommodative than church-like groups.

The Data

In order to test the propositions adequately, it would be necessary to have data on both commitment and belonging in early and later socialization. Such ideal longitudinal data were not available. However, data on young adults, who could be called the most recent graduates of early socialization, can offer some insights into the issues at hand. A city-wide sample of 708 young people, 15 to 24 years of age, was selected in Calgary, Alberta, in 1971. Respondents were selected randomly by enumeration area, block, household, and resident in household (only one youth per household was selected). As a result, the sample is representative of the city on a number of dimensions, including the age and sex composition of the city youth, the relatively high socio-economic composition of Calgary in relation to the rest of Canada, and the predominance of Anglo-Saxons.[5] The respondents also reflect the religious composition of the city; all major religious groups are proportionately represented. The Jewish population is so small that the sample did not contain an adequate number of Jews for analysis. In view of the important role of evangelical groups in the history of Alberta (Mann 1955), it is interesting to note that 20 such bodies were named by the respondents. Their total membership, however, forms only six per cent of the sample.

Methodology

Belonging was measured by the following question: "Are you a member of a particular religious group?" Socialization to belonging was measured by comparing the membership of the respondent with that of the mother: "What was the religion of your mother when you were ten years of age?" Three questions relate to commitment: "How strong was the religious climate in your home when you were growing up?" "How strong an influence was religion in your attitudes and behaviour when you were growing up?" "To what degree would you say religion *now* has an influence on your life?"

The first of the three questions gave an indication of the socialization to commitment by asking for an external measure, namely the religious climate in the home, while the last two questions were evaluations of the internal, personal religious commitment at two points in time. All three questions had a Likert-type response range of five: very strong, strong, some, slight, and none.

Of course, it is always dangerous to draw conclusions from single-item indicators. In defence of the validity of the items, it might be pointed out that the last item, the present influence of religion, had the following correlation with other scales: .64 with a four-item scale on religious beliefs, .57 with an eight-item scale on the present saliency of religious beliefs, and .60 with a question on the present importance of religious experiences. The single item was preferred for this analysis because, when used in conjunction with the question on the influence of religion when the respondent was growing up, it allows for a comparison to be made over a certain length of time.

A further methodological caution stems from the fact that the answers recorded only the respondents' personal perception of early socialization. Besides being subjective, they are dependent upon memory. As Berger and Luckmann (1967: 160) have pointed out so well, the past is always subject to dangers of reinterpretation in the light of the plausibility of one's present perception of reality.

Findings

1. Socialization to Belonging and Socialization to Commitment

While 56 per cent of Calgary youth consider themselves to be members of a religious body, 23 per cent say they were members in the past, and 12 per cent report they were never members.[6] The data indicate that a high proportion (75 per cent) of youth were socialized to belong to the denomination of their mother. This figure includes youth who no longer

TABLE 1. Home Religious Climate and Influence of Religion on Youth, by Denomination

(Percentages)

	PRESENT MEMBERS									PAST MEM-BERS	NEVER MEM-BERS	TOTALS
	Baptists	Evangeli-cals[a]	Lutherans	Roman Catholics	Presby-terians	United	Anglicans	Others[b]	Total			
	(18)	(33)	(26)	(125)	(15)	(102)	(64)	(10)	(393)	(166)	(87)	(646)
Home Religious Climate												
Very strong Strong	67	55	62	62	27	33	27	60	47	25	14	37
Some	28	30	8	26	53	39	41	30	32	37	26	33
Slight None	6	15	31	11	20	28	33	10	21	38	60	30
TOTAL	100	100	100	100	100	100	100	100	100	100	100	100
Influence of Religion When Youth Were Growing Up												
Very strong Strong	66	58	38	56	27	29	17	70	41	18	10	31
Some	17	27	38	26	47	33	38	20	31	26	26	29
Slight None	17	15	23	17	27	38	45	10	28	56	63	40
TOTAL	100	100	100	100	100	100	100	100	100	100	100	100

Influence of Religion Now

Very strong												
Strong	56	64	35	26	7	21	13	50	27	8	11	20
Some	22	15	23	36	33	28	25	20	28	20	20	25
Slight												
None	23	21	43	38	60	52	63	30	45	72	69	55
TOTAL	100	100	100	100	100	100	100	100	100	100	100	100

[a]Includes: Alliance Church, Christadelphians, Christian Missionary Alliance, Christian Reformed, Church of Christ, Dutch Reformed, Evangelical Free Church, Evangelical United Brethren, Full Gospel, Jehovah's Witness, Latter-Day Saints, Mennonite Brethren, Missionary Church, Moravian, Nazarene, Salvation Army, Seventh-Day Adventist.

[b]Includes: Bahai World Faith, Jew, Mediative (*sic*), Methodist, Moslem, Orthodox, Protestant, Reformed.

consider themselves members. Furthermore, 32 per cent of those who never belonged have mothers who did not belong when the youth were ten years of age, indicating that a certain socialization to non-belonging may have occurred as well. The data, which represent a wide variety of denominations, support Bibby and Brinkerhoff's findings that evangelicals, who stress conversion before belonging, tend to socialize to belonging as much as the more church-like groups.

A strong religious atmosphere in the home occurs far less frequently than socialization to belonging. Only 37 per cent of all the youth report the presence of a strong religious atmosphere (Table 1). As would be expected, a strong religious climate is more likely to have been the norm for present members (47 per cent) than for past members (25 per cent) or never members (14 per cent). Twenty-one per cent of present members and 38 per cent of past members report slight or no religious climate in the home.

It is useful to go one step further and try to estimate the success of early attempts at socialization to commitment. There is a possibility that, although the home religious climate was strong, young people may not consider that religion was influential on their attitudes and behaviour when they were growing up. This is, in fact, the case for some young people in the sample. The correlation between the two items is .66, indicating that one score can be predicted from the other 43 per cent of the time. The type of relationship found between perceived religious influence when a respondent was growing up and the home religious climate is predictable. Sixty-four per cent of those who report that the home religious climate was strong also indicate that religion was influential on their attitudes and behaviour when they were growing up; and 76 per cent of those youth who perceive religion to have been influential when they were growing up state that the home religious climate was strong.

While the attempt at socialization to commitment in the home was moderately successful, the home climate appears to be almost indispensable for any continuing success. In the remainder of this paper, socialization to commitment will refer to successful socialization as measured by the perceived strong influence of religion when respondents were growing up.

It should be noted that the low average of socialization to commitment is related to the large size of certain denominations in the city (Table 1). It also varies by denomination, and these variations do not simply follow the church-sect continuum. Roman Catholics, in particular, report relatively high socialization to commitment, along with the Baptists and evangelicals. The small sample size of a number of denominations leads one to interpret statistics for some groups with caution.

Table 1 further indicates that, on the one hand, socialization to commitment usually does include socialization to belonging. The few exceptions are those who were never members but who score high on socialization to commitment. On the other hand, belonging (present or past) involves strong early socialization to commitment in 34 per cent of the cases, but involves no socialization to commitment in 36 per cent of the cases. This raises the issue of the survival of belonging without commitment.

2. Survival of Belonging without Commitment

Looking at the total membership of religious groups, it would appear that accommodation, or belonging without commitment, is the norm rather than the exception for young adults (Table 1). Only 27 per cent of present members report that their religious commitment is now very strong or strong, while 45 per cent state that it is of slight or no influence. What needs to be clarified is whether the low commitment represents a decline or a simple lack of socialization to commitment. Forty-one per cent of present members report that religion was strong when they were growing up, whereas only 27 per cent find it influential now. Once again, the differences among the denominations are significant. Baptists and evangelicals represent the highest percentages reporting religion to be strong at both periods. Roman Catholics show the greatest loss between the two time periods.

This simple percentage comparison between the two time periods can hide the various types of change that occur for individuals. A comparison between the items for each of the respondents reveals that 41 per cent of the youth report no change (Table 2). Fourteen per cent have increased and 45 per cent have declined.[7] When we compare this table to the previous one, it is important to note that evangelicals did not decline substantially as a group because the 45 per cent who did decrease have been offset by another 27 per cent who increased in the same period. Baptists tended not to change at all (67 per cent) and to remain high. Catholics were far more likely to have declined than increased (58 per cent v. 15 per cent), yet the present influence of religion for them remains slightly higher than for the United Church members and Anglicans. For

TABLE 2. Extent and Direction of Change in Religious Commitment
(Percentages)

		CHANGE			
MEMBERSHIP	NO CHANGE	INCREASE	DECREASE	PER CENT TOTALS	FREQUENCY
Present Members					
Baptists	67	6	28	100	(18)
Evangelicals	27	27	45	100	(33)
Lutherans	35	15	50	100	(26)
Roman Catholics	26	15	58	100	(125)
Presbyterians	47	—	53	100	(15)
United	44	11	45	100	(102)
Anglicans	47	9	44	100	(64)
Others	30	50	20	100	(10)
TOTAL	38	14	48	100	(393)
Past Members	40	14	46	100	(166)
Never Members	55	15	30	100	(87)
TOTALS	41	14	45	100	(646)

the latter two groups decline was not substantial simply because there
was little room for decline. While an explanation for the performance of
Catholics is beyond the scope of this paper, it should be pointed out that
they are the only denomination in Calgary with a comprehensive school
system set up to support religious education in the home and the parish.[8]
But those Catholics presently in the Separate School System report
decline in religious commitment in very similar proportions to those who
are outside the school system.

Minor changes (e.g., from "slight" to "none"), and radical changes
(e.g., from "very strong" to "none") have been included in the above
measurement of change in commitment. There is some value in attempting to be more selective in assessing the impact of change, even though
this reduces the number of cases to such an extent that denominations
cannot be compared. Five groups can be extracted from the sample.
Youth can be classified as *always strong* in religious commitment if they
indicate religion was "very strong" or "strong" both when they were
growing up and at present. They can be classified as *always slight* if they
report religion was "slight" or "none" at both points in time. *Always
some* represents the youth who report "some" at both times. The *de-
creasers* and *increasers* are those who have moved from "very strong" or

"strong" to "slight" or "none", or vice versa. In other words, such changes are of at least two degrees and may be of four degrees.[9]

The independence of commitment and belonging becomes clearer when the new change categories are examined. It has already been established that belonging can survive without commitment, since most members report religion is not now influential in their lives. It can now be seen that belonging still survives for two-thirds of the cases who report radical decline in commitment (Table 3). The independence of belonging and commitment is further supported by the fact that slightly over half (52 per cent) of the youth who report that they have always been low in commitment have retained their belonging.[10] Although the number of cases is small, only 59 per cent of those who have radically increased in commitment are presently members. Finally, it is intriguing to note that belonging is more likely to survive radical decline in commitment than the continued absence of commitment (68 per cent v. 52 per cent). It is unfortunate that the number of radical decliners is too small to be adequately analyzed according to denomination. However, it is possible to determine which religious groups retain or lose members and relate that information to the loss or absence of commitment.

3. The Loss of Belonging

While Roman Catholics report the highest loss of commitment over time, they report the lowest loss of membership (21 per cent, Table 4). The United Church reports a much higher loss of members (37 per cent), while Baptists and evangelicals are close to the average loss for the sample (30 per cent). Why is membership retained in spite of loss or absence of commitment? It has already been indicated that such accommodation may reflect social pressure. Another explanation may be associated with theological heritage. Two statements express almost polar opposites of ecclesial theology: "No salvation outside the church", and, "Go to the church of your choice but go to church." While the first position historically has stressed the uniqueness and indispensability of the church, the other tends to see the church more as an elective vehicle which helps the individual to express his personal religiosity. It seems safe to say that the former statement is close to the Roman Catholic tradition and that the latter statement has developed within liberal Protestant settings. The data cannot prove that Catholic retention of membership in spite of loss of commitment is related to theology, but this is at least a

TABLE 3. The Survival of Belonging
Frequencies (in brackets) and Percentages

MEMBERSHIP	TOTALS		CHANGE IN RELIGIOUS COMMITMENT[a]			
		ALWAYS STRONG	RADICAL INCREASE	ALWAYS SOME	RADICAL DECREASE	ALWAYS SLIGHT
Present Members						
Baptists	(17)	(10)	—	(3)	(1)	(3)
Evangelicals	(25)	(16)	(2)	(2)	(3)	(2)
Lutherans	(16)	(6)	—	(3)	(1)	(6)
Roman Catholics	(75)	(23)	(2)	(14)	(23)	(13)
Presbyterians	(9)	(1)	—	(3)	(1)	(4)
United	(66)	(12)	(4)	(13)	(4)	(33)
Anglicans	(44)	(5)	(1)	(10)	(1)	(27)
Others	(7)	(3)	(1)	—	(2)	(1)
Total	(259) 58	(76) 89	(10) 59	(48) 67	(36) 68	(89) 41
Past Members	(119) 27	(4) 5	(4) 24	(14) 19	(16) 30	(81) 37
Never Members	(67) 15	(5) 6	(3) 18	(10) 14	(1) 2	(48) 22
TOTALS	(445) 100	(85) 100	(17) 100	(72) 100	(53) 100	(218) 100

[a]Only those youth who report the types of change indicated by the five categories are included in this table. For further explanation, see text.

TABLE 4.   Loss of Membership

DENOMINATION	PRESENT MEMBERS	PAST MEMBERS	TOTAL	PERCENTAGE LOSS[a]
Baptists	18	7	25	28
Evangelicals	33	17	50	31
Lutheran	26	12	38	32
Roman Catholics	125	34	159	21
Presbyterians	15	12	27	44
United	102	61	163	37
Anglicans	64	21	85	25
Others	10	2	12	17
TOTALS	393	166	559	30

[a]Percentage loss is calculated by $\dfrac{\text{Past Members}}{\text{Total Members}} \times 100.$

plausible proposition. Existing explanations for the retention of belonging without commitment stress the importance of belonging as a means of strengthening membership in a specific subculture. This is the position of Lenski and Greeley. It appears to be particularly applicable to Catholics in Calgary. The existence of the Separate School System means that the individual Roman Catholic has an intense association with the church during the schooling experience unless a formal break is made with the church.

In discussing reasons for retention of belonging, one should not lose sight of the fact that one out of every three Calgary youths who used to belong no longer does. This leads to some skepticism concerning Greeley's theory that Canada, like the United States, will remain a denominational society. Nevertheless, his treatment of the community function of religious belonging deserves to be taken seriously and perhaps could be applied to specific denominations within the society rather than to the society as a whole.

Discussion

The present sample has the advantage of being city-wide, but the findings cannot be generalized beyond Calgary. Further, the methodology has limitations which are readily acknowledged. Nevertheless, certain findings appear to be of substantive interest in the sociology of religion.

First, denominational affiliation, or belonging, clearly says very little about the religious commitment of Calgary youth. Secondly, in relation to the well-documented literature on the low level of religious commitment among youth, the study suggests that the lack of commitment may not [generally] arise from teen-age rebellion against parents and society in general. Rather, lack of commitment is frequently not an acquired "deviancy" but is associated with early socialization. Thirdly, the distinction between commitment and belonging may be useful in predicting the future religious involvement of youth. This author suggests that those most socialized to religion, both belonging and commitment, are most likely to have a religious commitment in the future. Fourthly, while there are strong and consistent differences between Baptists and evangelicals, on the one hand, and United Church and Anglican youth, on the other, Roman Catholic youth have characteristics which are difficult to categorize. Demerath (1965: 187) suggests that, more than other groups, Roman Catholics combine church-like and sect-like characteristics within the one denomination.

Another fruitful line of inquiry provoked by these findings relates to belonging independent of commitment. A number of urban sociologists are actively engaged in assessing the nature of and participation in the urban community. Janowitz (1967) and Greer (1962) use the term "community of limited liability" to express choice of involvement in local territorial communities. Physical or psychological withdrawal from the community can be of varying degrees. Sociologists of religion and of the city might well explore together the conditions under which various types of withdrawal from the community are likely to occur.

NOTES

1   Question 16 of the census is worded: "What is your religion?" Fourteen categories are provided, one of which is "no religion". The provincial totals range from 0.4 per cent in Newfoundland who report no religion to 13.1 per cent in British Columbia.

2   The question is worded as follows: "Did you, yourself, happen to attend church or synagogue in the last seven days?" It is regrettable that because church attendance polls have been taken so rarely in Canada (three times since 1946) one can legitimately question their validity. The American Gallup Poll asks the question ten times a year and reports the average. While the

trend has been one of decline in both countries since 1958, lack of data does not allow one to state whether there was an increase in attendance in Canada from 1950 to 1957 as reported in the United States. In 1970, however, two percentage points separated the countries, with the United States reporting [a higher] average of 42 per cent attending weekly.

3   Cf. Millett's application of the "minority church" concept of Canada which indirectly addresses itself to this phenomenon.

4   Some recent literature suggests that Glock and Stark's particular dimensions of religiosity are questionable.

See Gibbs and Crader (1970), Nudelman (1971), and Clayton and Gladden (1974).

5　For details concerning the sampling procedures and representativeness of the sample, see Currie (1973).

6　An additional nine per cent did not answer the questions adequately and will not be included in the analyses that follow.

7　"No change" means the respondents checked *exactly* the same category for both questions. Any change was coded as either an increase or decrease.

8　The Catholic Separate School System in Alberta is somewhat unique in North America. The number of schools, the staff, and the school budget are proportionate to the size of the Catholic population in the area. The quality of the system is considered to be comparable to that of the public school system. At the time of the survey, Catholic youth attending school were required by law to attend the Separate School System from grades 1 through 12. The information on the religious attitudes and values of Catholics, then, should be of particular interest to those who consider school to be an answer to the problem of maintaining religious commitment among youth.

9　For both increase and decrease, 90 per cent of the changes were of one or two degrees, 8 per cent were of three degrees, and 2 per cent were of four degrees.

10　To arrive at 52 per cent, it was necessary to exclude the "never members" from the calculation.

REFERENCES

Allport, Gordon W., James M. Gillespie, and Jacqueline Young
1948　"The Religion of the Post-War College Student." *The Journal of Psychology* 25 (January): 3-33.
Berger, Peter L., and Thomas Luckmann
1967　*The Social Construction of Reality.* Garden City: Doubleday.
Bibby, Reginald W., and Merlin B. Brinkerhoff
1974　"Sources of Religious Involvement: Issues for Future Empirical Consideration." *Review of Religious Research* 15 (Winter): 71-9.
1973　"The Circulation of the Saints: A Study of People Who Join Conservative Churches." *Journal for the Scientific Study of Religion* 12 (September): 273-84.
Bouma, Gary D.
1973　"Recent 'Protestant Ethic' Research." *Journal for the Scientific Study of Religion* 12 (June): 141-56.
The Canadian Institute of Public Opinion
1965　August 18
1970　April 25

1972　September 9
1973　July 12
Clayton, Richard R., and James W. Gladden
1974　"The Five Dimensions of Religiosity: Toward Demythologizing a Sacred Artifact." *Journal for the Scientific Study of Religion* 13 (June): 135-44.
Currie, Raymond F.
1973　"Religion and Images of Man Among Calgary Youth." Unpublished doctoral dissertation, Fordham University, New York.
Demerath, N. J., III
1965　*Social Class and American Protestantism.* Chicago: Rand McNally.
Durkheim, Emile
1965　*The Elementary Forms of the Religious Life.* New York: Free Press.
Gallup, George A.
1972　*The Gallup Poll, 1935–71.* New York: Random House.
Gibbs, James O., and Kelly W. Crader
1970　"A Criticism of Two Recent Attempts to Scale Glock and Stark's Dimensions of Religiosity: A Research Note." *Sociological Analysis* 21 (Summer): 107-14.

Glock, Charles Y., and Rodney Stark
1965   *Religion and Society in Tension.*
       Chicago: Rand McNally.
Greeley, Andrew
1972   *The Denominational Society,*
       Glenview, Ill.: Scott Foresman.
Greer, Scott
1962   *The Emerging City.* New York:
       Free Press.
Hoge, Dean R.
1969   "College Students' Religion: A
       Study of Trends in Attitudes and
       Behavior." Unpublished doctoral
       dissertation, Harvard University,
       Boston.
Janowitz, Morris
1967   *The Community Press in an
       Urban Setting: The Social Ele-
       ments of Urbanism.* 2nd ed.
       Chicago: University of Chicago
       Press.
Lenski, Gerhard
1961   *The Religious Factor.* New
       York: Doubleday.
Mann, W. E.
1955   *Sect, Cult and Church in Alberta.*
       Toronto: University of Toronto
       Press.
Millett, David
1969   "A Typology of Religious
       Organizations Suggested by the
       Canadian Census." *Sociological
       Analysis* 30 (Summer): 108-19.
Moberg, David O.
1962   *The Church as a Social Institu-
       tion.* Englewood Cliffs, N.J.:
       Prentice-Hall.
Nudelman, Arthur E.
1971   "Dimensions of Religiosity: A
       Factor-Analytic View of Pro-
       testants, Catholics and Christian

Scientists." *Review of Religious
       Research* 13 (Fall): 42-56.
O'Dea, Thomas
1966   *The Sociology of Religion.*
       Englewood Cliffs, N.J.: Prentice-
       Hall.
Parsons, Talcott
1960   "Some Comments on the Pattern
       of Religious Organization in the
       United States." *Structure and
       Process in Modern Societies.*
       Glencoe, Ill.: Free Press.
Rapport Dumont, Le, Commission
       d'étude sur les laïcs et l'Eglise
1971   *L'Eglise du Québec: un héritage,
       un project.* Montreal: Editions
       Fides.
Stark, Rodney, and Charles Y. Glock
1968   *American Piety: The Nature of
       Religious Commitment.*
       Berkeley: University of Cali-
       fornia Press.
Statistics Canada
1971   Population by Specified Religious
       Denominations (92-763).
Vernon, Glen
1968   "The Religious 'Nones', A Neg-
       lected Category." *Journal for
       the Scientific Study of Religion*
       7 (Fall): 219-29.
Wuthnow, Robert, and Charles Y.
       Glock
1973   "Religious Loyalty, Defection
       and Experimentation Among
       College Youth." *Journal for the
       Scientific Study of Religion* 12
       (June): 157-80.
Yinger, J. Milton
1970   *The Scientific Study of Religion.*
       London: Macmillan.

Adolescents, Religious Affiliation, and the Use of Drugs*

Paul C. Whitehead

Blum *et al.* (1969) contend that there is a greater tendency for the "irreligious" to use drugs. Mauss (1969) found that "lack of religious affiliation" is related to marijuana use among a sample of twelfth-grade students in California. Since the original version of this brief paper was written, a number of other studies have appeared which report findings similar to those noted below. For a description of these see Pearlman *et al.* (1971). The concern of this research note is with the relationship between professed religious affiliation and the use of ten types of drugs. For a discussion of other aspects of this survey, see Whitehead (1970), and for an overview of further investigations along these lines, see Whitehead (1971, 1974) and Smart and Whitehead (1974).

*Appeared first in Paul C. Whitehead, "Religious Affiliation and Use of Drugs among Adolescent Students", in the *Journal for the Scientific Study of Religion* 9 No. 2 (Summer 1970): 151-4. Published here in revised form with the kind permission of the author and the publisher. The data reported are part of a larger study concerned with the behaviour and attitudes of Halifax adolescents toward the use of drugs, supported by the Youth Agency of the Province of Nova Scotia, the Dalhousie University Faculty of Graduate Studies, Research Development Fund, and the Welfare Grants Division of the Department of National Health and Welfare, research project 552-21-3.

Methodology

Subjects

A 25-per-cent random sample of classes in each of grades seven, nine, eleven, and twelve in the Halifax School system completed a questionnaire concerning their use of drugs. The actual sample accounted for 63 classes from 26 schools (N = 1, 606 students).

Instrument

A slightly modified version of the self-report questionnaire used by the Addiction Research Foundation in its Toronto study (Smart and Jackson 1969) was used as the data-gathering instrument for this study. This 144-item questionnaire seeks various types of information: demographic (e.g., age, sex, nationality, religion, occupation of parents, sibling); behavioural (e.g., practices regarding tobacco, alcohol, marijuana, glue, barbiturates, and opiates); attitudinal (e.g., reasons for using various types of drugs); and estimates of the extent of drug use in the students' classes.

Procedures

Research assistants administered the questionnaires to all classes. In general, all classes at each school completed the questionnaire during the same class period.

Teachers were not in the classroom while the students completed the questionnaires. Research assistants promised anonymity and confidentiality to all students. Further, they indicated to the students that they could choose not to answer the questions by (a) not taking a questionnaire in the first place or (b) handing in a blank answer sheet. Only two students refused to take a questionnaire and nine students handed in blank answer sheets. Five per cent of the answer sheets were not included in the analysis because of gross incompleteness or obvious lack of cooperation.

Validity of Self-Report

All data are self-reports of behaviour. However, we have much confidence in the credibility of our data for several reasons. First, there was little opportunity for students to develop a scheme for sabotaging the study, since they did not know in advance that they were to participate. Second, there was little opportunity for students to interact with one another while completing the questionnaire and no opportunity to interact with those who had already completed it. Third, self-report questionnaires like this one have been used to ascertain deviance not only in terms of drug use but also with respect to a wide variety of crimes and delinquences (Wallerstein and Wyle 1947: 107–12; Nye and Short 1957: 326–31; Dentler and Monroe 1961: 733–43).

Studies aimed at measuring validity and reliability have been few, but their results have been encouraging. For example, Whitehead and Smart (1972: 83–9) used different measures of establishing the validity of self-reported rates of drug usage and concluded that self-reports seem valid, with little tendency toward overreporting. A preliminary attempt by the same authors to ascertain reliability of such drug use items produced comparable results.

In addition, Clark and Tifft (1966: 516–23) have used polygraph ("lie-detector") and interview data in the validation of self-reported deviant behaviour. Clark and Tifft had only one item (out of thirty-five) that dealt with the use of drugs. They found that 92.5 per cent of the responses concerning having "used or sold narcotic drugs" were "accurate", with only a slight tendency toward underreporting. Further, Hackler and Lautt (1969) examined systematic bias in measuring self-reported delinquency, and reported encouraging results for the use of self-report measures for typical high school populations.

Results

Catholics and Protestants report significantly less drug use than Jews and nonaffiliates (see Table 1). There is little difference in the rates of drug use between Catholics and Protestants, and between Jews and nonaffiliates. The higher rate of drug use for nonaffiliates confirms studies mentioned at the beginning of this paper. High rates of drug use among Jews have also been noted (Goode 1969: 48–64). It would seem that the socio-cultural factors that protect Jews from abusing alcohol (Snyder 1958; Blacker 1966: 51–80) offer no such protection from drug abuse. These data concerning Jews and nonaffiliates might be viewed cautiously because the sample includes only 27 Jews and 35 nonaffiliates. However, surveys similar to this one conducted in Toronto (Smart and Jackson

TABLE 1.   Percentage of Students Who Reported Using Drugs at Least Once in Last Six Months

	RELIGIOUS AFFILIATION			
DRUG	CATHOLIC (N = 811)	PROTESTANT (N = 707)	JEWISH (N = 27)	NON-AFFILIATES (N = 35)
Tobacco	50	46	43	47
Alcohol	39	41	52	41
Marijuana	5	7	13	20
Stimulants	6	7	9	21
Tranquillizers	6	6	17	9
Glue	3	3	13	9
Barbiturates	3	2	4	6
LSD	2	3	4	6
Other hallucinogens	1	3	4	9
Opiates	1	2	4	9

1969) and Montreal (Laforest 1969) have found comparable patterns of drug use for the four religious groups examined.

The religious groups do not show different patterns of preferences among the drugs. The rank order correlations of drug preferences among religious groups are all significant and range between 0.76 and 0.89. Similarly, it was previously found that the rank order correlation for drug preference between males and females in this sample is r = 0.87 (Whitehead 1970).

Discussion

A recent paper has attempted to account for the higher rates of drug use among Jews by pointing out that Jewish youth tend to be overrepresented in a variety of social categories that are characterized by elevated risk to use drugs. Specifically, Leffler (1973: 319) points out that drug use is an "urban-suburban malady" which corresponds to the residential patterns of most of the Jewish population. He also feels that economic considerations play a role in that Jewish youths come from upwardly mobile families where fathers devote much of their efforts to economic pursuits and mothers to other community activities at the cost of close relationships with their children. These factors produce a syndrome of drug abuse characterized by a rejection of "the materialistic world of their parents" (Leffler 1973: 320). Leffler points to a third risk factor as being "college bound". He cites studies which indicate that middle-class drug users are frequently college bound, and other studies which demonstrate that Jewish youth have significantly higher rates of orientation toward going to college than the general population (Leffler 1973: 320). Many of these same factors likely apply as well to religious non-affiliates, and may account for the higher rates of drug use among these collectivities in comparison to Protestants and Catholics who actually comprise most of the general population.

REFERENCES

Blacker, Edward
1966 "Sociocultural Factors in Alcoholism." *International Psychiatry Clinics* 3, No. 2 (Summer):
51–80.
Blum, Richard H., Lauraine Braunstein,
and Alma Stone
1969 "Normal Drug Use: An Explora-
tory Study of Patterns and Correlates." In Jonathan J. Cole and
J. R. Wittenborn, eds., *Drug
Abuse: Social and Psycho-
pharmacological Aspects.*
Springfield, Ill.: Charles C.
Thomas.
Clark, John P., and Larry L. Tifft
1966 "Polygraph and Interview Validation of Self-reported Deviant
Behavior." *American Sociological Review* 31 (August):
516-23.
Dentler, Robert A., and Lawrence J.
Monroe
1961 "Early Adolescent Theft."
American Sociological Review
26 (October): 733-43.
Goode, Erich
1969 "Multiple Drug Use Among
Marijuana Smokers." *Social
Problems* 17 (Summer): 48-64.
Hackler, James C., and Melanie Lautt
1969 "Systematic Bias in Measuring
Self-reported Delinquency."
*Canadian Review of Sociology
and Anthropology* 6 (May):
92-106.
Laforest, Lucien
1969 *The Incidence of Drug Use
Among High School and College
Students of the Montreal Island
Area.* Quebec: Office de la
Prévention et du Traitement de

l'Alcoolisme et des Autres
Toxicomanies.
Leffler, William J.
1973 "Middle Class Drug Abuse and
Jewish Youth." *Journal of Drug
Issues* 3, No. 4 (Fall), 318-21.
Mauss, Armand L.
1969 "Anticipatory Socialization
toward College as a Factor in
Adolescent Marihuana Use."
Social Problems 16 (Winter):
357-64.
Nye, F. Ivan, and James F. Short
1957 "Scaling Delinquent Behavior."
American Sociological Review
22 (June): 326-31.
Pearlman, Samuel, Anthony F. Philip,
Lillian C. Robbins, Edwin S.
Robbins, Elsa E. Robinson, and
Barbara Schmitter
1971 "Religious Affiliation and Pat-
terns of Drug Usage in an Urban
University Population." Pre-
sented to the First International
Conference on Student Drug
Surveys. Newark, September.
Smart, Reginald G., and David Jackson
1969 *A Preliminary Report on the
Attitudes and Behavior of Tor-
onto Students in Relation to
Drugs.* Toronto: Addiction
Research Foundation.
————, and Paul C. Whitehead
1974 "The Uses of an Epidemiology
of Drug Use: The Canadian
Scene." *International Journal
of the Addictions* 9, No. 2:
185-204.
Snyder, Charles R.
1958 *Alcohol and the Jews.* New
Brunswick, N.J.: Rutgers
Center of Alcohol Studies.

Wallerstein, James S., and Clement
     Wyle
1947   "Our Law-abiding Lawbreakers."
       Probation (April): 107-12.
Whitehead, Paul C.
1970   "The Incidence of Drug Use
       among Halifax Adolescents."
       British Journal of Addiction 65:
       159-65.
1971   "The Epidemiology of Drug Use
       in a Canadian City at Two Points
       in Time: Halifax, 1969–1970."
       British Journal of Addiction 66
       (December): 301-14.

1974   "An Epidemiological Description
       of the Development of Drug
       Dependence: Environmental
       Factors and Prevention." Pre-
       sented to the 5th International
       Institute on the Prevention and
       Treatment of Drug Dependence,
       Copenhagen, Denmark, July.
———, and Reginald G. Smart
1972   "Validity and Reliability of
       Self-reported Drug Use." *Cana-
       dian Journal of Criminology and
       Corrections* 14 (January):
       83-9.

The Religious Experience of Youth in Quebec*

Robert Sévigny

This article is taken from a larger study of religious experience and the psychological process of self-actualization.[1] Within this perspective, religious experiences are analysed by taking into account some fundamental concepts related at the same time to the notion of the "religious" and to the theory of self-actualization, as proposed by Carl Rogers. The analysis of religious experiences is based upon such questions as these: Are these experiences emotional or rational? Are they individual or collective? Are they experiences in personal or impersonal relationships? What are the values related to these experiences, and, more specifically, are they experiences of autonomy or of constraint? How is the process of integration of various experiences or of different regions of the psychological field carried out?

Interviews were conducted with students in Montreal in a classical college (Philosophy 1)[2] and in the scientific section of the twelfth grade in a secondary public school. Afterwards, a questionnaire of the Q-Sort

*Appeared first in English in Christopher Beattie and Stewart Crysdale, eds. *Sociology Canada: Readings* (Toronto: Butterworth and Co., 1974). Translated from Robert Sévigny, "La conception de l'expérience religieuse", *Sociologie et Sociétés* 1, No. 1 (mai, 1969): 7-21. Published here with abridgements with the kind permission of the author and the publisher.

type was prepared from the answers given in the interviews and this was distributed to a second sample drawn from the same settings: fifty students in Philosophy 1 and fifty students in the scientific section.[3]

In the first part of this questionnaire, the informant indicated on a scale with nine ranks whether each statement described "very little" or "very well" the image he had of his own religious experiences. In the second part, he indicated on a scale of the same type what was for him the ideal religious experience.

The form of the questionnaire implied the notion of degree rather than the notion of type. Moreover, when gathering the data, the nine-rank scale raised few technical problems and approximated quite closely the informants' way of thinking. We have regrouped these ranks to arrive at three categories made up of the first three, the last three, and the three middle ranks of the scale. Since each item was usually situated on one or several bipolar dimensions, we can consider that the first and the last third constitute two opposite poles.

[Percentages were calculated which describe] the proportion of the answers situated in the first and the last third [ranks]. These answers also deal with the image of the actual experience and the image of the ideal experience. They allow the exploration of the following aspects of religious experience: the general feeling of religiosity, God and Christ, the Church and the priest, practices in worship, and morality.

1. The General Feeling of Religiosity

The items of the questionnaire expressing a general feeling of religiosity show that at least half of the students are placed at the "religious" pole: 49.5 per cent consider that the phrase "I don't have a religious feeling" (item 1) describes them very little; 47.5 per cent judge that "religion has an important place in [their] life" (item 10); 55.7 per cent say that they like to "discuss religion" (item 31); 76.3 per cent feel they are very well described by item 22 which asserts, "In my religious life, I try as much as possible to clarify my thinking."[4] Yet, this percentage falls to 40.1 per cent for an adequate understanding of religion. For item 37, "I have not yet really understood what religion is", the informants distribute themselves in an approximately equal way at the two poles of the scale (35.1 per cent and 40.1 per cent).

If one puts the question in terms of the evolution of religious attitudes, a smaller number of informants place themselves at the "religious" pole. Thus, item 25, "I am less religious than before", is judged by 45.4

per cent as describing them very well. On the whole, nearly half of the informants define themselves as having a religious feeling, but a still larger proportion define themselves as being less religious than in the past and as not having a very great understanding of religious matters. Considering the ideal self, the proportion of those at the "religious" pole is much larger, and this holds for all the items (1, 10, 22, 25, and 37). Between 56.4 per cent and 75.3 per cent define themselves as having very religious ideals.

2. God and Christ

Let us look first at the items which express an emotional attitude towards a divine world. Seventy-seven per cent judge they are very well described by item 4: "God appears to me as an understanding person with whom you can get in touch." Nearly 58 per cent are situated at the "religious" pole for item 40: "I often think about the salvation of my soul." But 46.3 per cent have "the impression of not knowing much about Christ" (item 13); in fact, for this last item, only 26.8 per cent are placed at the "religious" pole.

The most significant result is perhaps the gap between the item on God and the one on Christ. The notion of God is much more important for the informants than the notion of Christ. We will see that this result corresponds to their conception of the Church and the priest.

If we look now at items 7, 16, and 28, which measure more explicitly the rational attitude towards religious beliefs, we see that the informants place themselves at this "rational" pole which, in the scale, is opposed to the religious pole. Nearly 62 per cent of the informants say they distinguish, in their belief in God, "that which comes from [their] individual reflection and that which comes from faith". Personal reflection plays an important part for them. Responses indicate a certain tension between the domain of emotion and that of rationality.

This tendency is still more evident in the answers to item 16: "I try to arrive at intellectual certainty in relation to the problem of eternity and the soul." Nearly 59 per cent of informants think that this statement describes them very well, while only 20.6 per cent consider that it describes them very little. Thus, there is quite a clear tendency to adopt a rational attitude towards religious belief. This is what we also find for item 28: nearly half of the informants (47.4 per cent) approach a belief in Christ from a logical or historical perspective.

Let us consider now the students' images of ideal religious beliefs.

For each item, the proportion of those who situate themselves at the "religious" pole is greater in the case of the ideal image than in the case of the actual image. On the whole, the informants believe they should be more religious than they are now. But it is significant to see that the largest gap between these two images is found in item 13, which deals with knowledge of Christ. While only 26.8 per cent think they have quite good knowledge of Christ, 53.6 per cent judge that ideally they should have.

3. The Church and the Priest

The Church as a Religious Institution

In response to item 43 ("I think that the Church is more a human institution than a religious institution"), a large number (40.2 per cent) said that this statement describes their view very well. Even at the level of their ideal image of religion, 32.0 per cent of the informants answered in the same way. This is the modal response, for the other informants are equally distributed between the two remaining categories. We may conclude that at least 40 per cent of the informants do not see in the Church an institution which primarily symbolizes the existence of God. The Church does not have an essential relationship with their religious experience. However, a third of the informants take a more traditionally "religious" view of the nature of the Church.

Individual or Collective Experience

If this tendency not to see in the Church the existence of divine reality does come through with certainty, we should also find a large proportion of informants for whom religious experience is individual and not collective. If we examine the answers to items 6, 15, 36, and 42, we do reach this conclusion.

For item 6, "I believe that my religious life would not have any meaning out of the Church", an equal proportion of informants is placed at each of the two poles of the scale (38.1 per cent). Even at the level of their ideal religion, 36.1 per cent judge that this statement does not describe them well; however, a majority think that this statement well describes their ideal (47.5 per cent).

For item 15, 44.3 per cent agree with this statement: "I place less importance on worship organized by the Church than on the prayers I offer by myself." Item 36 takes up again the fundamental question but in a positive form: "I place more importance on collective prayers (in the church, family, etc.) than on prayers I offer by myself." Only 8.3 per cent of informants think that this statement describes them well, whereas 68.0 per cent judge that it describes them poorly. Again we can see a rejection of religious experience which would take a collective form. We find the same tendency in additional answers. Interestingly, 73.2 per cent of the informants think that item 42 ("For me, religion is above all a personal dialogue between God and me") describes well their conception of religion. This proportion goes up to 87.6 per cent for the ideal image of religion.

Therefore, on the whole, the Church is an institution that is not highly valued by the informants. They tend more towards a private religious experience, oriented towards personal communication between themselves and their God. This orientation has an influence on their attitudes towards the dogmas of the Church.

The Teachings

From the point of view of this research, the teachings are rules proposed by the Church to its members. These rules deal as much with basic beliefs (e.g. God in Three Persons) as with norms prescribing certain practices or elements of Catholic worship (e.g., rules related to mass or to various sacraments). In so far as the Church is little valued by many informants, we can presume that the beliefs proposed by the Church do not constitute an important element of their religious experience. This does not necessarily mean that the informants do not hold any religious beliefs, or that the beliefs they hold are not beliefs proposed by the Church. It may mean that the informants have a tendency to choose between the various dogmas proposed by the Church and that this choice is a function of the personal conception that each one has of religious experience. The fact that a dogma is proposed by the Church does not ensure the adherence of the students.

Item 19 deals explicitly with teachings. It is not surprising to find that only 16.4 per cent of the informants think that "in [their] religious life, the teachings are the most important thing." The modal tendency is situated at the other extremity of the continuum, since 50.4 per cent believe that this statement describes their attitude very poorly. Item 41 deals with beliefs relative to mass: "Going to mass often brings me to think about the teachings concerning the mass, the Eucharist, etc." We find here the same tendency: only 27.8 per cent of the informants think that this item describes them very well, while 46.3 per cent judge the contrary.

Item 20 ("I find that a weekday mass has as much value as a Sunday mass") relates to the definition of Sunday as the Lord's Day and as the commemorative day of Christ's Resurrection. Again, 67.0 per cent of the informants agree with the statement and thus move away from the official position of the Church.

The Priest

Only one question deals directly with the conception of the priesthood, item 34: "In my own religious life, the priest is more a man like any other than a representative of Christ." The proportion of the informants who find that this statement describes them well is larger than the proportion of the informants that reject it (43.3 per cent as against 28.9 per cent). This tendency, as we see it, is logically in agreement with their conception of the Church. This does not signify that the priest is perceived or defined as a person not at all symbolizing a religious value. But the value of the priest is related to his capacity to enter into a profound human relation with the layman.

4. The Practices of Worship

We refer here especially to public worship, that is, to the practices proposed by the Church and implying collective participation.

Worship in General

The response to item 5 shows that 52.6 per cent of the informants think "that religious worship (mass, confession, etc.) is the least important aspect of religion", while only 26.7 per cent reject this statement. The modal tendency is not to attach a very great value to formal worship. As high school is a time evolution, we measured the same attitude in terms of change. Item 35 reads: "Religious worship has for me less and less meaning." An approximately equal proportion of informants accept or reject this statement (41.2 per cent and 37.0 per cent). If we take into account these two statements, we may conclude that among those who concede relatively minor importance to worship, for at least 10 per cent

(52.6 per cent less 41.2 per cent) of the informants this attitude has been established for some time.

Worship and Beliefs

For most believers, the mass is the symbol and expression of certain religious beliefs, like the death and the resurrection of Christ, or of the teachings about the communion of the saints. The minor importance of the mass in the view of many students may reflect their view that it is not symbolically associated with the world of religious beliefs.

The Mass: Individual Experience of Dialogue

The affective value of the mass, however, may be explained by the feeling that the mass is a privileged moment that allows one to be in touch with God. This feeling of being in the presence of God assumes a belief in God. But the fundamental point here is not so much the relation between the different expressive movements which characterize the mass (prayer, consecration, etc.) and the beliefs relative to God, as the fact that the mass is the occasion of a personal contact between the individual and God.

The notion of a dialogue expresses well, in the minds of the informants, the experience we are describing here. Responding to item 14 ("For me, Sunday mass is a way to continue a dialogue with God"), approximately equal proportions of informants accept and reject the statement—about 40 per cent. But, again here, there is a very large gap between these answers and the ones relating to the ideal image of religion. While only 39.2 per cent of the informants believe that this statement describes their position very well, 67.0 per cent judge that it describes very well their religious ideal. Thus we can logically presume that a good part of the negative attitudes towards mass corresponds to an absence of a feeling of dialogue during the formal ritual.

There is a relation between this tendency to conceive the mass as a privileged moment of dialogue between God and the individual and the tendency to favour the weekday mass as much as the Sunday mass. To the extent that the mass is defined as a means of personal dialogue between God and the individual, it matters little whether it takes place on a Sunday or on a weekday. The same reasoning is valid for item 21, which deals with the choice between confession to the priest and direct confession to God.[5]

Importance of Personal Motivations

Our analysis so far has shown a widespread tendency to place more value on beliefs or practices which concern personal experience. Students tend, for example, to reject the practices which do not conform with their personal beliefs. They tend to place some value on the mass in so far as it is an occasion for dialogue with God. They tend to retain beliefs which have integrated with their personal system of beliefs and they do not accept a belief merely because it is proposed by the Church. The analysis of items 9 and 24 will permit us to test this interpretation.

Item 9 reads: "I say to myself that the more I pray, the more I have merit." Only 10.3 per cent of the informants believe that this statement describes them very well and 72.2 per cent say the contrary. Item 24 states: "I prefer (or I would prefer) sometimes not to go to mass on Sunday rather than going without it meaning anything to me." The modal tendency goes in the same direction as the preceding item: 57.8 per cent of the informants think that this statement describes their attitude very well. Thus we may say that students seem to place importance on the intent or the individual motivation as a source of merit.[6]

We can summarize in a few propositions the tendencies relative to worship: Worship tends to be less valued in relation to the other dimensions of religious experience. But at the level of the ideal conception of religion, the informants in much greater proportions take positions at the "religious" pole; that is, they place more value on the practice of worship. Worship is one of the areas in which there is a large gap between the actual image and the ideal image: this corresponds with the tendency to value more the personal contact rather than collective contacts with God. Religious practices, and especially the mass, are not indispensable for a religious experience. This attitude is related to the tendency that some informants have to reject experiences the meaning and value of which they do not perceive.

5. Morality

We will analyse at first one item dealing with the general attitude towards morality. Afterwards, we will distinguish general morality from specific morals.

(a) *Morality as a Whole*

The following item permits us to give a general judgment about morality. Concerning the statement, "I rarely think about the problems of religious morality (sexual morals, political morals, etc.)", 23.7 per cent accept the position and 50.4 per cent reject it. Thus, half of the informants are situated at the pole supporting a religious morality. We will ask now what generalizations are possible based on these findings.

The modal tendency is to conceive of religion as related to a system of moral norms or values. The fact of defining it as religious should normally have some repercussions for human relations and behaviour (studies, work, relations with family and friends, etc.). On the whole, students accept the general principle of such a relation between religion and morality, as proposed by the Church. But they seem to accept to a lesser degree specific moral norms put forward by the Church.

(b) General Morality or Specific Morals?

Four items deal with general morality, that is, essentially with the idea that religious beliefs serve or must serve as the basis of a system of values encompassing all human experience. From this perspective, religious values establish the criteria of good and bad for all the main areas of life. This general statement deals with this idea: "Religion must influence my whole existence." The theme reappears in items 2, 32, 38, and 44.

TABLE 1. Percentages of Responses Comparing Students' Self-Images and Their Images of Ideal Religion

ITEM	STATEMENT	SELF-IMAGE OF RELIGION	IMAGE OF IDEAL RELIGION
2	My religious ideal really influences my everyday life.	24.8	70.1
32	What I do in my family, in my work (or my studies), etc., is done for God.	19.6	61.9
38	The fact of going to mass does not change the different areas of my life very much.	14.5	60.5
44	The things to which I attach the most value in my life are not related to my religious ideal.	35.1	56.4

At the level of self-image a low proportion of informants is situated at the pole of the integration of moral values: 24.8 per cent for item 2, 19.6 per cent for item 32, 14.5 per cent for item 38, and 35.1 per cent for item 44. Over all, few informants believe that their religious experience "really influences [their] everyday life".

However, in expressing their ideals, the young people are generally situated at the pole of the integration of moral and religious values: 70.1 per cent for item 2, 61.9 per cent for item 32, 60.5 per cent for item 38, and 56.4 per cent for item 44. The model tendency is to consider religious values as being related in one way or another to the whole range of activities. This implies that religion provides a moral direction in life: it does not necessarily imply adherence to a series of specific moral norms.

Specific Morals

Some religious norms specify certain practices of worship or prescribe proper behaviour in a wide variety of situations in everyday life. The most striking example—and one which the informants would talk about willingly—is sexual morals. In most interviews, informants recalled that in the name of religion, various agents of religious socialization (clergy and family, for the most part) proposed (and often imposed) very strict sexual morals. Item 3 ("I have some difficulty in not equating sexuality with sin") bears directly on this state of mind. Although only 26.8 per cent thought that this statement described their position very well, most would agree that this attitude was proposed to them and that they held it at one time or another. A large number have the feeling of being freed from religious sanctions regarding sexual behaviour and some believe that the norms of the Church are changing in this matter.

Another area is work and studies. This area is the one judged most often to be related to religion. Indeed, 72.2 per cent accept the following statement: "For me, to be honest and competent in my work (or my studies) is a way to respect Catholic morals" (item 27).

(c) Modal Tendencies

REJECTION OF INSTITUTIONALIZED MORALS

The rejection of specific norms, as in the case of norms related to sexuality, probably constitutes a rejection of what appears in the eyes of informants to be excessive institutionalization of religious experience. They accept the general framework proposed by the Church for religion and morals but they deny that the Church can define solely how general principles must be applied.

MORALS AND AUTHENTICATION

The acceptance of the general morality related to religious experience also appears as a form of authentication. Religious experience would not have a profound meaning if it were isolated from general human experiences. Taking into account religious values in everyday experiences satisfies a need for coherence and authenticity. The morality of a person becomes the most concrete sign of his religiosity. Responsible behaviour indicates that adherence to belief is not superficial and is authentic.

RELATION BETWEEN RELIGION AND MORALS

It is possible, on the one hand, to conceive of religion and morals as being related to each other but differentiated in tension, and, on the other hand, to conceive of this relation in terms of identity and integration. For most of the students in our sample, it does not seem that either mode has priority. This is what emerges from answers to item 12: "I think that if I relaxed my Catholic morals, I would come to abandon all my religious life." While 44.3 per cent of the students think that this statement describes them very well and they do not differentiate sharply between morals and religion, almost as large a proportion (34.1 per cent) think that this statement does not describe them very well.

There is no support, however, for an inference that the majority of the students, in establishing a relation between religion and morals, necessarily reject the existence of other foundations for a system of morals. No item dealt with the existence of morals which would not have religion as their foundation. Nevertheless, the analysis of the answers shows that a large number of informants accept the notion of human or natural morals. This is not necessarily a contradiction or an inconsistency. On the one hand, the students can recognize the existence of a multiple foundation for morals. On the other hand, they consider that religion must express itself in moral concern without going so far as to assert that all morals must have a religious base.

NOTES

1 Robert Sévigny, "L'expérience religieuse et l'actualisation de soi." Doctoral dissertation, Québec, Université Laval.

2 In Quebec, the classical college was a private college. The class "Philosophy 1" was equivalent to third-year [at such a] college [or secondary school].

3 The questionnaire was distributed in 1964.

4 This item was meant to measure the rational attitude towards religion,

but it is most probable that those who agreed with this phrase generally expressed their tendency to consider religion as a serious matter.

5   For Item 21, 56.4 per cent declare that they would prefer to confess directly to God rather than to a priest. The answers to this item can be explained by many aspects of the confession experience, for example, the relation with a priest who would not symbolize God, the recognition of our sins, etc. But it is plausible that the answers were also influenced by an orientation towards individual religious experience.

6   The lack of congruence between response to items 9 and 24 reveals a certain confusion, reflecting the ambiguity of what is proposed by the Church. The content of these two items also expresses this ambiguity.

List of Contributors

Asen Balikci, Department of Anthropology, University of Montreal
John W. Bennett, Department of Anthropology, Washington University
Reginald W. Bibby, Department of Sociology, University of Calgary
Frederick Bird, Department of Sociology, Concordia University
Philip K. Bock, Department of Anthropology, University of New Mexico
Merlin Brinkerhoff, Department of Sociology, University of Calgary
Stewart Crysdale, Department of Sociology, Atkinson College,
    York University
Raymond Currie, Department of Sociology, University of Manitoba
Leo Driedger, Department of Sociology, University of Manitoba
Jean-Charles Falardeau, Département de Sociologie, Université Laval
Robert Gaudet, Centre de recherches en Sociologie religieuse, Université Laval
John W. Grant, Emmanuel College, University of Toronto
Harry H. Hiller, Department of Sociology, University of Calgary
Everett C. Hughes, Department of Sociology, Boston College
Robert C. Kaill, Department of Sociology, University of Guelph
Warren E. Kalbach, Department of Sociology, Scarborough College,
    University of Toronto
Evelyn Kallen, Department of Anthropology, York University
Rex A. Lucas, Department of Sociology, University of Toronto
Lynn McDonald, Department of Sociology, McMaster University
W. W. McVey, Department of Sociology, University of Alberta

W. Edward Mann, Department of Sociology, Atkinson College, York University

Henry Milner, Department of Political Science, University of Quebec, Montreal

Sheilagh H. Milner, Department of Political Science, University of Quebec, Montreal

John S. Moir, Department of History, Scarborough College, University of Toronto

Hans Mol, Department of Religion, McMaster University

Colette Moreux, Département de Sociologie, Université de Montréal

Roger O'Toole, Department of Sociology, Scarborough College, University of Toronto

Jacob Peters, Department of Sociology, University of Manitoba

William Reimer, Department of Sociology, Concordia University

Robert Sévigny, Département de Sociologie, Université de Montréal

Mitsu llege,

Un

Date Due

Paul ⸺ de recⁱⁱ⸺ ⸺⸻ igieuse, Université Lava

Frank G. Vallee, Department of Sociology and Anthropology, Carleton University

T. Rennie Warburton, Department of Sociology, University of Victoria

Kenneth Westhues, Department of Sociology, University of Waterloo

Paul C. Whitehead, Department of Sociology, University of Western Ontari

M